Life and Death
with
Liberty and Justice

Life and Death with Liberty and Justice

A Contribution to the Euthanasia Debate

Germain Grisez and
Joseph M. Boyle, Jr.

UNIVERSITY OF NOTRE DAME PRESS
NOTRE DAME   **LONDON**

Library of Congress Cataloging in Publication Data

Grisez, Germain Gabriel, 1929–
  Life and death with liberty and justice.

  Includes index.
  1. Euthanasia—United States. 2. Right to die—
Law and legislation—United States. 3. Right to die.
I. Boyle, Joseph M., 1942–   joint author. II. Title.
KF3827.E87G75   344′.73′041   78-31249
ISBN O-268-01262-8

Manufactured in the United States of America

This book is dedicated to

Marie Rita Grisez, R.N. (1913–1936)

and to

Mary McGuckin Dean, R.N. (1898–1976)

and to all of the other members of the nursing profession who help persons who are ill, declining, and wretched to live with dignity even as they die.

Contents

Preface with Acknowledgments

In 1970 one of the authors of this book, Germain Grisez, published a work on abortion: *Abortion: The Myths, the Realities, and the Arguments*. In some respects the present work updates and extends the earlier one. However, the euthanasia debate is far more complex than that concerning abortion. The chief contribution we hope to make by means of the present book is to clarify the issues and examine the arguments in the rather confused euthanasia debate.

We hope that this book will contribute to the protection of life. At present there is considerable confusion among the friends of life; to some extent they are working at cross purposes. We hope that our work will provide a unified strategy for defending human life as effectively as possible: with a jurisprudence basing its arguments squarely upon liberty as well as upon justice, in accord with the American ideal of liberty and justice for all.

This book is complicated in various ways, and so readers may find parts of the work useful even if they do not wish to study the whole of it. Many different topics are treated. The table of contents together with the index will help locate topics in which a particular reader is interested. Topics dealt with in a jurisprudential mode in chapters three through nine are considered again from an ethical point of view in chapter twelve.

In the jurisprudential chapters the question toward which inquiry focuses is: What ought the law to be on this matter? Topics are considered systematically, beginning with a clarification of the issue, a criticism of various positions, formulation of criteria for a sound resolution, and—in many chapters—very specific proposals concerning what we think the resolution ought to be. Some readers might be interested in little more than our criticisms of other positions; others will press further with us. We believe that few who are interested in the subject matter will find the book wholly disappointing, although we do not expect anyone to be completely satisfied with it. We are not *completely* satisfied with it ourselves.

There are many questions in the fields of medical law and medical ethics which we consider outside the field of this study. We are not concerned with

xi

problems concerning experimentation, with issues concerning honest communication between physicians and patients, with the fairness of the health-care system as such, or with problems about the nonmedical care of dependent persons. The problem of legal competency is relevant to this study, but a good treatment of it would take us too far afield, and so we decided to leave this topic to others. Our central concern is with euthanasia. We consider other matters only insofar as they relate in one or another way to euthanasia.

Research on this book was substantially completed by August 1, 1977. Few new items were examined after that date. Moreover, the volume of materials covered was so great that in many cases we found it necessary to set limits to our research which will strike specialists in a given area as quite arbitrary. Our only apology is that this book is the first really comprehensive examination of the whole set of issues in the euthanasia debate.

Readers may wish to know which of the coauthors contributed what to this book. The project originated in a contribution which Grisez wrote by himself for the anthology edited by Dennis Horan and David Mall: *Death, Dying, and Euthanasia*. After completing his own essay and reading the anthology as a whole, Grisez decided that a more adequate, systematic treatment of the jurisprudence and ethics of euthanasia and related questions is badly needed. After collecting much material and forming some initial ideas, but with little plan for the organization of the book, Grisez sought Boyle's help in working out the outline and all the main arguments of the book. This was done in a fully collaborative effort. Since the primary business of philosophers is to argue issues, the work became a collaboration at this point.

Grisez then completed almost all of the research and much of the drafting by himself, although Boyle gave a substantial assist to drafting chapters eleven and twelve, and to redrafting certain other chapters and sections. The coauthors worked together over the first draft of chapters one through ten. At this point, the rectification of mistakes and the amendment of arguments was fully collaborative, with a more substantial contribution by Boyle. Finally, Grisez put the manuscript into shape for publication. Boyle did not examine the final version, which embodies some minor changes, before it went to press. Thus, while both coauthors share responsibility for the work as a whole, some propositions and arguments in it were not authored by Boyle; for them Grisez alone is responsible.

The debts incurred in the production of a work of this sort are many and various. The Canada Council and Campion College provided generous financial support for the research. Campion College also permitted extensive use, without charge, of stationary and copying facilities.

Joseph McPherson, a very capable student of law at Georgetown University, provided law-clerking assistance. Many individuals gave advice, provided materials, or contributed helpful comments on one or another chapter or section. Among them were Carl Anderson, William B. Ball, Virgil Blum, Robert M. Byrn, Francis Canavan, Philip Devine, Randy Engel, John M. Finnis, James McHugh, Robert G. Marshall, Marjory Mecklenburg, Albert Moracezewski, Richard Stith, and Robert M. Veatch.

The librarians at the University of Regina, Georgetown University, Georgetown Law Library, Catholic University Law Library, Library of Congress, and the specialized library of the Kennedy Center for Bioethics at Georgetown were very helpful. Of all the librarians those who staff the interlibrary loan service of University of Regina are most to be commended. Without their very efficient work this volume simply could not have been done. The MEDLARS service of National Library of Medicine also made an important contribution to the research.

Last but not least, Barbara Boyle and Jeannette Grisez supported the project in many ways and suffered it with nearly inexhaustible patience. The latter also typed the final manuscript, helped to prepare the index, and helped with proofreading.

Germain Grisez has enjoyed the friendship and support of Campion College and all its members since 1972. This will be his last publication as a member of this community of scholars. He hopes that his colleagues will find enjoyment and profit in this work, which their friendship did much to nurture and encourage.

Campion College, University of Regina
8 May 1978

1: Introduction

A. The Complexity of the Euthanasia Debate

Across the United States and throughout the English-speaking world an intense debate concerning euthanasia is underway. In many ways this debate is reminiscent of the debate over abortion. The participants are much the same, and the lines of argument advanced by each side invoke familiar basic principles and strategies. However, the issues related to euthanasia are far more numerous and complex than are the issues related to abortion.

The complexity of the euthanasia debate is obvious as soon as one considers together and attentively various facts which have been mentioned in the news at different times in recent years.

On the night of April 15, 1975, Miss Karen Ann Quinlan, a twenty-two-year-old New Jersey resident, stopped breathing for some minutes. She was taken to a hospital by friends and at first seemed completely unresponsive. But within a few weeks her condition changed. She did not regain normal consciousness, but she did show two different conditions: a sleeplike and an awakelike unresponsive state. In the awakelike state Miss Quinlan responds to light, to loud noises, to painful stimuli; she yawns, blinks, grimaces, cries out, and makes chewing motions. But she seems totally unaware of anyone or anything about her.

Miss Quinlan seemed to require the help of an artificial respirator to breathe. After many months Miss Quinlan's father, Mr. Joseph Quinlan, reached the painful decision that the respirator ought to be discontinued. He, a Catholic, believed this course to be morally correct and was assured by his spiritual advisors that it is consonant with Roman Catholic moral teaching. On March 31, 1976, nearly a year after Miss Quinlan became unconscious, the Supreme Court of New Jersey appointed Mr. Quinlan legal guardian of his daughter, an act clearing the way for him to remove her from the care of the physicians who believed that the respirator had to be continued.[1]

As it turned out, the experts were mistaken in their opinion that Miss

1

Quinlan could not survive without the respirator, for she was successfully weaned from it, and—as this is written in March 1978—she continues to breathe.

Yet on October 2, 1975, Mr. Quinlan's attorney made a statement, subsequently retracted, in a document setting forth "Factual and Legal Contentions of the Plaintiff," that "under the existing legal and medical definitions of death recognized by the State of New Jersey, Karen Ann Quinlan is dead."[2] And so from the outset the case of Miss Quinlan seemed to many to revolve around the question: When is a person dead? In popular discussion the issue was sometimes formulated bluntly: Why keep a vegetable alive? As we shall see, the real issues in this case are complex and difficult. It is not easy even to formulate them accurately and clearly.

Another case illustrates the question of the determination of death. On May 24, 1968, Mr. Bruce O. Tucker, a fifty-six-year-old black laborer in Richmond, Virginia, fell and seriously injured his brain. He was taken to the Medical College of Virginia Hospital. Efforts were made to care for him, but by the next day his attending physician decided that Mr. Tucker would not recover and that death was imminent. In the same hospital a heart-transplant team had a patient to whom they wished to attempt a transplant.

Mr. Tucker was examined by electroencephalogram (EEG, or brain-wave recording), and it was determined that there was no evidence of activity in his brain. He breathed with the help of a respirator. The machine was stopped for five minutes, and Mr. Tucker did not breathe spontaneously. He was declared dead, the respirator restarted, and his heart subsequently removed with the permission of a medical examiner.

Mr. William Tucker, the patient's brother, was not far away in the same city, and his name and address were in the patient's wallet. But the brother was not contacted. He subsequently concluded that the "donor," Mr. Bruce Tucker, had been wrongfully killed, and so he sued the transplant team. Dr. David M. Hume, the head of the team, welcomed the jury's decision finding in the team's favor by saying: "This simply brings the law in line with medical opinion."[3]

The issue in this case clearly was: Was Mr. Bruce Tucker dead when his heart was removed? But even this issue is not simple. What is it to be dead, and how can one tell that death has occurred? Should the law allow what the transplant team did? And if the law concerning the determination of death is to change, ought this to be done by allowing medical opinion and practice to set precedents which afterwards will be approved or limited by decisions of juries and judges?

Willard Gaylin, a psychiatrist, has proposed that death be defined by the irreversible cessation of specifically human functions, that "personhood" and "aliveness" be separated in the adult as they have been in the fetus. By redefining death in this way, spontaneously breathing human individuals might be maintained for months or years, and these bodies used and harvested for various medical purposes of benefit to others.[4]

If it would be acceptable to remove a still-beating heart for a transplant, can Gaylin's proposal be ruled out by law? If so, what principle distinguishes the cases? If Gaylin's analogy between the fetus and the adult were accepted and the present law of abortion granted as a point of departure, one might conclude that people who cannot take care of themselves and who will never, or never again, be able to function in a specifically human way are already dead, even if still conscious and responsive in some of the ways an animal is.

B. D. Colen has reported that at the Maryland Institute of Emergency Medicine (commonly called the Shock Trauma Unit) in Baltimore, where victims of accident and violence from all over Maryland and contiguous areas are flown by helicopter for intensive care, treatment has been discontinued for patients who were not in coma. Colen states:

> In fact, officials of the unit told me in 1974 that it was their policy to turn off respirators sustaining the life of quadrapalegics, patients completely paralyzed from the base of the skull down but patients who were, none the less, able to see, hear, think, and (but for the respirator tubes protruding from their throats) speak. These doctors rationalize that such patients can never live off the respirator, can never function for themselves in any way, are devoid of such basic reflexes as that involved in swallowing, and will almost inevitably succumb to infection and die within a few months of discharge from the unit. So rather than pass the buck to the patient's family, or a nursing home, the physicians in the unit allow the patient to die there.

And Colen makes clear that treatment is discontinued without the express consent of the patient, although the patient in these cases is capable of communication.[5]

Hardly anyone who commented upon the case of Miss Quinlan argued that she should have been maintained indefinitely on the respirator. However, many people probably would object to the discontinuance of treatment in cases such as Colen describes. How are these sorts of cases to be distinguished from each other? Is the critical factor the impossibility of asking Miss Quinlan what she wants and the possibility of asking this question of the patients in the Shock Trauma Unit? Or is an individual's exercise of liberty important? When a choice would be a very hard and painful one for a patient to make, is the only important factor the avoidance of prolonging a life artificially under adverse conditions and with poor prospects for future worthwhile activities and experiences?

B. Complex Factors Generating the Issues

Not only are the issues related to euthanasia highly complex but so are the motives and causes which are making these issues so pressing. It would be disastrous to oversimplify the roots of the movement for euthanasia. There are legitimate concerns which must be dealt with. Those with good motives for seeking changes in the law must be heard sympathetically.

It is often said that medical advances themselves create many of the problems. There are several senses in which this is true.

First, the use of the respirator can create a state of affairs in which some of the traditional criteria for death are clearly met while others clearly are not met. The question then arises: Is this patient dead or not?

Second, improved forms of treatment maintain the lives of many very weak individuals who would in the past have died. For example, antibiotics prevent infections which formerly carried off many severely malformed infants and many inmates in public institutions for the retarded, the mentally ill, and the aged. Yet the prevention of death from infectious diseases does not restore such persons to full health. Society thus is faced with a larger proportion of individuals who continue to live but cannot function well.

Third, the development of any new form of treatment raises the question of whether or not it is to be used in specific sorts of cases. So long as nothing can be done, no decision has to be made. When something can be done, one must decide whether to do it or not. Thus, for example, when surgical intervention became possible to treat infants born with spina bifida cystica, a congenital defect resulting from the spinal column's two sides not unifying perfectly, physicians had a new power to treat or withhold treatment in each case. The problem of whether a new treatment is to be used in a particular case is especially difficult when the treatment is first introduced. For then physicians might have doubts about the value and side effects of the treatment; they also have little medical tradition to guide their judgments.

Besides these rather direct ways in which technical advances in medicine are creating new problems there is another, less direct, psychological way in which progress puts pressure on traditional attitudes toward death, sickness, and defectiveness. The more medicine has become an efficient technique, the more patients and physicians themselves expect of treatment. In former times medicine was expected to guide people to more healthful living, to help the body to heal itself, to help the patient to live with chronic disease and defect, and to relieve symptoms. Today, while much of a physician's work is necessarily still directed toward the traditional goals, there has been a revolution of rising expectations.

Just as one expects a mechanic to fix one's automobile or major appliance, to make it run according to specifications, so one is likely to expect one's physician to intervene with a cure. For certain acute conditions dramatic interventions are possible. But the expectation is unrealistic for the dying, the chronically ill, the incurable, the irremediably defective. If an automobile or a major appliance cannot be restored to standard functioning, it is scrapped and replaced with an improved model. This mentality makes many people feel that the severely defective, the permanently insane, the declining aged are like abandoned vehicles, which no longer belong with the rest of us on the road of life.

Another way in which technical advances contribute to the problems related to euthanasia is that progress in medicine is one factor which continues to increase the price of medical care. Between 1950 and 1975 American health expenditures (public and private, social and personal) increased almost ten-fold in dollars, from slightly over 12 billion to nearly 118.5 billion dollars. Part of this increase was due to inflation, but even as a proportion of gross national product, American health expenditures rose from 4.5 percent of GNP in 1950 to 8.2 percent of GNP in 1975.[6] Some of this increase was due to technical advances; some to other factors, including federal programs of Medicare and Medicaid.

Regardless of the cause of escalating health expenditures the fact of this escalation cannot be evaded. Even American wealth, vast as it is, remains finite. Resources are scarce and there are many legitimate demands for them. Health expenditures cannot continue indefinitely to consume a larger and larger share of the gross national product. This state of affairs is bound to lead to the question: Should not care be withheld from those who stand to benefit but little from it? If the answer is affirmative, the next question is: Should not those who are to be denied care be helped to die quickly, especially if they volunteer?

The fact that medicine has become less a personal art and more an impersonal technique, together with the increasing costs of treatment, leads in another way to demands for changes in laws related to euthanasia. In times past many patients trusted their physicians, the dying felt secure and cared for, hospitals were for acute care and not for the dying patient. Today many patients have little or no personal relationship with their physicians, do not trust them, and feel exploited when charged heavily for impersonal treatment. The dying often feel abandoned and betrayed. As more and more patients die in hospitals and other institutions,[7] dying and the conditions of dying often seem an affront to the dignity even of those who die first class. The demand to facilitate the exercise of patient autonomy is an understandable enough reaction.

Another factor which is generating pressure for euthanasia is that persons who cannot care for themselves are today a burden and are likely to be unwanted in ways in which they were not unwanted in the past.

On the one hand the nuclear family is changing. It is less stable due to rising divorce rates, more mobile due to economic demands and opportunities. The nuclear family is less likely to include an extra child who devotes a good many years to the care of other members who cannot care for themselves. The wife and mother is more likely to be working outside the household. Thus the family does not provide its own, built-in nursing service as it once often did.

On the other hand the very concept of nursing service seems to have lost much of its appeal. A normal, healthy child can be irritating enough; cleaning and feeding it every day, comforting it when it is ill, and putting up with its constant demands tax a parent's patience. But most parents still receive a good deal of satisfaction from the normal, healthy child and have high hopes for the unfolding person. Any dependent person other than a normal, healthy child makes greater demands, gives less satisfaction, and holds out less promise. Only a person who finds fulfillment in service to the bodily needs of another wants such a dependent.[8] Thus, understandably enough, whether rightly or wrongly, there is strong temptation to look for a final solution to the problem of the burdensome and unwanted person, who must otherwise be accepted as someone's charge and given someone's service.

When the family provided much of its own nursing service, the nearby community helped the family with a certain amount of charitable aid. Often this aid was not sufficient, and as the family changed and urbanization continued, voluntary charity became less and less adequate to the need for social assistance. Thus, largely due to genuine humanitarian concern, voluntary charity was more and more replaced by public welfare, and partly due to mass demands expressed in the democratic process, public welfare has more and more become the welfare state, further and further removing those who contribute from those who benefit, and separating the two sides by a vast bureaucracy. In the United States, the involvement of the federal government with the welfare of the aged and the disabled dates only from the 1930s.[9] The cost is immense.

C. The Mounting Burden of Public Welfare

The point can be seen clearly by considering escalating expenditures under public programs for social welfare, comparing 1950 with 1975. Here we exclude expenditures for veterans programs and for education; we include social insurance, public aid, health and medical programs, housing, and other social welfare.

In 1950 all levels of government in the United States spent a little less than 10 billion dollars for social welfare; this was 3.73 percent of GNP and 15.94

percent of all government outlays. In 1975 expenditures exceeded 191 billion dollars—13.3 percent of GNP and 39 percent of all government outlays.

In 1950 the United States federal government spent less than 4 billion dollars for social welfare; this was 1.52 percent of GNP and under 10 percent of federal outlays. In 1975 the United States federal government spent more than 140 billion dollars for social welfare; this was 9.75 percent of the GNP and 46.57 percent of federal outlays. (This compared with 1950 defense expenditures amounting to 4.7 percent of GNP and 29.1 percent of federal outlays, and with 1975 defense expenditures of 6 percent of GNP and 26.7 percent of federal outlays.)[10]

It is generally believed, and we shall provide some evidence for the belief, that the rising costs of welfare were a potent factor in the legalization of abortion. Killing the unborn who would otherwise become welfare recipients is one way of limiting increasing welfare costs. But the problem of welfare costs points beyond abortion to changes in the law which will expedite the death of dependent persons, especially of the aged and dying.[11]

D. A Proposal for Easing the Burden

As we shall show, defective infants already are being selected for nontreatment, sometimes for active nontreatment, which means the withdrawal of all food and fluids.[12] Many of the mentally retarded residing in institutions are afflicted with multiple handicaps.[13] Among these there surely are numerous individuals in worse condition and with poorer prospects than some of the infants who are being selected for nontreatment. The line between the mentally retarded and the mentally ill is not always a clear-cut one; the two groups often are mixed together in the same institution.[14] A large part, perhaps the majority, of aged nursing-home patients have psychiatric symptoms. In recent years many of the aged who formerly lived in mental hospitals have been moved to the cheaper nursing homes.[15] Thus, there is a practical continuum between the defective infants now being selected for nontreatment and the aged millions who are dependent upon public welfare expenditures of one sort or another.

In 1972 Walter W. Sackett, testifying before a United States Senate committee conducting hearings on "death with dignity," stated that severely retarded, nontrainable individuals in public institutions should be "allowed to die." In two institutions in Florida, he said, there were fifteen hundred such individuals, and it would cost the state 5 billion dollars to keep them alive artificially for a period of fifty years. He did not explain what was artificial about the means used to maintain these individuals. But he did extrapolate his figures to the nation as a whole, to claim that in the same period the cost would be 100 billion dollars.[16]

If Sackett were correct, it would cost 66,666 dollars to maintain each such individual per year. Actually, maintenance cost per individual in public institutions for the mentally retarded was 5,537 dollars in 1971. Even if allowance is made for the capital cost of buildings and equipment, Sackett's estimate was ten times too high.[17] Still, at the end of 1971 there were 180,963 residents in public institutions for the retarded in the United States. Some of these undoubtedly were temporary residents, but more than 75,000 such residents at the time of the 1970 census were at least twenty-five years old and had been resident for at least fifteen months.[18] Even at a reasonable estimate the cost of maintaining 75,000 persons in institutions would amount to one-half billion dollars per year.

Moreover, the 1970 census counted 393,460 persons in public mental hospitals, 277,453 resident for at least fifteen months. At the end of 1975, due to new modes of treatment, there were only 191,395 resident patients in such facilities. But the cost of their care is high—perhaps 1,000 dollars per resident per month.[19] At this rate, to maintain even 125,000 permanent residents would cost 1.5 billion dollars per year.

The maintenance of the aged is an even more costly proposition. In 1973–1974 there were nearly one million aged persons in nursing and personal care homes. The average monthly resident charge was 479 dollars. Nearly half of this was paid by Medicare and Medicaid, and another 11.4 percent by other public assistance. About two-thirds of these persons were over seventy-five years old. In fiscal year 1976 Medicaid charges alone for this purpose reached 5.3 billion dollars nationwide.[20] Clearly, the monthly charge was continuing to escalate.

To maintain dependent persons in institutions is extremely costly. And it is universally held that most institutions fail to provide minimally decent human living conditions.[21] Moreover, many dependent persons probably are maintained outside institutions only at considerable public cost and private difficulty.

For example, it is estimated that in 1970 there were 200,000 persons in the United States with Intelligence Quotients of 0 to 24, and 490,000 more with IQs of 25 to 49; more than one-half of these persons were over twenty years of age.[22] Again, among the aged it is estimated that there are twice as many bedfast and housebound persons living outside institutions as in them, and ten times as many aged persons living in poverty outside institutions as in them.[23]

If euthanasia were accepted as a solution to the problem of dependency, the public contribution to the support of all these persons could be terminated. Those without private means of support could be processed into public institutions and allowed or helped to die at minimal public cost.

It is hardly likely that the social costs of the dependent will be ignored in the political unfolding of the euthanasia movement. Every citizen would do well to consider these costs and their relevance to the euthanasia debate, because the vast majority of today's population is potentially involved.

E. The Future Social Insecurity of the Elderly

Some may think themselves secure because they participate in private pension arrangements which seem sound and adequate. But inflation eats away at the value of annuities. Millions who built up sound and adequate funding for retirement in the 1920s and 1930s found themselves among the aged poor in the 1950s and 1960s. After World War II, retirement plans based upon equity investments (stocks) were developed; they held out great promise for a time. But in recent years the stock market has not kept pace with inflation, and many retirement funds, no matter how invested, have lost value in terms of constant dollars.[24]

To provide for one's old age in the face of inflation it would be necessary to save *more* during one's working years than one expected to spend during one's retirement, to take account of the negative effect of inflation which overbalances apparent earnings on investments. Invested money has never lost value over a long term; it seems impossible that the present situation will long continue. However, it is just possible that the very modern phenomenon of massive investment for retirement is going to falsify expectations based upon previous historical experience and seemingly sound theory.

Many people suppose that Social Security, which is now indexed, at least will provide a secure, minimum income for the elderly. United States Social Security was devised during the depression years of the mid-1930s as an attempt to prevent desperate poverty in old age, such as many then experienced. As originally devised, the plan mingled elements of insurance and of gratuitous public welfare assistance.[25]

However, the plan is altogether unlike insurance in two vital respects. First, participation for most people is not voluntary. Payments must be made, and are taken from the payroll, like other taxes. Second, there is no significant fund to balance the huge liabilities which Social Security has toward persons who will retire in the future. For all practical purposes the system is on a pay-as-we-go basis. The taxes collected each year are fully used in paying current benefits.[26] This system has worked until now because of the continuous economic and population expansion the United States has experienced from 1937 to 1977. But will workers in the future be willing to continue to pay the price?[27]

Already Social Security takes about 40 percent of *all* taxes on individuals— this figure includes the portion nominally paid by employers, since both portions ultimately are part of payroll costs from the economic point of view.[28]

In the 1930s there were 9.5 persons aged 20–64 for every older person; in 1975 the ratio had dropped to 5:1; in 2050, it is predicted, the ratio will have dropped still further to 3.5:1.[29]

Moreover, not all persons aged 20–64 are earning a taxable income. Currently there are about one hundred employed persons for each thirty retired persons, but those born during the baby boom of 1940–1965 will begin retiring in 2005. By 2030 there will be forty-five retired persons for every hundred who are working, an increase in burden of 50 percent. To finance this burden Social Security taxes will have to increase 50 percent over their present levels, perhaps to reach 20 percent of gross income. Such an increase would be especially burdensome to the middle class, whose marginal tax rate on an income (in current dollars) of 12,000 dollars would increase from 36 to 46 percent.[30]

The widespread fraud in Medicare and Medicaid, which are recently added public assistance programs of Social Security, threatens to erode public confidence in the whole program.[31]. Moreover, many people regard Social Security as radically unfair, and the public at large is likely to begin to share this view as the burden becomes greater. There are three main complaints.

First, Social Security taxes are at the same rate on the first dollar of the poorest worker's earnings as they are on the first dollar of the earnings of the wealthiest wage earner, and the total tax paid each year by the middle class worker is exactly the same as that paid by the wealthiest. Second, a retired wage earner must really retire to receive full Social Security benefits; a wealthy person can receive the full benefit together with an unlimited amount of unearned income from rents, investments, and other sources. Third, these characteristics might be justified if Social Security truly were insurance. But many charges against these funds cannot be rationalized as insurance.[32]

The facts about Social Security being what they are, no one should be confident that the program will do as much for the elderly in the coming forty years as it has in the past forty. At some point a large part of the currently employed might decide that they must look to their own future security and that they cannot count upon their children for it. This loss of confidence is likely to come about if the increasing burden of the retired leads to a reversal of the trend to improve their standards of living and health care. If wage earners project a downward trend to their own retirement years, the employed might decide to discontinue the intergenerational transfer payments of the Social Security system. The elderly, of course, would strongly oppose such a breach of faith—as it would seem to them. But they might not win.

As Robert N. Butler, director of the National Institute on Aging, has stated: "Americans suffer from a personal and institutionalized prejudice against older people."[33] In a youth-oriented society many older persons are forcibly disengaged from life and shunted aside. Burdened with increasing personal problems, they are expected not to be a burden to the young. Rather than being expected to grow and to contribute from the wisdom of their years, the elderly often are expected to be quiet, to go away, to decline and die quietly.[34]

Some point out, with a certain resentment, that elderly people, who are 10 percent of the population, receive 25 percent of expenditures on health care, while children, who are 38 percent of the population, receive only 9 percent of health care expenditures. Public programs, it is noticed, supply nearly 20 billion dollars of health care for the elderly—nearly two-thirds of their total health-care costs. The elderly receive per person about three times their proportionate share of the health-care service given the population as a whole.[35]

As one commentator has pointed out: "From the standpoint of social priorities, without regard for humaneness, the aged as beneficiaries of a public program and as recipients of public services (Medicare) represent a poor investment." He predicts that as pressures build up, side effects might include "a weakening of the taboo on the 'right to die.' " The chronically ill aged who need total care are likely to be shunted aside.[36]

Thus there are many factors which are making the issues related to euthanasia pressing. Not least among these factors is the growing burden of public welfare. But this factor is a double-edged sword. If Americans in the present generation begin to accept euthanasia as a means of lightening the welfare burden, they might just find that they have signed their own death warrant.

F. Killing as an Option No Longer Unthinkable

Killing on a massive scale has become a very common final solution to problems in the twentieth century.

World War I was fought brutally; it probably was the most destructive war in history up to its time. Under Lenin and Stalin, Soviet Socialism used mass killing as an instrument of political control and social transformation. Under Hitler, Nazi Germany adopted similar policies, adding the genocide of Jews. The Soviet Union was the first Western nation to legalize abortion; legalization has spread to much of the Western world, and is being carried to underdeveloped nations as a form of foreign aid.

World War II was fought even more brutally than World War I. Both sides used terroristic tactics, particularly strategic bombing, culminating in the American use of the atomic bomb on Japan to bring about unconditional surrender.

Guerrilla warfare and attempts to suppress it since World War II have refined terrorism, torture, and indiscriminate killing of military and civilian populations. Vietnam is only one example. Meanwhile, both the Soviet Union and the United States have developed and maintain in readiness capabilities for thermonuclear war, which might in a few hours destroy a large proportion of the world's population. The American strategy is one of deterrence; the hope is that thermonuclear war will never be necessary. Close observers of the Soviet Union doubt that the commitment to deterrence really is mutual.[37]

Yet there is no reason to think that humankind is becoming less morally responsible. Indeed, much twentieth-century killing has been done in the name of high moral ideals. The communist nations, for example, declare that they are trying to liberate humankind from oppression and to establish a good and just society. Despite the cynical scepticism of liberal democratic commentators on the world scene, there is little ground to doubt the sincerity of many communists or their genuine dedication to the marxist ideal. The liberal democratic nations, likewise, declare that they are trying to protect individual liberty against totalitarianism; motives doubtless are mixed, yet there is genuine idealism here too.

How can high moral idealism lead to mass killing? The Indo-European religious tradition stressed the sanctity of human life. Life as such somehow participated in the divine; human life in particular was considered sacred through its close affinity with spirit, and with the ultimate principle of meaning and value in reality. This ultimate principle was taken to be timeless; humankind and human history were thought to go on within an established framework, whether or not this was understood as the providential plan of a personal God.[38]

Modern, post-Christian thought has a very different world view. An impersonal, spiritless, mindless universe of mass and energy is believed to evolve by natural necessity, void of meaning and value until life capable of cognition and desire emerges under the impetus of blind forces. Significance and purpose only emerge fully in humankind, where there is self-consciousness and the ability to undertake purposeful transformation of the universe. Hence, there is no objective realm of principles to which humankind must conform its plans and desires, no divine law to which human law must look for its principles. For post-Christian men and women the principles of human law are *human* desires and interests, needs and satisfactions, joys and hopes *alone*.

Human desire and satisfaction alike have their primary locus in consciousness. Self-consciousness is what distinguishes humankind. The body and its processes are of a piece with nature, except to the extent that the body and its functioning can be controlled, transformed, dominated, and reduced to obedience by technique. From this post-Christian perspective human bodiliness and human personhood are two very distinct realities; personhood is comprised only of what is distinctively human.

It follows that human individuals who have not had an opportunity to develop distinctive personalities—or who have lost the power to exercise their distinctive personalities—hardly have the character of persons. The unborn, for this reason, seem to many only potential persons.

Likewise, from a marxist viewpoint the oppressed masses are so far deprived of personhood that mass killing for the sake of a future just society is not absurd; those killed now are only so many individual human bodies that can be used and destroyed so that the true men and women of the future can emerge. And from the liberal, democratic viewpoint the victims of totalitarianism are depersonalized; the people of southeast Asia, as well as the populations on which the missiles and their hydrogen bombs are targeted, are not persons because they do not have the liberty to develop significant personal lives.

Thus, for modern, post-Christian thinkers mass killing is acceptable as a final solution to human problems. Human life in itself no longer has sanctity. What is important is the quality of life, the extent to which an individual's life contributes instrumentally to the attainment and enjoyment of specifically human and personal values. Whenever some human individual's life is not of sufficient quality—whether measured from the individual's own perspective or from the perspective of society or both—that life becomes a disvalue. Such a life is unwanted because it is useless; it is evil because it is unwanted; it must be destroyed because it is evil.

To those who still believe in the sanctity of life the modern, post-Christian conception is unreal, almost incredible. It is hard to believe that a society which has committed itself so heavily to social welfare could turn about and systematically seek to limit and reduce the burden of welfare by mass killing. But the legalization of abortion is a fact. And abortion has been legalized on the basis that the unborn are not persons and can be destroyed if they are unwanted by the women who bear them and by society at large. Others who are unwanted differ but little from the unborn.

G. Public Confusion and the "Right to Die"

Thus far we have shown that the euthanasia debate is complex, far more so than the debate over abortion was. We also have shown that there are a great many social factors which make euthanasia a contemporary issue and which are likely to make it an even more intense issue in the future. Furthermore, there are aspects of the contemporary attitude toward human life which point toward the adoption of killing as a solution to social problems. In this state of affairs there is a real danger that proponents of euthanasia will reach their objectives before those inclined to seek other solutions have managed to sort out the issues, work out consistent and defensible positions on them, and advance attractive alternatives to euthanasia as a solution to problems.

In dealing with public opinion the clarification of the issues will be essential if legalization of mercy killing is to be prevented. This can be seen from the results of two polls, one by Gallup and one by Harris, both taken in 1973.

The Gallup question was: "When a person has a disease that cannot be cured, do you think doctors should be allowed by law to end the patient's life by some painless means if the patient and his family request it?" The response was 53 percent affirmative, an increase of 17 percent to the same question since 1950. (It is interesting to note that only 47 percent answered a 1974 Gallup poll that they favored the United States Supreme Court's ruling on abortion; the ruling was described in the question: "The U.S. Supreme Court has ruled that a woman may go to a doctor to end pregnancy at any time during the first three months of pregnancy.")

The Harris euthanasia poll asked two questions. "Do you think a patient with terminal disease ought to be able to tell his doctor to let him die rather than to extend his life when no cure is in sight, or do you think this is wrong?" To this question, 62 percent replied it ought to be allowed, 28 percent that it is wrong. Harris also asked: "Do you think the patient who is terminally ill, with no cure in sight, ought to have the right to tell his doctor to put him out of his misery, or do you think this is wrong?" To this question, Harris received only a 37 percent response that it ought to be allowed, while 53 percent said it is wrong.[39]

The different result of these two polls makes clear how a majority against active euthanasia can be converted into a majority in favor of it merely by submerging the distinction the Harris poll called to attention. One might imagine that the distinction between a patient's refusal of useless treatment, on the one hand, and, on the other, the application of deadly means by a physician at a patient's request would be clear to everyone. But this is not so. Proponents of euthanasia are making the most of such confusions.

In the United States a Euthanasia Society was founded in 1938. In 1967 it was making no progress toward its goal of legalizing at least voluntary euthanasia for adults. Members set up a new unit, the Euthanasia Educational Fund, to disseminate information. At or about the time this was done, Luis Kutner suggested the "living will"—something not as objectionable as mercy killing to the public at large, although not exactly what proponents of euthanasia had always sought.[40] The "living will" is a form letter, to be signed by adults, directing family and physician in case of terminal illness to avoid heroic measures or extraordinary means of treatment, and to give palliative care and permit natural death.

The Kutner proposal received much favorable publicity. Literature on death, dying, and euthanasia quickly began to burgeon. After the United States Supreme Court decisions on abortion early in 1973, much of the thrust behind the movement to legalize abortion seemed to pass over to the movement to legalize euthanasia.

At the beginning of 1975 the old Euthanasia Society was reactivated as the Society for the Right to Die, an action unit to press for legislation.[41] The Euthanasia Educational Fund and the Society for the Right to Die share the same office, and fifteen of the seventeen members of the officers and board of the latter organization in 1976 were among the officers, board, or committees of the former organization in 1974.[42] In 1975–1976 the Quinlan case was much in the news. This was what was needed to break the dam against legislation. The Society for the Right to Die vigorously promoted legislation for "death with dignity," advancing its own model bill.[43]

In 1976 California enacted the first such legislation, but the California law explicitly excludes mercy killing, extends only to competent adults, and asserts not a right to die, but only the right to refuse treatment so that nature can take its course.[44] However, in 1977, when more or less similar bills were introduced in the legislatures of forty-one states, seven additional states enacted legislation.

New Mexico and Arkansas were among these seven. Their laws do enact a right to die, extend the exercise of this to minors by means of proxy consent by a parent or guardian, and do not explicitly exclude (although they do not authorize) mercy killing.[45] The New Mexico statute is patterned on the model proposed by the Society for the Right to Die.[46] Even the more conservative California statute appears to be modeled upon the voluntary euthanasia bill which was debated by the British Parliament in 1969.[47] With only some simple amendments the California statute can become a law permitting and regulating killing with the consent of the one to be killed.

Many who doubt the wisdom of legalizing such killing believe that the proper course of action is to oppose the enactment of any legislation along these lines. Yet in California there was in the end little serious opposition to enactment of the statute. Most of those who opposed the legalization of abortion saw clearly what they wanted and did not want, and so they were able to react with vigor and unity, at least with respect to objectives. But now many of the same persons and groups are not sure where to draw the line with respect to euthanasia. The claim that people should have a way of controlling what is done to themselves is hard to reject as unreasonable. How can this claim be distinguished in theory and separated in practical politics from the legalization of killing with consent, and the authorization of absolute parental discretion concerning the nontreatment—and perhaps even the killing—of infants?

H. From Voluntary to Nonvoluntary Euthanasia

Even before the 1973 abortion decisions there was discussion of actual cases in which parents had refused treatment for their infants necessary to preserve their lives, and physicians and hospitals had refrained from the treatment on the basis of the parental refusal, although the necessary treatment would otherwise have been given as a matter of course.

One such widely publicized case was at Johns Hopkins University Hospital; it occurred in 1963 but was not publicized until later. The infant was afflicted with Down's syndrome (mongolism) and needed a surgical operation, simple enough in itself, to remove an intestinal blockage. The parents refused consent; the physicians and hospital sought no court order; the baby starved to death in about two weeks.[48] A somwhat similar case occurred in a Catholic hospital in Decatur, Illinois, where a chaplain advised that there was no moral duty to undertake the extraordinary means of surgery upon an infant lacking a normal esophagus.[49]

Almost exactly nine months after the United States Supreme Court's abortion decisions two important articles appeared in which physicians at the University of Virginia Medical Center and Yale-New Haven Hospital described in some detail and defended their own practices of withholding treatment from newborn infants suffering from a variety of defects. The arguments for these practices were that the prospects for "meaningful life" were very poor or hopeless, that considerations of quality of life may in such cases prevail over what others would regard as the infant's right to life.[50]

An intense discussion, which we shall summarize in chapter nine, unfolded beginning about the same time concerning the selection for treatment and for neglect of infants born with spina bifida cystica. Untreated infants may nevertheless survive and, if they do, be in far worse condition than had they been treated intensively from the outset. For some who engaged in this discussion the implication was clear that neglect must be total: The infant selected for nontreatment must not be fed, although it was able to ingest food in a normal manner.

As early as May 1972 John M. Freeman of Johns Hopkins argued that if infants were to be neglected, their death should with better kindness be actively hastened.[51] The physicians at Yale-New Haven Hospital also subsequently argued that choices for death, also by active means, ought to be legally permitted.[52] Writing in the same prestigious medical journal in which the physicians publicized their practices of letting babies die, philosopher James Rachels argued that the distinction between active and passive euthanasia is unsound.[53] Some commentators who think the selective nontreatment of defective infants to amount to homicide by omission agree that in this case, at least, letting die is simply a method of killing.[54] On this view, nonvoluntary euthanasia is being widely practiced, admitted, and ignored by legal authorities in America and England today.[55]

Joseph Fletcher has argued that it is wrong—immoral and irresponsible— not to back up abortion with the measures required postnatally to end damage in cases in which a child is born with Down's syndrome.[56] He published this view nearly five years before the United States Supreme Court's decisions concerning abortion. Since then more and more of those who argued vehemently that abortion was a very different matter from infanticide have proceeded from acceptance of the former to defense of the latter. The two practices do have a great deal in common.

Further, in the case of severely deformed infants maintained in custodial institutions, it has been argued that the alternative to kindly killing is banishment to a living death in a warehouse for human beings who are effectively reduced to a state of nonpersonhood by brutality and neglect.[57] Fletcher has pressed the view that individuals with an Intelligence Quotient below 20, perhaps also those with an IQ below 40, do not qualify as persons.[58] Again, as we shall see in chapter eight, others have joined him in this position.

Many who would not readily accept nonvoluntary euthanasia in other cases may be willing to accept it in the case of infants, for they are in a condition in which no adult ever again will be, and killing them—especially when the violence is concealed by the use of the method of calculated neglect—does not seem much different from abortion. Moreover, perhaps there are cases in which the omission of possible methods of treatment is morally acceptable and is, or should be, sanctioned by law. But if there are such cases, how can they be distinguished from others in which the neglect is simply a method of homicide, chosen merely because this method is not easily prosecuted as a crime?

Some who would reject nonvoluntary euthanasia even in the case of severely defective infants have a much more difficult time judging whether voluntary euthanasia might not be allowed for competent adults who give their informed consent to it. Clearly, here, a just respect for the person's right to life no more demands that euthanasia be forbidden than it demands that suicide and attempted suicide be considered criminal. For all practical purposes, suicide and attempted suicide are no longer held criminal in the English-speaking world. Why must those who choose to bring about their own deaths be required by law to do so by their own hands, when others who would willingly help could do the job more surely, more quickly, and more gently?[59]

However, if voluntary euthanasia is legalized, court decisions could extend the benefits of such kindly killing to children and other persons who are not legally competent. The argument would be that equal protection of the law forbids the limiting of the boon of being put out of one's misery to persons legally competent to give informed consent to the procedure. Substitute consent already is used to justify transplants from a noncompetent person.[60] And an important aspect of the New Jersey Supreme Court's resolution of the Quinlan case was the determination that Miss Quinlan's father could act on her behalf:

If a putative decision by Karen to permit this non-cognitive, vegetative existence to terminate by natural forces is regarded as a valuable incident of her right of privacy, as we believe it to be, then it should not be discarded solely on the basis that her condition prevents her conscious exercise of the choice. The only practical way to prevent destruction of the right is to permit the guardian and family of Karen to render their best judgment, subject to the qualifications hereinafter stated, as to whether she would exercise it in these circumstances.[61]

Of course, the New Jersey Supreme Court is not dealing with killing, and does not declare any right to die. Nevertheless, if the legislature were to hold voluntary euthanasia licit on the basis of a right to die, a court accepting this line of reasoning—which would be very difficult to reject—would be compelled to hold that the only practical way to prevent the destruction of the right in the case of noncompetent persons would be to permit others to render judgment on their behalf.

I. The Approach of This Book

Most discussions of euthanasia and related issues combine—or never begin to distinguish—questions about what is morally right and wrong with questions about what the laws should be if a democratic nation is to live up to its ideals of liberty and justice for all. When these two distinct kinds of questions are not mingled, the ethical issues are treated first, and recommendations concerning legislation are derived from the ethical conclusions. Also, in many cases the ethical discussion of issues is shaped by theological assumptions or by antireligious prejudices. An example of the latter is the work of Glanville Williams, who seems to think that showing a position to have had religious origins is enough to discredit it.[62]

In this book we try to distinguish and clarify the various issues related to euthanasia. We carefully examine arguments for changes in existing law. In working out what we believe to be a consistent position, we examine the demands of liberty and justice.

In the work that follows we carefully exclude theological considerations. We exclude them, not because we consider them unimportant, but rather because we intend this work to be a contribution to the common, public debate, in which no one's religious beliefs or antireligious prejudices can be legitimately taken as premises for conclusions about the formation of public policy. Theological considerations must be presented to a distinct audience: those who share the faith which the theology articulates and defends.

Also we distinguish questions concerning what the law should be from questions of what is morally right and wrong. Most of this book is devoted to examining and arguing questions of the former kind, which we call "jurisprudential." And we deal with the jurisprudential questions first, in chapters two through ten. Only after having completed our treatment of these matters do we briefly examine the ethical questions concerning what is morally right and wrong. By treating jurisprudential questions first, we have forced ourselves to limit our approach to these issues by excluding much of our own ethical position.

Specifically, in chapters two through ten we do not assume the sanctity of human life as a principle. In other words, we do not try to settle any jurisprudential issue by invoking the principle that one should never kill the innocent. Rather, we argue from the common principles of liberty and justice which have not yet been repudiated by any substantial segment of any liberal democratic society.

The basis for our jurisprudential treatment of the issues is presented in chapter two. There we articulate what we believe to be the American conception of liberty and justice, and show some of its implications for legality. On this basis the issues in subsequent chapters are treated.

Chapters three through nine contain our jurisprudential treatment of the substantive questions. In chapter three we argue that the legal definition of death does need to be clarified, and suggest how this might best be accomplished. In chapter four we consider the problem of how persons who are legally competent might more effectively control the treatment they will receive. Neither in chapter four nor anywhere else do we take up a problem which does deserve serious work: How is legal competency to be demarcated? This problem is not specifically related to euthanasia; it would require a sizable study by itself. Thus we decided to leave it to others.

In chapter five we examine the law concerning suicide. Libertarian considerations argue strongly for wide scope for individuals to control their own treatment; the same considerations argue for caution in active interference with persons who of set purpose wish to commit suicide. In chapter six we proceed to one of the central issues: Should voluntary euthanasia be legalized? Here we reach a negative conclusion. The implications of liberty and justice are more complex here than has been recognized either by proponents or by opponents of euthanasia.

As we explained at the beginning of this introduction, questions regarding the definition of death, the liberty of persons to refuse medical treatment, suicide, and voluntary euthanasia often are muddled together. Our treatment sorts out these issues and addresses them with considerations proper to each. Similarly, we separate the jurisprudential issues concerning self-regarding acts, which are treated in chapters four through six, from the jurisprudential issues concerning other-regarding acts, which are treated in chapters seven through nine.

In chapter seven we examine the question: To what extent do forms of killing traditionally held to be justifiable—for example, killing in self-defense or as capital punishment—provide a precedent for the euthanasia of those whom some consider would be better off dead? In chapter eight we directly confront the issue: Whether nonvoluntary euthanasia can be justifiably legalized? Our response is negative, for legalization of such killing would, we argue, deny to those to be killed the equal protection of the law. Finally, in chapter nine we complete our jurisprudential consideration of substantive questions by a discussion of the very difficult problem: How can the law ensure that persons who are not legally competent are not unjustly overtreated or deprived of treatment—especially not deprived of treatment to bring about nonvoluntary euthanasia by omission?

The consideration of substantive jurisprudential issues brings into the open some important defects in American constitutional law, as it presently stands after decisions of the United States Supreme Court in recent years. These matters of constitutional law are treated in chapter ten. In the first place we believe that justice requires the clear establishment, as a matter of constitutional principle, of the legal personhood and right to equal protection of the law of homicide of every individual who belongs to the species homo sapiens. In the second place we believe that liberty requires that religious and nonreligious worldviews be treated without prejudice, and that the latter not be assumed to have legitimacy as secular principles of jurisprudence denied by the First Amendment to the former.

Chapters eleven and twelve contain our examination of issues from an ethical perspective. Chapter eleven deals with ethical principles and defends the method of normative moral judgment we employ. This chapter also argues for the position that human life is an inherent, not merely instrumental, good of human persons, and so is not rightly treated as a mere means, but ought to be respected as inherently personal. Chapter twelve applies the normative ethical theory articulated in the previous chapter to the main issues discussed in the jurisprudential chapters, but now the question is what morality requires, regardless of what the law requires happens to be. This ethical consideration makes clear that legal standards and moral standards, as we see them, do not perfectly coincide.

Finally, in chapter thirteen we compare our own view of the relationship between law and morality with the view most commonly held by those who favor the legalization of euthanasia. We also attempt to show that the ethical theory we have articulated does offer a rational foundation for the jurisprudence assumed as the American proposition. If we are correct, sound ethics itself demands that public policy on euthanasia and related issues be formulated, not on the assumption of the sanctity of life, but rather on the principles of liberty and justice which Americans—as well as citizens of other liberal democratic nations—claim to uphold.

This book is addressed to all thoughtful persons who are willing to consider the jurisprudential and ethical questions related to euthanasia with open minds. We have developed our own positions, of course, but did not come to this subject matter with a set of ready-made positions. In the earlier stages of the inquiry we thought there might be considerably more room for the legalization of killing of competent persons with their consent and of restriction of treatment to noncompetent persons than we now consider defensible. Hence, throughout this work we make every effort to articulate counterpositions forcefully and fairly, and we try to deal with them straightforwardly and on the basis of principles which those whom we criticize ought also to accept if they are to remain consistent with their own professed ideals.

Because our conclusions will be found most acceptable by persons who doubt the wisdom of legalizing any killing of one person by another not now permitted by Anglo-American law, we hope our work will be especially helpful to such persons. We have tried hard to distinguish what ought to be conceded from what must be defended. If opponents of euthanasia cannot quickly come to agreement on these matters, we believe that proponents will attain their objectives much more easily and quickly than the merits of their case would otherwise permit.

J. The Task of the Movement for Life

There is a special urgency in acquiring a clear grasp on certain issues and in attempting to obtain legislative action which would protect liberty and justice while blocking the movement toward mass killing as a solution to the problem of social welfare costs. In chapter three we argue that the matter of the definition of death would be a proper subject for action by the United States Congress, using its enforcement power under the Fourteenth Amendment to define and protect the boundary of legal personhood for the dying. In chapter four we argue for legislation at the state level, in some ways much broader than recently passed "right-to-die" legislation, which would preempt the position now being occupied by proponents of euthanasia but would make no concessions to the ideology of their movement. In chapter eight we again suggest that the Congress might act to block legalization of nonvoluntary euthanasia by state legislatures. Finally, in chapter nine we urge legislation at the state level to put a stop to the present widespread and increasing practice of killing noncompetent individuals, especially defective infants, by omission of necessary treatment. Obviously, only some of the states offer a political opportunity to the legislation we think necessary at a state level. Still, whatever might be achieved will help save lives.

Although jurisprudential issues are to be argued on the basis of liberty and justice, not on the basis of sanctity of life, many opponents of euthanasia will be more concerned with saving lives than with liberty and justice, although not insensitive to the demands of these principles. If, as we fear, the movement for euthanasia is likely to gain considerable ground in the United States and other English-speaking countries during the next few years, such opponents of euthanasia are likely to become disheartened, as many opponents of legalized abortion became disheartened after the United States Supreme Court decisions of 1973. It is important for such persons to realize that the movement for life has saved and continues to save many lives, even if many more are lost. And according to their own perspective, these friends of human life should be spurred on by what they have accomplished, for every human life is precious.

Moreover, if we are correct in thinking that the most basic principles of a good society—liberty and justice—are critically at stake in contemporary issues about life and death, then work to enact laws or to maintain laws consonant with these principles, even when such work is unsuccessful, has value in preventing the corruption of political society. As long as society includes groups who struggle to vindicate its principles, they are not wholly lost; the basis for reform still exists.

Furthermore, the movement for life has a value in the education of members of the society which is especially important when the support of the law is lost. By working for human life those who strive to resist legalization of euthanasia will keep alive some consciousness of the horror of killing. This consciousness will prevent many people from carrying out the killing which the law would permit; they would have to make a very determined choice to do so as they are forcefully reminded of the true significance of what they are about to do.

The educational value of work on behalf of human life is not least significant for members of the movement for life themselves. This is especially clear in the case of young people. A young man or woman who has worked to defend the unborn and to prevent the killing of the dependent is far less likely than another person to embrace killing as a solution to their own problems when these become pressing.

Proponents of euthanasia will say, as proponents of legalized abortion have said, that those working for human life are hypocritical if they strive only to maintain criminal sanctions against killing and do nothing to change the social conditions. This charge is sophistic, for even if those who object to killing with legal sanction do not fulfill every other social responsibility, still their position retains its intrinsic validity.

However, in euthanasia and issues related to it, for reasons we have already explained, the shirking of social responsibility toward dependent persons and the approval of killing as a solution to the problem of welfare costs will go hand in hand. So must the defense of life and the acceptance of responsibility for the dependent. And when society at large shirks this responsibility, true friends of life must stand ready to shoulder voluntarily as much of it as they can. Thus the collapse of public programs based upon humanitarian idealism will make way for a rebirth of familial responsibility and neighborly charity.

To prepare for this eventuality, those who are friends of life ought even now to work hard to strengthen their own family ties, especially ties between generations and with close relatives beyond the nuclear family. They ought also to work to build up forms of practical cooperation and mutual assistance in the voluntary associations, such as local churches, to which they belong. Such associations were important media for charity in times past, nor did they always limit their help to their own membership. This function must be reactivated if as many dependent persons as possible are to be saved from the fate of those who are perceived as a public burden, and who are likely to be judged better off dead and publicly assisted in attaining this better condition.

It is very difficult to believe that the capability for thermonuclear war will continue to exist indefinitely in a divided world and never be put to use. It is even more difficult to believe that such a conflagration will be avoided as terrorism and extortion spread throughout the world, and as more and more centers of decision have some atomic weapons at their disposal. Under these conditions the use of such weapons even by a minor power or a private terrorist group could by error or escalation upset the all too delicately balanced equipoise of terror, which the United States, at least, wishes to maintain.

We do not doubt that those who survived a nuclear holocaust would be able to look back on our time and see clearly the intimate connection between the various ways in which liberty and justice are being violated in contemporary society and human life held cheap. If those who work for life, liberty, and justice cannot prevent disaster, they nevertheless should bear in mind that no disaster is total, and no future new beginning will be without roots in today's world. Thus men and women of today, even accepting as probable the most pessimistic prognosis for contemporary society, still are called upon to do what is now possible to lay the foundations for a future society in which life, liberty, and justice will be respected more perfectly and loved more purely than they are today.

2: Law, Liberty, and Justice

A. The Purpose of This Chapter

In chapters three through nine we shall be asking what the law ought to be in respect to suicide, the definition of death, the liberty of competent persons to refuse medical treatment, and the various forms of euthanasia. Such questions cannot be answered without invoking some standards which good laws meet and which bad laws fail to meet. In the present chapter we try to clarify some of the standards we shall assume and apply in subsequent chapters.

Our treatment of standards for good law will be limited in two ways.

First, we make no attempt to articulate a complete political philosophy or philosophy of law. Rather, we assume that there is a working consensus underlying American government and legal practices. We shall try to articulate this underlying consensus—which can be called "the American proposition"—and to present considerations which will lend initial plausibility to the standards of good law which it implies.

The ethical theory which we shall present and apply in chapters eleven and twelve will make it possible for us to provide a more adequate defense of these standards in chapter thirteen. It is worth noting that the standards of good law implicit in the American proposition differ little from those generally accepted in liberal-democratic nations which enjoy a jurisprudence formed by the tradition of British common law.

Second, there are many questions about the nature of law and about standards for good law which will not be crucial for settling the issues to be discussed in this book. For example, a good law must be a general rule or a directive issued in accord with one or more general rules; it cannot be a mere ad hoc imperative. A good law must be communicated effectively to those who are to be guided by it; it should not be retroactive; it must be clear, not vague; it must be consistent with other legal rules in force; it must require those who are to be guided by it to do only what is humanly possible; it should be constructed to last, not to be in need of constant tinkering; and it must be susceptible to effective and consistent practical application. We assume that such standards, while in need of explanation, are noncontroversial. They have been discussed by others.[1] We also assume that most philosophical controversies about the ultimate nature of law have little relevance to the problems we are going to consider.

Stated affirmatively, our main business in the present chapter is merely to articulate the notions of liberty and justice which will be crucial in almost every discussion in chapters three through ten.

Because of our limited purpose, we are interested in only one part of the theory of justice—namely, the justice a fair constitution should embody and will communicate to laws made in accord with it. There are many injustices in the society at large which are not the concern of the state; we will not be concerned with them, for good laws touch only on the justice which is the concern of the state. Even within this limit we attempt in the present chapter to articulate only a few common propositions which will be in play throughout subsequent discussions. These common propositions will be supplemented in connection with the construction and criticism of arguments on each issue.

B. Just Law and the Consent of the Governed

The people of the United States, like the people of any other nation, live together; they share a common life, cooperate together, and sometimes get into more or less serious conflict with one another. Laws are an important type of rule for directing the behavior of individuals and of various sorts of groups, such as families, corporations, and unincorporated voluntary associations, insofar as this behavior contributes to or potentially impinges upon the common life. The legal system, considered as a whole, claims authority to provide comprehensive and supreme direction for human behavior in the nation, and to give public validity to all other normative arrangements affecting members of the nation and its guests.

Obviously, not all norms of behavior are laws. There are moral norms which are not part of the legal system. Moral rules such as people help their neighbors who are in need, be grateful to friends who do favors and give gifts, and shape their feelings and attitudes in altruistic ways are not and cannot be laws. Such rules are beyond the power of law to enforce; the requirements of generosity and gratitude are too fine and too diverse to be specified and adjudicated, and the private character of feelings and attitudes puts them beyond the effective jurisdiction of law, at least of law which stops short of inquisitorial methods.

It often is thought that what is characteristic of law is that it is an order backed up by the coercive power of the state. But not all rules backed by coercive sanctions of one sort or another are laws. Apart from the orders and threats of employers and parents directed towards employees and small children, there are other examples of orders backed by threats which fail to have the character of law although they are issued by the dominant power in a certain territory.

For example, if the Mafia gains control of a certain region and manages it by terrorism, its orders fall short of the character of law; there are no general rules which define and limit such officers and their powers, and so there is no stable social order to which both the terrorist chiefs and their victims are subject. Similarly, if a powerful nation gives orders directly to the citizens of an adjacent nation and backs these orders with threats, such orders do not have the character of law, although those who are commanded might comply for fear of the consequences if they fail to do so.

Law, in short, presupposes that there is a political society, that those directed by law are members of the society or guests living within it, and that those directing by law are officers of the society, with powers defined and limited by the legal system itself.

The governing body of a political society at least claims legitimacy—that is, a status of right to rule which makes its power have the character of authority rather than of mere brute force. The claim of legitimacy implies that laws are proposed as rules which deserve respect and obedience. Every government claims that its laws have a reasonable basis which makes them worthy of moral respect in a way that arbitrary orders backed up by threats never can be—even though the prudent person respects terrorist threats. The latter respect is pragmatic and prudential, not moral. In claiming legitimacy a government claims that *virtuous* citizens will respect its authority.

To the extent that Americans think of their government as legitimate, then, they think of the laws as making a moral claim upon their minds and hearts. What do they suppose to be the basis of this moral claim?

They do not consider the moral claim of the law to be analogous to the moral claim of rules laid down by parents for the guidance of their children. Parents are naturally in a better position to direct their children than are the children themselves. Children ought to obey because parents know better and because, presumably, they have their children's interests in view when directions are given.

But among competent adults insofar as they function as members of a political society, none are naturally the superiors of others. This point provides a basis for understanding the principle of equality enunciated by the Declaration of Independence: All men are created equal. The equality asserted is not in natural endowments, in possessions, in achievements, or in virtue, but solely in political competency: No one is naturally a ruler, no one is naturally a subject, and there are no natural slaves.

If these positions are accepted—that is, if one agrees that the legitimacy of government is not analogous to parental authority and is not a function of the prerogatives of innately superior individuals—then the original question stands. What is the basis for the legitimacy of government according to the American conception of it?

The American proposition suggests the answer: Governments obtain legitimacy from the *consent of the governed*. We believe that this position can be understood in such a way that it is defensible as the right answer to the question. But there are many ways to misunderstand "consent of the governed." To avoid these misunderstandings, we must say something about consent. In particular we must consider briefly four points: (1) the scope of consent; (2) the normative element involved in consent which gives legitimacy; (3) those whose consent is required; and (4) the mode of voluntary acceptance which counts as consent.

First, the view that the legitimacy of a government depends upon the consent of the governed should not be taken to imply that each and every act of government requires consent of the people. If such were the case, a nation would be no more than a group of people acting together only when and just so long as each member of the group saw fit to participate. Political society would have no more stability than a group of children playing voluntarily together in a park.

Thus, when particular acts of government are in question, one does not determine their legitimacy by asking whether they directly have the consent of the people. One rather asks whether these acts are lawful. And ultimately questions about the lawfulness of the government's own acts must be resolved by appeal to the supreme law of the land: the Constitution. The consent which makes a legitimate democratic government is consent to the constitutional system, which provides the basic political organization of society, lays down basic rules and procedures, defines the most important and permanent offices, and determines how power is to be allocated and legally checked.

Thus the Preamble to the Constitution of the United States makes fully explicit the dependence of this basic law upon consent, and also makes clear the locus and the effect of this consent: "We the People of the United States . . . do ordain and establish this Constitution for the United States of America."[2]

Second, the consent of the people to a constitution which gives a government legitimacy—that is, moral authority—cannot arise from the mere fact that people do accept it; the acceptance also must have a certain moral quality. An agreement such as a mere social contract, adopted under a threat of one sort or another, could determine what a group of people will do together. But such an agreement of itself could not give legitimacy to the government and its laws. One cannot derive an "ought" from an "is." The mere fact of consent, if it is a fact without some inherent moral force, would not turn power into just power, into authority.

Consent given by someone who is not competent, by someone acting on the basis of ignorance or error concerning what is being approved, or by someone acting under psychological coercion is valueless. Such consent provides no moral basis for government. Moreover, if one consents to something to which one ought not to consent—for example, to do something wrong in itself—the consent, even if wholly voluntary, gives no color of morality to what is effected. So the consent which gives legitimacy to government is only such personal compliance as members of the society ought to give and do voluntarily give.

Many people comply with the demands of the law because they fear punishment. And many people accept a constitutional arrangement because they want for themselves protection of certain goods, such as life, liberty, and what Jefferson called "the pursuit of happiness." (This latter can be understood, in accord with the dictum that happiness means different things to different people, as the doing of those things by any individual which that individual considers to be inherently worthwhile.) People want protection of these goods against the behavior of others—other people in the society and other powers outside it—which would render them insecure. In other words, many people accept a constitutional arrangement because they do not want to be killed, raped, enslaved, beaten, deprived of their possessions, and so on.

The vulnerability of most persons, even of those who are personally very strong, to harm by other individuals or groups, together with the limits of the ability of the strong to protect those for whom they care, makes clear why most people do consent to a constitution. Almost any government is better than none at all. But these facts do not show that people ought to consent. And, as we have argued, legitimacy does not depend on the fact alone, but only on the fact of consent together with its quality as a morally justified act.

The moral justification for consent begins to appear if one notices that there is nothing irresponsible or arbitrary in the concern of people for basic goods such as life, liberty, and the pursuit of happiness. Security in such goods is no mere subjective demand. It is a requirement entailed by reasonable care about them, not only as they pertain to oneself but also as they can be shared in by others—including in "others" both those for whom one specially cares, as one's family and friends, and also those for whom one has no more but also no less than the respect for any fellow human being from whom one would wish a like respect towards oneself.

Thus as soon as the focus shifts from the fact that people want certain things to the inherent goodness of some of the things which are wanted, the claims of reasonableness come into play. Concern for the basic goods is a response to their inherent appeal. Thus, the concerned person can give a justification for his or her concern; consent to government is not a brute fact. "Why do you consent to a constitution?" Not merely "Because I *want* protection," but "Because my responsibility for my own life and other goods, and for the security of others for whom I care, demands that I obtain protection."

If consent is justified in this way, the principle of one's concern extends to all others who can enjoy these goods and who need security in them. Human life and the other basic goods are no less exigent in whomever they happen to be at stake than they are in oneself and in those to whom one is specially attached. This is the point we meant to suggest by saying that reasonable care about goods must extend to those whom one merely recognizes as fellows in the community of mutual human respect for the dignity which attaches to every person as such.

Thus, justified consent which provides the basis for legitimate government arises not merely from a coincidence of individuals' concerns about their own security and welfare (and that of those dear to them) but also from a truly common concern about goods recognized as having an inherent and common appeal to reasonable persons.

From the vantage point of this insight it is clear that the idea of fundamental rights and the idea that one's consent is necessary for the legitimacy of government are closely related. One *ought* to consent to government because it is more than a device for getting what one wants, more even than a common facility by which all living in a certain place can obtain together what they want individually. Government is required to secure rights. Rights are grounded in goods of persons which are prior to their merely factual desires— "prior" in the sense that the goods make the desires reasonable as well as stimulate them psychologically.

These goods deserve to be recognized, appreciated, respected, and promoted whether people are disposed to do so or not. Of course, all who are sane are disposed to do so when it comes to themselves, and to those for whom they specially care. But hardly anyone is consistently disposed to do so when it comes to others, to strangers or competitors. Then the inherent and common appeal to reasonable persons of life, liberty, and the pursuit of happiness takes on the exigence of a duty demanding respect for a right. Hence, the Declaration of Independence does not say that everyone *wants* security in life, liberty, and the pursuit of happiness. This factual premiss would be inadequate for the argument. The Declaration asserts that every person is endowed with an unalienable *right* to these goods.

The introduction of a normative element into the definition of the consent which is required for the legitimacy of government implies that there can be constitutions which deserve consent and those which do not deserve it, constitutions which make a moral claim and those which fall short of making a claim or which make only a false claim to the moral approval of the people. It is clear that people can either consent or refuse consent to a constitution of either sort. Thus, there are four possible situations. There are constitutions worthy of consent which receive it; those worthy of consent which do not recieve it; those unworthy of consent which nevertheless receive it; and those unworthy of consent which do not receive it.

In our view it is only in the first of these cases that there is a morally legitimate government which is established by the constitution in respect to those people who do consent to it. This situation alone determines a central, paradigmatic sense for "government," "political authority," "law," and "rule of law." All of these expressions, of course, are used in ordinary language of regimes which fall short of morally legitimate government. But the American proposition is that valid laws must meet the test of constitutionality, and that the constitution must be such that it deserves and receives the consent of the governed, which alone gives government legitimacy.

The second and the third possibilities raise interesting questions. One can imagine an instance in which very difficult circumstances limit the possibilities of effective government. A strong but benevolent group takes control, perhaps in the wake of some man-made or natural disaster, and establishes a rudimentary but just regime. In the circumstances people ought to consent. But perhaps many do not. In such a case power is exercised justly by the ruling group, and those who oppose the regime will be in the wrong. Yet in the absence of consent this arrangement which deserves consent falls short of the status of legitimate government. There is not yet a political society, for those who are ruled do not consider themselves in community with those who exercise power, though power is exercised justly and for good purposes.

Again, and more easily, one can imagine a regime which does not deserve consent. There seems to have been very widespread consent to the Nazi regime in Germany, not only in the early stages when Hitler was careful to preserve the formalities of constitutional rule but even in the later stages when many people realized that the regime was thoroughly criminal. The immoral ideology and systematically unjust practices of the Nazis destroyed the legitimacy of their regime, which no longer preserved the rights for which governments are instituted among men. Yet the consent of the governed continued to be given, and the Nazi regime derived power—although not just powers—from this support.

The case of a constitution which is unworthy of consent and which does not receive it can be illustrated—if we accept the argument of the Declaration of Independence—by the regime of the British Crown over the American colonies which revolted. The king had been a legitimate ruler, but his own lawlessness and disregard for rights destroyed his legitimacy. The colonists had consented to British rule, they then withdrew their consent. The bonds were dissolved and a new set of politically independent states formed, to be governed internally by their own constitutions and in respect to one another and other nations by their federal constitution.

The introduction of a normative aspect into the consent which is required to make government legitimate raises at once the third of the questions we listed above: Whose consent is necessary? In any society there are two classes of people who are not likely to consent to a just constitution insofar as it is such.

First, there are those who are not competent for such a voluntary act: children, the severely retarded, and so on. These present no serious problem for a theory of legitimate government. They can be treated as if they were citizens in the fullest sense by an extension to them of the rights and duties of which they are capable, but government acts toward them in a quasi-parental fashion rather than in a fully political fashion.

Second, there are those who are competent to consent but who do not choose to consent, even though the constitution is just. Such persons usually will acquiesce in the operation of the constitution and comply to a great extent with the laws. But they do so out of self-interest. They do not respect law; they do not distinguish between just power and mere force.

The question is: Does a government lack legitimacy because it does not have the consent of such persons? In our view the lack of the moral support of those who care little or nothing about morality in no way detracts from the legitimacy of government. It is the consent of those, the upright, who care about justice and are interested in the issue of the government's legitimacy which is decisive. In the fullest sense only they are governed by laws; only they are directed by lawful authority. Citizens whose involvement in political matters is based on self-interest rather than on justice are governed by law only in a derivative and imperfect sense. The lack of their consent is irrelevant to the moral claim of the law upon the minds and hearts of persons who are responsive to moral claims.

Morally speaking, persons who acquiesce in the operation of the constitution and conform to the laws out of mere self-interest are aliens to the political society. If they live in it with the status of citizens, they nevertheless function as if they were not committed to the rights which true citizens respect because of their response to the appeal of basic common goods, such as life, liberty, and the pursuit of happiness.

There is, finally, the question of the sort of voluntary acceptance which constitutes consent. Clearly, that sort of voluntary acceptance which is mere acquiescence and conformity out of self-interest does not constitute consent. Acceptance of an unjust regime out of morally upright concern for peace and various other human goods also is insufficient to constitute consent. There is even the possibility, already mentioned, of a benevolent dictatorship, a rudimentary but just regime which establishes order in a disaster situation; good persons might comply without having any opportunity to participate in deliberation and decision making. Here, compliance would not be consent, and no government in the full and unqualified sense would exist, although such a situation could easily unfold into a just constitution which would receive the consent it deserved from upright people.

What would be necessary to transform a benevolent despotism into a truly just government, its edicts into laws in the fullest sense? All that would be needed would be the consent of those subjects concerned about justice. One can imagine their consent being given explicitly, by some sort of referendum which approved the regime's effort, to unite all who accepted it into a political society. But such an explicit act of consent would not be necessary.

One also can imagine the regime beginning to articulate general rules, to make clear its purposes and guarantee its own self-restraint in the interests of justice. Those subject to the regime then might respond beyond the requirements of mere self-interest or moral concern about the goods directly at stake, but in accord with the need of the regime for willing cooperation with its purposes and projects. The extension of such willing cooperation would imply that one accepted the regime as such, and wished to consolidate and develop it. This implication in the acts of upright people agreeing with the regime's purposes would constitute consent to it.

Obviously, if the regime were able to provide possibilities for specifically political acts, such as voting for representatives who would make laws, then participation in the political process by upright persons who viewed their participation as cooperation, not merely as action required by the objective situation to minimize evils, would constitute consent.

However consent was given, once it was given, the regime would become a legitimate government in respect to those who consented. For others in its territory it would function in some ways as a government, but the full character of lawful authority would not be present, even though it might exercise power toward others than its full members—including children, aliens, citizens uninterested in justice, and upright citizens who had not yet had occasion or opportunity to do anything which would constitute consent.

If consent is to be taken seriously, there always must be assumed a possibility of nonconsent. Usually consent theories of legitimate government suggest two possibilities of nonconsent. First, even if one is a citizen by birth in a certain nation, most people are free to emigrate, and thus can remove themselves from the jurisdiction of their native land. Immigrating into a country—assuming one is concerned about legitimacy and accepts one's new homeland for the sake of its just constitution—certainly would imply consent. Not emigrating when one might—with the same assumptions—also would imply consent. Second, people can rebel or can initiate the first steps toward rebellion. In the context in which the Declaration of Independence was written, the

alternatives of consent and refusal of consent were clearly marked, to separate the loyalists from the revolutionaries who founded the American nation.

But the preceding analysis of consent makes clear that there is a subtler
alternative which can distinguish consent from nonconsent. When morally
upright persons—the sort of persons who are concerned about the legitimacy
of government—face the laws, they have a choice between regarding them as
a set of facts which must be taken into account prudently and regarding them
as reasonable guides to the common political life of the society and its common purposes. If upright persons regard the laws as mere facts ignored at
peril, then they do not consent. If they formerly consented and now no longer
do so, their behavior might not change much. But they lose respect for
government and the laws; they participate, not as cooperators in a process to
which they are committed as worthwhile in itself, but as independent actors
who must live with realities from which they have become alienated. The
possibility that the acceptance of unjust laws with respect to euthanasia and
related questions would lead to this sort of withdrawal of consent on the part
of morally upright citizens of the United States is an important one we shall
consider in later chapters.

The preceding considerations about consent make clear in what sense it can
be held that the consent of the governed provides the basis for the moral
claim which is embodied in the laws.[3] Moreover, these considerations show
that governments are legitimate—they derive their just powers and exercise
authority which is quite distinct from mere force—only if they receive consent from the relevant persons and in the relevant way.

The main objections normally proposed against consent theories can be
briefly indicated and answered.

First, consent is said to be a fiction, since no explicit contract ever is made.
Our reply is that consent can be and often is implicit in cooperation with a
regime when cooperation goes beyond necessity—beyond dealing with the
reality of government power or the acceptance of an unavoidably bad situation—and amounts to moral recognition of the government as legitimate.

Second, mere acquiescence is obviously possible without moral significance, since people can acquiesce from motives of self-interest or to minimize
evil without making any commitment to cooperate. We agree. Not all acquiescence constitutes implicit consent. But, as we have explained, certain kinds
of action which involve acquiescence do imply that consent which gives
government legitimacy.

Third, consent is impossible unless there are real alternatives, and it is
argued that often there are none. We deny that there are no alternatives to
consent. The possibility of acquiescence without commitment to the regime is
the most important of these and always available to the people. Released
from a moral bond to the laws as such, people in this situation might still

conform, but they will do so on principles other than those of the law-abiding citizen who considers the government legitimate.

Fourth, consent is never unanimous. This is admitted. A government which in some ways is one and the same thing with respect to all subject to its jurisdiction is morally different things to different people. If it is a just government for some who do consent to it, it also can be a just substitute parent for some incompetent to give consent or to refuse consent, a just host for some who are guests, a just enemy for some who are outlaws, and so on.

It is clear, of course, that there might be many just constitutional arrangements to which people have consented and do consent. For our present purposes, however, it is necessary to consider only one type of constitutional arrangement: that of the United States and of polities similar to it. Our next question, then, is: To what do Americans consent, and how do they justify their consent?

C. The Common Good

In what we have said thus far, little has been said about the coercive power of the state. Yet as a matter of fact, every political society uses force to back up its regime, whether or not this regime is a legitimate government. So much is this the case that—as we mentioned above—a monopoly on coercive power is often considered to be the defining characteristic of the state. On our account this characteristic is less important.

Yet it is not insignificant. Governments are instituted to protect unalienable rights—life, liberty, and the pursuit of happiness. In a world in which there always are domestic outlaws and foreign enemies prepared to violate these rights, an important function of the state is to protect them not only by the rule of law but also by force. If government is legitimate, force is used lawfully in the service of justice. It is certainly part of the American proposition that it is the business of government to establish justice and to provide for the common defense, by using proportionate force when necessary to protect rights against outlaws and enemies.

But it also is clear that there is consent to government for the sake of promoting and protecting a wider range of goods than those which fall within the narrow boundaries of security. The phrasing of the Declaration which refers to a right to the "pursuit of happiness"—a positive if personalized set of goods and activities—already suggests this. And the Preamble to the Constitution mentions the promotion of the general welfare as one of the purposes for which the fundamental law is established.

Some have held that it is unjust to use governmental authority beyond the minimum ends of guaranteeing peace and security, law and order—protecting life, bodily integrity, physical liberty, and property. But no such suggestion ever has been seriously entertained by the American people or by the people of any other modern, democratic state. Indeed, the very concern for political equality which entails the demand that government be by consent of the governed also tends to generate a demand for the extension of government into those areas of social and economic relationship where exploitation of the weak by the strong is likely to occur—even without overt violence—if the state does not foster institutions more responsive to a fair sharing of human goods than to the mere satisfaction of selfish or arbitrary demands.[4]

For Americans, then, the common good or the public interest is not limited to protection against overt violence and security in possessions. Our common political purposes comprise other goals than these, and so we consent to a government with authority to promote wider purposes. These purposes are a set of goods which Americans do in fact reasonably care about and do not believe capable of being promoted effectively except by means of the apparatus of the state, under direct control of the government.

The various goods which comprise the common good include some which are considered to be inherently worthwhile by many members of the society. The protection of human life is one such good; education is another. Yet some, perhaps increasingly many, members of society consider these goods to be in themselves of merely instrumental value. There are other goods included in the common good which are universally considered merely instrumental. For example, the provision of public roads, of a system of weights and measures, of a postal service, of a monetary system, of a legal form of bequest—all these are in the purely instrumental category.

Thus, an important part of the general welfare is the facility provided by law for members of the political society to carry out their private purposes in ways which the authority of government will recognize and its power, if need be, support. Besides legal facilities for contract and bequest, civil law provides a whole apparatus for private transactions, for holding and using property, for settling private disputes peacefully and impartially, and so on. And material facilities which are provided by government to promote the general welfare are not limited to economic and fiscal ones; public hospitals also are such a facility, and even amenities such as public parks and museums are developed and maintained for the sake of the general welfare.

From the preceding considerations it is clear that the common good of American society is not made up of an invariable set of intrinsic and instrumental goods. The human condition clearly requires that considerations of security and protection against violence remain a basic purpose of political society, and therefore that the power of government be used or available for use for this purpose. Certain less fundamental purposes also are likely to remain constant: for example, provision of a monetary system. But the commitment of American society to other goods has varied in the past and can vary in the future. Our nation has been less committed than it now is to promoting health, education, and welfare; one can imagine a future in which it will be less committed to these purposes than it is at present.

However, such changes in the goods which political society pursues do not change the fundamental character of the American proposition. We did not become a new nation when the Social Security Act was passed; enactment of a thoroughgoing program of socialized medicine would not radically alter the basic law of the land. Likewise, citizens who consent to the constitution do not alter their consent each time the government concerns itself with some new area of public interest.

In short, the actual content of the common good has varied to some extent and could vary much more. Such variation does not alter the nature of the state or affect the consent which the people give to the constitutional system. This conclusion raises two questions. First, are there any limits to what might be regarded as pertaining to the common good or the public interest? Second, if the particular goods which comprise the overall purpose of the state do not themselves serve as the object of consent—that is, are not themselves that to which the people make the common commitment which knits them into a unified political society—then what is the object of consent?

The answer to the first of these questions is that there *are* some limits as to what may be rightly considered to be part of the public interest or common good—and thus part of what people consent to when they consent to the regime as just, and in this way give it the legitimacy of a government which exercises just powers with the consent of the governed.

The very notion of a *common* good or of a *public* interest suggests that there is a contrasting category of goods which are *individual* or *private*. The Declaration of Independence listed liberty as one of the goods to which men have a right, and also listed the pursuit of happiness, which can hardly be understood except in a way which leaves room for a plurality of individual life-styles and private conceptions of what is intrinsically worthwhile. The Preamble to the Constitution likewise takes as one of the fundamental purposes of government to "secure the Blessings of Liberty to ourselves and our Posterity." If all goods were included in the common good, if all interests could be absorbed within the public interest, it would be hard to make sense of such a purpose.

In the *Federalist Papers* Hamilton explained that bills of rights usually are required in a state to make clear the privileges of subjects which are not to be infringed by the ruler. He maintained that such a statement of rights really is unnecessary in a constitution founded by the people themselves, precisely ordained by them to preserve liberty.[5]

Later, Madison argued for the amendments which became the Bill of Rights of the United States Constitution, but he did not deny Hamilton's libertarian argument and its assumptions. In fact, he admitted the force of the argument against the proposed amendments that by enumerating certain rights it might seem that others were disparaged. Madison sought to obviate this difficulty by means of a provision which became the Ninth Amendment: "The enumeration in the Constitution, of certain rights, shall not be construed to deny or disparage others retained by the people."[6]

The most notable example of the exclusion of certain purposes from the concerns of government, whereby these purposes are reserved in the domain of liberty for individual pursuit and for cooperative pursuit in nonpolitical, voluntary associations, is in the First Amendment: "Congress shall make no law respecting an establishment of religion, or prohibiting the free exercise thereof. . . . " While this protection of liberty originally applied only to the federal government, not to the States, it has been extended to the latter, and this exemplifies well the concern of Americans that their government be limited.

Reflection upon reasons for excluding religion from the domain of governmental concerns will suggest why the public interest must be limited, not only in this but in other matters as well.[7] We noted above that the common good includes goods which the political society as such can *effectively* pursue; religion clearly is not one of these. Experience had shown that the coercive power of government cannot effectively promote sincere religious faith, and that attempts to promote religion by state action lead to formalism as well as to strife, rather than to piety together with peace and security for all.

Furthermore, religion seems to be one of those goods which is inherently suited to pursuit by private, fully voluntary associations rather than by public institutions. The privilege of pursuing one's own ultimate destiny in one's own way, immune from public interference, seems to be a central element in each person's pursuit of happiness. Governmental interference in this area is regarded by Americans as an unjust infringement upon a basic zone of liberty.

It should be noted that some Americans favor what is said in the First Amendment about religion because it is a necessary implication of their own religious beliefs or disbeliefs. For example, some religious persons hold that religion is so much a personal and private affair, an encounter between the individual conscience and God, that no human agent can be anything but an obstruction. They thus reject government involvement because they reject anything like an institutional church. Some nonreligious persons hold that religion is so pernicious that the government must keep clear of it, or so much a matter of mere subjective feelings that there is no rational way to deliberate and decide about it—that anyone's religion is fine for him or her. On this basis, such people give their own theological—or should we say, "atheological"?—twist to the First Amendment.

Those who personally hold such beliefs and disbeliefs are, of course, entitled as Americans to do so, and they are free to favor the American system for their own religious reasons. But to insist upon any such reason as the necessary significance of the First Amendment would be, paradoxically, to read into it precisely the establishment of religion which it was intended to forbid. And any consistent juridical interpretation of the First Amendment in accord with the perspective of one or another specific theology or atheology would certainly lead to decisions which would inhibit the free exercise of alternative forms of belief, which the First Amendment was intended to protect.

Thus a nontheological—and nonatheological—understanding of the limitation placed upon government by the First Amendment is essential if it is to fulfill its own purpose consistently. The principle underlying American respect for freedom of religion is a very general one, a principle very basic to the American conception of political life. The principle can be stated as follows. The public interest extends only to those goods the cooperative pursuit of which gives political society the unity which it has. Since the common pursuit of goods in political society does not encompass all the goods which men and women can pursue and wish to pursue, there is a wide sphere of individual and social activity which lies outside political society, and thus outside the legitimate concern of government and direct regulation by law.

The exclusion of religion from the concerns of government both in the beginning and today is sufficiently explained and justified by the fact that many people who are ready to share in American political society reject religious faith, and many hold diverse faiths which cannot be rendered compatible without unacceptable compromise. Moreover, cooperation in political society for other purposes is possible—as proved by the American experience—without religious unity. Thus, government based upon consent cannot infringe upon religious liberty. Analogous arguments will make clear why there are other fundamental liberties which Americans consider nearly as inviolable as freedom of religion.

It follows from the preceding argument that it is a serious mistake to regard the public interest as the sum of all the private interests of those who make up the political society, the common good as the sum of all the individual goods of the members of the community. Private interests and individual goods account for diversity within American society. Such interests distinguish a variety of life-styles without necessarily throwing them into opposition with one another, that is, without making them political opponents and compelling them to organize political parties on religious or ideological lines.

Thus, by its very nature the public interest or the common good does not embrace all the goods pursued by members of the political society. It embraces only those goods to which they have a common commitment precisely insofar as they are all citizens of the same nation, members of the American polity.

Any attempt to extend the public interest or the common good to include activities which are properly private would lead to an unjust governmental infringement upon the liberty of members of the political society. This injustice is one which would never be consented to by upright members of any political society; it is one which Americans do not consent to.

In this way we reach the answer to the first of the questions posed above: Are there any limits to what may rightly be regarded as pertaining to the public interest or the common good? There are limits. The limits ultimately are drawn by the principle that all members of the political society should at all times be at liberty in all areas of life concerned with purposes which are not effectively pursued through the common activities of the political society. There will of course be dispute about the application of this principle. But where it applies, violation of it always will be gravely unjust and will detract from the legitimacy of government, which extends no further than the consent of the governed.

These same principles—liberty and justice—provide the basis for answering the second of the questions posed above: What is the object of consent—to what is it that Americans commit themselves together in a way which forges them into a single polity?

Since the particular goods which comprise the public interest are variable, it is the justice of the constitutional framework itself to which the members of a political society based upon consent of the governed primarily give their consent. Moreover, this very quality of the constitutional framework—the justice which alone makes it worthy of consent—demands that the liberty of the members of the political society be respected. To understand the thesis that according to the American proposition liberty and justice are the basic principles of legitimate government, we now consider the nature of liberty and justice, and the relationship between them.

D. Justice as the Chief Common Good

The conception of justice which is relevant here is justice as fairness. As we noted above, the reasonableness of pursuing common objectives by public means and governmental authority requires that the benefits of the pursuit be fairly distributed, and that the burdens of the effort also be fairly allocated. The normative element in the consent of the governed is based upon the distinction between merely wanting certain goods such as security and respecting these as goods which are as exigent for others—whom one merely regards as fellow humans with the respect one wishes from them—as for oneself and those close to oneself. Thus, laws get moral force from the common good only if they articulate a system of cooperation which, besides being effective, also is a fair system. Government may not pursue the common good by every expedient means, even by destroying some members of the polity for the sake of greater benefits to others. Such an approach would be unfair.[8]

This point, of course, raises the question what "fairness" means. It is tempting to suggest that "fairness" means "sameness" in the sense that all should be treated alike. But treating everyone the same would, if taken in all strictness, destroy the order of society in which different persons with different needs, abilities, tasks, contributions, merits, and risks cooperate together in one effort precisely by making the most of their diversity and complementing one another's limitations. The very differences among people are not negligible from the point of view of justice; it belongs to equal dignity that individual characteristics be appreciated and respected. This appreciation and respect is a most important part of the American proposition. It distinguishes the ideal of American polity from that of any society which loves liberty less than a form of equality which demands uniformity and conformity and forgoes the uniqueness of individuals for the sake of an egalitarian ideal of justice.

Thus, like "sameness," "equality" also is too easily assumed to be a helpful notion in understanding fairness. Actually, in political society the quantitative implications of equality generally are irrelevant. When the concept suggests anything very definite, it is likely to suggest something which is an impossible goal and a questionable ideal.[9] Of course, Jefferson assumes the principle that all men are created equal in the Declaration, but this principle must be understood as the exclusion of *inequality*—the inequality which obtains in a polity in which the constitution assumes natural castes, so that some are naturally rulers and others naturally subjects.

The concept of fairness which determines the consent of Americans to their basic law, the constitutional framework, can be clarified by considering a small private association or club. In such an association—assuming it to be voluntary at least in the way in which consent of the governed must be voluntary—it is easy to see what would be fair. Even if such an association were organized for immoral purposes, one could see that some ways of organizing it would be fair and others unfair to the members. Such a club will have its constitution and rules, even if these are not expressly formulated and written down. If these rules and procedures were understood, one would be able to tell at once whether the club was fair or unfair.

Would one who shared the commitment to the common purpose around which the organization was formed be willing to belong to it, accepting whatever role and responsibilities in it for which one was fitted? Would one be willing to have someone for whom one cared deeply—such as one's dear child—cooperate in the club (assuming there to be no objection to its purpose), accepting any position in it, abiding by its rules, dealt with by its procedures, to the extent of the reach of its constituting purpose? Considering the organization coolly and as a nonparticipant, would one who came to know and sympathize with each member be content with that member's lot in the club? If the answer to these questions is affirmative, the association has a fair constitution. But if the answer is negative, then the organization in some way lacks basic fairness.

Thus the fairness of a constitution means that the procedures and the rules and the limits of political society are such that reasonable participants would not feel exploited if they were in any role in the society, and they would be willing to have others with whom they identified by ties of affection or sympathy in any role in it. By "reasonable participant" here we mean one who is genuinely concerned about the common good—not one who uses the political process without commitment to the common purpose of political society. A reasonable participant, thus, is one who is neither motivated merely by self-interest nor by laudable desire to minimize evil in a bad situation, one whose motive is the intent of the goods embraced within the public interest, the disinterested intent which does to others as one would be done by, and which thus is able to confer authority and form community with all those who agree in working for and seeking to enjoy together these same goods.[10]

Another way of articulating the point we have just made is that the fairness which constitutes a political society in justice is no more and no less than equality in human dignity and mutual respect which is dictated by the golden rule or principle of universalizability. The difference between particular acts of individuals shaped by this moral principle and the justice of a constitution is that the latter systematically institutionalizes the principle, and thus presents an embodiment of it which can itself be understood as a good which is promoted, respected, shared, and enjoyed by the members of a polity who find their political association not merely useful but inherently good, personally fulfilling, gratifying to their personal need for harmony between their individual identities and social solidarity.

From the vantage point of this account of justice as fairness, one can understand and appreciate both the force and the limitations of other more specific principles which often are proposed in an attempt to define the demands of justice.

Does fairness demand that in an ongoing process of interpersonal relationship between two or more persons the interrelationship be equalized so that the benefits and burdens, the advantages and disadvantages, to each participant balance out? Often this is the case, for in many relationships, such as those involving contracts and torts, only such a balance provides a rule which reasonable persons will accept for themselves and so seek to impose on others. But in other relationships, such as the care provided by the strong and healthy for the weak and sickly, such equalization is out of the question and is not demanded by justice, since one would wish oneself, one's dear child, or any person for whom one felt sympathy to receive at least some support and assistance which could never be balanced by an equal repayment.

Does fairness then demand that each member of society contribute according to capacity and receive according to need? Again, especially when one thinks of the basic necessities of life and provision for them, fairness does seem to require equality defined by proportionality to principles of capacity and need. Yet there must be limits to the demand for contribution according to capacity or there will be nothing of an individual's own which can be used with liberty for the pursuit of happiness. And needs which go beyond the basic necessities, needs which are generated by the self-indulgence and self-destructiveness of some members of society, needs which are artificially created—the need for the latest toys—are needs that cannot expect the same respect as needs for minimally adequate diet, basic health care, shelter, clothing, elementary education, and the like.

Does fairness demand that members of the political society who contribute more than others to its well-being receive proportionately in recompense? Up to a point, certainly. Veterans programs for those who have risked their lives in a shooting war are seldom criticized. Yet perhaps certain civil officers contribute more than other citizens to the well-being of political society by making considerable personal sacrifices to enter and remain in public service. Still, it is not necessarily unjust if such persons are not rewarded as well for services rendered as the presidents of many large corporations or even as some star athletes.

Finally, in the allocation of the costs and losses of the common pursuit of political society some members foresee and accept avoidable risks for the sake of the common good, while other members have no opportunity to foresee and avoid (or at least insure against) these risks. Does fairness demand recognition of this willingness to contribute and to serve? In many cases an affirmative answer no doubt is indicated; those who volunteer for extremely hazardous duty in wartime, for instance, deserve something from their compatriots that others do not. Yet this principle cannot, any more than the others, be elevated into an absolute criterion of justice. Often members of society do not foresee risks only because they lack intelligence or information. If such persons accept the responsibilities which fall to them, they seem hardly less deserving than those who make similar contributions with greater foresight, which would have permitted them to avoid the risks they accept with greater voluntariness.

In short, a reasonable participant in political society, considering its basic law in the light of the moral principle of the golden rule (or universalizability principle), will sometimes think in terms of one, sometimes in terms of another, criterion in specifying just balance or proportion. And the selection and application of these specifying criteria, as well as their mutual limitation, is a work solely for the fair-mindedness of a person who respects others with the respect he or she wishes from them. Such a person also is prepared to give a public account of judgments in terms which will deserve and can be expected to receive approval as reasonable by other reasonable participants in the society.

If one understands fairness as we have explained it, one can readily understand why fairness often demands procedures which limit the government's effort to maintain law and order. Limitations on search and seizure, the requirement that a person be indicted, and the conduct of a trial with many protections for the accused (who is presumed innocent until proven guilty)—these provisions do not make for maximum efficiency in the processes of criminal justice. They do not promote law and order if this is understood merely as a state of affairs providing the maximum level of security for almost all citizens. But these protections contribute greatly to the fairness of criminal procedure. In this way they contribute to law and order insofar as this good is understood as an aspect of justice, as part of the object of the reasonable consent which gives government legitimacy and makes the legal process an exercise of lawful authority rather than of mere repressive power.[11]

Fairness in legal procedure and in the administrative procedure of government is essential, but it does not by itself constitute the fairness which legitimates just laws. Within limits, at least, one can imagine laws unfair as to their substantive provisions fairly administered and enforced. Thus, the laws themselves also must be fair. The purpose of any particular law—the mischief it is to remedy or the good it is to promote—dictates what classifications of persons may be made without arbitrary discrimination by which some are benefited or burdened unfairly in comparison with other members of the society. And, of course, if a law is to be fair, its very purpose cannot be discriminatory.[12]

Fairness in the laws themselves is part, at least, of what is meant by "the equal protection of the laws." If this phrase is considered not only as a legal standard to be applied by judges but also as a political standard to be respected by responsible legislators, equal protection also demands that the variety of projects undertaken by political society and the level of public commitment to various projects mandated by government power reach a balance which will be generally acceptable to reasonable participants in the society.

No single project undertaken by government makes equal demands or provides equal benefits to all. But a fair political process, with checks and balances working properly, limiting the power of majorities and the great influence of powerful minorities, should result in a mix of public activities satis-factory enough that reasonable participants in all the various roles in the society will find the whole package satisfactory. None will feel singled out for extraordinary burdens or ignored in the distribution of benefits, at least not in the long run, in a manner which would amount to being "picked on"— unfairly treated in comparison with society's "pets."

E. The Relationship between Justice and Liberty

But even the addition of the fairness required by equal protection of the laws to the fairness required by due process is not enough for the fairness needed to justify the laws of a polity which is based upon the consent of the governed. Another condition is necessary. As we have noted above, it is an injustice if government injects itself into matters which lie outside the common good. Such infringement is an unfair violation of the liberty of members of the polity. On this basis, the Fourteenth Amendment to the Constitution of the United States forbids every state to "make or enforce any law which shall abridge the privileges or immunities of citizens of the United States."[13] And the Ninth Amendment, as we have already mentioned, recognizes the rights retained by the people, the zone of liberty which lies outside the common good.

This aspect of constitutional fairness has several important implications in addition to the proscription of treating as public those matters which are properly private.

The first of these implications is that a fair regard for the liberty of persons forbids government to coerce citizens into cooperating in programs not essen-tial to the common good which they sincerely and reasonably believe to be seriously wrong.

We have inserted "not essential to the common good" in the preceding sentence because there are cases in which conscientious objections of some citizens must be overridden to prevent unjust harm to what all agree to be included in the common good. For example, defensive wars must be fought despite the objections of pacifists, and their participation cannot be altogether avoided to the extent that they remain members of the society whose re-sources and institutions are being employed for purposes which they deplore.

But when there is no such overriding public necessity, the liberty of citi-zens is at stake if the government embarks upon projects which offend the consciences of citizens. They should be able to remain good citizens without having infringed their liberty to stand aloof from what they detest as evil, and they cannot stand aloof if government wantonly disregards their misgivings, since these limit their consent, while they are drawn along willy-nilly with public policies and acts which they deplore.

A second implication of the libertarian aspect of the requirements for justice is that unless it is essential for the common good, government should not try to prevent citizens from doing those things which they regard as transcendently important. For example, deeply held conscientious convictions about what is ultimately true and good often are believed to carry with them an obligation to communicate these beliefs to others. On this basis, it seems to us, the First Amendment is sound in closely linking freedom of religion with liberty of speech and of the press, with the right to assemble peacefully and to petition for the redress of grievances. All of these guarantees protect the rights of conscience insofar as conscience is not only a standard of private morality for one's individual life but also a standard of one's personally responsible participation in various relationships with others, including the relationships of political society.

It also is worth noticing that respect for liberty of conscience is important for the effectiveness of a free polity. When many participants in a society regard themselves as conscience bound to do certain things, especially to communicate their deeply held convictions to others even at a grave risk to their own peace and security, then any attempt by governmental power to prevent such communication is likely to be self-defeating. While the liberties which are guaranteed by the First Amendment sometimes appear in the short run to have a disturbing effect upon American society, on the whole and in the long run respect for these liberties not only contributes very importantly to justice but also promotes stability in a practical way, by avoiding the unstabilizing effects of conscientiously motivated subversive activities.

A few additional remarks will help to clarify the relationship between justice and liberty.

First, it is not only the case that liberty must be protected by just laws; it also is the case that the formation and functioning of political society itself is a most important exercise of the liberty of its members. The consent of the members of the polity to the constitutional framework, their acceptance of particular laws, their participation in the political process by voting and accepting office, by protest and petition, and so on—all these are exercises of liberty. The real participation of citizens in the political process as an exercise of liberty gives meaning to the formulation of Lincoln that American government not only is of the people (as is any government) and for the people (as is any just government) but also is by the people.

Nevertheless, although justice and liberty mutually depend upon one another, they are not identical. Indeed, they are quite distinct.

Justice is an attribute of the polity insofar as it is a unity organized by its constitution, laws, and procedures, a unity formed by common consent in response to the common demand of the common good. Justice characterizes the single social order primarily and all its parts and aspects secondarily and derivatively insofar as the political order of society is founded upon the moral principle of universalizability—which dictates equal dignity and mutual respect—and not on mere power.

Liberty is a relation of individuals and groups within political society insofar as they are not *subject to* lawful authority. Liberty exercised for the common good becomes the working of political society, the activity of the people as governing rather than as governed. Liberty to act or to refrain from acting for other purposes is the scope for personal and social flourishing which is privileged against the demands of political society and immune from the coercive sanctions which government legitimately uses to protect justice when it is at stake.

F. Liberty and Justice as a Sufficient Standard

We believe that the foregoing discussion makes clear that justice—including fair respect for liberty—is the one component of the common good which is necessary and constant. Therefore, justice and liberty included in it together provide the standard by which the legitimacy of laws and proposed laws ought to be evaluated. Moreover, considering the diversity of deeply held positions on the questions to be dealt with in this book, we think that this standard is the only one which all parties to current debates must accept if they wish to argue as Americans committed to the American proposition.

The exclusive use by us of this standard to evaluate laws and proposed laws is likely to provoke objections from two quarters. First, some will deny that even these standards provide a moral basis for laws. Second, there will be those—including some who join in making the first objection—who will require either a different standard or a more ample one for evaluating laws.

Those who make the first objection might argue as follows. The preceding account of the standards which good laws must meet rests too heavily upon moral conceptions which may have been widely accepted two centuries ago but which no longer are supported by the consensus of the American people. The Declaration of Independence, in mentioning "unalienable rights," invoked a whole theory of natural law which today is widely rejected. Certain facts of the human constitution and condition which are contingent but not alterable by human effort do assure that people will seek peace and security. The interplay of diverse desires and the balancing of the pressures of special-interest groups do assure that most people will be patient with the workings of the contemporary welfare state. But facts such as these do not show that government has a moral basis in natural rights, rights which belong to all individuals antecedent to the rights which are bestowed by the law itself.[14]

In chapter eleven of this book we shall articulate a moral theory which stands on its own without the historical support of traditional theories of natural law, and which also can deal with the criticisms made against all of the more popular current theories of ethics. Having articulated this theory, we shall in chapter thirteen provide a properly ethical defense of the standard of good law which we have proposed.

But a brief response to the objection is appropriate here. To deny that liberty is a good which makes a moral demand is to admit that slavery might be morally acceptable—a proposition no one dares or seems even inclined to defend today. To deny that justice is a good which makes a moral demand is to admit that discrimination without basis in any difference which would be considered relevant by reasonable participants in the society could be morally acceptable—another proposition no one dares or seems even inclined to defend today. If the rights of people not to be enslaved and not to be discriminated against are rights which government ought to recognize and defend whether it does so or not, if these are rights not bestowed by any government but only recognized and enforced by some governments—those which are just—then there are natural rights, and all forms of legal positivism are gravely mistaken.

There is further reason why liberty must be admitted to make a moral demand. As we noted already, it is an injustice for the state to infringe upon legitimate liberties. This supposes that liberty is a great good, and indeed it is. Individuality and nonpolitical community are important goods which presuppose liberty—the scope for private action respected and defended by a just government. Autonomy ought to be respected sufficiently to allow a wide range of opportunity for private initiative.[15]

This is not to say, of course, that all who favor liberty do so out of regard for these goods. Some simply wish to be allowed to do as they please, whether for moral or immoral reasons. But the fact that people sometimes accept government for nonmoral or immoral reasons does not impugn the moral quality of the principle upon which government deserves consent. Such persons are not relevant in determining the moral legitimacy of government. Nevertheless, many people do seek to promote and protect liberty for all; they appreciate liberty as a good which always deserves concern and respect, whether that liberty is exercised by those with whom one agrees or not. All who take this attitude do treat liberty as a moral principle of law, and in so doing belie their own theoretical disclaimers of natural law and natural rights.

We turn now to the second objection: that some alternative or more ample standard than liberty and justice is required to evaluate laws and proposed laws. We already noted at the beginning of this chapter that there are many standards good laws must meet having to do with their workability as part of a legal system which does the job which law should do in guiding cooperation among members of the polity. These standards are not in question here; they are essentially noncontroversial. What is at issue here are suggestions of substantively different or supplementary standards for good law.

Of course, there is one other widely invoked standard which is quite distinct from the one we propose. It is the utilitarian standard of the "greatest good of the greatest number." Many who propose laws with respect to the matters considered in this book explicitly or implicitly appeal to this standard.[16] We shall scrutinize this standard from the perspective of ethical theory in chapters eleven and thirteen. In the latter chapter we shall show that utilitarianism does not and cannot account for the concern for liberty and justice for all which is fundamental to the American proposition. We shall show that utilitarianism leads to a merging of the public and the private; moreover, it cannot work as a public philosophy without imposing the moral beliefs of some upon others who regard such beliefs as false and their practical implications as thoroughly abhorrent. Utilitarianism, although accepted by many people today, is far from being a philosophy to which the American people as a whole have consented.

The objection that a more ample moral standard than liberty and justice is required to judge laws and proposed laws is a more serious one. Many people will object: Fundamental human goods such as human life itself are the foundation of both private morality and of the morality of law. Both individuals and societies, including political society and its government, ought to respect and promote these goods. In particular, government ought to protect life, for its protection is part of the basic purpose of any polity. Thus, it will be argued, moral respect for life by the political society is demanded, as the phrases "right to life" and "sanctity of life" suggest. Life, considered from this perspective, seems to be a direct, immediate, and absolutely essential part of the common good. How, then, can a standard for judging the adequacy of laws and proposed laws with respect to euthanasia and related questions neglect to focus upon this obviously relevant good?

We feel the force of this objection and well understand the insight of those who will make it. Nevertheless, we believe that there are several reasons why the good of human life should not be invoked as the standard for evaluating the laws and proposed laws to be discussed in chapters three through ten.

First, we admit that the protection of life is an important part of the common good. Nevertheless, it is not clear to us that the protection of life to which all upright people consent is proposed as part of the common good of political society precisely insofar as human life is a basic good of persons—that is, insofar as human life has sanctity. Many who are concerned to protect human life regard it as a most important instrumental value, not as an inherent good of persons which has the status of an absolute principle of morality. As we shall show in chapter eleven, section H, we consider this instrumentalist view mistaken. But we think it would violate the liberty of those who believe this proposition to demand that they accept the inherent goodness of human life as a direct, immediate, and essential part of the common good.

Second, we are convinced that almost everyone who is not already firmly opposed to euthanasia would regard as question begging the appeal to the good of human life as to a basic principle by which to settle the jurisprudential issues to be discussed in this book. If people can reasonably dissent from the position that the sanctity of life is an intrinsic component of the common good of political society, the charge of question begging would be justified. If those who would defend human life most effectively wish to show that there are arguments which are not question begging for their position, these arguments must be cogent; they cannot simply assume a principle which has been called into question.

The difficulty is intensified by the fact that the value judgment which is under fire is not simply that persons have an unalienable right to life, but also that the good of human life must be included in the common good of political society in such a way that the law will respond to life as to a principle so fundamental that it will require the overriding of conflicting claims of beneficence toward the suffering and liberty of those who wish to end their own lives voluntarily. We do hold that there is an unalienable right to life. We doubt that the other disputed judgment—that life is a direct component of the common good of political society in the required way—is defensible. If it is a sound proposition, it needs to be demonstrated, and we see no way to demonstrate it.

Whether or not this disputed proposition is true, we think it would be a mistake to try to use it as a basic principle in defense of human life in the debate over euthanasia and the related questions to be considered here. We shall show that the demands of liberty and justice are such that most of the proposals which tend to infringe upon the sanctity of life must be rejected *as bad laws* by the narrower standard we have proposed. Moreover, arguments which appeal to liberty and justice alone cannot easily be ignored in American political and legal debate. This standard is one which most people in our pluralistic society do accept; when they do not consistently accept it, they can hardly plausibly deny it.

Moreover, arguments in defense of life grounded in the standard of liberty and justice for all avoid even the appearance that those who would defend life simply are trying to impose their sectarian morality upon the whole society. Avoiding this false appearance will disarm the rhetorical weapon which has been most effectively used by those who would legalize acts destructive to human life. That weapon can be rearmed and turned about: In the euthanasia debate, as we shall show, it is those who advocate killing who are trying to impose their morality on the society as a whole.

It is very urgent that the debate about euthanasia be removed from the political arena in which it appears that competing special-interest groups are iply trying to impose their contrary moral opinions upon society. If this continues to be the level at which debate is conducted, those who would defend human life surely will lose most of the battles, even if they win an occasional skirmish. Those who would legalize euthanasia fully realize this fact. They have selected the arena and the weapons which maximize the chances of their own success. If one or another morality is imposed upon American society during the next few years, the morality imposed will not be that of the inherent sanctity of life.

The use of a narrower standard for judging laws and proposed laws, then, will tend to move the debate over euthanasia into an arena in which friends of life have some chance of success. For this reason, in the chapters which follow we do not ask: What should the laws be if they are to promote human life, respect its sanctity, protect the absolute right to life? Rather we ask: What should the laws concerning euthanasia and these other issues be if they are to be compatible with the fundamental American commitment to liberty and justice for all?

G. Privacy and Liberty

In recent years American courts have been invoking a right of privacy, giving it status as a fundamental right of Americans under the United States Constitution. This right served as a principle in the Quinlan decision and in certain other decisions touching on issues with which we are concerned in this book. It is likely to be invoked in many future cases concerned with these issues. Therefore, we wish to clarify what is meant by "right of privacy" and to show how this right is related to liberty.

The right of privacy as a principle for deciding constitutional issues first emerged in the United States Supreme Court decision in *Griswold* v. *Connecticut* (1965). In this decision the Court struck down a Connecticut statute forbidding the use of contraceptives.

In his opinion for the Court, which apparently was joined unreservedly only by Justice Clark, Justice Douglas argued that specific guarantees of the Bill of Rights have penumbras, formed by emanations from these guarantees. Hence, although nothing in the Constitution says that anyone has a right to use contraceptives, the various rights of privacy guaranteed therein somehow embrace the privacy or intimacy surrounding the marriage relationship in such a way that the states are prohibited by the Constitution from treating as a crime the use of contraceptives by married couples. Since the various rights from which the right of marital privacy emanates are fundamental, state laws forbidding the use of contraceptives by the married sweep too broadly and invade an area of protected freedom.[17]

Five other members of the Court wrote or joined in opinions concurring in the result supported by the opinion of the Court, but on somewhat different reasoning.

Justice Goldberg, joined by Chief Justice Warren and Justice Brennan, emphasized that the right infringed by the Connecticut statute was that of *marital* privacy. Douglas's rationale involving penumbras and emanations is replaced in Goldberg's opinion by an appeal to the Ninth Amendment, which reserves to the people unspecified rights not mentioned in the other articles of the Bill of Rights. Goldberg asserts that the Ninth Amendment means nothing if it does not protect fundamental, personal rights. Marital privacy, he argues, is among these rights and is infringed as much by a law forbidding the use of contraceptives as it would be by one mandating that couples be sterilized after having two children.

Fundamental rights are distinguished from the general liberty of citizens. Judges are to determine which rights are fundamental by looking to the traditions and collective conscience of the people, by considering the relationship of rights under consideration to the principles of liberty and justice which underlie all of the nation's civil and political institutions, and by taking account of the bearing of particular rights upon specified constitutional guarantees and the experience of a free society. By these tests Goldberg believes marital privacy to be a fundamental right. If a less-than-fundamental aspect of personal liberty were at stake, a state would have only to show that the law which infringed upon it was reasonably related to some permissible public purpose. But in the case of a fundamental right the regulatory effort of a state could stand as constitutional only if its infringement of the right were *necessary* to serve a subordinating public interest which is *compelling*.[18]

Justices Harlan and White, in separate concurring opinions, appealed to no right to privacy; they made no use of the distinction between liberty in general and fundamental rights. They approached the issue by way of the Fourteenth Amendment's guarantees of due process and liberty. The Connecticut law forbidding the use of contraceptives simply seemed to Harlan and White too arbitrary and unreasonable to be consistent with the constitutional guarantees of the Fourteenth Amendment.[19]

Justices Black and Stewart, joining each other in dissenting opinions, opposed the majority and would have held the Connecticut statute constitutional. While they considered the law a bad, even silly, one, they did not find in it any conflict with a constitutionally guaranteed right which would render the statute unconstitutional.[20]

In 1969 the United States Supreme Court held that one could watch obscene movies in one's own home; this action is protected from unwarranted governmental intrusions into privacy.[21] This decision hardly required appeal to the new concept of privacy; it could as well have been justified by old-fashioned, hard-core privacy.

In 1972 the Court struck down a Massachusetts statute forbidding the distribution of contraceptives to unmarried persons. This decision was based upon the decision in *Griswold* together with the guarantee of equal protection of the laws. In this way the right of *marital* privacy in the earlier decision was extended:

> If the right of privacy means anything, it is the right of the *individual,* married or single, to be free from unwarranted governmental intrusion into matters so fundamentally affecting a person as the decision whether to bear or beget a child.[22]

In the 1973 *Abortion Cases* the Court relied very heavily upon the right of privacy developed in these earlier cases. Admitting that the Constitution mentions no such right, the Court nevertheless maintains that it has itself long recognized certain areas or zones of privacy. The right of privacy might be located in the Fourteenth Amendment's protection of liberty or in the Ninth Amendment's guarantee of rights not specifically mentioned. Wherever found, the right of privacy, the Court asserts, is broad enough to cover a woman's decision to have an abortion. Still, the right is not absolute; it is subject to some limitations. It would have to give way to state interests when they become dominant. These state interests include the health of the pregnant woman herself during the second one-third of pregnancy and the life of the fetus once it becomes "viable." Still, as a fundamental right, only a compelling state interest could override the right to abortion embraced within the personal right of privacy.[23]

In a concurring opinion Justice Douglas distinguishes among levels of rights. Some, he holds, are absolute; among these are the rights guaranteed by the First Amendment. Others are not absolute, yet are fundamental. They are subject to regulation for the sake of a compelling state interest. Douglas divides these other fundamental rights into two groups, placing first those to do with marriage, procreation, the raising of children, and placing at the lowest level of fundamental rights a variety of liberties including the "freedom to walk, stroll, or loaf."[24]

It is not our purpose here to criticize the decisions which we have been summarizing. Our own understanding of the American proposition is such that the decisions prior to those in the *Abortion Cases* seem to us plausible, without reference to a specific or general right of privacy, in view of the Ninth Amendment and the privileges or immunities clause of the Fourteenth Amendment (although in present constitutional law the latter clause does not have the use we would assign to it in protecting liberty). We shall discuss the *Abortion Cases* in chapter eight, section G; our criticism of the decision in these cases is based on factors other than the right of privacy invoked by the Court. Also, in section D, above, we have argued that a fair regard for liberty forbids government to compel people to act against conscience or to prevent people from doing what they consider to be transcendently important unless such compulsion or prevention is essential to the common good. This principle would serve to distinguish fundamental rights from aspects of liberty which government might reasonably restrict when such restriction is helpful, although not essential, to the pursuit of some public purpose. Thus, we can make sense of the distinction between rights which are fundamental and other liberties which are not fundamental. But our principle for making this distinction probably does not coincide exactly with the principles assumed by any of the members of the Supreme Court, who make the distinction on their own diverse, and apparently incompatible, principles.

Our present purpose is to make clear what it means if courts appeal to the right of privacy to decide cases concerning euthanasia and the related questions to be considered in this book. In our view such an appeal is less a way of grounding a conclusion than it is a way of expressing a conclusion. There is no jurisprudential tradition behind the right of privacy which would determine how to extrapolate the implications of this right to issues to which it has not already been applied. But the determination of the United States Supreme Court that there is a right of privacy and that it is in some sense fundamental makes it possible for a court which decides that some aspect of liberty ought to be protected against any but an overriding or compelling state interest to express its decision by asserting that the liberty to be protected falls within the undefined scope of the right of privacy.

Respected legal commentators—both those who are satisfied with the Court's efforts to define new constitutional protections and those who are critical of these efforts—agree in considering the new right of privacy to be no more than a certain area of liberty or autonomy.

Louis Henkin does not think that the Court has gone beyond the bounds of proper judicial innovation. But neither does he think that the Court has provided a satisfying rationale for the zone of autonomy or immunity to regulation—the area of liberty—which it refers to by "right of privacy." Henkin makes clear that this is not privacy in any traditional sense and that it is being developed on an issue by issue basis in order to extend to certain other areas of life that kind of protection which hitherto was given to the rights mentioned in the First Amendment, rights considered in some special way to be fundamental. Henkin also points out that the Court has not clarified what a *fundamental* right is, and thus is forced to assert without cogent arguments that certain liberties have this status. Finally, he notes that the Court has not made clear what makes some state interests compelling.[25]

Clearly, not every liberty can be given the same jurisprudential status as the fundamental rights of freedom of religion and freedom of speech. John Hart Ely, who would not have opposed the legalization of abortion by statute, has argued very strongly that the Supreme Court crossed the bounds of proper judicial activity in its decision in the *Abortion Cases*. After quoting a passage in which the Court points out the difficulties a woman denied abortion might experience, Ely comments:

> All of this is true and ought to be taken very seriously. But it has nothing to do with privacy in the Bill of Rights sense or any other the Constitution suggests. I suppose there is nothing to prevent one from using the word "privacy" to mean the freedom to live one's life without governmental interference. But the Court obviously does not so use the term. Nor could it, for such a right is at stake in *every* case. Our life styles are constantly limited, often seriously, by governmental regulation; and while many of us would prefer less direction, granting that desire the status of a preferred constitutional right would yield a system of "government" virtually unrecognizable to us and only slightly more recognizable to our forefathers.[26]

Ely's conclusion is that the Court is legislating rather than adjudicating; he considers this wrong. Henkin, although his attitude is different, does not disagree with Ely's description. Henkin concludes his argument that the Court has provided no rationale by which to distinguish what is and what is not covered by the right of privacy by asking the rhetorical question:

> Is it, as some suspect, that the game is being played backwards: that the private right which intuitively commends itself as valuable in our society in our time, or at least to a majority of our Justices at this time, is called fundamental, and if it cannot fit comfortably into specific constitutional provisions it is included in Privacy?[27]

Whatever one thinks of the issue about which Henkin and Ely disagree—the legitimacy of what the Court is doing—there can be little doubt as to the point on which they agree: The right of privacy is not a new discovery so much as a new creation. (It is interesting, but for our present purpose only incidental, that the weight of legal commentary seems more to favor Ely's than Henkin's side of the issue on which they disagree.[28])

It might be suggested that the Supreme Court could simply maintain consistently that there are many rights reserved by the Ninth Amendment to the people and protected against abridgment by the states by the privileges or immunities clause of the Fourteenth Amendment. This approach would have the advantage of admitting the responsibility of the Court to protect liberty in its whole breadth, regardless of the mention or lack of mention of certain rights in the Constitution. Such protection would seem, as Goldberg argued in *Griswold,* to be in line with the intent of the Ninth Amendment. Unmentioned rights hardly can be disparaged more effectively than by being denied the protection given to those which are mentioned.

However, an approach along these lines would hardly require a compelling

state interest to be at stake to justify any limitation upon any of these liberties. In other words, if the whole scope of liberty were admitted to be the
iceberg of which the new right of privacy is only the tip, then the Court would
have to admit that a criterion must be articulated for considering some rights
embraced by privacy to be *fundamental* ones, which can be overridden only
by a *compelling* state interest. If some liberties are not shown to be fundamental, then they might be overridden by interests no more compelling than
those which justify statutes requiring motorcyclists to wear helmets, funda-
mentalists to forgo snake-handling, and both sadistic and careless persons to
treat animals kindly.[29]

Our conclusion is that none of the issues which are to be discussed in this
book can be settled by appealing to a right of privacy. If one becomes convinced that liberty and justice require that the state not interfere in certain
kinds of action affecting human life, one can formulate one's *thesis* by saying
that such acts are embraced within the "right of privacy." But this formulation will be question begging if it is used in an attempt to *establish* immunity
from state interference in any particular case. No one can say what the right
of privacy might embrace, except in the conclusion of an argument showing
what liberties ought to be respected more than others or in the conclusion of
an argument showing what the Supreme Court is likely to decide.

H. Law, Liberty, and Morality

To complete our discussion of the principles for judging laws, we must say
a bit more about the relationship between law and morality. The issue about
imposing morality needs some further clarification. This clarification will
bring out further aspects of the nature of liberty.

The main proposition concerning the relationship between law and morality
is that law cannot and ought not to attempt to enforce all of morality.[30]
Several considerations show why this is so.

First, law cannot reach the thoughts and decisions of persons to the extent
that these are not expressed in some overt way. Purely inner thoughts, attitudes, and choices are beyond the reach of evidence—unless one accepts the
use of the rack and the thumbscrew in interrogation. Attempts to regulate
purely inner matters lead to unenforceable laws. Nevertheless, this private
area is the primary locus of morality and immorality. Morality is of the heart,
in good will and ill will, in the deepest recesses of conscience. Thus, the
primary moral act, the act of choice, is beyond the effective reach of law.
Political jurisdiction certainly ends before one reaches the inner core of a
person where he or she is alone—or alone with God.

Second, law cannot in practice and ought not to try to establish justice in every aspect of intimate relationships, including the relationships between family members. For example, it certainly is unfair for parents to favor one child and to pick on another; it also is unfair for a friend to make a promise and then to renege on it without adequate reason. Ingratitude to a generous benefactor also is unfair. The law can reach none of these situations considered simply as such, although it can deal with gross child abuse and neglect, breach of contract, and literal biting of the hand that feeds one.

Third, there are moral responsibilities whose fulfillment is of little or no worth unless it is wholly voluntary. The obligation to be grateful is like this. So also are the obligations to repent one's sins, to adore God, to seek his kingdom and justification. The fact that legal coercion breeds hypocrisy which wholly blocks true piety and participation in the good of religion is by itself enough reason to exclude from the law rules requiring prayer, sacrifice, and other religious acts.

Fourth, if the law tries to impose a moral ideal, there are many situations in which the attempt will be self-defeating. For example, laws which prescribe what is contrary to the conscientious judgments of many people are likely to be self-defeating, inasmuch as these people will feel bound in conscience to disobey them. Government lacks the wholehearted support of those who are not conscientious; if it also alienates those who are, it loses a very important source of its legitimacy and effectiveness. Similarly, if law imposes a moral ideal which to most citizens lacks moral force—for example, in the prohibition affair—disregard of the law is likely to be massive and the law unenforceable.

This is not to say that there are no circumstances in which law may not require behavior which is considered by some citizens morally unacceptable, or prohibit some acts which are approved by most members of society. For example, laws forbidding racial discrimination are based upon a moral view which is not accepted by all and which is considered false by some. But the moral view in question is not a sectarian one held as a private morality by those who oppose racial discrimination. Rather, it is a basic demand of justice required by equal protection of the law. By contrast, a moral norm forbidding the use of alcoholic beverages or one forbidding private sexual immorality—acts in which many people choose to engage—cannot justly be enforced by law except to the extent that acts which are morally offensive to many members of society also offend public peace and order, or in other ways take on an aspect of injustice, and can be forbidden to the extent that they have this aspect.

Nevertheless, the relationship between law and morality is not such as to make unreasonable the public attempt to enforce by law a moral norm other than justice and respect for liberty when there is no significant disagreement on the matter among reasonable participants in the society, and when enforcement can serve some purpose. A project of enforcement of morals, under some conditions, can be as reasonable a governmental function as its more utilitarian activities of providing a monetary system or setting aside public parks. An appropriate basis for enforcing morality exists when there is a broad consensus that a certain type of act either is wrong or obligatory, and when those who would not spontaneously follow the norm do not regard its violation as a matter of deeply held conscientious conviction, but rather merely regard the norm as a demand they would personally prefer not to follow.

An example of a case which meets the requirement—where enforcement of the moral norm can be accepted as a welcome contribution to the common good—is in laws forbidding cruelty to animals, excluding bear-baiting, bull-fighting, and the like. Such laws are enforceable and do contribute to the common good by restricting impulses which interfere with the formation of dispositions of sensitivity and humanity which are widely held to be important for good character.

Inasmuch as law is limited and the domain of liberty not subject to law is very extensive, individuals and nonpolitical groups obviously are left by law at liberty to engage in many immoral acts. Every privilege carries with it a corresponding immunity, and every immunity entails a corresponding privilege. If law ought not to forbid certain immoral acts, then people have the privilege of committing these immoral acts. Thus a privilege often is a legal right, a license, to act in a morally irresponsible and wrongful way.[31]

However, such a right is no entitlement. It provides no basis for the person who is at liberty to act immorally to exact the cooperation of others, the support of society, or the use of public facilities in support of this liberty. If people do have a right to view pornographic films in the privacy of their own homes, this privilege is not an entitlement to the services of a professional moving-picture projectionist who prefers not to accept such work, nor is it an entitlement to the share one might claim for other uses of the municipal entertainment and recreation budget to purchase such films for the local library, nor is it an entitlement to a subsidy from the National Endowment for the Arts to help produce such films.

Finally, the commitment to respect very extensive liberty—and the act of legally recognizing and vindicating some particular liberty—is not rendered morally objectionable because those making the commitment or performing the legal act are morally certain that the privilege legalizes immorality and is certain to be abused by its immoral exercise.[32] This predictable consequence of liberty is but a side effect, foreseen but unsought, of the limitation of government which is demanded by justice. Like God, men and women who respect liberty intend a good and merely accept the very great evil of its immoral abuse. Political society cannot seek to suppress all immoral acts without seeking to extirpate liberty, which is totalitarian.

Totalitarianism is evil even if it seems necessary for the promotion of morality. The end does not justify the means. Totalitarianism in the service of moral fanaticism—as much as in the service of any other end—violates liberty and justice and offends the dignity of human persons. For the sake of justice and human dignity, the liberty to act immorally must be respected and protected by law, although this liberty need not be facilitated by law, since no privilege as such entitles one to the means required for its exercise.

To defend liberty even when it is immorally abused is true tolerance. To claim that every lawful exercise of liberty is morally acceptable for those who choose to adopt it is a false toleration, which implies ethical subjectivism. As we shall show in chapter thirteen, the latter in turn entails the principle required for a totalitarianism distinct from, but no less onerous than, that of the moral fanatic.

3: Definition of Death

A. Definition of Death and Euthanasia

Until the 1960s there was no legal problem about the definition of the death of a person. Statutes did not define death, because it was considered to be one of those facts too obvious to need definition. Case law presupposed a common understanding of death but wrestled with problems about determining the time of its occurrence. *Black's Law Dictionary* provided a definition:

> The cessation of life; the ceasing to exist; defined by physicians as a total stoppage of the circulation of the blood, and a cessation of the animal and vital functions consequent thereon, such as respiration, pulsation, etc.

The death of a person in this traditional legal view was a matter of fact; the occurrence and time of this fact could be established by medical certification or other competent evidence.[1]

In a living human body, as in other higher animals, life depends upon the coordinated functioning of the cardiovascular system, the respiratory system, and the central nervous system. If any of these three stops for long, the others stop shortly thereafter, and a process follows which everyone recognizes as characteristic of a dead body: unresponsiveness, lividity, frigidity, rigor mortis, decomposition.

Of the three interlocking functions that of the central nervous system, which is centered in the brain, is the most vulnerable. If the brain is deprived of fresh, oxygenated blood, one loses consciousness in a matter of seconds; irreversible damage to the brain begins in a few minutes, with parts of the brain required for conscious activities giving way more quickly than those parts which regulate nonconscious functions. But in fifteen or twenty minutes the brain no longer can signal the lungs to furnish more air. If nothing is done to force air into the lungs, the blood—even if it still circulates—no longer carries the oxygen necessary for muscle action, and the heart stops.[2]

Since breathing, blood circulation, and the functioning of the brain are so intimately related, and since a body is dead when these three functions cease, it generally has been accurate enough to identify death—the transition from the state of a living organism to that of a dead body—by cessation of breathing for more than a few minutes, by massive blood loss, by cessation of pulse and heartbeat, and even by abnormally prolonged unconsciousness from which an individual could not be roused to eat and drink. In the last case, as in those involving the heartbeat and blood circulation, breathing would soon cease, and then the process characteristic of a dead body would unfold.

However, modern techniques of intensive care loosen the connection between the cessation of vital functions. A brain destroyed to the point that the individual will never recover consciousness still can function sufficiently to continue to control nonconscious functions, including breathing. And if breathing continues, the heart can continue to beat and oxygenated blood flow to the brain. Although the individual cannot be roused to eat and drink, nutrients can be supplied by tube, and the body maintained in coma for a long period of time. This is the case with Miss Karen Quinlan after she was weaned from the respirator.[3] The ability to breathe spontaneously can be lost for a time or even permanently—for example, due to damage to the nerves between the brain and the lungs—in an individual whose conscious life goes on in a normal way, because the respirator can supplement or replace one's natural respiratory function. A heart-lung machine can replace both functions for a short time.

However, none of these techniques set off the current debate about definition of death. This debate was set off by the cases of individuals whose respiration is sustained by a respirator and who also seem to be in irreversible coma. If one turned off the respirator, the individual would surely be dead. But what is the situation before the respirator is turned off? Is such an individual already dead—inasmuch as there is neither consciousness nor spontaneous breathing—or is the individual still alive? One might think the latter to be so, because the heart continues to beat, and because the process characteristic of a dead body does not unfold. There may be reflexes in the extremities mediated by the spinal cord; the skin keeps its normal color and elasticity; the body is warm; rigor mortis does not set in; decomposition does not begin.

Clearly, if the individual is already dead, then there is no question as to whether treatment should be stopped. Turning off the respirator cannot kill someone who is already dead, and keeping it going obviously is pointless so far as the deceased is concerned. But being able to say with confidence that an individual is dead without turning off the respirator at once is not pointless so far as others are concerned. For under certain conditions such an individual's heart, kidneys, and other organs can be transplanted to other patients. To take the heart from a dying patient would be to kill that person; to take a heart from one obviously dead for some time would be to transplant a useless lump of dead and dying material, not an organ capable of sustaining the life of its recipient.[4]

Thus the issue is: Does the conception of death based upon the close interdependence of the functions of brain, lungs, and heart still hold when modern techniques of care make it possible to separate the termination of the three functions? Must the older conception of death be applied to individuals capable of neither consciousness nor spontaneous respiration when the termination of the three functions has been separated, inasmuch as the brain already is dead? Or may not such individuals be declared dead—even though the process characteristic of a dead body is not going on—so that their hearts and other parts might be used to benefit other persons without burdening the recipients and the transplant surgeons with the legal, moral, and psychological onus of conspiracy in homicide?[5]

One might wonder what this issue, considered in this way, has to do with the topic of our present study: euthanasia. How is the question of the definition of death more relevant to euthanasia than many other questions in legal medicine and medical ethics which will remain untreated here?

The relevance of the question of the definition of death to euthanasia is twofold.

First, if it is possible to correctly call "dead" certain classes of individuals which previously were considered living, and if it seems to many people appropriate to deal with these individuals as dead, then the law can approve what people consider appropriate without admitting homicide, for there is no homicide involved in treating the dead as dead. Thus, a correct definition of death, if it would eliminate some false classifications of dead individuals among the living, could relieve some of the pressure for legalizing euthanasia—in this case, pressure arising from a right attitude toward individuals really dead and only considered alive due to conceptual confusion.

Second, if it is possible to mistakenly call "dead" certain classes of individuals who previously were considered living, then the law can be made to approve homicide without seeming to admit it. Thus, a mistaken definition of death, if it would create some false classifications of living individuals among the dead, could achieve the objective of legalizing euthanasia without having to meet and deal straightforwardly with the questions of liberty and justice involved in such legalization. To take an example which goes well beyond any proposal we have seen: If anyone suffering from senile dementia can be classed as dead, then the dilemma of having either to care for such individuals or to kill them can be escaped. One can simply treat them as suits their condition.

Considerations of justice are raised in defining death by going too far in either direction. Obviously it would be unjust to those in fact alive to legally transform them into dead bodies by redefinition of death, for this would remove without due process all their rights as persons, deprive them of all their privileges or immunities, and leave them altogether without protection—let alone equal protection—of the laws. Less obviously it is likely to be unjust to others to class dead individuals as legally alive. The duties, including the duty of care, due to the living will be exacted inappropriately if required for those in fact dead and only held to be legal persons due to a mistake in the definition of death.

Still less obviously the rights of all who could benefit from the use of transplants of organs are infringed if the dead are mistakenly classed as living. Many persons have exercised their liberty to donate their remains or parts of their remains for the benefit of others by making use of procedures enacted into law by the Uniform Anatomical Gift Acts.[6] Although no one would have had any right to the remains of such persons apart from their gift, once they make this gift, those for whom it is intended have a right to receive it, just as persons who are lawful heirs have a right to their inheritance. Having provided for anatomical gifts, the law would be unjust to obstruct the execution of such gifts by mistakenly classing the dead as living.

B. Should Death Be Defined Anew?

Willard Gaylin sketched out in some detail the many ways in which the bodies of unconscious individuals—those in irreversible coma—might be used if such individuals can be considered legally dead. At present only those meeting the criteria for brain death in jurisdictions which have adopted this criterion can be used, and such individuals are encumbered with respirators. But Gaylin favors a definition of death which would include all decorticates now being treated as incurably ill. Gaylin calls individuals which he wishes to define as dead, although many signs of life still are observable in them, "neomorts." He suggests that rather than only one or another organ being taken from a neomort, it be maintained in a bioemporion—something analogous to the hospitals in which the living are maintained and the morgues in which cadavers are stored. Not only might vital organs be harvested as needed from neomorts but parts of the body which regenerate, such as blood, hormones, and skin, might be taken without ending the usefulness of the neomort. They also could be used for medical training and surgical practice. Neomorts could be used for the testing now done on prisoners, retarded children, and volunteers, as well as for sorts of testing not now done on human subjects. All sorts of experimentation could be done on neomorts, and they could be used to manufacture antibodies.[7]

Paul Ramsey objected to the updating of the definition of death or the procedures for diagnosing its occurrence for the purpose of facilitating transplants.[8] This objection is altogether reasonable if the updating is merely a matter of making an arbitrary change, for then the redefinition of death would amount to nothing more than a declaration that some legal persons are nonpersons so that they can be treated in ways which obviously would violate their rights if they were admitted to be persons. However, if the updating merely remedies the present vagueness of an insufficiently precise definition, then the possibilities of transplanting organs and making the other uses of neomorts which Gaylin outlines make it a matter of justice that the updating be done.[9]

It should be noticed that the question of defining death is different from the question of regulating the conditions under which treatment may be terminated. If an individual is dead, treatment obviously may and should be terminated. But, as we shall argue in chapter four, legally competent persons are at liberty to refuse treatment; if they have done so, then treatment ought to be terminated, although they are still alive and the termination of treatment will permit an existing condition of disease or injury to bring about their death. Also, as we shall argue in chapter nine, there are conditions in which the law ought not to mandate medical treatment for the legally noncompetent; in such cases those responsible for the care of the patient are at liberty to terminate treatment and allow the patient to die. Thus in order to deal with most of the problems about termination of treatment, it is neither necessary nor sufficient to redefine death.[10]

It also should be noticed that death can be defined in various ways. A definition of death in theoretical terms will tell what happens when an organism dies when this matter is considered within the framework of a general theory of life. A definition of death in factual terms will tell what observable or inferable state of affairs obtains if the theoretical concept of death is satisfied. A definition of death in operational terms will tell how to establish that the factual state of affairs obtains.

If, for example, one considers death to be permanent loss of consciousness, one needs a theory in which human life is defined in terms of conscious activity, and then the theoretical definition of death as permanent unconsciousness will follow. But this definition in theoretical terms needs to be supplemented by a definition in factual terms. What observable state of affairs must obtain if a body is to be declared permanently unconscious? Someone might assert that a necrotic condition of all or certain parts of the brain is sufficient to fulfill the conceptual requirement. Finally, this definition in factual terms needs to be supplemented by a definition in operational terms. How does one go about finding out that the relevant part of the brain (or the whole brain) is in fact in the specified necrotic condition? Certain tests must be prescribed and the method of interpreting their results specified. For example, it may be suggested that an electroencephalogram be made, and that if it reveals no electrical activity in the cortex of the brain, then one can be sure that the cortex is necrotic, provided that other possible and known causes of a flat or isoelectric EEG are ruled out.

There has been a good deal of disagreement as to whether there ought to be a statutory definition of death. In 1977 the Judicial Council of the American Medical Association continued to maintain that

> . . . this is neither desirable or necessary for physicians or patients, as it may result in confusion instead of clarification as advances in scientific capabilities occur. The physician is always ultimately responsible for the diagnosis he makes. Accordingly, death should be determined by the clinical judgment of the physician using the necessary available and currently accepted criteria.[11]

This position seems to assume that the only current problem is in regard to an *operational* definition of death, that this matter is within medical competence, and that there are adequate, currently accepted criteria.

In fact, the current problem primarily is in regard to the more basic theoretical and factual definitions of death. Indeed, many participants in the debate, as we shall soon see, do not consider that the theoretical question can be settled other than by an ethical or policy decision, which is no more in the competence of physicians than of other members of the society. Furthermore, once it is realized that the diagnosis of death terminates legal personhood, and that large questions of justice depend upon the correctness of this diagnosis, it is clear that even in the operational domain judgments by physicians in this matter need some regulation by legal guidelines, particularly inasmuch as there are no criteria currently and universally accepted by physicians in respect to the kinds of cases which gave rise to the current debate.

If the opinion of the Judicial Council were not based upon a misconception of the issue, it would be arrogant, for it would amount to a declaration that physicians alone can settle that certain individuals are legal nonpersons, and that no one has a right to question their judgments in so doing, although a debate about individuals of certain kinds has been going on for ten years among physicians, lawyers, philosophers, theologians, and others.

Some have granted that law must take an interest in the definition of death, but they have argued that statutes be avoided and judicial decisions sought to clarify the matter. The slowness and inconsistency of any development by judicial decisions argues against this approach. So does the lack of facility for the courts to investigate and hear evidence from all sides, and to consider the problem in general rather than within the problematics of a particular case. Most important, judicial decisions cannot guide action until they are formulated, and then they can guide action only for kinds of cases for which they would be adequate precedents.

Others have proposed similar and other strong arguments in favor of trying to settle the issue of the definition of death by statute.[12] Apart from the Judicial Council of the American Medical Association, we find little serious opposition to this conclusion. Therefore, we consider it settled. In any case, statutory definitions of death have now been enacted by at least eighteen states. Those who regard such definitions as undesirable ought nevertheless to be realistic enough to admit the value of considering what the law ought to hold on the matter if similar statutes are enacted in other jurisdictions or the statutes already enacted amended.

C. The Harvard Committee's Criteria

The first important attempt to redefine death was published in 1968 under the title "A Definition of Irreversible Coma: Report of the Ad Hoc Committee of the Harvard Medical School to Examine the Definition of Brain Death."[13] The chairman of this committee was Henry K. Beecher.

The title of the report betrays an ambivalence or confusion in the committee about its project, for "irreversible coma," "brain death," and "death" express distinct concepts, but the report proceeds on the unargued assumption that a single definition will suffice for all three. The committee does not define death in theoretical terms. However, in urging that redefinition be accepted to avoid great burden "on patients who suffer permanent loss of intellect, on their families, on the hospitals, and on those in need of hospital beds already occupied by these comatose patients," the committee seems to imply that those suffering permanent loss of intellect, although thereby burdened, are to be considered dead. Another argument in the report which only compounds the confusion is that because the termination of the use of extraordinary means to prolong life is morally acceptable—on the authority of Pius XII—"the moment of death is the moment when irreparable and overwhelming brain damage occurs."[14]

Lacking a definition of death in theoretical terms, the Harvard committee report nevertheless accepts as a definition in factual terms "a *permanently* nonfunctioning brain" or lack of "discernible central nervous system activity" or coma in which "function is abolished at cerebral, brain-stem, and often spinal levels."[15] On what basis was this factual definition accepted? The report does not say. But three years later Beecher expressed his own view in a paper vigorously defending the new definition against opposing views. Asserting that death has many levels, he says:

> At whatever level we *choose* to call death, it is an arbitrary decision. Death of the heart? The hair still grows. Death of the brain? The heart may still beat. The need is to choose an irreversible state where the brain no

longer functions. It is best to choose a level where, although the brain is dead, usefulness of other organs is still present. This, we have tried to make clear in what we have called the new definition of death.[16]

This statement makes clear that in one author's view the Harvard report was an attempt to impose one judgment of the need and of what is best upon some individuals previously classed by law as alive, and hence as legal persons with rights potentially at odds with the interests of those concerned with the usefulness of their organs.

The Harvard report itself was clear that it aimed to bring about a change in existing law concerning the definition of death. It proposed to accomplish this purpose by the adoption of its criteria by the medical community without statutory change in the law. It recommended that the judgment of the fulfillment of the criteria newly proposed be considered solely a medical issue. And it emphasized that individuals should be pronounced dead before being taken off the respirator:

> Otherwise, the physicians would be turning off the respirator on a person who is, under the present strict, technical application of law, still alive.[17]

Even if it is correct to maintain—as we shall argue—that an individual whose entire brain is dead is no longer a living person, the Harvard committee's approach seems to have involved a method in principle unacceptable: A private group here consciously attempted to effect the legal nonpersonhood of a class of individuals.[18]

The Harvard report proposed a definition of death in operational terms under the heading "Characteristics of Irreversible Coma." Absence of blood circulation or heartbeat are suggested as sufficient criteria of brain death. Given the continuation of this function, clinical (easily observed) signs were proposed:

1) Deep unconsciousness with no response to external stimuli and internal need. "There is a total unawareness. . . . "

2) No spontaneous movements and no spontaneous breathing. "After the patient is on a mechanical respirator, the total absence of spontaneous breathing may be established by turning off the respirator for three minutes and observing whether there is any effort on the part of the subject to breathe spontaneously."

3) No reflexes, except for those mediated only by the spinal cord. A flat or isoelectric EEG was suggested to be of "great confirmatory value." The depression of the nervous system by drugs or lowered temperature must be excluded. "All of the above tests," the report legislated, "shall be repeated at least 24 hours later with no change."[19]

The criteria proposed have been criticized as inadequate to establish the positive fact of brain death, although admittedly they do indicate serious brain damage. No one can show that an unresponsive patient is unaware, that inability to react to painful stimuli necessarily presupposes lack of perception of the pain. Three minutes off the respirator is not necessarily sufficient to establish the incapacity to breathe spontaneously; a damaged brain which is not yet dead will not be killed by deprivation of oxygen for this period. Signs which infallibly indicate death under normal conditions do not necessarily do so under unusual conditions of artificially maintained respiration. Hence, a sufficient operational criterion of the death of the entire brain would seem to require the positive establishment of a condition—such as deprivation of oxygen to the brain for a period of fifteen minutes or more—known to be incompatible with its continued functioning.[20]

D. Death as Process or Event

In 1970 Robert S. Morison advanced the argument that "death" and "life" signify not realities, but only reified and even personified abstractions. Death, he maintains, is a continuous process, not a clear-cut event. As life must be reduced to objects which undergo processes of growth, reproduction, and special ways of handling energy, death must be reduced to the limits and gradual ebbing of such functions, which happens not at an instant, but by gradual diminution. The complex interactions among the cells and of the organism with the environment give rise in the case of humans to the concept of "personality." But, Morison suggests, these interactions fail gradually, not with the termination of any one vital function. Thus, he concludes, the judgment required should be based not upon a definition in factual terms, but rather upon the comparative valuations of respecting or maintaining the residual level of interaction, and of terminating or hastening the decline of the process. In support of his proposal Morison appeals to the justification of abortion by those who argued that respect for the sanctity of life required that human decisions be made regarding the relative value of the potential of incipient life.[21]

Leon R. Kass criticized Morison's paper. He points out in the first place that while "death" is an abstract concept, it signifies a very real transition, and that Morison confused this transition from the condition of a living to that of a dead body with the quite distinct *process of dying* which goes on in a living body. Kass also points out that while parts of an organism can die while the individual as a whole survives and while parts can survive when the individual as a whole dies, thus to stretch out the phenomena of necrosis, the organic individual is an integrated functional unit, which from the point of view of a pathologist is dead when irreversible changes occur in certain vital tissues, especially those of the central nervous system. Finally, Kass makes clear that when Morison argues for the benefits of allowing the termination of life—especially the benefits to the individual involved—the argument presupposes that life still continues, although at reduced value, and that it would be justifiable to hasten a very definite terminal event: death.[22]

The distinction which Kass made clear in this argument between the parts of a human body—its various tissues and organs, which die at various times from conception until some time after the individual has died—and the whole human body is most important from the point of view of just laws. For the legal status of natural persons never has been recognized by law as belonging to any parts of a human body, whether living in the body or apart from it. Thus, for legal purposes the relevant question is not whether the heart has stopped or whether the brain is dead, but whether the human body as a whole is alive or dead. The condition of particular organs and functions is relevant only if it can be shown to provide a factual definition of the death of the whole organism.

E. A Stipulative Definition of "Death"?

In 1973 Roger B. Dworkin advanced the argument that attempts to settle a single legal definition of death were at best a waste of effort and at worst counterproductive. "Death" signifies a turning point of importance for a great many different legal purposes. The sensible thing, he urges, would be to define "death" in particular legal contexts, just as other terms are defined by law relative to the purpose of using them in each context. One might encourage transplantation of organs, if that seemed to be a desirable policy, by defining "death" broadly in the case of potential donors. Dworkin argues that the law has long recognized that death occurs at different times for different purposes. His evidence for this contention is that the laws of many states establish different presumptive death periods for missing persons for purposes of distributing their property and considering a spouse free to remarry. When these varying periods elapse, however, for each purpose an individual is legally dead—just as dead as one can be so far as the law is concerned.[23]

Alexander Morgan Capron replied to Dworkin by pointing out, in the first place, that although the law takes note of death for many diverse purposes, and although one might argue with the law's estimate of the importance of death in some cases, the law presupposes a familiar turning point called "death" and does not simply stipulate it. Further, legal *presumptions* of death are merely presumptions; they presuppose a familiar, factual state of affairs and merely indicate how to proceed when no one knows whether that state of affairs does or does not obtain. In fact, Capron points out, laws concerning the presumption of death take into account the possible counterfactuality of the presumption by making provision for cases in which it turns out to be false. In other words, one legally presumed dead is not as dead as one can be from a legal point of view—not, for example, so dead that it would be 'permissible to kill such an individual.[24]

Capron's reply is effective so far as it goes. He might have pointed out further that law cannot justly approach all problems of definition as if the purposes of particular policies could be allowed to control. In many cases this approach is unobjectionable. But in defining "death" the law is settling one of the boundaries of the legal personhood of natural persons, defining the limit at which, for example, the right not to be assaulted and cut to pieces, which is defined by laws prohibiting offenses against the person, ceases and a body is no longer protected against recycling.

Persons have a peculiar status in respect to the law, because they are the only entities it must recognize, the only entities it must serve. Wherever the boundary of personhood is established by whichever definition of death, those placed beyond the boundary are mere bodies outside all the purposes of the law. If not all in the society agree where the boundary is to be drawn, someone's particular opinion will be imposed and the opinion of others set aside if a precise boundary is established by law. And if no precise boundary is established, the rights and duties of all members of the society in the vicinity of the border are left unclear, with the result that the rights of many are put at risk, and the responsibilities of others are either rendered unenforceable or made to be enforced by unpredictable ex post facto judgments.[25]

In 1975 William C. Charron expressed concern that new definitions of death requiring total and irreversible cessation of function of the entire brain can impose unnecessary burdens upon those who care for permanently comatose bodies. He urges that a purely psychological definition of death in theoretical terms as permanent loss of consciousness be accepted, and that at the factual level the destruction of the cortex be taken as sufficient to establish the death of the person. In Charron's view this or any other definition of death is an expression of choice. He maintains that no definition expresses a truth, that every definition is a convention about the use of language. To serve its purpose, such a convention must meet a number of formal requirements and must be publicly acceptable. Charron thinks that psychological death would be a good choice. Although he is aware of the implications for legal personhood of defining death, he is not concerned about the fact that the new definition he proposes would contract the boundary of personhood for comatose bodies in the interest of relieving others of duties toward them.[26]

As a matter of logic, Charron's contention that all definition is stipulative is mistaken. Some definitions attempt to state facts about the uses of words; sometimes a claim is made that certain words of the same or different languages differ in form but agree in sense. Definitions of this sort can be true.

Other definitions claim that different expressions have the same reference—for example, "Rust is iron oxide" makes such a claim, which happens to be true, while "Rust is iron carbonyl" is false.

Charron points out that no appeal to intuition, no empirical data, and no a priori reasoning could establish the definition of death which he prefers. He takes this to show that no rational grounds can be given for considering *any* definition of death true, rather than merely a good choice.[27] However, he ignores the fact that the argument about the definition of death arose from a certain situation, that this situation revealed vagueness in the received concept of death for a certain set of new cases—those in which modern techniques of care separate the close connection of the termination of the various vital functions—and that definitions purporting to remove vagueness can be shown to be false if they fail to conform to already established uses of words so far as established usage goes.

To define death as permanent loss of consciousness—or even as permanent and irreversible loss of consciousness—is to make a claim which is simply false, inasmuch as it misrepresents established usage with respect to individuals who fall into coma outside the context of modern techniques of care. People do not treat such bodies as dead, because their condition is not known to be irreversible, and because the process characteristic of dead bodies does not unfold until breathing stops. If one abandons the common sense distinction between individuals who are in coma and bodies which are dead, one will have to introduce some neologisms—such as Gaylin's "neomorts" and "cadavers"—to make the same distinction. If one wishes to argue that the law should withdraw legal personhood from those in irreversible coma or that the law should permit such individuals to be treated as if they were dead while admitting their legal personhood, then one should assume the burden of defending one's thesis, not try to evade this burden by urging others to choose a definition of death which begs the question.

Underlying the proposals of Charron and others that loss of consciousness be accepted as definitive of death is a residue of dualism between self ("soul" or "ego") and body. This dualism is generally admitted today to be indefensible in theory.[28] But it is widely assumed in the context of ethics. Joseph Fletcher asserts dualism most clearly:

> Physical nature—the body and its members, our organs and their functions—all of these *things* are a part of "what is over against us," and if we live by the rules and conditions set in physiology or say any other *it* we are not *thou*. When we discussed the problem of giving life to new creatures, and the authority of natural processes as over against the human values of responsibility and self-preservation (when nature and they are at cross-purposes), we remarked that spiritual reality and moral integrity belong to man alone, in whatever degree we may possess them as made *imago Dei*.

> Freedom, knowledge, choice, responsibility—all these things of personal
> or moral stature are in us, not *out there*. Physical nature is what is over
> against us, out there. It represents the world of *its*. Only men and God are
> *thou;* they only are persons.[29]

Having taken this general position, Fletcher is not inconsistent when he maintains that when cerebral function is gone, "nothing remains but biological
phenomena at best. The patient is gone even if his body remains, and even if
some of its vital functions continue."[30] On this view the functioning of the
rest of the brain is irrelevant. A person is dead when there is "irreversible
loss of whatever component in his biological system holds the essence of the
person, and that component is the cerebrum in the brain, not the whole
brain."[31]

Hans Jonas correctly points out that a position of this sort denies the
extracerebral body its essential share in the identity of the person:

> My identity is the identity of the whole organism, even if the higher func-
> tions of personhood are seated in the brain. How else could a man love a
> woman and not merely her brains? How else could we lose ourselves in
> the aspect of a face? Be touched by the delicacy of a frame? It's this
> person's, and no one else's. Therefore, the body of the comatose, so long
> as—even with the help of art—it still breathes, pulses, and functions
> otherwise, must still be considered a residual continuance of the subject
> that loved and was loved. . . . [32]

We shall argue that the body Jonas describes is not always correctly considered to be alive. Nevertheless, Jonas seems correct—and we shall propose
additional arguments showing this in chapter eleven, section H—in rejecting
the dualism which identifies the person with consciousness and reduces one's
living body to the status of a mere object among objects in the physical world.
Only such dualism makes it seem reasonable to consider nonpersons those
who fall into irreversible coma outside the context of modern techniques of
care. Indeed, common sense regards even a dead human body as still partaking in the identity of the person; for this reason we do not—usually, at least,
up to now—treat human bodies as mere garbage to be disposed of.

F. Robert Veatch's Analysis

In 1976 Robert M. Veatch published a book-length study on ethical and
public-policy issues related to death and dying. His treatment of the problem
of the definition of death shows sensitivity to all the relevant issues and
distinctions we have been discussing up to this point.[33]

Veatch begins by offering a formal definition of death: "Death means a complete change in the status of a living entity characterized by the irreversible loss of those characteristics that are essentially significant to it."[34] This definition is used to shape the question which Veatch considers primary, namely the appropriate definition of death in theoretical terms. Or, as Veatch puts it, the basic definition of death is metaphysical, not factual. It is a question of ethical and other values. One must choose among the many elements which make human beings unique something whose loss amounts to the loss of humanness.

Veatch suggests four possible choices as plausible: (1) the loss of respiration and circulation of the blood; (2) the departure of the soul from the body; (3) the loss of the capacity for bodily integration; and (4) the loss of the capacity for consciousness or social interaction or both. In each case the loss must be irreversible to define a philosophical concept of death. (1) is only symptomatic; death happens to the whole organism, and particular vital functions are significant only to the extent that they indicate something about the whole. (2) cannot be translated into a definition in factual and operational terms unless it is reduced to one of the others. Besides, Veatch considers (1) to be "animalistic" and too base a function to define what is essential to the human and (2) to be a "relic from the era of dichotomized anthropologies."[35]

Veatch suggests that the capacity for bodily integration (3) includes all the integrating mechanisms possessed by the body, both for inner integration and for integrated interaction with the environment. This philosophical concept would translate into a definition in factual terms of death as the total and irreversible cessation of function of the entire brain, and Veatch tentatively accepts the Harvard criteria as indicating this factual state of affairs in operational terms.[36]

However, Veatch concludes that consciousness or the capacity for embodied social interaction (4) ought to be taken as the "truly essential characteristics." And of these, when he contrasts them, Veatch considers the capacity for embodied social interaction most important. However, Veatch does not wish to require that individuals manifest a capacity for rationality to be considered alive, for such a requirement might exclude infants, the senile, and the psychotic. One must avoid evaluating kinds of consciousness or social interaction lest one step out on the slippery slope of grading human lives by quantitative and qualitative considerations. So Veatch accepts the irreversible loss of any amount and sort of the capacity for embodied social interaction (which includes some form of consciousness) as definitive of human death.[37] This conceptual or theoretical definition translates into a definition of death in factual terms as the irreversible cessation of the functioning of the neocortex (outer surface of the upper part of the brain). Operationally, this criterion seems to translate into a flat EEG by itself as a sufficient indicator of death.[38] Any individual in a truly irreversible coma with no detectable activity in the neocortex would be considered dead, even though the coma might have begun and continued without any intervention of modern life-support techniques, and the individual to the ordinary person would appear merely to be in a deep sleep, still breathing without attachment to a respirator or any other tubes or machines.

Veatch fully realizes that the definition he proposes is incompatible with the received conception of death. He knows it is more than the refinement of an existing concept to resolve vagueness which has appeared due to modern techniques. Knowing this, he also sees that the replacement of the old concept of death with a new one raises a moral issue, inasmuch as it means that individuals will be considered dead who previously would have been treated as alive. He does not claim certitude that the new definition is correct. How can the moral question be resolved? It hardly helps, he notices, to invoke the interests of other persons. On the one side is the right of living persons to be treated as such. But on the other side, Veatch urges, is another moral consideration: "it is an affront to the dignity of individual persons to treat them as alive if they are dead."[39] Hence, he concludes, the situation is one of genuinely perplexed conscience, which people must resolve according to their best judgment.

This ethical conclusion with respect to the moral responsibilities of individuals must be translated into a public policy which can be enacted as general legislation. Veatch holds that legislation certainly is needed; he accepts the same sort of reasoning we outlined in section B above. But he thinks that in a "confused society" it would be well to make room for individual choice. Yet one cannot allow individuals or next of kin to draw any line they wish as death for themselves or for those for whom they are responsible, since sheer arbitrariness in this matter would open the door to absurd options, which would irrationally infringe upon rights (of the individual declared dead if the line were drawn too early) and impose duties (on others if the line were drawn too late).

Hence, Veatch proposes a statute which would determine legal death by the judgment of a physician, using as criteria traditional standards if artificial means of life support are not in use, but using irreversible cessation of spontaneous cerebral functions as a criterion if such supports are in use. Veatch does not specify how the latter state of affairs is to be determined except that it be "based on ordinary standards of medical practice." But to allow for individual choice, Veatch provides that anyone while legally competent may exclude the eventual use for their own case of the cerebral-function criterion of death, and the legal guardian or next of kin may exclude the use of this criterion for those who have not done so for themselves.

Veatch also attaches an interesting provision which would exclude any physician from pronouncing death—on any criterion—if there is significant conflict of interest with his obligation to serve the patient, such as an interest in other patients, in research, or in teaching which would benefit from pronouncing the patient dead.[40]

Veatch's treatment of the problem is sound in many respects. He rightly distinguishes the problems of theoretical, factual, and operational definition as the Harvard report did not. He also correctly insists that death is an event which happens to the organism as a whole. Seeing the ethical and legal question, he excludes the crude legal pragmatism of Dworkin and others. He does not suppose that the question of definition is a mere linguistic convention. Still, we find Veatch's treatment unsatisfactory in many respects.

In the first place, it is odd to define death formally as the complete change in the status of a living entity by which it irreversibly loses the characteristics essentially significant to it. If "essentially significant" were understood inclusively, then no organism could die, since every organism, insofar as it is a living *body*, has as its basic essentially significant characteristic bodiliness, and this is the one characteristic death does not remove.

Of course, Veatch does not take "essentially significant" in an inclusive sense; he rather means by it a characteristic of living humans which is chosen after an evaluation.[41] But then the formal definition merely becomes a vehicle for Veatch's articulation of his intuition that social interaction, even if the interaction be carried on at a level not uniquely human, is what is most significant about human persons. Moreover, even if one agrees with Veatch's choice of what is significant, one receives no reason for supposing that the loss of what is most significant about a person and the death of a person are one and the same. It would hardly be absurd to maintain that the capacity to think and to make free choices is what is most valuable about persons, but that there are many other significant aspects remaining even if this is lost. And many would hold that even an unconscious human body, which has not yet begun the process characteristic of a dead body, is an aspect of the person, partaking in personal dignity, and so deserving respect—even reverence. If they are right, no one may choose to consider such a body insignificant merely because it lacks more important human capacities.

In the second place, Veatch provides no reason for supposing that a capacity for embodied social interaction and consciousness always are lost together. It is not at all difficult to imagine a body which can no longer respond but which can still perceive—for example, which cannot move a single voluntary muscle but still can hear. This possibility cannot be proved to obtain, but neither can it be disproved. So much is this the case that some who consider the person to be a psychophysical whole and death to be loss of consciousness demand evidence of the death of the entire brain as the factual definition corresponding to their theory.[42] If incapacity for social interaction were accepted as a sufficient condition for one's death, individuals still conscious but unresponsive could become inmates of Gaylin's emporion for neomorts.

In the third place, Veatch realizes the dangers of embarking on the slippery slope of quantitative and qualitative determinations, and for this reason he is willing to settle for any minimum degree of the capacity for social interaction. However, by using the method of choosing what is significant on the basis of his own evaluation of various essential human characteristics, Veatch already has stepped onto the slope. The only way to avoid doing so—the way we ourselves adopt—is by limiting any new definition of death to a precision which respects established usage so far as it goes. Many more radical than Veatch in their views surely will demand that the function evidenced be specifically human, and the redefinition of death will become a final solution to many problems, a solution embraced without ever facing the issues which we shall argue in chapter eight. Surely if some are to be killed, the honest thing to do is to consider the question on its merits. (Veatch, himself, clearly does not disagree.)

In the fourth place, Veatch's effort to offset the moral question of the right to life by his counterconsideration—"it is an affront to the dignity of individual persons to treat them as alive if they are dead"—is very odd. Can one affront the dignity of dead persons? And if one can, does one do so by treating them as alive, provided that one does so only because one is not sure whether they are alive or dead and wishes to avoid treating them as dead if they are in fact alive? Moreover, even if there is some moral consideration here, it surely cannot be a question of justice. Hence, the law cannot reasonably take into account this odd moral consideration to offset what would seem a reasonable requirement: A human body ought to be considered alive unless one is certain beyond a reasonable doubt that it is dead. This requirement surely undergirds received standards for acting in doubtful cases—for example, seek help for accident victims (without presuming the apparently dead to be really so), give artificial respiration to those apparently dead from drowning or electrical shock, and so forth.

Perhaps Veatch's introduction of the point about the dignity of the dead is not merely odd, but even ad hoc, for he remarks: "It seems to me that only when such positive moral pressure is introduced on both sides of the argument can we plausibly overcome the claim that we must take the morally safer course."[43]

In the fifth place, Veatch's proposal that a statute allowing for cerebral death as a criterion for legal death should provide an opportunity for individuals to opt out seems to us unsound and unnecessary. It is unsound because it opens a boundary of legal personhood to an arbitrary choice which affects the rights and duties of others, and also because it requires an affirmative act to defend a basic set of rights—an affirmative act which many cannot be expected to get around to and which some, such as infants, never can do. Moreover, the limits of the option which Veatch chooses are indefensible against more radical proposals.

The statute Veatch proposes also contains a serious flaw which he very likely did not intend. Consideration of cerebral function only comes into play in the event an individual is on artificial life support. Two things follow. First, Veatch does not succeed in covering those he seems to wish to cover: cases in which respiration is spontaneous but the neocortex is nonfunctional. Second, while stating the traditional criteria, Veatch fails to take into account cases in which a patient is totally paralyzed from the neck down, but still fully conscious. Some polio and accident victims are in this condition; they need a respirator permanently. Read literally, Veatch's statute would allow them to be pronounced dead, something he surely did not intend.

G. A New Proposal for Defining Death

This brings us to our own attempt to refine the concept of death. In our view the current problem is one of vagueness in the concept which emerged when modern methods of intensive care rendered the result of using traditional criteria—the cessation of respiration and heartbeat for one-half hour or so—unclear as to its significance. If the vagueness is to be removed without radically altering the concept itself, the question to ask is: Why were these operational criteria taken to be significant? The answer seems to us to be that everyone observes the difference between a living body and a dead body, between a dying body and a decomposing body. Respiration and heartbeat are functions which are continuously present throughout life and observed from birth on. The process which is characteristic of a dead and decomposing body correlates very well with traditional criteria, not only as to occurrence but even as to temporal sequence. Clearly, something happened before the body began decomposing, at or about the time when breathing and circulation ceased. This "something" was the turning point at which a living body became a dead body. The turning point was called "death."

If we look at this situation from the point of view of biological theory, we can understand more clearly what the turning point is. Life often is said to be—in general—a certain kind of physicochemical process, and the life of an organism a collection of such processes. But an organism is more than a collection of processes; it is a coordinated system. From a thermodynamic point of view an organism is an unstable open system, but it continues because it is maintained in dynamic equilibrium by homeostatic controls. These controls are of various kinds, but in an organism which is complex enough to have a nervous system, this system coordinates and integrates the other control systems. This system is dispersed but centered in the brain; without some brain functioning, the whole system cannot be maintained. Thus when the whole brain ceases to function, the dynamic equilibrium is lost, the materials which were unified in the system begin behaving without its control, and decomposition begins.[44]

These considerations suggest a definition of death in theoretical terms close to one which Veatch considers and sets aside: Death is the irreversible loss of integrated organic functioning. Veatch speaks of a "*capacity* for bodily integration," but this is misleading, inasmuch as what is at stake is not a capacity, not a potentiality which a living body has, but simply is the unity which the living body has and maintains in its complex physicochemical set of processes. Moreover, Veatch introduces even in this definition the idea of social interaction. Unless "social" is taken merely to mean the continuing adaptation of the organism to the environment, however, it demands something essential, not to life, but only to certain special functions of certain kinds of living things. Even a carrot lives and dies.

If death is understood in theoretical terms as the permanent termination of the integrated functioning characteristic of a living body as a whole, then one can see why death of higher animals is usually grasped in factual terms by the cessation of the vital functions of respiration and circulation, which correlates so well with bodily decomposition. Breathing is the minimum in "social interaction." However, considering the role of the brain in the maintenance of the dynamic equilibrium of any system which includes a brain, there is a compelling reason for defining death in factual terms as that state of affairs in which there is complete and irreversible loss of the functioning of the entire brain. To accept this definition is not to make a choice based on one's evaluation of various human characteristics, but is to assent to a theory which fits the facts.

Someone might object that just as the functions of other organs can be supplied artificially, so perhaps the integrating function of the brain could be replaced by a computer. If the respirator does not maintain all of the organism intact, still it does maintain most of its parts in a working system, even when the whole brain is dead.

We notice, first, that the possibility of replacing the functioning of the brain is speculative. When the respirator maintains the organism, it is questionable whether there is complete and irreversible loss of the functioning of the *entire* brain. But this is a question to be settled by empirical inquiry, not by philosophy. Philosophically, we answer the objection by saying that if the functioning of the brain is the factor which principally integrates any organism which has a brain, then if that function is lost, what is left is no longer as a whole an *organic* unity. If the dynamic equilibrium of the remaining parts of the system is maintained, it nevertheless *as a whole* is a mechanical, not an organic system.

If death can be correctly defined in factual terms as the complete and irreversible loss of the functioning of the entire brain, then this definition can be accepted and translated into operational and legal terms without any radical shifts in meaning, arbitrary stipulations, or subjective evaluations. The problem which gave rise to the debate about the definition of death can be settled, and a good reason given for not proceeding to some other definition, proposed not to resolve vagueness but rather to alter the boundary of legal personhood in cases in which it has always been and still remains perfectly clear.[45]

What is an appropriate operational definition of death if it is defined in theoretical and factual terms as we have argued that it should be?

In most cases the criteria commonly used by persons of common sense and by physicians prior to 1968 remain sound and adequate. If a body shows no signs of breathing and heartbeat whatever for one-half hour or so, then one can reasonably assume death has occurred. Lividity, frigidity, and rigidity have considerable confirmatory value.

In the absence of traditionally accepted signs of death, persons having the relevant competence might be able to judge with certainty that there is an irreversible loss of functioning which is complete and throughout the entire brain. But such a judgment should never be made unless there are signs which warrant it beyond a reasonable doubt. Since there seems to be competent disagreement about the adequacy of the Harvard criteria, they cannot be regarded as sufficient in practice.[46] They could, perhaps, be sufficient. But if any with relevant expertise—which includes not only physicians specializing in neurology but also scientists in the field of neurophysiology—consider those signs *not to be* certain evidence that there is complete loss of functioning, which is irreversible and which affects the entire brain, then the expertise of such individuals provides ground for reasonable doubt that these signs are an adequate operational standard of death. For where experts disagree, those who are not expert have reason to doubt and have no basis to proceed with confidence in a matter which requires certitude beyond a reasonable doubt, when it is not absolutely necessary to proceed. And although it may be necessary to ignore the needs of some bodies, even live ones, it never is necessary to consider any body dead who might be alive.

H. A Model Statute

If what we have said about the definition of death is correct, how can this view be expressed in a statute? A good statute will clearly define death, so that the rights of the dying as living persons will be protected, and duties toward the living will not be exacted toward dead bodies. The statute must be drafted to clear up existing confusions as well as to provide immediate guidance for ordinary persons and physicians who must decide if someone is dead.

Thus, first, the definition of death in theoretical and factual terms ought to be stated, in order to make clear that all deaths are events of a single kind, and that the operational criteria employed should be directed toward determining the fact of the occurrence of an event of this type. Thus: "Death is the permanent termination of the integrated functioning characteristic of a living body as a whole. In human individuals beyond the embryonic stage of development death occurs when there is complete and irreversible loss of the functioning of the entire brain."

Second, the degree of certitude necessary in judging that death has occurred ought to be stated, in order to prevent injustice to those who seem to be dead but are in fact alive. Thus: "Every human body shall be considered living until it is clear beyond reasonable doubt that death has occurred."

Third, the criteria and procedure for judging death in ordinary cases ought to be stated, in order to provide clear guidance and eliminate carelessness and abuses which might exist or develop in the current atmosphere of confusion. In making this statement it is not necessary to speak about *spontaneous* functions and the absence of artificial life-support techniques, because the appearance of the normal phenomena of death are not produced, but rather are obstructed, by such techniques. A statute ought not to assume that a physician will be available to pronounce death and should not inhibit liberty unnecessarily by forbidding people to act if a physician is not available. Thus: "If during the period of one hour a body is still and unresponsive with no sign of breathing or pulsation, death probably has occurred. A licensed physician after careful examination of the body may so pronounce, and the body shall then be considered legally dead. In the absence of a licensed physician, the body should be watched for a period of twenty-four hours. If no sign of life appears during this period and if the body becomes stiff and if its temperature varies with that of its surroundings, the body shall then be considered legally dead. Death shall be deemed to have occurred at the moment when breathing stopped."

Fourth, the statute should state the criteria and procedures for judging death in extraordinary cases, in order to protect the rights of patients against application of arbitrary criteria and the use of procedures selected to further the interests of others. The statute should avoid specifying the technical methods to be used in determining that the factual definition of death is satisfied but nevertheless should regulate the activity of physicians to ensure that injustice is not done to anybody. The careful regulation of the activity of physicians does not imply that the law considers every physician to be under suspicion, but only implies that the law cannot consider every physician to be altogether above suspicion. Thus: "Even in the absence of the usual signs of death, the complete and irreversible loss of the functioning of the entire brain sometimes occurs. A licensed physician who has the expertness necessary to diagnose the occurrence of this condition may pronounce death in such cases provided that the following conditions are met: (1) The method used to determine that complete and irreversible loss of the functioning of the entire brain has occurred must be a method which all physicians and scientists whose special competence includes knowledge of the functioning of the brain agree to be certainly adequate to determine the relevant matter of fact beyond any reasonable doubt; and (2) The physician who pronounces death in the absence of the usual signs of death must have no prospect of benefit from pronouncing the patient dead, such as the use of the body for the benefit of other patients under his care or for teaching or research in which he is engaged. Death shall be deemed to have occurred at the moment when the functioning of the entire brain is estimated to have been lost completely and irreversibly."

Fifth, a statute defining death should make clear that it does not affect existing legal provisions concerning the presumption of death in the absence of an individual presumed dead. Thus: "Nothing in this statute affects provisions in existing law according to which absent individuals may be presumed dead under specified conditions for particular purposes. Such a presumption does not constitute a judgment that the absent individual has in fact died; except as provided by law, individuals presumed dead shall be considered alive."

The handling of dead human bodies is regulated by law. This matter need not be treated in a statute defining death, but the law concerning the handling of corpses should be reviewed and amended if necessary to assure that bodies pronounced dead by direct diagnosis of brain death will be dealt with in a manner consonant with the respect due to human remains, and also in a manner consonant with the expressed wishes of the individual deceased and next of kin.

I. Criticism of Existing Statutes

From 1970 to 1977 at least eighteen states have enacted definition of death laws. How does the proposed statute compare with these statutes? It does not seem worthwhile to review all of these statutes, but a few comments are in order.

Kansas was the first state to enact a definition of death.[47] The statute attempts to legalize the use of the Harvard criteria by adding to the traditional criteria a provision that under certain conditions "A person will be considered medically and legally dead if, in the opinion of a physician, based on ordinary standards of medical practice, there is the absence of spontaneous brain function. . . . '' The statute explicitly states that death is to be pronounced before artificial life support is withdrawn and organs removed for transplant.

This statute has been widely criticized.[48] But the two most important difficulties we see in it have been noticed seldom if ever.

First, this approach does not sufficiently specify the factual state of affairs constituting brain death, namely, complete and irreversible loss of the functioning of the entire brain. ''Spontaneous brain function'' shows confusion in the word ''spontaneous'' and dangerous imprecision in the unspecified ''brain function.'' ''Spontaneous'' is a sign of confusion because it is difficult to imagine what nonspontaneous brain function would be. ''Brain function'' without specification is dangerous because it is open to interpretation as cortical brain function and even as reversible loss of function.

Second, this statute provides no safeguards to assure that the standard for certitude appropriate for judging that a human body is dead will be met. ''Ordinary standards of medical practice'' assumes the existence of standards in a field in which they are not agreed upon; in practice, it permits the Harvard criteria and even other weaker criteria to be applied by any physician, even though there are competent physicians and scientists who consider these criteria inadequate.[49]

The California statute takes a different approach. It assumes the usual and customary procedures for determining death and says that a physician may use them as the exclusive basis for pronouncing death. It avoids claiming to propose a definition of death. In respect to brain death it adds a simple provision: ''A person shall be pronounced dead if it is determined by a physician that the person has suffered a total and irreversible cessation of brain function. There shall be independent confirmation of the death by another physician.''[50]

The word ''total'' is an improvement, but it would be better to say ''function of the entire brain.'' The requirement for a second opinion shows some recognition of the need for safeguards, but it is not adequate, since what is needed is guidance as to the method of judging to be used. Any physician is likely to be able to find *some* other physician who will agree with his opinion, and this is all the statute requires.

Capron and Kass proposed a definition which was intended to improve upon the Kansas model. Their proposal was followed more or less closely by several states, first by Michigan in 1975:

A person will be considered dead if in the announced opinion of a physician, based on ordinary standards of medical practice in the community, there is the irreversible cessation of spontaneous respiratory and circulatory functions. If artificial means of support preclude a determination that these functions have ceased, a person will be considered dead if in the announced opinion of a physician, based on ordinary standards of medical practice in the community, there is the irreversible cessation of spontaneous brain functions.[51]

"In the community" was not in Capron-Kass but was inserted by the Michigan draftsmen. The insertion is unwelcome, for it introduces an element of relativity appropriate in malpractice law but hardly desirable in the determination of brain death.

This type of statute accentuates a general failing of the new laws: The focus is upon the physician. No provision is made for cases in which a physician is unavailable, and the assumption is made that there are ordinary standards of medical practice which are adequate. Also, the defective phrase "spontaneous brain function" is retained from the Kansas statute. Finally, this statute read literally means that persons who are totally paralyzed from the neck down are to be considered dead, although they are fully conscious, if the use of a respirator does not preclude determination that spontaneous respiration and circulation has ceased, as it usually does not.

In 1975 the American Bar Association adopted a "current" definition of death as follows:

> For all legal purposes, a human body with irreversible cessation of total brain function, according to usual and customary standards of medical practice, shall be considered dead.

The word "total" was inserted in the draft before it was adopted by the House of Delegates.[52] However, the report of the Committee on Medicine and Law, published several months later, does not take note of the insertion.[53] The chairman, McCarthy DeMere, states in this report that the phrase "usual and customary standards of medical practice" covers

> . . . the situation where the standards are even different in the same hospital. In the intensive care unit the standard of medical practice of pronouncement of death could be the "lack of brain waves by the electroencephalogram."

In other parts of the hospital other appropriate standards would be used.[54] Since EEG *cannot* by itself evidence lack of function of the entire brain, the omission of "total" was perhaps significant, and DeMere's exegesis of "usual and customary standards of medical practice" is a substantial cause for concern that the way is being paved to set new boundaries of legal personhood, and in this way to deprive some persons of all their rights, without facing up to the fact that this is what is being done.

The Bar Association's current definition was not proposed as a statute, yet it nevertheless has been enacted, first by Tennessee in 1976, fortunately with the inclusion of the word "total" before "brain function."[55]

In 1977 North Carolina enacted a bill which simultaneously deals with the "right to natural death" and with "brain death." The substantive provisions of the statute are introduced by the statement that the "General Assembly hereby recognizes that an individual's rights as a citizen of this State include the right to a peaceful and natural death." The act explicitly excludes construction "to authorize any affirmative or deliberate act or omission to end life other than to permit the natural process of dying."

The main operative paragraph concerning brain death is as follows:

> (a) If a person is comatose and there is no reasonable possibility that he will return to a cognitive sapient state, and: (1) it is determined by the attending physician that the person's present condition is: a. terminal; and b. incurable; and c. there has been an irreversible cessation of brain function; and (2) there is confirmation of the person's present condition as set out above in this subsection, by a majority of a committee of three physicians other than the attending physician; and (3) a vital function of the person is being sustained by extraordinary means; then, in addition to any other medically recognized criteria for determining death, the person may be pronounced dead.

Following paragraphs specify conditions under which the extraordinary means to prolong life may be terminated *after death has been pronounced* or may be continued to facilitate the purposes of the Uniform Anatomical Gift Act.[56]

To evaluate this statute several factors must be noticed: the context of this statute within the framework of recognition of a "right to natural death," the language drawn from the New Jersey Supreme Court decision in the Quinlan case referring to a comatose person for whom there is no likely return to a "cognitive sapient state,"[57] the extraordinary requirement of confirmation by a committee, and the special provisions for terminating or continuing extraordinary means to prolong life *after death has been pronounced*.

All these factors strongly suggest that this statute is radically redefining death and thereby legislating the legal nonpersonhood of those in irreversible coma who have suffered *some* damage to *some* part of the brain and who require *some* use of *some* extraordinary means to sustain *some* vital function. The statute requires, not that there be irreversible and complete loss of the function of the entire brain, but only that "there has been an irreversible cessation of brain function," which is true in anyone who is irreversibly comatose. Also, since the statute does not specify what extraordinary means must be in use, and since an irreversibly comatose person ordinarily is fed by tube, it could easily be argued that every such person meets the specified criteria. By this statute Miss Quinlan could have been declared dead—something no one involved in the case maintained—before she was successfully weaned from the respirator.

Some may think it would be desirable to stop the special feedings by which Miss Quinlan's life is still sustained as this is written (March 1978). They could be correct; we shall consider the question of how far the law should go in mandating care for noncompetent persons in chapter nine. Meanwhile, it is not clear that Mr. Quinlan is constrained by law to have his daughter's life maintained in this way.

Others may think it would be desirable to continue the special feedings by which her life is still sustained but to pronounce her dead and transfer this neomort to an emporion to be used in ways beneficial to others. (This could be done only if the requirement of laws relating to anatomical gifts and the disposal of bodies were met.)

For reasons developed throughout this chapter, we think it would be a grave injustice to pronounce Miss Quinlan or anyone else dead while parts of their brain continue to function, or even where it is not certain that their entire brain has irreversibly ceased functioning. Hence, regardless of the intentions of those who enacted it—which probably were above reproach—we consider this North Carolina statute to be gravely unjust, and we consider it a very serious threat to the fundamental rights which flow from legal personhood of all the citizens of that state and of other states which might follow this model.

J. A Federal Definition-of-Death Statute?

What remedy might be applied to the inadequacies in the statutes we have considered? How might the rights of all citizens of the United States be protected, while there is solved the problem raised by the vagueness of the concept of death, the cause of the current controversy.

The Fourteenth Amendment to the Constitution of the United States (section one) provides as follows:

> No State shall make or enforce any law which shall abridge the privileges or immunities of citizens of the United States; nor shall any State deprive any person of life, liberty, or property, without due process of law; nor deny to any person within its jurisdiction the equal protection of the laws.

The same amendment (section five) provides: "The Congress shall have power to enforce, by appropriate legislation, the provisions of this article."

Since every individual's status as a legal person conditions his or her protection by all of the provisions of section one, and since any definition of death thus far enacted inadequately protects persons against a mistaken pronouncement of death which would terminate their status as legal persons, it seems to us appropriate that Congress should exercise its enforcement power under section five to affect the protection for all legal purposes of the rights of all persons under the jurisdiction of the Constitution, as these rights were intended to be protected by section one.

It might be argued that this matter is appropriately one which should be left to the jurisdiction of the states. There are practical reasons for not doing so. A great deal of federal funding is used for medical treatment, especially for research and teaching. Congress has a responsibility to assure that such activities, in which the federal government is involved, do not violate fundamental rights. Also, dying (or dead?) bodies have been transported from state to state; uniformity in definition of death and in standards for declaring it would be desirable. But much more fundamental than these considerations is the fact that the Fourteenth Amendment obviously is intended to limit the arbitrariness of the states; section five clearly is designed to empower the Congress to preempt matters previously within the jurisdiction of the various states just to the extent necessary to protect fundamental rights.

Finally, it might be urged that if the Congress were to attempt to protect the Fourteenth Amendment rights of all persons under the jurisdiction of the Constitution by enacting a uniform, national definition of death statute to preclude the danger that persons be deprived of their legal status by being declared dead mistakenly and prematurely, such an attempt would amount to an invasion of the province of the courts—especially of the United States Supreme Court—to which the power to interpret the language of the Constitution and to limit infringements by statute upon constitutionally guaranteed rights belongs. On this view, it would be argued, Congress could not act to legislate a definition of death unless the Court first took notice that inadequate definitions of death threaten Fourteenth Amendment rights.

The Supreme Court itself has answered this objection by asserting that neither the language nor the history of section five of the Fourteenth Amendment warrants such a construction, that congressional legislation to enforce the provisions of the amendment is authorized and contemplated, that the Congress is not limited to merely particularizing the "majestic generalities" of the amendment, and that congressional action need not await judicial determination that the application of a state law which is to be blocked violated this amendment.[58]

Our conclusion,then, is that the Congress has the power and the responsibility to protect legal personhood from infringement by enacting a statute defining death and regulating the methods for judging that death has occurred. Since the threat is clear and present, the need for congressional action is urgent.

4: The Liberty to Refuse Medical Treatment

A. "Euthanasia" and the Refusal of Treatment

In its etymological sense the word "euthanasia" simply means "good death." A word with such an origin can mean many things. For example, it could be taken to express the concept which some Christians express by "happy death," the concept of dying in Christ at peace with God. But in fact, until the last decade or so, "euthanasia" generally was taken to mean the act of putting to death someone suffering from a painful or prolonged mortal illness or injury.

In this sense euthanasia is mercy killing; it involves an activity: someone's doing something in order to bring about death. In recent discussion "euthanasia" in this sense often is called "active euthanasia." Active euthanasia might be done to persons *with* their consent, in which case it is called "voluntary active euthanasia," which we shall consider in chapter six; or it might be done to persons *without* consent on their part, in which case it is called "nonvoluntary active euthanasia," which we shall consider in chapter eight.

Distinguished from active euthanasia in much recent discussion is the withholding or termination of medical treatment when such treatment would be required to preserve or prolong life in someone suffering from a painful or prolonged mortal illness or injury, or in someone suffering permanent impairment considered to be incompatible with living a meaningful life. Such withholding or termination of lifesaving medical treatment has been called "passive euthanasia."

Passive euthanasia can also be distinguished according to whether it is voluntary or not. In chapter nine we shall consider the requirements of justice in the provision of medical treatment for noncompetent persons—that is, for persons unable to demand or forgo, to give or to refuse consent to treatment. If medical treatment needed to preserve or prolong life is withheld from such

86

persons or terminated in their cases, one might speak of "nonvoluntary passive euthanasia." In the present chapter we consider the liberty of persons who are competent to give or to refuse consent to medical treatment upon themselves. If this liberty is exercised to refuse treatment which would be lifesaving in order to avoid pain or hasten death or both, one might speak of "voluntary passive euthanasia." Voluntary passive euthanasia in recent discussion also has been called "natural death" and "death with dignity," although the latter expression sometimes is used to refer to other forms of euthanasia.

At the time of this writing (March 1978) eight states have enacted legislation—so called "natural-death" or 'right-to-die" laws—to facilitate voluntary passive euthanasia. In this chapter we shall consider this legislation and propose an alternative to it.

Accordingly, in the present chapter we shall not be considering the question of medical treatment for legally noncompetent persons—children, the severely retarded, the permanently insane, the senile, or, in general, those who are legally unable either to give or to refuse consent to treatment upon themselves—except to the extent that some such persons once were competent and while so might have made decisions about their own future treatment.

To put the point affirmatively, in the present chapter we are concerned with the liberty of persons to refuse medical treatment *for themselves*. This liberty is generally accepted when exercised by competent persons with respect to the present. We shall consider to what extent and by what means the law ought to facilitate the exercise by competent persons of this liberty with respect to the future when they may become unable to make decisions.

Much discussion of this problem is confused because the difference between moral questions and jurisprudential questions is ignored. Here we will not consider whether and under what conditions it might be moral for a person to refuse lifesaving treatment. We shall discuss this moral question in chapter twelve. In some cases acts morally wrong must be permitted by law, for the sake of just regard for liberty. Hence, in the present chapter we are concerned exclusively with the extent to which law should protect and facilitate the exercise of liberty; we are not concerned with the conditions under which one's exercise of the liberty to give or to refuse consent to medical treatment is morally good or evil.

B. The General Primacy of Patient Choice

Anglo-American law takes for granted as a rule that every competent adult is at liberty to seek medical treatment and not to seek it, and to give or to refuse consent to any treatment which is proposed. No police officer takes one to the doctor; one chooses to go. If one is negligent about one's own health, one cannot be charged with any offense or sued for damages by anyone else. If one does not like the treatment which physicians propose, one can dismiss them and find other physicians or one can refuse to follow directions, not take one's medicine, reject the suggestion that one go to the hospital, refuse to sign forms consenting to surgery—in general, be an uncooperative patient. The physician has no choice but to put up with one's uncooperativeness or to withdraw from the case.

In a 1914 New York case, Judge (later Justice) Cardozo stated this proposition clearly:

> Every human being of adult years and sound mind has a right to determine what shall be done with his own body; and a surgeon who performs an operation without his patient's consent commits an assault, for which he is liable in damages.[1]

The underlying concept is that a person has a basic right to bodily integrity and intangibility. Nobody can cut a person or even so much as touch a person who is not willing to be cut or touched without violating that person's rights and providing him or her with a legal claim to compensation for the violation. In principle, this claim is no less against a physician who treats a person without consent than it is against someone who attacks another in anger or with premeditated malice, for although the latter might be guilty of a crime of which the physician would be innocent, the *personal* offense is the same.

In effect, the law intends to enclose everyone in an invisible shield and to give to each person the right to decide when to lower the shield and when to keep it in place. The underlying theory, which surely is sound, is that bodily contact can be repugnant—if not harmful, distasteful—and that each person is the best judge of what contact is acceptable.

In the medical context the mere fact that one puts oneself into the hands of physicians does not mean that they can proceed as they see fit. They have a duty to explain what sort of treatment they propose and why, and to point out any significant risks or reasonable alternatives. They also have a legal duty to limit treatment to that to which one has consented. If they go beyond the boundaries, even for the patient's good and with good results, physicians violate the patient's rights.

For several reasons the basic legal situation with respect to the primacy of the patient's judgment is not as clear in most people's practical experience with physicians and hospitals as it is in theory.

In the first place, consent to the contact involved in medical treatment generally is implicit in the fact that one seeks treatment and cooperates in it; many persons do not realize that they have a right to be informed and to make decisions even after they have put themselves into the hands of a physician. Because talking with patients is time-consuming and can be a nuisance, physicians are not likely to make matters more explicit than necessary. Some legal decisions even have accepted the principle that physicians need not inform patients when the information itself might make the patient worse.[3]

In the second place, most people learn while children how to deal with physicians. Parental authority is transferred to the physician, who tends to remain a parent figure; the physician's technical skill adds reinforcement to this attitude, and the dependency one normally feels when ill and in need of care leads to childlike submissiveness in most patients.

Corresponding to the submissiveness of patients many physicians take a paternalistic stance. They hardly respect more than the law demands the right of patients to know what their condition is, what they are getting into with particular forms of treatment, and what the outlook is.[4] In defending their attitude physicians sometimes point out that they are not mere technicians, like auto mechanics or plumbers, who should be expected to do what patients want; physicians are professionals with their own judgment as to what is good and responsibility for carrying out this judgment. Indeed, even an auto mechanic or a plumber has some expertise. The status to which such physicians fear being reduced might better be compared to that of a simple laborer or servant: people who do no more than what they are told.

However, if physicians ought not to be viewed as mere servants (and they certainly ought not) and if physicians have professional knowledge and responsibility which a patient is rash to challenge and arrogant to invade (and any good physician has), still the patient must not be treated as a mere patient— that is, as an individual wholly incapable of action. Health and even life itself is only one good among many in which persons are interested. Individuals are at liberty to decide to what extent they wish to subordinate other concerns for the sake of pursuing this good. Hence, every patient has the right to set limits to the trouble, the inconvenience, the expense, the painfulness, the mutilation— in a word, the cost in the widest sense of "cost"—to be tolerated in even the soundest and most competent course of therapy.[5]

Any physician who cannot see and wholeheartedly accept this right of the patient is imposing a judgment not about a matter within medical competence but about the patient's hierarchy of values, which is a matter for moral and religious teaching and for personal decision. Of course, if a patient sets limits, the expectation of benefit from the physician's care must be limited correspondingly. And law must recognize this limit; it clearly would be unjust to hold a physician responsible for the poor health or death of patients who will not accept treatment which the physician proposes and which is in no way faulty from the point of view of medical judgment.

Moreover, if a physician proposes treatment and a patient is unwilling to accept the proposal and to cooperate with it, then the physician must be free to withdraw from the case. Legally physicians may do so provided they give sufficient notice to permit another arrangement to be made.[6] At the same time, if physicians use their right to withdraw as a lever to compel a patient to change a *nonmedical* judgment as to what is best, they act unfairly, unless the patient's judgment cannot be followed according to the physician's own good conscience.

C. Presumed Consent and the Physician's Liability

There is one very important and very common exception to the requirement that the physician proceed only on the basis of informed consent by the patient. The exception arises in the case of emergency, where the patient is unable either to give or to refuse consent. The physician may proceed provided the treatment supplied is medically appropriate and such that a reasonable person normally would consent to it, and provided the physician has no knowledge that the particular patient would not consent. In other words, when a patient cannot decide about treatment, the law establishes a reasonable assumption that the ordinary person who needs care would want the treatment a normally competent physician can give. Were this assumption not made, the intangibility of those few who would refuse treatment if they could do so would be held paramount to the actual desires as well as to the well-being of most people.[7]

Very often in emergency situations consent to proposed medical treatment by a spouse or other adult family member will be sought. In concept this procedure makes little sense insofar as the basic rights of the noncompetent adult are concerned, since no one else can exercise one's liberty on one's behalf and since one's need and incapacity to consent by itself is a sufficient basis for the physician to proceed with treatment.[8] However, by requiring consent by a close relative for treatment to a noncompetent adult the physician gains some protection against subsequent claims from the family and also some guarantee of payment of medical costs.

Once physicians begin to treat patients, they are held to carry on the treatment with the degree of care and skill usually exercised in the treatment of similar patients by the average physician under similar conditions. A specialist must meet the standards of the specialty; a physician working in a well-equipped hospital must use facilities as is customary there. The failure of one rendering medical treatment to act with that degree of knowledge, skill, and care commonly exercised in the same community under like circumstances by the average careful and reputable member of the profession is considered by law to be *malpractice*. Medical malpractice is a form of negligence; if the patient suffers any injury, loss, or damage—even if someone else whose interests depend upon the patient's being properly treated suffers in some way—the physician can be sued and the patient and/or others damaged can recover.[9]

The law's presumption of consent to treatment of a noncompetent adult in any emergency situation together with the constant concern of physicians to avoid anything which might be considered malpractice can combine to require physicians to proceed with great caution and inflexibility in caring for adults who are neither able to give nor able to refuse consent. In cases of this sort the physician does have primacy of judgment which would belong to the patient if the patient were able to decide. The wishes of the patient's family are not legally in control, except to the extent that each adult member of the family can relieve the physician of liability to himself or herself.

A physician might suspect from the patient's previous attitude and remarks that the particular patient would prefer that treatment be limited or terminated, but physicians cannot rely upon such suspicions, nor even on firmer evidence, since they cannot be confident that a court of law, which is the ultimate judge of evidence and legal responsibility, will reach the same construction of the patient's wishes. Moreover, in some jurisdictions the malpractice case law itself tends to press physicians toward meeting the ordinary standard of practice in order to avoid malpractice, even when they are quite sure that the patient would prefer treatment other than—perhaps much less than—the average careful and reputable practitioner in the community would provide under the circumstances.[10]

Some critics of natural-death or right-to-die legislation have argued that such legislation is wholly unnecessary, since patients now have primacy in deciding upon their own care. Such legislation, it is argued, somehow replaces patient primacy with an implicit supposition that physicians are masters of their patients unless patients take legal action in advance to limit what physicians may do. Such a supposition, on this view, tends to shift the locus of power in cases in which no legal action is taken in advance from the patient to the physician.[11]

In the light of the explanation we have given of the law's presumption of consent and enforcement upon physicians of the standard of practice common to their colleagues this argument is unconvincing. When an adult patient cannot decide personally, physicians are in control whether they wish to be or not, since they will be held responsible for the treatment they provide, and the extent to which their responsibility is limited by earlier wishes of the patient and by current wishes of the patient's family is at best marginal and doubtful. We shall consider later in the chapter a proposal to remedy this situation simply by assigning full and definite authority to the patient's family. But this is not the current state of American law.

Indeed, the case of Miss Karen Quinlan exemplifies the problem. Miss Quinlan was an adult, not a child legally under her father's parental care; she had been legally competent, but was no longer competent to give or to refuse consent to treatment; her earlier expressed beliefs and attitudes about the care she would wish under such circumstances were considered by the courts insufficient evidence of her nonconsent to treatment; the physicians caring for Miss Quinlan had assumed responsibility under circumstances of medical emergency with a noncompetent adult; the physicians believed that standard medical practice required that they *not* remove her from the respirator; the wishes of her family could *not* be considered determinative. Hence, Mr. Joseph Quinlan sought to be appointed legal guardian of his daughter so that his decision could control her care. The facts and existing law were perceived in the same way by the Superior Court and by the Supreme Court of New Jersey; however, the lower court did not grant Mr. Quinlan's request while the higher court did.[12] Regardless of what one thinks of the outcome, this case aptly illustrates the existence of a problem which so-called natural-death or right-to-die legislation is attempting to solve.

D. Limits of Patient Liberty

Apart from the problems which exist with respect to adults who have been competent but become noncompetent, there is some question in existing case law as to the extent to which even competent adults may legally refuse treatment *required to preserve life*. Several excellent studies have been done on the relevant cases, and so we shall not review these cases in detail. However, a summary of the results of the studies is in order.[13]

The leading case usually cited was decided in Kansas in 1960. In *dictum* the judge said:

> Anglo-American law starts with the premise of thorough-going self-determination. It follows that each man is considered to be master of his own body, and he may, if he be of sound mind, expressly prohibit the performance of life-saving surgery, or other medical treatment. A doctor might well believe that an operation or form of treatment is desirable or necessary but the law does not permit him to substitute his own judgment for that of the patient by any form of artifice or deception.[14]

Many of the cases have to do with the refusal of blood transfusions by Jehovah's Witnesses, who believe that receiving such transfusions violates a divine prohibition of eating blood. However, some cases are concerned with the refusal of other treatment, especially by elderly persons who prefer the consequences (including an earlier death) of forgoing life-preserving treatment to the pain and other disadvantages of accepting it. From the very general principle set down in the case cited one would suppose that all of these refusals of treatment by competent patients would have been honored and supported by the authority of the courts. But such is not the case.

In the first place, in some cases medical treatment is required by law in the interests of public health and safety. The leading precedent in this matter is a United States Supreme Court decision that the interest of a state in protecting it members from smallpox overrides the right of persons to refuse treatment—in this case vaccination—both insofar as this right is based upon bodily intangibility and insofar as it is based upon religious liberty and conscientious objection to treatment.[15] This case is followed by many others asserting the priority of the public interest to individual liberty, even religious liberty, in several matters that involve medical care, examination, and so on.[16]

In most cases the assertion of the priority of the public interest seems to us reasonable enough. In some cases, perhaps, liberty and especially religious liberty ought to be given more respect than sometimes has been the case. However, this problem is not especially related to euthanasia, and it must be argued on its own merits. Hence, in what follows we assume that any plan to protect the right of individuals to refuse treatment must allow for the right of legislatures by general laws and the courts by judgments in particular cases to order treatment in the interest of public health and safety even over religiously based objections to such treatment.

In the second place, courts have ordered medical treatment in some cases at least partly on the basis that without treatment patients probably would be incapacitated, by death or otherwise, to fulfill responsibilities to minor children. In one case the ground was that without treatment an unborn child might be harmed.[17] In other cases courts have not used this ground for ordering treatment, perhaps at least partly because the evidence did not show serious likelihood of harm to the children.[18]

This ground for compelling adults to accept treatment must be distinguished from the quite different question of the medical treatment of children themselves, which we shall consider in chapter nine. Commentators disagree as to whether courts ought to order the treatment of competent adults on the basis of their responsibilities to their dependents.[19] No one seems to have considered other cases in which an individual's responsibilities might be such that the public welfare would demand medically indicated treatment despite the individual's refusal. What, for example, might the public have a right to require if a Jehovah's Witness came to hold some high public office, required and refused blood transfusions, and in so doing imperiled a significant public interest in orderly government?

It seems to us that here the claims of liberty must to some extent be limited by other demands of justice. The specification of kinds of cases under which the public interest might reasonably require compulsory care hardly seems possible. To legislate the priority of the interests of dependent children to the liberty of parents to refuse treatment, especially if that refusal is religiously grounded, seems excessive, and yet there are some cases—for example, that of a pregnant woman in the late stages of pregnancy and that of a sole parent of children who might be left orphans with no support—in which the welfare of others establishes a public interest which seems very significant.

Hence, in what follows we assume that any plan to protect the rights of individuals to refuse treatment must allow courts by orders in particular cases to order treatment in the interest of the public welfare if lack of treatment probably would incapacitate an individual, by death or otherwise, to fulfill grave noncontractual obligations to others. In this area a refusal of treatment on religious grounds seems to warrant greater deference and so require a more compelling state interest to override than a refusal strictly on the ground of the right of bodily intangibility.

In the third place, in some cases courts have overridden the refusal of treatment by a person when competent on the basis that by the time of adjudication the individual had become incompetent; in some cases courts have expressed a suspicion that the person who was refusing treatment actually desired it.[20] No one seems to defend judicial opinions such as these. Such opinions suggest two requirements which any sound plan to protect the rights of individuals to refuse treatment should meet.

First, provision should be made to consider and act upon evidence that an individual when competent had made absolutely clear an unwillingness to accept certain kinds of treatment. For example, an individual who is well-known to be a Jehovah's Witness and who has made clear adherence to their belief and practice in respect to blood transfusions should not have blood imposed by a court order when an emergency arises on the ground that at that time the individual is noncompetent, hardly competent, unable to deliberate about the matter, really anxious to live, and so forth. (Of course, if a particular Jehovah's Witness gives some real sign of personal consent, that is another matter.) Second, provision should be made that the mere fact of refusing life-preserving treatment may not itself count as evidence of noncompetence.

A fourth class of cases in which courts have overridden refusal of treatment involved the basis that death resulting from such refusal would be suicide, and so contrary to public policy.[21] Legal commentators have been uniformly critical of the introduction of this consideration into issues about refusal of treatment.

In the first place, suicide involves both the intent to bring about one's own death and the setting in motion of the self-destructive process. When people refuse treatment of an existing condition, the intent often is lacking and cannot be presumed; the destructive process is not self-initiated. In the second place, whatever public policy considerations stand against liberty to commit suicide—a matter we shall discuss in chapter five—the liberty to refuse life-preserving treatment has an established legal status and reasonable ground which significantly distinguishes the refusal of treatment from suicide. The law must respect the liberty to refuse treatment even if it can be abused in some cases with self-destructive intent, but public policy considerations perhaps preclude equal respect for the liberty to commit suicide.[22]

Quite distinct from the case in which an individual simply refuses medical treatment is the case in which someone does in fact attempt suicide or self-mutilation and is in need of medical care to limit or repair the damage or injury accomplished. Generally speaking, existing law supports interference with genuine suicide attempts.[23] Since many who attempt suicide are reasonably assumed to be acting irrationally and without deliberate intent, the imposition of emergency medical treatment seems warranted, even if it must be given despite the express refusal of the patient.[24]

Physicians dealing with suicide emergencies cannot be expected to decide about the legal competence of the patient, nor should such physicians be subject to liability for any treatment they render with due care in such cases. Hence, we think that any plan to protect the liberty of individuals to refuse treatment must include a specific exception authorizing refused medical treatment if it is required by one who needs care because of an attempt at suicide or self-mutilation.

The fifth and last set of problem cases are those in which courts have ordered medical treatment partly on the basis that honoring the patient's desire not to have it would infringe upon the rights of the physician or the hospital or both.[25] The concern of the courts in these cases seems to be made up of two different considerations, confused with each other. First, as we have explained, physicians and hospitals are threatened by the law of malpractice. Potentially, they might be subject even to criminal charges if a patient dies due to criminal negligence. Second, the medical profession has its own standards of ethics, and physicians have their own conscientious responsibility. Legal commentators are agreed that neither of these considerations warrants the legal overriding of a patient's liberty to refuse care.[26]

Considerations of physician and hospital liability provide good ground for seeking judicial determination of a problem, and the courts should be readily available to make decisions in cases where there is serious doubt about grave responsibilities. But once a case reaches court, it is unreasonable for the court itself to use potential liability as a ground for overriding the patient's choice. The court can assume the liability and cannot be held for its mistakes.

The standards of ethics and the demands of conscience on the part of the physician are another matter altogether. The professional judgment of a physician cannot reasonably be held to override patient choice; to take that position would be to eliminate consent altogether and to absolutize the standard of good medical practice and the good of life and health on which it is based. If a physician has real conscientious objections to treating a patient within the bounds of the patient's willingness to be treated, however, the solution is to permit the physician to withdraw, not to compel the patient to accept unwanted treatment.

E. Privacy and the Refusal of Treatment

The Constitution of the United States and much other law seek in many ways to protect persons against unwanted intrusion by officials and even by other persons into matters which those protected wish to keep hidden, secret or confidential. These legal protections safeguard privacy, understanding "privacy" as it traditionally was understood. As we have explained in chapter two, section G, beginning in 1965, the United States Supreme Court has been withdrawing certain areas of liberty from regulation by criminal law—for example, the liberty to use contraceptives and to have abortions—and calling these immunities "privacy" in a new sense.

In 1973 a lower court in Pennsylvania considered the case of a woman who refused proposed surgery for possible cancer. Although confined to a mental institution as a chronic schizophrenic, the woman was ruled competent to give or to refuse consent to the treatment proposed. She had a number of reasons for refusing the surgery, among them a concern, based on the experience of a relative, that she might die as a result. The court vindicated her liberty to refuse treatment, stating:

> In our opinion the constitutional right of privacy includes the right of a mature competent adult to refuse to accept medical recommendations that may prolong one's life and which, to a third person at least, appear to be in his best interest; in short, that the right of privacy includes a right to die with which the State should not interfere where there are no minor or unborn children and no clear and present danger to public health, welfare or morals. If the person was competent while being presented with the decision which she did, the Court should not interfere even though her decision might be considered unwise, foolish or ridiculous.[27]

The novel element in this decision is its reliance on the new right to privacy and its extrapolation from privacy of a right to die.

The introduction of "right to die" into this decision is indeed strange. Dying was not the good protected, since the proposed treatment was not clearly necessary to preserve life; treatment was not refused with a view to death but in fact refused due to a possibly unwise fear of death. In an earlier case, involving a Jehovah's Witness, the Supreme Court of New Jersey also injected an irrelevant discussion of a "right to choose to die," which the court rejected, although it was not at issue; in that case the court proceeded to impose treatment because it denied the existence of any such constitutional right.[28]

In the context of the question of the liberty to refuse treatment, talk of a "right to die" is unnecessary and confusing. "Right to die" is ambiguous. In one sense it suggests a liberty to be immune from coercive interventions which would prevent death; in another sense it suggests an entitlement to the means, including an act by another, required to bring about death. The liberty to refuse treatment always has been protected without mention of any "right to die" in the first sense, and so in this context the expression is unnecessary. But it is used by proponents of euthanasia in an effort to lay the foundation for asserting a "right to die" in the second sense. Obviously, active euthanasia must be permitted by law if there is a right to die in this sense. But to assert such a right at the beginning of a discussion of active euthanasia is to beg the question, since the question whether active euthanasia ought to be permitted precisely is the question whether a person is entitled under certain circumstances to be killed.

In the Quinlan case the Supreme Court of New Jersey did not reverse its earlier view; this decision posits no right to die but posits only a right of self-determination to terminate medical treatment and allow Miss Quinlan's life to end by natural forces. Indeed, the court is careful to distinguish this liberty to let nature take its course from any sort of active killing.[29] However, the decision does rely upon the new right of privacy, which it contrasts with the bodily invasion of the means used to keep Miss Quinlan alive. The court denies that Mr. Quinlan's own right of privacy is involved; the sole right is that of the patient herself. The decision is that this right may be asserted on Miss Quinlan's behalf by her guardian:

> If a putative decision by Karen to permit this non-cognitive, vegetative existence to terminate by natural forces is regarded as a valuable incident of her right of privacy, as we believe it to be, then it should not be discarded solely on the basis that her condition prevents her conscious exercise of the choice. The only practical way to prevent destruction of the right is to permit the guardian and family of Karen to render their best judgment, subject to the qualifications hereinafter stated, as to whether she would exercise it in these circumstances. If their conclusion is in the affirmative this decision should be accepted by a society the overwhelming majority of whose members would, we think, in similar circumstances, exercise such a choice in the same way for themselves or for those closest to them. It is for this reason that we determine that Karen's right of privacy may be asserted in her behalf, in this respect, by

her guardian and family under the particular circumstances presented by this record.[30]

Thus the liberty to give or to refuse consent to treatment is unmentioned, and instead an appeal is made to privacy, with an argument from the universalizability of the decision to terminate treatment—this is what most people would choose in the circumstances—to the conclusion that *subject to qualifications* the privacy right can be exercised on Miss Quinlan's behalf by her "guardian and family."

If the new right of privacy is nothing but certain aspects of liberty, as we argued in chapter two, section G, then the common-law right of bodily integrity and intangibility, which always grounded the liberty to give or to refuse consent to medical treatment, is more a principle than a consequence of privacy. In any case, the liberty of individuals with respect to medical treatment was well established in the law long before 1965 and quite independently of any claim to privacy.

Moreover, one can question the wisdom of gathering long-recognized liberties into the new category. As matters were, the liberty to give and to refuse consent to treatment was at least something with which the law had a good deal of experience; the rules for playing that game were very well developed. If this liberty is now to be regarded as an aspect of the new right of privacy, the whole development must begin again.

The decision of the Supreme Court of New Jersey in the Quinlan case shows some of the difficulties of doing so. Had the case been treated in terms of the long-recognized liberty rather than in terms of the new right to privacy, the court might more fruitfully have confronted the real problem presented by the case: Under what conditions does the ordinary assumption that patients would desire and consent to treatment in accord with the usual standard of good medical practice give way? In other words, when must constructive consent—that is, the assumption that the patient would consent—to medical treatment be reconstructed in view of the special conditions of a patient which seem to make treatment no longer useful? This was in fact the question which the court sought to answer in its argument that almost anyone in that situation would want the respirator turned off.

The court did not explain how the usual assumption of consent can be reconstructed when physicians believe, as happened in the Quinlan case, that continuation of treatment is required and others concerned with a patient's well-being think the treatment should stop. The liberty of the patient to give or to refuse consent is crucial; what is needed is a sound way of determining what assumptions to make about the exercise of this liberty when the person cannot in fact exercise it.

The court suggested that a hospital ethics committee be consulted. If such a body existed and had authority to override the judgments of other parties to a dispute, it could resolve issues. But if it lacked such authority, any committee would seem simply to complicate the controversy by bringing into it an additional party. The authority of the proposed committee was not clarified.

F. Clarification of Standards a Partial Solution

Although the committee system enjoined by the Supreme Court of New Jersey seems to us misconceived, part of the problem of deciding what the noncompetent patient is assumed to consent to could be alleviated by committees of physicians, and the medical profession needs no new authority to deal with this part of the problem. As we have explained, physicians are not negligent provided they treat patients in line with the usual standard of good medical practice. Noncompetent patients are assumed to consent precisely to such treatment. It follows that if physicians who work together under similar circumstances can reach a consensus about how to handle certain sorts of cases, their consensus will shape the assumption of consent by the noncompetent to treatment in cases of those sorts.

We are not suggesting that physicians can or should arbitrarily change standards. The matter is not one for professional politics and it cannot be helped by taking votes. But a really representative committee of physicians in any locality might consider cases of sorts in which many people would consider the continuation of treatment to be futile and of no benefit to patients. If with discussion a genuine consensus is found to exist, and if this consensus is considered reasonable by competent colleagues in other localities, then the communication of the fact of this reasonable consensus to all physicians working in the community would be a useful guide to judgment in such cases. If one followed this guide in judging what treatment *was medically indicated* in a particular case, and if the judgment were challenged, one would have solid evidence that the usual standard of good medical practice had in fact been met.

Where consensus among physicians of average skill and carefulness is that a certain treatment is of no benefit to a patient, then consent to the treatment cannot be assumed. To continue the treatment in such a case is just as surely malpractice as to limit or terminate treatment which is usually given for the sake of its benefit—at least in terms of comfort—to the patient. For example, it is sometimes said that some physicians repeatedly attempt to resuscitate dying patients because they fear liability for malpractice. If they do the procedure repeatedly and do not regard the effort to be of any value to the patient, they are acting contrary to the consent which they should assume, namely, to treatment likely to help the patient. In cases like this discussion could clarify matters, for very likely in any given community of physicians there are some cases in which no one or hardly anyone would regard resuscitation as appropriate.

Physicians might hesitate to carry out the proposals we are making. But they do some of this work of looking for consensus already and should not shirk doing as much of it as necessary if they do not wish to have others intrude upon the sphere which properly does belong to medical judgment. Also, there might be hesitation to reduce standards of practice to a code which might inhibit rather than facilitate sound judgments in particular cases. But the consensus which is discovered need not be expressed in affirmative standards stated in general terms. It can instead be expressed in a way more familiar to clinical practice, by describing some actual cases and indicating kinds of treatment which by consensus are *not* required according to the usual standard of good medical practice in the community.

Such committee work would not have helped matters in the Quinlan case unless it had discovered and communicated a consensus that in a case such as Miss Quinlan's the use of the respirator was not *medically indicated*. Had such a consensus existed and been known to the physicians, their obligation to respect the boundaries of assumed patient consent—that is, its limitation to beneficial treatment in accord with the usual standard of good medical practice—would have led them to the conclusion that the respirator had to be discontinued.

In the absence of such a medical consensus—as well as in cases in which medical consensus does not settle the issue—there are only two ways to prevent similar cases. One is by clarifying the extent to which law ought to mandate the medical treatment of noncompetent patients. We shall consider this question in chapter nine. The other is by providing more effective ways for persons, when competent, to make known their own judgments in regard to their treatment during a future time of incompetency. This is the problem still to be solved in the present chapter.

G. A Critique of Existing Legislation

A plan for facilitating the exercise of one's liberty to give or to refuse consent to future medical treatment really will solve the problem only if it meets four conditions.

First, the liberty protected with respect to the future should extend precisely as far as the liberty an individual has at present. Thus, on the one hand, the limits upon refusal of consent set by the public health, welfare and safety, and other factors we discussed previously must be respected. On the other hand, to facilitate liberty in refusing treatment only when one's life is artificially sustained and one's condition is terminal hardly is adequate to protect those who wish to refuse treatment in other circumstances. For example, Jehovah's Witnesses hardly are treated fairly if others are helped by law to avoid unwanted treatment while unwanted blood transfusions are given them when they happen to be unconscious and this treatment is medically indicated. Other people might prefer not to have treatment they consider too costly, too risky, too painful, too mutilating; for all these reasons and others people might wish to make sure that the unwanted treatment will not be given if they happen to be unconscious, although not dying. If a liberty is to be facilitated for some, all have a right to have their lawful exercise of the same liberty facilitated. Bills which focus exclusively upon the terminally ill are discriminatory; they violate the right to equal protection of the laws.

Second, if physicians are to be restricted by a more effective exercise of the liberty to refuse consent, they must be relieved of liability for respecting the restriction as they are legally bound to do. It may be that there is no *real* liability to be relieved of, but that is not the point. In the concrete there are possibilities and probabilities, not clear-cut facts. Physicians have a right to know where they stand; they cannot be expected to take constant risks of incurring liability by walking an infinitely fine and unclear line between treating up to standard but beyond consent and treating within consent but short of standard.

Third, the interests of patients in being treated competently and up to standard when they do consent must be protected. Patients who refuse consent to certain treatment should not have to forgo legal protection against negligence in the treatment they do accept. The release from liability ought not to be a blank check. The patient must assume the risks of doing without the treatment refused, but it is wrong to make a patient pay for this by assuming risks for bad consequences which an average skilled and careful physician can take care of. In other words, the usual standard, adjusted by the refusal, must still apply when some treatment is desired and given. Moreover, there must be a very strong guarantee that the rights of patients who do consent or should be presumed to consent will not be violated by their being mistakenly treated as if they had refused consent to some treatment. Any plan which facilitates the liberty of some to refuse by undermining the security of others to receive the care which they want—which, in fact, most people want—sacrifices fairness to all for the sake of the liberty of some.

Fourth, a sound plan for facilitating the exercise of one's liberty to refuse consent to medical treatment for the future must provide a workable procedure. The refusal has to be expressed and communicated. The genuineness and validity of the communication must be certain. What is being refused must be definite, so that physicians will know just how far to go and where their responsibility and legal liability falls. The person who wishes to refuse consent must have open as many ways as possible of specifying what treatment is accepted and what refused.

With these four conditions in mind we can look briefly at some of the methods already proposed to facilitate the liberty to refuse consent. One approach is embodied in the so-called right-to-die or natural-death statutes which at the time of this writing (March 1978) have been enacted in eight states. The other approach is that individuals should be able to have a legally recognized agent or representative who can authoritatively give or refuse consent as treatment proceeds upon the noncompetent patient. The former requires a person to say beforehand *what* is refused; the latter only requires an advance decision concerning *who* can refuse. There are variations on these two main themes, but we do not think they need to be examined here.[31]

The first natural-death statute was passed by California in 1976; in 1977 seven other states—Texas, Oregon, Idaho, Nevada, North Carolina, New Mexico, and Arkansas—enacted such legislation.[32] The Texas and Oregon acts closely follow that of California and may be considered with it, as may the Idaho and Nevada acts, although they differ more significantly from the California model.

The California Natural Death Act proceeds on legislative findings that medical technology makes possible "the artificial prolongation of human life beyond natural limits." This "may cause loss of patient dignity and unnecessary pain and suffering." Persons have a right to decide about their own treatment, including the decision that when they are in a terminal condition, life-sustaining procedures will be withheld or withdrawn. Although the use of such procedures in such cases provides "nothing medically necessary or beneficial to the patient," physicians and lawyers are unsure of the legality of terminating their use even when a competent patient explicitly demands this. Hence, in recognition of the "dignity and privacy which patients have a right to expect" the act recognizes the right of a terminal, adult, competent patient to direct the physician to withhold or withdraw life-sustaining procedures.

The definitions in this act are important. A "terminal condition" is one which the physicians believe will cause death with or without life-sustaining procedures that would "serve only to postpone the moment of death." A "qualified patient" is one certified in writing by two physicians to be terminal. A "life-sustaining procedure" is a "mechanical or other artificial means to sustain, restore, or supplant a vital function, which, when applied to a qualified patient, would serve only to artificially prolong the moment of death" in the terminal patient.

The act authorizes persons to direct by means of a standard form that if they become incurable and terminal, then when death is imminent life-sustaining procedures shall be withheld or withdrawn so that they will "be permitted to die naturally." The directive refers to itself as the exercise of the legal right to refuse treatment. It includes a provision nullifying it in case of pregnancy. A special paragraph is completed only if the patient has been diagnosed as terminal at least fourteen days before the directive is made. The directive is in force for five years but may be reinstated or revoked by a competent person at any time, and competency cannot be questioned in case of revocation. If a person is noncompetent when the directive expires, it stays in force until communication is possible once more. Special requirements must be met if the person making the directive is in a nursing home. Any directive is valid only if witnessed by two persons not having a special interest.

Anyone involved in causing the withholding or withdrawal of life-sustaining procedures from a terminal patient is relieved of all liability for so doing provided it is done in accord with the requirements of the act. However, the physician is held responsible for making sure that the directive complies with the requirements of the act. If the patient is competent—a judgment the physician is held to make—the directive becomes irrelevant, for then the physician is required to ascertain the patient's current desires. If the patient did not make or reinstate the directive after the fourteen-day period after the patient became terminal and qualified, the directive becomes optional for physicians, who can take into account other factors as they see fit. Only if the directive was made after the fourteen-day period after certification of the patient as terminal and if the patient is noncompetent is the physician bound by it either to withhold life-sustaining procedures or to turn the patient over to a physician who will.

Compliance with the act does not constitute suicide, nor can it affect life insurance. People cannot be required to make a directive in order to obtain health insurance. The provisions of the act are not to be taken to lessen any right or responsibility lawfully to withdraw or withhold life-sustaining procedures which anyone had before the act. This last provision is an important one to prevent anyone's omission of the making of a directive from being interpreted as requiring treatment which would not be legally required had the act not been passed.

If someone purposely destroys or interferes with a directive to render it ineffective, this is a misdemeanor; if someone to hasten death forges a directive or conceals the fact that it has been revoked, this is homicide. Finally, the act includes a very important proviso: Nothing in it is to be taken to condone "mercy killing, or to permit any affirmative or deliberate act or omission to end life other than to permit the natural process of dying" in accord with the statute.

The Texas statute follows the California pattern closely. It requires that the directive be certified both by the maker and the witnesses before a notary public. Those withholding treatment are relieved of liability only if they avoid negligence. The physician need not judge the maker's compliance with other provisions of the act if the form complies with the act. The special provision for those in nursing homes is omitted.

The Oregon statute, like that of Texas, does not require the physician to assume the role of a judge of the patient's compliance with the provisions of the act. Oregon omits the clause nullifying the directive in case of pregnancy. The witnesses assume liability if they do not act in good faith. Within the context of a directive the patient's family may change physicians or hospitals if necessary to find one who will withdraw treatment.

The Idaho statute differs more significantly from the California model. A single physician can diagnose a terminal condition and need not certify it in writing. "Terminal condition" is defined rather loosely as an incurable illness "which reasonable medical judgment determines shortens the lifespan of the patient." But "artificial life-sustaining procedure" is defined strictly, as in California. The directive is to be made *after,* but at any time after, the terminal illness is diagnosed. The maker and witnesses must certify the document before a notary. There is nothing in this statute declaring that it does not authorize mercy killing—although it does not—nor specifying penalties for forging a directive, nor specifying what happens if a physician simply ignores the directive. One might argue that all these matters are implicitly covered by existing law.

The Nevada statute also differs significantly from the California model, but in other ways. "Life-sustaining procedure" is defined loosely to include any mechanical or artificial method of supplying or helping a vital function. The patient need not be diagnosed and certified as terminal; the act envisages declarations made in advance and mentions no waiting period. A "terminal condition" is an incurable condition such that the application of life-sustaining procedures serves only to postpone the moment of death. A directive under the act need not be in the prescribed form, and one section of the act seems to be intended to validate existing "living-will" documents. The prescribed form would put the directive into effect only when the patient is unable to communicate and death is imminent. The directive must be witnessed but need not be certified. Physicians are in complete control under the directive; they can take into account any other factors which seem to them important and can follow the directive or not, as they see fit. Physicians are relieved of all liability in either case.

Considering these statutes by the criteria we have stated and explained above, we find them highly unsatisfactory in many respects.

First, they do very little to facilitate the liberty to refuse treatment, since they apply only to life-preserving treatment in terminal illnesses—cases in which treatment probably could be withheld or withdrawn in accord with the usual standard of good medical practice without the statutes. Some of the laws make their provisions cumulative with existing rights and responsibilities, but others do not. Those which do not may be interpreted as restricting existing possibilities in the limited domain with which they deal. Moreover, all of these statutes give physicians more or less discretion which infringes upon the principle of the liberty of the patient.

Second, in general these statutes are generous in relieving physicians of liability, in some cases too much so. But in one respect they impose new duties, which are not medical ones. This is especially clear in the California statute which requires the physician to determine not only that the directive is in proper form but that the maker has complied with the substantive conditions of the act. This seems to require a decision more judicial than medical.

Third, in some of these statutes it seems that a person directing the withholding or withdrawal of treatment has to forgo the usual right to careful treatment, since the release from liability does not exclude negligence.

Fourth, despite attempts to define terms, exactly what is being refused is none too clear. Almost anything done to a person by a physician involves something artificial. Accordingly, the Nevada definition authorizes the total withholding of treatment. And the Idaho definition of "terminal condition" is loose enough to make any chronic illness terminal. Even the tighter definition of both expressions in the California statute cannot avoid vagueness in expressions such as "serve only to postpone the moment of death" and "death is imminent." The problem with such language is that patients may take it to mean one thing and physicians another. Perhaps the possibilities of misunderstanding are unavoidable, but here the terms are prescribed by statute, so that patients do not have their own choice among ambiguities and vaguenesses.

Finally, the requirement of a witnessed document, in some cases with the certification of a notary, clearly tends to protect persons against being allowed to die by malice or mistake. But such a document is easily destroyed, and care also requires that the conditions for revocation be easy and the punishment for false revocation relatively light. Thus the patient's own wishes could easily be defeated by any family member.

The North Carolina statute is not based on the California model. The key expression is "extraordinary means," which is defined rather loosely as "any medical procedure or intervention which in the judgment of the attending physician would serve only to postpone artificially the moment of death by sustaining, restoring, or supplanting a vital function." This would cover insulin and pacemakers. But action is triggered only by the opinion of two physicians that the patient's condition is terminal and incurable, although these words are undefined. A form is provided but need not be adhered to. The statute fails to specify at what age a person is competent to make a declaration, and it thus leaves open the possibility that a child's declaration would be considered valid. The act seems to intend to give legal force to "living-will" documents. However, the declaration must be witnessed by persons not having a special interest. And it must be certified by a clerk or assistant clerk of a county superior court. The latter provision is unique, and it assigns the clerk judicial functions in determining the genuineness of the document, especially if the witnesses are not available. There is nothing in the statute about what happens if the physician ignores the document and nothing about penalties for falsifying a document. There is an anti-mercy-killing paragraph, but nothing to indicate that the act is not to be taken as setting aside present patient's rights.

The North Carolina statute infringes on liberty as the others do and fails to facilitate the liberty to refuse treatment in most cases where this is really needed: where the means are ones a physician considers necessary for good medical practice. The effort to make sure that the document is genuine shows a reasonable concern for security, but the assignment of an important judicial function to a clerk or assistant clerk of a court is questionable. The key definition—that of "extraordinary means"—is deplorably loose. Most patients cannot be expected to know what this expression means, for it is current neither in the sense defined in the statute nor in the sense in which physicians are likely to take it—as referring to means not required for good practice.

The New Mexico and Arkansas acts differ from the rest in including provisions whereby declarations can be made on the behalf of minors—and in Arkansas of noncompetent adults. These aspects of these acts will be considered in chapter nine. These acts are also phrased in terms of a "right to die" rather than in terms of "natural death."

The New Mexico act turns on the definition of "terminal illness" as an "illness that will result in death . . . regardless of the use or discontinuance of maintenance medical treatment" and the definition of "maintenance medical treatment" as "medical treatment designed solely to sustain the life processes." Both of these definitions are loose. The declaration is to state that in case of terminal illness, maintenance medical treatment is not to be utilized. No prescribed form is provided for the declaration. It is to be made with the formalities for making a will. Terminal illness is to be certified by two physicians. The good faith of physicians is presumed, and they are relieved of liability unless it is proved they failed to exercise reasonable professional care and judgment. The act does not disclaim interpretation as an authorization for mercy killing. It does make its provisions cumulative with existing rights and responsibilities in respect to the termination of treatment.

This statute seems to us to have most of the disadvantages of those drawn on the California model, which, as we have seen, are concerned only with terminally ill patients. At the same time, its vagueness in definition and minimal requirements for judging the patient's wishes in terms of a witnessed but uncertified document, together with its great generosity in protecting physicians, begins to become dangerous. If the act were maliciously abused, it would be necessary to show that the physician had not acted in good faith in accord with the vague directive. The forger of a declaration, if found, could be punished. But a false document could easily be produced, its origin easily concealed, and anyone needing any sort of medical care to survive be done away with by two cooperative physicians, proceeding in a way which apart from this act would be gross negligence. Thus, in our judgment the New Mexico act not only seriously fails to protect liberty but also infringes upon justice by unnecessarily endangering the security of life of those whom it can be used to kill by omission.

The Arkansas statute is the shortest of all. It asserts the right of every person "to die with dignity." Anyone can at anytime execute a document with the formalities required for a will refusing and denying the use by anyone of "artificial, extraordinary, extreme or radical medical or surgical means or procedures calculated to prolong his life." No certification of terminal illness is required. Anyone acting or refraining from action in compliance with such a document is relieved of all liability.

This statute comes close to saying that anyone can refuse any medical treatment at all, since all medical treatment could be included under one or another of the four vague words: "artificial," "extraordinary," "extreme," or "radical." But persons signing such a document may not realize how broadly it could be understood, especially since it applies regardless of whether one is dying, terminal, or living with one's pacemaker. The lack of formalities beyond those required for a will opens up possibilities of abuse. The act does not even specify a penalty for the forging of a document. Thus, Arkansas has managed to go farthest in protecting the liberty to refuse treatment but has done so with a statute which—even more than the New Mexico statute—is open to dangerous abuses.

H. A Critique of Other Proposals

A quite different approach from that of the eight statutes we have been discussing is the legal establishment of provisions for an agent who would have the authority to make decisions on behalf of a person who is no longer competent to make them. Luis Kutner, who originated the proposal of a "living will," originally suggested that it be conceived as a revocable trust established by one over one's own body.[33] Scott R. Cox also developed a trust concept, apparently more with a view to limiting costs of terminal treatment than with a view to facilitating the liberty of persons to decide what care would be acceptable to themselves.[34] Judge Michael T. Sullivan urged that the law recognize a proctor, appointed by a court, to act for a dying person; in making this proposal Sullivan did not seem to envisage the situation in which a dying individual might be noncompetent.[35]

A very different approach suggested by Jeffrey Allen Smyth seems to accept the concept that once one delivers oneself into a physician's hands, medical standards prevail unless limited at the outset. Smyth, considering the patient-physician relationship insofar as it involves a contract, urges that the patient specify limits explicitly at the outset and thus provide that treatment be limited.[36]

Resisting the view that one's physician should also have the somewhat conflicting role of one's agent in deciding about the appropriateness in personal terms of medical care, Robert M. Veatch suggests that individuals might appoint a legal agent to refuse any treatment the agent considered inappropriate. Veatch also would have the agent for a noncompetent individual authorized to seek a court order to enforce a refusal if it were not honored. Veatch thinks persons appointing an agent with such a power might specify guidance for their agent's judgments or not, as they chose.[37]

Of these proposals only Veatch's moves from a limited consideration of the problem of the dying patient to the larger problem of facilitating the exercise of personal liberty in the decision about one's own medical care. All of these proposals involve some sort of transfer of authority to an agent of one's choice. The authors of all of them express doubt as to whether their proposals could be put into effect without legislation (or simply assume they could not be).

Sullivan's idea of a proctor has the very real advantage of requiring a judicial hearing and authorization, which would provide an opportunity to examine the evidence that the person for whom the proctor was to act really desired this representative; the court's authorization also would make the proctor's authority clear to everyone involved. Veatch's agency proposal does not include such safeguards; the appointment document would simply be a signed and witnessed statement. In view of the powers of the agent some sort of probate procedure seems to us to be needed.

After making the rather interesting agency proposal, Veatch goes on to propose legislation in some ways narrower, which would facilitate the refusal of treatment "on the grounds that the dying process cannot be morally prolonged." This bill would establish a hierarchy of authorized decision-makers for noncompetent persons, beginning with an agent appointed by the individual when competent. If no appointment were made, the spouse or a person of the first degree of kinship would have authority, and there would be rules to determine authority if there were several such persons. If there were no appointment and no family, the court would appoint a guardian. In determining the authority of the patient's representative a court would honor any document one executed with the formalities of a will when competent, in which one stated grounds for disqualifying a potential decision maker. The bill also would release physicians from liability when they act in good faith in accord with its provisions.[38]

In this proposed legislation Veatch does not make clear whether or not he thinks a court order would be required in each case. Without a judicial hearing, situations would easily arise in which someone would appear claiming to be an authorized agent, family members would begin acting individually, and physicians would be in doubt about whom they could accept as legally qualified. Veatch's proposal also might lead to decision-making in some cases by a family committee, which may be acceptable as an informal device but hardly seems attractive as a legal institution.

However, what is most unsatisfactory in Veatch's proposed statute is that it does nothing for the nondying person, for the person who could benefit from treatment but does not consent to it, for the person who wishes to refuse certain specific kinds of treatment or all treatment and does not want any committee or guardian. In other words, like the legislation recently enacted, Veatch's proposal facilitates liberty only within very narrow limits. His proposal is far more acceptable than many narrower ones, but it still discriminates in favor of people who trust agents to make ad hoc decisions and does little for those who know precisely what they want and what they do not want.

We have specified four conditions which good legislation facilitating the liberty to give and to refuse consent ought to meet. Nothing we have seen begins to meet these conditions. This is not surprising, for they are not easy to meet. Matters do not get easier, as we have explained, if one considers the entire field in which some persons might wish to reject medically indicated treatments during some period when they might become noncompetent. Dangers to persons who could be misrepresented as refusing consent must be guarded against, for it is unfair to everyone if new opportunities for homicide are created. At the same time, the ways in which consent can be refused for the future—by specific statements or through an agent—should not be limited. Any standard form which goes beyond necessary formalities seems to be an imposition on liberty. And in some cases even to insist upon a formal statement is too much. Individuals who have made their wishes clear—for example, that they wish no blood transfusions regardless of consequences—should expect these wishes to be determinative.

I. A Model Statute to Protect the Patient's Liberty

A good law must cover all of the various cases, solve all of the problems. To do so, we see no way but to require a judicial hearing in each and every instance in which a physician treating a noncompetent patient is to be limited from proceeding according to the usual standard of good practice. If the requirement of a hearing is established, then anyone can be at liberty to create, in any way he or she prefers, sufficient evidence to make clear what is to be done. The court, not the physician and not a clerk, must judge the evidence and direct the execution of what is determined to be the will of the noncompetent person. In this way, one's wishes cannot be overridden by someone's revoking a document which is the sole evidence of one's wishes. Those without families, people not in their home states, and others also can be treated equitably.

In practice, of course, individuals will not have to create their own evidence without assistance. Organizations have circulated the "living will." While a court might well refuse to accept such a document as evidence of anything, because it is too vague and ambiguous to be translated into operational terms, these organizations surely will be quick to suggest and publicize schemes for refusing treatment which courts will be able to interpret and make effective.

The proposal that there be a hearing and judicial decision for each case probably will be objected to on the ground that this procedure will create too much litigation. But every will is probated, every divorce passed on by a court, and even small claims get some sort of adjudication. To protect both the liberty of those who wish to refuse treatment and the security of everyone who does not wish to be mistaken to be a refuser of treatment, consideration of the evidence and a decision about one's wishes by a court seems a reasonable requirement. The hearing need not become complex and prolonged if the evidence is clear and the decision not disputed. And the necessary relief of the physician from liability need not extend beyond that for which he really is not responsible: limitation of treatment so that it conforms to the patient's lawfully exercised liberty.

A good statute might well begin with a statement of legislative findings summarizing the legal situation, the problem, and the solution along the following lines.

> The legislature finds that the liberty of competent adults to give and to refuse consent to medical treatment upon themselves has been recognized at common law from time immemorial and has in general been protected by the law of this State. This liberty is an aspect of the right of every person to bodily integrity and intangibility, a right closely related to the right to life. The administration to any person of medical treatment without informed consent is an assault upon that person. Such an assault is justified neither by the beneficent intentions of the one who commits it nor by any good result which might follow from it.
>
> The legislature also finds that the liberty of competent adults to give and to refuse consent to medical treatment upon themselves may be regarded as a right reserved to the people by the Ninth Amendment and as a liberty or immunity protected by the Fourteenth Amendment of the Constitution of the United States, as well as by_____of the Constitution of this State.

The legislature also finds that this liberty neither presupposes nor implies that any person has a right to die. Since every act which causes death or hastens it is a crime, no person can have a duty to do such an act, and so no person can have a right to die which would correspond to such a duty. There can be no right to die with dignity, although there certainly is a right to the protection of one's dignity from the very beginning of one's life until its end, including those times when one is sick, injured, and dying.

Moreover, if anyone attempts to commit suicide, then his or her liberty to refuse treatment may be lawfully ignored.

The legislature also finds that the liberty to give and to refuse consent to medical treatment is not an aspect of the right of personal privacy, which protects certain forms of behavior from criminal sanction. No criminal sanction ever has been attached to the exercise of this liberty. Moreover, this liberty was recognized in our law long before the right of privacy was extended to the protection of abortion and other behavior previously held criminal by our law.

Having clarified the nature and true foundation of the right to be protected, the legislative findings might continue with a statement of the need and purpose for legislation. This might be phrased along the following lines:

The legislature further finds that although the liberty to give and to refuse consent to medical treatment is well established in our law, certain problems require that this liberty be clarified and further protected by statute. Judicial decisions in some jurisdictions have imposed medical treatment upon persons despite their refusal of it, even when the refusal has been on religious grounds. Also, some doubt exists about the liability of physicians and health-care facilities when persons refuse consent to treatment yet do not altogether withdraw themselves from care. Moreover, there is a reasonable public demand that the liberty to refuse consent be facilitated, so that the personal decisions of individuals will continue to control treatment of them when they become noncompetent.

The legislature also finds that some people choose to refuse all or certain forms of medical treatment on religious and other deeply held conscientious grounds; that others choose to refuse or to limit treatment on grounds of cost, painfulness, or mutilating effect; that others choose to refuse treatment which might preserve life but which they consider to be futile; and that others choose to refuse treatment for other reasons.

The legislature finds that there are certain conditions under which the liberty of a competent person to give and to refuse consent to medical treatment may be justly overridden. Such conditions exist if the administration of treatment to a nonconsenting person is required by the public health, welfare, or safety; if it is required for self-inflicted injury, when the person must be considered temporarily unstable; and if refusal of treatment is likely to lead to incapacity to fulfill lawful responsibilities of a grave kind toward dependent children or others.

Apart from such exceptions, the legislature finds that all choices to refuse medical treatment upon oneself are lawful. The legislature considers itself bound as a matter of justice to protect and facilitate all lawful choices in a way which will afford equal protection of the law to all persons in this State. The legislature recognizes that some persons may abuse their liberty to refuse treatment by making foolish or immoral choices; nevertheless, the legislature finds that justice requires that this liberty be protected even if it is abused.

Having stated the purpose and need for legislation, a legislature might well make clear why the legislation it adopts is so different from that widely proposed and adopted by some other States:

The legislature also finds that no statute which would afford the equal protection of the law to all persons lawfully choosing to refuse medical treatment can limit itself to facilitating the wishes of those patients who happen to be terminally ill or who happen to especially dislike certain forms of treatment. Likewise, the legislature finds that it would be unjust to demand that people refusing treatment do so with certain intentions, since the intentions of persons exercising a liberty can be of no legitimate interest to the government. The legislature finds that proposals including such restrictions are unacceptable because they arbitrarily limit rather than protect and facilitate the liberty which citizens have enjoyed until now.

Although the statute will apply to the refusal by competent adults of treatment at the time treatment is proposed, the new and more important aspect will be its provision for effectively determining one's treatment during a future time when one may be noncompetent. This aspect may be explained in the legislative findings:

The legislature further finds that in the absence of evidence to the contrary most noncompetent persons must be assumed to consent to treatment provided that it is appropriate and rendered in accord with the usual standard of good medical practice for a condition of disease or injury from which they are suffering. Moreover, physicians and health-care facilities are required by law to proceed on this assumption.

The legislature therefore finds that if persons wish to refuse treatment which might be administered to them in accord with this assumption, then it is their responsibility both to provide evidence which will express and prove their choice beyond a reasonable doubt and to make sure that this evidence will come to the attention of physicians and health-care facilities which might provide unwanted treatment. The legislature finds and this act permits that persons might provide evidence of various chosen determinations about treatment in the event they become noncompetent: that regardless of their condition they refuse all or certain forms of treatment, that in certain circumstances they refuse all but palliative treatment, that they consent only to the treatment approved at the time of need by a certain designated person or persons, or that they limit the usual assumption of consent in some other lawful way. The legislature finds that it is the responsibility of persons who wish to make their choices legally effective under the provisions of this act to express their wishes in a sufficiently clear and definite form that there will be no doubt what their wishes are, and in a sufficiently certain and binding form that there will be no doubt that these are their wishes.

The legislature further finds that it would be unwise and unjust to ask physicians and the administrators of health-care facilities to assume a judicial role in cases in which a patient provides evidence that consent is refused to treatment otherwise necessary to meet the usual standard of good medical practice. The legislature also finds that it is not in the public interest to lessen the responsibility of physicians and health-care facilities to provide standard care on the untested evidence that the ordinary assumption of consent does not correspond to the desires of a particular patient.

Accordingly, the legislature finds that if there is evidence that a noncompetent adult patient may not consent to treatment otherwise medically indicated, and if there is any doubt about the legal duty of a physician or health-care facility toward such a patient, then the duty is to administer the treatment immediately required and to seek promptly a judicial determination of the doubt. Only such a determination will settle whether medical treatment is to proceed on the usual assumption or is to be limited in accord with the proved limits of the noncompetent person's consent.

So much for legislative findings. We realize that so lengthy a rationale for a statute would be unusual, but it also could be very useful, for the statute might be badly misinterpreted without this rationale, which embodies many concepts which have not been given much publicity in the last few years.

The statute itself will require a number of definitions, which must be supplied in accord with the existing law of each state. For example, "medical treatment" must be defined as treatment provided by certain classes of persons and institutions acting professionally. One of the more important definitions will be that of "the usual standard of medical practice." A definition along the following lines would be appropriate:

> "Treatment according to the usual standard of medical practice" in this act means medical treatment appropriate for an existing condition of disease or injury carried out in all respects in the manner in which a person practicing with the average professional skill and carefulness would carry it out in any case in which all of the relevant circumstances were the same or similar. Any limitation imposed upon a practitioner or health-care facility by refusal of consent to treatment which otherwise would be medically indicated shall be considered a relevant circumstance.

By this definition refusal of consent *changes* the usual standard of practice but does not release anyone from liability for failing to meet the standard.

Physicians thus will be required to take the patient's decisions as determinative in deciding how to proceed but will be held to do well whatever process of treatment is undertaken.

The statute also must make clear that it applies only to persons of an age judged to be the appropriate age for competency in consenting to medical treatment. We are not going to discuss the problem of the proper age of competency for this purpose, but it is worth noting that in recent years for many particular purposes the age of competency has been reduced. Perhaps it would be reasonable to regard young people as able to make decisions regarding health-care in general at an age younger, maybe even much younger, than eighteen.[39] Whatever the proper age for competency is judged to be, a clause along the following lines will be needed:

> The existing law of this State with respect to all the conditions for lawful medical treatment of persons under_____years of age and persons who have been declared legally noncompetent is in no way modified by any provision of this act, except insofar as a person declared legally noncompetent has made known his or her wishes concerning medical treatment during some prior period of competency.

This phrasing also takes care of the problem of persons who have been committed; their situation is a special problem which requires other legislation if it needs to be altered from the way it stands at present.

The statute also should contain a section excluding several likely misconstructions. These include misconstructions of its purpose and of its intended effect upon the existing situation. Something along the following lines might do:

> Nothing in this act is to be construed
> (a) as introducing or recognizing any right to die; or
> (b) as authorizing any person to do or to refrain from doing anything in order to bring about the death of any person; or
> (c) as creating any new obligation that a physician administer treatment above and beyond that required by the usual standard of medical care; or
> (d) as causing any treatment to be required by the usual standard of medical care if such treatment prior to the enactment of this statute was commonly considered futile and useless by competent and careful physicians; or
> (e) as impairing or superseding any legal right or responsibility which any person would have had prior to the enactment of this statute to bring about the withholding or withdrawal of medical treatment in any lawful manner; or
> (f) as requiring physicians or health-care facilities to seek judicial determination of their duties in cases in which there would have been no doubt as to their liability if they failed to respect a patient's wishes had such cases occurred prior to the enactment of this statute.

Our intention in proposing this phrasing is to keep the present situation as much as possible just as it is for people who are satisfied with it.

The statute also must contain provisions regarding insurance. We doubt that the law can justly require that persons who limit or refuse consent be treated in all respects the same for insurance purposes as those who do not. This would unfairly impose the voluntary risks of some persons upon others, who do not choose them. But the statute definitely must include a provision excluding as unlawful any attempt to make a person refuse or limit care as a condition for granting an application for health or disability insurance and the like.

The statute also should contain severe penalties for forging or tampering with evidence as to any person's wishes in regard to his or her own medical care. In particular, the misrepresentation that a person refuses treatment on which life might depend should be classed as attempted first degree murder, and as first degree murder if the misrepresentation causes or hastens death.

The four main sections of a statute would be embedded in the middle of it, but for convenience we number them here as sections one to four. The first affirmatively states the liberty to refuse treatment and gives it all possible clarity:

> Section one. It is a violation of the bodily integrity and intangibility of a person, subject to criminal and civil liability established in existing law of this State, to administer to any person without his or her personal, informed consent any medical treatment except in the cases specified in section two of this act unless such person be a minor or noncompetent person excluded by section_____from the provisions of this act.

> Whenever a physician-patient or other medical treatment relationship is initiated and whenever explicit consent to medical treatment is sought, the person initiating the relationship with or seeking consent of the patient must if the patient be competent clearly and explicitly state that the patient is at liberty to give or to refuse consent to treatment. Evidence of the failure to inform the patient of the right to refuse consent shall be evidence of negligence which if willful and deliberate shall also be criminal.

The liberty is not only affirmed in its whole breadth but also defined and enforced by the requirement that patients be informed of it. The second section states and limits exceptions to the liberty to refuse treatment:

> Section two. Notwithstanding the liberty of every competent person_____years of age or older to give and to refuse consent to medical treatment, no physician and no health-care facility shall be deemed to have administered medical treatment without consent if one or more of the following conditions is fulfilled:
> (a) the treatment is authorized by statute to be administered without the consent of the person treated for the protection of the public health or safety; or

(b) the treatment is appropriate to remedy a condition of bodily injury or harm which the person treated has brought upon himself or herself in attempting suicide or self-mutilation; or

(c) the treatment either is ordered to be given by a court of law or is consented to by a guardian appointed and authorized by a court to act in the matter; or

(d) the treatment is administered to a person from whom consent cannot be obtained because of his or her inability either to give or to refuse consent to treatment, and the following three conditions also are met: (i) the treatment is an appropriate remedy for an existing condition of disease or injury; and (ii) the treatment is carried out in accord with the usual standard of medical practice; and (iii) there is no evidence known to persons administering the treatment or to administrators of any health-care facility in which it is carried out which a reasonable person would take to be sufficient to call into question the ordinary assumption that the noncompetent patient would consent to treatment which is medically indicated; or

(e) the treatment is administered to a person from whom consent cannot be obtained because of his or her inability either to give or to refuse consent to treatment, and the following two conditions also are met: (i) the treatment provided is immediately required to preserve the life or protect the health of the patient pending judicial determination of the case; and (ii) judicial determination is promptly sought.

Having limited the conditions in which consent can be overridden and created a situation in which any evidence putting in question the usual assumption of the consent of the noncompetent person to indicated treatment will provide a strong incentive for taking the case to court for determination, the statute must go on to direct interested parties to a suitable court and to indicate to courts what is required of them:

Section three. Upon a petition by a patient under medical care or by a representative of such a patient, by a relative of such a patient, by a physician or health-care facility responsible for such a patient, or by any other interested party, any court of_____of this State shall promptly schedule a hearing and give notice of it to all interested parties. At the hearing the court shall receive and examine all evidence produced by any party concerning the nonconsent of the patient to proposed treatment or to treatment already in progress.

Evidence considered may include but need not be limited to expert testimony concerning the probable utility and benefit of the treatment; anything which might show that the patient rejects all or certain kinds of medical treatment on the basis of religion or other deeply held conscientious convictions, that under specified conditions the patient refuses all but palliative care, or that the patient desires decisions to be made on his or her behalf by some designated person or persons.

In assessing the evidence the court shall consider the presumption of consent to be in possession and shall not alter this presumption unless a different conclusion is established by the evidence beyond reasonable doubt. The refusal by any person of consent to medical treatment shall not itself be considered evidence of the noncompetence of such person.

If the court determines that one or both of the following conditions is met, then it shall direct that medical treatment be administered in accord with the usual standard of medical practice unrestricted by lack of consent: (a) if treatment of the patient is required by the compelling state interest of the public health, welfare, or safety; or (b) if the usual assumption that a noncompetent person does consent to treatment to which a reasonable and competent person usually would consent should stand in the present case, either because the evidence presented does not establish beyond reasonable doubt that the patient when competent exercised the liberty to limit or refuse consent, or because the evidence presented does not sufficiently show what limitation, modification, or termination of treatment would give effect to the patient's wishes.

In finding that treatment of a nonconsenting patient is required by the compelling state interest, the court must find that lack of treatment would be likely to result in substantial harm other than harm to the patient's own life or health. Such harm might include but is not limited to the probable resulting incapacity through death or otherwise of the patient to fulfill responsibilities to dependent children. If the patient's refusal of treatment is based on religious or other deeply held conscientious convictions, then the prospect of harm which grounds the state interest must be such as to constitute a clear and present danger.

If the court finds that neither condition (a) nor condition (b) is met, then the court shall cause treatment of the patient to be limited, modified, or terminated in accord with the proved will of the patient. In giving effect to the will of the patient the court may act by its own order or by appointing and authorizing a guardian to act on behalf of the patient or by both of these modes.

The court's assignment is to examine evidence about the patient's consent. This keeps the focus where it ought to be. Nevertheless, the usual assumption is that the patient consents to treatment in accord with the usual standard of medical practice, and such treatment is limited to that which is somehow of use and benefit to the patient. Hence, the court could consider expert testimony which would show that the treatment was not of use and benefit, and on this basis rule that nonconsent must be presumed.

The final section of the statute, as we have projected it, would be the limitation of liability:

Section four. Whenever medical treatment is restricted and delayed in conformity with section 2(e) or is limited, modified, or terminated in accord with a judicial decision under section 3, the provisions of this act and what is done in accord with it shall be a material and relevant circumstance in determining the usual standard of medical practice. Neither physicians nor health-care facilities shall incur any civil or criminal liability for acting in accord with the usual standard of medical practice as determined with this circumstance taken into account.

If a physician proposes a medical treatment which would be in accord with the usual standard of medical practice if the patient consented to it, and if the physician is prevented from proceeding with such treatment because of refusal of consent in accord with the provisions of this statute, then the physician shall not be deemed to have abandoned the patient if the physician withdraws from the case provided that due notice of withdrawal is given to the patient or to others concerned with the patient's interests.

By this provision nothing in the way of protection of the patient's rights is given up, yet the physician and the hospital are given the assurance they need to do the best they can for a patient within the limits set by the patient. If a physician, because of reasons of conscience or other concerns, objects to working under such limitations, the statute provides a way out.

As philosophers we do not pretend to be legislative draftsmen. We have articulated our proposed alternative to "death-with-dignity" legislation in a formal mode, to give definite embodiment to our proposed alternative to the statutes now being enacted.

J. Replies to Some Objections

Many objections are likely to be made against any proposal along the lines we are suggesting. We conclude by considering some of them.

First, it is likely to be suggested that minimum and purely formal conditions be established for a written statement if it is to count as evidence at the judicial hearing. The difficulty with this is that in some cases an individual will not have met specified conditions but will have left enough evidence to establish beyond reasonable doubt what his or her wishes are. Either the specified conditions will become an obstacle to giving effect to such a person's intent or exceptions will be made. In the latter case the formal conditions will be only advisory, and such advice—which would be very useful—can as well be given apart from the statute. Decisions of courts made on a case by case basis also will begin to indicate very quickly what formalities are accepted as giving evidential weight.

Again, it is likely to be suggested that a line of authority be established if an individual has not made his or her personal position known. For example, it might be stipulated that in the absence of evidence about the noncompetent adult's wishes a certain family member would be presumed that person's choice to act, and the court would so order. This idea has its appeal but involves the difficulty that it would alter the existing situation in a way which is not necessary for the purpose of the statute. Such an alteration ought not to be made unless it becomes clear that most people desire it. If the majority of citizens of a given State wish this or some other assumption established by the statute, there would be nothing unjust in including it.

Some might object that no new approach is needed at this time to deal with the liberty of competent persons to refuse treatment. Even legislation such as we are proposing will be open to amendment in the direction of facilitating voluntary euthanasia. The answer to this objection is that the movement favoring euthanasia has been gaining momentum consistently; it has not suffered a serious setback since 1967. In the battles up to 1973 opponents of abortion were able to appeal to a residue of traditional sentiment. Opponents of euthanasia will be able to appeal mainly to self-interest. A picture of a normal, unborn twenty-week baby has emotional impact; so, unfortunately, does a picture of a defective child, a psychotic, a senile person. Identification with such persons is more difficult for most of us than is identification with the infant. Self-interest can be served by limiting nonvoluntary euthanasia to the noncompetent in institutions. Therefore, some new strategy is needed. We believe that legislation along the lines we are proposing will be less open to revision to facilitate euthanasia than will the common-law situation which still exists in most states, and will be a substantial obstacle to euthanasia in comparison with the natural-death or right-to-die legislation which provides both an ideological framework and some legal safeguards necessary for euthanasia.

Some might object that the legislation we propose will encourage people to make decisions about future treatment when they are considering death abstractly and at a distance, but those decisions might well be different when the consequences of refusing treatment are imminent. The answer is that under the legislation we are proposing people could leave the future decisions to be made as they are now or could assign responsibility to someone they trust to make them at the time. Moreover, there is nothing in the proposed bill to prevent people from changing their minds. Besides, we see no reason to suppose that a person's desires or hypothetical desires at the time treatment is needed are more likely to express his or her true self than the same person's free and deliberate choice made at some earlier and calmer moment.

Some might object that it is unwise to give people so broad a right to refuse treatment. The answer is that legislation along the lines we are proposing is not giving anyone a right; it is only recognizing and facilitating a liberty which people in principle already have. Of course, the proposed statute would help people make their wishes in respect to their own future more effective than is now possible. However, we can see no justification for limiting people's liberty with respect to the future which would not equally justify limiting it with respect to the present.

While the state does have a duty to protect children and the permanently noncompetent from themselves and from the irresponsibility of others, it is of the essence of liberty that competent persons be able to make decisions about their personal lives and to have these decisions respected not only at the time they are made but also during the whole time to which they are meant to apply. Liberty may be exercised foolishly and even immorally, yet it must be respected. The alternative is a paternalism which might be benevolent but which cannot be just and is bound to be odious.

Some might object that if the liberty to refuse treatment is protected to the extent we propose, some people will abuse this liberty even to the point of using it to commit suicide, and that in consequence there will be further lessening of respect for human life. The answer is that nothing in our proposal lends color of lawfulness to suicide. On the contrary, we suggest provisions to make clear that suicide is against public policy. Still, someone might commit suicide by refusing treatment—understanding "suicide" in a moral sense. But this possibility already exists. The statute we are proposing only extends this possibility as an unwanted side effect of extending the just protection of the genuine liberty of persons to choose and refuse medical treatment. The grounds of this liberty are, not in any supposed right to die, but rather in the right of persons to bodily integrity and intangibility, which is closely related to the right to life itself.

5: Suicide and Liberty

A. Introduction

The relationship between suicide and euthanasia is not difficult to understand. On the one hand, suicide can be self-administered euthanasia. Even if the law does not permit physicians or others to kill at their request persons suffering from prolonged or painful illnesses, still it cannot stop such persons from trying to kill themselves.[1] On the other hand, some argue that if suicide ought not to be treated as criminal, then euthanasia, which can be considered assisted suicide, ought not to be treated as criminal. Why should it be wrong to help others do what they themselves are free to do?

Our concern with suicide in this chapter is limited to a discussion of what the law ought to be with respect to suicide, assisting suicide, and preventing suicide. We are not concerned here with the morality of suicide. The latter topic will be considered in chapter twelve. Just as it was too quickly assumed in the past that the proper legal position on suicide was settled by a widely accepted moral condemnation of it, so it is sometimes too quickly assumed today that the proper legal position on suicide should be settled by a widely accepted moral approval of it (or, at least, by the absolving as guiltless of those driven to it).[2] But moral judgments are not *directly* relevant to what the law in respect to suicide ought to be. The question is rather what our basic principles of liberty and justice demand.

In discussing suicide we assume that euthanasia, even of a voluntary sort, is a special problem. Moreover, in the present chapter we assume that all active euthanasia is excluded. If subsequent examination shows that voluntary active euthanasia ought to be permitted under certain conditions, its permission would be by way of amendment or exception to the general provisions of law in respect to both homicide and suicide, to the extent that these provisions are incompatible with voluntary euthanasia. In proceeding in this way we are not begging the question about voluntary euthanasia; we simply reserve this question for discussion in chapter six.

In common use all who deliberately kill themselves are called "suicides." In law the word is used in a narrower sense. People who kill themselves are suicides only if they are legally competent and act with self-destructive intent, voluntarily and intentionally doing something which causes their own death.[3] Thus children, insane persons, and those whose deaths occur in the course of some risky undertaking are not legally considered suicides even though they might be called "suicides" in common use if they act purposely or recklessly in a way which leads to their deaths.

B. The Changing Law on Suicide

Why is the legal concept of suicide narrower than the popular one? The reason is that in Anglo-American law suicide was considered a crime, a form of murder. The suicide was a *felo-de-se*—a felon or evildoer in respect to himself or herself. If killing a person is a great evil, killing oneself was not considered to be an exception; the identity of the agent and the victim was incidental. In British legal practice the suicide was punished after death by an ignominious burial and by forfeiture of property; the latter was part of the punishment for many serious crimes. American legal practice was not so severe. In some jurisdictions suicide probably never was a crime, although even in these it perhaps was considered a public wrong and unlawful.[4]

Thus, one could not be a legal suicide unless in killing oneself one met all the conditions one would have to meet to make the act of killing murder if it were done upon another person. Since children and insane persons cannot commit crimes and since reckless and self-destructive behavior would not be self-murder (but, at most, self-reckless homicide), some self-killings fall outside the legal concept of suicide.

Robert M. Byrn explains the attitude of the common law toward suicide in a most illuminating way by recalling the objections against suicide stated by a sixteenth-century judge and then by transposing these objections into more contemporary concepts and language.

The four bases on which suicide was considered unlawful four centuries ago were (1) that it is an unnatural act which violates the natural tendency of self-preservation, (2) that it is a breach of the divine commandment prohibiting killing, (3) that it is a kind of mutilation of the king, since it destroys one of his subjects, and (4) that it also is against the king, since it runs counter to his intention to prevent bad example.

Byrn translates (1) into the modern language of rights: suicide can be seen as a self-defeating claim to a right to destroy life which is the precondition of all rights. He translates (2) into the value of human lives simply as human lives: suicide seems to treat life as if it were property at one's own disposal.

He translates (3) into the modern concept that it is an inherent function of government to protect life, so that a person cannot lawfully commit suicide or consent to being killed by another. He translates (4) into the concept that it is legitimate public policy to bar conduct which would encourage suicide. In each case the translated basis for considering suicide unlawful has some support in recent case law.[5]

Now, the fact of the matter is that gradually, over the last century or so, suicide and attempted suicide have lost the legal status of crimes. With the disuse of forfeiture and ignominious burial as penalties suicide itself simply could not be punished. A successful suicide is like a successful revolutionary in standing beyond the reach of the law. And while persons attempting suicide were occasionally punished until the last few years, this practice also fell into increasing disfavor.[6]

Undoubtedly, part of the reason for the disfavor was that modern conceptions of responsibility have tended to support the view that even if the typical person committing or attempting suicide is not legally insane, still such persons are somehow not themselves and do not deserve to be dealt with as criminals. As criminal prosecution of persons attempting suicide declined, efforts to treat such persons as ill increased; indeed, the main use of statutes forbidding suicide attempts seemed to be their leverage in bringing about commitment of persons considered to require treatment for their suicidal tendencies.[7]

But there is more to the decriminalization of suicide than the changing conception of responsibility. After all, changed conceptions of responsibility have led to changed attitudes toward crime and criminals in general, and especially toward those committing the more unusual and more violent crimes.

But there is no general trend toward the decriminalization of crimes such as treason, murder, and rape. Such crimes are frightening to a large part of the public; they involve obvious injustice. The threat of criminal prosecution probably has a very substantial deterrent effect—not, of course, on those who do commit crimes, but on those many persons who are selfish and cruel enough toward others in ways unregulated by law to suggest that they would not stop short of crimes such as murder or rape were they not led by self-interest to respect the threat of legal punishment.

Suicide is different. It upsets and perhaps appalls others but does not frighten them for their own safety. It does not involve any obvious injustice to the victim, although the suicide may be regarded sympathetically as a victim of some injustice. And this act hardly seems likely to be deterred by any criminal sanction.

Suicide *always* differed from crimes against others in these ways. But, as the sixteenth-century judge quoted by Byrn makes clear, suicide formerly was sufficiently similar to other crimes to be considered a form of criminal evildoing, since it violated life, broke a divine command, and offended the king. Even with Byrn's translation of the objections into contemporary terms, however, the older rationale for considering suicide criminal seems to have lost its cogency.

A suicide need not make a self-defeating claim to a right to destroy his or her rights, but only a claim to a liberty to bring about his or her own death—the destruction of rights being accepted along with the loss of certain other good things as an unwanted but inevitable side effect. And the suicide need not suppose that his or her own life is property or make the rather obvious mistake of thinking that it can be alienated as property can be; yet the suicide may think that life itself is only instrumentally and not inherently good, and that death at times also can be instrumentally good, as a last resort to solve otherwise intractable problems. As for the suppositions that suicide infringes upon the concern of law to protect life and to prevent bad example, the exclusion of any other acceptable grounds for considering suicide unlawful leads many people to regard these suppositions as weak or as question-begging.

Central to the change in attitude toward suicide, we think, is a widespread decline in the belief that human life has sanctity which deserves reverence, or at least absolute inherent dignity which deserves respect without exception. Life is valued, but its value is widely believed today to be a function of its serving as a foundation for conscious experience. On this view, if conscious experience is rich and desirable, then life is valuable; but if conscious experience is impoverished, repugnant, lacking in the satisfaction of fulfilling relationships, then life is no longer "meaningful." In other words, the value of life is considered to be a function of the quality of life.

As we pointed out in chapter two, section F, because of this change many today do not accept the view that there is anything like a naturally given unalienable right to life; they do not consider life itself to be among the goods which of themselves ground the legitimacy of the legal claims of a political society upon its members. For this reason, as we have explained, we do not think that our present, pluralistic society can base legislation precisely and directly upon the sanctity or inherent absolute dignity of human life. (At the same time, as we shall make clear in chapters eleven and twelve, our own *ethical* position is that life is of itself an inherent personal good which ought never to be directly violated.)

Consequently, we think that the decriminalization of suicide reflects a change in the consensus—which constitutes our political society and gives government the moral basis for using power. When justice is violated, then life can be protected. For example, the lives of the unborn, if they were admitted to be persons, could be protected by law on the ground that it is unfair to protect others and to abandon them. But in the case of suicide, even if *morally* speaking the right to life is unalienable and even if one grants that *morally* speaking people can violate their own unalienable rights, justice certainly is not violated. Thus the traditional ground for regarding suicide as a crime has been removed. Unless there is some other basis for considering it such, respect for liberty demands that suicide be left outside the scope of criminal law.

C. Liberty and a "Right" to Suicide

As soon as one says that people must be at liberty to do any sort of act, many quickly draw the conclusion that a "right" has been posited to do that sort of act. And if a right, then there will be advanced at least a claim to protection from all public or private interference, and at most a claim to the necessary means to exercise the right.[8]

However, not every liberty entails a right in any strong sense. For example, religious liberty does not carry with it an entitlement to the means necessary for the exercise of religion. And the liberty of parents to disappoint their children by breaking promises made to them, to damage their children psychologically by playing favorites, to cause them pain by severe punishments—this liberty is no more than immunity from public intervention into the relationships of the family. Parental misbehavior is tolerated by political society, even though it may carry with it some damage to the common good, provided it remains within certain limits. And so while a parent is at liberty to be a bad parent, no parent has any right to be a bad parent.

Even if the criminal law should not be concerned with suicide and attempted suicide, such acts remain in many ways socially disturbing and costly. Many people who are not well balanced can be influenced by the example of others who kill themselves; if suicide became widely accepted, this influence could become more significant than it now is. A suicide sometimes leaves dependents uncared for and other duties unfulfilled. An individual who commits suicide often endangers others directly, by causing risk for those who try to help. Sometimes there is a significant indirect danger to others who are wrongly held responsible or blamed for the suicide's act.

If persons in difficult circumstances committed suicide fairly often, their doing so would create a social expectation that persons in difficulty need not be helped; they can solve their problems without the assistance of others by killing themselves. Moreover, the costs to the public of handling suicide cases can be considerable, for each such case is an instance of sudden and violent death which requires some investigation.

Finally, it is possible for a murderer to arrange things so that murder appears to be and is mistakenly taken to be suicide. No single suicide bears responsibility for creating the possibililty of deception. But if there were no suicides, such deception could not occur, and the more suicides there are, the easier such deception is likely to be, as each case which initially appears to be suicide must be subjected to less exacting scrutiny.

This last point, we think, is extremely important. That there are some instances of genuine suicide creates a danger which would not otherwise exist to every person who might be murdered and the murder made to appear a suicide. This danger is well known and generally recognized. But the responsibility of suicides for this danger is unremarked in discussions of suicide.

Probably there are two reasons why this factor is ignored. First, no single suicide creates it, and no single abstention from suicide would mitigate it. Second, many suicides do make an effort to leave sufficient evidence—for example, an explanatory note—to prevent confusion about the cause of their deaths. Still, if treating suicide and attempted suicide as criminal could eliminate this danger, there certainly would be a plausible basis in added security for the lives of others to forbid suicide. Of course, potential suicides are hardly likely to be deterred by any law forbidding suicide regardless of the purpose such a statute is intended to serve. Moreover, many of the other disturbances and social costs of suicide can be offset, even if the law not only considers suicide no crime but even treats it with a somewhat more permissive attitude than at present.

In recent literature some legal commentators have suggested that the right of privacy which was introduced by the Supreme Court of the United States in declaring laws forbidding the use of contraceptives unconstitutional and used most importantly in nullifying all of the statutes against abortion might be broad enough to encompass a "right to die."[9] In chapter four, section E, we said that privacy is irrelevant to the liberty of competent persons to refuse medical treatment. The right of privacy might seem more relevant to suicide, for here the subject is behavior which has been regarded as criminal. Since the right of privacy is said to be a fundamental right which can be overridden only by a compelling state interest, the establishment of the view that this right encompasses suicide would dictate a policy of minimum regulation.

However, as we argued in chapter two, section G, the right of privacy is nothing more than certain aspects of the liberty which is reserved to the people by the Ninth Amendment and protected by the privileges or immunities clause of the Fourteenth Amendment of the United States Constitution. Clearly, not every liberty can be given the status of the fundamental rights of freedom of speech and of religion.

The Supreme Court has suggested various grounds on which a liberty could be considered fundamental. But the liberty to commit suicide does not seem to be fundamental on any suggested ground. This liberty is not commended by the collective conscience of the American people; it is not one of the fundamental and pervasive elements of liberty and justice; it is not connected with any explicitly recognized right. Suicide rather is an act considered either wrong or pitiable, depending on the psychological condition of the person who commits it. The liberty to kill oneself thus seems to be nothing more than immunity from criminal prosecution and from such interference as would have no rational relationship to any legitimate state interest. Hence, we see no ground for holding that there is a fundamental right to kill oneself—a right which could be overridden only by a compelling state interest.

D. Restraints on Attempted Suicide

The most plausible basis for some authorized interference with suicide attempts is that many of them do not seem to be seriously intended; others, if seriously intended, probably are not carried out by individuals who are fully themselves. Although technically and legally sane enough, most people who kill or attempt to kill themselves probably are in a state of unusual stress, a state often compounded by alcohol or other drugs.[10]

Thus most people reason: People in their right minds do not seriously harm themselves, but that is what is going on here; therefore, the individual probably is not himself or herself; and so interference to prevent self-destruction and to limit harm as much as possible is appropriate. As Glanville Williams states it:

> . . . the law should allow some right of interposition to prevent a suicide. Self-destruction is frequently the outcome not of the settled philosophical determination of a balanced mind but of a passing impulse or temporary depression. The natural and human thing to do with a person who is suddenly discovered attempting suicide is to interpose to prevent it. This interposition, where only mild force is used, cannot be accounted a battery upon the would-be suicide.[11]

We have found no one who disagrees with this view.

Thus a sound legal policy will authorize the use of force—short of that force which would be likely to cause serious or permanent injury—to prevent a person from committing suicide. In chapter four we proposed for the same reason that the general liberty to refuse medical care should not extend to emergency treatment required to remedy a condition caused by an attempt at suicide or self-mutilation. Such persons must be presumed to be in a disturbed state of mind, and physicians should provide necessary treatment even over the express refusal of these patients.

Existing statutes in various states take somewhat different approaches to the problem of authorizing force to restrain someone from suicide. New York treats the use of force as justifiable under the following circumstances:

A person acting under a reasonable belief that another person is about to commit suicide or to inflict serious physical injury upon himself may use physical force upon such person to the extent that he reasonably believes it necessary to thwart such result.[12]

The Arkansas statute on this subject is similar, except that it adds the qualification—certainly harmless and probably desirable—that the force be non-deadly.[13] Substantially following the Model Penal Code of the American Law Institute, Pennsylvania law is:

The use of force upon or toward the person of another is justifiable when the actor believes that such force is immediately necessary to prevent such other person from committing suicide, inflicting serious bodily injury upon himself. . . .

The statute also provides that such force must be nondeadly.[14]

In one respect the Pennsylvania formulation is superior: It makes clear that the necessity to use force must be immediate. But in another respect this formulation seems to us inferior to that of New York: It conditions justification on the mere belief, not the *reasonable* belief, of the person using force.

It must be remembered that although these provisions ultimately intend the protection of persons from themselves, their immediate focus is upon legal justification of a person who forcibly interferes with another. Taken strictly, the Pennsylvania formulation would permit someone who forcibly restrained another to claim that the force was used in the *belief,* sincere although perhaps unreasonable, that it was immediately necessary to prevent a suicide attempt. What anyone believes is hard to prove and what anyone claims to have believed is hard to disprove. Thus this formulation is open to abuse. It would be better to require that the belief be reasonable: "when a reasonable person in the circumstances would believe. . . . "

Washington treats together the lawfulness of the use of force to prevent suicide and to compel a person to accept treatment. Force is lawful:

Whenever used by any person to prevent an idiot, lunatic or insane person from committing an act dangerous to himself or another, or in enforcing necessary restraint for the protection of his person, or his restoration to health, during such period only as shall be necessary to obtain legal authority for the restraint or custody of his person.[15]

Here the legitimation of the use of force is conditioned upon the fact that the one upon whom it is used is an idiot, lunatic, or insane.

Probably most persons who attempt suicide do not fall into these categories if they are taken in any very strict sense, and it is hardly reasonable to expect someone who is confronted with an apparent suicide attempt to ascertain the facts about the state of mind of the individual before trying to stop the attempt. Very likely in practice the conditions would be understood broadly if one intervened when the suicidal act was imminent, going on, or completed, and if one acted only to the extent required to obtain care for the suicidal person or to gain time in which to summon the help of the police. The explicit authorization of force in medical treatment of the attempted suicide together with the limitation of restraint or custody to the time necessary to obtain legal authorization seems to be a sound provision.

Glanville Williams urges that a person who has attempted suicide should not be restrained without a magistrate's order, and that the order of detention should have a very short time limit and not be subject to renewal until after the lapse of a substantial period intervening unless the individual is committed.[16] David F. Greenberg makes a very persuasive argument against the nonvoluntary civil commitment of persons considered suicidal, but he also holds that immediate restraint is justified by the fact that most who attempt suicide will be grateful subsequently for having been prevented.[17]

We agree with Greenberg that there is no justification for infringing on the liberty of many persons who are mistakenly considered or maliciously claimed to be suicidal in the process of restraining persons by nonvoluntary commitment merely on the ground that there is some danger of their committing suicide. Of course, if one who attempts suicide is observed to have other symptoms which would justify commitment even apart from the suicide attempt, then the fact that these symptoms are observed when treating the individual after an attempt at suicide should not interfere with necessary nonvoluntary commitment.

On the assumption that suicide and attempts at it ought not to be considered crimes we think a good statute concerned with suicide should include the following provisions with respect to its prevention. First, any person should be permitted to use immediately necessary nondeadly force to restrain another from an act which a reasonable person in the circumstances would believe likely to cause death or serious bodily harm to the one acting; however, if the need for restraint is not immediate, a private person should be required to turn the matter over to the police without delay. Second, a physician should be permitted to treat a person who appears to be suffering from an attempt at suicide or self-mutilation even over the protest of the patient provided that the treatment is immediately necessary. Third, neither the police nor a hospital should be permitted to restrain any person—that is, hold a person in custody despite his or her protest—without obtaining a court order promptly. And any such order ought to be limited to a short, definite period, such as twenty-four hours. Fourth, nonvoluntary civil commitment should not be carried out merely because someone has attempted or is threatening suicide.

Conditions such as these ought to be sufficient to protect typical suicidal persons without infringing unduly upon the liberty of individuals who make a deliberate, rational decision to kill themselves. As Glanville Williams points out, most people living in normal conditions do not need a protected "right" to commit suicide. If circumstances are arranged which are private and which will forestall interference by others, and if a means is used which is not likely to endanger or unduly inconvenience others, the liberty to kill oneself will be adequately protected by a legal situation which prevents the unsuccessful attempter both from being punished and from being unwillingly committed.[18]

Even if voluntary euthanasia remains illegal, proponents of such killing will not be wholly frustrated as long as the liberty to commit suicide is protected. People can kill themselves by drugs or drowning, or by other methods that do not present the danger to others involved in jumping from high places, smashing an automobile into a solid barrier, or shooting oneself. Persons who deliberately attempt to kill themselves in ways which endanger others or create a public nuisance should be punished, but various existing laws— disturbing the peace, reckless driving, firing a gun within a city, and so forth—are likely to be applicable in such cases.

The situations of persons who are confined in institutions and are subject to continuous custodial care presents a distinct situation. Someone who is in a hospital and too ill to leave, in a home for the aged or the incompetent, or in prison cannot so easily commit suicide. Still, even such persons can do so if they really wish to.[19] In the institutional context the institution and its personnel are likely to be held responsible if they do not do what is reasonably possible to prevent suicides.[20] For the protection of persons who are not attempting to execute deliberate, rational suicidal choices, institutions can hardly be relieved of liability if they allow inmates or patients to kill themselves.

However, there is some reason to think that too many restrictions do not benefit typical suicidal patients.[21] On the basis that persons in institutions also have rights, we think that the law ought to limit institutional liability if special restrictions, restraints, and surveillance are not imposed upon residents, patients, or inmates merely because they have attempted suicide, and if persons suspected of suicidal tendencies are nevertheless permitted the modicum of privacy and liberty to move about which most persons in their condition would desire.

There is one method of committing suicide which is available to anyone sufficiently determined to use it: the refusal of all nourishment. If an individual refuses to eat, force-feeding can be carried out. But this procedure not only overrides the liberty to kill oneself but also significantly violates bodily intangibility. We think that due respect for liberty would exclude the force-feeding of any person over that person's refusal unless the person were a child or were declared noncompetent by a court. If any person has the persistence to starve to death, many of the objections to other modes of suicide fail.

Moreover, in a case of this sort there is ample opportunity to talk with the suicidal person and to seek the intervention of a court if the person seems to be acting irrationally and indeliberately.

E. Assisted Suicide

There are special legal problems about suicide pacts and about cases in which someone incidentally harms another while attempting to commit suicide.[22] Neither of these sorts of problems is especially relevant to euthanasia, and so we omit treating both. The relevant problem is that of the legal status of a person who helps another to commit suicide.

Obviously, if it ought in general to be permissible for one person to help another to commit suicide *and* if killing another at the request or with the consent of the person killed is considered assistance in suicide, then the issue concerning voluntary euthanasia is solved. However, we think neither that criminal law should permit assistance in suicide nor that the distinction between assisted suicide and homicide with consent should be eliminated. We deal with assisted suicide here to the extent that it affects cases other than those in which euthanasia would be involved; we have reserved the consideration of euthanasia for chapter six.

Superficially there might seem to be very little difference between assisted suicide and homicide upon request. What difference is there, for example, if one person hands another a gun with which to commit suicide or if the first takes deadly aim and fires the gun at the request of the second?[23] Ethically it is difficult to think of any difference, and this is so regardless of the system of ethics one applies to the two cases. However, assisting suicide and committing homicide with the consent of the victim have often been legally distinguished, and we think that with respect to the technical question of the definition of the offenses this is as it should be.

On the one hand, where the evidence is that one person has killed another, the case ought to be tried as homicide. Even if the consent of the victim is to be considered a mitigating factor, the burden of proof for establishing this circumstance should fall on the accused. Otherwise the prosecution would be burdened with establishing that the victim did not consent; making the proof of this element necessary to establish murder would make things much too easy for murderers and much too risky for potential victims.

On the other hand, where the evidence is that a person has committed suicide, then the prosecution can be reasonably required to establish that another has helped if this is to be considered criminal.

Consequently, even if the penalties for homicide with consent and for assisting suicide were to be made equivalent—which we consider would be reasonable in view of the equivalence of the malice of the two forms of action—the two should continue to be treated by criminal law as technically distinct offenses.

But why should assisting suicide be considered a crime? There is one kind of case which borders on assisted suicide in which no one is likely to argue that the act should not be a crime. The Model Penal Code deals with this kind of case:

> *Causing Suicide as Criminal Homicide.* A person may be convicted of criminal homicide for causing another to commit suicide only if he purposely causes such suicide by force, duress or deception.[24]

Some states have adopted this provision or something similar to it.[25] The idea surely is reasonable. A person who brings about the death of another by the other's own but nonvoluntary hand is committing virtual homicide, not merely assisting suicide. But this provision is not broad enough to include many closely related cases which are more properly called "assisted suicide" and which ought also to be covered.

One who is a competent adult and who instigates and assists the suicide of a child, especially a child under fourteen or another legally noncompetent person, is equally engaged in homicide. There is a hazy borderline in this matter. What are we to think of cases in which a person in order to facilitate inheritance urges and assists an intoxicated or debilitated relative to commit suicide? It seems to us that if some cases of assisting suicide should be considered murder, the general rule ought to be that to assist suicide is to commit murder. Only such a rule offers adequate protection for those who do not bring about their own deaths with full voluntariness. This general rule might be qualified to permit mitigation when the defendant can show that the suicide was competent and acted voluntarily, no duress, force, or fraud having been exercised.

If this were the general rule for cases of assisted suicide, the question remains why genuine assistance should be a mitigated offense rather than no offense at all. We think there are several reasons for taking this position.

In the first place, if assistance with a genuinely voluntary suicidal act is considered no crime at all, then at least in practice the burden of proof will fall upon the prosecution to show that the suicidal act was not wholly voluntary.

In the second place, even if we grant that people ought to be at liberty to commit suicide, still there are enough reasons for regarding suicide with reserve—the socially disturbing effects and costs of such behavior which we mentioned in section C—that there are plausible reasons for trying to inhibit suicide by treating as crimes acts intended to help others to kill themselves.

In the third place, the fact that a person who commits suicide acts in many cases with mitigated responsibility and the fact that the criminal law cannot touch such a person are excellent reasons for not considering the act of self-killing a crime. Also, the typical diminished responsibility of the attempter together with lack of effective deterrent effect are good reasons for not considering suicide attempts criminal. But one who assists another to commit suicide need not be acting with reduced responsibility, and in many cases the prospect of legal liability will restrain the accessory.

In the fourth place, individuals can be induced in some circumstances to do things damaging to themselves and contrary to public policy without their own fully voluntary cooperation being eliminated. Prostitution is a case in point. The law certainly is not irrational if it considers criminal at least those who exploit others and induce them to act contrary to their own interests and dignity. If assisting suicide were no crime—and especially if homicide with consent were treated for purposes of punishment as equivalent to assisted suicide—wholly repulsive practices of ultimate exploitation and degradation would be legalized. In ancient times some individuals did kill themselves or sell themselves to be killed for the amusement of others as a way of obtaining money to provide for dependents. If assisted suicide were legal, an individual in need of money might agree to a proposition to fight wild animals, or to play Russian roulette, or to engage in some other type of self-destructive behavior for the amusement of spectators. The prospect of such an abuse is perhaps not great at present, but one can think of cases which differ in degree rather than in kind from such gross instances of exploitation. Certain professional sports verge upon gladiatorial combat.

Without engaging in prostitution individuals give sexual favors in situations which more or less approach the model of outright sale of oneself. Similarly, one committing suicide might be subjected to varying degrees of psychological leverage if the instigation and assistance of suicide is considered noncriminal. Since the liberty to kill oneself is not one which sound public policy must regard with complete neutrality, it seems to us altogether legitimate that the instigation and assisting of suicide should be held criminal to provide a context in which there will remain a line of defense for those who would be subjected to pressure to kill themselves.

The point is illustrated by a British case. By the Suicide Act of 1961 the law by which suicide was a crime in England and Wales was abrogated. However, the offense of assisting suicide was created and made an option to prosecution for murder or manslaughter:

> 2.—(1) A person who aids, abets, counsels or procures the suicide of another, or an attempt by another to commit suicide, shall be liable on conviction on indictment to imprisonment for a term not exceeding fourteen years.
>
> (2) If on the trial of an indictment for murder or manslaughter it is

proved that the accused aided, abetted, counselled or procured the suicide of the person in question, the jury may find him guilty of that offense.[26]

Early in 1977 Yolande McShane was convicted under this provision and sentenced to two years in prison.

In March 1976 Mrs. McShane had visited her eighty-seven-year-old mother, Edith Mott, in a nursing home. McShane was in debt and stood to inherit $70,000 upon Mrs. Mott's death. McShane gave her mother fifteen Nembutal tablets and urged her to take them with whiskey. A concealed police camera filmed the scene as the two women talked:

> "How many have you brought?" asks the mother.
> "Fifteen."
> "But does it take fifteen?"
> "For most ten are fatal, but if you take them with whisky, five are enough."
> "It is a mortal sin."
> "People are doing it left, right and center. It's not a sin anymore. It's nothing nowadays. But it's up to you."
> "But is it cowardly to do it?"
> "No, it isn't cowardly. If you had a dog in this state, you would take it to the vet, wouldn't you?"
> "A dog hasn't got a soul."[27]

After a visit of three and one-half hours, McShane departed and was arrested; the nursing sisters found the pills hidden in a bag of candy.[28]

If assisting and counseling suicide were not a crime, many reluctant persons would face such badgering, and often those in a debilitated condition would finally yield. In some ways creating the context for the badgering itself is even more repugnant than permitting the consequent deaths.

F. Criticism of Some Present and Proposed Laws

The suicide provisions of the Model Penal Code would treat McShane's act as a misdemeanor, because, unlike the British statute, the provision proposed by the Model Penal Code distinguishes between cases in which an attempt at suicide is actually made and those in which no attempt is made:

> *Aiding or Soliciting Suicide as an Independent Offense.* A person who purposely aids or solicits another to commit suicide is guilty of a felony of the second degree if his conduct causes such suicide or an attempted suicide, and otherwise of a misdemeanor.[29]

This is more protective than many existing laws.

New York, for example, defines the crime as "promoting a suicide attempt" and imposes the penalty only if one "causes or aids another person to attempt suicide."[30] Obviously, McShane only tried but did not succeed in getting her mother to attempt suicide, and thus she did not cause or aid any attempt. Other states define the crime in such a way that even if Mott had attempted but did not succeed in suicide, McShane would have been guiltless. Florida, for example, provides: "Every person deliberately assisting another in the commission of self-murder shall be guilty of manslaughter. . . . "[31] California, on the contrary, appears to include any form of advice or encouragement to commit suicide with assistance in a successful attempt: "Every person who deliberately aids, or advises, or encourages another to commit suicide, is guilty of a felony."[32]

These statutes do not seem to be well thought out. It is hardly likely that there is any reasonable explanation for their differing provisions.

To forbid anyone to encourage another to commit suicide would be to treat as a crime the writing of a philosophical or theological essay urging suicide as a legitimate way of solving one's problems. Freedom of speech demands that the crime be defined more narrowly.

It seems to us that even to forbid the advising or counseling of suicide violates liberty of speech and invades privacy in the strict sense by forbidding forms of personal communication which may not be morally defensible but which hardly offend any legitimate public interest in the way that assisting suicide does. For these reasons we think the language of the California statute and even of the English Suicide Act too broad. The Model Penal Code's "aids or solicits" comes nearer the mark, for behavior begins to have a potentially causal and objectionable role in a particular suicide attempt only when it becomes practical by inciting a specific act, providing directions for doing it, and perhaps also supplying some material means for carrying out the plan.

However, the Model Penal Code proposal does not distinguish between cases in which aiding and soliciting suicide leads to death and cases in which it only leads to an unsuccessful attempt. Perhaps from a moral point of view the two kinds of act differ little or not at all, but the law frequently distinguishes successful from attempted crimes and treats the former as worse, perhaps partly on the basis that success often is a sign of more planning and determination.

However that may be, aiding and soliciting someone who actually commits suicide is much more serious than similar behavior which does not result in death, for when death results the situation is not always easy to distinguish from murder and from the cases of causing suicide which, as we have argued previously, should be treated as murder. But when aid and solicitation does not result in death, the person who might have committed suicide is able to testify concerning what happened, and so the unsuccessful accessory does not present as dangerous a problem.

At the same time the Model Penal Code proposal makes a sharp distinction between cases in which the aid and solicitation results in an attempt and cases in which it does not. Not only are these two kinds of cases indistinguishable on any ethical theory we know of, but they also are very alike in their undesirable aspects so far as the public interest is concerned. Thus we see no good reason to distinguish between them.

In Switzerland the criminality of assisting suicide has turned upon the presence of a selfish motive.[33] Glanville Williams supports the acceptance of this approach in Anglo-American law, although he admits it would be novel; he also would merge assisting suicide with homicide with consent, and recognizes that doing this would cause a danger of false evidence but brushes aside this danger.[34] We think that the commentator on the draft of the Model Penal Code was correct in pointing out that motives often are mixed and that it is preferable to allow them to be taken into account at the sentencing stage.[35] As we have pointed out already, in cases in which death results it is important to avoid defining the crime of assisting suicide in a way which with Anglo-American (though perhaps not with Continental) legal procedures would result in setting too high a burden of proof upon the prosecution in cases which sometimes are not distinguishable from cold-blooded murder.

G. Recommendations for a Statute on Suicide

Present American law with respect to suicide is none too definite nor is it any too rational.[36] It seems clear to us that careful recodification is needed in this area to protect liberty and justice for everyone concerned. What needs to be done will vary somewhat from one jurisdiction to another, depending upon technical problems and the present state of the law in each. However, the following summary of the conclusions reached in this chapter indicates what shape we think the law of suicide should take in the areas which we have considered.

First, criminal law should explicitly state that suicide and attempted suicide are not crimes. This provision would eliminate any danger that a suicide attempt would be used as leverage to obtain a civil commitment not otherwise obtainable.

Second, criminal and civil liability should not fall upon anyone who does what is immediately necessary to restrain an agent or to mitigate the harm in circumstances in which a reasonable person would judge that another might kill or seriously harm himself or herself.

Third, criminal and civil liability should fall upon anyone who restrains another longer than necessary to call upon the police, and police and hospitals should not restrain people for their own good without promptly seeking a court order. A temporary court order for an individual's own protection should be limited to a very short time. Nonvoluntary civil commitment solely on the grounds that individuals have attempted or are expected to attempt suicide should be excluded. Forced feeding also should be excluded.

Fourth, criminal law should provide that anyone who supplies or offers aid, or solicits and urges another, to commit suicide shall be guilty of attempted manslaughter regardless of whether the intended suicide makes an attempt or does not make one. Here the criminality of the act must hang upon the intent that what is provided or said should bring about the suicide of the particular individual, and upon the fact that a reasonable person would expect that what is provided or said might have the intended result.

Fifth, criminal law should treat as a principal in murder anyone who aids another in actually committing suicide. Here—where a death occurs and the charge is murder—"aids" should be defined narrowly to exclude even practical directions and urgent solicitation. What must be prevented is the sort of behavior which creates the serious problem of false evidence. In cases of this sort evidence provided by the defense to show that force, duress, or fraud was not used, and that the person who committed suicide was a competent adult acting without special pressure or exploitation from the side of the defendant, should be considered in mitigation, and thus taken into account in sentencing. The burden of proof to show that aggravating conditions are present must not be on the prosecution.

If the law were arranged in this way, the liberty of those who deliberately and rationally choose to kill themselves would be protected to a considerable extent. Those who consider suicide appropriate can say so and can distribute information about how to proceed most efficiently by using various techniques. Mere general recommendation of suicide or even advice to an individual would not by itself be criminal. Those who fail in a first attempt at suicide will not be prevented, if they are determined, from promptly making another attempt. Even those in institutions who really wish to kill themselves will be able to do so.

At the same time strict provisions will tend to protect the public at large by discouraging persons from committing murder and trying to make the death appear a case of suicide. Also, the right to life of those who might be caused to kill themselves by a nonvoluntary or seriously pressured act will be protected; the law will be solicitous as it should be to protect the weak. Yet anyone who can establish factors mitigating guilt for assisting another's death will obtain consideration in sentencing.

Under such a statute many of those whose conditions arouse great sympathy for the argument in favor of legalization of voluntary euthanasia could solve their problem, if they wished, by self-administered euthanasia: suicide. In practice it would even be possible for others to provide substantial assistance. Persons contemplating suicide who considered it acceptable could discuss their condition with like-minded friends and receive moral support to carry out a decision to kill themselves without imperiling such friends; encouragement would not be solicitation. A physician could provide a patient with drugs suited to deaden pain or promote sleep or emotional tranquility, while he warned the patient to avoid a fatal overdose. A warning given in the hearing of witnesses undoubtedly would suffice to protect the physician provided that the patient really was competent and in such a condition that a reasonable person would expect such a patient to be able to understand the advice and to heed the warning.

Still, it will be argued, not everyone can bring about a desired death either by refusing treatment or by personal, suicidal action. Some need help, because they are too weak to help themselves, perhaps too closely cared for in an institutional setting to die otherwise than by self-starvation, which can be slow and difficult. For those who need such help proponents of voluntary euthanasia urge beneficent killing at the patient's own request. We turn now to this central problem.

6: Voluntary Active Euthanasia and Liberty

A. "Voluntary Active Euthanasia" Defined

At the beginning of chapter four we distinguished voluntary active euthanasia from other types by defining it as the deliberate bringing about of the death of someone with the consent of the person killed. Now we must refine this definition.

First, active euthanasia, whether voluntary or not, is the deliberate killing of one person by another. We use "Agent" to refer to anyone doing such a killing and "Patient" to refer to anyone undergoing such a killing—that is, being killed in this way. A deliberate killing is euthanasia only if three conditions are fulfilled. (1) Patient either is suffering and dying, or is suffering irremediably, or at least is irremediably subject to some disease or defect which would generally be considered by reasonable persons to be grave and pitiable. (2) Agent sincerely believes that Patient would be better off dead—that is, that no further continuance of Patient's life is likely to be beneficial for Patient. (3) Agent deliberately brings about Patient's death in order that Patient shall have the benefit of being better off dead—that is, not continue to suffer the condition (1) under supposition (2).

Second, active euthanasia is *voluntary* only if Patient is legally competent and gives informed consent to being killed by Agent. We distinguish active euthanasia which is not voluntary according to whether Patient is capable of consent or not. If Patient is not competent to give informed consent and if Agent assumes that Patient would consent if Patient were competent, then Agent's euthanasia killing of Patient is *nonvoluntary* on Patient's part. If Patient is competent to give informed consent and does not give it or if Agent assumes that Patient would not consent if competent, then Agent's euthanasia killing of Patient is *involuntary* on Patient's part.

Involuntary euthanasia involves an element of imposition by Agent upon Patient, since Patient's own judgment is not consulted or Patient's judgment or assumed judgment is overridden. As we shall see, most who advocate legalization of euthanasia support voluntary and nonvoluntary euthanasia—the latter, for example, for seriously defective infants. But no one is advocating involuntary euthanasia. Our primary concern in this chapter is voluntary active euthanasia; we mention nonvoluntary euthanasia only incidentally here and treat it fully in chapter eight.

Our statement of the conditions for active euthanasia above is intended to specify the conditions common to cases of "euthanasia" or "mercy killing" as these expressions are commonly used in news reports and popular discussions. The individual killed in such cases is not always terminally and incurably ill, although these requirements often are built into proposals for legalization of euthanasia. For example, Lester Zygmaniak's killing of his brother who had been paralyzed from the neck down in a motorcycle accident was called "euthanasia" or "mercy killing" although the patient was not dying; John Noxon's electrocution of his mongoloid infant son was called "euthanasia" or "mercy killing" although the baby was neither dying nor suffering.[1] What is common to all cases is simply that the patient is subject to some serious, permanent condition which most people would consider very sad.

Marvin Kohl claims that "mercy killing" is synonymous with "active beneficent euthanasia," and he defines these expressions by saying that "both refer to the inducement of a relatively painless and quick death, the intention and actual consequences of which are the *kindest possible treatment* of an unfortunate individual in the actual circumstances."[2]

Our condition (2) does not say anything about whether or not the killing is in actual consequence kind treatment; we require only that the killer believes the patient would be better off dead. To define "mercy killing" as Kohl does builds in a question-begging moral evaluation and blocks discussion of the question whether it ever makes sense to believe, as mercy killers do, that someone is better off dead. That death should be induced painlessly and quickly is not specified in our statement of the conditions for euthanasia, not that we exclude this element, but that we suppose it to be implicit in the agent's beliefs and motive that *relatively* painless and quick death will be sought.

Our statement of the conditions for *voluntary* euthanasia hinges upon the legal competency and informed consent of the person killed. Very often "voluntariness" is defined by the request of the patient, but persons who are under a misapprehension as to their condition and prospects as well as persons who are not competent to consent might request euthanasia without such a request expressing any voluntary act of theirs. Most proposals for legalization of euthanasia attempt to provide some assurance of voluntariness by safeguards designed to protect persons from being killed without their informed consent.[3]

Kohl has suggested that euthanasia be called "noninvoluntary" if either the patient gives informed consent or a parent or guardian consents on behalf of the patient; more recently he has urged that euthanasia with either personal or substitute consent might be called "voluntary."[4] In most actual cases there has been no question of substitute consent; in many of these cases, of course, the one killing a noncompetent individual has been the parent. As even Kohl himself admits, calling cases "voluntary" in which substitute consent is given is likely to be confusing. Thus, we would class as nonvoluntary both cases in which substitute consent is given and cases in which the consent of a noncompetent individual is presumed by the killer.

In her unpublished doctoral dissertation Sissela Ann Bok examines more carefully than anyone else has done the problem of defining voluntary active euthanasia.[5] We think her work supports our analysis, although she encapsulates the conditions for active euthanasia much more briefly, mainly in the simple statement that "the act must be motivated by mercy for a suffering person."[6] Bok goes on to point out that voluntary active euthanasia includes only a restricted class of cases and that proponents of legalization of euthanasia usually further restrict this class.[7] It is important to notice what voluntary active euthanasia does not include.

As we have already said, the condition of voluntariness excludes cases in which a noncompetent individual is killed and cases in which a competent individual is killed without informed consent. Since most cases of reported mercy killings either are the killings of infants or persons mentally defective or are killings of someone unconscious without prior consent, only a few cases—such as that of Zygmaniak in which the paralyzed brother begged to be killed—could possibly qualify as voluntary. And even in this case voluntariness is questionable to the extent that the expressed desire might not have deliberately been affirmed had the patient fully been informed about his prognosis and the possibilities, however thin, of some degree of rehabilitation.

Active euthanasia also excludes many acts and omissions often confused with it. The termination of the support of the functioning of organic remains after a person as a whole has died, which we considered in chapter three, would not be euthanasia because no one is killed. The omission of life-sustaining treatment which a person has refused or which a physician for some other reason has no duty to provide would not be active euthanasia. And the administering of analgesic drugs to relieve pain is not active euthanasia even if life is shortened provided that the patient's death is not deliberately brought about. Suicide, which may be regarded as self-administered euthanasia, is not active euthanasia as defined above, although we shall suggest that assisting suicide under certain circumstances can be assimilated to active euthanasia.

Insofar as the termination of maintenance of organic remains, the omission of life-sustaining treatment, the administering of analgesics, and suicide are already permitted by existing law, these activities in many cases can be licit alternatives to the active killing which proponents of euthanasia wish to have legalized.

B. The Present Law and the Basic Argument for Change

At present according to the law of English-speaking countries active euthanasia is criminal homicide. Usually there is premeditation, and the euthanasia killing meets the conditions for murder in the first degree. The consent of the victim, when given, is legally irrelevant to the criminal aspect of an act. The maxim "No injury is done to a willing party" holds in tort law—one cannot both consent to something and then sue the person who does it with one's consent—but not in criminal law. A crime is an offense not only to its victim but also to the public at large, and so consent of a victim to a crime does not justify the criminal act.[8] Thus, if one person kills another in a duel, the killing is criminal homicide even though the victim was a willing participant. The same holds for mercy killing.

The motive of mercy—that the killer acts in the belief that the victim will be better off dead—also is legally irrelevant. Murder presupposes "malice," but legal maliciousness is not in a subjective motive of hatred but in the factual intent to bring about death unlawfully, and so a mercy killer is legally malicious by deliberately killing without legal justification or excuse even if he or she is morally beneficent in trying to benefit a person sincerely believed to be better off dead than alive.[9]

In practice neither those who do mercy killings at the patient's request nor those believed to have acted with similar motives in killing noncompetent individuals and even competent individuals without their express consent are legally treated as typical murderers. Such killers might not be indicted, might be tried but permitted to plead not guilty and acquitted, might be acquitted by reason of temporary insanity, might be found guilty of a lesser charge but punished very lightly—for example, by a fine, a suspended sentence, or being placed on parole—or at the very worst might be convicted of murder but compelled to serve only a few years in prison.[10] As Yale Kamisar points out, two cases resulting in a conviction and imprisonment had features which distinguished them: in one the testimony of other relatives for the prosecution and in the other a hardly credible defense of accident.[11]

Clearly, voluntary euthanasia and assisted suicide are very similar. Between the two there appears to be little difference in effect, in intent, or in motive. In some cases there will be little difference in the objective evidence. In a 1920 Michigan case Frank C. Roberts was convicted of murder by poison. He had mixed poison and placed it within reach of his wife who took the poison herself and died as a result. The assisting of suicide in this case was treated as murder by poison, even though suicide was not held a crime in Michigan at the time.[12]

In chaper five, section E, we argued that apart from cases of euthanasia criminal law ought to treat as a principal in murder anyone who aids another in actually committing suicide, but that evidence that force, duress, or fraud was not used and that the person who committed suicide was a competent adult acting without special pressure or exploitation from the side of the defendant should be considered in mitigation. The burden of proof would be, not on the prosecution to show that mitigating conditions were absent, but on the defense to show that these conditions were present, and the mitigating circumstances could then be taken into account in sentencing.

Cases of euthanasia apart, it seems reasonable that criminal law should deal with homicide with consent in the same way we have argued it should deal with the assisting of suicide, because the two crimes are so similar. (Nevertheless—as we also argued in chapter five, section E—these crimes ought to be defined as distinct offenses for technical reasons having to do with burden of proof.) Applied to homicide with consent, the way we suggested the law should deal with assisted suicide seems close to present law-enforcement practices.

It will follow that, apart from the necessary technical distinction, voluntary euthanasia can be viewed as the same problem as assisting suicide when the condition of the one committing suicide is grave and pitiable and the motive of the accessory is to assist another sincerely believed to be better off dead. Discussion of the two kinds of acts together seems reasonable because it matters little who pushes the plunger of the hypodermic needle or who puts the tablets in the patient's mouth if the one being killed is legally competent and gives informed consent in either case and if the conditions and motives of the parties are otherwise the same. Moreover, if homicide with consent were legalized in cases in which it is voluntary active euthanasia, presumably a method which permitted patients to administer the cause of death to themselves would have to be accepted. And if assisting suicide in cases in which it is self-administered euthanasia were legalized, it would be difficult to maintain more than a conceptual distinction for technical purposes in such cases between assisting suicide and homicide with consent. Therefore, throughout the remainder of this chapter our discussion is intended to apply equally to cases in which someone assists self-administered euthanasia and to cases in which someone carries out voluntary euthanasia upon another without any causal behavior on the patient's part.

Here and there in the arguments of proponents of euthanasia one encounters the suggestion that appropriate candidates for euthanasia are persons who are in any case almost dead, or who are dead ''for all practical purposes,'' or who are mere vegetables beyond recovery.[13] Some remarks of this sort perhaps are based upon lack of clarity about the definition of death, a problem we discussed in chapter three. If the total brain is dead, then the person truly is dead, not practically dead. Some remarks of this sort perhaps are intended only to support a policy of terminating active treatment, a problem we considered in chapter four with respect to competent persons and we shall consider in chapter nine with respect to noncompetent persons. Anyone who might plausibly be meant by references to those almost dead and so on would not usually be in a state to consent to euthanasia. Even if one were to seek the informed consent of one's garden vegetables before harvesting them, one would not be likely to obtain it!

If proponents of euthanasia really hold that the appropriate candidates for mercy killing are those who consent validly and who are certainly in a terminal state, then they are referring to a subclass of the killings (our definition does not specify that the patient be terminal) with which we are concerned here. Within this class some who volunteer to be killed will be nearer death than others; no clear line can be drawn dividing the more from the less proximately dead, since proximity to death varies continuously by infinitesimals. The law makes no distinction based on such degrees; as long as life remains, it is a crime to destroy it.[14] Where active euthanasia is in question, the inherent vagueness of ''almost dead'' precludes the use of proximity to death in itself as a legally significant criterion of permissible killing.

Proponents of euthanasia often argue that since the withholding or termination of lifesaving treatment can be permissible, the active termination of life should also be permissible, since the distinction between killing and letting die is of little if any importance.[15] In answering this argument it is essential to keep a clear distinction between morality and law. We are not here concerned with morality; the ethical question will be discussed in chapter twelve. It will suffice here to suggest that whether the distinction between killing and letting die is morally important is related to whether the morality of actions is determined by their consequences or by other factors.[16] From a legal point of view there is a fairly clear and significant distinction between killing and letting die. Several commentators have explained and defended this distinction.[17]

Legally one could commit murder by omission, but one's omission is a legal act only if one has a clear legal duty to act, one is not prevented from fulfilling the duty, one omits to fulfill the duty, and the omission is the immediate and direct cause of the consequence which one is legally forbidden to bring about. For a death-causing omission to be murder rather than negligent manslaughter the malicious intent required for murder also is necessary; in other words, the omission has to be deliberate in order to cause death.

As we saw in chapter four, sections B and C, the physician's legal duty is limited to treatment to which the patient consents or to which consent is presumed, and does not extend beyond what is beneficial to the patient. It seems that there never has been a criminal prosecution of a physician for homicide by omission, and the reason is easy to see. Even if physicians do commit euthanasia—for example, of defective infants—by omission, legal proof of the elements of the crime would be very difficult.[18]

Whether a physician's legal liberty not to prolong life in many cases ought to be extended to a legal liberty (or perhaps duty) to terminate life at least in some such cases is precisely the topic of the present chapter. To attempt to settle the question of whether voluntary active euthanasia ought to be legalized by arguing against the ethical significance of the distinction between killing and letting die is to confuse morality with law and to beg the question as to whether there are sound jurisprudential grounds for maintaining the present legal distinction between the duty not to treat without consent and the prohibition to kill even with consent.

Considered from the point of view of law and law enforcement, killing and letting die at least differ in respect to the cause of death. This difference means that states of affairs for which there is evidence in cases of killing (even killing considered justifiable or excusable) are not easy to distinguish from states of affairs everyone agrees the law must attempt to control (cold-blooded murder), while states of affairs for which there is evidence in cases of letting die (even letting die which actually is murder by omission) are not easy to distinguish from states of affairs everyone agrees the law must not interfere with (the withholding of treatment out of respect for a person's legitimate exercise of the liberty to refuse consent to it). As we shall see shortly, serious jurisprudential problems about proposals to legalize euthanasia arise in part precisely from the difficulty of making and maintaining in practice the distinction between the killings which would be authorized by the legalization of euthanasia and those which would remain forbidden as murder.

The argument in favor of legalizing euthanasia, at least in cases in which informed consent would be given by a terminally ill patient, is not difficult to understand. By hypothesis such a patient wishes to die; hence, the killing would not be an injustice to the person killed. The suffering of the patient—perhaps supplemented by a consideration of the suffering of others and the cost of continuing care—provides some ground for considering the desire to die a reasonable one.[19] Pain relievers may not be wholly effective in eliminating pain and other sources of personal discomfort, embarrassment, and humiliation arising from the illness.[20] In our present pluralistic society many persons do not accept the principle of the absolute sanctity of life which is grounded in traditional moral and religious conceptions.[21] Hence, the argument concludes, the request of such persons to be killed and the liberty of persons willing to perform voluntary euthanasia should be protected by law.

To maintain the legal prohibition of voluntary active euthanasia is cruel to those who are made to suffer needlessly and is an infringement upon the liberty of those persons who would choose to be killed or to kill in order to prevent needless suffering.[22]

Opponents of the legalization of euthanasia can point out that those who wish to die can refuse all treatment except palliative care or can even kill themselves. However, proponents of legalization will respond that a certain proportion of candidates for euthanasia cannot solve their problems without the active help of another person. To maintain the legal prohibition of voluntary euthanasia, opponents must show that legalization would somehow be contrary to the common good.

Since the death sooner rather than later of a person dying in any case does not seem to harm society, how can it be contrary to the common good? If one could maintain that the good of human life is directly and of itself a concern of political society, opponents of euthanasia could base their opposition on the sanctity of life. But we have granted, at least for the sake of the arguments in this book, that in our present pluralistic society the good of human life itself is not to be considered a direct and immediate foundation of legal rights and duties. The question therefore is whether liberty and justice are served by the present prohibition of euthanasia or would be served better by permission of voluntary active euthanasia.

C. Other Arguments by Proponents of Legalization

Sometimes proponents of euthanasia seem to argue that since mercy killings already are done by the medical profession, the law ought to sanction this practice.[23] As a general principle the premiss of this argument can hardly be sustained. Lawyers often suborn perjury; merchants often defraud their customers; chiefs of state often obstruct justice. None of these acts should be legalized merely because they are done. Moreover, it is not clear that physicians to any great extent engage in active voluntary euthanasia. Evidence that they allow patients to die and evidence that they give substantial quantities of drugs to eliminate pain even if life is thereby shortened is not evidence that they engage in active euthanasia or give their approval to it.[24]

Glanville Williams suggests that in a 1936 debate in the British House of Lords two members who were also leaders of the medical profession—Lord Dawson of Penn and Lord Horder—and the Archbishop of Canterbury approved the practice of euthanasia by the medical profession while they opposed legalization of this practice.[25] Lord Dawson of Penn did make statements which taken out of context support the interpretation Williams offers. However, near the end of his speech Lord Dawson said: "We have not in mind to set to work to kill anybody at all. What we say is, if we cannot cure for heaven's sake let us do our best to lighten the pain."[26] The Archbishop of Canterbury clearly supported the termination of treatment in some cases and the use of means which might also shorten life to assuage pain; he expressly denied that such practices would be criminal and nowhere supported active euthanasia.[27] Lord Horder summed up the common position by saying:

> In conclusion may I repeat my main thesis? The two extremes of dying in pain and being killed do not exhaust the possibilities of the stricken patient, because there is a middle position created by a kindly and skillful doctor who gives assistance to an equally kindly nature, and that is what is at present implicit in the patient's question: "You will stand by me, won't you?" and the doctor's assurance: "Yes, I will."[28]

When the same issue was debated again fourteen years later in 1950, Lord Horder maintained and repeated the same position.[29]

Lord Ponsonby of Shulbrede, in introducing and supporting the 1936 bill, had been the one who urged that narcotics necessary to relieve pain shortened life, and had quoted supporters of euthanasia for the position that what competent physicians did for dying patients bordered upon or crossed the border of illegality.[30]

As a matter of fact these concerns seem to be unreal. Very substantial doses of opiates are required to kill patients, and increasing tolerance affects their action not only upon pain but also upon the brain center which controls respiration.[31] In one case reported in a proeuthanasia work an individual debilitated from advanced cancer and attempting suicide used more than twice the maximum dose normally required to kill without dying.[32]

Moreover, physicians do not incur criminal liability by using pain-killing drugs which incidentally shorten life. A British physician was acquitted of murder although he had administered excessively high doses of morphine, heroin, and other sedatives to a patient, and although circumstantial evidence suggested that his motives in doing so may have been questionable.[33]

In the face of these facts Williams recently has admitted that physicians can kill pain without killing patients and that they can kill pain without legal risk. However, he takes this situation to support rather than to undermine his argument for legalization of euthanasia, on the ground that the facts eliminate the ambiguity which—according to his own earlier myth—permitted physicians to kill with impunity.[34] This recent argument of Williams also is fallacious, since it not only continues to use unproved factual assumptions but also begs the question by taking for granted the acceptability of euthanasia.

Sometimes it has been suggested that the law may be kept as it is and physicians trusted to practice euthanasia in appropriate cases despite its illegality.[35] We by no means subscribe to this view. Rather, if the law ought to remain as it is, then every effort ought to be made to enforce it; if euthanasia ought to be permitted, then some way of legalizing it ought to be developed. However, perhaps some of those who urge that the law be maintained and the practice of euthanasia permitted do not clearly distinguish between active euthanasia and other practices which either are legal or are difficult to distinguish from legitimate practices of terminating treatment, killing pain, and providing a patient with drugs for proper uses which can also be abused by a patient who happens to be suicidal.

Someone might suggest that it would be desirable to legalize—"for the sake of removing any possible doubt"—legitimate practices short of active euthanasia which physicians now sometimes engage in. This suggestion seems to us to lack compelling grounds. The legal treatment of physicians does not show that the present situation subjects them to any undue threat of criminal prosecution.

Furthermore, where boundaries are now unclear, any attempt to specify them by statute would involve numerous vague terms. If practices expanded in view of the vagueness of a new statute—which is not unlikely—then not less but more doubt about the criminal liability of physicians would arise. Experience with statutes concerning abortion shows that it is more honest and more realistic to face the question of legalization of euthanasia directly; any attempt to clarify the law will substantially alter it or at least make a first step toward so doing.

Several legal commentators have suggested that the present discrepancy between the legal theory that active euthanasia is murder and the legal practice of treating mercy killers mercifully demands that the statutes be brought into conformity with practice. Different reasons are given for thinking that a change is necessary: Some claim that the discrepancy is detrimental to public confidence in the law and respect for it, while others urge that the irregularity of the present situation deprives either those committing euthanasia or those killed by it of equitable treatment or equal protection of law.[36]

Several points may be made in response to this suggestion. First, it is by no means clear that the present law does not prevent many mercy killings, a large proportion of which would be nonvoluntary and would not be legalized if strictly voluntary euthanasia were legalized. Second, most of the mercy killings which are presently dealt with by law are not voluntary; unless new statutory provisions are made with respect to nonvoluntary euthanasia, any present inequality in the treatment of the victims or the perpetrators of these crimes will continue. Third, criminal law in general involves some discrepancy between theory and practice; even apart from mercy killings not all homicide victims are protected equally and not all murderers are dealt with equitably. But this is no reason to repeal the law of homicide. Fourth, it may be possible to bring theory and practice closer together by enlightening judges and potential jurors with respect to the justification—assuming there is one—

for treating active euthanasia as a crime and also by permitting the mitigation of punishment for this crime without legalizing mercy killing.[37]

D. Some Legitimate Interests Opposed to Euthanasia

There are certain inevitable disadvantages which the legalization of voluntary active euthanasia will work upon persons who do not wish to be killed. How much weight these disadvantages ought to be considered to have and whether the imposition of them upon those who do not wish to be killed and do not want euthanasia legalized would be in itself unjust will be a matter of argument. Nevertheless, it is worth noticing these disadvantages because they provide a counterweight—even if it is not judged sufficient in itself— against the suffering which proponents of legalization wish to prevent.

First, as soon as one is able to choose to be killed provided that one gives one's informed consent to this decisive treatment, many people who do not wish to be killed will be given much more information about their condition and prospects than they care to have, with a view to allowing them to exercise their liberty to choose euthanasia. Our point is not that there is anything wrong with the requirement of informed consent for all medical treatment, especially for euthanasia. Our point is merely that other treatments to which one is asked to give informed consent offer some hope; the alternatives may be grim but the prospects are not altogether black.

Someone being asked for informed consent to euthanasia must be told that his or her case is utterly hopeless, that every alternative course of treatment is so repugnant that quick death might seem preferable. Such information need not be hard to bear if one is willing to accept the alternative of euthanasia. But many who do not wish to accept this alternative will be informed very fully, frankly, and horrifyingly of what the days, weeks, months, perhaps even years ahead hold in store. Some of this information they would have to receive bit by bit in any case if they were to make choices about their treatment during each stage of dying. But the possibility of euthanasia cannot be properly proposed without all of the bad news being spelled out at once.[38]

Proponents of euthanasia are likely to object that persons who are willing to consider a possibility must bear the burdens of considering it, while those who are not willing to consider the possibility of euthanasia can make this fact clear and be spared their physician's informative account. But this logical division between the willing and the unwilling is hardly likely to hold up in practice. Physicians might be forbidden by law to raise the possibility of euthanasia with their patients and might be limited to informing patients who demand information. Even if this limitation were not deemed an infringement upon free speech, it would help matters very little.

A friend, a relative, a patient in the next bed who accepted euthanasia would be sure to begin telling most patients what they believed was in store for them if euthanasia were not chosen. Supplied with such distressing information, few patients could resist the temptation to seek verification or correction from a competent person. And so a great many people who do not wish to be killed would be burdened with information which they would prefer not to have and which need never be given for fully informed consent to medical treatment as long as euthanasia remains an option excluded by law.

Hardly anyone seems to have considered the unnecessary suffering which will inevitably be caused by the provision of information necessary for valid consent to euthanasia. Many opponents of legalization do mention a second factor: Once the euthanasia option is available, those who do not wish to exercise it will have to resist it. Relatives, health-care personnel, social workers, friends, and mere acquaintances will more or less urgently suggest that certain persons, despite their reluctance, ought to consider and accept the euthanasia option.

Most people find it difficult to reject flatly any request and even more difficult to cut it off before giving it a hearing—a fact well known to door-to-door salesmen. And almost anyone who is weakened by illness and under psychological stress will be swayed by urgings that euthanasia be considered. Persons who do not wish to be killed will feel such solicitation to be a personal affront to their dignity, an affront difficult to prevent and impossible to redress.[39]

The need to resist the euthanasia option not only will take the form of rejecting the urgings of others but also will take the form of a painful conflict within oneself for some—perhaps for a great many—persons. Many who regard euthanasia as morally excluded in principle and yet who confront a grim prospect will be tempted to violate the principle. Even if one considers the conviction of such persons erroneous, their suffering will be nevertheless real.

Moreover, the temptation to accept euthanasia although one does not approve it may arise not only from selfish but also from altruistic motives. Many who are mortally ill worry that they are a burden to others, feel guilty for the care they need, apologize when they must ask for some service. These feelings will be increased and amplified by the awareness that all of the costs to others—emotional and economic as well—might be cut by one's own choice if one only felt that such a choice would be right.

Anxiety will be a further inevitable cost of legalization of euthanasia to those who do not wish to be killed. Legalization of voluntary euthanasia may be hedged about with more or less stringent safeguards. If the safeguards are less, the level of anxiety will be high and well grounded. If the safeguards are more, still many people will be anxious.

It is all well and good to say that reasonable persons will not worry that they will be killed without consent merely because others are being killed with consent. But not all persons in hospitals, in nursing homes, and in other institutions are reasonable. Many are at least slightly paranoid. Even limitations upon active treatment can generate anxiety when a policy of limiting treatment is known. But if the policy of limiting treatment is justified, this anxiety has to be accepted. The added anxiety which will be generated if active euthanasia is legalized need not be accepted unless the new policy is justified, and this anxiety is a cost which weighs with others against the fairness of the policy to those who do not wish to be killed.

Proponents of legalization often urge that the option of euthanasia would protect the dignity of persons who wish to take charge of their own dying rather than to play a completely patient role in the process of dying. This contention has some plausibility, we think, chiefly because the typical atmosphere of a hospital does not conduce to patient autonomy. Every patient tends by the very technology of modern medicine to be reduced to the status of a malfunctioning object which needs to be repaired. Patients have little active role in their own treatment. The dying are deprived of dignity in this situation largely because *everyone* who is subjected to it is deprived of dignity. But those who can look forward to getting well and resuming normal activities can stand the affront much better than those who have no such hopeful prospects. In section J of this chapter we shall suggest how this problem can be met otherwise than by euthanasia.

The point we wish to make at once, however, is that legalization of euthanasia for those who choose it will not at all improve matters for those who do not wish to be killed. In fact, the dying who do not accept euthanasia are likely to be treated with somewhat less sympathy and respect than is now the case. If they are a burden to themselves and to others, that will be their own fault. If the technically efficient solution of euthanasia is rejected, a dying patient will have rejected the last, most efficient treatment which modern medicine will have to offer. Health-care personnel and social workers who personally accept euthanasia are likely to treat those who persist in dying naturally with about as much respect as nonbelievers now tend to treat those Jehovah's Witnesses who desire health care but refuse blood transfusions.

If euthanasia is legalized, some of the most difficult cases requiring palliative care will be disposed of. As we shall show in section J, the techniques and facilities for palliative care have been improving steadily; improvements in pain-relieving drugs are but one example. Still, there is always room for research and further improvement. The incentive for such work will be lessened if legalized euthanasia takes care of those who would otherwise most benefit from such work. Thus, all who do not choose to be killed will lose the advantage they would otherwise obtain from further work in this field.

A final inevitable cost of euthanasia will be the added sorrow of those who do not approve of euthanasia when the option is chosen by persons they love. Once more, one can say that those who disapprove should not be pained by the exercise of liberty on the part of friends and loved ones. The fact is that many people will suffer more severe grief after a death induced by euthanasia just as many people suffer more grief after a death caused by suicide than they would have suffered had the death been natural. There is some reason to think that it is psychologically very important that those who must undergo the parting of death reach the stage of acceptance of this inevitable parting.[40] Those who choose euthanasia are likely to act not in the acceptance but in the defiance of death, and to leave loved ones to struggle alone for acceptance. Acceptance will not be easy if those who are bereaved also believe that their loved one's last act was an immoral one.

All of the preceding costs of the legalization of euthanasia to those who do not approve of it deserve some consideration. As we have said, it is hard to know how great in fact such costs would be; much would depend upon the complex social conditions of different groups. The costs might be mitigated to a great extent by careful legislation, but we do not think any of them could be eliminated entirely.

Proponents of legalization are likely to disregard such costs, because they largely result from the beliefs and attitudes of those who consider euthanasia immoral. But our argument here has nothing to do with the value of such beliefs and attitudes. The fact is that they exist and will continue to exist for a long time in a large part, perhaps in the majority, of the population. So long as there are people who do not wish to be killed and do not wish euthanasia legalized, they have a reasonable self-interest in avoiding such costs which weighs against the reasonable self-interest of those who wish to be killed in avoiding the suffering of terminal illness.

From the point of view of sound jurisprudence the self-interest of the opponents of euthanasia can no more be excluded from consideration than can the self-interest of its proponents. If the legalization of euthanasia would serve some very substantial public interest—for example, if it would stop the spread of a plague or something of that sort—then the self-interest of opponents would not count for much, for the public interest would stand against it. But as long as all that is proposed is the legalization of voluntary euthanasia, the legalization of euthanasia is not proposed to serve the public interest, because voluntary euthanasia will have little impact upon any important public interest. Nonvoluntary euthanasia, of course, might be promoted to save the cost of caring for the permanently institutionalized. But purely voluntary euthanasia is not promoted as a way of reducing public costs.

Hence, the legalization of voluntary active euthanasia is promoted almost exclusively on the basis of its possible service to those who would choose to be killed rather than to suffer needlessly. This interest is a personal and private one. Other personal and private interests, no matter what one thinks of the beliefs and attitudes which give rise to them, deserve equal consideration from the law, which may no more despise the moral convictions of those who would not wish to be killed than it may despise the moral convictions of proponents of euthanasia. Therefore, the law may no more disregard the interests of the former group in avoiding suffering especially repugnant to themselves than it may disregard the interest of the latter group in avoiding the suffering otherwise inevitable in waiting for natural death.

E. Argument against Legalization: Possible Injustice

The preceding considerations go far toward neutralizing the central argument in favor of legalizing voluntary active euthanasia. Yet these considerations do not prove that legalization must be excluded. We proceed now to an argument against legalization based upon the jurisprudential principles of justice and liberty. We believe this argument is decisive.

The argument can be stated summarily as follows. If voluntary active euthanasia is legalized without regulation, those who do not wish to be killed are likely to become unwilling victims; this would deny them the protection they presently enjoy of the law of homicide. And since the denial is to serve a private interest, it will be an injustice. If involuntary active euthanasia is legalized with close regulation which will involve the government in killing, those who abhor such killing will be involved against their wishes, at least to the extent that their government and institutions will be utilized for this purpose. Since the government's involvement will be required only as a means to the promotion of a private interest, this state action will unjustly infringe the liberty of all who do not consent to mercy killing as a good to whose promotion state action might be legitimately directed. A solution involving a compromise between legalization of voluntary active euthanasia without regulation of the practice and legalization with close regulation which will involve the government in mercy killing would mean some degree of lessened protection together with some degree of governmental involvement, a situation which will result in injustice partly due to the reduced protection of the lives of those who do not wish to be killed and partly due to the unwilling involvement of those who do not wish to kill. Since the stated conditions are all the possible conditions under which voluntary active euthanasia could be legalized, legalization is impossible without justice. Therefore, the legalization of voluntary active euthanasia must be excluded.

The conditional premises which form the first and second disjuncts of this dilemma require proof. In the present section we argue that legalization of euthanasia without regulation would endanger the lives of persons who do not wish to be killed. In section F we shall argue that legalization with the close regulation which would involve the government in acts of mercy killing would infringe the liberty of the many citizens who abhor such killing.

Perhaps the best previous argument against the legalization of voluntary active euthanasia is that articulated by Yale Kamisar. In a famous and widely reprinted article Kamisar argued that since physicians are always fallible, misdiagnosis is not uncommon, and so the decision for euthanasia in a "hopeless case" might be the sole factor which made the case hopeless.[41]

It seems to us that such considerations are reasons which would tell very strongly against the rationality of consenting to euthanasia if it were legal, but they do not tell nearly so strongly against the legalization of euthanasia. Presumably, part of the information which would have to be imparted to someone considering this terminal treatment would be that the diagnosis could be mistaken, the outlook could turn out to be better than expected, and so on. If patients nevertheless elected to be killed on despairing but realistic probabilities rather than to continue on the assumption that as long as there is life there is hope, then the risks of error involved would be part of the evil they voluntarily accepted in order to avoid what they regarded as the greater evil of suffering unto a natural death.

Still, Kamisar's point about the fallibility of physicians does have some weight. The dangers involved in this fallibility can only be assumed voluntarily by the patient if the patient is fully aware of the risk. But the physician who is informing the patient is not likely to stress the fallibility of physicians. And so there will be some built-in bias in favor of underinforming patients about this factor. Such underinformation will be a more or less significant factor in erroneous decisions to die, and to the extent that the voluntariness of such decisions is negated by the lack of information which ought to have been given, such patients will have been done some injustice.

It may be objected that whenever a major operation is done there is danger of an error, whenever someone is buried or cremated there is danger that a living person is being buried or cremated.[42] We admit that such dangers are unavoidable. The point is that in the case of voluntary euthanasia persons are likely to be led to consent without being fully informed of dangers, and this treatment is a preventable injustice: It is not necessary to legalize voluntary active euthanasia to promote any important, commonly accepted public purpose. To reduce the effective protection of the lives of some citizens in serving the personal and private interests of others who would choose euthanasia after being fully informed cannot be justified.

Furthermore, if voluntary active euthanasia is legalized, some persons will be killed on the basis of what will be accepted as their genuine, informed consent. But individuals can easily be pressured into consent. They might be only marginally capable of deliberation and yet fulfill the legal formalities required to authorize their being killed. They might misunderstand a well-intentioned but inadequate attempt of a physician to provide information, and choose euthanasia when they would not do so were more adequate information given.[43]

Once more, it might be argued that pro forma consent to major surgery, to abortion, and to other forms of medical treatment including self-commitment usually is presumed to be adequate. The capacity of the patient to consent, the possible effects of drugs, the motivation by outside pressures, and the possible inadequacy of information given are seldom called into question. And a physician who holds a pro forma consent is seldom if ever prosecuted for acts which would be criminal without informed consent. Why, then, should there be more concern in the case of euthanasia?

The answer is that in this case a defect in consent will lead in every instance to an unjust killing. How are potential victims to be protected against the consequences of their inadequately informed consent? "In the end, the most reliable and the most practical safeguard against abuse of this admittedly liberal consent provision," two authors say about a provision of their proposed euthanasia statute, "is the good judgment and the humanistic motivation of all concerned."[44]

As a group, doctors surely are as prudent and well-motivated as lawyers, merchants, and chiefs of state. But one cannot stake one's life on the good judgment and humanistic motivation of *every* member of any of these respected groups. Perhaps, indeed, too much confidence is reposed at present in the validity of pro forma consent to major surgery, to abortion, and to self-commitment. However, in most cases an inadequate consent can be challenged later on by a surviving patient. No one will survive to challenge the injustice done them by active euthanasia carried out on the strength of an inadequate pro forma consent.

Moreover, while medical judgments as to what is appropriate surgery are likely to cluster in view of recognized therapeutic aims, judgments—no matter how humanistic—as to when someone is going to be better off dead are likely to diverge, precisely because the standard here is an aspect of subjective well-being which falls outside the usual objectives of the medical art. Hence, only the person to be killed would be in a position to criticize the judgment of the physician who decides to proceed on the strength of a pro forma consent with euthanasia.

Normally, other physicians can criticize a medical judgment to proceed with major surgery, quite apart from considerations of the patient's consent. Admittedly, this is not so in the case of elective abortion, but here the only person recognized by the law to have a vital interest, the pregnant woman, usually will survive the operation and can challenge the validity of her own consent. This fact induces some caution in medical abortionists. There would not be the same ground for caution in a practitioner of euthanasia.

Thus far we have been considering cases in which persons would be killed on the basis of a pro forma but invalid consent to active euthanasia. Various sorts of safeguards might be considered to limit these dangers. Requirements for more than one declaration, more than one medical certificate, a waiting period, an interview by a public official, and so on are intended to obviate these dangers. Such safeguards would help. We think that they would have to be extremely stringent, for the failure of the safeguards to do their job would mean in each case that someone would be deprived of life nonwillingly, with color of legality but without due process of law.

Indeed, since the right which will be violated if active euthanasia is carried out when it is not truly voluntary will be the right to life, security in which is at present protected by the criminal law forbidding murder, no set of safeguards which omits a judicial hearing in each and every case of euthanasia would seem nearly adequate. Unless it is publicly established beyond all reasonable doubt that a certain person has given informed consent to being killed, the killing of the person should never be permitted.

Careful legal controls also would be required to ensure that there would be no mistakes about the identity of the individual who is killed. Even with the utmost care mistakes do occur in hospitals; occasionally the negligence is so gross that the courts do not require expert testimony to establish it.[45] For the sake of receiving care, which everyone desires, the public must run this risk. But if euthanasia is legalized, the public at large cannot reasonably be expected to assume any new and avoidable risk. So the carrying out of each and every euthanasia killing would have to have many of the formalities of an execution of capital punishment, and especially very great care about identity to preclude killing someone by a simple mistake about identity.

The euthanasia bill which was debated in the British House of Lords in 1936 included fairly careful safeguards. The individual to be killed had to be suffering from a terminal illness and had to make written application on a specified form; the nearest relative had to be consulted; a special quasi-judicial public official (called a "euthanasia referee") had to conduct an inquiry into each and every case before issuing a permit; the relative could take the case to court before the permit became valid; only the medical practitioner named in the permit could kill the patient, and was required to do so in the presence of an official witness.[46] Despite these safeguards, some participants in the debate pointed out possible defects in consent which would invalidate it.

In 1950 euthanasia again was debated in the House of Lords, although on this occasion no new bill was put forward. The Lord Chancellor, Viscount Jowitt, argued against legalization by urging that one could not say for certain that specified conditions were met. Having discussed competency to consent and other conditions, he concluded:

> None of these things can be asserted, and I ask your Lordships to say that the introduction of a Bill would be wrong, no matter what the safeguards might be, because there can be no adequate safeguards where one human being is allowed to start killing another.
>
> There must be no failure to apprehend the truth. Such a Bill would allow murder in certain circumstances; and the confines within which it is allowed can never be so clearly defined that we may not have people stepping outside them.[47]

Some proponent of euthanasia might object that this argument is question-begging insofar as it characterizes euthanasia as "murder." But such an objection would be to miss the point. The point simply is that what would be legalized *at present* falls into the category of murder. If it is legalized, euthanasia will be permitted by way of exception to the general prohibition of acts of homicide. Thus, any transgressing of the line between legalized euthanasia and the residual category from which it was drawn would be murder.

Proponents of euthanasia seem to pay too little attention to this fact. They argue as if they were still dealing with some other question, such as the sexual relationships of consenting adults in private or abortion. In such cases many proponents of legalization were not greatly worried about the boundaries, for they were prepared to see an entire category of previously criminal behavior made legal. No one can take this attitude with respect to the criminal law of homicide.

Even a proponent of euthanasia must bear in mind that a permit to carry out euthanasia might someday become the death warrant of a person who had not in fact given fully informed consent. That person could even be a proponent of the legalization of euthanasia. Proponents of abortion legalization could not be confused with unborn individuals; laws forbidding abortion could be simply abolished. But laws forbidding homicide cannot be. The safeguards could be extremely stringent, but no safeguards would be perfectly adequate. If euthanasia is legalized, some murder will be done which otherwise would not be done.

One proponent who clearly does not understand this situation is Glanville Williams. Eager for the legalization of euthanasia and frustrated by arguments about safeguards—which were objected to by opponents both as inadequate and as intolerable interference in the sickroom—Williams made a breathtakingly simple proposal. He urged that the law merely be amended to permit physicians a wide discretion. Having asserted erroneously that members of the House of Lords in the 1936 debate approved active euthanasia, Williams claimed his proposal would merely clarify a position which medical practice already approved. He said the proposal would merely acknowledge a practice already widespread and beneficial, remove from physicians a burdensome fear of the law, leave the matter to individual conscience, and introduce no danger whatsoever.[48]

Williams formulated the part of his proposal concerned with voluntary active euthanasia as follows:

> It shall be lawful for a physician, after consultation with another physician, to accelerate by any merciful means the death of a patient who is seriously ill, unless it is proved that the act was not done in good faith with the consent of the patient and for the purpose of saving him from severe pain in an illness believed to be of an incurable and fatal character.[49]

This formulation may not sound dangerous until one recalls that what is being proposed is an amendment to the law forbidding murder. Once this fact is taken into account, the danger is obvious.[50]

Any two physicians dealing with a seriously ill patient could kill the patient. They could be convicted of a crime only if the prosecution could prove *beyond a reasonable doubt* that they did not act *in good faith* or that they did not *intend* to save the patient from pain or that they did not *believe* the illness to be incurable and fatal. However, once a patient was dead, it would hardly be possible to disprove *beyond reasonable doubt* the physicians' good faith or intent or belief or claim that the patient had consented. Anyone who proposed to murder someone would need only to find a cooperative physician with a cooperative colleague in order to execute the murderous plan.

The point is that criminal law does not merely allow what it does not forbid. It also allows what it does forbid—that is, criminal law allows in practice what it literally forbids—to the extent that what it forbids cannot be proved beyond reasonable doubt to be done with criminal intent and in violation of the law.

The bill debated in the British House of Lords in 1969 did not put forward Williams's simple proposal. It included safeguards: a written certificate by two physicians, a written or oral declaration by the patient attested by two witnesses, a thirty-day waiting period, and a general provision authorizing the Secretary of State for Social Services to regulate the practice of euthanasia. The latter regulations would have included some limitation of those who could be killed and of those who would do the killing, the custody of declarations, and so on.[51] As we pointed out in chapter four, section G, the California Natural Death Act of 1976 incorporated many of these regulations and safeguards.

The Earl of Cork and Orrery, who led the opposition, pointed out that due to inevitable vagueness all of the safeguards in the bill really come down to trusting the two physicians. The witnesses might never be traced and in practice coud hardly be held liable, although the bill provided for their liability. As to the possibility of an oral declaration he said: "These words provide a loophole big enough for murder."[52] The point was made with regard to the written declaration by Baroness Serota:

> Even if all the practical difficulties of ensuring that all the safeguards incorporated in the Bill were complied with, it would be by no means certain that even these safeguards would be adequate against abuse. Supposing, for example, euthanasia were administered on the basis of a declaration which was afterwards alleged to be forged, or signed under circumstances which rendered it suspect, the Bill would appear to protect the doctor who in good faith administered euthanasia, but it might in practice also protect those who had been responsible for the false declaration. The vital witness would in many cases be the patient himself, and once he had died it might be virtually impossible to prove whether the declaration had been genuine or not, particularly if the witnesses could not be traced; and even if there were strong grounds for suspecting that the declaration was not genuine, it might be difficult to prove who had been responsible.[53]

Earl Ferrers pointed out that the bill would not prevent unscrupulous people from bringing about the killing of the unwilling but would only make them proceed with care in accomplishing the objective.[54] Lord Strabolgi suggested that the elderly would be especially vulnerable to trickery. He also mentioned that a strong argument against the death penalty is that it can be applied to the wrong person, and the same argument stands against legalizing euthanasia.[55]

Proponents of active voluntary euthanasia simply do not face up to this argument. When they come near it, their responses are not to the point and at times appear evasive and disingenuous.

Arval A. Morris, for example, proposes legalization with a safeguard of repeated witnessed requests and a thirty-day waiting period. Still, he admits, "The possibility of a conspiracy against the patient by the doctor and relatives, or by several doctors, probably cannot be fully guarded against by any voluntary euthanasia statute (or any statute at all)." But he claims that a properly drafted statute can minimize risks. He then proceeds to the irrelevant point that physicians can keep patients alive in order to increase their fees, and that a voluntary euthanasia statute will combat such an abuse and offset present malpractice laws. Before the reader has a chance to wonder whether this implausible statement has any relevance, Morris observes, "Ultimately, the best protection against dishonest, conspiring doctors lies in the ethical integrity of the medical profession."[56] He gives no reason for thinking that the ethical integrity most of us would grant to the profession as a body extends to every individual physician.

Walter Sackett, testifying before a committee of the U. S. Senate, brushed aside the suggestion that legalized euthanasia would mean that many people could get together and do evil things: "If those relatives have evil in their heart and they are going to kill him, they are going to kill him with something. It could be a gun, a knife, medicine. You know that, you are not so naive as to think there is only one way of killing a person."[57] Sackett simply does not seem to realize that euthanasia killing would provide potential murderers with the opportunity and temptation of a new method, which would have the advantage of great similarity to a legal act. The corpses of those who were willing to be killed would be very similar to the corpses of those who were not.

Under present homicide statutes only the possibility of concealing homicide by making it appear suicide has comparable possibilities for abuse. As we argued in chapter five, section C, these possibilities of abuse are surely sufficient to warrant a negative public policy toward suicide; if the law had the means to prevent suicide, the dangerous similarity of suicide to homicide would in itself be sufficient to justify the use of such means.

Kamisar points out that while Williams is most concerned about the liberty of the dying to die painlessly, Kamisar himself is more concerned with the life and liberty of those who would be needlessly killed in the process. He argues that the number wrongly killed would not be small.[58] Bruce Vodiga claims that in making this argument Kamisar "questions whether the premature and unnatural death of but one individual by mistake is worth relieving the pain and suffering of any number of others." Vodiga goes on in a footnote to suggest that here Kamisar "betrays the moral underpinnings of his analysis" to be theological.[59]

Apart from the fact that Vodiga, not Kamisar, set the proportion as one against an indefinite multitude, one must wonder what is theologically colored in this argument. Most people, if asked whether they would mind being killed by mistake if it would relieve the pain and suffering of numerous others, would answer without any theological reflection, in line with simple self-interest. "Indeed, I would mind." And why should anyone accept such a risk? It seems clear enough that to pass a law requiring one innocent person, chosen at random, to die for the benefit of numerous other individuals—especially when the benefit is relief of pain, not protection of life—is unfair.

Marvin Kohl comments on the argument that one ought not to legalize euthanasia because there is evidence that people who ought not to die will die and that this is unfair. Kohl says:

> . . . I would agree that one should ask: is it fair that people who ought not to, will die because of mistakes and abuses? But fairness is a double-edged sword. One must also ask: is it fair that those who ought to die will not be allowed to do so? Better yet: is it fairer to prevent the many who ought to die from doing so in order to protect the few who ought not to? And at what point does one draw the line? Would it be fairer to let one thousand,

ten thousand, or one hundred thousand suffer in order to prevent the unjust death of, let us say, one man?

He suggests that the question is a difficult one and that fairness demands that both sides be weighed.[60]

Kohl's formulation of and answer to the problem is prejudicial in several ways.

First, he talks about people who ought and ought not *to die,* but the problem is about people *being killed.* If the objection and response are formulated uniformly in terms of being killed, Kohl clearly is begging the question by assuming his own judgment as to the morality of killing: Those who wish to die ought to be killed. But in a jurisprudential argument the proponent of euthanasia is no more justified in assuming this morality and attempting to impose it upon the public at large—especially people who do not wish to be killed—than the opponent of euthanasia is justified in assuming a morality of the inherent sanctity of life.

In the second place, Kohl falsely assumes that the refusal to legalize euthanasia prevents people who wish to die from being killed. It does not. They can commit suicide. They can kill themselves by refusing treatment and even by refusing food. And no law prevents a physician from keeping comfortable people who are killing themselves by supplying them with adequate narcotic drugs until death occurs.

In the third place, Kohl provides no evidence for his suggestion that the proportion between those who will be killed against their wills is insignificant. And he takes no account of the universal and inevitable consequences, including anxiety, inflicted upon those who will not be wrongly killed but who will be made to suffer because some other people's wish to be killed is facilitated by the law.

Glanville Williams also ignored Kamisar's point about the danger of euthanasia when the former answered the critique of the latter. Kamisar had pointed out that legalization in accord with the suggestion of Williams would be dangerous and that the safeguards also would make euthanasia anything but quick and easy.

Williams answers by saying that the problem posed by the alternative of intolerable formalities and a dangerous lack of formalities is not an "ordinary logical dilemma." Williams proposes a parable to clarify what he takes to be the fallacy in Kamisar's argument. The parable concerns a mythical state of Ruritania from which citizens are not permitted to emigrate. A proposal is made to permit emigration, but its proponent is aware "of the power of traditional opinion, and so seeks to word his proposal in a modest way," including many safeguards. An opponent attacks the safeguards as an intolerable imposition upon a free Ruritanian citizen who wishes to emigrate. Williams states that this attack is only legitimate if the opponent of the safe-guards is willing to go further than the original proponent of legalization in permitting emigration.[61]

Williams ignores the fact that the safeguards are to protect those who do not wish to emigrate from being permanently exiled against their will. He also begs the question by using emigration as an analogy, since no one doubts that this practice ought to be legal and that where it is not, liberty is seriously infringed upon. Williams also smuggles in his own moral position, which is not that of most opponents of euthanasia, that mercy killing can be a good thing. Like other proponents, Williams is intensely sensitive to any attempt to impose a traditional morality of the sanctity of life upon those who reject it, but he is very ready to impose the morality of utilitarian killing upon those who reject it.

The foregoing considerations make clear that the legalization of euthanasia, no matter what the safeguards, would impose serious burdens and costs upon those who do not approve of euthanasia and those who do not wish to be killed. In our view such burdens and costs would make legalization unjust to all who do not wish to be killed. However, it must be admitted that with very strict legislation and careful legal control much of the risk could be removed. At the very least proponents of euthanasia ought to grant as a fair demand the requirement that the strictest controls would have to be imposed to prevent serious and unnecessary risks and widespread anxiety.

As a matter of fact, many proposals for euthanasia have included the re-quirement of a court hearing in each case, or at least the requirement of the direct involvement of a quasi-judicial official, as the euthanasia referee of the British bill of 1936. Except for Glanville Williams, leading proponents of legalization have seemed to recognize the need for judicial control.[62]

Probably the most adequate control would require that a person to be killed by voluntary active euthanasia be certified by a court, transported under police supervision to a special facility—perhaps a hospital attached to a prison—and there put to death by a public official especially authorized for the task. A procedure like this would allow the court to ascertain beyond reasonable doubt that valid consent had been given, allow the police to make certain that only persons licensed by the court to be killed were delivered to the executioner of euthanasia, and would restrict the practice of mercy killing to a small group of specialists who could do such killings only during their working hours. Safeguards like these would not be omitted in the legalized killing involved in capital punishment; we see no excuse for the nonchalant attitude of proponents of euthanasia reflected in their failure to propose safe-guards of this sort for legalized mercy killing, which would be far more extensive and dangerous to innocent and unwilling persons than capital pun-ishment is.

F. Legalization of Euthanasia and Liberty

But making euthanasia killing into a public process—whether by the more modest involvement of officials and courts usually projected by proponents of euthanasia or by the more extensive and justly required involvement of public institutions we have just now outlined—raises a new difficulty. Many people in this society still consider euthanasia killing a grave moral evil: They want no part of it. A system which would make such killing a public function not only would demand that such persons tolerate the exercise by others of liberty in a manner morally abhorrent to themselves but also would demand that the public at large become involved in such killing.

Even if the law were carefully constructed to assure that no individual and no private institution opposed to euthanasia were ever forced to participate directly in such killing, that no public funds were expended in support of the activity—for example, by requiring that the petitioner pay the cost of the hearing and of the other services—making euthanasia a public function would still force every member of society to cooperate in the minimal sense that public institutions and facilities would be used for a purpose to which many people take grave objection—an objection which must be respected as legitimate even if it is regarded as erroneous.

Such persons will regard the public institutionalization of mercy killing as a corruption of the political society, which is grounded upon and justified by their willingness to consent and participate. Governmental involvement will infringe upon the liberty of those who wish no part in killing to remain entirely clear of it. They never meant to enter into a compact for mercy killing. Now they shall find their institutions and facilities turned to this purpose. When suicide is made legal, the liberty of such persons to stand aloof is not infringed, for suicide remains a private act. But if euthanasia becomes a public function, the liberty of persons who abhor it to stand aloof from such killing will be infringed.

We expect that this argument will be objected to on the ground that very often society compels its members to participate, at least to the same extent, in activities which many find abhorrent. We now turn to objections along these lines.

Consider war. Even with a broad conscientious objection clause many citizens who consider all war or a particular war immoral are forced to cooperate insofar as war is a public activity, is carried on with tax funds, and so on. Those who have been in the position of dissent from the Vietnam war know how outrageous involvement by the United States in it seemed to them. It would still have seemed so even if all who objected to the war had been exempted from the draft and even from paying taxes to carry on the war, for the national involvement would have meant that those who considered the war a moral outrage and corruption still would have been involved because their country was involved.

Those who consider mercy killing morally repugnant would feel the same way about it, but if the government can be involved in Vietnam against the conscientious objections of many citizens, why can it not be involved in mercy killing despite the conscientious objections of many? A proponent of euthanasia very likely would add that mercy killing would be more like World War II than like Vietnam—a public activity without so many objectionable aspects and one in which most of the society could concur.

In reply to this objection we point out that war under any conditions is different from publicly institutionalized euthanasia in one vital respect: War is directed toward the promotion of a substantial public interest. Even if one holds that the means—war in general or particular wars—is thoroughly evil, one is committed to the common purpose of national security and one must admit that those who authorize, support, and conduct the war do so in the name of this common purpose. The most extreme pacifist also wishes the society to be peaceful and secure, understands that war is directed to these goods, and objects to violence only insofar as it seems to be a vicious means to a good public purpose.

If society were not able to involve its pacifist members at least minimally in its common action of self-defense in cases such as this, most people believe there could be no society. The liberty of the pacifist to stand aloof from violence must be limited by the general public consensus that there is a substantial public good, that some means must be used to promote and defend it, and that this means is essential (even despite public recognition that use of violence is damaging to the community to the extent that it is divisive because some so strongly and sincerely oppose it).

The standard of a substantial public good, an apparently necessary means, and general consensus about its acceptability should be used in passing laws and in testing their constitutionality to the extent that they impinge upon equal and ordered liberty. Mercy killing serves a private interest in avoiding pain and suffering. There are other means suited to this goal: the refusal of care and suicide. And there is no general consensus that this means is acceptable.

Consider capital punishment. How does it meet the stated criteria? Many object to it and yet are forced to participate in such killing. Our reply is that capital punishment might not meet the stated criteria.

It could be justified only if the public good at stake were substantial. The arguments against retributive punishment by death precisely seek to show that the substantial public good of justice is not directly at stake. If the good at stake is the public safety and prevention of crime, the arguments regarding the failure of capital punishment as a deterrent tend to show that it is not a necessary or even an effective means to this admittedly legitimate goal. And there is no real consensus that killing criminals is an acceptable means of enforcing law. For these reasons it seems to us quite plausible to argue that the continuation of capital punishment violates the liberty of all who regard it as morally repugnant to stand aloof from this sort of killing.

Someone will object that health care certainly has been accepted as part of the general welfare. May not the help which some desire to die with dignity be considered a legitimate part of health care? Not on the definition of "health care" which is commonly admitted by existing consensus. Euthanasia would stipulate a new definition of "health care" and thus alter a common purpose over the objections of opponents. In other words, proponents of euthanasia cannot claim it as part of health care without trying unilaterally to amend a public purpose. This is precisely the point at which the violation of the liberty of opponents to stand aloof occurs.

If euthanasia were to be justified by being incorporated in some substantial public interest, it would have to be shown that liberty to obtain help in being killed is directly and of itself involved in the common good. Then concerns about the protection of unwilling victims and liberty to stand aloof would be of marginal importance. But if the sanctity of life cannot be defended by its proponents as a direct component of the common good, neither can being killed painlessly be defended by its proponents as having such a status. Of course, we do not deny that the mitigation of the pain and suffering of individuals is a good and a very significant one; we merely deny that it is directly and in itself a matter of public interest. It is a private interest, however important.

What proponents of euthanasia need to show is that their liberty either overrides the right of opponents not to be killed unwillingly or the liberty of opponents not to be involved in a practice from which they wish to stand aloof. In other words, those who favor legalizing euthanasia must show that the demand of opponents to have their lives and liberty to stand aloof respected somehow amounts to an unjust exploitation of those who wish to be killed for their personal and private interest in avoiding pain and suffering. When Kohl suggests that fairness requires that the interests of both proponents and opponents of euthanasia be weighed against each other, he ignores the fact that safe euthanasia would require public authority, and that on libertarian principles the scale is tilted against those who desire public involvement in a practice for private benefit on whose acceptability there is no consensus.

Another objection is that government often is used to promote interests which are essentially private—for example, it provides education which primarily benefits the individual. The reply is that promoting such private interests is acceptable to the extent that there is a general consensus that it is a necessary means to a common good, in this case the general welfare. The general welfare is a whole set of conditions which most everyone needs to pursue their private interests in their own ways.

While extreme libertarians wholly oppose the welfare function of the state, state involvement in a practice such as euthanasia is repugnant in a way in which welfare state functions in general are not, for a practice such as euthanasia is abhorrent to the consciences of many citizens who regard it as evil and corrupting. As we have explained, were the state to participate in legalized euthanasia, such citizens would become unwilling participants in acts they reasonably, even if erroneously, consider to be murder, and their liberty to stand aloof would be seriously infringed.

Still, it will be objected, the public system of education is not really so different from the publicly institutionalized arrangement for safe mercy killing. Many people do have conscientious objections to what the school system is doing—for example, in promoting what they consider to be a secularist value system and in teaching children a morality which is in conflict with that of their parents. Others contend that the present public system of education chills their exercise of religious liberty, for it maintains a monopoly upon public funding of lower education while it offers an educational experience which is shaped by the deeply held conscientious convictions or beliefs of one part of the population and which is incompatible with the convictions and religious beliefs of other segments.[63]

The answer to this objection is that even if some people think that what the public schools are doing is immoral and would like to be at liberty to stand aloof, it is difficult to see how the general welfare could be promoted without some public system of education. If some public education is provided, then equal protection of the laws demands that a rather extensive system be provided to avoid discrimination against those who cannot privately arrange educational facilities.

It might be true that in many places the present system of public education favors secular humanism just as public education in the past favored common Protestant Christianity. But no school system can carry out an educational process without in practice adopting some philosophy of life, some religious or nonreligious world view as the foundation and framework for intellectual formation and for the social interaction in the school which shapes character. Perhaps the present arrangement does chill the exercise of religious liberty, but this could be remedied without doing away with publicly funded education. We shall discuss this issue further in chapter ten, section D.

Another objection is that government is deeply involved in the distribution and sale of alcoholic beverages, which many consider to have no moral use. It is obvious that the use of such beverages serves no substantial public interest and is, if anything, contrary to the public health and safety. Our reply is that in this case government is only trying to control and restrict the abuse of the private activity of drinking.

But cannot the same view be taken of necessary government involvement in euthanasia? No, because in the case of alcoholic beverages there was a law against the manufacture, sale, and use of them (Prohibition), and it was agreed to repeal this general law, not only out of respect for liberty but also to avoid evils consequent upon the law itself. Proponents of the legalization of abortion succeeded partly by arguing on the analogy of the repeal of prohibition. But in the case of euthanasia the general law against homicide cannot be repealed.

Government involvement in the distribution and sale of alcoholic beverages followed repeal in an attempt to provide some continuing protection for the public interest which had justified Prohibition: Everyone realizes that society would be far better off if most *other* people did not drink at all or drank less than they do. Government involvement in euthanasia would be necessary only because of an amendment to the law of homicide. But the public interest does not require that this be done. Moreover, state involvement in the liquor business serves a substantial public interest in regulation, an interest best recognized by those who prefer Prohibition. Regulation of euthanasia will not be required to protect the public interest unless euthanasia is legalized, and whether it should be legalized is precisely the question at issue.

No doubt, if euthanasia is legalized, then many of those upon whose liberty state involvement will infringe will prefer to accept this infringement upon their liberty to stand aloof than to suffer the injustice of running the risk of being murdered. But the willingness of opponents of euthanasia to accept a lesser evil rather than a greater if this practice is legalized does not mean that legalization would not do them evil, and so does not undermine the argument that legalization without government involvement in the practice of euthanasia would be unjust to those who would be killed unwillingly and that legalization with government involvement would infringe upon the liberty of those who find mercy killing morally abhorrent to stand aloof from a practice they regard as evil and corrupting.

Just as Kohl argued that fairness to those who ought not to die (that is, to be murdered) must be weighed against fairness to those who ought to die (that is, who demand help in being killed), so proponents of euthanasia will argue that the liberty of opponents of euthanasia to stand aloof from such killing must be weighed against the liberty of those who desire euthanasia to be killed and to assist in such killing. But there is no agreed upon principle by which these two liberties can be weighed against one another; the weighing will be wholly arbitrary. Hence, the preference for the liberty of those who approve euthanasia which would be embodied in legalization would infringe upon the basic principle that society is limited by an affirmative common consensus. Mercy killing is no part of this common consensus.

For the sake of liberty euthanasia by refusal of treatment and by suicide must be tolerated. Such acts do not pose any substantial threat to the public which could be avoided if these practices were not allowed, and so these practices do not demand public involvement in acts widely regarded as immoral. The liberty to remain aloof is an aspect of that liberty to which free societies are dedicated. The liberty to be killed cannot be protected, so far as active euthanasia is concerned, without being drawn from the private into the public sphere. There is no consensus that it ought to be.

Consequently proponents of euthanasia face a dilemma. Either they must advocate the legalization of euthanasia without state action in the killing, but this would unjustly endanger the lives of those who do not wish to be killed; or they must advocate legalization with public institutionalization at a level which would mitigate dangers as much as possible, but this would infringe upon the liberty to stand aloof from such killing of those who abhor it; or they must advocate legalization with some degree of state action short of the institutionalization which would mitigate dangers as much as possible, but any such compromise would to some degree and in some proportion both unjustly endanger the lives of those who do not wish to be killed and infringe upon the liberty to stand aloof from such killing of those who abhor it.

In any case, the fact that the interest of those who wish to be killed is a private one cannot be ignored. As we showed in section D, even the most careful safeguards could not altogether eliminate the imposition of new burdens and costs upon those who do not wish to be killed, and these weigh against, whether or not they outweigh, the suffering which active euthanasia could prevent. The one private interest deserves as much consideration as the other.

G. How our Argument Differs from Yale Kamisar's

The argument we have presented against euthanasia legalization in many ways is like that proposed by Kamisar but is different in one respect. Kamisar also confronted Williams and other proponents of euthanasia with a dilemma, the first leg of which emphasized the danger to those who would be unwillingly killed. But the second leg of Kamisar's dilemma was merely the consideration that safeguards are cumbersome and obnoxious.[64] The weakness of this consideration makes Kamisar's argument rest almost wholly upon the inevitably or probably harmful results of legalization no matter how carefully safeguarded.

As we have shown—and as anyone who reads Kamisar's article carefully will see in much richer detail—a case strictly upon this basis is by no means weak. But our argument emphasizes the dilemma by pointing up something objectionable about safeguards which has more jurisprudential weight than their mere burdensomeness: They also infringe upon the liberty to stand aloof. Opponents of euthanasia up to now have not focused attention upon this aspect of the matter. We believe that it deserves attention.

Proponents of legalization naturally have been sensitive to their own interest in the libertarian aspect of the issue. They do not wish to be forbidden to kill and be killed as they think fit. Often they argue for euthanasia as if they were arguing once more about the liberty of consenting adults to engage privately in sexual activity of their preference. We have tried to bring out the disanalogy between the legalization of such practices and the legalization of euthanasia.

Society can officially ignore what Doe and Roe do sexually with each other in private provided that they are both adults, that they really do consent, and that they do not cause each other lasting bodily harm. However, if Roe and Doe engage in sadistic practices upon Oe, even with her consent, such that her life is endangered or her body seriously injured, then the situation is more like voluntary euthanasia. If the state, to protect persons who are not masochists, must regulate and institutionalize the consensual practices of Roe, Doe, and Oe—for example, by issuing licenses to certain public houses in which these practices will be permitted and by providing a legal process to certify the consent of Oe—then a jurisprudential problem arises which is even more like that involved in legally regulated and publicly institutionalized voluntary active euthanasia.

Does the public have a liberty to remain aloof from sadomasochism? We submit that the public does have such a liberty, and that such practices could not be safely legalized without public involvement by way of regulation and institutionalization, which would violate the liberty to stand aloof. Our new contribution to the argument against legalization of euthanasia has been that the public has a liberty to stand aloof from the killing of human beings. This consideration, together with the already well-argued point that even voluntary euthanasia cannot be legalized without undue danger or extensive public involvement, poses a very serious dilemma for proponents of legalization.

Proponents of legalization stress libertarian considerations in favor of their view. They ought also to attend to the libertarian aspect of the opposing position. How can a policy be regarded as liberal if it facilitates the liberty of some citizens to kill and be killed by involving in activities repugnant to many citizens the legal processes and institutions in which all participate willy-nilly? Genuine liberals must be careful lest they press for a society in which only secular humanists can live and die comfortably. Such a "liberal" society would be one from which those who abhor killing, even in the context of voluntary euthanasia, would be profoundly alienated.

The moral justification of euthanasia, as we have pointed out, is part of one competing world view among others; some people believe in this world view and are committed to putting it into practice, so far as possible, in their own lives. Society must respect this world view as a secular religious belief. But proponents of this world view will cease to be liberals and will become totalitarians if they continue to urge its acceptance as a secular, established religion. Society can no more justly become involved in the rites of mercy killing (or sadomasochism) than it can become involved in the rites of religious worship (or snake handling). Although those who accept these rites do so for diverse reasons, those who reject them agree in considering any governmental involvement in practices they abhor to be a serious infringement upon liberty.

So long as mercy killing is limited to suicide and the refusal of treatment and so long as sadomasochism is limited to activities which do not cause serious bodily harm, society can tolerate these exercises of liberty. But when the safety of others begins to be endangered by mercy killing which involves the activity of a person other than the one killed, or by sadomasochistic activity which might result in the injury or even death of nonconsenting persons, then society can limit these dangers in the interest of the public safety, just as it forbids snake handling and enjoins blood transfusions for the children of Jehovah's Witnesses over the objections of their parents. Society has no obligation to legalize snake handling and to make it into a publicly regulated and institutionalized activity in order to protect those not willingly involved in it. No more has society an obligation to legalize euthanasia and make it into a publicly regulated and institutionalized activity.

Nor will it do to say that the liberty of those who abhor mercy killing to stand aloof would only be slightly infringed by governmental involvement in this practice. Reading a few verses of the Bible each day in the public schools is only a little establishment of religion. But that little is too much for those who take conscientious objection to it.

In his article Kamisar proceeded from the short-range view of voluntary euthanasia to a long-range view of the dangers that legalized active euthanasia would not remain entirely voluntary. This part of his argument contains two sections: first, a consideration of the likelihood of the spread of euthanasia to at least some cases in which it would be nonvoluntary; second, an argument based upon the prospect that legalized euthanasia could end in genocide, as it did in Nazi Germany.[65] The second of these points, the Nazi experience, we will consider in chapter eight, section H. But here we shall assume what we will try to prove in chapters seven and eight: Nonvoluntary and involuntary euthanasia ought not to be legalized. If this is correct, any evidence or reasons which would show that voluntary euthanasia cannot be legalized without legalizing nonvoluntary euthanasia as well will confirm in a very important way the conclusion we think we have established already without reference to this longer-range view. Hence, we turn now to it.

H. From Voluntary to Nonvoluntary Euthanasia

Kamisar pointed out that proponents of euthanasia themselves, while urging the legalization of voluntary euthanasia, do not carefully and consistently restrict their consideration to euthanasia of the voluntary sort. From its beginnings many involved in the movement to legalize euthanasia have favored the legalization of nonvoluntary as well as voluntary euthanasia, sometimes even favored the legalization of nonvoluntary euthanasia over the legalization of voluntary euthanasia. But the leadership of the movement restricted proposed bills, for the most part, to strictly voluntary euthanasia and explicitly said that proposals had to be limited because the public was not ready to accept the broader principle. So one must begin by opening the door, one must proceed step by step, and so on.[66] This policy of incrementalism is still being followed.[67]

Kamisar also pointed out that most of the killings commonly called "mercy killings" and frequently discussed by proponents of voluntary euthanasia have been instances or potential instances of nonvoluntary euthanasia—cases in which infants or other noncompetent persons have been killed, even cases in which competent adults have been killed without consulting them.[68] Kamisar's article was published in 1958; a survey of more recent literature produced by proponents of voluntary euthanasia reveals that they still rely heavily upon examples of the nonvoluntary sort.[69]

The use of such examples is significant; it manifests the real interests and concerns of proponents of legalization. If in their own minds they made a sharp and critical distinction between voluntary and nonvoluntary euthanasia and if they were committed as a matter of principle to the legalization of the former and against the legalization of the latter, then either they would never mention examples of nonvoluntary euthanasia at all or they would mention these examples only to distinguish such killing from the killing whose legalization they propose. The use of irrelevant examples would only be confusing and would be carefully avoided.

But as a matter of fact proponents of the legalization of voluntary euthanasia use, not merely mention, examples of nonvoluntary euthanasia. Part of the logical and rhetorical weight—in some cases a very substantial part of it—is placed on these examples. If they prove anything at all, they prove that the practice they exemplify ought to be accepted. And whether they prove anything or not, they unquestionably reveal the belief of those who use such examples: nonvoluntary euthanasia ought to be legalized and a limitation of present proposals to voluntary euthanasia is merely a tactical maneuver in the long-range strategy of legalizing the killing of all who "ought to die."

Kamisar pointed out that proponents of euthanasia often favored the killing of defective children.[70] Leading proponents of legalization—such as Joseph

Fletcher, Glanville Williams, Marvin Kohl, and Walter Sackett—continue to include infanticide in their euthanasia projects, and the same is true of many less well-known authors writing on the subject.[71]

Proponents of the legalization of euthanasia will object that to insist upon the longer-range view beyond the legalization of voluntary euthanasia to the future legalization of nonvoluntary euthanasia is to commit the fallacy of a wedge ("slippery slope" or "camel's nose under the tent flap") argument.

When Williams originally criticized a so-called wedge argument, it was an instance of utilitarian argument to the effect that even if voluntary euthanasia were perfectly acceptable in particular instances, it would be bad to allow it as a general practice. Williams disposed of this objection easily by pointing out that the practice to be generalized was intended to be a particular one which would be justified in each relevant case.[72]

Kamisar does not argue in this fashion. Rather, his point is that the proponents of euthanasia are engaged in a movement, that there is a likely second step consequent upon the projected first step, and that this second step can be prevented only if the first is carefully avoided. One of the most telling points Kamisar makes in defense of his form of the argument is that defenders of civil liberties constantly use it, on the principle that civil liberties can very easily be seriously eroded unless great care is taken to prevent the first step infringing upon them.[73]

Williams also recognizes a psychological version of a wedge argument, according to which the danger in permitting some killing is that it would habituate people to doing and to accepting killing in general. Although this premiss is no part of Kamisar's argument, Williams seems to suppose that it is and easily produces examples which indicate that not every practice tends to become more and more generalized once it is permitted.[74]

Kohl also considers the wedge argument. According to Kohl what underlies it is the belief on the part of the opponents of euthanasia that proponents are concerned with economic utilitarian advantages alone and that all utilitarian theories are the same as those of the Nazis.[75] Arthur Dyck answers Kohl by pointing out that what worries opponents and gives rise to wedge arguments is not the concern which Kohl mentions, but rather the appeal of proponents to some notion of dignity to justify killing. Since there is no agreement upon what constitutes dignity, no one can tell in advance just what is justified when a right to die by mercy killing is justified on this principle.[76]

We believe that Dyck's rejoinder to Kohl is essentially correct. However, not all proponents of the legalization of euthanasia appeal to "dignity." But even when they do not, they appeal to some principle which would justify nonvoluntary euthanasia at least in some cases if it could justify voluntary euthanasia in any cases at all. Sometimes the principle is formulated in terms of quality of life or meaningful life. Sometimes it is formulated in terms of the naturalness and goodness of death and its utility for the species. Sometimes it is formulated negatively and brutally by talking about certain noncompetent persons as vegetables or cabbages and talking about the institutions in which they live as warehouses or mausolea.[77]

Moreover, the kind of argument proposed by Dyck is not correctly classified as a wedge (or slippery slope) argument. Rather, Dyck is noting that the movement from voluntary to nonvoluntary euthanasia is required by a consistent application of a principle which those who advocate the legalization of voluntary euthanasia appeal to in support of their view. The logical implications of one's principles are not like the probable psychological or sociological consequences of adopting certain policies or engaging in certain practices. Reasonable persons are necessarily committed to all the logical implications of the principles they accept. But a reasonable person can adopt policies or engage in practices while hoping that possible consequences—even consequences which are highly probably—will never come about.

Thus, if one holds that certain sorts of people would be better off dead and would be kindly treated by being killed, it matters little whether these people are competent to consent or not. Their competency to consent would be an important matter only if their informed judgment that they would be better off dead were a condition required for it to be true that they would be better off dead and so a condition that justified killing them. In any other case any characteristic of a person by which that person would be better off dead could be an attribute which might belong to noncompetent as well as to competent persons.

Clearly, proponents of the legalization of voluntary active euthanasia have not restricted themselves to premises drawn from libertarian considerations—as we, for example, restricted ourselves in chapter four, where we defended the liberty of competent persons to refuse treatment, without introducing any consideration based upon our own views about what would be beneficial to such persons. Rather, proponents of the legalization of euthanasia regularly use premises which reflect their conviction that under some conditions people are better off dead, that their lives are too poor in quality to be endured, that their lives lack meaning, that their survival offends human dignity, that they deserve the compassion shown a sick beast, that they are mere vegetables, and so on and on. Thus advocates of the legalization of voluntary active euthanasia do not use examples of nonvoluntary mercy killing by an absentminded slip on the psychological or sociological slope of their humane project. The premises used by proponents of voluntary euthanasia logically entail nonvoluntary euthanasia. To stop short of killing all those whom they sincerely believe would be better off dead would be a completely irrational and arbitrary limitation upon the unfolding—according to its own inner dynamics—of their well-intentioned project of beneficent killing.

To say that proponents of the legalization of euthanasia will not be satisfied with voluntary euthanasia is to make, not a prediction, but merely an observation. This is the importance of what we noted above: Williams, Kohl, Fletcher, and others can denounce wedge arguments all they like, but they continue to argue in accord with their principles for nonvoluntary euthanasia, especially in the case of defective children. The traditional position grounded an unalienable right to life in a conception of the sanctity of life; advocates of euthanasia reject this position in its entirety. But for strategic reasons they seek the concession of the sanctity of life first in the approval of voluntary euthanasia; the right to life of those who are unable to assert this right is reserved for a later agenda.

Williams can assure us that he is not prepared to approve the killing of the elderly at the present time; Kohl can assure us that he only approves killing he regards as kindly; Fletcher can assure us that all who meet his indicators of humanhood will continue to be protected so far as he is concerned. But all of them are drawing jurisprudential conclusions from their own moral principles and failing to pay attention to the jurisprudential implications of the method by which they proceed. Every member of society has his or her own moral principles which must be given as much respect as those of Williams, Kohl, and Fletcher. Hence, it if is once conceded that some people ought to die because others think they would be better off dead, then in practice it is conceded that the law must sanction the killing of anyone whom the majority of citizens sincerely believe would be better off dead.

Special moral conceptions of individual welfare could be excluded altogether; an advocate of the legalization of euthanasia could argue on strictly libertarian grounds that individuals who wish to be killed should be allowed to have the help of other individuals who wish to help them.[78] An approach of this kind would exclude the killing of noncompetents and would emphasize the purely individualistic aspects of dignity—namely, the value inherent in persons asserting themselves in the face of death rather than awaiting it patiently.[79] This kind of approach would remedy to some extent the implausibility of efforts of proponents of euthanasia to limit the practice to those who are dying of a physical illness; if liberty is the ground justifying the legalization of killing with consent, then there is really no reason to restrict such killing.[80] It would, in fact, be discriminatory to permit death with dignity for those suffering and dying, yet not permit it for persons who are simply fed up with life, for those who wish to commit hara-kiri, for those whose concept of honor requires that they engage in duels, for those who would like to play games of hunting human quarry (by mutual consent), and so on.

The obvious difficulty with a purely libertarian approach is that certainly the legalization of killing with consent on this basis could not possibly be hedged with safeguards which would protect persons who do not consent. All of the dangers in legalized euthanasia return in an even stronger form.

Their writings indicate clearly enough, in any case, that proponents of legalization of euthanasia do not take a strictly libertarian approach. For example, frequently in the literature favoring the legalization of euthanasia one encounters the argument that society should have as much compassion for its members as people are held to have for animals. All approve and indeed desire that an animal which is in misery should be killed mercifully. Must not as much kindness be shown people as horses?[81] Of course, the killing of animals is nonvoluntary euthanasia. Moreover, they are not always killed for their own interest; they are also killed for the interest of humans who own them. Thus, anyone who argues for the legalization of voluntary active euthanasia by appealing to the model of veterinary euthanasia reveals a commitment to principles which extend beyond voluntary to nonvoluntary euthanasia.

There is still another reason why the legalization of active voluntary euthanasia is certain to lead to the legalization of euthanasia for noncompetent persons. In law, parents or guardians of minors or other noncompetent persons can give substitute consent for the handling of the property and affairs of such persons. The consent is considered valid only if the action authorized is in the best interests of the person on whose behalf it is given. In recent years this doctrine has been extended to allow organ transplants from noncompetent persons to their relatives on the theory that such transplants in some way would be in the interests of the noncompetent individuals themselves.[82]

In the Quinlan case the Supreme Court of New Jersey used the doctrine of substitute consent in deciding that Miss Quinlan's right of privacy could be exercised on her behalf and that such exercise by another was necessary lest the right be destroyed.[83] In 1977 the Supreme Court of Massachusetts applied the doctrine of substituted judgment in justifying the refusal by a court-appointed guardian of treatment for acute leukemia to Mr. Joseph Saikewicz, a mentally retarded resident of a public institution. In reaching its decision the Massachusetts Court held that precisely in order to protect the human dignity of noncompetent persons, the law must recognize and protect in them all the rights and choices it protects in competent persons; the law must not proceed on the absolute assumption that the best interests of a noncompetent person will be protected by ordering that treatment be carried out.[84]

We shall discuss these decisions in chapter nine, section L. We mention them here neither to criticize them nor to suggest that either decision in any way justifies active euthanasia of the noncompetent. They clearly do not. But the principle of substituted judgment asserted and applied in these decisions could not be denied or withheld from application without serious inconsistency in any closely analogous case.

If voluntary active euthanasia is legalized, one can be sure that many courts—perhaps including the United States Supreme Court—will assert and apply the doctrine of substituted judgment to extend the law to cover non-competent persons. The decisions would hold that equal protection of the laws requires that the right to the supremely kind treatment of being killed when one would be better off dead must be accorded the noncompetent as well as those who can give personal consent. To deny the right of the non-competent to die, the courts would argue, would be to disregard their equal personal dignity. The case would be most plausible with respect to infants who are born defective and who would have been aborted had their defects been anticipated. If they are not beneficently killed, it would be argued, such infants will have to be allowed to die more slowly and more painfully by deliberate neglect.[85]

Between such infants and many other children, between them and adults who have never been competent, and between them and the permanently insane or senile there are no clear boundaries at which to limit the continuous extension of the right to die. Thus no statutes will be needed to legalize nonvoluntary euthanasia; the courts will enter where legislatures might fear to go.

Yet, if legislatures do not take the first step by legalizing voluntary active euthanasia, courts are not very likely to take this step. To do so, the courts would have to assume the legislative function and could not help being obvious about doing so. The United States Supreme Court could strike down all laws against abortion, but no court can strike down all laws forbidding homicide. Voluntary active euthanasia cannot be legalized except by writing an exception to existing statutes forbidding homicide. The defining of such an exception depends upon many policy considerations and the expression of the exception would require a statute. Hence, the battle over the legalization of voluntary active euthanasia will be fought in the political arena, and the effect of the work of proponents and opponents of euthanasia upon legislatures not only will settle the issue of voluntary euthanasia but also will determine the legal life-or-death decision with respect to many noncompetent persons.

I. From Individual Liberty to Public Policy

Those who argue for the legalization of voluntary active euthanasia at times appeal to the liberty of individuals, although they do not restrict themselves to this appeal. We have been arguing that premises which assert that some persons would be better off dead entail the movement from voluntary to nonvoluntary euthanasia. Utilitarian calculations concerning public welfare are likely to lead from voluntary euthanasia to government programs to solve the problem of dependency by killing at least some of the dependent: primarily those residing permanently in public institutions and wholly dependent upon public funds for survival.

Some proponents of the legalization of euthanasia say they wish to exclude crass economic considerations from their weighing of the costs and benefits of beneficent killing.[86] We do not question their sincerity. But in American society during the past twenty years developments initiated on the basis of individual liberty and personal privacy have grown into public programs on the basis of utilitarian calculations concerning the costs and benefits of various forms of public welfare expenditure.

The argument for liberty in the field of contraception prevailed (in our view, correctly as a jurisprudential matter). By 1976 the federal government was attempting to find ways of promoting contraception more effectively among teenagers, and the public interest in doing so was spelled out in terms of cutting social costs and welfare dependency. Any requirement for parental consent was a mere obstacle to be removed.[87]

The argument for abortion legalization prevailed (in our view, incorrectly as a jurisprudential matter). The decision made only a passing mention of the social concerns about population growth, pollution, and poverty.[88] However, the liberty to abort became at once a right to abortion, which many courts ruled had to be provided in public and even private hospitals and paid for with public funds.[89] (In this process little respect was shown for the liberty to stand aloof; one federal court struck down the entire conscience clause in a state abortion statute, even that part pertaining to individuals.[90]) The U. S. Supreme Court held unconstitutional the efforts of states to allow parents to veto the abortion decisions of children.[91]

In 1977 the Court relented slightly by holding that the states are not constitutionally *compelled* to provide abortions.[92] Still, Medicaid funding of abortion continues in many places. Nationally and internationally Planned Parenthood and other private organizations heavily supported by public funding divert a substantial part of their resources to abortion.[93]

The underlying public interest is seldom stated explicitly. Yet it has been operative. For example, Harriet F. Pilpel, testifying in 1966 on behalf of the New York Civil Liberties Union before a New York State Assembly committee considering the partial legalization of abortion, gave first place in her attack to the tremendous social cost of illegitimacy. While admitting that it would be simplistic and callous to view the problem merely in monetary terms, she first presented the claim that the nationwide cost of supporting the "unwanted children" born during a single year could run to a public expense of 17.5 billion dollars over a seventeen-year period. She also argued that women have a right to abortion and that the fetus' competing interest in life might be regarded as "highly insignificant."[94]

Similar factors are operative and powerful in the matter of the legalization of euthanasia. In a law journal article Richard Delgado points to the economic aspects of the utilitarian view of the public interest involved in abortion and urges that the same interest is involved in euthanasia[95] In testimony before a committee of the U.S. Senate, Walter Sackett urges that if the severely retarded who are not trainable were "allowed to die," the State of Florida could save 5 billion dollars over a period of fifty years, and a nationwide saving of 100 billion dollars over the same period could be attained.[96]

Robert A. Derzon, Administrator of Health Care Financing in the U. S. Department of Health, Education and Welfare, points out in a memorandum to the Secretary on "Additional Cost-Saving Initiatives—ACTION":

> The cost-savings from a nationwide push toward "Living Wills" is likely to be enormous. Over one-fifth of Medicare expenditures are for persons in their last year of life. Thus, in FY 1978, $4.9 billion will be spent for such persons and if just one-quarter of these expenditures were avoided through adoption of "Living Wills," the savings under Medicare alone would amount to $1.2 billion. Additional savings would accrue to Medicaid and the VA and Defense Department health programs.[97]

Derzon, of course, is not talking about active nonvoluntary euthanasia. If he were, he would be able to project far more substantial savings and to do so with far greater plausibility.

J. Alternatives to Legalizing Voluntary Euthanasia

Some have suggested that short of legalization of euthanasia, the motive of the person committing homicide could be taken into account to reduce the charge or to mitigate punishment.[98] This approach might have the value of reducing the discrepancy between the law on the books and the law in practice. However, we doubt that it would be good policy to make any such change with respect to nonvoluntary mercy killing. If a provision for such killing were made, this might well become a stepping stone toward legalization. Moreover, it is not clear that justice would be served by encouraging people to apply their personal judgments that someone else would be better off dead to the extent of killing the other person without consent.

Nevertheless, we think it would be quite reasonable to make informed consent be a factor which could be established by the defense, and if it were established, a principle for the reduction of the finding of guilt from that of murder to manslaughter. This approach is in line with that which we suggested for assisted suicide. In either case the genuine willingness of the person killed would mitigate substantially the evil of killing by removing its injustice. The act would remain criminal solely for the protection of the public, which benefits from the reduction to the greatest extent possible of any act which is likely to be difficult to discriminate from murder.

Opponents of the legalization of voluntary active euthanasia ought to give thought to alternatives to legalization compatible with their attitudes toward human life, liberty, and justice. In previous chapters we have proposed legislation in harmony with our own view of the issues considered. Here, we believe, no new legislation will be of much help. Yet proposals to legalize euthanasia would hardly appeal to responsible people if there were not certain genuine needs which deserve consideration. Unless alternatives are developed which are responsive to these needs, those who oppose euthanasia will seem to be confined in a purely negative position in respect to the issue, including the underlying needs.

"Death with dignity" has been one of the most appealing slogans of those promoting euthanasia. We believe that reflection upon the meaning of this slogan and the reason for its appeal will help to clarify at least one area in which authentic, positive alternatives to legalized euthanasia are possible and urgently needed.

In a perceptive essay Paul Ramsey points out that the concept of "death with dignity" is paradoxical: Death is always an indignity, the ultimate indignity, and no talk of its naturalness and appropriateness changes this fact. In making this point Ramsey also attacks the conceptions underlying the belief of proponents of euthanasia that some people ought to die quickly because they would be better off dead.[99]

Ramsey's points are well taken. The slogan "death with dignity" puts a challenge or a question: "You do not wish to die without dignity, do you?" One is inclined to answer without too much thought: "No." But this is like answering someone who asks whether one has stopped beating one's spouse by affirming that one has. The question is not one question but two. Nobody wants to die without dignity, but most people do not want to die at all. Dignity, whatever exactly it is, is no doubt a good thing; by coupling dignity with death the proponent of euthanasia gives death excellence by association which it does not have in itself.

Nevertheless, we feel that there is an important truth which ought not to be overlooked expressed in the slogan "death with dignity." One cannot believe that the slogan could have gained such currency if it was not saying something significant which seemed correct to people. What is this core of significance? One looks in vain in the works of proponents of euthanasia for a clear explication of it. They fail even to try to define the key word "dignity."

Dignity is worth, not worth for something, but inherent worth. Dignity pertains to persons. It is not an achievement but an endowment, something one has which is very close to one's simply being what and who one is. To the dignity of one person corresponds the attitude of respect on the part of others.

The concept of dignity can perhaps be understood most easily if one considers its significance in an aristocratic society. Dignity is the excellence of those who are born superior to others. The qualities of self-possession, coolness, ability to command which are required for the exercise of the role of a superior come to be associated with and taken as signs of dignity. If superior persons, members of the upper classes, undergo or suffer something which makes clear that they are not so very different from the vulgar mob, then their dignity is offended. Often loss of respect due to dignity follows. Degradation can seem to remove dignity altogether.

In Christian thought all humans have an immense dignity insofar as they are created in the image of God and called to become members of the divine family. Post-Christian conceptions in democratic societies maintain something of the Christian democratization of dignity. Every person has dignity, is entitled to respect. The notions of basic political equality and of liberty and justice for all follow upon this democratic concept of dignity. But there also is a personalistic dimension to post-Christian ideas of dignity. Each person is unique, and respect for dignity demands that the uniqueness of the individual and the irreducibility of anyone to the status of a mere case of a class or a mere functionary in a system be recognized, accepted, and acted upon.[100]

Even in a democratic context the concept of dignity keeps many of its aristocratic connotations. If a child acts very grown-up for her age, adults will remark that she is a very "dignified" little girl, the assumption being that adults are inherently superior to children. If aspects of functioning which humans have in common with other animals are observed, an individual feels humiliation and loss of dignity, since at least there is the natural superiority of all humans to other animals. Members of society who for one reason or another are treated with unusual deference or respect—for example, high public officials—are regarded as having a dignity which attaches to their office. Etiquette maintains dignity by carefully excluding vulgarity—oftentimes distinctions are made purely for the sake of distinctiveness.

With these clarifications one can understand the significance of the notion of dignity in the euthanasia debate.

In the context of refusal of treatment it would be an offense against dignity, because an offense against liberty and justice, to impose unwanted treatment upon a competent adult. To the extent that such impositions occur the individual is no longer regarded as a person and is reduced to the status of a malfunctioning organism which is to be dealt with according to the values and standards of others—the medical technologists. Conversely, to seek the informed consent of patients is to respect their dignity.

Even the allowing of persons to exercise their liberty wrongfully by deliberately killing themselves—whether by refusal of treatment or by active suicide—is a respecting of their dignity. An individual's self-determination and individual wishes are allowed to control, which would be senseless if selfhood had no inherent worth. At the same time, to carefully avoid injustice to anyone and to refuse to impose upon noncompetent persons the judgment of others that they would be better off dead also is to respect their dignity: They are viewed as unique persons, not merely as suffering animals.

In many ways the typical hospital situation infringes upon people's sense of dignity and self-respect. The individual becomes a mere case and a mere patient. Class distinctions vanish in the common dress of the hospital gown and the common misery of disease. Differences between human beings and animals are less important in certain respects than what all sentient creatures have in common. In any case, what persons have in common with animals becomes manifest, often embarrassingly so, and cannot be ignored.

Intense pain is a great equalizer; one's animality takes over and dominates one's consciousness and behavior. Helplessness humiliates; the impatient patient would like to take charge and do something. And many hospital situations add further insults by failing to provide privacy for the carrying on of baser functions, by failing to listen to patients and to inform them about their own condition and prospects, by using cases as material for clinical study and instruction, by subordinating many aspects of the unique personality of each patient to the overriding demands of technically efficient treatment.[101]

The dying patient usually undergoes all of these experiences which take away one's sense of dignity.[102] Those observing dying patients—especially those not emotionally absorbed, who can gaze upon the dying with personal detachment—are intensely conscious of the loss of dignity. (Those who are more personally involved are more concerned about the life and health than about the dignity of the patient.) The observer says: How pitiable is a man or woman dying! And the thought is colored by unavoidable anxiety: And I too shall suffer this indignity.

As long ago as the ancient Stoics, at least, it was considered appropriate to commit suicide in order to avoid loss of dignity. The conception of the suicide of honor in many cultures, especially in military castes, is closely related to this view. Undoubtedly, a voluntary and quick death can prevent indignity.

But there remains the question whether it makes sense to die in order to protect this sort of dignity. There also is a manifestation of dignity in accepting suffering with courage and patience, in maintaining one's uniqueness against the power of suffering and death. Suffering and death is a challenge most people must face sooner or later; dealing with this challenge in a properly human and uniquely personal style can be a triumph which protects and manifests the genuineness and depth of one's dignity. A person with great self-respect grounded not upon superficial appearances of excellence but upon real and unalienable specifically human and uniquely personal worth will not be unduly humiliated by a recalcitrant organism.[103]

In recent years a number of authors have studied dying with a view to improving the care of persons who are dying rather than with a view to hastening death. Their work points to some simple and obvious truths: Dying persons need and can benefit only from care which is appropriate to them both insofar as they are persons and insofar as they are dying.[104] Psychological help for dying patients and their families and the use of special techniques such as hypnotherapy have received more attention.[105]

But by far the most hopeful development has been the establishment and success of care facilities specially dedicated to appropriate care for dying persons. One of the most outstanding of such facilities is St. Christopher's Hospice in London, whose medical director, Dr. Cicely Saunders, has provided a model of what care which respects fully the dignity of the dying can and ought to be.[106] Lord Raglan, sponsor of the euthanasia bill debated in the British House of Lords in 1969, had recently visited St. Christopher's, and he admitted in the debate, "It might be said that if everyone could spend his last days in such surroundings there would be no need for this Bill."[107] But he observed that there are not enough such places, and that some people would prefer a quick death even to dying with excellent care.

What is so different about a hospice? Its first principle is that the patient is a person. Dying persons must be listened to, and what they wish to know must be told them with gentle honesty. Personal tastes, needs, and interests must be catered for. And persons are not merely patients; they can participate in care, can help to make a valuable community. Community is prior to technology. Visiting takes place freely; families come to help. Patients can come and go, visit home if they are able, and return when they wish. The routines and rules and disciplines of an ordinary hospital or even an ordinary nursing home are mostly ignored.[108]

Secondly, a dying person is dying. Hence no irrelevant and meddlesome treatment is given. But alcohol and pain relievers flow freely. The hospices have made great progress comforting the dying; their work has made clear that the dilemma either of dying in a drugged stupor from a finally fatal dose of morphine or of dying in misery is a false one. Patients can be made comfortable while being kept functional.[109] Moreover, drugs are used freely not only to block pain but also to improve the patient's mood and to treat symptoms. Those who provide care in a hospice never take the attitude that a case is hopeless and there is nothing to be done. Every dying patient has the hope of a "fair and easy passage."

But, thirdly, perhaps the greatest work of the hospices has been in dealing with the psychological, social, and spiritual suffering which is unavoidable when one is dying. Care requires presence and contact; patients are not allowed to suffer and die alone, without human touch and a compassionate presence. Cooperation with the family helps the social aspects. The dedication and commitment to the dignity of dying patients of all who participate in care, the belief that each dying person is irreplaceable, and the assumption that living, even while dying, can be and ought to be good and meaningful mitigate suffering in these other human aspects.

The evidence of what has been accomplished already in developing good care for the dying is so impressive that anyone who examines it is likely to be convinced that there certainly can be dignity in dying without voluntary active euthanasia. If the legalization of voluntary active euthanasia is to be rejected in the interest of protecting the lives and respecting the liberty of members of society who do not wish to be killed and to kill, then this alternative to death by active euthanasia must be promoted. Indeed, it seems to us, there is some duty of society to make available to all quality palliative care.

There are several aspects of terminal care which could be helped by public action. First, grants could be distributed in a way which would encourage research and education in the more effective alleviation not only of pain but also of various forms of discomfort and inconvenience suffered by dying patients. Second, public and private health-care programs could be amended to encourage care for the dying at home or in facilities especially dedicated to such care. Third, a special program of subsidies for the establishment of hospices or palliative-care units could be designed, in order that examples of such facilities would be available in more places. Fourth, public health programs could provide seminars and special courses to retrain physicians and nurses for better care of the dying even in ordinary hospitals.[110]

There is no necessity that any person die in misery, deprived of human dignity. To recognize the evil that this happens in some cases is to manifest human sensitivity and compassion. To press for active voluntary euthanasia as a solution to the problem is to adopt the technically easiest and most efficient solution, the solution most in line with those aspects of health administration and medical practice which least comport with the dignity of persons. To provide appropriate and excellent care for the dying is to respect fully not only the dignity of those who are terminally ill but also the dignity of all of their brothers and sisters who must someday join them in death, but who are in no hurry to do so by someone mistakenly or maliciously administering "death with dignity."[111]

7: Killing Which Is Considered Justified

A. An Economic Argument for Nonvoluntary Euthanasia

Not all killings of one human being by another are held by the law to be crimes. In some cases killing is excused. For example, some who kill lack criminal intent: one who kills another by accident and without recklessness, one who kills another while sleepwalking or by a reflex act, and one who kills another while incapable of distinguishing right from wrong—such incapacity is always assumed in the case of very young children. Such excusable killings are neither forbidden nor permitted by law; they simply fall outside the concern of the law. For this reason they will be of no interest in what follows.

But there are cases in which a killing is intentional, yet the law does not hold the act and intent criminal since the killing is considered justified. The most obvious categories of justified killing are those which are authorized by the law itself—for example, capital punishment which executes a legal sentence and acts of war carried out under lawful authority. Under certain conditions modern Anglo-American law also considers killing in self-defense and in the arrest and detention of criminals to be justified. Finally, even when abortion has been considered homicide—the killing of one human being by another—abortion to save the mother's life was permitted as justified either by a statement of exception in the statute or by the common law exception on the ground of necessity.[1]

The question to be examined in this chapter and in chapter eight is whether nonvoluntary euthanasia might not under certain conditions be assimilated to other killing considered justified, and under these conditions legalized to the extent that it would be in the public interest.

In chapter six we considered the argument for voluntary euthanasia, assuming that nonvoluntary and involuntary euthanasia must not be permitted. The argument for voluntary euthanasia has its greatest plausibility when it maintains and stresses the requirement of voluntariness, since the liberty of those who wish to be killed and of those who wish to kill them demands

184

respect. Our argument was that respect for this liberty ought to prevail neither over respect for justice to those who do not wish to be killed nor over respect for the liberty of those who wish to stand aloof from euthanasia killing. We also argued that voluntary euthanasia will not be legalized without at least some nonvoluntary euthanasia also being legalized—especially the killing of defective infants. And we noted that most proponents of voluntary euthanasia hold principles which would justify nonvoluntary euthanasia if these principles justify voluntary euthanasia.

It might be supposed that if there is a sound jurisprudential argument against voluntary euthanasia, then a fortiori there is a solid argument against the nonvoluntary sort. But this does not follow. Why it does not may be seen by considering the position of Foster Kennedy, a physician and member of Cornell University who was also President of the Euthanasia Society of America prior to World War II. Kennedy recognized that the killing of persons who had been functional could not be legalized without permitting the killing by mistake of many who would have recovered. However, he favored the killing of congenitally defective and nontrainable children, for in these cases he considered a foolproof system of diagnosis and prognosis to be possible.[2]

Kennedy did not propose that infants be killed at or shortly after birth. His idea was that all children should be given a chance to develop and to display their potentiality. But when children reach the age of five, competent medical personnel can tell whether they will be trainable or not. So Kennedy suggests that when persons five years of age or older seem to be hopelessly unfit, then their guardians might apply to a legally authorized medical board. The board would examine the individual at least three times at four-month intervals. If the board decided that there was no hope that the congenitally defective child could be trained, then he or she should be relieved of the burden of living. In making reference to guardians Kennedy does not mean to exclude an application by the parents of a defective child being cared for at home. But he seems to have in mind primarily those cared for in institutions, whom "we hustle out of sight."[3]

It seems clear that if euthanasia were limited to cases of the sort which Kennedy had in mind, procedures could be developed adequate to exclude almost entirely the killing of others by mistake or by malice. Just as we suggested in chapter six that perhaps a safe system of voluntary euthanasia could be set up if there were sufficient public involvement, so Kennedy's proposal could be developed into a system which would eliminate the nontrainable without putting others at grave risk. The medical board could be required to give its testimony before a court, any interested party could be permitted to try to show that the individual proposed for euthanasia might in fact be trainable, the decision for death could be made only when the nontrainability of the individual was established beyond a reasonable doubt, the individual to be killed would be taken in police custody to a special place where the killing would be done by a public official who would act only in execution of the court's order. If a system along these lines were first developed to dispose of nontrainable children, it later could be extended to cover all persons requiring permanent institutional care at public expense.

Of course, many people would object even more strongly to the involvement of public institutions in such nonvoluntary euthanasia than to the institutionalization of voluntary euthanasia. But an argument can be made that the overriding of liberty to stand aloof from such killing can be justified inasmuch as it could promote a public interest. The interest in question is a financial one. The congenitally defective who are not trainable, the permanently insane, and the senile often are cared for in public institutions for many years at considerable expense.

Walter W. Sackett, testifying before a committee of the United States Senate, put this argument as follows:

> We have training institutions for the less severely retarded who are trainable. I am all for those, but in these two institutions for the severely retarded in Florida, we have 1,500 residents, some with heads as big as buckets, some small as oranges, grotesque and drawn up in contracture. According to present-day cost and the fact that you can keep these individuals alive artificially to between 50 and 60, it's going to cost the State of Florida for 50 years $5 billion.
>
> Translated roughly this means it's going to cost the various States over this same period $100 billion, and when one thinks of what one could do with this money in other fields, the less severely retarded, the mentally ill, our jails, in our homes for delinquents, it is most revealing. . . . It is a question of cost benefit.
>
> Now, where is the benefit in these 1,500 severely retarded, who never had a rational thought. . .?[4]

As we pointed out in chapter one, section D, Sackett's estimated savings are not correct. But, as we also explained, it is true that a considerable amount might be saved if certain groups of individuals who require constant, permanent care were put to death.

Statements as frank as Sackett's are not prevalent, but neither are they rare. Forty years ago, William G. Lennox, who had previously been a medical missionary and was then a professor at Harvard Medical School, argued bluntly in economic terms that funds not be wasted on monsters, congenital idiots, the permanently incurable and institutionalized. To the objection that society would not countenance planned murder, he replied that society countenances war in which the best are killed, while it prolongs the lives of the worst. Lennox was an expert on epilepsy, and he especially deplored the care given to forty thousand epileptics in public institutions; most of these patients and others who are cared for at home "are physically or mentally incapable of self-support and will be a burden as long as they live."[5]

More recent authors sometimes endorse similar views. Robert H. Williams specifies candidates for euthanasia:

> There are various levels at which one can consider the indications for euthanasia: (a) a group of individuals who will soon be encountering death; (b) a group with such severe mental damage as to be unable to express proper judgments with respect to termination of life, and (c) a group with varying degrees of cognizance, but with disabilities so incapacitating and so common as to produce great hardship on society. At the present time it is important to deal predominantly with the first group.[6]

In another work he suggests that euthanasia might be considered as a method of population control, although a deplorable one.[7]

Similarly, Richard Trubo, reporting with sympathy the views of Fletcher, Sackett, and others, stresses economic considerations. Trubo claims that it cost (1973) $1.5 billion per year just to care for all the children with Down's syndrome.[8]

Glanville Williams protests that the idea of euthanasia for the aged *in present society* would shock him as much as anyone, but he projects a future situation in which people, although not able to function, might be kept alive until they were one thousand years old. Williams argues that under such conditions it would be inappropriate to maintain "hospital-mausolea" for such persons.[9]

Even Marvin Kohl, who is careful to separate himself from some advocates of euthanasia who have written as if economic considerations are paramount, is not willing to deny such considerations a lesser role subordinate to the chief consideration of doing what is kind and loving:

> Indeed, if a society is too niggardly to allow its members to live with dignity, then allowing or helping them die with dignity should strike even the most economically-minded of individuals as being a great bargain.[10]

Although his endorsement is lukewarm, Kohl cannot forbear to state this economic argument.

As we saw in chapter one, section E, the costs of Social Security are mounting so rapidly that it is not at all implausible that society will be prepared to allow and to help the elderly to die "with dignity" long before the horrible fantasy of Williams could ever come to pass.

These economic arguments for nonvoluntary euthanasia present a challenge which is distinct from the challenge presented by typical arguments for voluntary euthanasia, which we examined and answered in chapter six.

Those who argue for nonvoluntary euthanasia on economic grounds can point out that this practice would not have to be dangerous to the public at large. The criteria for selection could be comparatively clear-cut—for example, residence for a certain length of time in a public institution or in a private one wholly at public expense. People are placed in such institutions on the basis of their objective condition and are hardly likely to be maintained in them for years if their condition does not warrant it.

At the same time the condition of such people which causes them to be institutionalized generates the substantial economic liability of the cost of their long-term care in the institution. The arguments of the various authors we have quoted imply that this economic liability generates a substantial public interest in cutting costs. If the liberty of those who abhor mercy killing to stand aloof from it cannot be overridden by the private interest of those who volunteer to be killed to avoid suffering to themselves, it can be overridden—so the argument for nonvoluntary euthanasia can go—by the public interest in relieving society of the burden of the permanently dependent.

Opponents of euthanasia are likely to object that in some cases the killing of institutionalized persons would constitute not only nonvoluntary but even involuntary euthanasia. Some permanently institutionalized persons are legally competent, and although some such persons might be willing to be killed, others would reject the idea very firmly. Killing them thus would conflict with their own expressed and competent decisions.

Proponents of euthanasia for the dependent would argue that in general killing such persons would be kindly, since their institutional existence generally is wretched and their quality of life miserable. To kill those who would be better off dead is a kindness, not an injury—the argument goes—and so satisfies the concept of euthanasia. Yet even proponents of euthanasia must admit that killing such persons *against* their wills hardly would be "euthanasia."

The law could provide that institutionalized persons would only be killed after a legal process which determined either that they were not competent or that they gave their informed consent to the procedure, and that the other conditions established by law were met. Given such an arrangement, most of the burden of the permanently dependent could be eliminated, since the non-competent could be killed without their consent and some of the competent with their consent. No one would be killed involuntarily—that is, against an expressed and competent decision.

Proponents of strictly voluntary euthanasia are likely to object that if an argument for overriding the liberty to stand aloof of those who abhor euthanasia killing must be entertained on the ground of the public interest in saving the cost of caring for the permanently dependent, then a fortiori the case for overriding this liberty should have been entertained when we considered voluntary euthanasia, because the legalization of voluntary euthanasia under strict controls also could save public money—that used to pay for the costs of medical care for competent persons, particularly the elderly. The memorandum of Robert A. Derzon, which we quoted in chapter six, section I, points in this direction, although he explicitly refers to 'Living Wills'' and does not mention active euthanasia.

Our response to this objection is that in chapter six we did not consider an argument for overriding liberty to stand aloof based upon the public interest in cutting costs of care because economic considerations clearly do not support a case for both legalizing euthanasia and restricting it to instances in which it would be strictly voluntary. Rather, the potential savings from purely voluntary euthanasia would be limited and can hardly be expected to be great in comparison with the predictable, substantial savings from nonvoluntary euthanasia of the permanently dependent. Moreover, while a simple hearing could determine fairly easily that a person to be killed was not resistant to the proposal, no simple procedure could establish that a person was competent and genuinely willing to be killed. Hence, if economic considerations are accepted as a basis for legalizing euthanasia, the argument will be irresistible for legalizing nonvoluntary as well as voluntary euthanasia.

The manner in which proponents of euthanasia themselves argue confirms our point, for those who emphasize economic considerations argue for nonvoluntary as well as voluntary euthanasia, while those who make a serious effort to exclude killing which is not purely voluntary carefully avoid trying to justify euthanasia by the potential public interest in saving money.

Furthermore, although there clearly is a public interest in saving public funds, this public interest is of a peculiar sort, as we shall argue in chapter eight. While we are ready to consider for the sake of argument that economic considerations might override the liberty of persons who abhor killing to stand aloof from it, our conclusion will be that a jurisprudence which justly respects liberty would not permit it to be restricted pragmatically for purely budgetary reasons.

Opponents of euthanasia will object to any proposal of nonvoluntary euthanasia primarily on the ground that such killing would be unjust to those killed. The right to life of the permanently institutionalized would be violated, it will be argued, if they were killed in a program of legalized nonvoluntary euthanasia. Such killing cannot be justified, the objection will conclude, even if it is granted for the sake of argument that saving the costs of caring for such persons is in the public interest.

But those who favor such a program of nonvoluntary euthanasia can argue that if the relevant public interest is granted, then killing can be justified. After all, the law does not altogether exclude killing; the right to life never has been held to be an absolute. As we have noticed at the beginning of this chapter the law not only treats certain deadly deeds as excusable but even considers killing in some circumstances justifiable. The cases of killing in war, in self-defense, as capital punishment, and in the extreme cases in which abortion was permitted even under the most restrictive statutes seem to provide some precedent for killing in a program of nonvoluntary euthanasia. In each case some important public interest seems to have been recognized by Anglo-American law as sufficient to justify killing despite the general presumption of the law against it.

If the instances in which killing traditionally has been considered justifiable do provide precedents for legalizing nonvoluntary euthanasia in the public interest, then those who oppose such killing face a dilemma. Either they accept these precedents or they do not.

If they do not accept them, opponents of euthanasia show themselves even more absolutist in asserting the sanctity of life than the traditional jurisprudence which did allow killing in these cases as justifiable. Such absolutism in asserting the sanctity of life would make clear that opponents of euthanasia adhere to a sectarian morality, and that they wish human life to be treated as a direct and intrinsic component of the common good of political society. In other words, rejection of all killing—even in cases in which the law traditionally has regarded it as justified—would make clear that proponents of euthanasia are correct in claiming that opponents wish to impose their morality upon society at large.

In fact most opponents of euthanasia are prepared to admit that killing in some cases is justified; only total pacifists deny the public the right to defend itself against unjust aggressors and criminals. Moreover, those who held traditional views even agreed that in some cases innocent lives might justifiably be taken, for although there was no agreement about the extent and justification of abortion to save the mother's life, no major group excluded such killing in every single instance.[11] The admission that killing in some cases is justified leads to the other horn of the dilemma: If it is admitted that killing is justified in other cases, then nonvoluntary euthanasia also might be justified if the public interest is served by it.

Of course, this dilemma has force only if cases in which killing has traditionally been considered justified are genuine precedents for the killing in the public interest which is advocated by proponents of nonvoluntary euthanasia. If there are nonsectarian jurisprudential grounds for rejecting as unjustifiable some instances of killing traditionally considered to be justifiable, then killing in these instances at least will provide no precedent for legalizing nonvoluntary euthanasia. Moreover, if there are important jurisprudential differences between instances in which killing has traditionally been considered justifiable and the killing which would be carried out in a program of nonvoluntary euthanasia, then an opponent of the legalization of nonvoluntary euthanasia could admit that killing might be justified in the kinds of cases traditionally accepted and yet deny without any inconsistency that nonvoluntary euthanasia would be justified, even if it were granted to be in the public interest.

In the remainder of this chapter we shall show that all of the instances in which it is generally agreed that killing can be justified differ from legalized nonvoluntary euthanasia in significant ways, so that proponents of legalization are mistaken in regarding killing in war, as capital punishment, in self-defense, and in abortion to save the mother's life as precedents which show that it would be justifiable to kill the dependent in order to relieve the public of the burden of caring for them. Incidentally, we also shall show that even those who hold that human life must be protected as inviolable by law are not inconsistent in accepting killing as justifiable in the cases in which it traditionally has been accepted.

In chapter eight we shall argue that killing people without their consent is incompatible with the principle of justice upon which Anglo-American jurisprudence is based. To be specific, we shall show that nonvoluntary euthanasia would violate the requirement of equal protection of the law.

B. Killing in War

It is undeniably part of the American consensus that killing in war can be justified. Consent to the constitutional purpose of providing for the common defense implies that some killing is accepted. But beyond this very general proposition there is little consensus either about the conditions under which war can be justified or about the sorts of killing which can be done legitimately even in a war considered to be justified.

Sometimes proponents of euthanasia point out how much killing has been done in wars considered justified. For example, in World War II, in Korea, and in Vietnam civilians were purposely killed on a large scale in the carrying out of the policy of strategic bombing, and in the last war little effort was made to avoid the killing of helpless civilians.[12]

However, no one considers all wars to be justified and no one who seriously thinks about the matter considers all acts done in any war to be justified. Furthermore, there always has been considerable disagreement about the conditions under which war might be justified and the limits within which it might be justly fought. Certainly there is no agreement on any such general proposition as the following: Soldiers are legally justified in killing whenever this killing would be in the public interest.

First, soldiers are considered legally justified only in killing those who are designated "the enemy," and the enemy includes only persons who are foreigners or rebels acting outside of and against the domestic legal system. Moreover, not even all who are associated with the enemy are considered justifiable targets of military action. Although the immunity of noncombatants often has been violated, the principle of limiting military action to enemy combatants is part of the traditional law of war.

Second, many people who share in the general public consensus which accepts some killing in war as justified hold that there are very narrow limits of just warfare. According to the views accepted by such people the fact that killing in war is in the public interest is a necessary but by no means a sufficient condition for considering such killing justifiable. The other conditions necessary for a just war would not be met by a program of nonvoluntary euthanasia. Hence, even if it is granted that a program of nonvoluntary euthanasia might be in the public interest, the justification of killing in war would provide no precedent for concluding the justifiability of killing the dependent for the sake of the public interest in saving the cost of caring for them.

To make clear our point that one can provide a jurisprudential justification of war which is consistent with the Anglo-American legal tradition and which involves several conditions in addition to the requirement that the killing be in the public interest, we briefly consider the conditions Thomas Aquinas articulated in his classical statement of just-war theory. We are not concerned here with the moral question with which Aquinas himself was directly concerned, nor are we arguing that his account is in any way authoritative in defining the public consensus concerning the limits of just war. Our only point is that his analysis is a possible rationale for accepting some killing in war as justifiable without admitting any broad principle which would make the justification of killing in war a plausible precedent for the justification of nonvoluntary euthanasia in the public interest.

Aquinas lays down three conditions without which killing in warfare cannot be just. First, war must be conducted under public authority, since individuals always can appeal their private quarrels to such authority. Second, there must be a just cause; the enemy cannot be opposed unless there has really been a wrong done which must be opposed by force. Third, the intention of those fighting must be upright. Aquinas quotes Augustine with approval in condemning "the desire to harm, the cruelty of revenge, a vindictive spirit, the rage of self-defense, the lust of power, and the like."[13] This position absolutely excludes that a war can be fought without one side, at least, being fundamentally and clearly in the wrong. Only defense against injustice begins to justify war, and even then an upright intention would limit violence to that which is absolutely necessary to stop or to mitigate the injustice.[14]

Such a limitation means that if it were possible to oppose the injustice with nondeadly force, then that would be necessary to justify resistance. However, warfare unfolds when at least one party uses deadly force unjustly. The other must either offer no resistance at all or must resist with force adequate to defend so far as possible the lives of those resisting the unjust attack. Thus in all war there is a threat to life which is generated by the attacker to enforce an unjust demand which otherwise might be thwarted by nondeadly modes of resistance.

Now, although the theory of just war proposed by Aquinas by no means defines the American public consensus concerning the justifiability of killing in war, it is a fact that developing international law during the twentieth century—especially under the auspices of the United Nations Organization in its effort to restrict warfare since World War II—approximates very closely to the conditions Aquinas articulated.[15] And it certainly is well within the bounds of the American consensus to take a position which would permit as legitimate only wars which conform to the most stringent conditions of international law. Thus, the killing in warfare which must be accepted as justifiable by those who stand within the American consensus does not seem to go beyond killing which meets the following conditions:

1) One side is being attacked or about to be attacked by the other; those attacked are unwilling victims and they have done nothing wrongful to provoke the attack.

2) The aggressor cannot be brought to justice by appeal to a higher authority recognized by both sides, nor does the defender have an alternative—such as retreating from the confrontation and seeking a peaceful settlement—which would not permit the aggressor to attain its objectively unjustified objective.

3) Those responsible for the defense cannot succeed using only nondeadly force, since the attackers use or are about to use deadly force.

4) Those killed are actual agents of the attack (not noncombatants or prisoners) who still pose a real threat (not an already defeated enemy) which the killing is likely to help to frustrate (not an already victorious enemy).

Understood in this way, justifiable war must be defensive. To seek by force to overcome an opponent who is not using or about to use deadly force is to act aggressively. The use of terror, torture, and reprisals is not justified. The killing of noncombatants or the indiscriminate killing of noncombatants and the agents of attack alike is unjustified.

The jurisprudential justification of killing in war thus seems to require one to concede only this much: that actual agents of an unprovoked attack may be killed to protect the rights threatened by the attack provided there is not some alternative way of protecting these rights and provided the killing seems really necessary and useful to protect these rights.

In war those whose killing is jurisprudentially justified are either foreigners or revolutionaries, and in either case are individuals whose lives are not under the protection of the law which authorizes their being killed, since they refuse to recognize its authority. The only alternative to war within the stated limits is for the rule of law to yield to the rule of brute force. Pacifists themselves understand the objective which is sought by the defenders in a jurisprudentially justifiable war, and they do not disapprove of the objective. However, they reject the use of deadly force even to resist evil. Their liberty to stand aloof from the involvement of their societies in defensive war is overridden to the extent necessary—conscientious objection on an individual basis may be permitted—by the public purpose of the war together with the defense of the rights of those who would suffer unjustly and the liberty of others to seek to defend these rights.

The acceptance of the justifiability of killing in war under the conditions we have articulated clearly provides no precedent which would justify a program of nonvoluntary euthanasia. The dependent for whom nonvoluntary euthanasia is proposed are not aggressors; they use no deadly force. They do create a social burden, but there are ways of dealing with this burden short of killing those who constitute it. The dependent are not outlaws; their continued existence poses no threat to the rule of law. Moreover, those who oppose nonvoluntary euthanasia do not approve of the objective which would be sought by such a program.

The theory of just war also makes clear how those who accept it can without inconsistency hold that law must regard human life as inviolable. Killing in warfare which must be accepted as justifiable will be consonant with the purpose of the law insofar as such killing protects the right to life and other rights of those who are subject to the law against the brute power of those who do not respect its authority.

C. Killing in Self-defense

With respect to the right of individual self-defense a standard textbook of criminal law summarizes American law on the matter in the following terms:

> One who is not the aggressor in an encounter is justified in using a reasonable amount of force against his adversary when he reasonably believes (a) that he is in immediate danger of unlawful bodily harm from his adversary and (b) that the use of such force is necessary to avoid this danger.
>
> It may be reasonable to use nondeadly force against the adversary's nondeadly attack (i.e., one threatening only bodily harm), and to use deadly force against his deadly attack (an attack threatening death or serious bodily harm), but it is never reasonable to use deadly force against his nondeadly attack.
>
> There is a dispute as to whether one threatened with a deadly attack must retreat, if he can safely do so, before resorting to deadly force, except that it is agreed that he need not retreat from his home or place of business.[16]

Unlike killing in war, killing in self-defense occurs within an established social context. But like killing in war, and by contrast with the killing which would be involved in a program of nonvoluntary euthanasia, killing in self-defense is considered justifiable only because the usual protection of rights provided by the law is unavailable. If it were available, resort to self-help would be excluded.

Moreover, killing in self-defense is considered justifiable only if the aggressor is doing or about to do something which is not only threatening but also of a type which is unlawful insofar as it is likely to harm the other in a forbidden way. The one who resorts to self-defense thus is justified only insofar as an attack is repulsed or prevented which would violate rights, whether or not the agent of the attack is in a condition of being criminally responsible.

The law's distinction between deadly and nondeadly force is vital but must be understood as a practical rule, not as a theoretical dividing line. In practice one facing a threat cannot distinguish between cases in which the threat is to life and those in which it is only to bodily integrity. For example, someone threatened with a gun does not know what the attacker will do with it: shoot to kill or only to wound. Similarly, one using defensive force cannot distinguish very well between means likely to cause great harm and those likely to cause death. To the extent that the law allows *the intent* to cause the attacker's death, the legal conception of intent must be assumed: one knows the means used is likely to cause death and intends the means to be effective.

A merely sincere belief that there is a necessity to use deadly force in self-defense is insufficient to justify the legal use of such force. The belief also must be reasonable: one a reasonable person would hold in the circumstances. Yet the belief can be false without undermining the justification. The attack must be immediate or imminent, for otherwise there is an alternative to self-defense: resort to public authority. Ordinarily the aggressor has no right to self-defense, but there are exceptions. An attacker who uses obviously nondeadly force can defend against an excessive response; likewise, an aggressor who has withdrawn can defend against a retaliatory attack.

Retreat is not required where nondeadly force is all that is involved. Many jurisdictions do not require one who is attacked to retreat rather than use deadly force, but some do, and so no more than this needs to be explained for a reasonably adequate jurisprudential justification of that killing which is done in self-defense. However, one who is attacked in his or her own home or place of business is not held to retreat even if this could be done safely before using deadly force to repel deadly force. The concept here seems to be that one's home is one's safest retreat; probably also the law assumes that an aggressor who also is a trespasser normally does not attack with deadly force and permit the one attacked to retreat safely unless the purpose of the attack is to infringe seriously upon property or other rights of the one attacked.

The principles of law with respect to the defense of another person are very similar to those with respect to self-defense. In some jurisdictions private defense of strangers has been excluded; where it is considered justified—which would seem reasonable enough—there have been some difficulties in dealing with cases which arise from errors made about who deserved protection from whom.[17]

The principles of law with respect to defense of property vary somewhat from jurisdiction to jurisdiction. The narrower view excludes the use of deadly force to protect property unless the circumstances are those in which deadly force also is justified in self-defense, or unless an intruder into an occupied home behaves in a way which is reasonably interpreted to show the intent to commit a felony, and the intruder ignores an order to desist.[18]

A police officer or one assisting an officer can use force to bring about an arrest. If the arrest is for a misdemeanor, only nondeadly force may be used. If the arrest is for a felony, then deadly force may be used, but only if necessary to bring about the arrest or to prevent escape from custody.

A person, not necessarily a police officer, may use deadly force to prevent or terminate the commission of a felony, but only if such force is necessary and only if the felony is dangerous, such as murder, arson, robbery, burglary of a dwelling, kidnapping, or forcible rape. The underlying principle is that dangerous felonies may cause death or serious bodily harm, and so deadly force is reasonable to prevent them.[19]

There have been suggestions that the justification of the use of force in arresting and detaining prisoners be limited even more, so that in effect deadly force could be used only where there was some likelihood that the person not arrested or not detained through nonuse of force would seriously violate someone's rights.[20]

The legal conditions for justifiable killing in self-defense and in law enforcement thus are quite narrow. They are very similar to the conditions outlined above in which at a minimum killing must be justified in warfare by a nonpacifist. Agents of nonprovoked attacks may be killed to protect the rights threatened by attack, but only if there is not some alternative which would adequately protect these rights. The aggressor can always obtain immunity by withdrawing from the attack. Law enforcement claims precedence over the right of innocent persons to resist; their protection is in legal processes. Yet the lawful use of force in law enforcement is narrower than usually thought, and there is a tendency to restrict it even more. In any case, compliance with the orders of arresting and detaining officers protects one from the use of deadly force except insofar as one may be subjected to capital punishment.

The acceptance of the justifiability of killing in self-defense and in the process of criminal law enforcement clearly provides no precedent which would justify a program of nonvoluntary euthanasia. Killing considered justified in these instances certainly is held to be in the public interest. But the public interest which is at stake is the protection of basic rights and the carrying out of public duties required to protect these rights. As in the case of warfare, moreover, there is no inconsistency in considering killing justified in these instances yet in holding that the law must regard human life as inviolable; for, at least in jurisdictions where it is more limited, killing is justified in self-defense and in law enforcement only when the alternative would be to allow the rule of law to be overcome by the rule of force, and the lives of those who respect the law to be at the mercy of those who refuse to submit to its authority.

D. Killing as Penalty

Since killing traditionally has been considered justifiable as punishment for serious crimes, especially for murder, it seems to offer a stronger precedent for considering a program of nonvoluntary euthanasia justifiable. Unlike killing in war, in self-defense, and in the course of law enforcement activities, capital punishment is not essential to protect rights and to defend the rule of law against the brute force of those who will not submit to it.

Of course, criminals do attack innocent victims, and it is reasonable to suppose they will continue to do so unless hindered. Mutual protection against criminal acts certainly is one of the purposes of political society, and no government can set this function aside. But by the time capital punishment becomes possible, the criminal has been identified and is in close custody. Defense of the rule of law in this case seems quite possible without the use of deadly means, particularly today when the state can hold criminals in maximum security prisons. Thus it would appear that capital punishment can be justified only by the public interest in terminating the careers of criminals without going to the inconvenience and expense of maintaining them in prisons for life. A justification along these lines is not so far removed from an argument for a program of nonvoluntary euthanasia on economic grounds.

However, we do not think that the practice of capital punishment provides the precedent for euthanasia which it at first appears to provide. In the first place there is no longer a consensus in Britain or America that capital punishment is justifiable. Hence, without violating the principles which are accepted in common, those who oppose euthanasia can reject an argument in justification of it based on analogy with capital punishment simply by taking their stand with those who deny the justifiability of this type of killing.

It is true some of the opposition to capital punishment is based upon the assumption that human life as such is sacred. A pamphlet published by the American Civil Liberties Union states, ''Executions in prisons gave the unmistakable message to all society that life ceases to be sacred when it is thought useful to take it.. . ."[21] Clearly, arguments along these lines cannot be accepted by a jurisprudence appropriate to a pluralistic society in which there no longer is a consensus upon the sanctity of life. To exclude capital punishment on this basis would be to impose a sectarian morality which depends upon assumptions which lie outside the commonly accepted principles of liberty and justice.

Nevertheless, as we already suggested in chapter six, section F, a more acceptable argument against the death penalty is possible. In American society today there is widespread abhorrence of this practice. The public good which is served by it is not clear, for it is not established that the threat of death deters criminals.[22] The involvement of society in this sort of killing therefore seems to violate the liberty to stand aloof of those who object to it on conscientious grounds.

With public attitudes toward the death penalty in the state they are, opponents of euthanasia can simply deny the justifiability of capital punishment and thus undercut its use as a precedent for euthanasia without putting themselves outside the American consensus. However, even if the justifiability of capital punishment were universally accepted, there are some important disanalogies between this practice and the killing which would be involved in a program of nonvoluntary euthanasia. Capital punishment can be defended on a narrow rationale—indeed, it is most plausibly defended on a narrow rationale—which stops far short of justifying killing whenever it happens to be in the public interest.

The chief disanalogy between capital punishment and euthanasia is that the former is limited to persons who have been convicted of serious crimes. Criminals are not merely a burden to society; they have defied the rule of law and inflicted grave harm upon other members of society who respect the law and look to it not only for the protection of their rights but also for the vindication of their fair claims to retribution. Hence, one can argue for capital punishment on a basis which is quite independent of any assumption that it is an effective deterrent or an efficient way of disposing of criminals. The argument is that some crimes, especially cold-blooded murder, warrant death as a penalty and are not justly punished if this penalty is not inflicted.

A rationale for capital punishment along these lines clearly provides no precedent for a program of nonvoluntary euthanasia. Permanently dependent persons who would be the primary candidates for nonvoluntary euthanasia have not defied the law and have not harmed others unless indirectly and with no malicious intent. Thus, there is no public interest in exacting death to vindicate a demand for just retribution against the dependent. The burden they impose upon the public is purely one of caring for them. The public interest in killing the dependent would be strictly economic.

Justifications of the killing done in war, in self-defense, and in law enforcement are based upon the necessity for such killings if the rule of law is to be protected against brute force. A plausible justification for the death penalty also must appeal to the demands of justice in fair punishment. In all of these cases those who are to be killed select themselves by their own unlawful acts. In none of these cases is the quality of life of the persons to be killed a relevant consideration. Hence, opponents of euthanasia can without inconsistency accept killing in all of these cases without admitting any principle which would justify a program of euthanasia, even if it is granted for the sake of argument that nonvoluntary euthanasia of dependent persons would be in the public interest.

E. Abortion as Legally Justifiable Killing

In recent years many nations in the common law tradition have legalized abortion in a more or less extensive set of instances beyond the traditionally accepted cases in which it is necessary to save the mother's life. Most extreme was the decision of the United States Supreme Court in 1973 in the *Abortion Cases,* since this decision in practice permits abortion at any stage of pregnancy whenever the pregnant woman and the physician agree to it. In the earlier stages of pregnancy no question of motive can be raised; even in the latter stages the mother's health—defined to include all aspects of her well-being—is deemed sufficient to justify the killing of the unborn.[23]

Since the interests which are accepted as justifying abortion can be merely private ones, the legalization of abortion seems to provide a very strong precedent for the legalization of nonvoluntary euthanasia, which would be carried on not for mere private interests but for the public interest (granted for the sake of argument) in saving the costs of caring for permanently dependent persons. However, the legalization of abortion does not provide the precedent which it might appear to do for legalizing euthanasia.

In the first place abortion has been legalized on the basis of the exclusion of the unborn from the status of legal personhood. This exclusion is explicit in the U. S. Supreme Court decision and is implicit in the statutes passed in the United Kingdom and other countries. Although the justice of this exclusion is arguable, it has a certain foundation in the common law, since the unborn never have been protected by the same law of homicide which protects everyone else. The legalization of nonvoluntary euthanasia would differ from the legalization of abortion, for a public program of nonvoluntary euthanasia would be aimed at individuals whose lives at present are protected by the law of homicide—individuals whose past and present status as legal persons is beyond doubt in any nation within the common law tradition.

Furthermore, there is no consensus in America or in any other English-speaking country upon the justifiability of abortion except in cases in which it is necessary to save the life of the mother. Those who oppose nonvoluntary euthanasia very often also oppose abortion and consider abortion which is not strictly necessary to save the mother's life to be nothing else than nonvoluntary euthanasia of the unborn. Whether the opposition to abortion is considered correct or not, proponents of nonvoluntary euthanasia beg the question if they appeal to abortion as a precedent, when the justifiability of the latter practice is just as much in question as that of the former.

Hence, if the legal justification for that killing which is done in cases of abortion is to serve as a precedent for legalizing nonvoluntary euthanasia, the argument must proceed from the narrow class of cases in which abortion was generally agreed to be justifiable prior to recent changes in the law. At the very least, cases which are not granted by at least some who oppose nonvoluntary euthanasia cannot be taken as a precedent for legalizing other killing. But if abortion is considered justified only in some very narrow classes of cases, it provides little plausible ground for legalizing nonvoluntary euthanasia.

However, any concession that abortion is justified—even if only when it is strictly necessary to save the mother's life—does raise questions which are not raised by the acceptance of killing as legally justified in war and in the other kinds of cases considered thus far. For this reason it will be informative to examine the grounds on which abortion to save the mother's life might be justified. This examination will show that one can consistently accept such abortion as justified and reject the use of this type of killing as a precedent for legalizing nonvoluntary euthanasia.

The justification of killing in war and the other cases considered previously depends upon the fact that those killed stand outside the law, and killing them is necessary to protect rights and to vindicate justice. Abortion to save the mother's life cannot be justified jurisprudentially as a necessary means to protect rights against attack and preserve the very order of law itself. The situation of the unborn in such cases of abortion does present a threat to the mother's life; she is unwilling to die and did nothing wrongful to bring about the threat; and there is no alternative to killing the unborn if the mother's life is to be saved. But the unborn individual is not the agent of a wrongful act; what the unborn poses as a threat is, not a type of behavior which has been declared unlawful precisely as threatening to another, but an accidental and inevitable consequence of its merely living and developing naturally.[24]

It follows that if opponents of the legalization of euthanasia concede the justifiability of abortion even in this narrowest class of cases, they must concede something more than is conceded as justified in accepting killing in war and the other cases already considered. They must concede that killing can be justified not only by the compelling public interest in protecting rights and the rule of law itself but also by what appears to be an essentially private interest in the protection of another's life.

To see just how much must be conceded if abortion to save the mother's life is to be given a plausible jurisprudential justification, we begin with the most restricted case: abortion which may save the mother's life in circumstances in which the alternative to abortion is that both the mother and the child will die. In this case there is a threat or grave danger to the life of the mother, she is unwilling to suffer the threatened harm, she did nothing wrongful to bring the situation about, and killing is necessary if life is to be saved. In these respects the case is similar to justifiable self-defense. The difference is that here there is no aggressor; the threat does not arise from a type of behavior which is unlawful. But in place of this the condition of an especially repugnant alternative to killing is given: Not to do the act of killing will turn out (by hypothesis) with no survivor at all.

In abortion in such a case life is certainly taken without the justification that the rights of the one threatened are protected against attack. But is the *right* to life of the unborn violated in this case? Those who regard this right as unalienable might say so. However, if the right to life is based, not upon the status of life as a substantive component of the common good, but rather upon fairness in protecting each person's real interest in his or her own life, then it seems reasonable to say that the right to life is infringed if and only if an act of killing unfairly reduces one's share in the protected good of life. But on the assumption that the unborn will die whether or not an abortion is done, killing of the unborn to save the mother's life does not reduce the child's share in this protected good. Therefore, whatever one may think from a moral point of view of such killing, jurisprudence can allow the killing of the unborn in this kind of case without either conditioning the right to life upon quality-of-life considerations or admitting that the right to life of the unborn can be weighed against and outweighed by the interests of the mother.

Of course, the laws which permitted abortion to save the life of the mother were not restricted to cases in which the alternative in view was the death of both mother and child. What justification can be given for abortion which is necessary to save the mother's life when the alternative is that the child could survive if the mother were permitted to die?

There probably are concrete cases which would be described abstractly in the preceding language—due to prejudice in favor of the mother—where an objective statement of the situation would be that while the abortion might improve the mother's physical health, there is reasonable probability that both mother and child would be saved if the killing of the child were postponed, good care were given, and the pregnancy were brought to term. Those who grant no more than the justifiability of abortion to save the mother's life do not have to justify killing in cases such as this; they can recognize that it will occur if the law permits any abortion at all, but regard killing in all such cases not as justified but as an unjustified abuse of the legal exception.

If there is not a reasonable probability that care can save both the pregnant woman and her child, then it usually is reasonably certain that prompt action will more probably save one or the other—either the child or the mother. This is usually the situation when a craniotomy is performed. If nothing is done, then there is a real and increasing probability that both the mother and the child will die. But if action is taken quickly, it is easier and more certain to save one life if the child is killed. Conceivably the mother might be cut apart to release the child, but this would take time during which the child's condition might deteriorate to the point that both would be lost.

In a case like this the mother's right to refuse treatment on her own behalf becomes an important consideration. If she does refuse treatment, then the baby cannot be killed for her benefit. Indeed, if she approves, the effort to save the baby can be made even if this increases the probability of her own death to practical certainty. The abortion will destroy the child, however, and so her agreement to accept this treatment is not sufficient in itself to justify it. The principle relevant to the child would seem to forbid harming it as a violation of its right to life.

However, this situation is odd. The probability of survival is (by hypothesis) less on the side where the right *as so far defined* lies. But the principle that no one may be attacked in a way which would violate his or her share in the protected good of life envisages a more common situation: one in which preference for one or another individual's life would depend upon discrimination on some principle other than equal protection of life itself. While this general principle of protecting all lives equally is likely to be adopted as just when no further circumstances are specified, still if it is clear that everyone would accept some restriction of the principle in special circumstances, then such a specification can be accepted by a sound jurisprudence. To see what is just, then, one must consider the problem in terms such that it can be examined behind a veil of ignorance, to ensure that temptations to discriminate on irrelevant criteria are excluded.

Let the specification of circumstances be as follows: An equal number of lives is at stake whether action (killing) is taken or not, but there is a greater probability of saving life by action (the killing of some) than by nonaction (the letting die of others). If the inviolability of life is not introduced here to bar killing and to approve letting die, then anyone putting himself or herself in the various roles would prefer that the course be taken which offers the greater probability of survival on the average. Thus fairness seems to demand that killing be permitted when it is necessary to provide the greater average protection of each person's share of life in case not all lives can be saved.

On this specified principle abortion to save the mother's life is permissible not only when otherwise both lives would be lost but also when otherwise the probability of saving at least one life would be lessened. In this case the infant killed loses its chance (which is a lower probability than the mother's chance) of life. But the loss of this share of the good of life is not a violation of the right to life of the child, since the right is only to a fair share, and fairness demands that preference be given to that life which more probably can be saved.

Of course, if the general principle which justifies abortion when the killing of the unborn is more likely to save one life is accepted, the same principle will justify the killing of the mother, even against her will, in case the child has a better chance of surviving if the mother is killed than the mother has if the child is killed or allowed to die. In case the mother must be killed to maximize the chances of one surviving, she loses some share in the good of life but her right to life is not violated, for the specified rule demands as the standard of fairness preference for the life which more probably can be saved.

What is to be done if the probabilities of survival are equal whether action (killing) is taken or not? In this case it might seem that killing must be excluded, for it will not offer any greater protection of the good of life and to permit killing would prefer the claim of one not in possession of a good to the claim of one in possession. Here, it seems, the law ought to prefer inaction. It is to be noticed that although theoretically a perfect balance between the probabilities of survival might be unlikely, in practice the uncertainty of such difficult situations is sure to make the probabilities indistinguishable in some cases.

We think that the answer to this question is that the law should not make rules which can never be enforced. The facts of a situation which is at all close will not be such as to establish that the probabilities were precisely equal. Of course, if a physician were to announce that he considered the probabilities equal and yet that he had killed the child out of preference for the life of the mother, the principles thus far stated would condemn his act as a violation of the infant's right to life.

Thus it seems that the exception which permits abortion to save the life of the mother can be justified jurisprudentially if it is taken to mean that abortion is permitted when probably otherwise both mother and child will die and when otherwise the child will more likely die than the mother. However, if the exception were formulated in these terms, it would in practice permit abortion whenever it was not clear that otherwise the child would more likely survive than the mother.

F. Abortion for Health and in Cases of Rape

What we have said thus far raises the question: What other classes of killings will be justified if abortion can be justified in the way explained? If the preceding analysis is right, then killing will be justified in other sorts of cases only if there is some further nondiscriminatory modification of the general rule that equal protection of life means that no one ought to be killed. A nondiscriminatory modification would be one which every reasonable person, considering the matter while excluding from consideration nonrelevant descriptions of the individuals involved, would be ready to accept and to apply to his or her own case.

Of course, in considering any proposed modification one ought to formulate the rule (as has been done here) in a fashion which could cut both ways. Otherwise, the intuitions of a majority, perhaps a very great majority, based upon their own distinctive interests will prevail over the interests of a minority—interests of a sort which the majority could not share in fact and may not be able to identify with imaginatively. Considerable care is needed to avoid developing rules of law which are in reality discriminatory although they seem fair enough to most people.

If abortion can be justified to save the mother's life, could it also be justified to protect her health?

Before answering this question, one ought to bear in mind that the distinction between protecting life and protecting health will not fall at the same point in a jurisprudential as it would in an ethical consideration. Ethics is concerned primarily with helping individuals arrive at sound moral judgments for themselves. Thus the question of health comes into play as soon as the danger to life is not imminent if the matter is considered from an ethical point of view.

But on a jurisprudential view the question of protecting health only arises when it is *clear* that the danger to the mother's health is not and will not become a danger to her life. If the danger to health is not one a reasonable person could and would distinguish from a threat to life itself, then abortion to save the mother's life already includes a certain margin of abortion to protect health. Thus the question which is raised in a legal context when it is asked whether abortion ought to be allowed to protect the mother's health is the question whether killing ought to be permitted to prevent harm to another when the harm will clearly be short of death.

If the matter is considered in general terms, the question is whether an individual who is the agent of no wrongful act may be attacked with deadly force in order to prevent harm to another individual—harm clearly short of death. The answer surely is obvious. No one is going to admit a rule in these terms if it is assumed that the rule would apply generally, so that anybody might be in the position of being killed to prevent harm to another.

Of course, many people would be willing to accept the principle if it were specified in qualitative terms, making clear that the individual to be killed would always be unborn. But such a qualitative specification, which makes clear that those considering the matter will not be in the role of victim, clearly is a discriminatory appeal to interest rather than an appeal to impartial intuitions about fair play. Hence, the acceptance of abortion as justified to save the mother's life along the lines sketched out above cannot be extended to abortion for reasons of health.

What about abortion in the case of rape? The state of affairs in which a woman is pregnant as a result of rape is a continuing violation of her liberty, but it is not as such a threat to her life. The situation is caused by a wrongful and unlawful act, but not by any act of the unborn individual who would be killed by the abortion. The continuation of the pregnancy does not as such violate the mother's rights or harm her except insofar as it is a continuation of an infringement upon her liberty.

There also is to some extent an alternative way of compensating the woman for her loss of liberty rather than permitting the killing of the unborn to end the infringement upon it. Society could pay for the service of continuing pregnancy in such cases in order to protect the right to life of the unborn. Such compensation would seem reasonable, especially since the law has failed to protect the woman who has been raped and so should mitigate consequential damages to her.

No principle accepted thus far would justify killing the unborn conceived by rape. A candidate for a general rule which would permit abortion in such a case might be the following: It is permissible to kill one person when there is no other way to terminate a continuing infringement upon the liberty of another, although the one killed has done nothing wrongful and although the loss of liberty might be partially compensated in some other way. Even with the last phrase excluded, we hardly think anyone would accept a general rule along these lines. Certainly, no one who opposes euthanasia must or would accept it.

Judith Jarvis Thomson proposes an imaginary situation which she uses especially to argue for the justifiability of abortion in cases of rape, even on the assumption that the unborn is a person with a right to life. One wakes up to find oneself hooked up in bed with a famous violinist, so that his blood circulates through one's own veins and is purified by one's kidneys. This has been done by a Music Lover's Society to protect the violinist's life until he recovers in nine months from a kidney ailment which will be fatal to him otherwise. One has been chosen because no other way is possible for saving the violinist's life; no one else has exactly the right blood type. The hospital director sympathizes with one's plight but claims it would be wrong to unplug the violinist, now that the situation exists, since this would kill him. However, it will only last nine months.

Thomson says it would be nice if one were to accede to the situation but denies there is any obligation to do so. Much less, she adds, would there be an obligation if the situation were to go on for nine years or for the rest of one's life rather than for nine months. Her conclusion is that while everyone has some sort of right to life, this right is not unlimited and unproblematical. One has no claim upon others for everything which one would need to stay alive. Nor, she asserts, has one any absolute inviolability, for the act of unhooking oneself from the violinist would kill him, yet this act seems clearly to be justifiable.[25]

The disanalogy between abortion in the case of rape and in Thomson's imaginary case can be pointed out. The violinist will die from a cause from which death would otherwise be inevitable had the person used to save his life not been imposed upon. The infant dies from a battery which would have been impossible had its mother not been attacked by a third party who violates both her liberty and her right to bodily intangibility. Legally, to unhook oneself from the violinst is not to kill him, for one has no legal duty to be hooked to him and unhooking oneself is not the legal cause of death. Aborting the unborn is the legal cause of its death. Thus, one's unhooking cannot possibly be a violation of the violinist's right not to be killed. But aborting could be a violation of the unborn child's right not to be killed, unless it is assumed that unlike others, the unborn child has no such right, especially because in the case of rape it came to be as a result of an unlawful act—but one in which it was in no way involved.

Thomson's analogy would be closer if one could not unhook oneself from the violinist except by dismembering him. Cutting the violinist to pieces would be the legal cause of death, and the one who did it would have committed homicide. Moreover, because the violinist was passive in the process, one could not defend one's homicidal act by claiming it to be an instance of self-defense, especially since the violence to oneself was both nondeadly and already completed. In a case like this sympathetic prosecutors probably would not prosecute, the grand jury probably would not indict, and so on. Still, one who cut the nonoffending violinist to pieces in order to unhook oneself from him would be technically guilty of murder.

This conclusion would be rendered more acceptable—and the plausibility of legally justifying abortion in the case of a pregnancy resulting from rape less so—if the analogy between the violinist and the unborn conceived in consequence of rape was made closer in several respects than Thomson makes it.

First, we should assume that the Society of Music Lovers did not purposely hook one to the violinist in order to save his life. Rather, the Society attacked one, and the violinist happened to become hooked to one as a result of their attack, although he had no part in it.

Second, we should assume that the violinist was not in such a condition that he would have otherwise died, but rather that his condition of temporary dependence rose from the attack itself, so that he is as much a victim of the attack as the person to whom he is hooked.

Third, we should assume that the burden of being hooked to the violinist is not greater than that of pregnancy; one can very likely go about one's normal activities, not be compelled to stay in a hospital bed for nine months, much less for nine years or the rest of one's life. (Thomson here perhaps alludes to the fact that a parent has a long-term responsibility for children, but this long-term responsibility is not analogous to being hooked to the violinist and need not be accepted by the woman who conceives as a result of rape.)

Fourth, we should assume that one's condition of being hooked to the violinist was not a unique state of affairs, but an instance of a common type—that people regularly become hooked to others in this way, but usually only as a result of an act to which they consented—except that one is hooked to the violinist without the usual prior consent on one's own part.

With all of these modifications in Thomson's analogy, would it seem reasonable that one be regarded as legally justified in cutting the violinist to pieces in order to unhook from him? We do not think so. Moreover, such a justification could not be established by any principle of traditional Anglo-American jurisprudence. Rather, the proper outcome of a trial for murder would be guilty, but with considerable mitigation of punishment due to the extenuating circumstance that one was trying to free oneself from a condition into which one had been put by a most grave violation of one's liberty and bodily intangibility.

Our conclusion thus is that apart from cases of killing in war, self-defense, and law enforcement, individuals can be regarded as having an equal right not to be killed which protects their fair share in the good of life. Abortion to save the mother's life can be legally permitted on principles which are both reasonable and so narrow that they do not even extend to the justification of abortion in other very difficult cases. The rationale for abortion to save the mother's life need only be that this action carries with it the *greater probability* of saving at least one life—that of the mother. If abortion does not do this, it is not really "to save the life of the mother," and laws forbidding abortion except to save the life of the mother—such as existed in the United States until 1973—strictly construed would not have permitted it. As long as no discriminatory principle is introduced, the old statutes provide no precedent for killing which is not required to maximize the chances of survival of some involved in a difficult situation. Thus they provide no precedent for nonvoluntary euthanasia, and so the abortion permitted by the old statute can be consistently admitted as just by those who oppose the legalization of nonvoluntary euthanasia.

G. Justifiable Killing in Cases of Necessity

The conclusion reached in the previous section might be challenged by proponents of euthanasia. In addition to cases of abortion to save the life of the mother there can be other cases in which the killing of someone who has done nothing to offend the law might be necessary to save the lives of others. Like cases ought to be treated alike, and so the killing of some members of a group ought to be considered justifiable whenever such homicide carries with it a greater probability of saving life. Might not a legal rule adequate to justify such killing also justify nonvoluntary euthanasia?

A consideration of some examples and the formulation of a rule adequate to cover such cases will show that the justification of killing in such cases need provide no general justification for killing in the public interest. Considerations of fairness alone will provide sufficient rationale for a legal rule permitting as justified that killing which might be required in cases of necessity, at least to the extent that Anglo-American law has even approached admitting the justifiability of such killing.

There are few real cases which might be covered by such a rule of law. But there are some plausible, imaginary cases which also can be considered to show the adequacy and limits of the rule we shall formulate. We consider the actual cases first.

In 1841 a sailor, acting under orders of the mate, threw passengers overboard to lighten a floundering lifeboat in the icy North Atlantic. The survivors were subsequently picked up and brought to Philadelphia. The mate and other crew members quickly dispersed, to leave this one sailor, Holmes, to be arrested and tried.

The grand jury refused to indict for murder, so Holmes was tried for manslaughter. The judge told the jury that in a case of this sort seamen must give way to passengers except for those sailors needed to operate the boat. Then, if there were time to do so, the persons to be thrown overboard should be chosen by lot. This had not been done. The jury found Holmes guilty but recommended mercy, which he surely deserved because he had acted responsibly throughout the ordeal. He was sentenced to six months at hard labor in addition to the time he had already spent in jail waiting trial.[26]

About forty years later four sailors were adrift in the Atlantic. After about three weeks, when their food and water had run out, two of the men, Dudley and Stephens, killed the cabin boy, who was the youngest and weakest of the four. The three consumed the body and survived for several more days, when they were finally rescued. The survivors were taken to England, and the two tried for murder.

The jury found as to the facts by a special verdict that the men probably would not have survived had they not killed the boy, that the boy probably would have been the first to die, that at the time of the killing there was no reasonable prospect of relief, that the accused killed the boy because they thought all would starve unless someone were killed—thus that the killing was necessary and was done out of necessity to save life, but that there was no greater necessity to kill the boy than any of the other three men.

This verdict was referred to the Queen's Bench Division for a judicial decision as to the relevant law. The judges found that the law does not justify killing even when necessary to save life and judged the accused guilty of murder. They were subsequently reprieved, and their sentence commuted to six months imprisonment without hard labor.[27]

The defense of necessity which is admitted at common law permits a finding of not guilty in respect to an act done in violation of criminal law under the following conditions: (1) the act is done in an emergency situation under the pressure of physical circumstances, not human pressure; (2) compliance with the criminal law in the circumstances would have resulted in greater harm than was reasonably expected from the violation; (3) the situation was not brought about by the fault of the one who did the act in question. The reason for permitting this defense is not that the actor lacks criminal intent, nor was it traditionally that the law would not be effective in such circumstances in deterring the forbidden behavior. Rather, this defense was allowed because the purpose of the law is to protect and promote the human goods of society at large and of its members; if in an unusual case conformity to the law would defeat its very purpose, then the letter of the law must be set aside in order to fulfill its purpose.[28]

A classic example of necessity which is found throughout the philosophical tradition is the case in which the law forbids the opening of a city's gates between sunset and sunrise, but the city's militia is pursued by a more powerful enemy force and seeks admission during the night. The gates are to be opened to save the militia who can better defend the city from inside its walls than from outside them. As in this case, the defense of necessity can be invoked only when the peril is immediate and there is no alternative. Also, the defendant's belief that the act is necessary is not controlling; the court will judge the belief reasonable or not and the harm avoided sufficient or not. Moreover, if the law already specifies what is to be done in the circumstances, then one cannot defend violating its specification by pleading necessity.

This was the defense which the British court rejected in the case of Dudley and Stephens. That the defense might apply to other kinds of cases was admitted, but to the taking of life only in the case of self-defense. And the court denied that the pressure on Dudley and Stephens was what the law ever had called necessity. Self-preservation may not be regarded as a higher and prior law. No one can judge the comparative value of lives. In this case the youngest, the weakest, and the most unresisting was chosen to be killed. There definitely was no more necessity to kill him than one of the grown men.[29]

An imaginary case is that of the cave explorers. A group of explorers is trapped in a cave in immediate peril of drowning from rising waters. There is one way out, but an extraordinarily fat man pushes into it, becomes stuck, and so blocks the exit of all the rest. The group has sufficient explosive to blast the fat man out of the exit while every other effort to dislodge him fails. One may assume either that the fat man is headed out of the cave and will survive although his larger number of companions will perish if he is not blasted out, or that he is headed inward so that all will perish if nothing is done. Here the life to be sacrificed is clearly specified by the circumstances. Can killing the fat man be justified in either case?

Other imaginary examples are a case in which the only way to stop an electrician from mistakenly throwing a switch which will bring about a disaster is to kill the electrician, thus to save countless others; a case in which drowning persons struggle for a plank, perhaps with one already in possession; and a case in which one mountaineer must be cut loose to prevent a whole party or a greater number from falling to their deaths.

Various rules of law might be proposed to guide action in cases such as these. Statutes have formulated the common law defense of necessity to some extent but do not clearly indicate a rational principle for applying the theory to cases involving the taking of life, although they do not absolutely preclude the possibility of justifying homicide by necessity.[30] What we wish to propose here is not necessarily the widest justifiable rule which would permit the taking of life, but a rule wide enough to cover the relevant cases and general enough to exclude discrimination. Such a formulation will make clear what must be admitted by opponents of euthanasia who regard abortion to save the mother's life and the killing in analogous cases of necessity as justified, and thus will show whether or not the rule which is necessary to permit these killings also will permit euthanasia.

We propose the following as an apparently adequate rule. An act which otherwise would be considered homicide shall be judged justified if (1) two or more persons are involved in a single state of affairs; (2) this state of affairs was not caused by any wrongful act or omission of any person; (3) the act which caused death was believed to be necessary and would have been regarded by a reasonable person in the circumstances to be necessary to alter the state of affairs in a manner which would prevent the deaths of everyone involved, or of a larger number of those involved, or of an equal number whose chances of survival were greater than the chances of survival of those who were killed; (4) the intent of the person or persons acting was to maximize the average probability of survival of all involved; (5) the principle by which the person or persons killed were selected was settled either by the necessities of the state of affairs, or by the antecedent duty of those killed to lay down their lives if necessary for the protection of the others, or by lot, or by some principle accepted by all who were killed, or by some combination of these factors; and (6) either (a) a hearing was held by a suitable court of law in which due process was accorded to those to be killed and a judgment reached that the preceding conditions were met, or (b) a trial of those doing the killing is conducted afterward on a charge of murder or a lesser charge and the defense establishes by preponderance of evidence that the preceding conditions were met.

The statement of the first condition avoids any qualitative discrimination among the persons involved. Nothing is said about whether they are old or young, good or bad, beautiful or ugly, strong or weak.

The second condition might be thought to be included to exclude abortion in the case of rape. But this is not the point. We are narrowing the rule to avoid admitting cases in which emergency circumstances might be engineered in order to allow as justifiable killings which otherwise would be murder.

The third condition embodies the reason underlying the justification of killing in these conditions. Most people desire to protect their own share of the good of life, and fairness demands that there be no discrimination of some in favor of others. But in case all lives cannot be saved, rational persons would desire to secure the best chance of protecting their own lives and the lives of others. Thus the best chance becomes the fair share which the law must protect. The rule proposed accomplishes this and so appears to be just.

The fourth condition merely specifies that the mental element of the act must be in accord with the justification, for if it were not, then the killing would have been done with murderous intent and ought not legally to be justified. In practice, excluding murderous intent directs attention to the principle which justifies killing out of necessity and thus limits the killing to that which the rule accepts as justifiable.

The fifth condition specifies all the ways of selecting those to be killed which appear to be fair. In some cases the circumstances indicate who must be killed; this is so in abortion to save the mother's life. In other cases antecedent duty is the determining factor; the court in *Holmes* indicated that the unnecessary sailors should have been sacrificed before the passengers. In other cases selection might be by lot, as the court also suggested in *Holmes*. Or, finally, those involved might all agree upon some principle of selection— for example, that the first person in the lifeboat to stop bailing would be the first to be thrown overboard and so on.

The sixth condition of our proposed rule envisages cases in which, as in most abortions, there would be time to carry out a hearing before the act was done, and other cases in which there would be no time to adjudicate the issue until after the fact. A trial of each case of killing justified by necessity does not seem an unreasonably burdensome requirement, for such cases must be discriminated carefully from those not justified. The burden of proving the deed otherwise criminal would remain with the prosecution; the defense would bear the burden of showing necessity, but only the burden of proving it reasonably credible, not the heavier burden of establishing it beyond a reasonable doubt, since innocence is to be presumed unless guilt is proven.

The rule we have formulated covers the verdict in the case of Holmes. Sailors not required to operate the boat should have been sacrificed before the passengers, and then the passengers only to the extent necessary to save the rest and by a fair principle of selection. One could argue that the heaviest passengers should have been thrown overboard first, since fewer persons would thus be killed to lighten the boat sufficiently. The verdict in the case of Dudley and Stephens also is covered if it is assumed that there really was no more necessity to kill the cabinboy than one of the adults.

In this case, too, an argument could be made for killing the biggest individual, since the rations would be thus increased to the greatest extent possible with only a single death. However, if one assumes that the average probability of survival really was greater by the killing of the cabinboy—the supposition would be that he was so far gone that he probably would not have survived in any case—then the rule would justify killing the boy. The court obviously did not believe the latter supposition, and on the evidence its judgment seems correct.

The case of the cave explorers presents fewer problems than the real cases. The fat man is designated by the circumstances, and the case always is sketched in such a way that more will survive by blowing the fat man out of the way than by refraining from the act. Even if the fat man is assumed to be headed out of the cave so that he would otherwise survive, the average probability of survival is increased if he is blasted out.

In the struggle for the plank the drowning persons if in possession have no problem of justifying the repulsing of attempts to take the plank away—this is simply self-defense. In many such examples, too, the fact that maintaining possession of the means of survival does not itself kill the one repulsed must be taken into account. Presumably someone repulsed might be able to find other flotation.

The mountaineer cases present no problem when the situation designates who is to be allowed to fall, whose line must be cut. In some such cases there may be accepted responsibilities which will determine what may and may not be done in case of accident. These rules would be binding.

The rule which we have outlined is sufficiently broad to cover abortion to save the life of the mother, but not other cases of abortion. It also would cover the actual and imaginary cases in which killing might be permitted upon a plausible justification based on necessity. But this rule clearly does not cover nonvoluntary euthanasia.

The killing which would be permitted by the rule would be limited to that done when people find themselves in tragic circumstances in which not all can survive. In these circumstances killing would be permitted only to the extent that it could be justified by a rationale based on protecting the good of life fairly to the maximum possible extent. By contrast, the alleged justification for nonvoluntary euthanasia is that it would be in the public interest in cutting the cost of caring for the dependent. This interest, if allowed to prevail, would sacrifice the lives of those killed to the economic interests of the public at large.

From our consideration of this problem and the other cases of justifiable killing in previous sections we conclude that none of the cases in which the law has permitted killing provides a plausible precedent for nonvoluntary euthanasia. All of these cases do have a regard for the public interest, but each limits killing by other necessary conditions which would not be fulfilled if the dependent were killed to cut the burden of caring for them.

Moreover, opponents of euthanasia are by no means inconsistent if they admit as jurisprudentially justified killing in war, in self-defense, as capital punishment, and in abortion (and analogous cases of necessity) where killing maximizes the average chances of survival. Even if some such killings are regarded as immoral, they can be accepted by a system of law without unfairness to those who are killed.

Of course, our argument in this chapter has not shown that nonvoluntary euthanasia necessarily is unjust. All we have shown thus far is that the *argument* for nonvoluntary euthanasia fails to the extent that it is based upon claiming other types of legally accepted killing as precedents to justify this type of killing. A position supported by a bad argument might still be true. In chapter eight we directly confront the question: Can the killing of certain persons who pose no threat to the rights of others and the rule of law be justified, on the ground that they would be better off dead and that the public interest would be served by killing them? Our conclusion will be that such killing cannot be justified.

8: Nonvoluntary Euthanasia and Justice

A. Introductory Considerations

In chapter seven, section A, we summarized an argument, based on the public interest, which is offered for legalizing nonvoluntary euthanasia. Part of the argument was that the kinds of killing generally regarded as justifiable by Americans, including those who oppose euthanasia, seem to provide a precedent for killing those who are a burden upon society, in the public interest of cutting the costs of this burden. In the remainder of chapter seven we examined the various kinds of killing which have been considered juris-prudentially justified in Anglo-American law. We found, in summary, that all of the cases in which killing has been legal until now have been instances in which killing is necessary either to protect the rights of other persons and the rule of law from being overridden by brute force or to provide the best average possibility of survival when some members of a group must be sacrificed to save the lives of others.

The public interests invoked in these justifications of killing are very specific ones. Neither of these justifications provides a rationale on which euthanasia might be justified. Neither would euthanasia prevent acts which if unopposed would violate rights protected by law nor would it vindicate the rule of law against those who reject its authority. Nor would euthanasia killing serve the common interest by protecting to the maximum extent possible every individual's fair share in the good of life when not all locked together in some tragic situation can survive.

The rationale for permitting euthanasia is different. Presumably this type of killing ends lives which are no longer worth living. The assumption is that sometimes individuals would be better off dead, in other words, that sometimes a quick and painless death is preferable to continued life, and that continued life in such cases would be a disvalue. Nonvoluntary euthanasia thus is defended precisely as a form of *euthanasia*—that is, on the basis that it would be beneficial, not harmful, to the individuals killed. And the liberty to stand aloof of those who abhor such killing is said to be outweighed by the public interest in cutting the costs of caring for certain classes of individuals, especially those who require permanent care in institutions at public expense.

As in previous chapters we are concerned here with the question of what the law ought to be, not with the question of the morality of nonvoluntary euthanasia apart from the law. Also, the subject here is whether killing ought to be legalized, not to what extent treatment ought to be legally required. What the law should demand in the way of treatment for noncompetent individuals will be considered in chapter nine.

Still, from a legal point of view homicide can be committed by omission as well as by positive behavior. In certain hospitals at present defective babies are not given treatment with the expectation that they will die. It has been argued that there is a legal duty in at least some such cases to give the treatment which is not given and that a basis exists for prosecution.[1] While homicide by omission might be difficult to prove beyond reasonable doubt, the distinction between such homicide and homicide by positive behavior is irrelevant to the questions of principle to be discussed here.

Thus what follows is relevant to any cases in which nonvoluntary euthanasia is carried on, whether by positive behavior or by omission. Some proponents of euthanasia have asserted that omission avoids the problem of the consent of the person killed.[2] This is not true in general. It is true only if one omits what is not a legal duty or omits without the intent of bringing about death. If one fails to fulfill a legal duty to someone with the intent that the individual will thereby die, one commits homicide by omission.

Glanville Williams points out that law—in particular, a law forbidding homicide—is a social necessity; society would collapse if people could murder with impunity. However, he maintains, there are forms of murder or near murder, including infanticide and abortion, which it is not socially necessary to forbid. These, he holds, are forbidden as a result of a "philosophical attitude," not for reasons of public security. And Williams strives to convince his readers that euthanasia can be condemned only by a religiously grounded belief in the sanctity of life. He thinks that this fact is sufficient to require that the prohibition of euthanasia be removed from criminal law.[3]

Of course, there have been societies in which types of killing have been legally permitted which are forbidden by Anglo-American law. And it may well be the case that Anglo-American law is as solicitous as it is to protect human life for reasons having historical roots in Christian thought. However, many other elements of our criminal law arguably have the same religious roots—for example, the solicitude of law to avoid convicting the innocent. Such a policy perhaps is not required by social necessity or public security. Even so, its derivation from Christian conceptions can hardly be sufficient to require that this policy be abandoned, and a policy making for greater efficiency in law enforcement be adopted in its stead.

In this chapter we argue that nonvoluntary euthanasia cannot be jurispru-dentially justified. The classification of individuals' lives by qualitative stan-dards which would be essential in any program of nonvoluntary euthanasia would violate the requirement of justice that no one be denied equal protec-tion of the laws. We are not arguing here against nonvoluntary euthanasia on the assumption that human life is absolutely inviolable. Opponents of such killing need not take that tack. Instead, we argue simply that since a law of homicide is indispensable, justice requires that it protect the lives of all.

Social necessity and security as a practical matter demand that the class of those to be protected include all whose being killed would create conflict and significant disturbance of the peace. But another principle requires that those protected by the law of homicide not be limited to this special group, and this principle, despite what Glanville Williams says, is by no means a religious one. Equal protection of the laws demands that the prohibition of homicide extend from the protection of the strong and those with strong friends to the weak and friendless. If laws are not extended to benefit the weak and friend-less, then they regulate power in the interest of the powerful, and the concept of what is fair becomes wholly unnecessary.

The concept of fairness which underlies equal protection does not alto-gether exclude rational classifications from the laws. Rational classification is present when a law extends equally to those who are similarly related to the good or the harm which the law is intended to promote or to prevent. How-ever, classifications which exclude any person from the equal protection of basic human and civil rights are highly suspect and can seldom if ever be defended as rational.[4]

When a law aims at the promotion of some good, the principle of rational classification often is held to permit the exclusion of some persons, even though they might be able to benefit, since there always are various sorts of limits to what can be done to promote any good. However, the law of homi-cide does not protect human life in every possible way. It does not require, for example, that subsistence be provided to all who are in need or that a rescue effort be carried out for all who are in peril. The law of homicide requires only a forbearance: that every person refrain from killing others. The principle of rational classification thus cannot be satisfied in the case of the law of homicide if some persons are excluded from the protection it offers as if there were a practical impossibility in extending this protection to every person.

As we have explained in chapter seven, the principle of rational classifica-tion does permit the exclusion from the protection of the law of homicide of those whose acts gravely threaten legally protected rights. It also permits the exception by which some may be killed to maximize the average chance of survival. But in general every individual is similarly situated in respect to the good of life which is protected by the law of homicide's prohibition of killing. Therefore, in general the law of homicide is fair only if it extends beyond what is socially necessary to protect the lives of all persons, including those who are so weak and friendless that someone's killing them would not detract from the security of society.

To overcome this argument, proponents of nonvoluntary euthanasia must do more than show that Anglo-American legal conceptions of justice, which are embodied in the requirement of equal protection of the laws, have religious roots. Whatever the roots of such conceptions, they are an essential part of the consensus upon which the legitimacy of American government rests. Furthermore, no advocate of euthanasia has challenged the requirement of equal protection of the laws. Thus it is incumbent upon proponents of nonvoluntary euthanasia to show that this practice would not involve the mischief which a fair homicide law seeks to prevent: unjust infringement upon the good which each member of society has in the secure possession of his or her own particular life.

While proponents of the legalization of nonvoluntary euthanasia have not explicitly formulated their arguments in this framework, the manner in which they argue for their proposals shows that they are seeking to meet the requirement of equal protection of the laws with respect to the law of homicide. There are two main ways in which it may be argued that the euthanasia killing of an individual would not infringe upon the good of life in a way which violates justice.

First, it may be argued that the killing is a benefit rather than a harm, for life in the circumstances is a burden rather than a boon. No one is deprived of anything unfairly if something harmful is taken away. Thus if nonvoluntary euthanasia takes away life which is no longer of worth, it is justified. In other words, the argument is that no one harms others by killing them when those killed are better off dead.

Second, it may be argued that certain individuals who are members of the human species nevertheless are not members of society and cannot be legal persons, for they fall short of the conditions necessary for an individual to be a person. This second argument was accepted by the United States Supreme Court with respect to the unborn when the Court declared that the unborn are not legal persons, although the Court concealed the significance of its holding by suggesting that the unborn are only potentially alive and by ignoring the fact that unborn individuals are members of the human species.[5]

Sometimes proponents of nonvoluntary euthanasia seem to propose both that those to be killed would not be harmed and that they are nonpersons, a view suggested by the frequent use of the analogy between such killing and the disposal of animals. Very seldom do proponents of nonvoluntary euthanasia appeal mainly to societal interests in killing some individuals without trying to show either that this killing would benefit those killed or that the killing might be considered the disposal of substandard individuals who can be considered nonpersons.

B. Proposed Criteria for Denying Equal Protection

Marvin Kohl argues that killing can be a benefit rather than a harm and that euthanasia should be considered justified in case it is a benefit. He does not attempt any general statement of the conditions under which someone who does not volunteer to be killed would be better off dead, although he does attempt to deal with the objection that one cannot tell by empirical evidence that a person who does volunteer would really be benefited by being killed. In this latter case one has the evidence provided by the individual's own expressed preference.

Kohl provides hardly any description of those for whom death without their own consent would be, as he calls it, "the kindest possible treatment." He offers only an example of a child born with some severe defect such as blindness or deafness, with death not imminent as long as care is provided, such that "although unable to move a muscle, he suffers no pain."[6] (Kohl does not explain how anyone would know that someone unable to move a muscle was suffering no pain.) Kohl carefully stipulates that unwanted kindness is still kindness, just as unwanted fire is still fire.[7] Thus he seems to imply what he surely would not assert: that not only nonvoluntary but even involuntary—that is, explicitly refused—euthanasia might be justified, in case someone killed those who would be better off dead but who stubbornly refused to accept what was in their own best interests.

Glanville Williams clearly accepts a quality-of-life justification for euthanasia. He holds that an assertion of the value of human life "in the absence of all the activities that give meaning to life, and in the face of the disintegration of personality that so often follows from prolonged agony, will not stand scrutiny."[8] This formulation is provided in a context in which Williams has voluntary euthanasia in mind. But in another context he urges that it cannot be right to save spina bifida babies; the quality-of-life description Williams gives is that such children may be paralyzed and incontinent or retarded, or all three together.[9]

A. R. Jonsen and others report discussions at a 1974 conference held in California which apparently reached substantial agreement that life-saving treatment is harmful to an infant if it cannot participate even minimally in human experience, and that such an infant might be killed under various conditions—for example, if it is affected by gross physical anomalies and is unwanted by the parents and unneeded by society.[10] What does "participation in human experience'' mean? The authors say that it is a matter of presence or absence of a capacity, not a matter of degree of variation from a statistical norm, and that the capacity is "to respond affectively and cognitively to human attention and to develop toward initiation of communication with others." The authors refuse to quantify or to describe in detail the relevant levels of activity but think that a baby with Down's syndrome would meet the criteria while one with trisomy 18 would not.[11]

Richard A. McCormick had argued for quality-of-life criteria for letting babies die by suggesting potentiality for human relationships as a criterion. When it is thought that an individual totally lacks this potentiality or that it will be wholly subordinated to the struggle for survival, life can be said "to have achieved its potential"—that is, to be worthless.[12] Jonsen and his coauthors quoted McCormick, and the latter has returned the compliment by quoting from their conclusions and endorsing them as similar to his own proposal, which he is willing to formulate in terms of potentiality for "meaningful life." He admits the latter phrase to be packed with implications; he insists that the individual still has a value but urges that life may not be worthwhile if the individual does not stand to gain from it.[13] McCormick writes in terms of letting die rather than of killing and is more concerned with moral than with legal considerations. Still, his approach is one which in a legal perspective would justify killing if it justifies the intentional bringing about of death by calculated omission.

The preceding approaches do not deny the personhood of those to be killed, but rather claim that killing in some cases makes no difference to an individual or is a real benefit. The alternative approach is to deny the personhood of those to be killed and in this way to remove them from the scope of the law forbidding homicide.

Joseph Fletcher is an outstanding example of those who prefer this approach. He has written on the matter more than once.

In 1968 Fletcher maintained that humanness requires self-awareness, conscious relationship to others, and rationality sufficient to support some initiative. He held the difference between man and brute to be a matter of degree, but still a real difference. On this basis he maintained that one who would prolong the life of an infant afflicted with Down's syndrome would be guilty, but not one who killed such an infant: "True guilt arises only from an offense against a person, and a Down's is not a person."[14]

In 1972 Fletcher proposed various indicators of humanhood, among them a standard of minimal intelligence: "Any individual of the species *homo sapiens* who falls below the I.Q. 40-mark in a standard Stanford-Binet test, amplified if you like by other tests, is questionably a person; below the 20-mark, not a person." This would hold either before minimal intelligence is achieved or after it is lost irretrievably.[15] By 1974, although not retracting his previous statements, Fletcher claimed that neocortical function is the chief criterion of humanhood. He does not mention that this necessary condition is hardly sufficient for the performances he still considers necessary for real humanhood.[16]

Michael Tooley denies that infants at or shortly after birth are persons—that is, human individuals with a serious right to life. Tooley dismisses as irrelevant to the consideration of their rights the fact that such individuals are living members of the human species. He claims that an organism is not a person until it has a concept of itself as a continuing subject of experience. What has such a self-concept to do with having rights? Tooley claims that there is a conceptual relationship between having rights and being able to desire that others respect one's rights. But why should this be the case? Tooley says that the obligations of others corresponding to one's rights are conditional, since an individual can waive rights. This position, however, demands too much, for it would mean that when an individual is irrational or asleep or has been duped into not wanting something, then the individual has no right to it. So Tooley modified his requirement to avoid such cases. But he maintains that one who has never had the appropriate desires can have no rights; otherwise, he maintains, a reproductive system would embody a right to life which would render contraception as much a violation of rights as abortion or infanticide.[17]

H. Tristram Engelhardt, Jr., argued in 1973 that infants with defects might be considered persons with a negative quality of life, such that they would have a right to die.[18] By 1976 Engelhardt argued that life is only a value, not a principle of morality, and that only persons who are moral agents deserve respect such that treatment of them must not be contingent upon their value. If this position is accepted, Engelhardt says, then "it would follow that we do not have obligations to fetuses, infants, animals, and the very senile in the way that we do to normal adult humans, for only normal adult humans are persons in the strict sense of being necessarily objects of respect." Englehardt refers to Kant as authority for this position but supplies no real argument for it; he simply assumes that rights belong to members of a community and that no one should count as a member of a community who cannot function as such.[19]

C. Critique of the Proposed Criteria

In appraising such proposals as attempts to show how killing some individuals would not violate equal protection of the law of homicide, one must bear in mind what proponents of euthanasia must show. It is not enough for them to establish that many individuals are suffering from conditions which are bad, deplorable, or pitiable. No one wants a defective baby in one sense: Everyone prays or hopes for a sound and healthy one. Similarly, no one supposes that senility in itself is a desirable condition. Some might argue that an exceptionally high intelligence is not an unmixed blessing, but no one thinks it is a cause for regret if one's intelligence is in the normal rather than in the exceptionally low range. Hence, everyone confronted with descriptions of various wretched individuals will be saddened by their condition.

But advocates of euthanasia must show that some individuals would be better off dead, or that they are nonpersons. Merely showing that people are in bad shape does not prove that they would be better off dead nor does showing that some individuals are so defective that they seem alien to human activities prove that they are nonpersons.

Furthermore, proponents of nonvoluntary euthanasia will say quite sincerely that if they themselves had been or were in the deplorable condition of some other individual, then they should not have wanted to live and would not have minded being killed. If voluntary euthanasia were in question, willingness to be killed would be decisive with respect to the individual expressing it. But liberty precisely means that individuals are entitled to be unwilling where others are willing, and to be willing where others are unwilling. And so proponents of euthanasia must show by some nonarbitrary principle that those who are to be killed nonvoluntarily would be better off dead or are not persons. Otherwise, the practice of nonvoluntary euthanasia would amount to no more than either the imposition upon those to be killed of the subjective preferences and value judgments of others, or the imposition upon them of the world views of others who consider themselves qualified to judge that some human individuals really are not persons.

Glanville Williams is no doubt sincere in saying that he would not have minded being killed had he been in the condition of a spina bifida child, paralyzed and incontinent, or mentally retarded, or all three.[20] But the question remains whether he is entitled to impose this personal preference upon children who happen to be in that condition. Richard Lamerton objects strenuously to the common tendency of advocates of euthanasia to classify damaged persons as vegetables; he also points out that in many cases the prospects of an individual depend very heavily upon the nursing care which is given.[21] This obviously is so with respect to many spina bifida babies.

Jonsen and his coauthors report the agreement of participants in a conference that life is meaningless if there is not potential for human relationships and some prospect of individual initiative. They admit the vagueness of the criterion. John A. Robertson points out that in many cases the potentiality for communication is not necessarily excluded by congenital conditions but is rather blocked by inadequate care. He also urges that there is no ground to demonstrate that an unproductive existence is necessarily unhappy. Even in the most extreme cases, in which an individual's prospect is life in a crib in an institution, no one else has a valid basis to conclude that if the individual were able to speak, consent to being killed would be given. The standards of others perhaps have little relevance for such individuals. "Life, and life alone, whatever its limitations, might be of sufficient worth to him."[22]

Even if one grants McCormick that some infants have achieved their potential if they have no prospect of participating in human relationships—whatever precisely this means—there remains a question why having achieved their potential would be a relevant criterion for denying that such infants have some good life to be protected. Many middle-aged men perhaps have achieved their potential, are more a burden than a consolation to those with whom they live, and in later years produce nothing equal in quality to what they produced when young. Some people might say that such men have achieved their potential and no longer enjoy human relationships of any significance. Even if this were conceded, it does not seem to be a reasonable ground on which to modify the law of homicide. McCormick can only be sure that someone does not stand to gain from life by assuming that his personal conceptions of a life worth living must apply to others.

Kohl argues that people should be free to choose to die. But when an individual is not capable of choice, Kohl thinks that a responsible individual or, if necessary, the state should be allowed to choose for him or her. In Kohl's view this application of substituted judgment would be in accord with libertarian principles. His explanation of this claim is so remarkable that it deserves quotation:

> The fundamental value of liberty is that it diminishes the risk of injustice and gives men the sense of dignity they need. It is not always easy to know when a person is not free to choose, nor should the transfer of this obligation be taken lightly. However, when fanatical insistence on consent only brings with it continued or increased misery, and when it is clear that neither justice nor dignity is being served, then we must choose and act on behalf of the interests of the individual. It may be concluded, therefore, that this part of the L-P [libertarian] proposal is consistent with the principle of beneficence, and that all men concerned about human welfare ought to subscribe to it.[23]

Kohl seems oblivious to the fact that liberty is important because it allows other people to have a different theory of morality from his and a different conception of what is kindly.

Liberty for Kohl is merely a means to ends which he happens to approve; practical resistance to this reduction of liberty—and also of justice—to Kohl's conception of beneficence seems to him fanaticism. This is the reason why Kohl is able to argue at length in favor of nonvoluntary euthanasia as kind treatment without it ever occurring to him that he ought to attempt to show that everyone must agree about what is kind and agree with him in regarding euthanasia as kind. People who would consider anyone else's killing them a violation of their rights and dignity no doubt would seem fanatics to Kohl.

Engelhardt's earlier position, which admitted that those he proposes to kill are persons, appealed to lawsuits which attempted to establish a cause of action for wrongful life. Engelhardt did not point out that the courts declined to hold that causing life is a tort, because, as was expressly stated in some cases, there is no rational way of comparing life with defects to nonexistence and demonstrating the latter preferable to the former.[24] A court cannot grant an award in a lawsuit unless there is a rational way to determine the existence and worth in damages of a harm done.

There has been considerable discussion in recent years about the possibility of setting a monetary value upon human lives—for example, in the context of discussions about whether more money should be spent on preventing disasters than upon aiding victims after disasters occur. With respect to such discussions it is important to notice that valuations reflect only the choices people make; they provide no objective standard which has unarguable validity as a principle for making quality-of-life judgments. Indeed, even in the economic sphere attempts to solve problems in which human life is at stake—ordinarily by being at greater or lesser risk of accident—run into the difficulty that there is no accepted way of making interpersonal comparisons of utility; such attempts also must disregard nonquantifiable interests and concerns which nevertheless may be taken into account by individuals in setting their own preferences.[25]

Fletcher's various and inconsistent proposals for excluding some human individuals from the status of personhood obviously are arbitrary; the very inconsistency of these proposals reveals their arbitrariness. Fletcher's assertion that a Down's is not a person also is arbitrary. It would not be accepted by individuals with Down's syndrome who could read and understand what Fletcher says about them.[26] Similarly, Fletcher gives no reason for accepting his view that those with an IQ 40-mark or below are "doubtfully persons." Evidently Fletcher has a special standard of personhood which seems as obvious to him as Kohl's personal conception of kindness seems to him.

Tooley apparently confuses the fact that one can waive certain of one's rights *if one is legally competent*—the rights which one can waive do *not* include the right not to be a victim of homicide—with a quite different proposition: one must be in a position to claim one's rights to have any rights at all. He asserts, not the latter proposition, but only a weakened and qualified version of it. But there are no reasons given for not adding further qualifications to the ones which Tooley admits.

Tooley's suggestion that affirming rights for every human individual would imply a right of a reproductive system not to be contraceptively interfered with is a pure figment of his own imagination. No one has ever posited such a right, and the law of homicide is concerned only with those who are individuals and members of the human species. Why species membership should be irrelevant to having rights Tooley never explains. Tooley, it appears, decided that the unborn and infants are not to be regarded as persons, and on this basis he formulated and stipulated a definition of "person" suited to achieve his purpose.

Engelhardt explicitly appeals to Kant's philosophy for authority to support his own position. Kant's philosophy is only one among many others, and it is one which hardly anyone today attempts to defend. Many criticisms can be made of it.[27] There seems to be no reason suddenly to accept it as a reasonable basis for denying the personhood of large classes of human individuals who are not normal adult humans. Once more, as with Tooley, one has the strong suspicion that Engelhardt's real reason for using the criterion he adopts is that it yields the conclusions he wants.

The diversity of proposals for declaring some human individuals nonpersons points up the arbitrariness of all such proposals. They reflect the special ideals and/or interests of those who advance them. Even if a substantial segment of society were to adopt one or another such proposal, it would remain an expression of the bias of that segment, an expression of its particular world view, from which other members of the society remain at liberty to dissent. Why should it be assumed that those who happen to be incapable of joining in the disagreement by either assenting or dissenting would agree with the world view which would make them nonpersons, extinguish all the legal rights they now enjoy, and smooth the way for themselves to be killed?

As has been pointed out often enough by others, the declaration that some human individuals are not persons is a prelude to mistreatment and killing, for it generates an attitude of indifference in which what is done seems no more significant than what is acceptable in the treatment of animals. Advocates of euthanasia often appeal to the mercy humans show to animals as a ground for permitting nonvoluntary euthanasia of humans. Animals, of course, are not members of society, and they are not presumed by law to have any rights. Hence, law allows human beings to deal with animals according to human conceptions of what is beneficial or harmful to animals (and in the interests of humans). The proponent of nonvoluntary euthanasia similarly wishes to deal with some human individuals as if they were not persons, so that they can be treated in accord with the conceptions of others who decide that these "nonpersons" would be better off dead—or that it is expedient for society to be relieved of the burden of treating them as persons.

D. Arguments Based on an Alleged Public Interest

In chapter seven, section A, we reviewed economic arguments put forward by Sackett, Lennox, Robert Williams, Trubo, Glanville Williams, and Marvin Kohl which might seem to provide a foundation for overriding the liberty to stand aloof of those who abhor killing by establishing a substantial state interest in ridding society of the burden of providing for members who are not and never will be productive. Economic arguments of this sort do not themselves hinge essentially upon quality-of-life considerations, but because the proposed killing is advocated as a type of euthanasia, quality-of-life and economic considerations are intermingled both by authors who emphasize economic considerations and by those who minimize them.

In considering economic arguments one must distinguish between factors which might set an upper limit to the legal duty to provide care for some individuals—a matter we shall consider in chapter nine—and conditions which are urged as good reasons for killing some individuals. Omitting care amounts to homicide by omission only if there is a legal duty to provide care. Glanville Williams's fantasy of individuals living to one thousand years of age and requiring extensive care through most of this life span projects a situation in which it would be impossible to provide the needed care. In such a situation no legal duty to provide care could fall upon anyone, since no one can be bound to do what is impossible.

To help those to die "with dignity" whom society is too niggardly to help to live with dignity might be a great bargain, as Kohl suggests, but it also clearly would be an unjust imposition of the strong upon the weak. Homicide laws provide a minimal protection of each person's individual share of the good of life by requiring everyone to forbear killing. This forbearance is always possible. Hence, there seems to be no reason why those who are not to be cared for should be considered a special class from whom equal protection of the law of homicide could be withdrawn without injustice.

Of course, proponents of nonvoluntary euthanasia will argue that those who are not to be cared for will be better off being killed if the natural causes which would bring about death would be painful: "Would it not be better kindness to substitute human agency?"[28] In other words, society should at least help those to die with dignity whom it is too niggardly to help live with dignity.

Richard Trubo develops this theme at length by describing the miserable conditions in which many individuals who are permanently institutionalized now exist. In some institutions for the retarded less is spent for a patient's food each day than a pet owner would spend to feed a cat; in one hospital understaffing is so severe that patients were left unfed, forced to obtain drinking water from toilets, and generally neglected.[29]

However, either better care is owed such individuals or it is not. If it is, then killing them would merely avoid a lesser injustice by committing a greater. If better care is not owed such individuals, still killing them can be judged better kindness only if conceptions of others are used to judge that they would be better off killed at once than neglected or badly cared for.

Proponents of euthanasia will attack as insignificant the distinction between killing and letting die.[30] The distinction certainly makes no difference in many cases—for example, homicide by omission of care which one has a legal duty to provide is as much homicide as is killing by a positive performance.[31] However, the law does distinguish between acts of omission to which one is not legally obligated—here there is no crime even if the omission results in preventable death—and acts of commission. The basis of this distinction is not irrational, since everyone can forbear to kill others, and demanding this forbearance provides a great deal of protection for each individual's share of the good of life. There also is the practical consideration that if one omits to save another, the other may survive even so, perhaps with the aid of some third party; while if one kills another, alternative possibilities for preserving life are eliminated at a stroke.

In the argument for nonvoluntary euthanasia outlined in chapter seven, section A, the public interest in saving the cost of caring for the permanently dependent, it was argued, could override the liberty to stand aloof from euthanasia of those members of society who abhor such killing. We promised to show in the present chapter that the public interest in saving money is not the sort of interest which a jurisprudence which justly respects liberty would permit to override liberty to stand aloof. We are now in a position to keep this promise.

As it has now been made clear, the killing of permanently institutionalized noncompetent persons and others whose care is a burden to society is not a *necessary* means to easing this financial burden. Society might also cut costs simply by ceasing to provide the care which it now provides. This alternative would leave those from whom care would be withdrawn to die of neglect or to survive by private charity. Such a withdrawal of support from the dependent would be a drastic step, and one we by no means advocate. The point is that it would be a step no more unjust to those abandoned than killing them would be, and a step which could be taken without overriding anyone's liberty.

In fact, such a withdrawal of support from members of society who now depend on it for survival would simply limit the objectives of political society to those which it pursued before the evolution of the modern welfare state. In general, whenever there is a genuine public interest in saving money, the problem can be solved in a similar way: by limiting the role and activities of the state.

Money is only a means, not a substantial public purpose in itself. The

Preamble to the Constitution of the United States mentions justice and liberty, public tranquility and the common defense, civil unity and the general
welfare. It does not mention saving money. The limits of the money available
to government for public purposes are an expression of the limits of the
common will to pursue these purposes. In other words, if a government is
compelled to save money, it is being told by the people that there are limits to
what they are willing to have the government do. Such limits are a signal not
to act but to limit action.

Hence, budgetary considerations as such never offer a compelling reason to
override the liberty of citizens, and a jurisprudence with a just respect for
liberty will provide no rationale for any government to undertake activities
abhorrent to citizens for the sake of cutting the cost of public programs.
Rather, reducing or eliminating some of the costly programs will be the solution of choice.

If economic arguments cannot justify euthanasia in the public interest, still
there are noneconomic considerations with respect to the public interest
which might seem to justify the legalization of such killing.

One can imagine a possible situation in the wake of disaster in which not all
could be cared for and it might seem better kindness to kill some than to let
them die.

Perhaps in a very difficult situation some would have to be killed to protect
others—for instance, from the spread of disease. The latter possibility might
fall under the generalized rule which we formulated in chapter seven, section
G, according to which it is justifiable to kill some when this is necessary to
improve the overall average probability of survival provided that those to be
killed are chosen by some fair principle. Thus if it were necessary to kill some
to protect public health, neither their prospects for a certain quality of life nor
their personhood nor their burdensomeness to society would have to be taken
into account. So the justification of such killing would not entail the justification of nonvoluntary euthanasia.

As to the carrying out of a program of nonvoluntary—or even of voluntary—euthanasia in a disaster situation, acceptance of such a measure would
only entail acceptance of killing if the program involved killing rather than
merely the selection of some for care and treatment in a situation in which
care for all is impossible. To admit active killing in a confused and difficult
situation would be extremely dangerous. Those allowed to do such killing
could in practice kill almost anyone they wished with impunity. Moreover, it
is hard to see how the use of scarce personnel and resources to carry out
killings could be justified when these same personnel and resources could be
employed in more positive ways.

If in less disastrous circumstances it is justifiable to omit care and treatment, the alternative to killing need not be to allow death to occur with

excessive misery. The pain might still be mitigated with drugs. For example, even if it is granted—something we do not concede—that it is justifiable to omit lifesaving surgery in the case of an infant afflicted with Down's syndrome, those who have custody of the infant need not choose between killing it and allowing it to undergo severe suffering as it dies. They can administer palliative care as they would to any other dying patient.

Proponents of euthanasia might argue that in a disaster situation they could state a criterion by which some might be selected for death without unfairness: Those to be killed should be the individuals who are most burdensome to sustain. But it must be noticed that everyone is a more or less grave burden to society. An advocate of euthanasia will respond that the intended criterion is not merely burden but net burden—that is, the burden which is not offset by a contribution. The economic argument for killing those who are permanently institutionalized is not that the cost of their maintenance is great—the cost of maintaining the leading members of society undoubtedly is far vaster—but that this cost is not offset by any contribution.

But who is to judge the worth of various contributions? In a disaster situation one person might think that helping the least afflicted to survive would be a very important contribution, another might think that vengeful retaliation against an already victorious enemy in accord with the plan of deterrence which has failed must take priority, another might think that consoling the dying would be nobler and more worthwhile. A Roman Catholic might believe that the activity of a priest administering the sacraments would be the greatest contribution of all. Clearly, it is impossible to weigh these different contributions and to determine which are worthwhile and how much each is worth without taking for granted some particular world view, some special set of ideals and interests, as a premiss. And so it is equally impossible to determine the net burden.

An advocate of euthanasia on economic grounds will argue that in our present circumstances it is not impossible, nor even difficult, to calculate the net burden to society imposed by those whom Sackett and others describe, for their contribution is nil. But this is to assume that having needs and requiring care and compassion is not itself a contribution to others. Not everyone will accept this assumption; it is far from self-evident and it presupposes a particular world view.

It is particularly odd to maintain that the contribution must be economic in a society in which many people accept the burden of caring for pets for the sake of the noneconomic contribution which pets can make to one who cares for them. The noneconomic contribution of helpless humans to society can be much more significant if it not merely generates psychological satisfactions but provides an occasion for exercising moral qualities of compassion and fairness. Of course, this proposition *also* rests upon a particular world view.

However, the question is: Why should it be fair to impose one of these world views rather than the other upon helpless individuals? Equal protection of the law of homicide ought not to be modified to leave some class of individuals unprotected on the ground that on one or another world view—perhaps even a very widely held set of ideals and interests—such individuals contribute nothing.

Further, if net burden were to be used as a criterion, one should notice that on many conceptions of what is valuable leading members of society are a much greater net burden to society than is any individual who happens to be a permanent inmate of a custodial institution. The wealthy consume tremendous amounts of scarce resources. Whether their contributions begin to approximate the costs they impose upon society is an ideological issue.

Many living in underdeveloped nations and in communist societies would deny that the rich and powerful leaders of developed liberal democratic nations make any worthwhile contribution to human well-being. Perhaps they are right. If so, a criterion of net burden might indicate that a Rockefeller or a justice of the United States Supreme Court imposes a greater net burden on society than does any defective child. Whether they do or not is not a question which can be settled by objective calculation. It all depends on the value one places upon the contributions of such persons and how one appraises the costs they impose upon society.

Of course, there is no likelihood that nonvoluntary euthanasia will be extended to the rich and powerful on the ground that permitting them to live is excessively costly. Being rich and powerful, they can take care of themselves and can see to it that the law will not withdraw its prohibition of homicide insofar as it applies to them and to those whom they want to have protected. But this consideration, while important, has to do with mere power, not with justice. The demand of equal protection of the laws is a matter of justice; according to this standard mere power may well bring about changes in the laws, but it cannot warrant withdrawing protection from anyone who would otherwise be entitled to it.

E. Injustice of Criteria of Selection for Euthanasia

Up to this point we have considered various proposals by advocates of nonvoluntary euthanasia which might seem to justify withdrawing the equal protection of the law of homicide from some individuals who are to be killed if the proposals are accepted. Some proposals emphasize quality-of-life considerations and embody a belief that some people would be better off dead. Other proposals would restrict personhood and rights to some limited class of human individuals by assuming that the excluded individuals share insufficiently in characteristics which are essential if one is to be a person. And still others emphasize the social costs of caring for some persons who are assumed to make no worthwhile contribution to society.

We have pointed out that all of these proposals involve arbitrary standards. Those who advocate nonvoluntary euthanasia hold one or another world view—embracing a certain set of ideals and interests—which seems to them to justify removing the protection of the law forbidding homicide from a larger or smaller number and variety of human individuals. All persons are of course entitled to hold whatever world view seems right to them. This liberty to hold one's own preferred ultimate conception of things is a very important one which is protected in the United States by the First Amendment's prohibition of the establishment of religion and interference with free exercise of one's fundamental beliefs.

However, although proponents of euthanasia are entitled to hold their own conceptions which might seem to justify killing some other human individuals, they are not entitled to impose upon those they wish to have killed their peculiar conceptions of quality of life, of personhood, and of worthwhile contribution. Indeed, as we shall argue in chapter ten, section A, the effort of proponents of euthanasia to establish their peculiar conceptions as legal standards is an attempt to establish a religion in violation of the First Amendment. Other members of society are at liberty to hold diverse world views. In particular, those whose death is proposed cannot fairly be assumed to accept the views which underlie proposals to kill them—views upon which there is no social consensus.

We come now to another consideration which argues against all of the attempts to justify withdrawing the protection afforded by the law of homicide from some human individuals. All such attempts appeal to various criteria: defectiveness and normality, paralysis and mobility, retardation and intelligence, inability to communicate and potential for relationships, mutilatedness and integrity, unawareness of one's own good and sufficient awareness to demand one's rights, lack of a sense of justice and ability to apply principles of justice, dependence and independence, inability to care for oneself and autonomy, or some other criterion.

The proposals of advocates of nonvoluntary euthanasia appear to offer a workable criterion for deciding whom to kill only because they contrast extreme instances of a negative condition with standard instances of a preferred contrary condition. Thus, Fletcher, for example, contrasts extreme instances of mental retardation with standard instances of intelligence within the range of statistical normality. But let us suppose that some such criterion were adopted to justify allowing nonvoluntary euthanasia, whether on the ground that those to be killed would be better off dead, or on the ground that they are not really persons, or on the ground that they do not contribute enough to offset the burden they impose upon society. How would any such criterion work? And what would be the implications of adopting it and using it as a basis for allowing some individuals to be killed?

In practice the criterion would have to be applied to draw a line within a continuum of cases, for all of the suggested criteria refer to properties which vary in degree. Cases can be found along the continuum which differ so little that even experts would disagree whether one or another individual was more retarded, more defective, and so on. This problem is concealed by the reticence of most proponents of the various standards concerning the methods of reducing their ideas to operational terms. Clear-cut cases can be given as examples in a theoretical discussion, but borderline cases also will have to be dealt with in practice. If euthanasia were legalized, a line would have to be drawn, and life-or-death decisions made by applying the criteria established to all the cases, including the borderline cases.

Under these conditions any drawing of a line within the continuum of cases inevitably will be arbitrary and thus unfair. Some individuals would be killed while others hardly distinguishable from them would receive the full protection of the law of homicide. The two groups would be separated at the borderline, not by any rationally defensible principle, but only by arbitrary judgments.

There would be a tendency to set the standard somewhat high and then to select for death only those individuals who clearly fall short of the standard. But this strategy would not help matters. The standard in theory makes a cut where there is really no intention of making it in practice. In practice the cases which clearly fall short of the theoretical standard are adjacent to cases which only slightly less clearly fall short of it.

Those who advocate the legalization of nonvoluntary euthanasia might object that this argument is a fallacious wedge or slippery slope argument. But this objection would miss the point entirely. We are not (yet) arguing that the criterion will not stay at the level at which it is initially set. Rather we are pointing out that at any selected level—for example, at any designated degree of retardation or insanity or senility—any criterion used to select those to be killed will inevitably require arbitrary distinctions between very similar cases, and these arbitrary judgments will send some to death who differ by a hardly measurable and surely insignificant degree from others whose lives will be spared.

But, it will be objected, the law draws arbitrary lines all the time— to settle that an individual below a certain age is legally noncompetent and an individual driving above a certain speed is guilty of an offense. We concede that lines drawn in such cases are arbitrary. The same is true when it comes to a teacher's passing and failing borderline students. But all such cases differ from nonvoluntary euthanasia.

In the first place, in many cases the line itself is drawn arbitrarily but—as in a legal age of competency—judgments are clear-cut and not arbitrary. The criterion for euthanasia would involve both an arbitrary cutoff point and the arbitrary discrimination of borderline cases. Moreover, in other cases rights as fundamental as the right to life are not at stake.

Furthermore, usually laws and procedures with arbitrary cutoff points and judgments of borderline cases are *necessary* for purposes which are generally agreed to be legitimate. (Although it is not easy to convince a student who has failed a course of this point if a classmate whose performance was only a single percentage point better passed the course.) The arbitrary discrimination of those to be killed in a program of legalized, nonvoluntary euthanasia can be wholly avoided. It is unnecessary unless such a program is adopted. And there is no consensus upon any important public purpose which nonvoluntary euthanasia would serve.

It will not do to suggest that the problem of making life or death judgments here is no different from problems which courts of criminal law regularly face, especially when the death penalty is used. For the courts at least are looking for something which is not a matter of degree: legal guilt or innocence. Assuming there is guilt, then the degree of it comes into consideration in sentencing, with results which hardly provide grounds for complacency about the use of a similar procedure in any other field. At least where capital punishment has been involved, however, Anglo-American law has not been compelled to settle life or death issues on the basis of a criterion which is no more than a certain degree of some property which is present in only infinitesimally distinct degrees in a multitude of adjacent cases.

Even if there were a criterion which would permit fine discriminations to be made and used as a basis for selecting for euthanasia some persons judged too deficient in a certain quality to deserve to live, still a further difficulty would emerge. Once those who fall short of the original criterion were eliminated, there would be a tendency for standards to rise.

Joseph Fletcher, for example, by one of his stipulations has decided that those below an IQ 20-mark certainly are not persons. Once those who failed their IQ tests at the determined level were killed, it would seem rather foolish to stop the process. Some will have barely passed the required test; as we have pointed out, they will differ very little from individuals already killed. It would hardly seem sensible at this point to forbid the killing of those Fletcher already has deemed doubtful persons—those with an IQ above the 20-mark but below the 40-mark.

Intelligence quotient itself is based upon the average of a test group which is chosen to be representative of the population as a whole. Each time the tests were revised and recalibrated, the new form would always locate a group with an IQ below the 20-mark.[32] Of course, this particular problem might be avoided, unless it is an intentional part of the program of some proponents of euthanasia, by specifying a criterion in such a way that it would not *automatically* result in constantly higher standards as more deficient groups were eliminated.

However, since the deficiencies are a matter of degree, rising standards would be very difficult to avoid. The most deficient extant instances in comparison with any ideal always seem to be extreme cases, since expectations are determined by the median of instances in comparison to the ideal as much as by the paradigm itself. Every teacher is familiar with this point: The better the group of students with which one is used to dealing, the poorer a given student seems to be. If at first those who are blind and deaf and lacking all four limbs are considered too defective and are legally killed, next those who are blind and deaf and who lack three limbs and part of the fourth will be considered too defective. And so on.

It might be thought that these operational difficulties could be avoided simply by treating as justified only the killing of individuals who have a certain social status. For example, perhaps only the permanently institutionalized should be permitted to be killed. This approach would conform to the franker proposals which emphasize economic considerations. But it would hardly afford any lasting resolution.

Many wholly dependent individuals cared for privately are in a condition as bad as that of those in public institutions. Moreover, most of these individuals are more or less dependent on public financial aid. The law hardly could permit the killing of the institutionalized without extending equal protection of the right to be killed to those under private care. Any individual's chances of surviving infancy and childhood and of being spared whenever in a condition of helpless dependence would depend upon the extent to which sufficiently strong and solvent protectors stepped in to protect life.

There is yet a further implication of accepting criteria based upon properties subject to degree for legalizing the killing of some individuals. Any criterion which would be used must be widely regarded as related to a positive attribute or ideal which is of central human significance. Otherwise deficiency hardly would be a basis for legitimating the killing of defective individuals. Already those who are quite deficient in some of the suggested respects are regarded as inferior; in many ways their rights are afforded minimal respect. When those deficient below a certain level are judged by law to be better off dead or to be nonpersons or to be useless consumers, this judgment certainly will have an effect upon the respect which will be given to other persons who are deficient, although not so deficient as to be candidates for nonvoluntary euthanasia.

The implication is particularly clear in the case of positions which would deny personhood to some individuals in order to withdraw the protection of the law of homicide from them without seeming to restrict unfairly equal protection. On the one hand, if an IQ 20-mark and below means that one is not a person and an IQ 40-mark and below means that one is doubtfully a person, an IQ 60-mark and below means that one is somewhat less a person than the average. On the other hand, geniuses are more persons than others.

The underlying thesis is that if one is only a person by having a certain minimal degree of some property which persons have in various degrees, then one is more a person the more one has of that property and less a person the less one has of it. Thus the criteria proposed to justify nonvoluntary euthanasia will lead to a legally recognized caste system, which can hardly be limited to the single area of decisions about whose life will be unprotected by the law of homicide.

Certain proponents of beneficent euthanasia will protest that not all proposals for legalizing nonvoluntary euthanasia depend upon the denial of the personhood of those to be killed and that their own proposals would depend upon no such denial. Rather, the idea is to kill those who would be better off dead, not out of disregard for their dignity and their rights, but rather out of respect for those whose lives have become a burden to themselves and whose deaths will be a positive boon.

However, when this judgment is made for one person by another and nonvoluntary euthanasia administered, this is tantamount to a denial of personhood; the views of others are accepted as an adequate ground for exterminating those whose lives are considered not worth living. Moreover, the legal establishment of quality-of-life criteria for killing will give an officially sanctioned status to such criteria, so that application of them to make other discriminations will be irresistible even if the discriminations are not formally made on the basis of more and less personhood. All will be persons, but some more deficient than others in a property which the law admits to be so important that a certain level of deficiency in it renders human life officially not worth living.

The preceding argument is a very powerful one against using qualitative criteria to select certain human individuals for the status of nonpersons or to select them for the status of persons so deficient in a quality that they might be denied the protection of the law of homicide. But the point of this argument must not be misunderstood and overstated. We are not arguing that the use of qualitative criteria for such purposes *logically entails* that others, who are permitted to live although more or less deficient in the quality which serves as a criterion for legalized killing, must be considered persons in various degrees according as they participate the relevant quality.

John Rawls has shown that it is logically possible both to hold that one has the status of personhood by virtue of certain capacities which depend upon the presence of a certain degree of qualities which vary according to more and less, and to hold that all who qualify as persons should enjoy equality in their basic personal and civil rights. According to Rawls only individuals capable of having a notion of their own good and a sense of justice qualify as moral persons and need be considered persons before the law, yet all such persons, once they do qualify as such, ought to enjoy equality before the law. (It is important to note that Rawls understands "capable of" in a broad sense, so that at least most infants and perhaps even most of the unborn would have the relevant capacity.)

Rawls suggests that the inequality of persons would follow from making personhood depend upon qualities which vary in degree only if one accepted certain additional assumptions, which he does not accept. The additional assumptions are those of a theory of ethics according to which the rightness of action depends upon its efficiency in maximizing good consequences. Given a theory of this sort, individuals who have a greater degree of qualities considered desirable are bound to be treated unequally, since right action will pursue the better consequences of making the most of the possibilities of those individuals who are regarded as the best. Rawls holds a very different ethical theory. On his view, fairness to every individual who qualifies as a person and equal opportunity for all persons to make the most of themselves are far more important in determining what is right and wrong than is getting a maximum of good results. Hence, persons ought to be considered to have equal rights even though they vary in the degree to which they share the qualities by which they have the capacity required for them to be persons at all.[33]

We partly agree with Rawls. It is true that even if individuals qualify as persons by having the level of intelligence and other qualities required for a capacity to understand what is good for themselves and to have a sense of justice, still one can consider personhood as the defining characteristic of a class of entities—namely, that class of individuals who have legal rights and duties—and can hold that all persons have equal rights. Any given individual must either be a member or not be a member of a class of this sort.

The logical point Rawls makes is clear in respect to natural kinds: Natural species are distinguished by their natural capacities, which depend upon qualities subject to degree, and yet one does not regard individuals of such kinds as if they were only more or less the kind of thing they are. For example, humankind is distinguished by the capacities to think and choose, and yet one does not regard different individuals as more or less human depending upon the level of their ability to think and make choices.

However, while evidence of the ability to think and choose sometimes is useful for recognizing humans—for instance, in examining the remains of primitive cultures—other criteria also are ordinarily used to recognize individuals as human. One usually can recognize another as human on sight; one always could do so by a careful study of the individual's genetic makeup, since all human individuals belong to the same interbreeding population and are genetically similar. Hence, although *humankind* is distinguished by the evidence in some of its members of the abilities to think and to choose, *individuals* are classed as human by their membership in the human family, not by their individual ability to think and to make choices.

It follows that if more is required to qualify for personhood than that one be a living human individual—for example, if one qualifies as a person only by having a certain degree of a quality such as intelligence—then some human individuals will not be persons. Persons will not be individual members of humankind which is distinguished by human capacities to think and choose; persons will be individuals *directly* distinguished by the potential for a certain level of thought and action.

At this point we can see how the approach Rawls takes will run into difficulties. If persons are directly distinguished as such by their *individual* capacities, how are these capacities to be known? The only way to know an individual's capacity, once reasoning about one individual from its resemblance to other members of its family is excluded, is by waiting to see what the individual can do. Hence, if personhood depends upon the presence of a certain degree of a quality which human individuals have in diverse degrees, then one will not be able to recognize any individual as a person until the required degree of the relevant quality actually is displayed.

Even so, one might insist that once the required degree of the relevant quality is displayed, all who reveal it will be considered equal. This position remains logically possible. But we do not think it would be psychologically possible to hold in practice to this position. Even without assuming the sort of ethical theory which Rawls rejects (rightly rejects, as we shall argue in chapter eleven, section C), one who began calling others "persons" only when they actually showed a certain level of intelligence and action would inevitably consider personhood something which comes to be gradually and is achieved more or less perfectly. It would follow that the subnormal would be considered inferior persons and the above normal would be considered superior persons—that is, inferior and superior *precisely as persons*—and between superior and inferior persons there would be differences of status which would place each group in its proper caste.

F. A Just Criterion: Membership in the Human Species

Proponents of euthanasia are likely to object to the preceding argumentation that if no quality-of-life criteria are admitted, than one must hold that all lives are inviolable regardless of their quality. After all, there are intelligent porpoises, parrots which talk, apes which seem to be able to use some simple tools, and so on. If qualitative considerations are excluded, an unqualified philosophy of reverence for life would require the protection of bacteria against penicillin.

But this objection presupposes the qualitative criteria—sharing in certain abilities to some degree—which the preceding argument has criticized. The opponent of euthanasia need not defend any philosophy of absolute reverence for life. The argument begins with an existing law forbidding homicide. The issue is whether that law ought to be modified to permit some human individuals to be killed whose lives until now have been protected by the law's prohibition. The opponent of the legalization of euthanasia need only defend as reasonable the line drawn by the existing law of homicide or a more inclusive line than that drawn by present law.

The line drawn by the existing law of homicide in Anglo-American jurisdictions protects every living human individual from birth, with the exceptions discussed in chapter seven. Being a human individual is an all-or-none property, not a quality in which one can share in various degrees. Human individuals are members of a well-demarcated biological species. They are easily recognized by their familial relationship with other members of the species, regardless of their individual performances.

Of course, not everything which pertains to human life is a human individual. For example, one's left arm is not a human individual; it is only part of an individual. Similarly, although one's sperm or ovum is alive, human, and an individual cell, it is not a human individual, but only part of some individual. The human individual is the whole organism of the species homo sapiens. In chapter three, section D, we distinguished between the death of such a whole and the death of its parts. Only the death of the whole is the death of a person.

Human individuals are the only natural persons recognized by Anglo-American legal systems. There is nothing else which all those now recognized as protected by the law of homicide have in common beyond the fact that they are members of the human species who have been born alive. Since the preceding argument shows that there is no way to protect some of those now protected while excluding others without introducing unjust principles of discrimination, the conclusion is that the law ought to continue to protect all human individuals without discrimination.

Drawing the line at this point is not at all unreasonable. As Rawls and others have pointed out, the legal system is made by humans for humans. By it human individuals regulate their relationships to each other so that these relationships reflect not merely the interests which humans share with other animals but the peculiarly human ideals of liberty and justice in which other animals do not participate. Still, to qualify for legal personhood and to have one's basic rights protected, in particular one's right to life, nothing beyond the common property of species membership can be required, or else the problems of quality which varies by degrees will emerge.

As to allowing nonhuman animals the status of legal personhood and the protection of basic rights which attend this status, this theoretical possibility is hardly a point which deserves serious consideration. Existing laws which protect animal life are based upon conceptions of human interests and ideals—for example, conservation for use, prevention of immoral cruelty, and the like.

In practice law cannot undertake to protect any large segment of nonhuman animals by making them legal persons, and there is no significant body of public opinion which would support such an innovation. If nonhuman animals were to be regarded as individuals due respect and in possession of their own rights, then either lines would have to be drawn on some arbitrary basis or even viruses would be included—something obviously unworkable.

G. Legalized Abortion a Violation of Justice

But what about the requirement that human individuals be born alive before being accepted as legal persons? This dividing line excludes from legal personhood a subclass of members of the species, the unborn, which are in reality whole organisms and distinct individuals. At present the law in the English-speaking countries does not consider the unborn to be legal persons, and the law of homicide does not forbid killing unborn individuals. This is true even where laws forbidding abortion provide some protection for such individuals; antiabortion laws are not based upon the assumption of the full legal personhood of the unborn, for if that assumption were accepted, the ordinary homicide laws would apply to them.

Two points may be made by way of jurisprudential defense of the present exclusion of the unborn from protection by the law of homicide.

First, this exclusion is based upon a status which is not a matter of degree. To this extent, using birth as a necessary condition for legal personhood is not legally unworkable in the way that using quality-of-life criteria is. Or, to put the point another way, the repeal of the laws forbidding abortion does not open the door to the killing of an indeterminately large class of individuals other than the unborn from whom this repeal withdraws legal protection.

Second, the exclusion of the unborn from protection by the law of homicide is not *in itself* a novel discrimination introduced as a practical application of one particular world view. As we have pointed out already, antiabortion laws were necessary to protect the unborn precisely because the commonly received legal view was that the unborn are not protected by the law of homicide which protects those who are already born. To permit nonvoluntary euthanasia would be a more radical step than to legalize abortion, for the legalization of nonvoluntary euthanasia would mean the withdrawal of protection from individuals until now protected by the same law of homicide which protects everyone. Those killed in a program of nonvoluntary euthanasia, whether declared nonpersons or not, would be individuals whose personhood before the law has been universally accepted in Anglo-American jurisdictions until now.

Nevertheless, we think that unborn human individuals ought to be considered legal persons and that the restriction of the law of homicide by which it protects only those who have been born alive ought to be abandoned. The case for this position has been stated at length elsewhere and need not be repeated in full here.[34] However, a few comments are in order.

First, until modern times no one knew when human life begins. It was commonly thought that it began from nonliving materials sometime during pregnancy. But by 1800 it was known that while new human individuals begin, human life as such does not begin but is transmitted continuously. Further, law generally stays close to common sense. From a common sense point of view there is something lacking for the full reality and personhood of an individual until birth occurs and one can begin to interact with the separate and distinct body of the infant. Between the time when spontaneous movement of the fetus is felt (animation) and live birth a common sense view is that the unborn is alive and growing—the baby *is coming*. Hence, there is a tendency to count the unborn as being in an intermediate state between nonbeing and being, between lifeless material and the fully real, liveborn infant. Law also has very important problems with evidence. No one can be held guilty of killing until it is certain that life is present, until it is clear that the act was the cause of death, and so on.

Under these conditions Anglo-American law would have found it extremely difficult to attempt to consider unborn individuals as legal persons whose lives would be protected by the laws forbidding homicide. Some clear dividing line was essential, and birth was quite naturally chosen. At the same time unborn individuals were protected by special laws, already to some extent at common law and later by statutes which were enacted beginning early in the nineteenth century when the real status of the unborn began to be understood more accurately.[35]

In its decision repealing laws forbidding abortion the United States Supreme Court accepted false historical claims by proponents of abortion which called into question the fact that abortion was a crime at common law and which denied that antiabortion statutes were intended to protect the lives of the unborn.[36] A more responsible effort by the Court to discover the relevant history of the law would have revealed the situation summarized in the preceding two paragraphs.[37]

Second, Anglo-American law never has taken a consistent position either that the unborn are not legal persons or that they are legal persons. In different areas of the law different solutions were reached at different times and places, solutions always recognizing the impossibility of completely excluding the unborn from the human community but never simply affirming their unqualified membership and rights. Nevertheless, if any recognition was to be given at all, it was very difficult not to give increasing legal status to the unborn. The reason for this is simple and obvious enough: If there is a claim of justice, less than full and unqualified recognition of the claimant is injustice. And so until the proabortion movement reversed a long-term trend, Anglo-American law tended for more and more purposes to regard the unborn as already existing legal persons in possession of rights before the law, some of which were actually enforced prior to birth.[38]

In its abortion decision the Supreme Court distorted this state of affairs in two ways. It suggested that there existed disagreement concerning when life begins and it proposed to avoid settling this disputed issue. It then noted that the law did not consistently regard the unborn as legal persons, minimized the respects in which personhood was in fact accorded the unborn by the law, ignored the trend toward fuller recognition, and summed up the situation by saying, "In short, the unborn have never been recognized in the law as persons in the whole sense."[39]

Third, inconsistency in the law with respect to the status of individuals as persons is intolerable. Law can deal with most things in different ways for different purposes. But persons are not simply something within the subject matter of legal concern. Persons are those for whom the law exists. If one is a person, one deserves the whole service of the law; if not, none of its service. The case of the unborn is not the only historical instance of legal inconsistency on this matter. Slaves and Indians also were treated inconsistently, being recognized as persons for certain purposes and denied personal status for other purposes.[40]

The controversy over legalization of abortion forced a decision which would settle the status of the unborn, for if they were persons, then the demand for abortion could not be admitted; while if they were not, it could not be resisted. The issue was not a matter of policy on which consensus or lack of it could be decisive, because the putative right of persons to live was at stake. Nor was it a matter on which a decision could be avoided.

The Supreme Court held that if the unborn were persons, then the case would have to be decided in their favor. But instead of facing the responsibility of settling this crucial issue the Court maintained that the case for personhood was not proved and thus that the unborn should not be considered persons. The question was what consistent policy ought the law to adopt; the Court begged this question by assuming that if the unborn were not already fully recognized as persons, then such recognition could not be given them.[41]

Fourth, the dividing line of birth is not particularly significant either with respect to the status of human individuals as members of the species or with respect to their status as individuals involved in human society. There is very little difference between an infant about to be born and a neonate. And the developments in the law made clear that in many respects the unborn are involved in society—for example, by owning property which must be managed, by needing the support of their fathers, by suffering negligent damage and death, by requiring medical care which a mother might reject for herself on religious grounds, and so on. Also, the quickly developing movement to allow nonvoluntary euthanasia of defective newborns clearly extends the acceptance of abortion to the class least distinct from the unborn.[42] Moreover, the unborn could be recognized as legal persons without any legal impracticality.

To insist upon birth in addition to membership in the human species under these circumstances—taking into account what has been known for more than a century—is discriminatory. Hence, all living human individuals should be considered legal persons; the same law of homicide should protect the lives of all equally.[43]

However, the Supreme Court claimed that killing the unborn must be permitted because they are only *alive* on one debatable theory—a patent absurdity. Still, the Court admitted that there is some sort of life which is other than life "as we know it": a potentiality of life, or potential life, or fetal life. At the point of viability a state can give some protection to this so-called potential life "because the fetus then presumably has the capability of meaningful life outside the mother's womb."[44]

In taking this position the Court implied that the life of all those who survive either spontaneous or induced abortions but who are too young to survive the neonatal period is not meaningful, although such individuals certainly are legal persons and are citizens of the United States according to the Fourteenth Amendment. Thus in its decision on abortion the Court itself began the trend toward belittling the significance of the life of infants already born which is now unfolding in the movement to legalize killing some such persons, whether on the theory that such life is not meaningful and that such persons are better off dead, or on the theory that such individuals should be excluded from personhood, or on the crass view that whether such individuals are persons or not, they simply should be disposed of if they cost more than they are worth.

Our conclusion is that legalized abortion, except to save the life of the mother, is a violation of justice. Equal protection of the laws demands that the unborn be considered legal persons, and their lives be protected by the same law forbidding homicide which protects other persons. We shall return to this subject in chapter ten, section B.

H. The Nazi Experience with Euthanasia

In his article on euthanasia Yale Kamisar argued, as we saw in chapter six, that voluntary euthanasia would lead to nonvoluntary euthanasia. In this connection he suggested that the Nazi action was an example of the "parade of horrors." We omitted this aspect of Kamisar's argument from consideration in chapter six because the Nazi program did not begin with voluntary euthanasia. However, the Nazis did proceed from more to less restricted nonvoluntary euthanasia, and they proceeded from nonvoluntary euthanasia to genocide. Hence, the analogy of the Nazi action deserves consideration here, where the subject is nonvoluntary euthanasia and where the problems of drawing and maintaining firm lines have been discussed.

In discussing the Nazi action we do not intend to rest our case upon this historical analogy. However, Germany is the only nation in modern times which has undertaken a program of nonvoluntary euthanasia about which we have any real information. (Perhaps nonvoluntary euthanasia is practiced in the Soviet Union or elsewhere, but we have been unable to find any significant evidence on the matter.) Hence, the Nazi action deserves some consideration.

At the same time the differences between Nazi Germany and the Anglo-American nations of the 1970s require caution lest one press the evidence of this past experience too far. Certainly, if there were no objection to nonvoluntary euthanasia *except* that based upon the Nazi action, the argument would not be strong. But the preceding arguments have shown that nonvoluntary euthanasia would involve a very serious injustice right from the beginning. Since the Nazi action and the nonvoluntary euthanasia proposed today would share the common characteristic of injustice from the outset, consideration of this analogous instance is instructive.

Proponents of euthanasia have attempted to neutralize the force of the Nazi experience with euthanasia by four diverse lines of argument.

First, it is sometimes maintained that the Nazis were racists and that their euthanasia programs were a means to purification of the Aryan race. Since the end rationally required the means of genocide, this means was used. But since no advocate of the legalization of nonvoluntary euthanasia in an English-speaking nation espouses racism, there is no reason to suppose that this type of killing will get out of hand and lead to the excesses that it did in Nazi Germany.[45]

Second, it is sometimes maintained that the Nazis did not engage in mercy killing at all. What they did was really cruel, strictly merciless murder. Kohl protests vehemently that beneficent euthanasia is intended to be kind, that it does not rest upon a principle of utility, and that its sole point would be to minimize misery and maximize loving treatment. Thus because present society so loathes Nazi atrocities, it must avoid cruelty and indifference, and so accept beneficent euthanasia.[46]

Third, it is argued that Anglo-American tradition and law are so different from the totalitarianism of Nazi Germany that there is no reason to fear a repetition of Nazi horrors if nonvoluntary euthanasia were legalized in these democratic and liberty-loving nations. Glanville Williams, for example, points out that American laws permitting sterilization were little used and that men trained to kill in World War II did not return home after the war and continue killing.[47]

Fourth, it is sometimes argued that the Nazi action is not a historical precedent because of the ideological character of Nazi objectives. Their racism was not simply discriminatory; it was totally impractical, a mere abstract ideal. Euthanasia in Anglo-American society would be pragmatic, a matter of rational, cost-benefit calculation. The benefit to society would be a real one, measurable in tax dollars and cents.[48]

As to the first point the authorities whom Kamisar quotes make clear that euthanasia began in Germany quite apart from the anti-Jewish policies of the Nazis. German Jews were at first excluded because it was believed that the blessing of euthanasia should only be granted to "real" Germans. The roots of the program antedated the coming to power of the Nazis, in a propaganda barrage which established the proposition that there is such a thing as valueless life.

Early in the program a protesting official of the Domestic Welfare Council of the German Protestant Church asked, "Where is the borderline? Who is abnormal, antisocial, hopelessly sick?" But persons in institutions were killed, and their relatives were sent a form letter saying, for example, "Because of her grave mental illness, life was a torment for the deceased. You must therefore look on her death as a release." Precisely because the killing of the sick had become somewhat acceptable, the Nazis, using psychiatric certificates as a basis, carried out political killings under the guise of euthanasia.[49]

Frederic Wertham describes at length the unfolding of the euthanasia program in which mental patients and others in institutions were killed. Thousands of German, non-Jewish children were killed by starvation and by drugs. In the early stages only infants suffering serious defects were killed. But the project did not end until allied troops overran Germany, and as time passed, the children became older and the indications slighter—for example, "badly modeled ears," bed wetters, and "difficult to educate."[50] In all, an estimated 275,000 persons who had been in nursing homes, hospitals, and asylums were killed; this number included some indeterminate proportion of foreign workers.[51]

In 1920 two respected professors, Karl Binding and Alfred Hoche, published a booklet defending euthanasia.

Binding, a doctor of jurisprudence and philosophy, began his section of the work by emphasizing that there was no question of recognizing any right to kill; what was at issue were merely the conditions under which, in addition to emergencies, the destruction of human life might be permitted. He went on to argue for *death with dignity* for those desiring it. But he did not stop with voluntary euthanasia. Incurable idiots, whether congenital or not, may be regarded as mere caricatures of real persons. Parents or heads of institutions should be allowed to apply on their behalf for euthanasia; if the latter, a mother might wish to object, and in that case the child could be returned to her care. Ideally a committee should consider each case in advance, but this might not always be desirable. Errors undoubtedly would occur, but only a life of little quality would usually be lost by mistake.

Hoche, a medical doctor and psychiatrist, argued that an individual could lose so many human characteristics that life would be devoid of value. Incurable idiots can be regarded as mentally dead, but they may be able to live for many years with considerable costs for care. Such persons cannot respond to love and do not participate effectively in human relationships. The purpose for destruction of such valueless lives is not primarily pity, since they do not suffer to any great extent, but rather a rational consideration of social interests, for example, in making the best use of scarce hospital and health-care facilities.[52]

The preceding evidence clearly indicates that the Nazis began by endorsing existing proposals for euthanasia. The project was not in the first instance racist. But neither was it based on voluntariness. Rather, the emphasis was on the good of society. The principle seems to have been that when there are individuals who are better off dead or for whom life and death make no difference, then the burden of institutional care for such persons can hardly be justified.

As to the second point—Kohl's argument that beneficent euthanasia has nothing to do with the Nazi action—two things need to be noticed.

First, Kohl's conviction that insistence upon voluntariness is fanatical when the killing would be kind according to Kohl's own view is not reassuring. Many people would hold that killing of a nonwilling person never can be kind. The basic arrogance of judging some human lives not worth living, as if that judgment were an objective fact when it is only an expression of subjective opinion, is common to Kohl and to Hoche and Binding.

Second, as we have seen, the arguments for euthanasia on grounds of social utility are too common to ignore. Kohl talks as if economic considerations are insignificant in the movement of nonvoluntary euthanasia. But, as we showed in chapters six and seven, considerations of costs of care are not a small part of the argument for euthanasia just as they were not a small part of the argument for legalizing abortion. The weak and helpless who are dependent are equally unwanted persons—and likely to be declared nonpersons—whether they happen to be unborn or not. Kohl himself cannot forbear to mention economic considerations. But the most important point is that Kohl is quite ready to impose his conception of kindness upon nonconsenting individuals to justify killing them, just as Fletcher is quite ready to impose his conception of personhood upon some until now considered persons to negate their right to life.

As to the third point—that Anglo-American traditions are very different from Nazi totalitarianism—the distinction no doubt is real and important *up to now*. The question is whether it will continue to be so. To assume that it will is precisely to beg the question which is at issue when it is suggested that the legalization of euthanasia in Germany paved the way to genocide. The German people also had a tradition which rendered the Nazi atrocities incredible. Yet German physicians, even leading members of the medical profession, cooperated quite willingly and enthusiastically in the euthanasia program and in human experimentation. They were not terrorized into what they did. Rather, Nazism gave them an opportunity which they seem to have been waiting for.[53]

Kamisar points out that no one would have expected the United States to mistreat Americans of Japanese ancestry as it did during World War II. A number of other examples are relevant. During World War II Great Britain and the United States carried out terroristic bombing raids. These culminated in the atomic bombing by the United States of Hiroshima and Nagasaki. The terroristic strategy of nuclear deterrence emerged from this experience. The existence of the deterrent overarches American military strategy.

In 1960 many Americans believed that the United States would never carry out antiguerrilla warfare with terror, torture, and reprisals, and with the obliteration of the distinction between combatants and noncombatants, as the French had done in Algeria. It was widely believed that French officers were corrupted by their colonialism and that they were so inept as to be unable to carry out a surgical strike against the enemy's military power. But then there was Vietnam, endless escalation, pacification and cruelty, the "mere-gook rule," and Mai Lai. Any nation which considers itself incorruptible is already corrupt.

Moreover, the United States and nations like it could be even more vulnerable than a totalitarian society to an orgy of murder. At least in a totalitarian society there is some central control, some tendency to limit murder when the national interest is at stake. But a democratic society in which liberty becomes license and the rights of the weak are overriden by claims of privacy by the strong can slip into anarchy. Even when the security of the nation is threatened, even when the majority wish to call a halt to killing, it may not be possible to do so. Near the surface of contemporary democratic societies there is a tremendous reservoir of aggression, which rioting and civil strife of recent years has only begun to uncover.[54] To remove any of the present inhibitions with respect to killing would be foolhardy indeed.

As to the fourth point—that Nazi euthanasia was ideological while Anglo-American euthanasia would be pragmatic—it is not clear that this distinction, even if it is assumed to hold, makes a great difference. When the way is opened to killing, ideological fanaticism and individual greed can be equally effective motives. But the distinction is not even clear.

As we have explained already, Nazi euthanasia was not at the outset racist. C. P. Blacker quotes with credit a statement by a prominent Nazi, Hermann Brack:

> Hitler's ultimate reason for the establishment of the euthanasia programme in Germany was to eliminate those people confined to insane asylums and similar institutions who could no longer be of any use to the Reich. They were considered as useless objects and Hitler felt that, by exterminating these so-called useless eaters, it would be possible to relieve more doctors, male and female, nurses and other personnel, hospital beds and other facilities, for the Armed Forces.[55]

This concern seems no less pragmatic, rational, utilitarian, and well-grounded in cost-benefit analysis than do the arguments of Walter Sackett, Robert Williams, and others, or the memorandum, which we quoted in chapter six, of Robert Derzon to the United States Secretary of Health, Education, and Welfare. The last, of course, was not advocating active, much less nonvoluntary, euthanasia.

Furthermore, Anglo-American arguments for euthanasia, especially the killing of defective infants, are continuous with arguments for abortion, and the latter simply unfolded the ideology of the birth-control movement. This movement always has involved an ideological commitment. The first American Birth Control Conference passed a eugenics resolution stating that "we advocate a larger racial contribution from those who are of unusual racial value."[56] Margaret Sanger herself strongly supported this view in urging that the procreation of the diseased, the feebleminded, and the poor should be stopped.[57]

This eugenicist coloring persisted in the birth-control movement from its beginning in the 1920s into the mid-1930s.[58] But by the late 1930s the eugenics movement came under a cloud, and the argument was shifted into more democratic terms: It was important to avoid having a disproportionate part of the population come from segments with the least economic opportunity in which healthy development and acculturation of children is impossible.[59]

Population growth, pollution, and poverty—cited by the United States Supreme Court as complicating factors in its abortion decision—can mark out matters of legitimate public concern. But in much debate of the past two decades these factors have been used to project an ideology of the common welfare which especially conforms to the conceptions of the upper classes as to what is necessary both for their own pursuit of happiness and for the kindest possible treatment of the multitudes of poor people crowding into public parks and drawing sustenance from Aid to Families with Dependent Children and other relief programs.

In sum, there remain important disanalogies between the Nazi situation and the situation which shall come into being in any Anglo-American jurisdiction which legalizes nonvoluntary euthanasia. But the disanalogies are not as great as proponents of euthanasia claim. And it is entirely possible that the legalization of killing within any of the ideological frameworks used by proponents of euthanasia would unfold into a reign of terror even more severe than that of Nazi dictatorship, because it would lack totalitarian restraint and be characterized by the degradation of democratic liberty into anarchic license.

Nevertheless, it also is possible that at least in self-interest the citizens of any Anglo-American jurisdiction would not go beyond killing the weak and unprotected, so that some semblance of law and order would remain. In this case the extremes of cruelty in the awful horror of Nazi genocide might never follow even if nonvoluntary euthanasia is legalized and extended far beyond what anyone would expect at the outset.

Much would depend upon the speed with which killing began and spread. From this point of view the legalization of nonvoluntary euthanasia by a decision of the United States Supreme Court comparable to the abortion decision would be especially dangerous, for this would preempt the normal operation of the political processes in each state and would make it extremely difficult to withdraw or limit the legalization of killing when restraint began to deteriorate seriously.

I. Concluding Remarks

As we pointed out in chapter three, section J, the Congress of the United States has enforcement power under the Fourteenth Amendment whereby it can act to protect basic rights of persons by appropriate legislation. We believe it would be desirable if Congress would enact legislation guaranteeing the protection of the laws of homicide in all jurisdictions under the Constitution to all persons, except in the cases of capital punishment and self-defense, thus to exclude by preemption the legalization of nonvoluntary euthanasia by the various states. An attempt to enact such legislation would, at the very least, be a positive step which would force the euthanasia debate to unfold somewhat faster than proponents of euthanasia might prefer.

Proponents of euthanasia very likely would resist such an effort by claiming that it amounted to an attempt to impose one view upon the whole society, in which there is no longer any consensus regarding the absolute inviolability of human life. After all, democratic government and law is based upon consensus. In this respect there remains an important difference, proponents will insist, between legalizing nonvoluntary euthanasia in a democratic society and in a totalitarian state, since the majority rules in the former society while a few vicious men determine what will be done and enforce their will by terror in the latter.

But this argument would be fallacious. Consensus does extend and limit the purposes to which government can properly direct the common resources and activities of political society. Thus, if there is no consensus that the protection and promotion of human life in itself should be an object of state action, then one must concede that the concept of the sanctity of life cannot be assumed in jurisprudence as a principle.

However, whether all persons shall equally be protected by the law of homicide and whether all human individuals should be considered persons are not questions about purposes. These are not issues about ideals and interests which can be settled by a consensus which would either include protection of rights and recognition of personhood within the sphere of common concern or leave these matters in the domain of liberty outside the field of appropriate state action. Whether society extends the protection of the law of homicide equally to all and whether it recognizes all human individuals as persons are matters on which one position or the other inevitably must be taken, with decisive results for the individuals concerned.[60]

It remains possible, of course, that a majority of citizens with the color of legality will choose to set aside the standard of equal protection of the laws or will choose to declare some until now recognized as persons to be nonpersons, thus to attain the same result. But if this happens, consensus with regard to justice itself will be gone. The acts of government then will be a reflection merely of power, resolving competing interests in a mutually acceptable way. Minority rights will no longer exist, because "rights" will mean no more than what is conceded to members of the group by the dominant part of it.

Such a condition would be, in reality, no more a political society cooperating under law than was the German state under the Nazi regime. For what is lawless about dictatorship is not the fewness of those in power but the arbitrariness with which they exercise power, unrestrained by the requirements of equal liberty and justice for all—that is, for the weak as well as the strong, for the deficient as well as the normal, for the burdensome as well as the productive. What is obnoxious about racist discrimination is not that the principle is race but that the discrimination is unjust. Careful exclusion of racial principles for discrimination of lives too meaningless to live, of human individuals too unintelligent to be persons, of persons too burdensome to protect from being killed will not make the discrimination just.

In an article arguing for the standard of membership in the human species as sufficient for legal personhood, Joseph L. Lewis has pointed out:

> In a country where racial, social and ideologic tensions between various groups and the state become greater daily and more profound every decade, that neither membership in the human race nor the right to life is to be determined by arbitrary socio-political standards is a good point to have clear, both for the safety of the persons comprising dissident and minority elements and for the safety of those persons comprising both the state, as society, and the governmental state. Not only is it a good point to have clear in general, but it is a good point to have constitutionally clear, in the form of unequivocal written law.
>
> If one group of Homo sapiens can, in the course of history, be singled out and as a class have their right to life and liberty suspended, then in a historic context appropriate to the action, another group of Homo sapiens may be singled out and as a class have their right to life and liberty suspended. Because of the neatness with which society continues to function through its rational systems and established procedure, it is hard to perceive that the Supreme Court's abortion decision has declared a rationalized state of nature among the groups, classes, and individuals of American society. The Supreme Court decision represents a social Darwinistic doctrine of survival of the fittest, and the Supreme Court has arrogated to itself the rationalizing power to say who is the fittest.[61]

Because we agree with Lewis that the unborn surely ought to be recognized as legal persons and their right to life protected, we also agree with him that the Court's decision was a radical injustice to this minority. And the tendency of the present legal situation with respect to the unborn does follow logically: to terminate the rule of law and to substitute the rule of brute force.

However, we think Lewis is mistaken in supposing that the corruption of legality in the United States Supreme Court decision on abortion—and in the more or less extensive legalization of abortion in other jurisdictions within the common law world—totally corrupts legality and throughout society substitutes a struggle for survival for fair cooperation toward common purposes, with respect for liberty beyond the field of common action.

The power of the United States Supreme Court, even the power of the British Parliament, is not so great that a single act on its part can utterly destroy lawful authority in an entire political society. Moreover, the claim of justice in the case of abortion, while clear enough for those prepared to see it, is not so patently clear that those responsible for recognizing it can not have overlooked it, thus perhaps engaging in an exercise of self-deception but not necessarily in an exercise of dissimulation and solemn mockery.

Further, a large part of the society does recognize the injustice and is working for its rectification by lawful means, for example, by seeking an appropriate amendment to the United States Constitution. Many other citizens, we believe, would support this cause if they understood more clearly what is at stake.

Of course, if nonvoluntary euthanasia is legalized and especially if it becomes widely accepted, then the corruption of legality which Lewis is talking about will not be so restricted, especially because in this case it would be very difficult to make a mistake about what is just even with the help of self-deception. And, as we have said, if the legal order as a whole becomes corrupt, formerly democratic societies would no more remain communities under law than was the German state under the Nazi regime.

In such a circumstance even those persons comprising the state as a society and high government officials would no longer be safe, as Lewis points out. Acts intended to defend innocent lives from destruction under the color of legalized nonvoluntary euthanasia might cause great tensions, as judges and lawmakers who decreed the practice and physicians and others who administered it might come to be viewed—whether rightly or wrongly—by those most dedicated to the defense of the right to life as unlawful attackers.

Yet even if those in power were able to keep themselves safe while they killed the powerless, this would not change the fact that such killing would violate justice—the justice which the American people always have hoped to establish in their common life. All of those killed without their consent will be denied equal protection of the law, whether they are killed by the arbitrary judgments of others that they would be better off dead, by the arbitrary imposition on them of criteria which would make them nonpersons, or by the brutal decision to solve finally the problem of dependency by killing the dependent.

Advocates of euthanasia often point out that in certain primitive tribes which lived in very hard environments there was a practice of abandoning the elderly and others who could not keep pace with the group. Even in such a practice, imposed by cruel necessity, there was respect for the dignity of persons who were left behind. The dependent who were killed in a program of nonvoluntary euthanasia would enjoy no such respect for their dignity. They would be deprived at once of life, of liberty, and of justice with the approval of the law of a land which has made its proud boast: liberty and justice for all. And they would be disposed of like refuse by a nation unwilling to care for them, although it is the richest and most powerful nation the world has ever known.

9: Justice and Care for the Noncompetent

A. The Need for Legislation

In chapter four we considered the liberty of competent persons to consent or to refuse consent to medical treatment. To the extent that some such persons make decisions about their own future care which will be legally effective when they are noncompetent, the problem to be considered in the present chapter is mitigated. For here we consider the question: To what extent and by what means must the law, if it is to be just, require that medical care be supplied to persons who are not legally competent?

Among such persons, of course, there are many, such as infants and children below the age of consent (whatever the law determines this age to be), who never have been competent. Thus the issue to be considered here is unavoidable, no matter how many persons who are legally competent make effective decisions about their own later care. No system of "living wills" or designated agents solves the problem of what to do about the infant who never has been in a position to make a living will or appoint an agent.

Our primary concern in this chapter is how much care the law should require for noncompetent persons, particularly in cases in which care is necessary to save their lives. The reason for this emphasis is that the most serious injustice which can be done the noncompetent is to withhold care as a method of killing them.

There often will be levels of care above and beyond what the law can mandate which will be beneficial to persons and no imposition upon them. We must likewise be concerned to limit care so that noncompetent persons are not subjected to overtreatment, which also at times can be a serious injustice. Moreover, there are problems about the supply of care to noncompetent persons when it is needed for their health and well-being, even though not at all demanded to preserve life. The legal solution we shall propose toward the end of the present chapter will be of some help in dealing with all such problems, although we will not focus upon them in the course of the discussion, since problems in which life is not at stake are only remotely connected with euthanasia, the focus of this book.

In chapter eight we argued against nonvoluntary euthanasia. If we are correct in holding that the law may never justly permit this practice, then neither can the law tolerate homicide upon noncompetent persons effected by the withholding from them of medical care. Homicide by omission is just as grave an injustice as is homicide by deadly deed, and the law forbids the former just as completely as it does the latter.[1]

However, it is much more difficult to recognize and to prove that a crime has been done by omission than that a crime has been done by commission. Not acting to save life is not always homicide, for it may not be possible to act; if it is possible, one in a position to act may not be aware of the need to do so. Even if one is aware that one could act to save a life and that this life will be lost if one does not act, there still will be no legally significant omission unless there is a legal duty to perform the act which one fails to perform.[2]

Generally speaking, parents are legally bound to care for their children, physicians for their patients, and so on. Such duties provide the foundation on which a prosecutor could argue that the withholding of care known to be possible and necessary to save life constitutes murder or another form of homicide by omission.[3]

However, there can be no duty to provide care—even care possible and necessary to preserve life—if that care would be such that no reasonable person would consider it appropriate and of real benefit to patients in their actual condition. On this basis there is no homicide in omitting to resuscitate a dying patient over and over again, for such efforts are not demanded by the ordinary standard of due care and probably violate this standard. In such cases physicians do not have a duty to do everything possible to keep patients alive, and so their nonaction is not an illegal omission, even though they could act and know that the patient surely will die if they do not.

It follows that the determination by law of what care will be required for noncompetent persons will be a determination of what neglect will be homicide. In times past, when hardly anyone was prepared to approve nonvoluntary euthanasia, special efforts to see to it that persons would not be homicidally neglected were unnecessary. Now, however, many favor active euthanasia, including nonvoluntary euthanasia, as we saw in chapter eight.

The law lacks adequate provisions and machinery to cope with the new situation, and so until now it has not defined very precisely the duty to provide care. Thus, persons are dying, as we shall show, by the unjust withholding of lifesaving medical care, but no prosecutions are taking place. The law must be concerned about such potential victims of homicide just as much as it is concerned about others who might be killed by deadly deeds. Otherwise the requirement of equal protection is unfulfilled in respect to these persons. What is needed is a method of specifying before it is too late for the individual concerned what care cannot be withheld without homicidal neglect.

Children suffering from Down's syndrome sometimes are born with an intestinal blockage which will be fatal if not repaired by surgery, but which can be corrected by a fairly simple operation with a very high rate of success. In some cases in recent years surgery has been withheld from such children, although it is given routinely to babies needing it who are not unwanted by their parents. Legal and ethical commentators generally have regarded this withholding of care as unjustifiable discrimination against these infants.[4] Yet there is evidence that many physicians tend to ignore this consensus about what is due care for children afflicted with Down's syndrome; one survey indicated that half the pediatricians in Massachusetts would recommend nontreatment of the intestinal blockage when it is noted in such infants.[5]

Another fairly common kind of case which has been much discussed in the medical journals and elsewhere is that of the infant suffering from spina bifida. Spina bifida is a congenital defect resulting from the failure of the spinal column's two sides to unify perfectly, so that the child is born with a split in the column which may permit the spinal cord to protude, causing a hump on the back and preventing its normal closure. This defect results in damage to the nerves and lack of normal function in the part of the body below the site of the damage. Without treatment many such infants die from infection or from hydrocephalus, which is very often connected with the spinal defect.

In recent years it has become possible to close the opening in the back surgically and to treat the hydrocephalus. When full treatment is given, some of these children nevertheless die. However, many survive to grow up and are seldom severely retarded. Yet such persons suffer from many serious problems, usually including paralysis of the lower body, lack of bladder control, and other handicaps.[6]

Until the late 1950s not much could be done for children born with this defect, yet some survived. During the 1960s, as the new techniques became available, many centers having the facilities and expertise to use them vigorously treated almost all such children. They left untreated only those who were dying or whose condition posed technical obstacles to treatment. The percentage of survivors increased, but the burden of caring for children who survived and the handicaps under which they would still suffer became more apparent.[7]

Beginning around 1970, many physicians adopted policies of selective treatment, giving vigorous care only to infants whom they believed would survive and be able to enjoy a comparatively high quality of life. But there was no unanimity upon the standards for selection.[8] Moreover, at some centers infants excluded by the selection procedures seemed to be dying more quickly than would have been the case before treatment was possible—although in those earlier days large numbers of such children were reported as stillborn who somehow probably would have been live births during the years when intensive treatment was the rule.[9]

Some advocate that nontreated infants should be given only normal nursing care and protected against suffering. Tube-feeding, oxygen, and antibiotics would be denied, but pain-killing drugs and normal feeding would be ordered. Treatment for hydrocephalus would be excluded absolutely, because "progressive hydrocephalus is an important cause of early death."[10]

Others advocate periodic reevaluation of infants with spina bifida who survive early neglect, in order to prevent continuing survival of an infant in a condition growing constantly worse due to continued neglect.[11] Half-treatment can result in survival in much worse condition than would have been the case if treatment had altogether been excluded.[12] Consequently, some urge that active measures to bring about death be legalized as the only solution for infants excluded from vigorous treatment.[13]

Although some physicians put great stress on the distinction between killing and letting die, those who favor active euthanasia as a treatment of choice regard this distinction as a mere quibble.[14] From this point of view early death is sought as a management option, sometimes by the "active" withdrawal of treatment, a policy by which even fluids are withheld so that death will come quickly.[15] Others insist that nurses cannot be expected to lower their standards of basic care for a spina bifida infant, yet the nurse "has to be inspired to do the right thing" and not to save babies excluded from treatment by the selection process.[16]

Some physicians are beginning to express severe reservations about the whole effort to select infants for treatment and the consequences of this effort.[17] One thing is clear. The problem presented by infants suffering from spina bifida is not unique.[18] Similar problems arise with respect to patients of every age, when the prognosis with vigorous treatment is not for the attainment or restoration of healthy, normal functioning, and yet the prognosis without treatment includes the possibility of a prolonged and more severely damaged survival, which can be excluded with assurance only by withdrawing even normal feeding.[19]

It is often said that the problem of the extent to which the noncompetent ought to be given care has arisen because of the development of new medical techniques. These techniques make it possible to keep many persons alive today who only a few years ago would have died no matter what anyone tried to do for them. This explanation is partly correct, because every new power raises a new question concerning the conditions under which it is properly exercised and properly reserved.

But a far more important factor in the problem about care for the noncompetent—a factor which clearly would have given rise to this problem even had there been no progress in medical techniques during the last decade—is the shift from the older ethics based upon the sanctity of human life to the newer ethics based upon the quality of life.[20] Even some who accept legalized abortion regard as a legal fiction the denial of the personhood of the unborn by the United States Supreme Court. The transparency of this fiction leads directly from the legalization of abortion to the conclusion that infanticide also should be legalized, although a few strive to maintain a significant distinction between the killing of defective children before and after birth.[21] The view that unquestioning deference must be given to the parents' wishes with respect to the nontreatment of an already born child which is unwanted because of its defectiveness clearly is an extension of the view that a woman has a right to abort an unwanted pregnancy.

Examples such as that of the children suffering from spina bifida make clear that some sort of legal policy is needed to distinguish cases in which treatment ought to be required from cases in which it should be optional or even forbidden.

At present an infant or a person who has a legal guardian most often is treated in accord with the wishes of the parent or guardian, usually with these wishes shaped by physicians but ultimately respected by them. Some argue that this situation is quite satisfactory and that the law should remain aloof from it.[22]

The question of the noncompetent adult who has no guardian is less clear, for treatment now usually depends upon consensus between the attending physician and the patient's near relatives, but cases such as that of Miss Karen Quinlan reveal the limits of this arrangement. If the legislation we propose in chapter four were adopted, the physician clearly would have primary authority unless either a patient previously competent had established some control or a court overruled the physician's judgment or appointed and authorized a guardian to do so.

However, even if the locus of decision-making authority were clarified, there would still be a question whether the unchecked judgment of the parent or guardian and of the physician—even when the noncompetent patient's physician and family are in complete agreement—should determine the giving and the withholding of medical care. If in some of these cases—for example, that of the mongoloid child with intestinal blockage—there ought to be a legal duty to treat, then leaving matters as they are makes it almost impossible to prevent or punish this type of homicidal omission. By such an omission a person's life might be taken without due process, just as would be the case if active euthanasia were used as the method. Hence, the first problem is to determine what the law should be with respect to the substantive issue: To whom is care due and under what conditions does it cease to be due? Only after this question is answered can one reasonably appraise various possible procedures for protecting the rights of everyone involved.

B. Inadequate Solutions Criticized

Someone might argue that the proper course is to assume the consent of all noncompetent patients to treatment which would preserve or prolong their lives. However, this approach oversimplifies the problem by overlooking the fact that there is a duty to give care only when it is appropriate, and treatment is appropriate only when it is in the patient's interest.[23] In all the literature which we have seen concerning the case of Miss Quinlan there is a clear consensus—in comments both before the respirator was withdrawn, when it was generally expected she would die as a result, and afterwards— that such treatment was not appropriate. The New Jersey Supreme Court also reached this conclusion and thus gave a clearer legal status to the duty not to continue lifesaving medical treatment of noncompetent persons under certain circumstances.

While cases precisely like Miss Quinlan's are rare, the decision is being implemented in respect to a range of more or less similar cases.[24] Many patients on chronic hemodialysis find the treatment distressing both physically and psychologically.[25] Probably a person suffering from paranoia would find such treatment especially distressing. Would it be a duty to provide the treatment regardless of the distress? A recent Massachusetts Supreme Court decision, which we shall discuss in section I, upheld the refusal by the guardian of an adult with Down's syndrome to accept life-prolonging therapy for leukemia.[26] Some might criticize this decision, but hardly anyone will argue that an infant who is so badly deformed that death is inevitable regardless of treatment must be treated to prolong life as long as possible.[27]

Another proposed solution is based upon the use of the distinction between ordinary and extraordinary means of treatment.

In 1957 Pope Pius XII stated in an address to a group of medical specialists that while there is a moral obligation to use ordinary means to preserve life, there is no obligation to make use of extraordinary ones.[28] This distinction has been widely quoted in the literature concerning the limitation of treatment, and it played some part in the *Quinlan* decision. It also appears in the 1977 Arkansas statute which allows a member of the family or guardian to refuse the use of "extraordinary means" of medical care.[29]

However, as Paul Ramsey and Richard McCormick have pointed out, the distinction proposed by Pope Pius does not conform to the medical distinction between what is ordinary and what is not, and the force of the papal distinction is normative rather than descriptive.[30] Hence, to appeal to this distinction in the legal context is of little use, for this appeal merely raises once again the question what treatment is appropriate for a patient in a given condition, considering the patient's overall legitimate interests.

Moreover, the introduction of the ordinary-extraordinary distinction into law seems undesirable for another reason. Since the distinction comes from a religious context, it lacks a proper legal history. If it is to be used in law, then the body of traditional Catholic moral theology will have to become a source for legal judgments. This situation could be considered a violation of the First Amendment's prohibition of the establishment of religion.

Sometimes it has been suggested that the method of triage, which is used in military and disaster situations, should be applied for the selection of patients for medical care, with the implication that in this way defective and abnormal individuals might be justly excluded from treatment.[31]

In military medicine attention at times has been given to those sick and wounded soldiers who would be restored to active duty, while more seriously damaged soldiers were ignored. Clearly, this system treats individuals as means to the military objective rather than as patients who deserve equal respect for their personal needs. It is understandable enough in the situation in which persons are treated as expendable, but only a totalitarian society could make a general practice of such a method, and even then could do so only by clearly specifying the objectives for which persons were to be used.

In disaster situations a somewhat similar system has been used to select patients for care: Those are treated first for whom the physician can do a great deal of good with a minimum of effort. Those in very poor condition and who would require a large part of the available resources to survive are not cared for unless they survive until after those likely to benefit from fast treatment have been cared for. This method makes sense when there is an immediate shortage of facilities and personnel for care, since it distributes what is available in a manner most likely to save the largest number of lives.

However, the denial of care to noncompetent individuals is never argued for on such grounds; the justification is their prospective quality of life, or the impact of their care upon others or society at large. Clearly, disaster medicine is a special situation which would cut across the lines between competent and noncompetent, and require no special justification for ignoring anyone less likely to benefit significantly from quick treatment. When immediate pressures are not imposed by an unavoidable situation, the factors which require the special approach of disaster medicine are no longer present. The adoption of patient-selection methods suited to a disaster situation for the open world of normal society would be no more reasonable than the adoption of emergency-relief techniques as national economic policy.

Of course, many who advocate the selective nontreatment of defective infants and other noncompetent patients urge that consideration ought to be given to the interests of the species, of society, and especially of the individual's family when a determination is to be made about treatment.[32] Those who advocate active euthanasia on the assumption that some human individuals fall short of criteria for personhood or on the assumption that the right to life of some persons can be extinguished by the conflicting interests of others obviously would support this line of argument.[33]

But if assumptions which would justify active euthanasia are excluded from consideration, then the impact of an individual's survival upon society or the extent to which an individual's family desire the individual to survive can hardly be accepted as just standards for limiting the duty to provide medical care.[34] If such standards were accepted, then the lives of some persons who happen to be noncompetent would be subordinated to less pressing interests of others. Such subordination would violate the due process and equal protection rights of noncompetent persons. These rights are recognized for the mentally ill and retarded no less than for other persons.[35]

Recent legislation in the United States requires that institutions and facilities receiving federal funding make the adjustments necessary to accomodate handicapped persons.[36] Also, there have been widespread efforts to make better provision for the education and training of exceptional children. In the face of these developments, it would be patently discriminatory to select any group of noncompetent patients for nontreatment in the interests of society or their families.[37]

The problems of families are touching and truly serious when they are faced with long-term responsibility for an infant or other family member who requires unusual care and who perhaps will never (or never again) be able to live a normal life. Yet families can obtain a good deal of public assistance and in other ways be helped to bear their burden.[38] Rather than legalize the exclusion of some noncompetent persons from treatment, additional assistance could be provided. In extreme cases parents can give up their parental rights and responsibilities.[39] In the past this process usually has led to institutionalization in a public facility. But in recent years much has been done in providing foster home care for individuals whose families could no longer care for them. Children with spina bifida have been accomodated in this way.[40]

In considering the unfairness of selection for nontreatment on the basis of the impact on society and the family if an individual survives with defects, it is instructive to review the experience of selection of patients for hemodialysis when such treatment was in very short supply. Some programs attempted to select by a committee decision based upon considerations of the social value of various candidates for treatment.[41]

It quickly became clear that committees tended to select according to their own middle-class standards. The approach was strongly criticized and finally abandoned by at least one of the important facilities which had used it.[42] Random selection by taking patients on a first-come basis has been accepted as a fairer procedure.

Age also has been used and sometimes been imposed by law as a criterion for selection for hemodialysis. But this limit can be understood as an application of the disaster-situation method of triage if the specific modality of treatment is limited and life-expectancy from treatment is the decisive consideration.[43] In the absence of such medical indications and a real necessity to work within limits the use of age as a criterion seems to be an unusual case in which a group has been excluded from treatment on a discriminatory basis.

C. Toward a Solution: The Demands of Justice

Generally, those who argue for the application of criteria based upon social and family interests to exclude some noncompetent persons from treatment also urge that the prospective quality of life of such individuals ought to be taken into account.[44] Moreover, some who do reject exclusion from treatment on the basis of the interests of others nevertheless urge that the potentiality of an individual for some level of human functioning must be present if the individual is to merit treatment necessary for survival.[45]

Against this view the same arguments we proposed in chapter eight against nonvoluntary euthanasia tell. We shall not repeat these arguments here. The crux of the matter is that different people have different quality-of-life standards. No one is able to judge fairly what a day of life is worth to some other person.[46] It would be arbitrary to accept quality-of-life standards as a basis for providing less protection for the lives of certain classes of individuals. Moreover, all of the injustices in the use of qualitative criteria uncovered in chapter eight, section E, will occur if these criteria are used in selecting persons for nonvoluntary euthanasia, whether the killing is accomplished by deed or by omission.

Sometimes it is argued that to refuse to select for nontreatment on the basis of prospective quality of life is to treat the disease in disregard of the well-being of the person afflicted with it.[47] However, as the literature on spina bifida makes clear, the adoption of such criteria amounts to a judgment that individuals with certain disabilities would be better off dead.[48] Once this principle is adopted, moreover, the distinction between nontreatment and active euthanasia can hardly be maintained, since efficiency in attaining the objective prescribed by the principle demands active euthanaisa.[49]

It is worth noticing that if the infants being killed by neglect were slightly older when their prognosis became known, there would be much greater hesitation about denying them treatment. It is easier for a family to reject a newborn whose prospective quality of life is as poor as that of the average child afflicted with Down's syndrome or spina bifida than it would be to refuse treatment for a four year old who was injured in an accident and had a similarly dim prognosis.[50] Many middle-aged competent persons are far from being perfect specimens; they do not refuse medical care for themselves on that basis.[51] In view of this fact it is hardly fair for them to refuse the treatment required by their newborn children.

It is often argued that toward life's end people become mere vegetables, who ought not to be kept alive. But it is prejudicial to classify some persons in this way. Moreover, there is a variety of types of persons who are considered to be in persistent vegetative condition.[52] Further, many of the elderly who are considered senile really are suffering from some condition which could be treated if sufficient attention were given to careful diagnosis.[53]

Richard A. McCormick argues that the alternative to appraising the value of care in terms of prospective quality of life is to treat all patients with every means available. He further suggests that the criterion of extraordinary means can be translated into considerations of quality of life.[54]

But this argument overlooks the fact that individuals who are competent can refuse treatment upon themselves without the intent to end their own lives, which would be the motive if they appraised their future prospects and decided they would be better off dead. Such refusal of treatment, including treatment without which life will be shortened, can be based upon objectionable features of the treatment itself, its side effects, and its negative consequences. An individual who has no desire to die can take such factors into account and decide that life without treatment, so long as life lasts, will be better than life with it. Such a decision is not a choice of death.

If justice is to be done to noncompetent individuals, an effort must be made to make such a decision on their behalf when they cannot make it for themselves. In this way the noncompetent will be protected from having treatment imposed upon them which they probably would reject if they were able to do so. Likewise, justice demands that no judgment be made on anyone's behalf that he or she would be better off dead. Not only would it never be possible to know with reasonable certitude that a noncompetent person would make such a suicidal choice, but the implementation by others of such a choice would violate the jurisprudential principles which argue against legalizing assisted suicide and voluntary euthanasia, discussed in chapters five and six.

The basic requirement of justice with respect to care for noncompetent persons is easy enough to state: The noncompetent person ought not to be denied that care which any reasonable person who was competent probably would desire in similar circumstances, and the noncompetent person ought not to be given care which any reasonable person would refuse in a like case. The factor of noncompetence as such simply is irrelevant to one's need for care and the duty of others to provide it. If this factor is taken as an excuse to treat noncompetent persons otherwise than they would be treated if they were competent, an injustice is done.

The difficulty with this basic requirement is that clear as it is in theory, in practice its application is not at all clear.

The problems which arise with respect to treatment of noncompetent persons always or almost always are grounded in conditions causally related to, although distinct from, their very noncompetence—for example, in a condition of serious deformity, or of retardation, or of a poor medical prognosis, or of serious debility. Reasonable persons usually have not been in such conditions, although in some cases there is a class of individuals who have been and could express an opinion. For instance, many who suffer from spina bifida grow up and have normal or near normal intelligence. Also, while no one has been in Miss Quinlan's condition and is now able to express an opinion about what is appropriate treatment for one is such a condition, people can project a state of affairs in which they might be in such a condition.

Yet even when some individuals have been in one condition and many can imagine themselves in another condition, the requirements of justice cannot be settled by an opinion poll, although such polls might have some relevance. Competent persons can refuse not only inappropriate treatment but also appropriate treatment, and can refuse treatment without a good reason—for example, if they wish to commit suicide by omission.

Noncompetent persons cannot exercise their liberty; no one else can commit suicide for them. Therefore the wishes we can project for the noncompetent will only help determine what is just to the extent that these wishes conform to the public policy which does not favor suicide, but which only permits it out of respect for liberty. Thus what one would want if one were in the place of a noncompetent individual will point to what is just treatment of such an individual only if one's desires are not only intelligible but also compatible with a nonsuicidal intent. This distinction was unnecessary in chapter four but will be indispensable here.

Furthermore, even reasonable persons who reject both nonvoluntary euthanasia and suicide will not easily agree in all cases that medical care or other care either certainly must be supplied to or certainly must not be imposed upon a legally noncompetent patient. There will be many cases about which persons who are altogether reasonable and in no way willing to accept active euthanasia or suicide will disagree when it comes to setting the standard of care of noncompetents.

This is so because individuals who are not suicidal can quite reasonably disagree in very similar circumstances concerning the extent to which they themselves wish to accept medical or other care. About all that one can be certain of is that anyone would wish palliative care—to kill pain and to minimize the discomfort of an unhealthful condition—as well as ordinary nursing care, and that anyone would refuse experimental treatments, those with a minimal chance of success, and those which would prolong the process of dying without giving at least some increased opportunity for action.

While these implications of the basic requirement of justice in respect to the noncompetent are very little, still they are enough to suggest that the withholding of all care—even including the comfort of fluids—to promote quick death must be regarded as prima facie unjust. At the same time the termination of active life-support systems maintaining the life of a dying and unconscious person must be regarded as prima facie just.

Although the Supreme Court of New Jersey invoked a supposed constitutional right to privacy in its resolution of *Quinlan,* it is important to notice that the court's decision in this case also rested upon the assumption that Miss Quinlan was dying.[55] Moreover, the court argued that most people would make a similar choice for themselves and for those closest to them.[56] No one, the court believed, would wish to endure the unedurable, to be held back from inevitable death for a few months, when there was no reasonable hope of being restored to consciousness and some degree of human activity.[57]

Every person receiving medical care is entitled to care in accord with the ordinary standard of medical practice—that is, the good care which a reasonably prudent physician of normal knowledge and skill would provide in similar circumstances. This standard of care has been given a certain precision through judgments in cases involving malpractice.[58] One might suppose that it would be helpful in defining the physician's duty toward noncompetent patients.

However, this standard is of little help. For, in the first place, the malpractice cases do not involve the withholding of care which causes the patient's death; they generally involve defects in what a physician does. Second, what constitutes due care is at least partly defined by that to which a patient consents or would consent, as we explicitly specified in chapter four, section I. Hence, the problem of determining what patients should be assumed to want cannot really be settled by the standard of due care except when this standard makes clear what anyone would want. Third, many cases of kinds with which we are primarily concerned in this chapter are too different from other cases to apply standards of due care, which depend upon analogies in which all the relevant circumstances are the same. Fourth, physicians would easily argue that the practice of withholding care *precisely in order that* patients will die is becoming accepted as standard medical practice.[59]

Perhaps cases in which children afflicted with Down's syndrome have been permitted to die would be judged to be instances of malpractice; surely they would if the parents desired good care for the child and the physicians failed to perform the necessary surgery. However, as things stand, the physicians rely upon the refusal of the parents to consent, and the possibility of malpractice toward the infant patient, whose rights can hardly be reduced to the rights and interests of the parents, remains unexplored because no one with standing to sue for the wrongful death of the infant comes forward to do so.

D. Inevitable Economic Limits and Justice

In some discussions of the extent to which there is a duty to provide medical care it is pointed out that care can be very costly.[60] Can at least some classes of noncompetent individuals—for example, children who are born afflicted with severe defects due to spina bifida—be denied care on the ground that care for them simply would be too expensive? To answer this question it is necessary to consider the prior question as to what is each individual's fair share of medical care. For this we must consider what medical care is.

Ordinary nursing care and medical care must be distinguished from each other. Ordinary nursing care includes those things patients would do for themselves if the strength and will to act were not absent; in the case of infants it includes those things which a mother would do for her child. Thus nurses see to it that their patients are fed, kept clean, kept warm, changed in position from time to time, and so on. A professional nurse provides in addition to ordinary nursing care medical care under a physician's direction and in this capacity functions as an assistant physician.[61]

Medical care is the application of means of preserving life, promoting health, and easing the pain and discomfort of disease and injury when the means applied require the special training, knowledge, and skill of a person whose profession it is to engage in such work. The province of medical care is to examine with trained skill, to diagnose on the basis of expert knowledge and professional experience, to plan and prescribe treatment in accord with the state of the art, to perform tests and treatments using equipment and instruments which might endanger patients if they were used without special skill and care, and so on. What is medical care in a proper sense should be defined in terms of the concept of health, and health itself must be limited to the well-functioning of a person—in the present context, to organic well-functioning.[62]

Because of the distinction between ordinary nursing care and medical care it would be unfair to argue that noncompetent persons must be denied whatever is their fair share of medical care on the ground that the total cost of their care, including nursing care or maintenance in a public institution, will greatly exceed the average amount which can be spent for each member of society for medical care. If anyone wishes to argue that society cannot afford to feed nonproductive consumers, that argument should be proposed in a straightforward way, without confusing the cost of other necessities of life with the cost of medical care. Exceptionally bright and able children also are expensive to bring up, and exceptionally well-to-do persons also consume a great deal more than the average share of the gross national product.

In the allocation of resources America has large and unsolved problems concerning the priority which ought to be given to medical care in general and to various modes of medical care. At the level of delivery of care there sometimes are problems as to the allocation of limited facilities—for example, kidney dialysis machines or transplant operations.

In general, we are not concerned here with such problems, for they affect the competent as well as the noncompetent and are only remotely related to euthanasia. However, we shall briefly discuss the need to limit medical care at some level and the manner in which this might be done without unfairness to noncompetent persons or to others who happen not to be in a strong position to obtain care which would be of benefit to them.

Many criticisms have been made of the existing health-care system as a whole. Some doubt that health-care ought to be treated as a commodity; it is argued that physicians have achieved a monopoly such that they exploit patients by charging for their need. Others urge that the allocation of medical resources is faulty—for example, in putting so little stress upon preventive medicine.[63] We are not concerned here to argue these issues. Whatever the injustices in the present system, they affect the competent as well as the noncompetent. Our concern here is with the special issue of justice which is involved if noncompetent persons are taken advantage of so that treatment due them is withheld or treatment a competent person would reasonably and legitimately refuse is imposed upon them.

It is clear that society has some common commitment to the provision of medical care. Public funding is devoted to health in many ways, and society recognizes, licenses, and supports the medical profession—and does the latter at a very high level. Still, there are many other purposes, such as national defense and education, to which the society also must direct its scarce resources. It will never be possible to do everything possible in any one field. As medical technology develops and evermore expensive forms of treatment are devised, the inevitability of an absolute limit on expenditures, even when life is at stake, will become even clearer.[64]

There already has been some experience of this situation with the introduction of kidney dialysis, which is too expensive for most people to afford. Not all who could benefit were treated; various methods of selection were developed. In some cases ability to pay was a disqualification for admission to a program. United States government funding of dialysis was widely criticized on the ground that other, similarly expensive treatments would not be able to be made available with public funds to all who might benefit from them.[65]

Given the system of health-care delivery which actually exists, a fair share of health care available to individuals seems to be based upon need—which seems to be a very reasonable principle—limited by ability to pay.[66] All physicians can refuse to accept any noncompetent patient for care if they are unwilling to provide service without payment and if there is no source from which payment might be expected. Anyone having care of a noncompetent person in need of medical treatment is innocent of neglect if every effort is made to obtain treatment, but none is available because there simply is no way to obtain it. But this situation obviously does not justify what we are mainly concerned with in this chapter: the purposeful withholding of medical care from noncompetent patients who are *already* patients of some physician.

It is worth noticing that cases discussed in the literature in which care has been withheld so that individuals would die do not seem to have hinged upon immediate financial problems. One reason for this might be that when care is not obtained because of financial difficulties, this situation does not appear to anyone to involve an ethical problem which requires an argument in its defense. Another might be that although the medical costs involved in caring for defective infants and other noncompetent individuals often are substantial, much of this cost can be reimbursed from public funds and from insurance.[67]

At the public level there are limits on what can be allocated for medical care. Yet up to the present there never has been a policy by which a particular group has been defined and systematically denied a share in available medical resources.[68] If, as some fear, advancing medical technology threatens to absorb an ever-increasing share of scarce resources, limits can be established without selecting particular groups for discriminatory treatment.

There would be many ways to accomplish this purpose. One would be to set dollar limits to the total amount of public funds which could be paid to or on behalf of any single individual to reimburse medical and hospital costs during a year and/or during a whole lifetime. These same limits could be applied by statute to the total which could be received or paid on one's behalf from ordinary health and major medical insurance, including all group insurance. If individuals wished to spend more, either on an item by item basis or by buying special individual insurance to supplement the limited policies generally available, they could of course do so. However, no one would be considered to have a legal duty to pay for anyone's care beyond the established limits.

Arrangements such as these would prevent the situation which is often projected as a specter: a cure for cancer which costs millions of dollars for each patient or a means of keeping people alive for hundreds of years.

E. Nonsuicidal Reasons for Refusing Treatment

Both nondying and dying persons might have reasons for considering the refusal of treatment without which life cannot be saved or prolonged. However, such considerations are far more likely to appeal to a person who is dying. Hence, any legal policy with respect to the refusal of treatment on behalf of noncompetent persons must be based upon a clear concept of the condition of dying or the process of terminal illness. How can this concept be defined?

Sometimes it is suggested that everyone is dying from the very beginning of life.[69] But while it may be true that the decline of vitality is a lifelong process, to identify this process with the condition of dying is to defy common sense and the ordinary use of language, which notes an important distinction between aging and dying. Again, it is urged that to determine whether an individual is dying one must know that individual's previous history.[70] A patient's history may be helpful in diagnosing an existing condition, but extreme ill health and debility compared with a prior condition of well-being and vigor is not by itself enough to determine that one's condition is terminal.

Again, dying is sometimes confused with the condition of incurable illness.[71] But many conditions such as diabetes are incurable, and yet not every diabetic is dying. Nor will it do to say that dying is a condition intermediate between full life and full death.[72] Many who are declining and debilitated might be said to lack full life, but such persons are not dying; in another sense, as long as one is alive, one has full life, since being alive is not a matter of more and less.

If we consider the conditions under which we say that someone is dying, we find that generally this is not said unless one knows some cause which is already at work in the individual and is expected to be fatal. For example, a friend may seem very ill and rapidly declining, but is not said to be dying until the cause is diagnosed as a condition which cannot be reversed—for example, an invasive and inoperable carcinoma of a vital organ. At the same time, if such a cause is known to be engaged in its inexorable operation, a person who seems quite vigorous can be called "dying," although not perhaps "terminally ill." The cause which is identified must be one which cannot be removed or counteracted by any treatment available under the actual conditions.

A process which is potentially fatal and irreversible will not lead to the judgment that the individual is dying if there is still any significant possibility that the individual will die by the unexpected intervention of another cause such as an accident or another disease. In effect, to say that someone is dying is to make a prediction with considerable assurance that a condition already known to exist will be fatal—will be listed as at least the underlying cause of death on that person's death certificate.

On this conception not everyone who has an incurable condition which normally is eventually fatal should be said to be dying. In many cases there is a prospect of prolonged life with good treatment, so that there is a significant probability that an unrelated factor will cause death. Thus, someone afflicted with a form of cancer which can be held at bay for several years would not be considered dying even if the condition will kill if something else does not do so first, because such an individual can also die of a heart attack, an automobile accident, or some other cause. Moreover, decline and debility, particularly if it is appropriate to an individual's age and life history, would not be considered a process of dying; "old age" is no longer an adequate explanation of anyone's death.

Nevertheless, there are times when one can be certain a person is dying without being able to specify a precise cause of death. These are cases in which an individual's condition is so extremely debilitated and so rapidly worsening that an observer can be certain that *some* fatal cause is at work. For legal purposes cases of this sort will not be very important, since usually physicians can diagnose the condition of which anyone is dying; if the condition cannot be diagnosed, they will assume a patient is dying only at a point at which the withholding of treatment which would prolong life could not be considered unlawful, and the imposition of such treatment could hardly be considered due medical care.

The concept of dying has an inherent vagueness, and the criteria for recognizing a person as dying are not always easily applied. The vagueness of the concept arises because it depends upon the probability that some existing condition will be the cause of death, and this probability is not precisely specified. The criteria for recognition can be difficult to apply because misdiagnosis is not uncommon; treatments considered ineffective sometimes succeed. Dying patients sometimes recover and live for years.[73]

From the point of view of the problem we are concerned with in this chapter the distinction between persons who are dying and those who are not is important for two reasons. First, as noted above, considerations on the basis of which a person might choose to refuse medical treatment which is available are far more likely to appeal to a dying person than they are to one who is not dying. Thus law must take into account the fact that an individual is or is not dying if appropriate refusal of treatment or consent to treatment is to be constructed on his or her behalf.

Second, although someone who could provide care and who has duty to do so will be negligent if such care is not provided, such negligence could hardly be held to be homicidal unless it could be shown that a reasonable person could predict and the negligent person did foresee that death would result—that is, that the negligence would *cause* death.[74] Depending upon the conceptions of causality which are adopted, a court would find it more or less difficult, or even impossible, to find that negligent care of an already dying person caused death or even certainly hastened it.

Even a dying person might desire medical treatment of various sorts. One surely would desire palliative care to limit suffering and discomfort, to remove annoying symptoms. One might also desire more active treatment if it held out the promise of a remission of the process of dying sufficient to allow one to do or to experience something one wished to do or to experience.

Ordinary nursing care also would be desired, both because lack of it would increase suffering and because the personal aspects of such care generally are a comfort to one who is dying. Even here, of course, there would be limits. If being fed caused a dying person considerable discomfort and no apparent satisfaction, and if the pains of hunger could be allayed without these untoward consequences, then it would not be unreasonable to assume that such a person would prefer not to be fed.

But while a dying person might desire various forms of care, such a person also might well choose to refuse therapy of a more active sort, even if aggressive treatment could prolong life considerably. Several considerations might be regarded as adequate grounds to refuse treatment.

First, sometimes treatment is experimental or otherwise risky. A person who is dying, just as one who is not, might prefer to avoid treatment which carries with it some danger of bringing about an unexpected result, such as immediate death, increased discomfort, or an alteration of one's disposition.

Second, some treatment is itself painful or brings about other experienced conditions which are undesirable. One who is dying might well choose not to undergo pain, to prefer a somewhat shorter but more pleasant life.

Third, in many cases the requirements for the application of medical care would interfere with the activities and experiences which one desires during the time remaining. For example, one might well refuse care which would take one away from one's family or one's work. One might prefer to spend one's last days in a pleasant retreat rather than to spend one's last months in an intensive care unit.

Fourth, many people object to certain forms of care on the basis of some principle. A Jehovah's Witness might refuse life-prolonging or even lifesaving blood transfusions. Anyone might refuse a heart transplant if the heart had to be taken from another not already dead.

Fifth, there are a variety of reasons why persons find medical care psychologically repugnant. Those who are not dying generally overcome this repugnance; those who are dying might well consider such feelings adequate ground for refusing life-prolonging treatment. Among the factors which make medical treatment repugnant are shame or embarrassment at being seen and touched by others, humiliation at being dependent upon other people and even on machinery to carry on one's vital functions, impatience with treatment which does not yield felt benefits, resentment against physicians and other persons administering care who seem too detached and insensitive or too professionally cheerful and optimistic, and irritation at being aroused, fussed over, and disturbed. Such psychological repugnance to treatment provides much of the content of the concept of indignity which lends plausibility to the slogan "death with dignity."

Sixth, in many cases medical care for one individual makes very severe demands upon others—for example, the depletion of a family's financial resources or the tying up of medical facilities which could actually be put to use for the benefit of others. Persons who are dying might well prefer not to impose such burdens on others. Here we are considering, not costs and resource allocation as an excuse for neglecting the care of individuals, but the probable legitimate desires of the individuals themselves which only indirectly reflect these factors.

F. Reasonable Presumptions for the Noncompetent

Although in general persons who are legally noncompetent can be presumed to consent to care in accord with the ordinary standard of medical practice to the extent that such care will preserve or prolong life, this presumption admits of exceptions. While the preceding argument shows that considerations based upon an individual's prospective quality of life if he or she survives ought not to be allowed to weigh against providing care—since this would amount to the judgment that the person would be better off dead— considerations on the basis of which the person would themselves probably prefer that treatment not be administered cannot be ignored without unjustly imposing upon the noncompetent person.

It might be urged that the limitation of care where appropriate will be assured if the ordinary standard of medical practice is properly understood and followed. But except to the extent that this standard itself takes into account the circumstance of the patient's personal consent to or refusal of treatment—the very circumstance here under consideration—the ordinary standard of medical practice often will indicate that treatment be continued in cases in which from the patient's viewpoint limitation would be appropriate. This discrepancy might arise because the present standard of medical practice in respect to certain forms of treatment is to continue applying them as long as there is any possibility that they will prolong life. It might also arise because the reasons why a patient would prefer not to have certain kinds of treatment continued are personal ones which lie beyond the physician's normal perspective and competence to evaluate.

If a noncompetent person is dying and permanently unconscious, then the reasonable presumption is that medical care to prolong life is inappropriate, since most people would find care under such conditions psychologically repugnant and inconsiderate of others. Still, most people would wish to be treated as living persons until they actually die—and to have their bodies treated with decent respect afterwards. The provision of ordinary nursing care, to the very limited extent to which it can be given without medical expertise to use special equipment and techniques, seems to be required for due respect to even permanently unconscious dying persons, considered as living persons until they die.

If a noncompetent person is dying but is not always unconscious, then in addition to ordinary nursing care there is a reasonable presumption that palliative medical care is appropriate. Whether life-prolonging treatment is appropriate is a matter of judgment. On the one hand, the fact that an individual is dying may be enough to indicate that care would be refused for one or more of the reasons stated above. On the other hand, if an individual is able to engage in any activities or to have any experiences which he or she might wish to continue, and if none of the considerations on which a refusal of treatment would be based seems to apply in the particular case, then consent to treatment ought to be presumed, even though there is no likelihood of recovery to a point at which competency would be regained and even though many people would regard the quality of life of such an individual to be negative.

If there is a probability that patients will recover sufficiently to do things or to experience things which they might value, and especially if there is a significant possibility that patients will recover enough to become competent to make their own decisions about care, then the desirability of treatment increases. However, the considerations on which treatment might be refused also must be weighed, and the probable choice of the patient projected from the evidence available.

In most cases any permanently unconscious patient can be presumed to be dying. Generally the underlying cause of unconsciousness probably will eventually cause death either directly or by complications resulting from the continuing state of unconsciousness itself. However, inasmuch as a person is not dying if lifesaving treatment can reverse the probability of death from an existing condition, a permanently unconscious person is not necessarily dying.

Even in such a case it seems to us reasonable to assume that such a person would refuse medical treatment. Some considerations which weigh against treatment would appeal to most people. This appeal need not be dismissed as prejudiced because everyone could at some time find themselves in the condition described. Moreover, in a permanently comatose condition there is no opportunity for doing and experiencing, which most people would value, to offset the appeal of reasons for rejecting medical treatment.

It might be objected that the last point depends upon an evaluation of the quality of life of a permanently unconscious person. But this is not so. No judgment is made that the person would be better off dead than living in the given condition. However, the given condition of the patient must be taken into account to notice whether there are any positive aspects of the patient's life which a reasonable person would regard as outweighing those considerations other than suicidal ones on the basis of which a person might refuse treatment.

The process of weighing the alternatives against one another, moreover, is not an attempt to calculate the net value of each alternative; rather, it is an attempt to conjecture what choice people themselves would make. Here what choice most people who considered the matter would make with respect to themselves if they were ever in the condition described is relevant evidence upon which to ground the conjecture, especially if the common opinion is shared by persons who do not consider suicide and euthanasia legitimate.

If a permanently noncompetent person is neither dying nor permanently unconscious, the general presumption in favor of consent to lifesaving treatment according to the standard of good medical practice will usually stand as correct. Most competent persons who are not dying accept lifesaving medical treatment regardless of the aspects of the treatment and its effects which might make it repugnant, and there is no reason to presume that noncompetent persons would take a different view of the matter.

If a person is only temporarily noncompetent and is neither dying nor permanently unconscious, then the presumption in favor of consent to lifesaving treatment is even stronger, since the condition in which one would be able to make choices for oneself is likely to be valued both for the use of liberty itself and for other activities and experiences which one might enjoy.

Even in a case of this sort, however, considerations on the basis of which a person might choose to refuse lifesaving medical treatment cannot be wholly excluded. The prospective quality of life subject to limitations and handicaps is not a factor which should be taken directly into account. Any judgment that a person would be better off dead than surviving with limitations and handicaps is illegitimate, for refusal of lifesaving treatment projected on this basis amounts to suicide. The law can hardly accept the conjecture that anyone would commit suicide without accepting the practice as legitimate, not merely as something to be tolerated out of respect for liberty.

Although a prognosis of a life which would be considered by some to be of poor quality cannot be taken into account, yet the actual condition of a person must be considered in weighing the significance he or she probably would attach to various factors which might make the treatment itself seem repugnant.

Moreover, in many instances lifesaving treatment is only more or less probably going to succeed. In other words, in many cases a person who is not dying inasmuch as possible treatment could reverse the probability of death from a given cause nevertheless probably will die due to that cause. For example, a patient who has a condition which might be remedied with surgery which has a high mortality probability is not dying inasmuch as the surgery *could* succeed but will probably die due to the condition since the surgery *probably will not* succeed. When the likelihood that a possible treatment will succeed in saving life is low, a patient who would be considered dying except for the possible success of the treatment can reasonably be considered to weigh more heavily factors which would make the treatment repugnant than if the probable success of the treatment were high.

G. Application to Cases of Defective Infants

In terms of the preceding principles one can consider the judgments which ought to be respected with regard to some of the kinds of cases discussed in section A.

An infant suffering from Down's syndrome who needs a fairly simple operation to remove an intestinal blockage and who is otherwise in good condition certainly ought to have the operation. No one who was competent would refuse such a simple operation for themselves, and no normal child would be denied it. The undesirable aspects of the surgery itself and its consequences are slight and the prospect of success with the operation good, while death is inevitable if the surgery is not done. The only reason for denying the infant the treatment is the impermissible one of its antecedent congenital condition. The treatment is withheld only for fear that it will succeed, when it is assumed that the patient's life ought to be terminated either for the benefit of others or because it is considered better off dead.

Infants born with spina bifida present a more complex problem. Some are dying. For them the withholding of surgery and other medical treatment, except palliative and ordinary nursing care, would be acceptable. Others are not dying, for there is a probability that good care will be lifesaving. The presumption in such cases must be in favor of treatment. However, in cases in which an infant is in very bad condition so that the probability of survival although real is comparatively low and the expected course of treatment is unusually long and difficult, one might conceivably conjecture that a person in this condition would refuse treatment to avoid the pain, the interference with life, the disturbance, and the inconvenience to others which the treatment would impose.

The advice of individuals who have survived such treatment and who do not approve suicide and euthanasia would be of great value in making a reasonable conjecture in a case of this sort. If such persons considered the treatment, when its probability of success was not good, of sufficient worth to justify the adverse aspects of the treatment itself and its consequences, then one could say with confidence that a person in such a condition probably would prefer to be treated. This conclusion is especially compelling when one considers that failure to treat someone who is not then killed by withdrawal of ordinary nursing care is likely to lead to survival of the individual in a far worse condition than would have obtained if vigorous treatment had been undertaken at an early stage.

The literature which we reviewed on the problem of selection of children for medical treatment from among those afflicted with spina bifida makes clear that most—if not all—who advocate selection argue on the basis of social interests, family interests, and the prospective quality of life of the child who survives. Little weight in their argument is placed upon the considerations which might render the treatment repugnant to the afflicted individual. The fact that physicians do treat infants with spina bifida, no matter how poor their prognosis, if parents demand treatment also suggests that there is no strictly medical justification for withholding treatment.

The fact that most people who are competent would desire treatment for themselves or their already accepted children if an accident created a situation analogous to that in which the spina bifida is born confirms the conjecture that such an infant would consent to treatment. The analogous situation we are imagining would be one in which an accident put an individual's life in peril, but there remained a substantial chance of saving it by a rather long and difficult course of treatment, with a prospect of imperfect recovery to a life subject to many limitations and disabilities, sometimes even with reduced intellectual powers.

This is the kind of situation in which individuals every day urge physicians to do everything possible to save life, on the assumption that where there is life there is hope. No one gives up as easily upon his or her own life or upon the life of a wanted child as do the physicians who exclude spina bifida infants from care. It is clear that exclusion in most cases—except those in which the infant is dying—is based upon a judgment that the prospective life is not worth preserving.

H. The Case of Miss Karen Quinlan

As we noted previously, when the *Matter of Karen Quinlan* was heard by the New Jersey courts, the general assumption was both that she was permanently unconscious and that she was dying. On these assumptions it was not unreasonable to conjecture that in her condition she would refuse at least the intensive care she was receiving and to which her family objected. Psychological repugnance and consideration for others who might make use of the resources and facilities might have been sufficient considerations to warrant a reasonable choice against treatment in the intensive care unit. Also, although it was not established that Miss Quinlan held any principle which would have required her to refuse intensive care, it was plausibly argued that she accepted a position according to which the refusal of such care was a morally acceptable option.

Even if it had been believed that Miss Quinlan was not dying, a very plausible argument can be made that the considerations weighing against care would have prevailed in a reasonable judgment by her. An individual who stands to gain only the preservation of life from intensive care, with no prospect of recovery of abilities to act and to experience, might well prefer that others have the advantage of the resources and facilities used in this way, and might well consider intensive care so repugnant as to be unendurable. It also is worth noticing that many people would consider refusal of care in such a case morally obligatory on the ground that consent to it would express an attitude of clinging greedily to life, an attitude hardly compatible with a decent respect for the interests of other people.

Nevertheless, the Supreme Court of New Jersey can be faulted for not pursuing more carefully the question of whether Miss Quinlan was dying or not. It could be argued that the damage she has already suffered will very probably be the underlying cause of her eventual death. If so, then she is dying, and we doubt that the law ought to require that she be given any medical care at all. The use of antibiotics to fight infection and the feeding of a special formula by tube surely are forms of medical care. Ordinary nursing care probably would not keep Miss Quinlan alive for long, for even if she is able to swallow, the effects of malnutrition and infection probably would end her life in a short time.

But if the law cannot require that a person in Miss Quinlan's condition be given medical care if she is dying, it cannot forbid all such care and especially cannot forbid less aggressive forms of care if a person is not dying—that is, if the care really maintains life. Life is a good to which most people cling, and the less aggressive forms of care are neither so repugnant nor so incompatible with the interests of others in alternative uses of resources and facilities that one need assume that a person in Miss Quinlan's situation would refuse the medical treatment she now receives.

In other words, we think that Mr. and Mrs. Quinlan have made a judgment on their daughter's behalf which is well within the bounds of reasonable conjecture, although it is not the only reasonable conjecture which they might have made. It would also be reasonable to suppose that a person in Miss Quinlan's condition, even if not dying, might regard all medical care with repugnance and might consider even a minimal burden to others something to be avoided.

X. The Case of Mr. Joseph Saikewicz

The recently decided Massachusetts case, *Superintendent of Belchertown State School* v. *Saikewicz,* poses a different problem. Mr. Saikewicz was an institutionalized, sixty-seven-year-old man. He was so severely retarded that he could not communicate verbally. He had been in general good health but became ill. Acute myeloblastic monocetic leukemia was diagnosed.

This disease is considered incurable, although chemotherapy is regarded as appropriate treatment for it. Such treatment is painful, often has serious side effects, and requires some cooperation from the patient. Without therapy the patient dies without great pain or discomfort. With treatment the patient often dies in a short time due to complications of the treatment itself or, despite the therapy, due to the disease. But if the therapy is successful, a remission of the disease occurs. The remission might be as short as a few weeks or as long as several years. The prognosis for successful therapy is better in younger patients.

The Belchertown State School sought appointment of a guardian to consent to treatment on behalf of Mr. Saikewicz. A probate court appointed a guardian who investigated the matter and reported to the court that he did not believe the therapy would be in Mr. Saikewicz's best interests. The probate judge accepted the guardian's recommendation but also referred the case for appellate review. Review was granted by the Supreme Judicial Court of Massachusetts, which approved the lower court's decision on July 9, 1976. Mr. Saikewicz died September 4, 1976. A full opinion had been promised and was finally issued over a year later, November 28, 1977.[75]

The Massachusetts high court argues that the noncompetent person has the same rights with respect to care as has the competent person. Competent persons are held to have the right to refuse treatment; this right is an aspect of the right of privacy, conceived of as "an expression of the sanctity of individual free choice and self-determination as fundamental constituents of life."[76] The right to decline treatment might sometimes be overridden by a state interest in preserving life, in preventing suicide, in protecting the rights of other persons such as dependents, or in protecting the integrity of the medical profession. But the first interest does not obtain if the patient is incurable as Mr. Saikewicz was; the second and third were irrelevant; and the integrity of the medical profession was not threatened in this case, since the decision was based on medical advice.

The court also argues that a case such as Mr. Saikewicz's poses a special and difficult problem. On the one hand, the rights of such a noncompetent person must not be set aside. Since competent persons can decline treatment, the possibility of declining treatment cannot be excluded for noncompetent persons. On the other hand, choices for noncompetent patients must be made in such a way as to protect their own best interests. In reaching a substitute judgment concerning such patients' best interests all relevant aspects of their actual condition and circumstances must be taken into account. The question which had to be answered on behalf of Mr. Saikewicz, then, was what he himself would have considered to be in his own best interests had he been able to form and express a preference. Yet in answering this question his actual condition, including his present and future incompetency, could not be ignored.

The probate judge mentions two factors weighing in favor of treatment: the fact that most people want it and that it could prolong life. He lists six factors weighing against treatment: Mr. Saikewicz's age, the probable side effects, the low chance of significant remission, the certainty of immediate suffering, the patient's inability to cooperate in the treatment, and the "quality of life possible for him even if the treatment does bring about remission."

The Massachusetts high court holds that what most people want is not relevant; what Mr. Saikewicz would want is the issue. But his life could not be considered to be of less value than the life of anyone else, "the value of life under the law having no relation to intelligence or social position." The equation of the value of Mr. Saikewicz's life with the quality of his life is firmly rejected. The probate judge's use of the expression "quality of life" is benignly interpreted: The phrase is vague and perhaps ill-chosen but must be taken to refer to the condition of Mr. Saikewicz's life as he would have experienced it with the effects of therapy, *not* to his condition of mental retardation. The decisive factor in approving the guardian's judgment to decline treatment on Mr. Saikewicz's behalf was that in his condition he would not have been able to cooperate with the treatment; it would have meant a continuing state of pain and disorientation for him.[77]

In our view the substance of the opinion of the Supreme Judicial Court of Massachusetts in this case is almost wholly sound. Except for its reliance upon the supposed right of privacy, which we have criticized in chapter two, section G, the court's treatment of the liberty to decline treatment supports the same position for which we argued in chapter four. The principle of equality between competent and noncompetent persons in their rights to appropriate but not excessive treatment is the same principle upon which we are proceeding in this chapter. The grounds on which the court holds that care might be refused are some of the grounds we have articulated.

Most important, the court very clearly rejects any supposition that Mr. Saikewicz's life was inferior because of his severe retardation; it wholly ex-

cludes a quality-of-life justification for the refusal of treatment
thus refuses to assume that a person as retarded and ill as he w
off dead. In this respect the Massachusetts high court has full
potential damage of the probate judge's opinion and defended t
tion we have been defending.

It is easy enough to imagine other cases in which it would be reasonable to
project a refusal of lifesaving care by a noncompetent person whose noncompetence is caused by a condition which also would make the care especially
repugnant. Many people who are on kidney dialysis find it so objectionable
that they voluntarily discontinue treatment. To a great extent this repugnance
is psychological.[78] If a paranoid person required such treatment to survive,
the treatment might be experienced as a form of torture, and it might well
cause such a person extraordinary anguish. In cases of this sort one could
hardly doubt that it would be reasonable to conjecture that patients would
refuse such care if they were able. On this assumption the imposition of care
would be an injustice.

By contrast, it ought not to be assumed that everyone who is debilitated
and noncompetent would desire life without care in preference to life with it.
The often-repeated assertion that pneumonia is the "old man's friend" might
be true with respect to an elderly person who is dying. But even a person of
advanced age and in coma who is not dying ought not to be abandoned. The
question still remains whether there is anything especially repugnant about
the treatment such a person requires to survive. If there is not, then treatment
should be given, just as it would be provided for a younger and more productive member of society.[79] To assume that the elderly would be better off dead
is a form of discrimination based upon prejudice in favor of youth and potential productivity.

The Proper Locus of Decision-Making Authority

If the principles we have outlined are the correct ones on which to determine whether a noncompetent person should or should not be given medical
treatment, the question remains who will make the many judgments which are
involved and how the making of these judgments might be regulated in order
that noncompetent persons will neither be killed by neglect nor be treated in
ways they would reasonably refuse if they were able.

Present neglect statutes tend to require that those who have the care and
custody of noncompetent persons seek medical treatment for them when a
reasonable person in the circumstances would consider treatment necessary
and there is some way to obtain it.[80] These statutes could be clarified and
broadened, and we shall propose that this be done in the legislation we shall
outline in section M. But despite their limitations such statutes together with

prevailing customary practice tend to create a situation in which there normally are two parties involved in decisions about care for noncompetent persons.

If the noncompetent individual is an infant or has a legal guardian, the parent or guardian seeks necessary medical care, must consent to it, and can change physicians if this seems desirable. Still, physicians need not accept the decisions of a parent or guardian as determinative; they can appeal to the courts in the interest of the noncompetent person. Normally physicians shape the decision of the parent or guardian by the information and advice they give, and so they have no real difficulty in acting in accord with the decision which is made.

If the noncompetent individual is not an infant and has no legal guardian, then the locus of decision-making authority is less clear. However, the physician usually will be assumed to have the right as well as the duty to administer lifesaving treatment in accord with the ordinary standard of good medical practice. In most cases the next-of-kin of the patient will be informed about prospective treatment, and consent or release of liability will be sought. The attending physician is likely to take into account the views of a noncompetent patient's family. Thus in practice the treatment of the noncompetent adult who has no guardian as well as of the infant or noncompetent who has a legal guardian is likely to depend upon consensus between the attending physician and at least one member of the patient's immediate family or the patient's guardian.

The legislation which we proposed in chapter four would, if adopted, make even clearer that the primary locus of decision-making authority resides with the physician in case the patient is an adult who has no legal guardian; at the same time our proposal would facilitate decisions by competent persons in regard to their own future medical treatment and would make such decisions binding upon any physician who agreed to treat such persons.

If the parents or family and the attending physician of a noncompetent patient who is dying agree about what ought to be done in the way of medical treatment, then we see little reason why the law should authorize anyone else to intervene except to make sure that the patient really is dying. If the consensus favors what in fact will be overtreatment, then no great injustice is likely to be done, especially if persons who are at some time competent are able to decide effectively about their own future medical care and thus forestall unwanted treatment.

If the consensus errs on the side of withholding treatment that perhaps should be given, the fact that the patient will die regardless of neglect or treatment makes legal control difficult, since the causality of death will be unclear. Also, in the case of dying patients the considerations which might provide a basis for a reasonable refusal of medical care have considerable force, and the physician and family are probably in the best position to appraise the weight of these considerations and conjecture what the patient if competent would choose.

Again, if the parents or family and the attending physician of a noncompetent patient who is not dying reach a consensus that some treatment ought to be given, there is little likelihood that this consensus will lead to a seriously unjust imposition of treatment upon the patient. Furthermore, it would be difficult in such a case to establish an alternative approach as more reasonable and in accord with what the patient if competent would choose.

However, if a patient is not dying, then even if the parents or family and the attending physician agree that some treatment ought to be withheld, the correctness of the judgment reached by consensus is not beyond question. This is so because the parents or family and the attending physician might agree with each other that the patient would be better off dead and might be cooperating in implementing this impermissible consensus. Also, while only a remote possibility it is not impossible that an attending physician and a patient's family might conspire to kill the patient by calculated neglect, not in the supposed interest of the patient, but in the interests of the family and perhaps of the physician as well.

It follows that the consensus of the noncompetent patient's attending physician and family ought to be determinative if the patient is certainly dying or if the consensus favors treatment for a patient who is not dying. However, if their consensus favors withholding treatment from a noncompetent patient who is not dying, their judgment cannot be considered beyond question.[81] Furthermore, if these two primary sources of decision-making on behalf of noncompetent patients are in conflict, then some independent authority is needed to resolve the dispute.

The number of cases in which problems can arise will be reduced if laws such as we proposed in chapter four are enacted. Further, if legislatures deem persons competent to make decisions about their own care before the age of majority for other purposes, some decisions can be made by patients themselves which now must be made by others.[82]

Still, there will remain many cases in which a substitute judgment must be made, and the parents or family and attending physician disagree concerning what should be done, or they agree but their consensus might well be an agreement to commit homicide by neglect. What is to be done in such cases? Sometimes guidelines are suggested without any method for making or rectifying decisions.[83] Such guidelines are of little help.

Some suggest but others strongly oppose resting ultimate confidence in the physician.[84] If the issue were a merely technical one, this confidence might not be misplaced. However, since the judgment is one which goes beyond medical competence, the physician's advice, while indispensable, can be considered final neither when the parents or family of the noncompetent patient disagree nor when the justification of that very advice is called into question.

Others suggest that parents, at least, be given absolute decision-making authority in respect to their own children.[85] In most cases this would be very reasonable, but when the physician disagrees or when there is a possibility that the parents are abusing their authority, then there ought to be some way to protect the infant, just as there is a way to protect it against abuse and neglect of other kinds.

A committee of physicians has been proposed and sometimes used to help make decisions about giving and withholding care, but a committee has many of the disadvantages of the single physician and also diffuses responsibility, thus to make bad decisions easier.[86] A guardian who is not supervised also might easily make arbitrary decisions.[87]

It seems to us that the rights of noncompetent persons cannot be protected unless there is liberal access to the courts when the attending physician and the parents or family disagree, or when another interested party believes that the noncompetent individual is purposely being killed by the withholding of appropriate medical treatment. Only a court can guarantee due process for the noncompetent: hear all of the evidence, weigh it impartially, and apply an articulated policy to the facts.[88] The courts, of course, have no monopoly on fairness, but they do have a monopoly on the legal processes which ensure so far as possible that the legal rights of all persons are protected.

As in other cases, the work of the courts in this matter ought to be guided by carefully drafted legislation. If legislation is not enacted, the courts will be left to draft their own—a task for which experience indicates the courts are not particularly well suited.

In many cases decisions on acceptance or refusal of treatment will have to be made on the basis of a close examination of the details and will have to be changed from time to time as the patient's condition changes. Such judgments almost always would best be left by the courts to a guardian designated for the purpose and given both authority and general direction by the orders of the courts. The governing statute ought to make clear what sort of persons can be considered qualified to act as guardians for noncompetent patients.

In some cases it might be argued that the noncompetent patient's best guardian will be a member of the family. This view can be sound, for family members are likely to be in a good position to know what the patient would desire. However, if the interests or the attitudes of the family conflict with the interests of the patient or the standards required by public policy, then a guardian from outside the family will be a better choice. What such a guardian lacks in intimate knowledge of the relevant facts, he or she is likely to make up in objectivity in judging both the relevant facts, and the irrelevance of factors which ought not to be allowed weight.

K. Criticism of Arkansas and New Mexico Statutes

Two of the statutes regarding the refusal of treatment passed in 1977—those of New Mexico and Arkansas—include provisions for execution of a document by one person on behalf of another.

The Arkansas statute is predicated on the assertion of a right to die with dignity and provides for the making of a document with the formalities required for a will to refuse the use of "artificial, extraordinary, extreme or radical medical or surgical means or procedures calculated to prolong" one's life or, alternatively, one "to request that such extraordinary means be utilized to prolong life to the extent possible." Any person may make such a document for himself or herself. The third section provides for the making of a document on behalf of a minor or an adult who is somehow incapacitated from executing such a document. It must be executed in the form of a will:

> (a) By either parent of the minor; (b) By his spouse; (c) If his spouse is unwilling or unable to act, by his child aged eighteen or over; (d) If he has more than one child aged eighteen or over, by a majority of such children; (e) If he has no spouse or child aged eighteen or over, by either of his parents; (f) If he has no parent living, by his nearest living relative; or (g) If he is mentally incompetent, by his legally appointed guardian. Provided, that a form executed in compliance with this Section must contain a signed statement by two physicians that extraordinary means would have to be utilized to prolong life.

The fourth section of the act releases persons, hospitals, and other institutions from liability which might otherwise arise out of "failure to use or apply artificial, extraordinary, extreme or radical medical or surgical means or procedures calculated to prolong such person's life."[89]

This statute is an attempt to assure that there is a definite locus of decision-making authority in respect to the care of minors and noncompetent individuals. It opts for locating the authority in the family by designating in sequence various relatives who might make decisions. Probably the legislators were moved by the *Quinlan* case and wished to prevent control by physicians against the wishes of the family in a case very similar to that.

The legislation does not respond to the entire breadth of the problem, for it does nothing to remedy cases in which physicians and family agree to non-treatment in violation of the rights of a person whose life they believe to be not worth living. Moreover, the vague and unhelpful notion of "extraordinary means" is pivotal and is not defined in the statute.

In concept the law seems to assume that the patient would be in terminal condition when the document becomes effective, but this requirement is not expressed; therefore, attention is not directed to the very critical question of whether the patient is dying or not. The legitimate bases on which one might construct either consent or refusal of treatment are not stated. The formulation by the document of what can be done seems to assume that in any case only one decision is needed and that no one could reasonably wish to accept some forms of treatment while rejecting others.

The listing of persons who can act on behalf of a minor or noncompetent is likely to create confusion and uncertainty. Either parent can act, and a conflict will arise if they act inconsistently. If a spouse is unwilling to act, this unwillingness can be overridden by an adult child or by a majority of such children. Conflicts will arise if the spouse acts to require treatment to be continued and the children order that it be stopped, and also if an even number of children favor and oppose continuation of treatment.

Apart from the case of a minor, the statute leaves unclear when a person should be considered incompetent to the extent that another can act for him or her. What will happen if a patient is too weak to make a document but is able to speak with effort?

Finally, the statute makes no provision for a hearing before a court to hear evidence on factual questions and to assure that the rights of the noncompetent individual are protected.

The New Mexico statute turns on the definition of terminal illness as "an illness that will result in death . . . regardless of the use or discontinuance of maintenance medical treatment" and the definition of maintenance medical treatment as "medical treatment designed solely to sustain the life processes." The statute specifies no form for the directive to physicians. It does prescribe that the document is to state that in case terminal illness is certified, maintenance medical treatment shall not be utilized for the prolongation of life. The certification is to be by two physicians, one the patient's attending physician, in writing; physicians certifying terminal illness are presumed to be acting in good faith, and physicians acting in accord with a declaration are released from liability.

The fourth section provides for the making of a document for the benefit of a terminally ill minor. If the minor has a spouse who has reached the age of majority, then the spouse may act; if not, a parent or guardian may act. However, if the minor who is terminally ill gives "actual notice of contrary indications" or if action by a parent or guardian is opposed by a spouse or other parent or guardian, then the document may not be executed.

The document is ineffective without the certification of a judge of the district court where the minor is domiciled or maintained. The court must appoint a guardian ad litem for the minor, and judges are to certify the document only if they are satisfied "that all requirements of the Right to Die Act have been satisfied, that the document was executed in good faith and that the certification of the terminal illness was in good faith."[90]

Again, this legislation does not deal with the case in which treatment which ought to be given is omitted. The pivotal concept of terminal illness is introduced but not defined as clearly as might be wished, and the hearing is directed to investigate, not the question of fact, but only the good faith of the physicians certifying it. Legitimate bases upon which one might construct consent to treatment or refusal of treatment are not stated, and this legislation also assumes that only one decision is appropriate: either to continue or altogether to withdraw "maintenance medical treatment."

The requirement that a document not be executed if there is disagreement expressed by the minor patient, by a spouse if there is one, or by either parent or guardian, together with the requirement that the patient's own physician certify terminal illness, in practice would mean that lifesaving treatment should be withheld only when there is unanimity among those most intimately involved. Since the law deals only with minors, it makes no provision for a case like that of Miss Quinlan.

Moreover, although the parent or guardian of a minor could change physicians and thus secure agreement, the situation is confused by the requirement that the minor's own expression of wishes can block action. If the minor is considered competent to determine what must be done, then it is difficult to see why the minor's wishes should be effective only in the blocking of a declaration.

The judicial hearing and appointment of a guardian ad litem respond to the need for due process. But the deficiencies in the act prevent this hearing from being fully effective, because the court is not directed to consider vital questions of fact, is not provided with standards for constructing a reasonable decision on behalf of the minor, and is not directed to appoint a guardian qualified to decide about care on legitimate bases in case the parent or guardian and physician are proceeding on the assumption that the patient ought to be allowed to die because he or she would be better off dead.

Finally, the statute does not do anything to provide for cases in which the patient is not terminally ill but consent to treatment which is necessary to preserve life might nevertheless reasonably be refused.

L. The Decisions in *Quinlan* and *Saikewicz* Criticized

The decision of the Supreme Court of New Jersey in the *Matter of Quinlan* also must be considered as an attempt to legislate a solution to the problem of the construction of reasonable decisions concerning the medical care of noncompetent persons. The court conceives the problem as one which had arisen because of developments in technology making it possible to keep a person in Miss Quinlan's condition alive. The court admits that the physicians declined to discontinue treatment in accord with "then existing medical standards and practices." The legislative intent is then explicitly stated:

> Under the law as it then stood, Judge Muir was correct in declining to authorize withdrawal of the respirator.
>
> However, in relation to the matter of the declaratory relief sought by plaintiff as representative of Karen's interests, we are required to reevaluate the applicability of the medical standards projected in the court below. The question is whether there is such internal consistency and rationality in the application of such standards as should warrant their constituting an ineluctable bar to the effectuation of substantive relief for plaintiff at the hands of the court. We have concluded not.[91]

The court then proceeds to argue that the standard of medical practice permits termination of active treatment in the case of dying patients.

It had already argued that Miss Quinlan had a constitutionally protected right of privacy which would permit her to refuse treatment and that this right could be exercised on her behalf by her "guardian and family."[92] The court suggests that the problem lay in the possible contamination of medical judgments by the self-interest or self-protection concerns of physicians and proposes to take care of this possibility by the institution of a hospital ethics committee to share responsibility.[93] The court's holding in the case appoints Mr. Quinlan guardian of his daughter's person, explicitly saying that he might change physicians. Then the holding is stated:

> Upon the concurrence of the guardian and family of Karen, should the responsible attending physicians conclude that there is no reasonable possibility of Karen's ever emerging from her present comatose condition to a cognitive, sapient state and that the life-support apparatus now being administered to Karen should be discontinued, they shall consult with the hospital "Ethics Committee" or like body of the institution in which Karen is then hospitalized. If that consultative body agrees that there is no reasonable possibility of Karen's ever emerging from her present comatose condition to a cognitive, sapient state, the present life-support system may be withdrawn and said action shall be without any civil or criminal liability therefore on the part of any participant, whether guardian, physician, hospital or others.

The court then adds a footnote:

> The declaratory relief we here award is not intended to imply that the principles enunciated in this case might not be applicable in divers other types of terminal medical situations such as those described by Drs. Korein and Diamond, *supra*, not necessarily involving the hopeless loss of cognitive and sapient life.[94]

The testimony of the physicians referred to by the court merely indicated that
in some cases of terminally ill patients who are not already cerebrally dead
aggressive treatment might be discontinued, especially with the consent of the
family, on the ground that the patient "has lost human qualities" or that
treatment "does not serve either the patient, the family, or society in any
meaningful way."[95] The court concludes its opinion with the following:

> By the above ruling we do not intend to be understood as implying that a
> proceeding for judicial declaratory relief is necessarily required for the
> implementation of comparable decisions in the field of medical practice.[96]

In this way the court attempts to ensure that its judgment in the case will
serve not simply as legal precedent for courts but as effective legislation to be
followed, without further appeal to the courts, by those involved in decision-
making for the noncompetent and responsible for their care.

Like the legislatures of Arkansas and New Mexico, the Supreme Court of
New Jersey failed to grasp the amplitude of the problem of protecting the
rights of the noncompetent in the matter of medical care decisions. The court
attempts to legislate, but nothing in its decision speaks to the case of an infant
left to starve in a nursery because parents do not want it and physicians agree
that it would be better off dead. Indeed, the loose legislation which the court
has enacted will tend, if anything, to weaken the previously existing protection of such an infant.

In chapter four, section E, we criticized the court's use of the concept of a
constitutional right of privacy. One additional unfortunate implication of
framing the problem in terms of such a right is obvious here: The right of
privacy might protect a patient from overtreatment, but it does not call attention to the patient's right to a fair share of treatment, a share which those
responsible for noncompetent persons have a duty to obtain or to provide.
Since the rights to receive as well as to refuse treatment are not given equal
attention, the court's decision creates a danger that the equal protection of
the law of homicide will be denied to the noncompetent, who will be killed by
malevolent denial of due care.

Although the court realizes that medical standards cannot be altogether
determinative and that someone must decide on behalf of the patient, these
two matters are not clearly related to one another. The court apparently
considers medical standards to be unclear and inconsistent—which perhaps
they are—and assumes the task of amending them.

A much better approach would have been to recognize that physicians have
no right to treat patients except in accord with consent and that lack of such
consent is a relevant circumstance for determining what good medical practice demands. We argued this point in chapter four. Had the court taken this
approach, it would not have had to challenge the standards of the attending

physicians and would have focused attention upon the question of the patient's consent and the need for adequate standards for constructing a decision when the patient is unable to decide.

The court considers matters in the context of an assumption that the patient is dying. The careful definition of this condition is not investigated, nor was the question of fact fully examined. The problems which arise with respect to nondying patients are not touched.

The court refers to Miss Quinlan as comatose and unable to return to a "cognitive, sapient state"; these conditions are not precisely defined, although one might argue that the testimony at the trial by which the language was introduced into the record provides some definition. That testimony seems to indicate that something more than the consciousness characteristic of a normal infant is intended.

One physician explained "sapient" as meaning "perceptive, intelligent behavior, as opposed to vegetative responses, as opposed to vegetative expressions," while another defined "useful recovery" as a level of consciousness in which a patient "is able to function with discriminate senses, sapient sense, that is, to make judgments and to function in a humanistic sense."[97] This rather vague language could be construed to exclude defective infants, the severely retarded, the incurably insane, and the very senile. And the court's footnote indicates it wants its legislation also to apply to a wider range of cases of terminally ill patients.

The court lays down no qualifications for a person to be appointed as guardian with authority to make the substitute judgment. In fact, most remarkably, the court does not seem to realize that the key to the solution of the instant case is the appointment of Mr. Quinlan, who could not have put into effect his judgment on behalf of his daughter without the court's action. So there is no indication how other cases, which the court wishes to have settled without adjudication, will resolve the issue of guardianship.

At the same time the court mandates consultation with a hospital committee. This diffuses responsibility and infringes upon the rights of the patient, for if the proper position is that the guardian can act for the patient, then refusal of treatment on the patient's behalf ought to have removed authority for the hospital and physicians to continue that treatment, just as refusal by a competent patient ought to require a physician to desist from unwanted treatment. In other words, the court to some extent imposed continued treatment upon Miss Quinlan by setting requirements for the termination of treatment which undermine the principle that a person should not be treated without consent.

It is interesting to notice, moreover, that New Jersey hospitals did not have committees such as the court prescribed and subsequently set them up in response to the new legislation by the court.[98] The idea of an ethics committee to share responsibility had been suggested in a law review article, with qualifications which the New Jersey Supreme Court deleted.[99] We consider this idea objectionable. Ethics committees would add fresh complications, diffuse authority, and dilute the patient's rights without guaranteeing due process and equal protection to those patients who are being killed by omission.[100]

The Supreme Court of New Jersey is unduly concerned to keep cases out of the courts. The court holds that problems of the sort involved here can be distinguished from the commitment of noncompetents and other matters which must be processed through the courts.[101] Undoubtedly there are differences, but the court does not say what they are. Moreover, if a person's liberty cannot be limited without legal process, it is hard to see why life should be limited when there is a question about the legitimacy of so doing without a process.

The Court is no doubt worried about the limits of judicial competence in medical matters, but this worry is misplaced. The problem with noncompetent patients as with competent ones is not a need to review technical decisions within the expertise of the physician, although in some cases expert testimony might be needed to settle matters of fact, such as whether a patient is dying or not, and whether a proposed treatment is likely to have certain effects. Rather, the problem with noncompetent patients is to construct a reasonable decision on their behalf, in order that they receive the care which they deserve and would want and that they do not receive treatment they would not want.

Courts can and must determine that persons are not competent to decide for themselves when they are not, find whether the patient's condition would or would not support a presumption for or against treatment, and select a guardian and provide the guardian with guidance about the legal policy which must be borne in mind in deciding on the patient's behalf. No procedure which does not involve a judicial hearing can adequately protect the rights of patients in these matters when the ordinary decision-making process breaks down or seems to someone concerned to be yielding unjust decisions with respect to a particular patient.

Finally, the Supreme Court of New Jersey wants what it calls the principles it enunciates in *Matter of Quinlan* to be applied in other more or less similar cases without a judicial hearing. But what were these "principles?" Is the intention that treatment might be terminated whenever a patient is terminally ill and the family wishes treatment terminated? Does the court desire that a parent of an adult be accepted by others as a legal guardian without recourse to the courts? Does the court intend to exclude criminal and civil liability in all cases where treatment is terminated? No one knows.

In contrast to the effort of the Supreme Court of New Jersey in its decision in *Quinlan*, the Supreme Judicial Court of Massachusetts in *Saikewicz* affirms the responsibilities of the courts in deciding issues concerning medical care for noncompetent persons. The Massachusetts high court states that the case was properly brought to probate court, where the rights of Mr. Saikewicz could be protected. For the future the court calls attention to statutory requirements which ought to be followed. It directs that in a hearing on a petition for the appointment of a guardian for an alleged noncompetent person, the person also be represented by a guardian ad litem, an advocate who will press whatever case there might be for treatment.

The decision whether to give or withhold treatment regarding a person found noncompetent is reserved to the probate judge. This decision is to be made on the standards clarified in the instant case. The judge may seek expert advice as needed. If a hospital has an ethics committee or other consultative body, the judge will listen to its advice. But the authority to make decisions is not to be abdicated to any such body, and the directive in *Quinlan* to this effect is explicitly rejected. Questions of life and death deserve and require the due process for which the judicial branch of government was created. The responsibility is not to be shunted off to some other group representing the social conscience.[102]

The Massachusetts high court's treatment of the issues and procedural guidelines is much superior to that of the Supreme Court of New Jersey. Yet the Massachusetts opinion also raises certain difficulties. Does the decision mean that every single medical judgment with respect to a noncompetent person must be contingent upon the outcome of a judicial procedure? The court does not clearly exclude this interpretation, although it does state in a note that it does not intend to lay down general guidelines concerning emergency medical care for the noncompetent but leaves this task to the legislature.[103]

William J. Curran and Arnold S. Relman, in separate, brief articles in the *New England Journal of Medicine,* attack the requirements for a judicial hearing laid down in the *Saikewicz* decision by claiming that the court is invading the proper province of medical judgment, requiring unnecessary and time-consuming litigation, and showing an undue lack of confidence in the existing medical-care system. The nub of the critics' dissatisfaction with the decision, however, is most clearly revealed in Curran's observation:

> The Court seemed to want to make it clear that a mentally retarded person's life was fully worth saving. This ruling could mean that brain damage to an infant or very serious burns and disfigurement and limited bodily functioning could not be taken into consideration in offering or withholding resuscitation or intensive care to a patient. This interpretation could present very serious implications for medical decision making.[104]

Similarly, Relman cites the articles by Shaw and by Duff and Campbell published in 1973 in the same journal—articles which exposed and defended the practice of selecting infants for nontreatment on quality-of-life criteria. Relman claims these articles showed the complexity of the problem, but he says that few until the *Saikewicz* decision suggested that the physicians and next of kin could not be trusted to make these difficult decisions.[105]

George J. Annas, by contrast, in another journal comments favorably to the decision in *Saikewicz*. According to Annas the questions to which the Massachusetts high court directs attention are the correct questions. Moreover, while a legal procedure is difficult, it is the only way to guarantee both the noncompetent person's rights not to be treated excessively and not to be purposely killed by neglect.[106]

We believe Annas is correct, although the *Saikewicz* decision certainly leaves unclear the extent to which cases must be brought to court. Moreover, the criteria for decision are not spelled out as clearly and fully as they should be. Presumptions are not established in cases in which patients are not dying. And the qualifications of persons to be appointed as guardians are not considered. The court perhaps hopes that the legislature will address itself to all of these problems. If so, we think that the *Saikewicz* decision points precisely toward the proposal we now make.

M. Outline of an Adequate Statute

The previous discussion has shown that legislation is needed to protect the rights of noncompetent persons in receiving their fair share of medical care and in not having excessive care imposed upon them. We have proposed legislation in chapter four to take care of the right of competent persons to refuse treatment. Here we assume that this proposed legislation is enacted, and thus the number of noncompetent persons for whom choices must be constructed is somewhat reduced.

Also, in the legislation we outlined in chapter four the provision is clear that physicians have primary decision-making authority in respect to noncompetent persons who are not minors and who have no legal guardian. Unless directed otherwise by a court, a physician is to assume that the noncompetent person under care consents to appropriate treatment to remedy an existing condition of disease or injury. To some extent the legislation we are now going to propose will call into question the appropriateness of the treatment which a physician acting in good faith might give; consent might be construed to limit treatment which the ordinary standard of medical practice would otherwise require.

The legislative findings, on which the legislation we are about to propose might be grounded, could be along the following lines.

The basic principle is that every person has a right to a fair share of

available medical treatment, especially if such treatment is required to preserve life. No one can justly be deprived of medical care on the ground that
he or she has in prospect a life which some might consider to be of poor
quality.

It follows that those having care and custody of noncompetent persons
must obtain or provide for them so far as possible appropriate medical care
for any existing condition of disease or injury when a reasonable person in the
circumstances would consider such care necessary. Although economic limitations require that costly medical treatments be optional in certain circumstances, the costs of treatment cannot justly be accepted as a basis for limiting treatment of those considered by some to have in prospect a life of poor
quality if treatment otherwise would be obtained and provided.

It also follows that an injustice is done to noncompetent persons if medical
treatment is imposed upon them in circumstances in which any reasonable
and competent person would refuse treatment. Many reasons might be considered by a competent person sufficient to refuse medical treatment, and
quite apart from any intention of hastening death a person might prefer a
briefer life without treatment to a longer life with it. In unusual cases even
treatment needed to preserve life might be refused without suicidal intent by a
competent person who is not dying. The possibility that noncompetent persons might wish to refuse treatment if they were able to do so must be
recognized, and the right of noncompetent persons to avoid excessive treatment as well as to obtain appropriate treatment must be protected.

Another point which the legislative findings should mention is that persons
who are dying are far more likely than those who are not dying to have
reasons for refusing medical treatment, since the disadvantages of accepting
treatment appear greater as its probability of preserving life and restoring
health appears less. The question whether a person is dying is a matter of fact
to be determined by evidence.

Furthermore, a method of deciding on behalf of the noncompetent patient
whether medical treatment is to be accepted or refused is needed to protect
the right of such a person to appropriate but not excessive treatment. The
right to be protected neither presupposes nor implies any right to die. Nor is
this right properly considered an aspect of the right of personal privacy,
which pertains to liberty. Noncompetent persons cannot exercise their liberty, and no one can exercise a person's liberty on his or her behalf.

The problem to be dealt with by the legislation is that while in most cases
the rights of noncompetent persons are at present sufficiently protected, in
some cases these rights are not adequately safeguarded. Some people have
made their wishes known during a prior period of competence. Many are
suitably treated in accord with a judgment shaped by an attending physician
and concurred in by family members or others closely concerned with the

well-being of the noncompetent patient. But in some cases those who bear such responsibilities to the patient are unable to reach consensus, and in a few cases they reach a consensus which violates the rights of the person for whom they are responsible.

It is important for the legislature to point out that in some cases persons who would not have died with appropriate and available medical treatment have been deprived of such treatment for the benefit of society or their families, or on the theory that they would be better off dead. In such cases the crime of homicide is committed by omission, which is no less criminal than homicide by deed. Homicide by omission cannot be justified by asserting that the person killed in this way would have agreed to it, for such an agreement would have been suicidal in intent and would have been consent to homicide. Neither assisted suicide nor homicide with consent is lawful, and suicide is contrary to public policy.

Certain duties which already exist, but which are to be reinforced by the statute, should be summarized. Every person who has knowledge such that a reasonable person would suspect that homicide is being committed, whether by omission or by deed, has a duty to inform the police in order that life may be protected and the law enforced. Police and prosecutors have as grave a duty to prevent and punish crimes by omission as those by deed. Every person who believes that a noncompetent person is suffering grave mistreatment or neglect has a duty to call the matter to the attention of the public welfare authorities. These authorities have the duty to protect the welfare of noncompetent persons who otherwise would be deprived of the necessities of life.

The crux of the problem is that noncompetent persons including those whose quality of life is considered poor by others have the same right as any other person to due process of law and equal protection of the laws. Thus if there is doubt as to what decision concerning medical care ought to be attributed to any noncompetent person, this doubt should be resolved in accord with the provisions of law by a judicial hearing. Since the graver injustice will be done to a noncompetent person if life-preserving care is withheld which ought to be given, the initial presumption in any such case is that such treatment required to preserve life would be accepted. However, this presumption can be rebutted by evidence, especially in the case of a person who is dying, but even in certain cases of a person who is not dying.

A declaration of legislative findings along the preceding lines would summarize the conclusions for which we have argued in previous sections. Some might object to the requirement that anyone who knows of a suspected case of neglect or homicide by omission must report it. But this duty is implicit in existing law. Moreover, statutory requirements that physicians report child abuse are not uncommon.[107] The onerousness of the reporting requirement can be lessened for the person reporting if confidentiality is maintained. The results of reporting can be lessened for others involved if police and public health authorities undertaking any investigation of a report realize that what appears to someone to be homicide by omission or grave neglect might nevertheless be a reasonable effort to avoid excessive treatment.

The statute will require a number of important definitions, which must be supplied in accord with the existing law of each state. For example, "medical treatment" might be defined as treatment provided by certain classes of persons and institutions acting professionally and lawfully, to exclude forms of care and treatment which nonprofessional persons normally can provide to themselves or others in their care without prescription or special training and direction by a professional person. "Ordinary nursing care" might be defined as those forms of care which a person who is sufficiently alert and strong could and would provide for himself or herself, or which a mother could and would provide for her infant.

"Responsible persons" can be defined to include all who share in the responsibility of obtaining or providing medical care for noncompetent persons, including but not limited to attending physicians or nurses, administrators of hospitals or other institutions of which noncompetent persons are inmates, parents or guardians of infants and wards, family members sharing a common domicile with the noncompetent, and the spouses and offspring of noncompetent adults.

"Primarily responsible persons" would have to be defined with great care, for this expression would designate those whose judgments in many cases will be determinative. One of the primarily responsible persons will be the attending physician of a patient, or the physician primarily in charge of the medical care of a patient. In jurisdictions in which it is possible at present that a patient be under medical care without a particular physician being identified as the attending physician, provisions will be needed to prevent this situation.

The other primarily responsible persons, if any, will be determined by the status of the patient. Parents normally are primarily responsible for infants; either parent might be authorized to act if only one is present, but if both are present and not in agreement, then neither can act. For legal wards the legal guardian is primarily responsible. For noncompetent adults domiciled with their immediate families or relatives, some jurisdictions have definitions of "next of kin" which might be adopted or modified. A person domiciled with a spouse would have the spouse as primarily responsible; a person without a spouse domiciled with an adult child would have the child as primarily responsible—or the elder or eldest of two or more such children. For persons normally residing in institutions wholly responsible for their care and custody the chief administrator of such institution would be primarily responsible.

The most important definition in the statute will be that of "dying." A person is dying only if there exists in him or her a condition of disease or injury such that beyond reasonable doubt the condition will be at least an underlying cause of death, provided that no one is considered dying if available medical treatment can prevent death due to an otherwise fatal condition and that no one is dying who in the opinion of medical experts concerning the condition will not succumb to it regardless of treatment within one year. The last provision would exclude from the status of dying those persons who have contracted a disease known to be eventually fatal but which can be held at bay for a prolonged time by suitable treatment. Some such limitation seems to us necessary for legal purposes, although not essential to the idea of "dying person."

The statute will require a clear determination of those persons to whom it applies. We believe that with respect to minors the best solution is to draw a clear line by designating an age under which parents will be recognized as primarily responsible and authorized by law to make judgments which normally shall be binding upon physicians, just as when competent patients make a judgment in respect to their own care. The age to be set is a matter of dispute, and we leave it open here as we did in chapter four. The one essential point is that the age of competence to make medical decisions must be uniform both for the statute outlined in chapter four and for the one proposed here.

Apart from cases in which the noncompetent person is a minor or a legal ward of a guardian, the determination of competency is an instance of a general problem from which we prescind throughout this book.

Physicians will have decision-making authority according to the provisions of the law we outlined in chapter four, but they normally will act or refrain from acting only with the consensus of others primarily responsible for the patient. In case of disagreements the issues will have to be settled by a judicial proceeding, and the first issue in such a proceeding will be the question of competency of the patient if this question is disputed by anyone concerned.

Most jurisdictions already have statutes requiring parents to provide the necessities of life for their children and characterizing as neglect failure to do so. The statute proposed here might well begin its regulative provisions by broadening this obligation to include whomever shares responsibility for a noncompetent person in respect to the obtaining of medical care which a reasonable person would consider needed. But except for those primarily responsible, others could discharge their responsibility by calling to the attention of the public welfare authorities any case of apparent neglect.

Although certainly implicit in existing law, the statute ought also for the sake of clarity to require that anyone who suspects homicide by omission should inform the police of any facts upon which the suspicion is based. The police should be enjoined to investigate such reports with the same vigor as they would any other report of a homicide in progress. The welfare authorities and the police should be required to communicate information to one another, so that both will be able to act in fulfillment of their respective duties, regardless of which first receives relevant information.

In cases in which a parent or legal guardian refuses medical care for an infant or ward physicians should be held, not to seek a court order authorizing treatment, but to report the matter to the public welfare authorities. If there is any indication that the care refused would be appropriate, the welfare authorities should be required to seek the judicial hearing. The same will be the case if those primarily responsible agree in withholding care which might be appropriate. In cases in which the evidence is that excessive treatment is being administered to a noncompetent person those considering the treatment excessive would have responsibility for seeking a judicial hearing.

The heart of the statute would be the prescription of the issues to be considered by the court, the standards to be applied in adjudicating the issues, the presumptions which are to be considered in possession, the qualifications for a person to be appointed guardian, and the authorization of the guardian to act on behalf of the noncompetent person.

The court's first duty should be to determine whether the patient was in fact an infant, a legal ward, or an otherwise noncompetent person. The next issue would be whether the noncompetent person is dying or not according to the statutory definition of "dying." If necessary, expert examination and testimony would be sought to settle this issue. It should not be considered resolved by the stipulation of all parties that the patient is dying, but it could be resolved by their stipulation that the patient is not dying. The next issue would be whether the noncompetent patient should be presumed to have reasons for refusing available medical care, although the care could be considered by at least some physicians appropriate in the existing circumstances.

The court should proceed on the following presumptions. If a noncompetent patient is dying, then agreement between those primarily responsible for the patient concerning what care is proper should be presumed conclusively to express the choice of the patient. If the patient is not dying, then agreement between those primarily responsible for the patient that care or treatment be given to prolong life or preserve or restore health should again be presumed conclusively to express the choice of the patient. If a noncompetent patient is dying and those primarily responsible for the patient disagree concerning what care is proper, then the court should consider in possession the presumption that the patient's next of kin expresses the patient's wishes, but this presumption will be subject to falsification by the preponderance of the evidence. If a noncompetent patient is not dying and those primarily responsible for the patient disagree about whether care or treatment be given to prolong life or preserve or restore health, then the court should consider in possession the presumption that the patient would desire medical care. If a noncompetent patient is not dying and those primarily responsible for the patient agree that care should not be given, then the court must find whether the patient's life is likely to be shortened by omission of care; if so, the presumption in possession should be that the patient would desire care; but if not, the presumption in possession should be that the patient would refuse care.

Where conclusive presumptions are established, a case could be terminated with an order which would have the effect of legally establishing the patient's own decision concerning treatment, thus to free all concerned from the civil or criminal liability which they might otherwise fear if medical treatment were given or withheld in a state of uncertitude as to the patient's consent to or refusal to consent to treatment.

Where rebuttable assumptions are established, the court should hear evidence relevant to determining the probable advantages and disadvantages of available medical treatment for the patient. In the case of dying patients such evidence would be that treatment could prolong or enhance the patient's ability to act and to have experiences desirable to him or her, in comparison with evidence that treatment would be considered undesirable.

The grounds for considering treatment undesirable, articulated in section E, ought to be specified in some detail in the statute: the treatment is experimental or risky, it would be painful or otherwise experienced negatively, it would interfere with activities or experiences the patient might otherwise enjoy, it would conflict with some principle to which the patient adheres, it would be psychologically repugnant to the patient, or the patient would consider the financial or other impact of the treatment upon other persons a strong or even morally compelling reason for rejecting the treatment.

If a noncompetent patient is not dying, then the probability that available treatment might prolong life or preserve and restore health also ought to be considered to the extent that it can be determined by evidence in favor of prolonging treatment.

In hearing the evidence the court should be directed by statute to exclude carefully evidence concerning the patient's prospective quality of life except insofar as such evidence bears upon the patient's own probable lawful wishes concerning treatment. In other words, the court should be careful to rule out of order arguments claiming that survival would be undesirable due to the patient's condition of debility, age, declining strength, mental or physical handicap, or other disadvantage.

Where the court judges that the evidence presented preponderantly supports the presumption in possession, the case could be terminated. If the issue arose because of disagreement among those primarily responsible for the patient, then one of those whose initial position agrees with the decision which the court finds should be attributed to the noncompetent patient may be appointed guardian unless upon examination this person is found unqualified. If the issue arose because those primarily responsible agreed with one another contrary to the presumption soundly to be in possession, then another qualified person should be appointed guardian. In any case the guardian should be charged to make decisions in accord with the finding.

Where the court judges that the evidence presented does not preponderantly support the presumption in possession, a qualified guardian should be appointed and charged to make decisions in the light of the evidence and other information which the guardian obtains from time to time.

The decisions made by a court-appointed guardian, provided that they are made in good faith, should be final, just as a competent person's decisions with respect to his or her own care should be considered final. Moreover, such decisions should be considered a relevant circumstance in determining the standard of due medical care, so that physicians and hospital authorities will not be held liable for limiting or modifying care in accord with such decisions.

The qualifications for appointment as a guardian should include the following.

First, no one should be appointed guardian who does not agree with the public policy that assisted suicide and homicide with consent are acts rightly held to be criminal, that homicide by omission is as grave a crime as homicide by deed, that every person is entitled to a fair share of available medical care regardless of such person's prospective quality of life, that the refusal of life-prolonging medical treatment sometimes is reasonable and lawful, and that a person's own choice if he or she were able to make it should determine the limits of treatment to be given provided that such choice is not suicidal.

Second, no one should be appointed guardian who has a personal interest potentially averse to that of the patient in the results of decisions he or she is likely to be called upon to make.

Third, no one should be appointed guardian who lacks the knowledge and intelligence necessary to understand the condition of the patient, the possible benefits and disadvantages of treatment, and the legal policy which requires that decisions be made from the patient's viewpoint and in disregard of factors held by law to be irrelevant.

In terminating cases and appointing guardians the court should explicitly direct that if certain medical treatment is lawfully withheld from a noncompetent patient, there nevertheless remains an obligation to provide care and treatment suited to the patient's condition, including ordinary nursing care and such palliative care as may mitigate the patient's suffering.

In some jurisdictions it would be desirable to clarify the possibility and limits of a parent's being relieved of rights and responsibilities for a child. In cases in which lifesaving treatment is ordered for an infant unwanted by the parents removal of the infant from their care might be indicated. If so, the statute also should settle the question of financial responsibility. It seems reasonable that parents who are able should contribute at least to the extent of the normal cost of raising a child if they are to be relieved by the state of this responsibility.

Consideration ought to be given to the possibility of establishing a public office concerned with the medical care of the noncompetent. Such an office might be assigned the duties we have proposed be given to the public welfare authorities, including the receiving of information and the filing of cases on behalf of the noncompetent. The office also might have on its staff persons qualified to act as guardians; such individuals by increasing experience might be more able than others to assume the tasks of guardian when appointed to the role.

In addition, a public office concerned with the medical care of the noncompetent could perform quasi-judicial functions by carrying out preliminary investigations of complaints and attempting to bring about agreement in cases in which the difficulty is caused by misunderstanding or ignorance of the legal requirements. A well-designed procedure for resolving problems according to well-known principles with easily predictable results frequently would lead to a resolution without a court hearing of cases which could be resolved without testing presumptions in possession.

The statute ought to make clear that the liability of all concerned is limited by the legally established substitute consent of the patient but is not removed when the circumstance of the patient's consent to or refusal of treatment is taken into account.

Penalties for failing to report information on the basis of which a reasonable person would suspect that appropriate medical care is being withheld or inappropriate care imposed should be substantial but not so great as to deter their imposition. In one case—that of failure to report omissions which any reasonable person would consider homicidal—the one failing to report should be treated as an accessory or coconspirator. Similarly, perjury in a hearing which resulted in the withholding of care necessary to preserve the life of a person and caused the subsequent death of that person should be treated as homicide.

The statute when enacted should be called to the attention of physicians and hospital administrators, as well as studied by relevant public employees. The legislature might well provide for special promulgation by having an appropriate state official prepare and distribute a summary of the legislation and commentary upon it to assure that all concerned, including the courts, would be prepared to implement the legislation as quickly and effectively as possible.

10: The Constitution, Life, Liberty and Justice

A. Liberty and Justice in Jeopardy

Many of the most important public debates involving jurisprudential issues in the United States since World War II can be viewed as conflicts between parties who prefer as much liberty as possible and parties who prefer as much equality as possible, especially in matters involving important components of justice. Libertarian arguments have been offered against the growth of the welfare state, equalitarian arguments for it; libertarian arguments against going beyond the ending of legally enforced segregation to begin legally enforced integration of the races, equalitarian arguments for it; libertarian arguments against criminal laws protecting the lives of the unborn, equalitarian arguments for such laws.

As a comparison of the individuals and groups on either side of these and similar issues quickly makes clear, no one is consistently a libertarian or an equalitarian. Simultaneously respecting both of these basic jurisprudential principles is never easy. Moreover, as exemplified in the preceding chapters, there are considerations of either liberty or equality or both on opposite sides of many, if not of all, important jurisprudential issues.

In the course of our study we have noted many important respects in which—assuming our conclusions correct—liberty and justice are presently being violated or are threatened with violation in the immediate future.

The liberty of competent persons to consent and to refuse consent to medical treatment has been violated, and the law has failed to provide effective means by which persons can exercise this liberty with respect to a future time of noncompetence. The recently passed natural-death or right-to-die legislation is objectionable for many reasons, not least that it arbitrarily restricts the very liberty it is intended to implement. The liberty of persons who wish to commit suicide sometimes is infringed by excessive measures of restraint and

298

custody; such measures often infringe upon the privacy of persons who live in institutions. The liberty of members of society who oppose the death penalty to stand aloof from this form of official homicide seems to us to be violated by every jurisdiction which uses this method of punishment.

The liberty of members of society who consider abortion murder of the unborn to stand aloof from public programs which involve the state in this form of killing has been violated by every jurisdiction which has put public facilities and public funds at the disposal of those who engage in abortion. Similarly, if voluntary euthanasia is legalized and carefully regulated to the extent that it must be if it is to be safe, the liberty to stand aloof of all who regard as abhorrent such killing with the consent of the victim will be violated by the *institutionalization* of the practice. Everyone, nevertheless, will admit institutionalization to be necessary to protect the lives of those who do not consent to be killed.

The liberty of physicians to provide noncompetent patients with appropriate but not excessive medical treatment is violated to the extent that the present legal situation compels the physician to work in a context of uncertain liability, instead of facilitating a clear determination of the patient's constructive consent in cases in which there is doubt about it.

Not every limitation on liberty is a violation of it. Liberty is justly limited whenever all who are reasonable agree to its limitation for the sake of the common life they share, the social order which liberty itself creates. But every restriction of liberty without social necessity and every limitation of liberty which unfairly weighs on some for the good of others does involve injustice. The preservation of the blessings of liberty is itself a very important aspect of political society's constituting purpose.

Some proposed definitions of death would deprive living persons of their legal status as persons; such deprivation is a fundamental injustice which opens the way to a whole series of other injustices. At the same time to insist upon outdated standards for determining death is to compel the living to treat the dead as if they were alive, when the contrary can be established beyond reasonable doubt. This is unjust, especially when the dead person has made an anatomical gift which is interfered with. Competent persons are unjustly required to undergo and someone is required to pay the cost of unwanted treatment when the liberty to refuse treatment is insufficiently recognized and implemented. The noncompetent who are deprived of appropriate treatment or who have imposed upon them excessive treatment likewise suffer an injustice.

But most important is the unjust deprivation of life which is involved in the failure of the law to provide equal protection to this basic good. Those who are aborted before birth, those who are killed by omission after birth, and those for whom early death is sought as a management option are unjustly deprived of their lives. At the bottom of the present and growing tendency to deprive some persons of life is the ascendancy of one particular world view: secular humanism with its consequentialist ethics. According to this world view, one person can decide on behalf of another that he or she has a life or prospect of life not worth living, a life which does not merit preserving and protecting.

Secular humanists, of course, are entitled to affirm this world view and to seek to live their personal lives according to it, so long as they respect the interests of society and the rights of others. This is what liberty means. But in America today—for that matter, throughout the Western world—secular humanists are seeking to have their world view established as the exclusive legitimate framework for public policy.

Thus Western societies are moving very rapidly from a jurisprudence based upon the traditional religious morality of sanctity of life to the new morality of quality of life judged from a secular humanistic perspective. From the position of protecting every individual's life as inherently inviolable Western societies are moving directly to the opposite position of withdrawing legal protection from some individuals' lives considered as useless to themselves and others—as lives which ought not to have been conceived or which ought to be quickly terminated. The kindest possible treatment for such persons is to kill them, it is argued, for they will be better off dead.

The injustice of imposing upon a noncompetent person someone else's concept and standard of quality of life is patent. So is the injustice of imposing secular humanism as the established framework of public policy upon a whole society, many of whose members do not share the secular humanist faith. Indeed, as a matter of constitutional law, the use of the secular humanist perspective as a privileged basis for public policy—which was what happened in the legalization of abortion and is proposed in the argument for legalizing euthanasia—constitutes an establishment of religion in violation of the First Amendment of the United States Constitution.

Proponents of euthanasia no doubt will vehemently deny that they are attempting to establish a religion. Their own literature is filled with attacks upon the principle of the absolute inviolability or sanctity of human life precisely on the basis that this principle is rooted in a religious view which not everyone holds in contemporary pluralistic society. In effect, those seeking to justify nonvoluntary euthanasia are urging that instead of earlier religious principles, purely rational and humanistic principles ought to be accepted as a basis for public policy. According to these principles whatever policy will have the best social consequences, judged according to utilitarian ideas of what is best, ought to be adopted.

But in taking this position the proponent of euthanasia is saying in effect: "You may not legislate your morality, because I am going to legislate mine. And I have a right to do so, because mine is areligious while yours is religious." It has seriously been suggested that any legislation which enforces a religiously rooted morality, even in purely secular terms, amounts to an unconstitutional "establishment of religion"; on this view only legislation which serves an obviously rational, "independent, secular, utilitarian, social function" is acceptable.[1]

But can utilitarianism, with its consequentialist criteria for good policy, be made the final standard of the constitutionality of legislation without establishing secular humanism as the official religion of the United States? More generally, can any of the principles embodied in the arguments of proponents of euthanasia be admitted as a basis for excluding some human individuals from the equal protection of the law forbidding homicide without the establishment of the world view which would justify this exclusion and the imposition of this world view upon those to be excluded as well as upon other citizens who still hold to a different world view—for example, one which embraces some conception of the sanctity of life?

It may seem fanciful to suggest that the preference for areligious to religious world views in the determination of public policy issues constitutes an establishment of religion. After all, secular humanism, for example, is by definition *not a religion*. However, this point is not well taken.

The United States Supreme Court already is committed to the position that "secular humanism" is a religion despite its areligious character. In *Torcaso* v. *Watkins* the Court ruled that the State of Maryland had denied secular humanists the free exercise of their religion by demanding of them profession of belief in a Supreme Being as a condition of eligibility to hold the office of Notary Public.[2] In *United States* v. *Seeger* the Court held that a conscientious objector to military service should be considered as having an adequate religious basis for objection if his objection was based upon a belief which occupied in his life the same place as belief in God holds in the life of one clearly qualified for exemption.[3]

Still, in *Seeger* there remain suggestions that reference to something more than personal moral convictions is necessary for religion. But in a subsequent case, *Welsh* v. *United States,* the Court held:

> If an individual deeply and sincerely holds beliefs that are purely ethical or moral in source and content but that nevertheless impose upon him a duty of conscience to refrain from participating in any war at any time, those beliefs certainly occupy in the life of that individual "a place parallel to that filled by . . . God" in traditionally religious persons.[4]

In taking this view the Court had to contend with the fact that the statute excluded from exemption persons whose objection was based upon "essentially political, sociological, or philosophical views or a merely personal moral code." The Court held that this language does exclude those whose beliefs are not deeply held and those whose judgment is not a matter of moral principle but rests only "upon considerations of policy, pragmatism, or expediency." But a deeply held conscientious conviction, regardless of its source or any reference to a ground beyond human relationships, qualified as religious.[5]

Presumably, proponents of euthanasia will maintain that their views are deeply and sincerely held, at least by themselves, and that these views somehow have a basis which transcends mere policy, pragmatism, and expediency—a basis for evaluation which is more than a mere personal preference. They must maintain as much to try to evade the charge of arbitrariness which we have leveled against them. But in holding their beliefs to be deeply and sincerely held proponents of euthanasia will fulfill the requirements for their beliefs to be considered religious.

Principles which would justify the limitation of the law of homicide on the basis of quality-of-life considerations, restrictions of personhood, or evaluations of the worth of contributions by various members of society thus are just as much religious beliefs as are principles which would preclude on the basis of the absolute sanctity of life the arbitrary refusal of care for themselves by competent persons who think they would be better off dead and so wish to die. Thus, while proponents of euthanasia are at liberty to hold and to live their personal lives in accord with their own world views, they are not entitled to have some sort of common denominator of their world views accepted and established as the basis for settling which human individuals until now protected by the law forbidding homicide shall be allowed in the future to be killed. Such acceptance and establishment would amount to the establishment of secular humanism and its imposition upon all members of the society, especially upon those whose right to life would be annulled in accord with it.

Commenting upon the Supreme Court decisions we have summarized, Paul Ramsey concludes:

> A well-founded conclusion from this is that any of the positions taken on controversial public questions having profound moral and human or value implications have for us the functional sanctity of religious opinions. The question concerning non-religious positions is whether they any longer exist; and whether proponents of one or another public policy are not, whether they like it or not, to be regarded as religious in the same sense in which traditional religious outlooks continue to affirm their bearing on the resolution of these same questions.[6]

We agree with Ramsey in recognizing as religious in the constitutional sense views which are on their face purely secular and humanistic.

However, we differ from his view to the extent that it implies that there can be no nonreligious or neutral basis for resolving controversial public questions. There is such a basis in the commonly recognized principles of liberty and justice which we have appealed to throughout this book. These principles required us to forgo any appeal to the traditional principle of the sanctity of life; the same principles equally require proponents of euthanasia to forgo any appeal to contemporary conceptions of the quality of life, the requirements for personhood, or the value of various sorts of contributions to society.

It is clear that in certain contexts the United States Supreme Court has been ready and willing to recognize secular humanism and other nontheistic, deeply held foundations of personal morality as religious. This recognition cannot fairly be extended to adherents of such religions when it is to their benefit and them conveniently forgotten when the same Court undertakes to adjudicate on abortion and other matters.

As we pointed out in chapter eight, section A, advocates of legalized abortion and nonvoluntary euthanasia such as Glanville Williams argue that the alternative to retaining a traditional morality of the sanctity of human life as the basis for public policy is adopting a utilitarian conception of quality of life which would justify legalizing some forms of murder or near-murder forbidden in the past by Anglo-American law.

Against Williams, and without invoking a moral principle of sanctity of life, we argued that utilitarian, consequentialist conceptions of the social function of homicide laws ought not to determine to whose lives these laws will extend protection. The distinct and neutral principle of justice—equal protection of the laws—should settle the issue. Even legitimate public policy concerns about problems such as poverty, pollution, and population ought not to be allowed to be weighed in a consequentialist scale against the value of the lives of members of society.

Of course, in the *Abortion Cases* the United States Supreme Court pretended to maintain judicial neutrality and reserve, especially in regard to the question when human life begins. But the Court's professed uncertainty about this well-known matter of biological fact was exposed as a pretense when it legalized the killing of the unborn—by attributing to them only *potential* life, which at most is *possibly* meaningful if the live birth occurs, and by refusing even to consider their interest in life—while it balanced women's interests against various state interests which it held become compelling as pregnancy progresses.

In *Roe* v. *Wade* the Supreme Court of the United States did not maintain judicial neutrality. Rather, it adopted one religious perspective, established it, judged in accord with it, withdrew from one group of living human individuals the legal protections hitherto afforded their lives, and imposed a new constitutional provision on American society in violation of the liberty of all who do not share the secular humanist perspective.

Someone will object that the Court had to decide the case one way or another, to please one side or the other. Strictly speaking, this is not true.

The Court could have declared itself and other courts incompetent to decide the issue on constitutional grounds and unable to decide it on other grounds. Such a decision would have left all parties to the debate free to promote their positions by political means in the legislatures, including Congress, and also free to seek the amendment of the Constitution to bring it into harmony with their own understandings of the conflicting claims of liberty and justice.

Instead, the Court chose to exercise raw judicial power to amend the Constitution in a manner other than those ways provided for in the Constitution itself. The amendment consisted in giving the right of privacy of pregnant women an absolute constitutional status, so that the states would no longer be permitted to protect as they had done—in some cases for more than a century and one-half—the lives of the unborn.

John Hart Ely remarked that *Roe* v. *Wade* was not constitutional law and showed almost no sense of an obligation even to try to be.[7] The reason is that in this case the Court exercised the only legally recognized policy function which is superior to constitutional law: the deliberation and consent which creates and amends the constitution. The American conception of free government demands that this deliberation and consent be the supreme exercise of the liberty of the people: "We the People of the United States . . . do ordain and establish this Constitution." In usurping this function, the Supreme Court most grievously violated the liberty of the people. The legitimacy of American government is severely wounded; powers which are not *just powers* are exercised with specious authority.

Thus, although the United States today remains in many ways unlike Nazi Germany, in many ways which are very important it has become like that lawless regime of might claiming to make right. Moreover, discrimination which rationalizes killing is equally vicious whether it is rooted in an ideology of racial perfection or in an ideology of individualistic perfection, which asserts that no unwanted child should ever be born and no life below a certain standard of quality should any longer be protected.

What is more important is that—as we argued in chapter eight, section G— the Supreme Court could have decided the legality of abortion without assuming as established either the traditional morality based upon the sanctity of life or the new morality based upon quality of life. The question should have been one of whether the law, which had never been consistent in regarding the unborn either as persons or as nonpersons, would better accord with the basic, common principles of justice and liberty if it were rendered consistent in one or the other way. Since the only thing common to all already recognized by law as natural persons is membership in the human species, and since the unborn of human genesis are members of the species, no nondiscriminatory basis exists for excluding the unborn from legal personhood. Once the unborn be admitted to be persons, equal protection of the laws demands that a society which cannot exist without a law of homicide protecting its strong members and those defended by strong protectors should also protect its weak and unwanted members by the same law of homicide.

In the preceding chapters we have suggested many ways in which laws might be reformed without alteration in the Constitution to conform better to the requirements of liberty and justice. Death can be defined, thus to protect those at this margin from being unjustly considered dead when they are not and to protect the living from being required to treat dead bodies as legal persons. Once the significance and breadth of the problem is recognized, we think this definition would best be made by an act of Congress under its enforcement power of the Fourteenth Amendment.

The impositions on liberty in relation to those who have attempted suicide can be eliminated easily. The liberty of competent persons to refuse treatment and the rights of the noncompetent to appropriate but not excessive care can be facilitated and protected by appropriate statutes, which we have outlined in chapters four and nine. Capital punishment can be abolished by statute, for if the practice is not unconstitutional, neither is its abolition.

However, in the United States, at least, not all of the existing violations of liberty and justice can be remedied so easily.

The rectification of the injustice to the unborn of denying their lives protection will require either a reversal by the Supreme Court of its decisions in *Roe* v. *Wade* and *Doe* v. *Bolton* or a constitutional amendment to make clear the requirements of justice which the Constitution formerly respected and implemented but now—in the state of the law as it is after the Court's action amending the Constitution—ignores and blocks.

Moreover, the rectification of the violation of the liberty of the people involved in the establishment of the secular humanistic world view as the sole legitimate framework for the determination of questions of public policy will require either a reversal by the Supreme Court not only of the abortion decisions but also of certain others, which we shall discuss in section D, or a constitutional amendment to make clear the requirements of liberty in a pluralistic society with respect to every theistic and nontheistic religion, every world view which provides an ultimate foundation for any set of deeply held conscientious convictions by which citizens can live their personal lives within the common society.

B. Every-Human-a-Person Amendment

Various commentators on the Supreme Court's decisions in the abortion cases set forth the reasons why an attempt to amend the Constitution must be made in order to reverse the Court's denial of equal protection of their lives to the unborn. Various formulae of a possible amendment have been proposed.[8] Probably the simplest amendment which would reverse the Court's decisions would be one stating; "Nothing in this Constitution shall be construed as providing any foundation for any challenge to the laws respecting abortion which were in force in the year 1966, or to laws similar to them in protecting the lives of unborn human individuals."

Such an amendment would leave entirely open all of the questions which were raised by political efforts to modify the laws but would firmly exclude the courts from questioning the constitutionality of even the most conservative laws in force in 1966, before Colorado enacted the first of the so-called "liberalizations" of the antiabortion statutes. But an amendment of this sort would in fact be a form of states' right amendment and would have all the defects of that approach—defects we believe have been pointed out sufficiently by others.[9]

One difficulty with an attempt merely to turn the clock back is that the practice of denying the right to life of some persons already has extended, as we have shown, beyond the unborn to others, especially defective infants. We believe that the Supreme Court in *Roe* v. *Wade*—regardless of intent—laid the foundation for the extension of quality-of-life considerations to serve as a rationale for denying the right to life of persons already born when it said:

> With respect to the State's important and legitimate interest in potential life, the "compelling" point is at viability. This is so because the fetus then presumably has the capability of meaningful life outside the mother's womb. State regulation protective of fetal life after viability thus has both logical and biological justifications.[10]

The key expression here is "meaningful life." Implicit in the use of this expression is the concept that some lives are not meaningful, that some are so lacking in quality as not to merit equal protection of the law.

Someone will object that this reading of the Court's remark is unfair. All the Court intends in the context, it will be pointed out, is what could have been expressed as an explicit tautology: only when a fetus is developed sufficiently to survive after birth does it have the capability of surviving after birth. Prior to viability an aborted fetus by definition cannot live.

The objection probably correctly expresses what the Court intended. But the fact is that nonviable aborted fetuses do live for various lengths of time after they are born alive, since viability technically means the possibility of surviving not only birth but also the neonatal period—that is, the first twenty-eight days of life *after* birth.[11] Tiny embryos only about five and one-half weeks after conception have been delivered alive and lived long enough to determine by experiment that some reflex arcs already are established in the nervous system at this stage of development.[12] Some such individuals survive only for a few minutes, but more developed individuals survive for hours, days, or weeks, yet are considered nonviable after they die if they do not in fact survive twenty-eight days.

Now it is this life which nonviable infants live *after they are born* for any period up to twenty-eight days which the Supreme Court refers to as non-meaningful. But it is clear that these individuals are considered not only persons but also citizens by virtue of the Fourteenth Amendment. While courts have had some difficulty in deciding when a person is born, they have never questioned that birth of a live—not a stillborn—infant begins the condition of one who is a potential victim of homicide.[13] In other words, the killing or the intentional shortening of the life of a nonviable person and citizen is the same crime of homicide as the killing or the intentional shortening of the life of anybody else. A nonviable infant is in no different condition than someone who is dying at a later stage in human existence. It is no defense against a charge of homicide to say that one's victim was certain to die within twenty-eight days regardless of one's deadly deed.

Thus in *Roe* v. *Wade* the Court—regardless of intent—took the startling and unprecedented step of declaring not to be meaningful the lives of a certain class of citizens. While it did not in that decision declare these citizens to be unprotected by the law of homicide, it did predicate the state's interest in preventing their abortion on the possibility of their extended survival. Hence, when a fetus is aborted alive, the Court implied that the nonviable had no meaningful life. The Court thus suggested that such citizens might not be able to be significantly deprived of what they did not meaningfully have.

This construction of what the Court meant in *Roe* v. *Wade* would be highly implausible were it not for subsequent events. Even prior to *Roe* v. *Wade* there were widely published reports of the killing of aborted infants delivered alive. One of the states which attempted to ensure protection for such citizens was Missouri, which in its 1974 abortion statute provided:

> No person who performs or induces an abortion shall fail to exercise that degree of professional skill, care and diligence to preserve the life and health of the fetus which such person would be required to exercise in order to preserve the life and health of any fetus intended to be born and not aborted. Any physician or person assisting in the abortion who shall fail to take such measures to encourage or to sustain the life of the child, and the death of the child results, shall be deemed guilty of manslaughter.

In challenging this statute before the Supreme Court the appellant in *Planned Parenthood of Central Missouri* v. *Danforth* argued that the provision was intended to prevent all abortions. Despite the implausibility of this contention and the declaration by Danforth, Attorney General of Missouri, that the section was meant to protect the lives of infants already born, the Court held that the section could not survive constitutional attack, for, "It does not specify that such care need be taken only after the stage of viability has been reached. As the provision now reads, it impermissibly requires the physician to preserve the life and health of the fetus, whatever the stage of the pregnancy." Moreover, the court refused to sever the second sentence from the first, claiming that the provisions must fall as a unit. Then the Court added, "And a physician's or other person's criminal failure to protect a live-born infant surely will be subject to prosecution in Missouri under the State's criminal statutes."[14]

This final sentence might be taken to mean that the Court is working on the standard assumption that an infant born alive, whether viable or not, is protected by the same statutes as anyone else. However, in the context of the Court's renewed insistence on the importance of viability the sentence also could be taken to mean that a nonviable infant henceforth is not to be regarded as live-born even though it is living apart from its mother after the abortion is completed. This interpretation is supported by the fact that the Court refused to sever the provisions of the section. Also, the Court's statements here at least can be read as a bit of free legal counsel for abortionists; Make certain there are no live-born infants and you have our protection.

The United States Court of Appeals, Eighth Circuit, dealt with the 1974 Minnesota abortion statute shortly after the Supreme Court decided *Danforth*. The Minnesota Statute had two separate and distinct sections, one requiring a physician to choose methods of abortion when feasible which would protect the life of a potentially viable fetus, the other clearly and explicitly concerned with the live-born infant:

> A potentially viable fetus which is live born following an attempted abortion shall be fully recognized as a human person under the law.
> If an abortion of a potentially viable fetus results in a live birth, the responsible medical personnel shall take all reasonable measures, in keeping with good medical practice, to preserve the life and health of the live born person.

The court of appeals held that this provision could not stand because it incorporates "potentially viable" and so requires a physician performing an abortion after the twentieth week "to exercise the prescribed standard of care and use only those procedures and techniques calculated to preserve the life and health of the fetus."[15] One might charitably assume that the court simply was confused, but this assumption is hard to sustain, inasmuch as one of its own members dissented and also pointed out the sense of the provisions which were struck down, just as Justice White, joined by Justice Rehnquist and the Chief Justice, had done in *Danforth*.[16]

In any case, the Supreme Court's reference to meaningful life in *Roe* v.

Wade clearly implies that the lives of nonviable citizens are not meaningful. The reason why they are not, presumably, is that they are going to be short: at most less than twenty-eight days from birth. If this fact deprives these lives of meaningfulness, however, a similar value judgment will deprive of meaningfulness the life of anyone who is about to die. And once some lives are agreed to be meaningless, it will be very hard to distinguish from them many other lives which are widely thought to have no more worth than they do. On this basis one should not be surprised that infanticide has become an acknowledged practice since 1973.

Apart from what the courts have done, we saw in chapter eight that there already is a significant movement to deny the humanity or the personhood of certain individuals already born, on the ground that they lack what some regard as minimal qualifications for inclusion in the human community. As we showed in chapter eight, section E, even those advocates of nonvoluntary euthanasia who do not explicitly deny the personhood of those whose lives they consider to be of poor quality hold principles which in practice will lead to the establishment of a system allocating persons with lives of diverse quality to diverse castes.

Under these conditions we do not consider it a sufficient response to *Roe* v. *Wade* to declare the personhood and protect the lives of the unborn. We do not criticize the efforts already made to draft an appropriate amendment; several of these are excellent and deserve support. But we do think that since no amendment has yet been passed, a broader approach which will better meet the present and developing denial of the equal protection of the law of homicide would be preferable.

We think an amendment should make explicit the legal personhood of all members of the human species. It also ought to reject explicitly the subordination of the protection of anyone's life to any other public or private interest or right, for there are many who argue that the lives of persons must be subordinated. The amendment also should make clear that classifications based upon quality of life considerations are just as suspect as racial classifications. Furthermore, while an amendment can exclude discrimination against the unborn as a class, there will remain problems of detail concerning the beginning of life and concerning death. These issues seem to us more appropriately resolved by a legislative process than by constitutional enactment. So we propose an enforcement power which would explicitly include legislative determination of doubts concerning classes of entities which might or might not be individuals belonging to the human species.

Section one. Every living individual which is a member of the species homo sapiens whether born or not yet born shall be a person within the meaning of the word "person" in the Fifth and Fourteenth Amendments to this Constitution. No part of such an individual shall be a person even though such part be living, whether within or apart from the person of whom it is a part.

Section two. No private or public interest or right shall be deemed sufficient to subordinate any person's right to equal protection of laws respecting homicide, nor shall protection of any person's life be conditional upon a belief that such life is meaningful, worth living, or of use or benefit to the person whose life it is.

Section three. Legal classifications of persons on the basis of age, mental or physical normality, ability to take care of themselves, vigor, and strength shall be suspect, but shall be held permissible if such a classification is used to provide special advantages, privileges, or protections to persons who are not in the prime of life, are retarded, defective, deformed, dependent, declining, or weak.

Section four. Nothing in this Article alters the status at law and the rights of corporations and other nonnatural persons.

Section five. Congress shall have the power to enforce this article by appropriate legislation. This power shall include but not be limited to deciding disagreements which may arise in any jurisdiction subject to this Constitution concerning whether any class of individuals is a class of entities each of which is a member of the species homo sapiens.

We first explain the provisions included in this proposal and then indicate why some other possible provisions have been omitted.

Section one identifies the legal personhood of natural human individuals with the only thing they have in common—membership in the same biological species. It has been argued that those who supported the Fourteenth Amendment intended to do this.[17] We propose to make the point as explicit as possible. The second sentence, concerning parts of individuals, is added to make clear that only a whole organism of the human species will count as a natural person. Thus, the various organs which survive the death of a person are not persons; a man's sperm or a woman's ovum is not a person; one's cells growing in a culture are not persons. Neither is one's head or one's foot a person. This does not mean that a person's head cannot be legally protected. It and other parts of a person can be protected, but only in function of the protection of persons whose parts they are.

Section two attempts to establish equal protection of the lives of all persons against any and all supposedly conflicting claims, even claims based upon an individual's own interest in achieving the better condition of being dead rather than living a life of poor quality. We think that some formulation along these lines is essential if a right-to-life amendment is to be effective, since many are arguing that the right to life of some persons must yield to other's interests or the public's interest in avoiding a burden of welfare dependency, and many are arguing that for some persons death is a benefit.

Section three is intended to give the same protection to those whose quality of life is regarded by many as poor as the Fourteenth Amendment (as it is now understood) gives to those whose race is regarded by many as inferior. Classification which tends toward alleviating inequality is permitted, but classification for other purposes on such bases must be considered suspect and worthy of the closest scrutiny.

Section four is inserted only to avoid misunderstandings which might arise, since the amendment will define natural legal persons very carefully and might erroneously be understood to change the status of other legal persons.

Section five places an enforcement power in Congress, especially in order to be definite about where authority lies to settle doubtful cases. However, the enforcement power is not limited but is extended as far as the power granted Congress by the Fourteenth Amendment extends. For the most part the amendment as we have drafted it directs the courts and legislatures in their substantive work.

The first section does not limit itself to the right to life. We understand why proponents of other human life amendments have limited their scope. However, we think that logic and justice require that legal personhood be recognized where it reasonably exists and not restricted to certain purposes. Furthermore, we do not think that legal difficulties of any great magnitude will be created if the unborn are considered persons not only for the right to life but absolutely.[18]

The second section does deal with the right to life. However, we have put the matter not in terms of life itself, but in terms of equal protection of laws of homicide, to conform to our position that justice, not life itself, is the good directly at stake in political society. If a society could exist without any laws prohibiting homicide, then there would be nothing wrong in that society leaving all equally unprotected.

The approach by way of equal protection also avoids a serious difficulty, namely, that of either specifying a discriminatory exception allowing the subordination of the life of the infant to that of the mother or leaving open the possibility of even more extensive discriminatory exceptions.[19] Our approach, we think, would require any permission for killing to be formulated in a nondiscriminatory way, along the lines of the law we formulated in chapter seven, section G, which would permit killing when necessary to preserve the best chance of survival for the largest number of persons involved in a difficult situation.

It will be objected that our approach would require that every abortion be treated as first degree murder and that the woman undergoing the abortion be treated as a principal in the crime. We think that if the unborn are really to be considered persons, there is nothing unreasonable in considering killing them the same as killing other persons. But the usual requirements for proving someone guilty of murder would still apply. First, it would be necessary to show that a living individual had existed and been killed by the procedure. Second, it would be necessary that the intent and premeditation required for first degree murder were given. Furthermore, not all who are guilty of murder are punished with great or equal severity.

There would be nothing unfair in considering murder a crime which might be aggravated if the victim were deprived of other goods and if other persons and society were made to suffer other losses besides the life which every person stands to lose. Thus, the murder of a public official or of a person with dependents could be made a more serious crime, since in such cases more mischief is done than the killing itself. A law of homicide along these lines might provide equal protection of all against being killed, while providing supplemental protection to some lives in virtue of the related interests.

The third section is intended to protect the interests of those who are thought to have a poor quality of life against discrimination other than that which would permit homicide. It might be thought that this section is superfluous. Yet these persons are not always fairly treated, and a society which does not license killing them might well continue to neglect and mistreat them. Affirmative action programs cannot be written into the Constitution; different jurisdictions under varying conditions might have more or less ability to improve the condition of the disadvantaged. But the Constitution can make clear that any form of discrimination against these disadvantaged persons is excluded and can at the same time explicitly open the door to programs which would enhance the quality of their lives.

The fifth section, concerning enforcement, does not refer to laws prohibiting homicide. No one doubts that Congress and the state legislatures have power to make such laws for their respective jurisdictions, and no new grant of power is needed if such laws are to be framed in the terms the amendment specifies. However, Congress may need and would by this section be given the power to override discriminatory state legislation and to preempt the protection of the rights of the disadvantaged if the states fail in this respect. Moreover, some continuing authority is needed—and experience suggests that this authority had better not be the courts—to settle the problems which are bound to arise in borderline cases.

Even if one extends the protection of life to the unborn at every stage of their biological development or from fertilization on, factual issues still must be resolved—for example, whether a birth control device which prevents implantation is an attack upon a person or not, and whether cortical death is the death of a person or not. A uniform policy on such issues would be desirable, and a sound and uniform policy is more likely to be achieved by the Congress than by the courts or the state legislatures. Also, what is at stake here is legal personhood—as we pointed out in chapter three with respect to the definition of death—with all of the rights and privileges which attend it, not merely some part of these rights and privileges which are consequent upon citizenship at either the state or federal level, or both.

C. Need for Protection of Liberty

Although the enactment of a human life amendment along the lines that we or others have proposed might be difficult, the concept of such an amendment is easy in comparison with the concept of an amendment to remedy the infringements and threatened infringments on liberty which we have noticed. The difficulty here, primarily, is that the Supreme Court of the United States, which has itself determined that secular humanism and other nontheistic world views are religious, tends to treat the secular humanist view with its consequentialist ethic as if this view merely gave neutral form to the common principles of American society. In doing this—for example in *Roe* v. *Wade*— the Court, as we have argued, is establishing a religion and judging according to its sectarian tenets.

Leo Pfeffer, a professor of political science at Long Island University, serves as special counsel to the American Jewish Congress. He is a noted practitioner of constitutional law, especially in the domain of church-state relationships, and has argued many cases successfully before the United States Supreme Court, urging separation between religion and government, the exclusion of religion from the public schools, and the denial of public funds to nonpublic schools. In 1975 Pfeffer published a book concerning church-state relationships and the Court as referee in these relationships. This work is remarkable because of what it concedes from the point of view of a person who is both knowledgeable and friendly—or, at least, not hostile—about the direction which the Supreme Court has taken in recent years.

In chapter six, section I, we pointed out that government interests in the field of birth control and abortion go beyond a permissive attitude taken out of respect for liberty—invoked by the Court under the title of "privacy." In fact, the government has extensively promoted birth control, both at home and abroad; abortion also in various ways has become an instrumentality of public policy to deal with the welfare problem. Euthanasia already is seen by some as an extension of this approach to human problems.

Pfeffer offers a similar analysis of the Court's decisions concerning contraception and abortion.

The anticontraception laws were not a real obstacle to the liberty of persons who wished to use contraception. But they were an obstacle to a state policy encouraging contraception. Pfeffer notes:

> The middle income and the affluent, married and unmarried, use contraceptives; the poor have babies. When the poor, often racial minorities, are on the welfare roles, taxpaying Americans rebel and expect the state to do something about it.[20]

Other solutions being unacceptable, the practical way to limit the costs of public welfare programs was to get the poor to control births. Although the national government already was taking this approach in foreign aid programs, the states were obstructed by their own laws against contraception. Pfeffer speculates that the reason the Supreme Court struck down these laws as unconstitutional "may lie in the fact that the justices recognized the need to get the laws off the books" so that either the states themselves or private agencies could openly promote birth control. Pfeffer then adds a remarkable statement, which agrees entirely with the views of the most severe critics of the Court's decisions concerning abortion:

> In this respect the nine justices on the Supreme Court, being immune to political reprisal since they serve for life, may be performing a significant though quite controversial function; they may be compelling the people to accept what the judges think is good for them but which they would not accept from elected legislators.[21]

In other words, the Court is legislating, and in legislating is imposing on the people the justices' own conceptions of what is good and right. Pfeffer does not observe one important implication: that in so acting the Court is usurping a power which does not rightfully belong to it, to place itself above the law and infringe upon the liberty of the people.

Pfeffer extends his explanation of the Court's decisions from birth control to abortion. After mentioning other reasons why the Court may have legalized abortion, he adds:

> All this is true, yet it is probable that a major factor here, as in the case of contraceptive birth control, is the taxpayers' revolt against rising welfare rolls and costs. Legalization of contraception not having worked to an acceptable degree, and other measures . . . proving too Draconian for public acceptance, permissible abortion, encouraged by the state, is the next logical step.[22]

The Court's first dealing with the abortion law, in *United States* v. *Vuitch,* was inconclusive, because this decision allowed the laws to remain in force, although it limited their effectiveness. Apart from other inadequacies Pfeffer notes:

> . . . and perhaps more important, the decision did not meet the needs of the poor who receive their medical services from municipal and county hospitals and clinics. So long as an anti-abortion law was in the State's criminal code, the physicians and nurses were not likely to perform an

abortion or even counsel one where the only reason for it was that the mother was a welfare recipient with seven children and no husband.[23]

Again, after summarizing the argumentation in *Roe* v. *Wade* and *Doe* v. *Bolton,* Pfeffer says that it "is difficult to escape the conclusion that nonlegal factors significantly influenced the decisions: our socioeconomic situation calls for the availability of abortion as a birth-prevention technique . . . "; but, Pfeffer adds, the legislatures were unable to act to repeal the abortion laws because of the "image of Catholic political power."

Actually, as everyone involved in the matter knows, the opposition to repeal was broadly based, and by 1973 it was beginning to become effective in many places where the Catholic contribution was a negligible factor. However that may be, Pfeffer concludes that "the Court had to do what had to be done and did it." He concludes the discussion on abortion with a parenthetical note regarding a 1973 New York City study which indicated that abortion had kept 24,000 children off the city's welfare rolls.[24]

Subsequently, in considering the efforts to repeal antihomosexuality laws, Pfeffer, reiterating his explanation of the contraception and abortion decisions, says that in the case of homosexuality those who advocate decriminalization "lack the most potent motivating factor possessed by the abortion reform movement, the economic factor. Homosexuality is not a practical or effective means of curbing the fruitfulness of welfare recipients."[25]

On June 20, 1977, The United States Supreme Court decided three cases related to the institutionalization of abortion. A whole series of lower court decisions had compelled the states to fund abortion under Medicaid and public hospitals to provide facilities for performing abortions.[26] Two of the 1977 cases concerned a Pennsylvania statute and a Connecticut Welfare Department regulation which limited state payment for abortion to those cases certified to involve medical necessity, thus to exclude payment for elective, nontherapeutic abortions.[27] The third concerned a directive by the mayor of St. Louis prohibiting abortions in public hospitals in the city except when there was a threat of serious physiological—not merely psychological—injury or death to the mother.[28]

The lower federal court decisions would have compelled Pennsylvania and Connecticut to remove their restrictions on funding and St. Louis to facilitate abortions in its city hospitals. The United States Supreme Court reversed these holdings, to permit governments at the various levels to settle through the political process to what extent abortion would be carried out as a state action. Thus, the Court recognized the distinction between the liberty of persons to have and to do abortions without criminal sanctions and the supposed right of such persons to the cooperation of the public at large, including those who consider abortion to be the killing of unborn persons and who for that reason find it utterly repugnant. In other words, the Court refrained from holding that the Constitution *requires* everyone to participate in the killing of the unborn.

However, the Court did not reach its conclusions on the basis of the liberty of those who consider abortion abhorrent to stand aloof from such killing. Rather, the Court merely denied that equal protection of the laws *requires* that the public facilitate abortion to the same extent that it facilitates childbirth. On the Court's analysis Pennsylvania, Connecticut, and the city of St. Louis had adopted a policy favoring childbirth. The Court held that the public could adopt such a policy without violating the Constitution, but the Court also said that nothing prohibited the adoption of a public policy funding and facilitating abortion.[29]

Those who oppose both abortion and the drafting into cooperation with it of the public at large could take some satisfaction in the Court's refusal to impose the institutionalization of abortion as a matter of constitutional obligation on every jurisdiction in the United States.

However, despite their disappointment and frustration, proponents of abortion as an instrument of public policy did not lose much of what they gained by the abortion decisions of 1973. In many places abortion has become institutionalized and what has been done will not be undone. Furthermore, private agencies, such as Planned Parenthood, can devote much of their resources to funding abortion and seek increased governmental support to replace such funds diverted from their other activities.

At the same time the liberty of persons to have and to perform abortions is recognized and protected by the Court, while the liberty of others to stand aloof is ignored. Had the Court carried through an adequate and consistent libertarian treatment of the issues, even without reversing its 1973 decisions, it should have held that while the state cannot interfere with abortion, neither can it facilitate it. The former violates the liberty the Court has ascribed to pregnant women and physicians, but the latter, in the absence of an overriding public necessity, violates the liberty to stand aloof of all who consider abortion abhorrent and who in no way consent to its inclusion in the activities conducted by a government which must derive its just powers from the consent of the governed.

One of the most interesting aspects of the 1977 decisions is that they contain explicit statements in the dissenting opinions of Justices Blackmun, Brennan, and Marshall which support Pfeffer's interpretation of the 1973 abortion decisions.

Brennan's remarks are the least telling of the three. He merely states that the 1977 decisions "can only result as a practical matter in forcing penniless pregnant women to have children they would not have borne if the States had not weighted the scales to make their choice to have abortions substantially more onerous.''[30] Blackmun in a brief dissent denies the distinction between a liberty and a right to have an abortion, speaks of the plight of poor women, and attacks the people of St. Louis for electing a mayor who ran on a platform promising to close the city's hospitals to nontherapeutic abortion. The people of St. Louis, according to Blackmun, "impresses upon a needy minority its own concepts of the socially desirable, the publicly acceptable, and the morally sound, with a touch of the devil-take-the-hindmost." The Court had argued that jurisdictions have their own priorities and must be allowed to spend limited funds in accord with them. To this argument Blackmun replies:

> The Court's financial argument, of course, is specious. To be sure, welfare funds are limited and welfare must be spread perhaps as best meets the community's concept of its needs. But the cost of a nontherapeutic abortion is far less than the cost of maternity care and delivery, and holds no comparison whatsoever with the welfare costs that will burden the State for the new indigents and their support in the long, long years ahead.

Blackmun concludes his dissenting opinion by noting the existence of another world "out there," thus to appeal to the public policy considerations which apparently prevailed over the principles of legality in the 1973 decisions. He says, "And so the cancer of poverty will continue to grow."[31]

Perhaps it is not surprising that Blackmun accepts as a strategy for a public war on poverty the elimination of this cancer by the elimination of the poor who are its victims. Of course, this rationale is terrifying when one thinks of its application to the problems which we have been examining, because all of the human misery which is involved in conditions which some regard as constituting a poor quality of life can finally be eliminated only in one way, by killing the miserable and afflicted. This one perfect and final solution also has the essential cost-benefit feature which Blackmun points out in respect to abortion.

What is surprising, however, is that Marshall is no less clear on his views:

> The enactments challenged here brutally coerce poor women to bear children whom society will scorn for every day of their lives. Many thousands of unwanted minority and mixed race children now spend blighted lives in foster homes, orphanages, and "reform" schools. Many children of the poor will sadly attend second-rate segregated schools. And opposition remains strong against increasing AFDC benefits for impoverished mothers and children, so that there is little chance for the children to grow up in a decent environment. I am appalled at the ethical bankruptcy of those who preach a "right to life" that means, under present social policies, a bare existence in utter misery for so many poor women and their children [citations omitted].[32]

Marshall obviously *accepts* the evils he describes as inevitable and unaltera-
ble. He sees them as evils but fails to see them as challenges to be overcome.
Poor black people who exist in utter misery are to be saved from misery by
being killed before birth.

Someone who did not know otherwise might suppose that Marshall was
an unreconstructed racist. One who does know better must suspect that
while the United States Supreme Court is located only a few blocks from
the Washington, D.C., ghetto, a man who has achieved the status of a
member of the Court is so far alienated from the people of the ghetto that he
can burn with hatred at the evils from which the people suffer without ever
feeling true compassion for the people who suffer these evils, so that he has
embraced the solution of the upper-middle-class establishment, which has
set itself against the social change necessary if America is to be transformed
into a good and just society. Or perhaps Marshall speaks from some dark
depth of depression, disillusion, and despair, a melancholy which can no
longer believe that children who are scorned can yet receive the respect
they deserve, that children whose lives are blighted can yet know the love
of which they are deprived, that children who attend second-rate segregated
schools can yet enjoy the educational opportunities to which they are entitled, that children of poverty can yet be helped to grow in a minimally
decent environment, that those who live a bare existence in utter misery
need not even now be deprived of that bare existence to be redeemed from
that utter misery.

Whatever Marshall's personal views, his dissenting statement together with
the statements of the others provide fresh evidence that Pfeffer's explanation
of the 1973 decisions was a sound hypothesis. The Court has been "compelling the people to accept what the judges think is good for them." Fortunately in this instance the Chief Justice and Justices Powell and Stewart were
unwilling to impose public support of abortion to the extent that Brennan,
Marshall, and Blackmun would have imposed such support. However, Blackmun's resentment against the legitimate policy decision of the people of St.
Louis, who elected a mayor committed to excluding abortion from the city's
hospitals, means that citizens cannot refuse to cooperate in killing the children of needy minorities, because this refusal amounts to imposing the
people's "own concepts of the socially desirable, the publicly acceptable, and
the morally sound."

Blackmun obviously thinks that only the elite who sit at the bench of the
high Court, far above the mass of the people who live on the land below, are
entitled to impose their own concepts of the socially desirable, the publicly
acceptable, and the morally sound. And from the olympus of the Court these
few men have the power to hand down their personal convictions, shaped by
a secular humanist world view with its consequentialist ethic, not merely as

advice, not merely as ordinary law, but as constitutional requirements—as the supreme and very difficult to amend law of the land.

It is hard to know how best to proceed in trying to disestablish the world view which the Court is effectively establishing. Congress and the various states are forbidden to establish a religion, but the Supreme Court cannot be prevented from doing so while it pretends that the world view it accepts is no more than the commonly held principles of liberty and justice which constitute the minimal public morality without which government would lack legitimacy. Nevertheless, a constitutional amendment could make clear at least that secular humanism and other nontheistic world views are on a par with traditional religions and could direct the Court to avoid confusing the moral convictions of its own membership with the minimal public morality.

Further, as our discussion in chapter six, section F, of the liberty to stand aloof made clear, a truly pluralistic society must avoid so far as possible making into public activities in which all must participate modes of action to which many citizens take profound conscientious objection. In some cases society must act despite the conscientious objections of a minority of its members. But such action is only justifiable if there is a substantial public purpose, recognized as such even by the objecting minority, to which the mode of action they find abhorrent seems to be a suitable and even necessary means, and if the adoption of this mode of action is by a general consensus reached by the majority despite its awareness of and respect for the views of the dissenting minority.

These conditions were fulfilled by World War II, to which strict pacifists objected on grounds of conscience. They were hardly clearly fulfilled at any stage of the Vietnam war and clearly were not fulfilled by the end of 1966. The conditions likewise clearly are not fulfilled by the use of abortion to eliminate misery by eliminating the miserable. Yet abortion is more or less extensively done by state action throughout the United States.[33] And there is every reason to expect that euthanasia will deeply involve public action, primarily to make it safe for those who do not wish to be killed and who are powerful enough to ensure that the state will protect them, secondarily to make it effective alongside contraception and abortion as an instrument for solving the problems of those who live miserably in public institutions at great expense to productive taxpaying citizens.

Thus, it seems to us, there is a need for constitutional recognition of the liberty to stand aloof, a declaration of the narrow conditions under which the state should proceed with forms of action to which some citizens conscientiously object, and a provision for the protection of such citizens from any more intimate involvement than necessary in the actions they find abhorrent. The diminishing foundation of consensus about goods other than liberty and justice themselves makes increasingly necessary provision for conscientious objection if there is to be any possibility of maintaining social unity with a government having even a plausible appearance of legitimacy.

D. Life, Liberty, and the Education Establishment

In chapter six, section F, we admitted that it is difficult to reconcile the monopoly which the public school system has on public support of education with the implications of the principle of liberty which we there articulated. Many people have conscientious objections to what the public schools are doing; a great many have felt compelled by their deeply held conscientious convictions to provide an alternative means for educating their children. While the problem of educational freedom is too large a one for us to attempt an adequate treatment of it here, this problem is relevant to the issues regarding life, liberty, and justice with which this book is primarily occupied. The question of educational freedom must be given some consideration here, because such consideration will help to clarify the very important point that secular humanism does not offer a neutral approach to public policy issues.

Moreover, the public school system is being used to inculcate the principles appealed to by the supporters of most of the important public policy proposals bearing upon life and death which we have criticized throughout this book. Across the United States the children are being formed in the new quality-of-life morality, especially but not only in courses of sex education which have been promoted by organizations closely connected with the groups which have promoted contraception and abortion. Moreover, seizing the opportunity presented by parents and other concerned persons who are anxious about the moral formation of the young, a great many schools have established programs in values clarification, which very effectively undermines the claim of traditional moral standards to objectivity and prepares the minds of the young to be as receptive as possible to the consequentialist ethic which is the moral doctrine of secular humanism.[34]

The first thing to understand about the American public school system is that until the last few decades it did not even pretend to be religiously neutral. What it claimed to be was nonsectarian. In fact it was only nonsectarian in relation to various forms of Protestantism. By and large the public school system of the United States has been a publicly financed, common Protestant educational system. The Protestant version of the Bible was used in the schools for religious instruction, Protestant prayers and hymns were said and sung, Protestant ideals and standards inculcated, and very often Protestant interpretations of history, literature, and other sensitive subject areas were given, in some cases by Protestant clergy.

Anyone who takes the trouble to talk with elderly Catholics and other persons who were not like their Protestant peers in the schools of the early decades of the twentieth century will hear many stories which make clear what the situation was. But numerous court cases—none of them ever reaching the United States Supreme Court—also provide unquestionable evidence.[35]

Leo Pfeffer quite frankly summarizes the situation. American public education was initially Calvinist. As it spread, there were problems due to sectarian differences with other Protestants. The solution was to use the Authorized (King James) Version of the Bible as a textbook in religion but to exclude sectarian comment and interpretation. When Roman Catholics began coming to the United States in large numbers in the 1830s, they could not conform to the established arrangement:

> In some schools the teachers and authorities did not insist that Catholic children participate in the exercises, but in others Protestant fervor or anti-Catholic prejudice dictated a different course, and non-compliance by Catholic students led to corporal punishment, expulsion, and other forms of discipline.
>
> As a result Catholic parents brought many lawsuits in state courts. In these cases the legal issue was whether the King James Version of the Bible was a sectarian book and hence not permissible for public school use. Because most of the judges were themselves Protestants the decisions in most cases favored the status quo. The frequency of such decisions did much to encourage an exodus of Catholic children from public schools and establishment of Catholic parochial instruction, usually under diocesan auspices.[36]

Many state constitutions and statutes prohibited the funding of "sectarian" schools—that is, of schools other than the common Protestant system, which in this way gained a monopoly on public funding.[37] In short, the American public school system simply was a common Protestant school system.

In 1947 the Supreme Court of the United States—holding the First Amendment clause concerning establishment of religion applicable to the states by way of the Fourteenth Amendment—declared that there must be separation between church and state. Nevertheless, it approved as a service to the children rather than as aid to the schools the provision of bus transportation to pupils attending parochial schools.[38] In 1948, having laid the groundwork, the Court, deciding the case of *McCollum* v. *Board of Education*, held unconstitutional an arrangement by which Illinois children were released from other work for a time each week to receive religious instruction in classes approved by their parents and taught at the school by religion teachers who came in from outside at no cost to the school system.[39] Pfeffer indicates an important aspect of this landmark decision:

As indicated, all the pre-*McCollum* lawsuits challenging religion in the public schools had been brought by Catholics. With *McCollum,* the burden of litigation shifted to atheists (McCollum, Doremus), humanists (Schempp), Jews (Engel, Gluck), and occasionally liberal Protestants (Zorach).[40]

Following *McCollum* a series of cases were decided which purged the public schools of the vestiges of the old Protestant establishment. The most important of these cases were *Engel* v. *Vitale* (1962), in which the Court held unconstitutional the recitation of a short, public-school-sponsored prayer, and *Abington School District* v. *Schempp* (1963), in which the Court rejected as establishment of religion the vestigial devotional use of the Bible and the saying of the Lord's Prayer.[41]

What happened is clear enough. For about a century Catholics complained about the establishment of Protestantism in the public schools to little or no avail. The First Amendment restrained Congress but not the states, and the Supreme Court was uninterested in the problem. After World War II persons standing outside the common Protestant establishment attacked its privileged position in the public schools. The Court discovered that the First Amendment's prohibition of establishment does apply to the states, thus to give itself power to drive religion altogether out of the public schools. Presumably the result would be to make them religiously neutral.

But can this be done? Justice Jackson, dissenting in 1947 from the decision permitting the public to provide bus transportation for children attending parochial schools, strongly emphasized the religious function of the Catholic school system and contrasted it with the public school approach:

> It is no exaggeration to say that the whole historic conflict in temporal policy between the Catholic Church and non-Catholics comes to a focus in their respective school policies. The Roman Catholic Church, counseled by experience in many ages and many lands and with all sorts and conditions of men, takes what, from the viewpoint of its own progress and the success of its mission, is a wise estimate of the importance of education to religion. It does not leave the individual to pick up religion by chance. It relies on early and indelible indoctrination in the faith and order of the Church by the word and example of persons consecrated to the task.
>
> Our public school, if not a product of Protestantism, at least is more consistent with it than with the Catholic culture and scheme of values. It is a relatively recent development dating from about 1840 [citation omitted]. It is organized on the premise that secular education can be isolated from all religious teaching so that the school can inculcate all needed temporal knowledge and also maintain a strict and lofty neutrality as to religion. The assumption is that after the individual has been instructed in worldly wisdom he will be better fitted to choose his religion. Whether such a disjunction is possible, and if possible whether it is wise, are questions I need not try to answer.[42]

Although this contrast ignored the true history of the public schools and propagated a myth as to their neutrality—a neutrality Jackson interestingly characterized as "lofty," suggesting a position of superiority to religion—it at least makes clear that there is more to the matter of religion in schools than saying a short prayer or reading a few verses from the Bible.

Different approaches to education are grounded in different religious conceptions of faith. On a Catholic conception one receives faith as a member of the church to which he or she belongs; on a Protestant conception one chooses one's religion and subsequently may or may not associate with those who are like-minded in a church. Jackson is admitting that the public school system by its very "neutrality" favors the Protestant over the Catholic conception of how one receives Christian faith.

By the following year, when *McCollum* was decided, Jackson was ready to discuss the questions about the very possibility of neutrality which he had claimed characteristic of "our public school." Jackson concurred in the decision that released-time was unconstitutional, but he was worried about the Court's seeming readiness to lay down the sweeping constitutional doctrine as demanded by complainant: "to immediately adopt and enforce rules and regulations prohibiting all instruction in and teaching of religious education in all public schools." Jackson observed that there were 256 separate and substantial religious bodies in the United States, and that if the Court were to eliminate everything objectionable to any of these sects from the public schools it would leave public education in shreds, cause educational confusion, and discredit the system.

Perhaps some subjects such as mathematics, physics, or chemistry can be completely secularized, but most subjects cannot be sterilized of the religious, because everything in the culture worth transmitting is saturated with religious influences.

> One can hardly respect a system of education that would leave the student wholly ignorant of the currents of religious thought that move the world society for a part in which he is being prepared.
> But how can one teach, with satisfaction or even with justice to all faiths, such subjects as the story of the Reformation, the Inquisition, or even the New England effort to found "a Church without a Bishop and a State without a King," is more than I know. It is too much to expect that mortals will teach subjects about which their contemporaries have passionate controversies with the detachment they may summon to teaching about remote subjects such as Confucius or Mohamet. When instruction turns to proselyting and imparting knowledge becomes evangelism is, except in the crudest cases, a subtle inquiry.[43]

And so belatedly realizing that the schools could not maintain strict and lofty neutrality, Jackson urged the Court to proceed with judicial restraint:

It is idle to pretend that this task is one for which we can find in the Constitution one word to help us as judges to decide where the secular ends and the sectarian begins in education. Nor can we find guidance in any other legal source. It is a matter on which we can find no law but our own prepossessions.[44]

Unfortunately Jackson did not draw the appropriate conclusion: The monopoly of public funding enjoyed by schools which could not be thoroughly and loftily neutral amounts to establishment of religion, and this establishment chills the right of free exercise of all those who find the nonneutral public schools less consistent with their religious beliefs than would be their own, alternative system of openly religious schools.

The case of *Abington School District* v. *Schempp* (1963) is especially interesting because of the manner in which the Court carefully skirted the problem of the nonneutrality of the public schools. In *amicus curiae* briefs the American Ethical Union and the American Humanist Association expressed their interest in the issue, identifying themselves as religious in the constitutional sense which the Court recognized in *Torcaso* v. *Watkins,* where both Ethical Culture and Secular Humanism had been mentioned by name and identified as nontheistic religions.[45]

The Ethical Union brief makes clear that its nontheism is not necessarily atheism; members are at liberty to believe in a Supreme Being. What is essential is freedom of thought and privacy of judgment. Ethical societies take an attitude of strict neutrality toward worship, theism, and prayer; their positive thrust is toward the enhancement of ethical fellowship or human relations. The methods of religious formation adopted by this group are as follows:

> In their Sunday Schools, Ethical Culture Societies carefully avoid developing in their children a view of life that is dependent upon the dogma of the divine word or the worship of a Supreme Being. The program seeks to impart to the children instead an understanding of the religious and cultural heritage of other groups and of the dignity and worth of each individual in order that they may better understand their own Ethical and humanistic heritage.
>
> In part, the study by the children of the traditions of other religions is based upon religious literature, including the Old and the New Testament. The curriculum of the Sunday School of the New York Society for Ethical Culture states that: ''The Old and the New Testament are examined as literary documents with great ethical import which have exerted a far-reaching influence on Western civilization.'' [citation omitted] The study of the Bibles and the doctrines therein contained is made under the supervision of a Sunday School teacher who can aid the children in comparing one with another so that their similarities and differences may be brought forth as well as their religious and moral significance.

The Ethical Movement does not subscribe to the claims of any of the various Holy Books of mankind as being the ultimate word. Leaving to each of its members the personal decision as to their divine nature, Ethical Culture draws from various scriptures their moral and ethical principles. "It starts where the Jewish and Christian communions stop, seeing in the ethical precepts of the Old Testament and in those of the New, stages in the evolution of moral standards beyond which we are now to advance."[46]

The Humanist Association brief explains its view of religion:

As an approach to living, as a philosophy and a religion, Humanism is free from any belief in the supernatural and dedicates itself to the happiness of humanity on this earth through reliance on intelligence and the scientific method, democracy and social sympathy. . . .

It is not attempting to form another church but to supplement and relate the Humanists in various churches and to join them with secularists in common study and fellowship.

In 1933 "A Humanist Manifesto" was issued by 34 distinguished persons, including John Dewey, Robert Morss Lovett, John Herman Randall, Jr. and Charles Francis Potter, most of whom considered themselves religious in a non-theological sense. Religion to them meant the group quest for good life and the pursuit of the ideal, but unlike traditional theistic religions that ideal was grounded in nature rather than in the supernatural. Humanists endeavor to keep the human spirit free from binding dogmas and creeds and to search for truths rather than "The Truth".

It firmly believes in the fundamental American doctrine of complete separation between church and state and that this principle must be maintained in its broadest aspects.

It regards the public school as one of the most democratic American civil institutions and that its idea of secular education should not be compromised by using it as an agency for religious activities or instruction.[47]

On this basis the Humanist Association quite reasonbly found the reading of the Bible and the saying of the Lord's Prayer abhorrent practices in the public schools and demanded that they be excluded as unconstitutional mingling of church and state.

Both the Ethical Union and the Humanist Association considered themselves religions, and quite correctly in terms of the Court's acceptance of the position, which we discussed in section A, that anything which takes the place of religion in one's life is constitutionally a religion. One's ultimate concern, one's way of valuing most intensively and comprehensively, the source of one's deeply held conscientious convictions is one's religion, whether one belongs to any church, engages in any conventional religious practices, or even thinks of oneself as religious.[48]

The Ethical Union makes clear exactly how in its *religious* perspective the writings others consider sacred are to be regarded. They are to be treated with respect as great literary documents, studied with care for their human and ethical significance, but never accepted as the ultimate word.

The Humanist Association proudly declares its allegiance to democracy as it understands democracy. While it eschews any search for "The Truth," it "firmly believes" in the absolute separation of church and state and regards the public school as the most democratic of institutions.

One of the founders of the Humanist Association, John Dewey, articulated a tremendously influential educational philosophy, which has shaped the education of the teachers in many of the faculties of education in the United States and elsewhere for much of this century. Dewey considered the school a small-scale but actual democratic society in which children would learn by practice how to reform and humanize the larger society. The stress on problem-solving, on social adjustment, and on situational factors which is so characteristic of modern educational theory and public school educational practice is in no small measure indebted to Dewey's educational philosophy, which includes a psychology, an ethics, and a secular humanistic religious attitude.[49]

The decision of the Court in the case excluded devotional Bible reading and prayer from the public schools. In doing so the Court surely was correct inasmuch as these are religious practices and the public schools have a monopoly on public support, so that religious practices in them constitute an establishment of religion.

But the Court failed to face up to the issue of the nonneutrality of the residual educational system. It came closest in saying:

> It is insisted that unless these religious exercises are permitted a "religion of secularism" is established in the schools. We agree of course that the State may not establish a "religion of secularism" in the sense of affirmatively opposing or showing hostility to religion, thus "preferring those who believe in no religion over those who do believe." [citation omitted] We do not agree, however, that this decision in any sense has that effect. In addition, it might well be said that one's education is not complete without a study of comparative religion or the history of religion and its relationship to the advancement of civilization. It certainly may be said that the Bible is worthy of study for its literary and historic qualities. Nothing we have said here indicates that such study of the Bible or of religion, when presented objectively as part of a secular program of education, may not be effected consistently with the First Amendment.[50]

The Court certainly is correct in holding that the exclusion from the public schools of the vestigial religious exercises at issue in the case does not establish a religion of secularism.

But the Court ignores the fact that the public schools do in fact embody and put into practice deeply held conscientious convictions. To some extent these convictions are a generalized residue of Jewish and Christian religion and morality, a nondenominational residue which plays a part in American public life generally—for example, in the simple ceremony of the pledge of allegiance to the flag. This residue, which has been called "civil religion," is almost inseparable from the conventional patriotism and attitude of civic responsibility inculcated in the public schools in more conservative sections of the United States.[51] To the extent that all conventional religion, including American civil religion, is successfully excluded from the schools, they inevitably embody other deeply held convictions. In many schools a secular humanist educational philosophy, developed by Dewey and others, is in fact given the dominant position. In such schools, whether by forthright indoctrination or by the subtle communication of the organization of the educational experience, the methods of teaching, and the like, children are formed in secular humanism.

Perhaps the Court forgets its own extremely broad definition of "religion," which as we have seen was invoked by the Ethical Union in its brief. Nevertheless, the Court approves as the acceptable way of dealing with the Bible in public schools precisely the way in which the Ethical Union deals with it in the religious education of the children of its own members in the Sunday Schools conducted by their groups. Moreover, the Court misdefines "religion of secularism" as affirmatively opposing or showing hostility to all religion, so that this would be established only if the public schools actively propagated nonbelief in anything at all.

Obviously, they cannot do this, and the Humanist Association never proposed it. The Humanist Association is dedicated to the happiness of humanity on this earth through reliance on the scientific method and intelligence, democracy and social sympathy. Its founders considered themselves religious in a nontheological sense but with an ideal grounded in nature. This is the sort of religion which secular humanists want in the public schools, and with the support of the Court this is the sort of religion which the public schools propagate.

In a concurring opinion Justice Brennan argued that the public schools really are neutral:

> It is implicit in the history and character of American public education that the public schools serve a uniquely *public* function: the training of American citizens in an atmosphere free of parochial, divisive, or separatist influences of any sort—an atmosphere in which children may assimilate a heritage common to all American groups and religions.

Brennan then proceeds to contrast "public secular education with its uniquely democratic values" with forms of "private or sectarian education, which offers values of its own."[52]

This way of looking at the matter is deeply confused. If the public schools embody a unique set of values, they are teaching a religion. The supposition is that this religion is acceptable to everyone, because it is common to all American groups and religions. But, one wonders, what is this common body of values? We of course do not deny that there are common standards of liberty and justice. On particular points persons whose religious views differ greatly can come to agreement in moral intuitions—for example, that racial discrimination is unjust. By ending segregation and undertaking integation, by striving to develop a school community in which children of various races learn to live together in mutual respect and cooperation, the school system embodies this intuition without necessarily establishing a religion.

But teachers do have foundations for their deeply held conscientious convictions in this matter, and children are curious. Moreover, not all children are going to share the intuition that racial discrimination is wrong. What are teachers to tell them? Shall they say: It is wrong because the Supreme Court has said so, and that is all there is to it? This would be an extreme legal positivism, which is one religion among others—"religion" being understood as the Court has defined it. Some teachers might be tempted to say: Because God is our Father, and all of us are his children, and we ought to treat one another as brothers and sisters who share in his dignity. Clearly, to say this is religion—it is an example of the common, nondenominational religion which is called "American civil religion." The teacher can avoid this explanation, of course, but any alternative explanation also will manifest deeply held conscientious convictions and so, on the Court's own definition, will be religion of one sort or another.

And so we come back to the admission which we made in chapter six that the principle of liberty cannot be reconciled with the monopoly which the public schools enjoy. They try to contribute to the growth and health of children but must adopt one conception of maturity and healthiness rather than another.

If one is a secular humanist, sex education which helps children to understand and accept their sexual feelings, to appreciate the possibilities of sexual gratification, to avoid such undesirable consequences as venereal disease and unwanted pregnancy, and to be tolerant of persons with varying sexual preferences makes very good sense. If one's religion is not secular humanist, such sex education too easily accepts what must be dealt with cautiously, too quickly approves gratification over restraint and sublimation, too exclusively emphasizes public health considerations as the parameters of bad sex, and too quickly tolerates masturbation, premarital sex, adultery, homosexuality, and other forms of behavior which many parents still consider wrong.

More broadly, if one is a secular humanist, it makes good sense to invite children to clarify their own values by discussion of problems in a context of social interaction with their peers, for the secular humanist believes that all values ultimately emerge out of human social experience with concrete situations. Thus, problems such as abortion and euthanasia will be discussed, by using as material cases in which killing has some emotional appeal, and the children will be asked to give their own opinion: "Johnny, how do you feel about the Eskimo family leaving their grandma behind?"

If one's religion is different, courses in value clarification amount at best to indoctrination in a dangerous relativism which contradicts the objectivity of moral norms and the authority of their source—for example, in God. At worst, such courses more or less openly propagate secular humanist beliefs and attitudes, for example, by using materials which suggest on cost-benefit consequentialist grounds that those whose quality of life is poor ought to be "allowed to die."

Obviously, even if secular humanism is not inculcated, still schools must form the minds and characters of children if they are to educate, and any effort at formation flows from a source of values, for such formation is an exercise in the communication of values. Talk about health and growth is no less religious, taking "religion" in the sense the Court has given it, then talk about holiness and grace.

While the Supreme Court has excluded certain manifestations of conventional religion from the public schools while it evades the issue of their non-neutrality, it also has firmly been refusing to allow any substantial public assistance to nonpublic schools. As we saw, it permitted the states to fund bus transportation as a benefit to the children. Subsequently it allowed the furnishing of standard textbooks to nonpublic school students, on the ground that neither the purpose nor the primary effect of furnishing such books was to advance religion but rather was to advance the secular component of the education which children receive even in the context of a religious or other nonpublic school.[53] If this approach had been applied consistently, it would have opened the way to public financing for a substantial part of the education of children in nonpublic schools which met common standards for recognition as legitimate educational institutions.

However, in *Lemon* v. *Kurtzman* (1971) the Court held that programs enacted by Pennsylvania and Rhode Island to compensate church-related schools and their teachers for instruction of children in secular subjects violate the religion clauses of the First Amendment. The Court argued that the statutes would bring about excessive entanglement of religion and government, because the schools have a religious purpose, because the children are being formed in religion by the school, because the state would have to be involved in the schools to make sure the restriction of assistance to secular purposes was respected, because the state would have to audit the schools' books, because the grants would become a political issue and lead to political division along religious lines, and because any entanglement would be a step onto a slippery slope.[54]

In the opinion of the Court there were only mild suggestions of a point stressed very much in a concurring opinion by Douglas: The religious and secular aspects of education in a religiously oriented school cannot be separated in practice, religious principles permeate the curriculum and the operation of the school, and teachers cannot avoid dealing with even the most secular subject matters in a way marked by their profound beliefs.[55] Douglas ignored the fact that permeation by deeply held, conscientious convictions also is inevitable in public schools.

It is not altogether clear whether entanglement is establishment or interference with free exercise of religion. Perhaps it is both. The concurring opinion of Brennan suggests that the restrictions in the state programs would interfere significantly with free exercise.[56]

In a dissenting opinion White argues that the subsidies would not violate the establishment clause and that they could be viewed as required by the free exercise clause. His argument is that when the state undertakes to further education, considerations of free exercise tell against refusing support to students attending parochial schools merely because there they also receive instruction in the religion they are free to practice. But White also undertook to argue the implausible proposition that a strict separation between secular and religious activities within the schools was possible and could be carried out in practice.[57]

It seems to us that a stronger argument might have been made by suggesting that the subsidies could be paid without state involvement in the schools and an entanglement of any very real sort could thereby be avoided. The impossibility of teachers maintaining neutrality is not peculiar to parochial school settings, and so special surveillance of such schools would be unwarranted.

More basically, the Court has admitted the liberty of citizens to educate their children in a religiously oriented manner. The state requires all children to attend schools. It collects taxes and provides a school system, which naturally accepts the views of the socially dominant group and tries to mold all students in accord with them.[58] Those who dissent from the views of the dominant group nevertheless either submit their children to this molding process or they exercise their liberty by finding alternative means of education which meet common minimal standards. To deny public funding to such dissenting groups for their service to the commonly accepted educational purpose obviously chills the free exercise of religion and denies to those who dissent the equal protection of the laws.[59]

Many who would not accept this argument in the present context nevertheless presented a similar but far weaker argument for the public funding of abortions, which the 1977 decisions *accepted as permissible* although not constitutionally required. The argument for public funding of openly religious schools is stronger for at least two reasons. First, the public does compel children to go to school; it does not compel anyone to become pregnant. Second, although some dislike religiously shaped education and consider it harmful to children, no one regards the policy of allowing parents to educate their children according to their own world views as a grave injustice; many people find abortion not only repugnant but abhorrent as a grave injustice to unborn persons. Yet some who urge that the denial of public funding to impoverished pregnant women annuls their right to abortion also urge that the denial of public funding to impoverished religious parents is altogether compatible with their right of free exercise of religion. If they were free in the extreme case to keep their children out of school altogether, the argument might have some plausibility, but since the law will compel attendance if the parents do not send their children to the only schools they can afford—the publicly supported ones to which they conscientiously object—the argument is wholly lacking in plausibility.[60]

E. Freedom of World View Amendment

Thus, let us sum up our current discussion. We have been suggesting that a clarification of the Constitution is needed to point out the parity of secular humanism and other nonreligious world views with the traditional religions and to warn against treating the former as neutral and equivalent to the public morality of liberty and justice. We also explained why the right of conscientious objection is in need of formal, constitutional recognition without restriction to one or another narrow subject matter or area of public activity.[61] Now, with the discussion of the school question we have tried to clarify why the myth of public neutrality in education should go the way of the myth of separate-but-equal facilities for the races.

In education and other positive public programs—such as health care— public involvement may be essential for the common welfare, which is an aspect of the common good which serves a whole variety of goods of individuals and voluntary organizations. But when people with varying world views would take diverse approaches to forming such programs, respect for the liberty of all in a pluralistic society demands that any group which can develop its own alternative program receive public recognition and support to the extent that its program serves the common welfare. Otherwise, free exercise loses all practical meaning in the modern welfare state, and equal protection of the laws has a meaning only for those who share the dominant world view which manages to shape the public programs.

With these purposes in mind we propose the following "Freedom of World View" amendment as a point of departure for a discussion of this subject:

Section one. Neither Congress nor the legislature of any State shall make any law respecting the establishment of Secular Humanism or any other world view, nor shall the free exercise of any world view be prohibited. The liberty of free exercise hereby guaranteed shall be subject to the same limits as the liberty of free exercise of religion guaranteed by the First Amendment to this Constitution.

Section two. No court of the United States or of any State shall adopt as normative for the interpretation of this Constitution or the constitutions of the various States principles of the right and the good rooted in the world views adhered to by the judges themselves as distinct from the principles of liberty and justice about which there is general consensus among the people, despite their diverse world views.

Section three. Neither the United States nor any State shall engage in any activity repugnant to the deeply held conscientious convictions of the majority of its citizens; nor shall they engage in any such activity repugnant to a minority without declaring the necessity of the activity for a substantial public purpose. Upon making such a declaration, Congress and the legislatures of the various States in their respective jurisdictions shall provide means by which conscientious objectors can stand aloof so far as possible and be exempt from direct participation. The means provided shall avoid creating either an advantage or a disadvantage for conscientious objectors in comparison with other citizens.

Section four. Both the United States and the various States shall respect the equal liberty of all citizens to contribute to the public welfare by participating in institutions and programs of activity formed by their own world views. Congress and the legislatures of the various States in their respective jurisdictions shall not fund public programs directed toward health, education, and welfare without funding equitably privately organized programs directed toward the same purpose.

Section five. Congress shall have the power to enforce section two of this Article with respect to judges of the courts of the United States by the process of impeachment. Whenever one-third of the members of the House of Representatives petitions their Speaker for a vote whether to impeach any civil officer of the United States, the Speaker shall call the issue to a vote within thirty days.

We propose the preceding only as a sketch of the constitutional reform we think is needed. Clearly the matter is very difficult and requires a great deal of thought and discussion.

The first section would make explicit what the Supreme Court already has held but not consistently adhered to: All world views are on an equal footing. This means that nontheistic world views must not be treated as if they represented the common basis of the society and thus be given a status preferential to traditional religious views.

Our second section sets down an ideal for judicial neutrality between their own moral views and those of other citizens. The ideal is a high and difficult one. Probably it could be more clearly formulated. The ideal would have no legal force if it were not somehow enforced. We propose in section five that the power of impeachment be used to enforce judicial neutrality. In proposing this we also suggest that the process be expedited by requiring a vote on a possible impeachment—not only of judges but of any civil officer of the United States—whenever a substantial part of the House demands it. Apart from expediting this vote, the impeachment process would be no easier than it now is. The Senate would remain the ultimate court and would still convict only by the votes of two-thirds of those present.

This very likely would mean that judges would seldom if ever be impeached for their nonneutrality. But the possibility of impeachment would create a decent caution on the part of the judges and a beneficial scrutiny of their grounds for decisions on the part of their critics. Under such conditions *Roe v. Wade* might not have been ventured.

Our third section does three things with respect to conscientious objection. First, it establishes this as a constitutional right, which seems to us essential if a pluralistic society is not going to infringe constantly upon the liberty of many of its members. Second, it eliminates the restrictions of conscientious objection to a few isolated instances. Third, it requires that efforts be made to equalize the situations of conscientious objectors with other citizens.

Had a constitutional provision such as this been in effect during the Vietnam war, everyone who objected to it on grounds of conscience could have been exempted from military service but would have been required to accept equally onerous service in the public interest in some nonmilitary capacity. But by the same token all who served would receive similar benefits. If a provision like this would lead to a general refusal to serve in a particular war, that would be an excellent sign that the war did not enjoy public support.

Our fourth section goes beyond cases in which people wish to avoid an activity to which they take conscientious objection to cover cases in which groups of people wish to serve the public interest in their own ways—for example, by providing their own school or health-care facilities as an alternative to public programs. We have argued at length for the justice of such an arrangement in the case of the schools. The same principles would apply as well to health care and other fields of activity. This provision would go a long way toward making society truly pluralistic, not only at the level of individualism but also at the level of the subcultures which are far more significant for cultural richness than is individual idiosyncrasy. Individualistic pluralism is for an elite few; subcultural pluralism is something which can be enjoyed by the many.

Someone will object that provisions to protect the liberty of all to stand aloof from activities to which they take conscientious objection and to enable many people to enjoy the liberty of pursuing the public good in their own ways will be difficult to administer and will lead to waste and inefficiency. This may be true, but ease of administration and efficiency in pursuing the public good concern only means to it, while liberty and its just protection are very important components of this very good. An argument based upon ease of administration and efficiency, if taken to its ultimate implications, is an argument for a totalitarian state, which simplifies administration, pursues its ends with efficiency, and crushes liberty.

F. Concluding Practical Considerations

We have outlined two amendments: one to protect human life as it should in justice be protected and the other to insure liberty and enhance its exercise. Many have sought an amendment along the lines of the first of these for several years with little practical result. One might wonder whether the second has any better prospect of success, and whether it is worth the work of pursuing either or both of these lines of reform.

One point worth noting is that distinguishing the issues as we propose would have the advantage of creating two distinct movements which could share many common members but also could appeal to somewhat different groups. Progress toward the goals of either of these proposals would be very worthwhile and would mitigate significantly the dangers in which American society now stands. It would be a serious mistake to suppose that the establishment of secular humanism and its new morality is less a threat to the liberty of those who adhere to other world views than it is to the rights of those, for example, who are being killed because no one cares to protect them and many prefer to lessen the welfare burden.

Still, we are not optimistic about obtaining the passage of constitutional amendments along the lines of either of our proposals. Why, then, propose them?

First, the effects of both proposals could be achieved by new decisions of the United States Supreme Court itself. Neither of these proposals makes any substantial change in the Constitution; both merely make clear how the Court should be interpreting it. A reversal by the present Court of positions it has taken is unlikely. But the present Court is not immortal. There are only a few persons who are likely to be appointed to the Court in the future. The task is to try to learn who these persons might be, to try to educate them, to find which of them would join in judgments reversing the errors of the Court, and to seek the appointment of such persons.

Perhaps as things now stand persons who are eligible by virtue of their socioeconomic status and other qualities to be appointed to the Court are likely by these very same factors to be impaired in understanding the meaning and implications of the fundamental American commitment to liberty and justice for all. But times do change and nations sometimes suffer shocks which bring them back to their fundamental commitments.

Second, the movement for the reform of the Constitution must be a mass one and as such it needs a clear focus. Yet even if this goal is not reached, the movement can achieve a great deal. The Constitution cannot be effective in a vacuum. If the United States has an overreaching Court which imposes bad law, this is partly because people do not sufficiently understand what good law is, do not insist upon having it, are not eager to live under it, and are not willing to work to make it effective.

Laws must be understood, appreciated, and respected by the people subject to them if they are to be more than arbitrary rules imposed to govern behavior irrespective of the desire of members of a society to cooperate together in a truly common life. If by some miracle a properly astute Court were given America today, the present situation would change little without changes throughout the body politic. Yet even with an overreaching Court and some bad law the nation need not be wholly corrupt if people know what is just and continue to strive after it despite infringements upon their liberty.

Persons who are working hard to achieve a good are themselves less likely to yield to a temptation to violate that good. Young people who are committed to seeking just laws to protect the lives of the unborn are less likely than others to be tempted to share in unjust killing.

Thus infringements on liberty and justice can at least be slowed, and many human lives which otherwise would be lost can still be saved. For this all who love life, liberty, and justice may hope, and in the light of this hope work through the night which is our time.

11. Theories of Ethics

A. Why Ethical Reflection Remains Necessary

In previous chapters we have been concerned with jurisprudential questions—that is, with questions concerning what the laws ought to be—with respect to euthanasia and related matters. But upright persons not only wish to live under sound laws; they also wish to make morally right judgments.

Legal standards direct and regulate society and provide means by which members of society can pursue their purposes in orderly and recognized ways. Moral standards are primarily sought by persons to shape their own activities. It is a mistake to think of moral norms as if they formed an additional legal code. Upright persons undertake ethical reflection about moral questions not so much to settle controversies with others as to make sure that their own lives will meet the test of reasonableness, will be examined lives worth living by persons conscious of and grateful for the human capacity for rational reflection and self-criticism. Thus the question "Who is making these rules, and why should I accept them?" which always is appropriate when one is confronted with laws is out of place when one is seeking moral standards. A serious person regards any proposed moral standard as an appeal to reason and accepts it if no more reasonable alternative can be found.

There are a number of reasons why moral guidelines are necessary and legal standards by themselves are insufficient.

As we explained in chapter two, section H, not all of morality can be legislated. Thus law necessarily leaves open to individuals a more or less broad set of options, some of which are questionable from a moral point of view. Upright persons will wish to know which of the legally permissible acts are morally acceptable and thus to be seriously considered.

Moreover, upright persons tend to extend their ethical reflection to the law itself. The fact that laws are in force is no guarantee that they are just. Anyone who is concerned about moral goodness will wish to know whether present laws—or any proposed laws, including our proposals—are *morally* worthy of wholehearted support. This concern gives rise to two questions.

336

First, is the conception of government which is based solely upon the commonly accepted principles of liberty and justice morally defensible? In chapter two we articulated this conception as an expression of the American consensus (or, more broadly, of the form of liberal democracy common to the English-speaking nations). Throughout our treatment of the jurisprudential questions we have assumed that this conception of government is sound. Many readers may feel that government ideally should be somewhat less libertarian, that it should embody a commitment, for example, to the good of human life itself, not merely to equal protection of the law of homicide. The ethical theory which we will articulate in this chapter and the next will enable us to argue in chapter thirteen that the more libertarian conception of government is morally defensible not merely as a compromise in a society in which immoral persons participate but even as a sound principle for constituting community among persons who respect as fully as they deserve both human life and every other human good.

Second, in the preceding chapters we have considered, criticized, and rejected numerous proposals which would facilitate killing some persons or letting some persons die when others think they would be better off dead. Underlying these proposals are two assumptions. One of these assumptions is that human life is, not a good intrinsic to human persons, but merely a necessary condition of personal fulfillment. On this assumption life is an instrumental good at the material or biological level. The other assumption is that the rightness and wrongness of human acts depends strictly upon their measurable good or bad consequences for human persons. On this assumption, when continued life is of no benefit and its termination would prevent further suffering, then beneficent killing is morally required.

In the present chapter we are going to criticize the consequentialist method of ethical reasoning, propose what we believe to be a sound alternative to it, and argue that human life is a constitutive, not merely instrumental, good of human persons—a good which contributes directly to human fulfillment regardless of the quality of life a person enjoys.

B. Some Less Plausible Theories of Ethics

Before we criticize the consequentialist method of ethical reasoning, we consider briefly some other current approaches to moral questions. These approaches are generally considered less plausible than consequentialism, and the difficulties inherent in them lend consequentialism much of the plausibility it has.

Very often those who deal with difficult moral questions, including professional philosophers and others considered to have some expertise in critical reflection, proceed in an unsystematic and ad hoc way. They do not raise the question: What method of ethical judgment is sound? Instead they deal directly with the moral issues and proceed from assumptions which they expect readers or listeners to grant.

One very simple way to do this is to argue by analogy. A real or imaginary case which seems simple and clear is taken as a premiss, and the extent to which people's moral judgments about the case coincide is used as another premiss. The conclusion is then drawn that the same moral judgment should hold for a somewhat similar but less simple and clear case, concerning which moral judgments have diverged.

The analogy proposed by Judith Jarvis Thomson, which we criticized in chapter seven, section F, between abortion and disconnecting oneself from the violinist, is an example of this way of arguing. Our criticism of her argument makes clear why arguments of this sort are weak. If the instances which are compared are not alike in all relevant ways, then the analogy, although persuasive, loses its appearance of rational cogency. If the instances which are compared are alike in all relevant ways, the moral standard implicit in the judgment of the clearer case also will apply to the less clear one. But such arguments will be effective only when the principle itself is not in question. However, the issues considered in this book concern principles, not merely the application of standards to cases, and the same is generally true of important arguments about public policy issues. Thus, arguments by analogy cannot provide a rational ground for settling the issues in dispute.

Another approach to moral issues which avoids the problems of ethical theory is casuistry. Casuistry is a method of moral reasoning by which one applies an accepted set of principles to difficult cases by clarifying the peculiar features of these cases, making explicit all the principles which might be relevant, and comparing the difficult cases to simpler cases determined by each of the relevant principles. In law casuistry is indispensable, and it also will be used by anyone or any moral community which holds and develops a complex set of moral standards. But casuistry has its limitations. Like argument by analogy, it assumes that there are principles which are not in doubt. The application might refine or qualify an accepted standard but will not so radically alter it as to dictate contradictory decisions concerning cases previously decided by the standard.

The issues with which we are concerned in this book go beyond problems of difficult cases to be decided without abandoning accepted principles. The issues have become acute precisely because there no longer is a moral community in contemporary political societies concerning the good of human life and the practical implications of this good. Thus, to proceed as if the issues of principle were merely casuistic problems is to fall short of one's responsibility in the debate.

Marvin Kohl, for example, falls short in this way when he argues casuistically as if beneficent euthanasia were merely an application of the principle of
kindness which is generally accepted. Most people who have accepted the
principle of kindness would consider killing necessarily unkind. Kohl's interpretation is novel, and it would upset many judgments previously reached by
applying the very principle to which he appeals. Obviously the interpretation
of the requirements of kindness which Kohl requires must be argued for. But
while he answers various objections to mercy killing, *assuming it kind,* he
does not argue for his radical reinterpretation of what is required by the
principle of kindness. Thus, Kohl's treatment begs the question at issue. So
will every effort to handle issues of principle as if they were merely problems
of particular application to be dealt with casuistically.

Therefore, any adequate approach to the issues treated in this book must
confront the problems of ethical theory and provide an account of the way in
which moral standards themselves can be critically defended—that is, how
one can rationally prefer one to another candidate for the status of moral
norm when the candidates are incompatible with each other directly, not
merely in tension with each other in application to difficult cases.

One of the simplest ethical theories compares the source of moral judgments to the sources of factual and scientific judgments. Just as one knows
factual truths by observation or experience and develops science on the basis
of particular factual truths, so it is suggested one knows moral truths by
experience with the moral data and develops moral principles by generaliza-
tion from such experience. On this theory one might say that conscience is a
moral sense by which one intuitively perceives moral truths.

A slightly different version of intuitionism suggests that general moral
norms are grasped directly, somewhat as self-evident principles—for example, of mathematics—are believed by some to be grasped. Intuitionist theories of this second sort account for the universality and necessity which
many people believe to belong to moral norms.

However, appealing as intuitionism is, moral judgments do not seem to be
either like matters of fact or like self-evident general principles of any theoretical discipline. Moral judgments and moral standards are normative, not
theoretical. They say what ought to be, not what happens to be or what
necessarily is. Whether one thinks of intuition on the analogy of sense perception or on the analogy of insight into some sort of necessary principles of
the order of things, it is difficult, to say the least, to understand how one
could intuit what might or might not be, but ought to be.

Furthermore, both particular moral judgments and proposals of general
moral norms conflict. This conflict, as we have just explained, is what gives
rise to the need for ethical theory. Intuitionism seems to suggest that there
really should be no more conflict here than there is about matters of fact or

self-evident principles. But the conflict remains, and no one who holds an intuitionist theory is in a position to explain the fact of conflict or to suggest a rational method for resolving it. Intuitionists thus are reduced to what seems a bare and unsupported assertion of conflicting moral claims. Those who do not accept such claims are called "morally blind" or "morally muddled," but when such charges are laid mutually, discussion is at a standstill.

The failure of intuitionism has led many modern, especially twentieth century, philosophers to doubt that there is any rational way to vindicate any moral norm or judgment. Certainly, if claims to truth in the moral domain are mistaken—if there is no truth or falsity to be had in this domain—then moral norms and particular moral judgments will not be able to be vindicated rationally.

In this case moral judgments often are regarded as the expression of the feelings or attitudes or commitments of individuals or groups: Such things have a function in generating and shaping behavior but are themselves simply facts about persons or societies, not normative truths. The theory that moral judgments are facts of this sort is called "subjectivism"; as applied to societies and cultures, it sometimes is called "relativism." We shall simply say "subjectivism" to cover all forms of this theory.

Certain facts make subjectivism appealing. For one thing, some who are confident that they know the truth about morality are tempted to fanaticism; they may be harsh and intolerant toward others who disagree or who fall short of the standard of true morality. Another point is that people who hold differing moral views, provided that they are sincere, generally are considered morally upright only if they follow their own best judgment, so that different people are morally good in following conflicting moral judgments. Another point is that morality seems to be a matter of a person's free decision; if there were an objective truth in moral norms, then such freedom would seem to be excluded. Again, subjectivism gains some plausibility from the fact that very often people use moral language to do no more than express their feelings, attitudes, or commitments. Thus, often those who do not like a public policy say it is "unjust," because this is a very emphatic way of expressing one's negative feelings or attitudes or one's preference for some alternative approach.

However, intolerance does not follow necessarily from the belief that there is moral truth, nor does tolerance follow from subjectivism.

One can hold that there is moral truth but that it leaves room for a certain range of life-styles which ought to be tolerated whether one likes them or not. One also can hold that forms of behavior one considers incompatible with true moral standards ought to be tolerated for the sake of various human goods, such as liberty and justice.

Moreover, it is obvious that persons of sincere good will can disagree irreconcilably in regard to ethical questions and can consider themselves bound to follow courses of action which lead to tragic conflict with one another. Those finding themselves in such conflicts need not, and often do not, condemn as vicious those with whom they are in conflict.

Furthermore, one can embrace subjectivism and have completely intolerant feelings, attitudes, and commitments. And if one is a consistent subjectivist, one will consider such intolerance beyond criticism or reproach from any source. Those who embrace subjectivism must confront moral disagreement as a matter of fact to be dealt with according to their own feelings, attitudes, and commitments. Such persons might forbear to do all they would like, but not out of any respect for *objectively valid* principles of liberty and justice—for there can be no moral foundations for such values. Their validity extends no further than their effectiveness if subjectivism is correct. A subjectivist involved in a moral conflict cannot think an opponent sincere *but mistaken,* for there is no moral truth about which one can be mistaken.

The desire for tolerance surely is worthy, but it does not require subjectivism. Rather it requires a distinction between the viciousness or guilt of one who acts and the wrongness or evil of what is done, between the virtue or good will of one who acts and the rightness or goodness of what is done. People of good will can do what is evil by mistake or through weakness, and it also is possible for vicious people to do good despite their worst efforts.

All persons must follow their own consciences, for one's conscience is one's best judgment as to what one ought to do. Nobody is morally guilty who does his or her best to find out what is right and then acts according to this best judgment. But such a judgment, for all its sincerity, can be mistaken—that is, can be *in error* (if, contrary to subjectivism, there is moral truth). Thus, if one finds certain practices of others ethically indefensible, one need not pass a judgment of moral condemnation upon those who engage in or defend such practices. Tolerance of those who disagree with one's judgment, compassion for those who do what one judges to be evil (often in circumstances in which one might oneself do far worse evil), are fully compatible with a firm judgment that the practice one rejects is *truly* immoral, not merely inconsonant with one's own feelings, attitudes, or commitments.

Other facts which at first glance make subjectivism appealing also fail on closer examination to lend it rational support.

The suggestion that moral freedom entails subjectivism depends upon a confusion—one which is very widespread—between moral judgment and moral choice. Moral life, obviously, is not a matter of given facts. In the moral domain a person is no mere puppet moved by natural forces. Rather, as a moral agent, one determines oneself, writes one's own autobiography, creates one's own history. A person can say "No" to the world which presents itself and with that "No" can undertake to make a world more in accord with a moral vision. Thus moral life is the sphere in which men and women are superior to what is given in advance. How, then, can one submit to moral standards which do not reflect one's own decisions?

The answer is that moral decision is twofold. One is the choice of what one will do; the other is the judgment as to what one should do. Due to this ambiguity it makes perfectly good sense to say, "He decided that he would be doing something wrong if he killed his defective child, but he decided to kill the child to end the suffering of everyone concerned, including himself." The first "decided" refers to judgment, the second to choice. In neither sense is *decision* a fact of nature. But decision as judgment can have an objectivity as an expression of moral truth—if subjectivism is mistaken—which decision as choice cannot have.

If this were not so, there would be no morally wrong acts; the very fact that one decided to do something would make one's choice be right. If subjectivism were correct, there would hardly be room for immorality; immorality would at most be dissonance between one's actions and one's own feelings, attitudes, and commitments—a dissonance one always could remedy by changing one's feelings, attitudes, and commitments as well as by changing one's behavior. In any case, inasmuch as feelings, attitudes, and commitments are themselves merely one set of facts among others, a subjectivist theory does not account for the sense that moral life involves transcendence to the given. Rather, it renders this sense of transcendence inexplicable. A theory which leaves room for moral truth but distinguishes it as normative from the truths of fact and self-evident principle which are the model for intuitionist ethical theories will avoid the difficulties of intuitionism without falling into subjectivism.

Finally, it can be granted the subjectivist that people often do use moral language without intending by it to express more than their own feelings, attitudes, and commitments in a particularly forceful way. Some children call anything they dislike "unfair." This use of moral language is accounted for by the subjectivist theory, just to the extent that truth is no concern of those who talk this way.

But even here the subjectivist theory does not fully explain what is going on. Moral language as subjective expression has something which makes it preferable to a straightforward expression of one's feelings, attitudes, and commitments. Moral language makes an appeal to the reasonableness of others, while a merely subjective expression could at most appeal to sympathy. This special feature of moral language is understandable if, in fact, the cases in which it is used in a subjectivist way are parasitic upon standard uses in which something more is being expressed: a moral truth which deserves attention and respect *as well as sympathy* for the person—a fellow member of a moral community—who utters it.

In short, subjectivism is inadequate as an ethical theory. It puts an end to rational discourse about morality as surely as intuitionism does. It precludes justification of basic moral principles and reduces them to the status of facts. And it renders unintelligible the fact that one can be mistaken in one's moral judgments and be in need of correction. Moreover, subjectivism makes it very difficult to understand how anyone can do what is morally wrong, since immorality will merely be a matter of inconsistency which sufficiently energetic and ingenious persons always can try to remove by altering themselves or their culture rather than by conforming action to existing standards—which are only facts to be dealt with efficiently like any other obstacle to doing as one wishes.

Although few if any who engage in the euthanasia debate profess either intuitionism or subjectivism as an ethical theory, many popular discussions of these issues seem to presuppose an intuitionist or a subjectivist theory of morality.

More and more people try to support their diverse and incompatible moral views by an appeal to "experience," as if experience were a final and unanswerable argument. Actually it is no argument at all. People who appeal to experience often imply an intuitionist theory. This is so if they think that they discern moral truth in their experience. Otherwise they imply a subjectivist theory if all they mean is that their experience has contributed to their peculiar feelings, attitudes, and commitments, which are what they are, and neither need nor can have any more justification than any other fact, such as feeling depressed, liking Bach, or being committed to one's country right or wrong.

Again, polls showing changing public attitudes often are cited as if they indicated that traditional moral standards are surpassed and no longer valid. But mass public opinion—even if it reflects something more worthy of respect than the effectiveness of the opinion-making media—does not settle morality unless subjectivism is correct. And if it is, the new morality is no more true than the old one, and there can be no more justification for accepting the latest opinion than for holding to traditional opinions.

The history of twentieth-century ethical theory, apart from the articulation of various versions of subjectivism, is largely a series of attempts to find a way of getting beyond intuitionism and subjectivism.[1] If these views are untenable, most philosophers think, there must be some rational way to criticize and justify moral norms, even the most basic of them. How can one do this?

Many religious persons would answer that moral judgments are true simply because God has given his commandments to humankind, and these commandments can be reflected in human moral judgments, which thus conform to a standard which cannot be wrong.

Philosophers generally will not accept this account, partly because it depends upon religious faith and partly because it is difficult to discern the practical implications for difficult questions of the commandments traditionally believed to come directly from God. Thus some argue that euthanasia must be excluded as forbidden killing; others that it must be permitted as compassion toward a suffering neighbor.

However, a more basic problem with a divine-command theory of morality is that it seems to be another form of subjectivism, but one with God as the sole subject whose determinations constitute morality. Of course, on this account the norms are not truths and cannot be rationally defended. If one attempts to avoid this conclusion by providing reasons *why* God's commands *ought to be accepted* and followed in practice, then one appeals to a moral norm which claims respect apart from the fact that God commands anything.

Thus even those who hold that God does give certain commands which transcend human understanding and that these commands ought to be accepted in faith—a position we ourselves hold—preserve the possibility of rational defensibility for religious morality only if they can explain why one ought to believe and live one's faith. If one abandons the possibility of rational defensibility for religious morality, one forgoes the possibility of proposing faith with any sort of moral appeal. The alternative is to propose it as something either with no appeal or with an appeal to nonmoral interests.

One way to try to supply reasons why divine commands ought to be accepted is to appeal to human nature. Presumably, various kinds of action comport well or badly with human nature, considered as a whole.

The difficulty with this theory is that all possible human acts are consistent with human nature if this nature is considered as something which is given. Thus, viewed in this way, human nature provides no norm by which one can separate good from bad acts. However, if nature is considered not merely as a given but as a normative ideal, then naturalness is equivalent to what human persons ought to be. The appeal to nature thus becomes an appeal to intuition, or a merely question-begging attempt to articulate this intuition.

The ethical theory of Immanuel Kant is an attempt to find a moral norm in the nature of human persons themselves, while it excludes as immoral much of what men and women actually do. Kant argues that what is central to personal moral life is rational self-determination to action. Goodness attends one's action to the extent that it issues from principles which can pass reason's test of perfect self-consistency; evil attends one's action to the extent that it is elicited by one's given needs and interests, desires and fears, in a way which escapes or evades control by the rule of reason.

Kant surely has located a *necessary* condition of moral goodness. A person who is uninterested in principle, who is willing to make special exceptions in particular cases for no reason at all, clearly is unconcerned about morality.

But it is not clear that Kant has located a *sufficient* condition of moral good-ness. It seems possible for anyone to achieve rational consistency if he or she is ingenious enough at making distinctions.

Moreover, if as Kant suggests immorality attends action which flows from impulse unregulated by reason, then moral failings seem rather to be some-thing a person suffers than something a person does. But while people do fail morally through weakness, such failings seem less seriously immoral than those acts in which reason seems to play a larger role. In short, Kant does not show how a person, precisely as a *rational* agent, can be immoral (and in the moral sense "unreasonable"). The violation of rational principles such as the laws of logic leads to the total breakdown of rational functioning; the viola-tion of moral norms does not but rather represents a peculiar perversion which is only maximally possible if there is no breakdown in rational func-tioning. One of the data from which ethics begins is that there is a distinction between being immoral and being mentally ill. Kant cannot account for this distinction.[2]

The challenge to go beyond intuitionism and subjectivism, which is not adequately answered by the theories discussed thus far, is met more plausibly by those ethical theories which are called "teleological." A teleological the-ory also begins from some truths which are considered to be too basic to demonstrate—truths which are claimed to be self-evident or known by intu-ition after a reflective clarification. But these truths themselves are not pro-posed as moral norms. Rather, a teleological theory maintains that moral obligations are determined by what promotes human well-being or human flourishing. The basis for moral norms thus includes two kinds of proposi-tions. One of them characterizes certain goods—"goods" not in a moral sense but merely in the sense of things desired for their own sake—as con-stituents of human well-being or flourishing. The other kind of proposition specifies the manner in which human acts must be related to these human goods if the acts are to be morally right.

Teleological theories have considerable initial appeal. Morality does seem to be for persons, for their full development and true well-being. It seems mistaken to think that moral rules are mere restraints upon human desires and actions, mere limits which would prevent people from being all that they might become.

Moreover, the proposition that human well-being is to be promoted does seem to be self-evident. In arguments about what is to be done the disagree-ment is always about what will promote well-being, in what it consists, whether an action or policy which seems to promote it really—perhaps in the long run—does not do so. Thomas Aquinas, for example, argues that the first principle of practical reasoning is: Good is to be done and pursued, evil is to be avoided. And he holds this principle to be self-evident. Moreover, "good" here signifies, not moral goodness, but rather what contributes to human well-being or flourishing.[3]

C. Consequentialism: A Plausible but Inadequate Theory

For the moment we put aside the question of what constitutes human well-being or flourishing. This question, concerning what goods are basic to morality, we shall consider shortly. But first we wish to consider the theory of the method of ethical reasoning which we call "consequentialism." This theory has become extremely popular in modern times, both among professional moralists and among others who discuss moral and public policy questions. The influence of consequentialism upon the issues discussed in this book has been enormous.

According to the simplest consequentialist theory of moral reasoning the moral good or evil of human acts is determined by the results (consequences) of these acts. If an act has good consequences, then that act will be good; if it has bad consequences, it will be bad. Of course, most acts have consequences which are partly good and partly bad, and moral judgment is necessary only when one must compare alternative courses of action, among which one might choose, to determine what one ought to do. Consequentialism holds that the morally good act will be the one which on the whole gives the best results. All the alternatives, including not acting and delaying action, must be compared. If one can add up the good results expected of each possible course of action and subtract in each case the expected bad results from the good, then according to the simplest form of consequentialism the morally right choice is that alternative which will yield the greatest net good—or, in an unfavorable situation, the least net harm.

In other words, the consequentialist wishes one to think about what one might do in terms of its impact upon human persons—the extent to which it will benefit or harm them. The right thing to do will maximize benefits and minimize harms. Only the one best act will be morally good, and it will be obligatory. Other possible courses of action will be immoral, more or less seriously so depending upon the extent to which they are less beneficial or more harmful to someone than the morally right act.

A consequentialist theory of moral reasoning seems implicit in the ethical and political theories of a great many modern thinkers. Machiavelli and Hobbes, for example, seem to argue in this way for proposals which seemed radical in their day. Marx, when he justifies revolutionary action, seems to do so by pointing to its necessity to overcome alienation and attain a new level of human life, much better than the dehumanized existence in which human-kind has suffered until now. Even many contemporary Christian thinkers seem to offer consequentialist arguments, sometimes based upon an other-worldy conception of human flourishing, for their moral teachings. But more than any others in the English-speaking world, the utilitarian thinkers, including Jeremy Bentham and John Stuart Mill, explicated and defended consequentialism as a method of ethical reasoning. The consequentialist formulation which they made popular is: The right act is that which brings about the greatest happiness for the greatest number.

The utilitarians joined consequentialism with a theory of human well-being which was more or less frankly hedonistic. Hedonism equates what is intrinsically good for persons with pleasure or enjoyable experience, what is bad for persons with pain or undesirable states of consciousness. The utilitarian theory thus proposes that the morality of actions be judged by the extent to which they cause enjoyment and minimize misery. Obviously, consequentialism need not be tied to a hedonistic value theory; consequentialism itself perhaps is more plausible than this or that theory of value with which it has been connected.

Still, consequentialism with a more or less strong component of hedonism underlies many proposals for altering public policies and laws in ways which diverge from traditional morality. Justifications for mercy killing, for example, which invoke quality-of-life considerations generally evaluate quality in terms of the enjoyable activities and experiences an individual is likely to have in comparison with the pain and suffering the individual must undergo if life continues. Considerations of the interests of the family and society bring into account the relative costs and benefits to others, in accord with the utilitarian injunction to consider the good of all concerned. When it seems that the benefits of continued life for the individual and for others are overbalanced by the harms of suffering and burdens, then it is presumed such killing would be kindly and that it is morally permissible and even obligatory.

There are many different forms of consequentialism. We have described the simplest form.

It is direct. It locates the preponderance of value which determines the moral worth of each particular action in the particular state of affairs brought about in and through that action. More complex versions of consequentialism are indirect. They look to the overall state of affairs which will be brought about if one accepts a certain rule or other principle, and then the moral significance of particular acts is judged by their conformity to that rule or other principle.

Again, some versions of consequentialism are pure. They admit no moral value which cannot be judged by consequentialist considerations alone. Other versions of consequentialism are mixed. They hold that some or all moral values can be judged only if consequentialist considerations are supplemented in appropriate ways by nonconsequentialist ones—for example, by the limiting requirements of justice.

Act consequentialism and rule consequentialism do not seem to us to differ as much as is sometimes supposed. Act consequentialism admits that if a judgment is right in any particular case, then the same judgment should be made and followed by anyone who faces a similar set of alternatives with a like balance of good and bad consequences. Thus the judgment of the particular act, just insofar as it is a rational appraisal, is really universal and thus is a rule. And a rule consequentialist, when pressed, does not insist that rules must be maintained if on the whole and in the long run change in them would be for the better. Thus rules are qualified to permit all reasonable exceptions, and reasonableness is judged by the consequences of acts.

Rule consequentialists sometimes argue that their position takes account of situations in which it is harmless to the community and advantageous for each individual to act in a certain way but disastrous for all if everyone acts in that way. However, act consequentialism can justify making and enforcing rules—since the making of a rule is itself a particular act—to restrain everyone from contributing to a situation when the cumulative effect would result in a common disadvantage. Among the consequences of an individual act are the implications it has for the actions of others and the consequences it will have when joined with the predictable acts of others. Thus act and rule consequentialism seem to yield the same results.[4]

Even if some forms of consequentialism are not reducible to the simplest sort, every kind of consequentialism involves a common feature: They all require the weighing of values implicit in various alternatives, whether these alternatives be courses of action, rules, life-styles, or something else. We hold that precisely because of this feature, shared in common by all forms of consequentialism, it is an unworkable theory of moral reasoning. It cannot do the job for which it is intended by its proponents.

In recent years many philosophers have criticized consequentialism. Many of these criticisms have tried to show that consequentialism would yield moral judgments at odds with the considered moral opinions of most morally serious people. For example, it is often pointed out that consequentialism cannot justify common moral judgments about justice, because a consequentialist is concerned about the maximizing of the total benefit and has no way to assure fair distribution of goods.[5]

But a consequentialist has two ways to respond to objections of this sort. First, it can be argued that fairness itself is important because unfairness causes a great deal of misery and leads to conflict which breeds even more misery. If strict fairness is not required to avoid bad consequences and if some inequality in distributing benefits is beneficial on the whole, then the consequentialist will argue that it is fanatical to insist upon strict fairness.

Second, consequentialists can—and often do—regard their theory as a revisionist approach to moral dilemmas, as a new morality. If it does not account for prevailing moral opinions, that might be because these opinions are corrupted by the prejudices of ancient traditions. The consequentialist will urge that this new approach be adopted to put moral judgment, at last, on a rational basis, a basis similar to that adopted by science and other advanced forms of human thinking.

Our own critique of consequentialism does not depend upon an appeal to moral intuition for counterexamples to consequentialist judgments. Our position is, not that consequentialism gives wrong answers, but that it cannot rationally justify any moral judgment, because it is an altogether unworkable way to proceed from an appreciation of the basic human goods involved in human well-being or flourishing to judgments on the moral quality of human acts, humanly approved rules, or the like. The subject matter upon which consequentialists try to bring their theory to bear, we maintain, is such that no one can reason about it in the way consequentialism urges.

Consequentialism is a calculative method. It suggests that the good and bad effects of each alternative be tallied, that the total bad effects be subtracted from the total good effects of each alternative, and that the net results of each computation be compared with the others. The alternative which gets the best—or least bad—score is the one to be accepted.

This calculation simply cannot be done unless the values of the various outcomes are such that they can be measured against one another. But the good effects of one alternative—in the simplest case of one action—often seem to be simply different in kind from its bad effects. Moreover, the good and bad effects of each alternative often appear simply incommensurable with the good and bad effects of the other possibilities.

The appearance of incommensurability between various goods which are components of human well-being is revealed clearly by examples. A young woman has a choice whether to be a physician or a lawyer. Assuming that the decision is not settled by an existing resolution to take up the career which will probably yield a better income or something of the sort, the young woman will see that each profession is humanly worthy in its own way. A physician can help to promote health, cure disease, and comfort the dying. A lawyer can help people cooperate together, promote public order, and protect justice. One simply cannot add up the pro and con features of these ways of life and assess the worth of each. There simply is no neutral scale on which she might weigh in homogeneous units the good and bad aspects of the two professions.

Of course, if one assumes a prior commitment to some further good, a commitment which is not allowed to be put in question while considering these possibilities, then the comparison may be carried out with a definitive result. For example, if a young man is determined to follow that career into which he can enter with fewer years of time and fewer dollars for schooling, then a simple comparison will tell him to favor the law and avoid medicine. If he has made up his mind to follow as lucrative a career as possible, a study of his own talents and of the market situation will indicate, at least with a certain degree of probability, which alternative to accept.

But moral choices are not simply selections of the most efficient ways of reaching some antecedently established goal. Rather, moral choices are made in a context in which one recognizes multiple goals, accepts the possibility that some of these may be called into question, and does not preclude the need to accept constraints on the pursuit of some goals.

The incommensurability which appears in choices like the one just described also appears in choices which most people would consider paradigmatic cases of moral decision, as moral dilemmas very difficult to resolve. For example, if one must decide whether to undergo chemotherapy for cancer, one must consider the pain, disruption, expense, psychological repugnance of the treatment and its effects. One also must consider the obligations which would go unfulfilled if one dies sooner than necessary, the various activities and experiences one will miss out on. It is hard to see how any of these items could be rationally weighed against one another. The same thing is true in other cases. How, for example, is the value of the life of a severely defective infant to be weighed against the costs of treatment, the burdens to the child's parents and to society, and so on?

When consequentialists propose their theory, it seems overwhelmingly sensible. Choose the course of action which will yield the greatest net benefit to all concerned. If one disagrees, the challenge is: Do you mean that one ought to prefer an alternative which brings about more misery on the whole? Clearly, one cannot prefer this if it is really the alternative. But now we have shown, on closer inspection, that the comparison of alternatives does not appear to present one with instances in which any alternative is clearly and unambiguously likely to bring about either a greater net benefit or more misery on the whole. Rather, all of the morally interesting alternatives seem to embody incommensurable goods.

We hold that this appearance of incommensurability of the goods in the alternatives between which one must choose is veridical: The appearance is reality and cannot be overturned. These goods are either means to or components in human flourishing. That these human goods are incommensurable is implied by the fact that human individuals can make free choices. One can make a free choice only between options which embody incommensurable goods. If possibilities which initially seemed to offer significant alternatives turned out not to embody any incommensurable goods, then one's judgment would be determined and no choice would be necessary. Other possibilities simply would fall away in favor of the one which appeared best.

The point can be clarified in the following way. If goods were commensurable, then there would be no need for free choice, since in each case of deliberation between alternatives one could discover by calculation which possibility was the best. If one could discover which possibility was the best—using "best" in a single, uniform meaning—then it would be psychologically impossible not to take the alternative which one had discovered to be the best. Of course, if one were able to take what was known to be less good—using "good" in the comparison in a single, uniform sense—such a choice would be irrational. But the point we are making is even more basic. If one of the alternatives about which one deliberates were recognized to be determinately better than the other options, then it would be impossible to choose any of the others. Choice, after all, is for the sake of the good in what is chosen; choice of what is less good rather than of what is more good could not be for the sake of anything.

It is possible to choose unreasonably that which is less good than an alternative which one might choose—for instance, to choose unreasonably to do what is morally evil rather than what is morally required. But such unreasonableness is possible only because what is judged to be "best" is *not* discovered to have as much good—using "good" in a single, uniform sense—as any alternative and some more good besides. Rather, each eligible alternative is seen as having some special good—peculiar to itself and incommensurable with the good held out by the other possibilities—which will be attained only if that alternative is chosen and must be forgone if another alternative is taken instead.

If goods were commensurable as consequentialist calculation demands, then one of the options could be discovered to have as much good as the others and more good besides. The "as much" would replace or compensate for the good forgone in the alternatives not chosen; the "more besides" would make the best alternative irresistible. If goods were commensurable, there would be a common standard of goodness, and no alternative ever would hold out an appeal peculiar to itself. By the common standard one possibility would be found to have all the good, all the appeal, of any alternative possibility, and then some; the alternatives simply would not measure up.

The preceding, quite abstract argument can be confirmed by reflection upon experiences one has of making choices, particularly those choices of acts for which one feels morally responsible.

If we seek within our experience for the cause of the fact that we have actually done something for which we feel moral responsibility, we usually come back to a point at which we ourselves made a choice, at least a choice to "go along" with something. Prior to the choice itself we were aware of two or more possibilities, incompatible with each other and lying in the future before us. It seemed to us that none of these possibilities was bound to occur. We thought that only we ourselves could settle whether each possibility would or would not ever become real.

We therefore considered each alternative in turn by noting the pros and cons of each. These pros and cons were not altogether comparable. Although there may have been some common factors, we did not find that one alternative included all the pros and excluded all the cons of the other (or else they would not have appeared to be genuine alternatives). With some perplexity at the lack of any common standard by which to measure the various pros and cons, we acutely felt the need to settle the indeterminacy in the facts ourselves. In considering each of the alternatives from the point of view of the good and appeal peculiar to itself other possibilities seemed clearly inferior. But since every possibility seemed better after its own fashion, the quest for the altogether better was frustrated. The possibilities offered incommensurable goods; there simply was no way to measure the peculiar "better" of one alternative against the "better" of a diverse sort proper to another.

One's problem in choosing is like that of a person who is asked which is preferable, a dollar bill or a copper cent. So long as the credit of the government is good, the bill is worth more as money. But if one needs a bit of copper to bridge a gap in an electrical circuit, then a penny is preferable and the paper bill worthless. So it is when we choose: We must settle which of two or more possible "betters" we will realize.

Thus we determine ourselves by taking as a measure of good the standard by which one alternative will appear decisively better. And once we have chosen, the rejected alternatives seem to pale in appeal. No longer impartially considering all possibilities from the perspective of each of them in turn, we view the whole set of possibilities from the single viewpoint of the good proper to the one we have chosen.

Looking back on a choice already made, we always seem to have chosen the greater good—the alternative which appeared better—unless we have a change of heart, which happens, for example, when we repent of having done something immoral. Some argue from the retrospective experience of the superiority of what was chosen that we do not really determine ourselves but rather are determined by the facts to choose the greater good. They forget that before the choice was made, each alternative seemed better in its own way, and our perplexity in seeking the greater good was terminated only when we ourselves selected the single measure of good which we then applied to all the possibilities—a measure according to which one alternative only then became unambiguously better.

Consequentialism goes wrong by ignoring this fact: There is no "greatest net good" because goods are incommensurable. One's computer balks and says that this does not compute. Consequentialism logically must presuppose that while deliberation is going on, the choice already is made, the value standard already settled, so that there will be no self-determination. But in this assumption a consequentialist must ignore the facts of experience. We do determine ourselves, not by computation, as if there were commensurable goods, but by accepting one way of being satisfied rather than another as the standard by which we shall proceed in a given case.

Of course, the consequentialist can accept the conclusion that free choice entails the incommensurability of goods and try to escape the implication that consequentialism is unworkable in principle by denying that human persons make free choices. As a matter of historical fact most consequentialists have embraced some form of determinism. Those in the English-speaking tradition have usually held the form of determinism which is called "soft determinism," or "compatibilism." According to this view human acts are determined in a way which is compatible with their being imputed to the people who do them, for human agents remain free in the sense of being uncoerced even though their acts are neither uncaused nor self-determined but rather are determined by a cause. Often compatibilists are psychological determinists, who maintain that one necessarily chooses that alternative which seems best.

A consequentialist who accepts a deterministic account of human choice and action, however, merely relocates the difficulty which we have already pointed out in the consequentialist position.

If the factors which cause choices are nonconscious ones, then the effort of thinking about moral questions is futile, since one will choose as one is nonconsciously determined to choose.

If the factors which cause choices are consciously grasped reasons—that is, if psychological determinism is accepted—then a consequentialist ought logically to identify the sufficient condition of the choice with the result of the consequentialist calculus. In other words, what seems best will be what is discovered by calculation to promise the greatest net good. But this leads to a conclusion which the consequentialist cannot accept: What one ought to do will be identical with what one will do. This conclusion cannot be accepted because it is a fact, always taken for granted by ethical theory, that one can do what is wrong, that one can violate the requirements of morality.

A consequentialist might argue that even on a consequentialist theory which accepts psychological determinism a person still might fail by ignorance or miscalculation to discover what is right. Thus the objective norm will be established by consequentialist calculation properly carried out, the subjective choice will be determined, and the choice will be divergent from the norm. The consequentialist thus would be urging that there is one sovereign norm of morality: Calculate carefully! But to say that one ought to calculate carefully so that one's choices and acts will be determined by the greatest net good simply moves the question about freedom and morality to a different level of choice and action. Either one is free to calculate and not to calculate, and this choice is not determined and so not controlled by consequentialist considerations. Or one is determined to calculate and will do it as one is determined to do it—if consequentialism is relevant at all in precisely the way that one ought to do it.

Thus, whether persons can make free choices or not, consequentialism cannot provide guidance for morally significant choices. On the one hand, the commensurability of goods which consequentialism requires is incompatible with free choice, so if persons do make free choices, goods are incommensurable and consequentialism is not workable as a method of judging what the choices ought to be. On the other hand, if persons do not make free choices, they are determined to choose an act either in accord with or at odds with the consequentialist judgment. If at odds, then it is senseless to say that people ought to do what the consequentialist judgment says, for they cannot. If people are determined to act in accord with the consequentialist judgment, then it does not make sense to consider their choices and actions morally significant, for they cannot do other than they ought.

The consequentialist, therefore, must either accept the unworkability of his theory because of the incommensurability of goods, or admit the pointlessness of moral reflection because of the impossibility that one choose and act as one ought when one is otherwise determined, or deny a fact which all ethical theory presupposes: that people sometimes do what is morally wrong. We conclude, therefore, that consequentialism fails as a theory of moral reasoning.[6]

If the foregoing refutation of consequentialism is correct, any ethical theory which involves it fails just to the extent that the theory does involve it. Someone might object that it is hard to believe that so many serious philosophers and others hold a theory as bad as this. After all, the subject matter is not esoteric but is the making of moral choices, which everyone directly experiences. Our reply is that the very failure of consequentialism helps its proponents to feel that it is an important ethical theory well grounded in their own experience.

When consequentialists argue for the moral permissibility of certain kinds of action—for example, the permissibility of killing those whom they think would be better off dead—the possibilities are examined in the light of the consequentialist's own prior commitments. These prior commitments need not have involved personally adopting a proposal to kill anyone but might have involved condoning the acts of others. Moreover, the prior commitments need not have had to do with the specific kind of act under consideration provided that they had enough bearing on the goods at stake in the kind of act for which the consequentialist argues and the kinds of act alternative to it in the situation the discussion envisages.

Enough bearing for what? Enough bearing so that the consequentialist does not perceive the incommensurability of the goods, but perceives them according to a uniform standard, which allows the calculation consequentialism requires to be carried out after the manner of an intuitive estimate. One who has approved abortion, for example, might consider the case of a severely defective infant in terms of the good preferred to human life in the approval of abortion and on this consideration judge that life with defects is of such poor quality that the child would be better off dead.

Thus the consequentialist feels confident that "greater good" or "greatest net good" has a very clear and definite meaning. But these expressions, as consequentialists use them, mean no more than "the good which anyone *with my commitments* would prefer." Still, consequentialists want their judgment to be accepted as a moral judgment; they claim that their judgment expresses a standard which any reasonable person ought to accept. So consequentialists project their personal commitments upon the objective possibilities and then read off this projected set of preferences as if they were an objective description which any reasonable person would perceive.

In other words, although consequentialism is wholly unworkable as an ethical theory, it is quite serviceable both as a method of rationalization and as a form of persuasive discourse, by which one can commend one's personal preferences and prejudices in terms which suggest moral objectivity.

As a method of rationalization consequentialism is sufficiently subtle that it can be accepted by persons of fairly subtle intelligence who have a theoretical interest in moral questions and who are conscious enough of more vulgar methods of rationalization to find their arbitrariness unacceptable. As a form of persuasive discourse consequentialism provides a great deal of material which subjectivist theorists analyze quite accurately, only to miss the fact that like other parasitic uses of moral language, consequentialism is rhetorically effective only because there are standard, nonsubjectivist ways of using the language of moral evaluation.

Someone familiar with recent analytic ethics is likely to object that there is nothing unreasonable in the effort to combine arbitrariness and the willingness to universalize in the formation of an ethical theory. Such a strategy, after all, is that explicitly adopted by R.M. Hare and other prescriptivists. However, we think Hare is attempting to do what is rationally impossible—namely, to derive the moral "ought" from the premoral "is" of a combination of facts: facts about premoral desires, facts about linguistic usage, and facts about decisions. The interested reader is referred to a lengthier examination of Hare's approach published elsewhere.[7]

D. Legitimate Uses of "Greater Good"

Still, it will be objected, measuring, counting, and weighing of goods do have an important place in practical reasoning. When people are trying to decide what to do, they do make use of these operations. "Greater good" and similar expressions are used meaningfully. How can this fact be squared with our argument that consequentialism is unworkable?

Goods can be measured, weighed, and counted. But when they are, the context is either one of two kinds. In one kind a practical but nonmoral judgment is made. One calculates, not to determine what one ought to do morally speaking, but to determine what is better in some nonmoral sense of "better." In another kind of context one does reflect to determine what is morally right. But one does not measure, count, and weigh the amount of human good which is promised by each alternative, and *then* draw a conclusion of moral principle. Rather, one reflects within a framework of moral assumptions, which set a definite standard for the relevant goods.

It is easy to find examples in which comparative evaluations are made in reaching a practical, nonmoral judgment. Consideration of a few such examples will clarify how different this procedure is from consequentialist moral reasoning.

Sometimes people compare the extent to which goods in which they are interested probably will be realized by various possible courses of action. They notice that one possibility will lead to all the benefits to which another will lead, and more, and also notice that other things are equal. For instance, one seeking the best rate of government-insured interest might compare the rates available at various savings institutions and find that one offers a slightly higher effective rate than the rest and meets all the other conditions which have been set. In a case like this the possibility which maximally satisfies interests is taken.

But the practical judgment is not a moral judgment. At this point one has no choice except in a sense in which a computer also makes a choice. If one's investment decision is morally significant, this is in virtue of a prior judgment and choice which established the standard—for example, the best rate of government-insured interest—to the exclusion of other considerations.

If one finds out that the indicated institution discriminates against blacks or some other group in granting mortgages, one now confronts a possible moral choice. But the goods of maximum return on one's investment and of avoiding involvement in racial injustice are not one good, but two, and they are incommensurable.

In cases in which there is a definite standard and one accepts what is better by that standard one is attaining all the good one can in any other possibility by the one chosen, and then some. This is like killing two birds with one stone. Of course, a person can choose not to kill two birds with one stone, but only if some other good comes into consideration. For example, a hunter might wish to practice conservation. Malicious egoists can choose an act which benefits only themselves rather than a similar act which also benefits others, but only because egoists' malice can make it seem that denying a good to others is an additional good to themselves.

"Greater good" has a legitimate place in technical judgments. If one has a well-defined objective and knows the cost of various ways of attaining it, one can rate a certain means economically best. "Best" here simply means most efficient. Cost-benefit analysis yields judgments of this sort.

There is nothing wrong in being efficient. But neither does efficiency indicate moral acceptability. Whether what is efficient is morally acceptable depends on the moral quality of one's ends and the means chosen to pursue them. Thus whenever the moral acceptability of both ends and means is taken for granted, practical reasoning which is calculative does help one to discover the best—that is, most efficient—course of action.

Engineering regularly proceeds in this way. But the engineer's recommendation of the right alternative to choose is not a moral judgment. Medicine, as technique, involves many legitimate, nonmoral judgments of what is best. But the physician as a person also is interested in what is right and wrong. Here the consequentialism of technical reasoning is out of place and unworkable, unless it serves the illegitimate functions of a method of rationalization and form of persuasion.

Thus, if one's well-defined objective is the elimination of Jews, one can proceed efficiently. Waste of scarce resources would be wrong. One must look for the best way of carrying out the task. But "best" here refers to a technical, nonmoral value.

Expressions which signify comparative value also are used in contexts in which it appears that calculation leads to a moral judgment. We now turn to a few examples of such uses.

A morally upright person who is not a consequentialist, asked to help kill a defective child, might say: "No, I won't do it. What you wish to do would prevent much misery. But it also is an attack upon the child's life, which I consider to be a good that must be respected. The benefit here cannot outweigh the harm, so I cannot bring myself to help you."

Upright people do talk this way, and it sounds consequentialist. But we submit that upright persons who talk in this way do not mean that they have reached the moral judgment by weighing goods against one another without using moral standards—and this is what consequentialism requires. Rather, upright people use consequentialist language to express moral judgments reached in other ways. Believing that the act would be wrong, the upright person *thereupon* considers the good it would achieve to be less than sufficient to justify it. The estimate of the comparative goods is reached by way of the moral judgment; the moral judgment is not reached by weighing, counting, and measuring goods independent of moral standards.

There are several reasons why upright persons use language which sounds consequentialist. First, morally good people do not usually carefully distinguish moral from nonmoral uses of evaluative language. They consider all other values from a moral perspective and thus lend them a moral coloring. Second, everyone tends to use language as it is used. Calculative language is widely used legitimately in technical contexts, and it also is used in plausible rationalizations. In modern technical cultures technical thought tends to become a model for all rational discourse. Third, in contemporary culture many people who are morally upright are on the defensive. It is less embarrassing to give a consequentialist formulation of one's moral judgments than to say simply, "I won't help you because what you propose seems to me to be immoral." Fourth, a child learns the language of technical activity and evaluation earlier than moral concepts are developed. Even the child's initial concept of morality is technical: Knowing how to be a "good child" is a technique to be mastered. Thus, technical language naturally is a matrix for moral language.

Expressions signifying comparative evaluation also have a legitimate use in explaining moral judgments to the extent that "greater good" or "higher value" can refer to a difference relevant to moral judgment in the *kind* of value. Goods intrinsic to persons have relevance to morality in a way that extrinsic, merely instrumental goods do not. Thus, one can say that a human life ought to be preferred to the life of an animal, since the life of a person is a higher value. But this expression does not indicate the commensurability the consequentialist needs. Rather, this expression merely makes the claim that, morally speaking, human beings come first.

"Greater good" also is used meaningfully in the context of legal processes. Judgment reached by legal processes ought to be morally just, and legal processes obviously involve weighing, counting, and measuring. Justice is symbolized by a blindfolded person holding a scale.

However, a legal judgment has moral force only to the extent that the legal system has a moral basis and uses morally justifiable procedures. Conflicting claims and relevant facts, not human goods, are weighed in the scale of justice. This scale is not morally neutral, for it precisely is the morally normative principles of justice which are at the foundation of legality and governmental legitimacy. The scale of justice is what makes the authority of the law something other than mere power.

E. A Nonconsequentialist Theory: Human Goods

Consequentialism has achieved widespread acceptance. However, because of its inherent unworkability it should not be accepted. We have pointed out the essential reason why consequentialism is not really a theory of moral reasoning. Many other philosophers have shown that there are other unsolved problems for a consequentialist.[8] We believe the preceding considerations make clear that the problems not only are unsolved but are insoluble. Consequently a teleological approach to ethical theory must be nonconsequentialist if it is to be defensible. A defensible teleological theory must take fully into account the fact of moral existence revealed in our critique of consequentialism: the incommensurability of human goods. We begin an exposition of the theory we consider sound by discussing first the question of the goods to which teleological moral reasoning directs action.

Reflection on the motivations of human acts which are morally significant—that is, those done by deliberation and choice—reveals that some acts are done for their own sake. Play and recreational activities often are done for no purpose beyond the activities themselves. Such activities are not lacking in purpose and meaning; their purpose and meaning is within them. One might say they are done "just for the fun of it." Thus, these activities are considered inherently worthwhile. In saying they are good one is not making a properly moral judgment. Rather, one is saying that such activities are part of human flourishing; they perfect and complete human persons and give their lives some of the meaning they can have.

The immediate reason why one chooses in a particular case, however, often is subordinate to an ulterior motive. If one asks a laborer why he labors, he might answer: "To make money." If one asks why he seeks money, he might reply: "To feed myself and my family, because we get hungry." If one tries to push the inquiry beyond this point, one might find oneself none too gently rebuffed, not because the laborer is ignorant of a further purpose, but because apart from satisfying the basic conditions to survive, there simply is no further purpose here. To try to question the self-sufficiency of a purpose which is in fact ultimate as motive is likely to seem to simple persons a way of ridiculing them.

Thus, play and recreation, while inherently worthwhile, are not the only things human beings recognize as giving meaning to their lives. Knowledge of truth and appreciation of beauty also are recognized as good. Those who consider knowledge and esthetic activities merely instrumental are rightly considered philistines who do not appreciate the full potential of their own human personalities. Such persons, if not considered immoral, are pitied as individuals somehow defective in personal capacity for a fully human life.

As our example of the laborer suggests, life itself also is a good which people wish to preserve and protect for its own sake. So also is health, the perfection of the living body precisely insofar as it is an organism. Like the other goods we have mentioned, life and health can have an instrumental importance as well as serving as motives by themselves for human acts. But life and health can, and often are, considered to be instrinsic aspects of human flourishing.

This point is clearer in respect to health, since people seek to be healthy not only because they can thereby do other things they value but also because they consider health itself desirable. The same seems to be true of staying alive. Much of humankind over its history has struggled to feed and clothe and shelter themselves and to continue the race through children.

However, some deny that human life has the intrinsic worth and dignity we attribute to it. They attribute to life a merely instrumental value. Since the intrinsic worth and dignity of life is pivotal for the ethical determination of the issues with which this book is concerned, we shall devote section H of the present chapter to an extended response to the view that life is not an intrinsic good of persons.

There are still other inherently worthwhile activities which contribute in their appropriate ways to human flourishing. Human beings strive to establish harmony between various aspects of their own personalities, harmony with other people, and harmony with God. Friendship among people obviously is a human good for itself, although friends also must have a common interest, which will shape their action toward some one or many other basic human goods. Likewise, for those who believe in the divine, friendship with God is considered good for its own sake. Many religious people regard prayer not merely as an instrumental activity but as a part of life which is important simply because it is a way of being with God.

Self-integration, similarly, is considered worthwhile. As in other societies which have reached a level of abundance at which mere survival is no longer the primary concern of most people, many people in our society regard self-integration as a central purpose of their lives. People want to "get themselves together," to "find themselves and establish their identities," to be "happy." For those who do not consider themselves self-integrated, or as well integrated as they wish to be, many acts can be chosen as means to the pursuit of this good.

But this good itself can be realized in acts which participate in it. Just as there must be some specifying common interest which unites friends in a relationship they consider good in itself, so in activities by which a person pursues other goods in an integrated way the person can be motivated by the inherent goodness of his or her acts insofar as they embody in harmony all aspects of the personality fully alive: bodily powers, dispositions, emotions, beliefs, commitments, and so on. Thus, one can choose to act for one's own self-integration and can regard other human goods for which one acts as providing opportunities for the enjoyment of self-integration. The conception that virtuous activity is its own end exemplifies this notion of self-integration as an intrinsic component of human flourishing.

We have listed the goods which seem to us to constitute human flourishing. Perhaps the list is not complete. We have made no attempt to establish a

perfect classification. For the purposes of this book such precision is unnecessary. We only wish to make clear that there are several incommensurable
human goods, that human flourishing has many intrinsic aspects. Each of
these goods makes a peculiar and irreducible contribution to the complete
well-being of persons. While every person loves some goods more than
others, it simply would not make sense to say that participation in goods one
prefers makes the forgoing of others no loss, no limitation to oneself. If the
goods were commensurable, this would be so, but because they are not,
every choice is at once self-realization and self-limitation.

Our list might appear to have one glaring omission: Pleasure is not included
as a basic human good. The omission is intentional. Pleasure is an experience, and experiences are not actions, whereas human flourishing is constituted of acts. The human goods are not products of human acts or ideals at
which actions aim. They are realized within human acts by the very doing of
these acts—realized not exhaustively, but participated to a greater or lesser
degree.

Of course, the performance of actions worthwhile in themselves often is a
pleasant experience. But sometimes it is not pleasant to do good acts, and the
enjoyment which good acts do bring is rather their *felt* goodness than some
separate good participated in by them. Thus the enjoyment involved in friendship or knowledge or healthful eating is not a good and motive apart from
these goods but simply is their goodness consciously experienced.[9]

F. How Morality Depends upon the Human Goods

If what we have said thus far indicates the goods—or at least some of the
goods—toward which human actions ought to be directed, nothing we have
said thus far shows how one can reason from one's awareness of human
goods to moral judgments concerning what one ought to do. To approach this
question we recall that the method of moral reasoning we are articulating is
teleological but not consequentialist. A teleological theory justifies moral
judgments about right and wrong in terms of what is humanly good or worthwhile. Basing moral obligations on the well-being or flourishing of persons
surely is intuitively plausible. We hold that it also is theoretically defensible.

When a person considers that an action is right, this consideration makes a
demand upon the person: The action is regarded as one to be done. But no
action can be done unless it can be chosen, and no action can be chosen
unless it promises a good which makes it appealing. Unless the "is to be" of
the normative judgment is a mere extrinsic compulsion, which might elicit
servile obedience but no moral respect, the person who is called to respond
by action must perceive the demand as an intrinsic appeal—in other words, as

an expression of the goodness in the action which makes it interesting as a possibility.

Moreover, if choice is self-determination, then the goods one can choose must be considered as aspects of one's own identity. It follows that the rightness of moral choices must be based upon the well-being or flourishing of persons, for a moral agent can identify with this and find self-fulfillment in it. We do not deny that there are other principles of morality transcendent to human persons, but these principles must specify moral demands by way of human goods, for otherwise they would be alien impositions upon human flourishing, which would elicit resistance rather than respect from reasonable persons.[10]

Thus we hold that the basic human goods are the principles which are in some fashion expressed as norms for action by moral judgments—in other words, that "oughts" arise from "goods," that what makes some acts right and some wrong must somehow derive from what makes all acts possible: the appeal of the goods which makes possibilities live options for a human agent. But this raises the question: How does this normativity work? Obviously not all acts which are possible are right. How can the very principle of the possibility of some actions (those which are morally excluded) require that these possible actions not be made actual? The nature of this normativity of human goods for human acts can be clarified by the following considerations.

In the first place, nothing is considered good unless it is thought of as having a basic reality which can be more or less developed and perfected. To be a good entity of a certain kind is to be an entity of a kind which can be more or less perfectly, and which in fact is more rather than less perfectly. The possibility of degrees of perfection depends upon potentiality in the entity; goodness is realization of potential. But not every realization of potentiality is good. Sometimes an entity which can be more or less fully what it is will be deprived of its fuller and fullest realization on the whole by realizing only one potentiality.

The point can be illustrated by considering living organisms simply as such. The perfection of an organism is health. Health is a disposition for the exercise of the functions of the organism so that its whole repertoire of possible life will be unfolded. In this respect a healthy organism is one which is realizing its potentialities. But growing cancerously also is within the potential of an organism. This realization of potentiality is not good. The trouble with it is that it deprives the organism of its fuller and fullest realization on the whole. Hence, the good of an organism is a fulfillment of life potentialities which leads to further fulfillment and more abundant life. What is bad for an organism is a realization of some potentialities in its vital processes which tend to deprive it of continuing and more abundant life.

The same thing is true, analogously, in other realms. To think in ways that are inconsistent, muddled, unsure, and unsystematic is one way of realizing the human power of thought. But this actualization of potentiality is bad, not good. What is good is thinking which is consistent, clear, sure, and organized into schemes of explanation. Such thinking is good because it makes knowing flourish and expand. Bad thinking is self-limiting. Likewise, in the realm of fine art creativity is good because it is expansive of the realm of artistic entities. And in the technical sphere efficiency is a value because it is getting the most one can out of what one has.

Human goods are the principles of the possibility of all human acts. They establish moral norms insofar as acts flow from deliberation and choice. Every choice is both self-realizing and self-limiting. Insofar as any choice is self-realizing, the good which makes it interesting renders the choice possible for a person who is rational, not blindly or insanely driven to act. The good appeals to intelligence, not merely presenting itself as possible, but offering itself as a possibility to be realized through action. Thus there is a direct, normative appeal in every human good.

However, the direct, normative appeal of each human good is not yet moral normativity. Deliberation about the possibilities of self-realization through a morally evil act and choice of such an act also responds to this direct appeal. Indeed, the normative appeal of the good which is held out by a possible morally evil act is the content of the experience of temptation. Every teleological theorist recognizes that the pursuit of particular goods through particular acts can be immoral.

Still, although no single good provides a moral norm, the normativity of all the basic human goods together does give rise to a moral norm. For the goodness of the person as a human agent through deliberation and choice lies in realizing, not all potentialities for action, but rather in realizing those which are conducive to fuller and the fullest self-realization. Or, in other words, while every choice has an aspect of self-limitation, some choices are self-limiting in a way that others are not. Choices which are restrictive of the very principles upon which one can act humanly tend to stunt and constrict the person rather than make the person flourish. Thus such choices are morally bad. They are ones which, although possible because of their responsiveness to the appeal of some basic human good, are unnecessarily self-limiting because they are incompatible with a realistic appreciation of other goods and openness toward the possibilities these other goods hold out.

Of course, the moral normativity of all the human goods together cannot require that one simultaneously act for all of them or actively oppose all that threatens them. One can only do so much. Choices must be made; these will necessarily involve self-limitation in fact. Individuals and communities must commit themselves to something and forgo other possibilities. Yet one can forgo a possibility without altering one's appreciation of the good which gave rise to it. To alter one's appreciation of a good is to reject its normativity. An act whose choice involves this is morally evil.

Thus, the basic requirement of morality is that one choose and act for some human goods, while at the same time one maintain one's appreciation, openness, and respect for the goods one is not *now* acting for. A strong basic requirement which would demand something more specific is impossible in view of the plurality and incommensurability of the goods, and the limitations of human powers and opportunities, which together make choice necessary.

The preceding explanation of the basic requirement of morality is, we realize, very abstract. And a clear understanding of the relationship between the morality of acts and the basic human goods, which are aspects composing human flourishing, is central to ethical theory. Therefore, we are going to explain the same relationship again in a somewhat different way.

Any sound teleological ethical theory must be consistent with the fact that not every choice is morally evil, yet every choice responds to the appeal of the human goods promised by one possible course of action and leaves unanswered the appeal of the equally basic and incommensurable goods promised by one or more alternatives. That each of these goods is to be realized and protected is a starting point for deliberation about possibilities which would bear upon it. Such a starting point is a principle for practical reasoning about what to choose and to do. Corresponding to the whole set of basic human goods is the whole set of principles of practical reasoning.

This whole set of principles directs that all the goods be realized and protected. But even bad acts depend upon and respond to some of these principles. Therefore, none of the principles of practical reasoning is a moral norm merely by being a practical principle. The underlying assumption that human life ought to be preserved and respected, for example, does not of itself dictate that no one ought ever to be killed.

The distinction between moral good and evil according to the theory we put forth is primarily a distinction between ways in which proposed courses of action are related to all of the principles of practical thinking. Some proposals are consistent with all of these principles, although they hold out the promise of participation in only some of the basic human goods toward which these principles direct human interest and action. Other proposals are consistent with some of the principles of practical thinking—those which direct action to the goods promised by these proposals—but inconsistent with at least one principle of practical thinking. Proposals of the former sort are morally good, while those of the latter sort are morally bad.

Thus, for example, if a physician is considering whether to treat a certain patient or not, and to treat the patient in one way or another, the proposed courses of action about which he is deliberating can be related in two different ways to the whole set of principles of practical thinking which express the claims of the whole set of basic human goods. On the one hand, as the alternatives are understood, all the various forms of treatment might promise a benefit for the patient's health, and none of them might seem inconsistent with any other basic human good. On the other hand, as the alternatives are understood, while all of them promise a benefit to the patient's health, some of them might be rejected by the patient on grounds of conscience—for example, by a Jehovah's Witness who will not accept blood transfusions. Assuming that patients cannot justly be treated against their will, the physician must consider alternatives rejected by the patient differently than those the patient accepts.

Those rejected by the patient, while equally or even more conducive to health, are inconsistent with another principle of practical thinking: The liberty of patients must be respected. A consequentialist might argue that the greater benefit to health which is promised by the treatment involving transfusions outweighs the violation of the patient's liberty. We have shown, however, that consequentialism is not workable; a physician who reasoned in this way would merely be rationalizing the imposition of his own preferences on the patient. According to our view alternatives which are consistent with all the principles of practical reasoning will be morally acceptable; those incompatible with any principle of practical thinking will be morally wrong. Thus, if the liberty of others must be respected and if a certain treatment cannot be given without violating this principle, then the giving of such a treatment is morally excluded.

A morally evil proposed course of action is intelligible and interesting because of the good it promises. It can be adopted if one is prepared to regard the good with which it is inconsistent as a lesser good than the good it promises. It is possible to regard one basic human good as a lesser good than another precisely because the goods are incommensurable, and so any of them can appear to be lesser goods if they are judged by a standard of goodness specified by another mode of goodness.

However, it also is unreasonable to regard any basic human good as a lesser good than another simply because the goods are incommensurable. If one cares about all of them precisely insofar as they are goods, not insofar as they are particular modes of goodness toward which one has a special bias, then one will never judge any human good by a standard specified by one or more other human goods.

One who is about to choose in a morally right way respects equally all of the basic goods and listens equally to all of the appeals they make through the principles of practical thinking. Because of the incompatibility of practical alternatives—since one cannot do everything at once—choice is necessary. No single good, nothing promised by any one possible course of action, exhausts human possibilities and realizes the whole potentiality for humankind's flourishing. But just as two propositions having no common terms cannot be inconsistent with each other, so a proposed course of action is consistent with those principles of practical thinking to which it is merely irrelevant.

Thus, one can choose one possibility which promises certain goods and is irrelevant to other goods promised by an alternative without violating the practical principle which directs action to these other goods. In this case one remains open to these other goods. One does not adopt a restrictive standard of goodness. One's understanding of the various human goods, one's appreciation of their special potential contribution to the flourishing of persons, remains the same after the choice as before.

One who is about to choose in a morally wrong way does not respect equally all of the basic human goods and does not listen equally to all of the appeals they make through the principles of practical thinking. The proposal which one is about to adopt involves detriment to some human good. One is tempted to accept this detriment for the sake of the realization of another good which will thereby become possible. Such a proposed course of action is responsive to at least one principle of practical thinking, and it might be merely irrelevant to—and thus consistent with—some others, but it is both relevant to and inconsistent with the principle which directs one to promote and respect that good to which the action will be detrimental. Yet the principle which is to be violated is as basic as the one on which the proposed course of action is based; the good which is to be realized is no more an aspect of the flourishing of persons than the one which is going to be harmed.

A person in adopting such a proposal cannot remain open to the good promised by morally acceptable alternatives, for this good is going to be violated. In choosing to accept this violation one implicitly adopts a restrictive standard of human goodness. One's understanding of the various goods is affected by the choice. The good which is violated is no longer considered equally basic and incommensurable with the good to which it is sacrificed. The good which is violated now becomes a "lesser good," and the good for which it is violated becomes a "greater good." The choice, which is partially irrational insofar as it conflicts with some principle of practical thinking, is rationalized by reducing to the extent necessary a basic human good from its status as an intrinsic component of human flourishing to the status of a mere means.

If the preceding explanation of the relationship between the morality of acts and basic human goods is correct, still there remain two serious questions to be considered. First, is not moral good and evil something more personal and interpersonal than the relationship between human acts and their principles which we have been discussing? Does not moral evil involve a violation of the good of others? From a religious viewpoint must it not be seen as sin, as alienation from God and rejection of his love? Second, how does the basic requirement of morality take shape in concrete moral obligations to do or to avoid specific acts?

The answer to the first question is this: The central locus of the distinction between moral good and evil is in the relationship between choices and human goods, which we have been explaining. But the impact of morality and the reason for its importance is by no means limited to this relationship. It affects one's relationship to other persons, to God, and to one's own fulfillment.

If I choose with the attitude that my choices define and limit the good, I shall lack the detachment to appreciate the possibilities of others' lives, which would complement my own by realizing the values that I cannot. Their good, which I do not choose, will become for me at best a nongood, something to which I shall remain indifferent.

Egoism can decrease only to the extent that I remain open to the embrace of all the goods, those as well as these, yours as well as mine. The attitude of immorality is an unreasonable attempt to reorganize the personal and inter-personal universe, so that the center is not the whole range of possibilities in which humankind can share, but the goods I want and actually pursue through my actions. Instead of community immoral choices generate aliena-tion. The conflict of competing immoralities is reflected by incompatible per-sonal rationalizations and social ideologies, each of which seeks to remake the moral universe in accord with its own bias.

Those who understand immorality in religious terms cannot be expected to find any merely philosophical account completely satisfying. But the philo-sophical account we have proposed might coincide, so far as it goes, with a religious view. It certainly is impossible to maintain a fully open attitude toward all human goods, irreducibly diverse and incommensurable as they are, unless one accepts the reference of human conceptions of goodness to a real unifying source of goodness which is beyond human comprehension.

For if the goods which humans comprehend—which constitute a unified field for human choice and action—are not diverse participations in a unity beyond all of them, then they must be unified by reference to one another. In that case what one chooses will appropriate an absolute priority to which what one rejects must be subordinated—if it is to be regarded as good in any sense at all. However, if one accepts the reference of human conceptions of goodness to a reality beyond human comprehension, then openness to that goodness can count as love of it, although one does not make it by itself the objective of any particular action.

Such love of the good can be interpreted in a religious context as at least compatible with a response of human love to God's love. And if the goodness in question is identified with God, respect and openness to all human goods can be understood as human fulfillment by participation in a goodness which first of all is God's. An immoral attitude, by contrast, would exclude a real goodness beyond the goods humans can know and choose; immorality would refuse to seek human fulfillment as a realization by participation in God's own goodness. From a religious point of view any morally evil act, in which the good chosen is made more absolute than it is, will be an instance of implicit idolatry.

The principle of morality which we have articulated also can be seen as a basis of a personalistic morality aimed at personal fulfillment. The basic human goods against which one ought not to act are not impersonal; the moral norms forbidding violation of these goods are not mere legalistic rules. These goods each make their intrinsic and irreducible contribution to the flourishing of human persons. They do not transcend persons by subordinating their good to some higher, nonhuman purpose. The various goods only transcend persons as they are by drawing them toward what they are not yet but still can come to be by their creative efforts.

G. How the Principle of Morality Shapes Obligations

As we have pointed out, the fundamental moral requirement is that one respect and remain open to all of the basic goods. To respect a good is to treat it always as a good. Even when one does not pursue a good, as we have explained, one can acknowledge its special contribution to human life. At the very minimum this acknowledgement requires that one not direct one's action *against* any of the basic goods. This ethical principle articulates the classical maxim that evil may not be done that good might follow therefrom. It also is expressed, more loosely, in the saying that the end does not justify the means.[11] Thus there are absolute prohibitions of certain types of choice—that is, those which are directed against one of the basic goods. For example, one may not choose to kill innocent persons as a means to overthrowing an unjust ruler, since this action would be directed against the good of life.

The absolute negative norms which demand unconditional respect for the basic human goods are, not restrictions imposed to limit the flourishing of persons, but rather exclusions of arbitrary limits which would be placed on the principles of human action by the adoption of a proposal to act against a basic human good. To diminish in no way the full scope of these basic principles is to maintain an indispensable condition for human flourishing, for it is to preserve the possibility of all actions which might promote this flourishing.

Beyond one's immediate objectives there always remains an unlimited and unforeseeable possibility of something more, of human goods to be realized in oneself and in other persons. This something more will unfold as it might only if people in choosing remain creatively faithful to it, and such faithfulness demands respect for the goods which ground its very possibility.

A consequentialist, observing that any choice is relevant to two or more human goods, proposes that morality be determined by reference to all of the goods involved. However, consequentialism focuses upon the goods only as they are concretized in limited, prospective good results and confines the person within the limits of measurable goods, reduced to unity by the standard arbitrarily adopted for the occasion. The consequentialist might assert that morality must be for human fulfillment, but this theory demands that human fulfillment be like the perfection of a product which at some point is completed and no longer open to being more abundantly. Consequentialism thus not only demotes the ''lesser good'' from its proper status as an intrinsic component of human flourishing to the status of a mere means; it also demotes the ''greater good'' from its proper status as an inexhaustible aspect of the potential flourishing of human persons in always new and richer ways to the status of an attainable goal, an objective to be reached and then replaced by some new objective.

The ethical theory which we have articulated, no less than consequentialism, holds that morality is determined by reference to all of the intrinsic aspects of human flourishing. But this ethical theory, unlike consequentialism, reflects the complexity and richness of human flourishing and maintains openness to personal fulfillments beyond any measure even conceivable at a given moment in a person's life or in the life of humankind. Moral norms are not restrictive of personal fulfillment, for they only limit persons from limiting themselves more narrowly than is inevitable for limited beings.

We have now indicated one way in which the basic requirement of morality takes shape in concrete moral obligations to avoid specific acts. Respect for all the basic human goods demands that one never act directly against any of them, that one never adopt a proposal to realize some good by acting in a way detrimental to one or more of these goods, which are aspects of potential human flourishing. It follows that every kind of action which could be justified only on the basis that if evil might be done that good would follow is morally excluded.

But the basic requirement of morality generates other forms of responsibility, many of them more affirmative than negative in the direction they give to one's action. Several of these forms of responsibility are especially important for the problems considered in this book. They are ones which bear upon one person's treatment of others.

First of all, human beings, if they respect all that contributes to human flourishing, will be ready to cooperate with other persons in the realization of human goods. A person who loves what is humanly good, and is not fixated upon his or her individual participation in and enjoyment of good, will not stand idle while others starve, suffer, and die. Such a person will find intolerable the exploitation of others and will do what is possible to help them.

This form of responsibility has important implications for the treatment of dying patients. Persons who are morally good not only will refuse to make choices directed against human life but also will extend themselves to care for a dying person and to protect what goods one who is dying still can enjoy, even if they happen to have no contractual or other well-defined duty to such a person.

Second, persons who respect all that is good will never make themselves a special case. Morally good persons will recognize as a form of responsibility which must shape every choice the golden rule or principle of universalizability. Such persons do not regard themselves and those with whom they have special, close ties as "more equal" or more worthy of respect than other persons. Persons who act in accord with this form of responsibility will try to identify with other persons' concerns and will not fail to ask what they would want if the roles were reversed.

Such attempts to put oneself or those for whom one especially cares in the positions of persons who will be affected by one's acts will be very important in dealing with the senile, the defective, the insane, the comatose. In such cases there is no more direct way to determine one's obligations, which in other cases would depend on the patient's consent. There is a temptation to separate oneself from those in so different a condition, to begin to think of them as mere objects or organisms, as vegetables or nonpersons. This norm excludes all such ways of thinking about patients. It also excludes letting patients die of starvation and thirst. Who would wish themselves to be treated in such a way? Similarly, there are excesses of treatment which are excluded: those to which no one in the patient's place would consent.

Finally, all who respect all of the basic human goods recognize many specific duties to other persons. The readiness to promote and respect all the goods of persons leads to cooperative activity, to organized efforts by communities of people. The work is divided, the activity shared, and thus roles created and duties defined. Not everyone has the same obligations, since no two persons belong to all the same communities or have similar roles in the communities to which they do belong. But no one who is morally good can avoid making genuine commitments to many communities. These commitments are the proximate moral principle of the many specific moral obligations which are defined by one's duties. Thus, morally good persons regard their involvement in social roles not merely as a way of fulfilling themselves but as a way of responding to the appeal of human goods by working with others for common fulfillment, by serving others who cannot take care of themselves.

Moral obligations which stem directly from the requirement to respect and promote basic human goods do not depend upon common commitments.

They hold regardless of any special relationships among persons. For example, if human life must be respected, then possible courses of action which involve killing people for the sake of ulterior goods are morally excluded, regardless of who these people are and how one is related to them. And if one has a strict moral obligation not to kill someone, that person's life is morally protected; he or she might be said to have an unalienable right to life.

By contrast, moral obligations which stem from common commitments make special demands on members of the community toward one another. Those to whose role it pertains to do or to refrain from doing something have duties to fulfill which their roles require. Other members of the society, who would be affected in one way or another by nonfulfillment of the requirements of a role, have rights or entitlements that the role be fulfilled. Rights and duties of this sort are moral responsibilities, yet they are not absolute, for changes in the community and its definition of roles can alter one's duties or rights. Thus a patient whose right not to be killed is unalienable has only a conditional and perhaps alterable right to the care of a particular physician or hospital.

Still, it is very important to keep in mind that rights and duties which arise from community are not mere social conventions. They are mediated by a common commitment but are ultimately grounded in the normativity of the human goods which are the principles of morality. Hence, most of the moral requirements of a person's daily life are located in the claims which other members of the community have upon one's responsible service.

Thus, parents, having undertaken to generate children, have a duty to provide and to care for them, even if they are defective. Physicians have a duty to care for their patients, even if the patients in many cases are not pleasant, interesting, and rewarding.

In sum, we have articulated four forms of responsibility or modes of moral obligation by which the basic requirement of morality begins to take shape in specific moral judgments. The four are: never to act directly against any basic human good, to help others when possible, to consider impartially actions which will affect others, and to respect the rights of those to whom one has duties. These four modes of obligation are normative principles for the more specific moral norms concerning various kinds of action. Using these modes of obligation, we shall argue in chapter twelve for certain moral positions relevant to the problems considered in this book.

Before proceeding to this matter, however, we must keep a promise made earlier: to reply more carefully to the objection of those who hold that human life is not one of the intrinsic aspects of human flourishing but is only a means, of great but merely instrumental value, to the properly personal goods of human individuals.

H. Human Life an Intrinsic Personal Good

Those who claim that human life itself does not have the status of a constitutive aspect of human flourishing do not deny that life is very valuable to persons. Not only those who consider life an integral part of the well-being of persons but also those who consider it a merely instrumental value think that respect for life and protection of it are very important functions of law and morality. Those who deny that life is of itself a basic human good can explain the importance life has in law and in morality by pointing to a fact which everyone admits: Life is a necessary condition or essential means for the attainment of any other human good. The point of disagreement is whether life is only a necessary condition for realizing other human goods or is also an integral component of human flourishing, which should be protected and promoted on its own account.

Those who consider life only a necessary condition for the realization of other, specifically personal goods often suggest that to consider it inherently good would be to absolutize it and thus to distort its proper role in one's hierarchy of values. According to this view ethical theories which insist upon the sanctity of life defer too much to this value, so that instead of life serving the person and personal flourishing, it becomes a dominant consideration and claims an unwarranted mastery which is offensive to personal dignity. There are a number of arguments which render this view plausible.

First, those goods which are worthwhile in themselves are not merely given facts. Rather, they are presented in one's deliberations as goods which can be realized through one's actions. Life, however, is a given. It is presupposed by every deliberation. Hence, it does not seem to be an end to be pursued.

Second, most reflective persons regard life as subordinate to other, higher values. Among those who so regard it are those such as Socrates and Thomas More whom almost everyone would consider morally perceptive and unquestionably upright. Martyrs, whether religiously motivated or not, willingly die for truth, friendship, justice, and so on.

Third, life is not unique to persons. Animals have life and so do plants, including cabbages and carrots. Thus, life is not properly personal, and so it seems to constitute no part of what makes up the flourishing of persons as such.

Fourth, people do commit suicide, and suicides are not necessarily insane. Thus, it is quite possible for rational agents to treat their own lives as if they were not good at all. If life were an intrinsic good of persons, it seems that this would be impossible.

Plausible as these objections are, however, they are not compelling. Before proceeding to a constructive argument in favor of our own position, we answer these objections as follows.

In answer to the first objection, one must notice that although life indeed is a given—a fact presupposed by the activities of deliberating and choosing by which one pursues what is good—human life, even the life of the agent deliberating, is not merely a given. The reflexivity of human awareness makes it possible for a human agent to deliberate and choose about the very presuppositions of choice. One can consider killing oneself; one can consider doing things which will protect or destroy, lengthen or prolong, one's own life.

Also, choices which are morally significant bear not only upon the basic human goods realized in the agent but also upon their possible realization or protection in other persons. One clearly can make choices which affect the lives of others. One also may choose to hand on human life by having children or to prevent the beginning of new lives. So life is not merely a given. This fact also is recognized, at least implicitly, by those who consider human life a merely instrumental good of persons. Nothing is a means or instrument unless choices can be made so to use it.

In answer to the second objection, we concede that many good and heroic persons refuse to cling to their own lives as if the absolute good were in life itself. For such persons there are other goods which they consider far more important. But this hierarchy of values does not imply that life is not of itself an aspect of human, personal flourishing. To say that life is intrinsically, not merely instrumentally, good is not to say that life is the *only* intrinsic good of persons or that it is the good to which upright persons will normally direct much of their thought and effort.

According to the ethical theory we have outlined one can hold that life is inherently good and yet make morally good choices which one foresees will jeopardize one's life provided that these choices do not amount to an act directed against life as a means of promoting some other good. (We shall explain this point more fully in the next chapter.) A final point must be made in answer to this objection. A person who is good and upright can nevertheless be mistaken. It might be that Socrates, for instance, did not consider human life an intrinsic good of persons. If this was his view and it was sincere, then even if it is a mistake, this takes nothing away from his heroism.

In response to the third objection, we point out that biological life is specifically different in humans, in other animals, and in plants. This is not a matter of philosophical speculation but a matter of fact which any biologist knows well.

Although animals can perform many of the kinds of functions performed by plants, animals perform their functions in a way proper to themselves. Animals assimilate food, grow, and reproduce, but they do these so-called vegetative functions in an animal way. To be able to do some of the things a plant can do is not to be a plant; to be partly perfected by activities common to animals and plants is not to be partly a plant.

The same is true for human beings. Persons can do many of the things other animals can do and many of the things plants can do. But this does not imply that persons are nonhuman animals or plants or that any part of the kinds of functions persons can perform are a consequence of a nonhuman animal or plant portion of the human individual. It is obvious from a biological point of view that a human being is a certain, specific kind of organism. To be one kind of organism, by definition, is not to be any other kind. Also, any individual of a certain kind is through and through an individual of that kind.

Human life, then, is properly human, precisely because every aspect of it is specific to human individuals. There is no such thing as common life—this is a mere abstract concept—which becomes this or that kind of life by some added qualification. Similarities or analogies between various forms of life presuppose, rather than negate, their specific, real differences. Thus even a comatose person is no vegetable; biologically the remaining functions, however minimal, are such as no cabbage or carrot does, for they are still specifically human processes of specifically human organs.

In answer to the fourth objection, we notice that the intrinsic goodness of the basic human goods does not prevent people from treating them as if they were mere means or obstacles. For the ethical theory we articulated above the possibility of denying in practice the true status of any of the intrinsic aspects of human flourishing is tied to the possibility of acting immorally, and immoral acts are not completely irrational. Thus, selfish persons can treat justice and friendship as if these human goods were merely convenient devices to facilitate their systematic exploitation of others or mere practical obstacles to pushing systematic exploitation as far as they would like. This does not mean that justice is nothing more than the interest of the stronger and cleverer or that friendship is merely a sentimental idea in which weaklings indulge.

No doubt there must be some degree of rationalization or self-deception for a person to treat what is an inherent aspect of personal flourishing as if it were merely instrumental. But such self-deception obviously is possible. If human life is, as we hold, an intrinsic good of persons, those who consider it otherwise in practice also quite naturally convince themselves that life is merely an instrumental good, expendable for the sake of higher personal interests.

None of the arguments intended to show that human life is merely instrumental is successful. Nevertheless, the evidence which shows that human life is an intrinsic aspect of personal flourishing is not unambiguous. Whenever life is the object of choice, goods besides life could always affect one's consideration, for even in the worst situations one who can deliberate can be anxious to preserve life at least partly insofar as it is a necessary condition for the pursuit of other goods. A person who fights the onslaught of a fatal disease not only wants to survive but also wants to watch television, to visit with loved ones, to pray, and so on. Persons who willingly undertake to hand on human life to children not only desire that their children live but also that they enjoy many other human goods.

According to our own view it is good to be alive not only because life enables one to do other good things, but also because human life itself is good. Still, the data need not be interpreted in this way. Those who maintain that life is only an instrumental good for persons interpret the data otherwise.

Hence, a less direct argument is needed to establish the thesis that human life is an intrinsic personal good, a constitutive aspect of human flourishing. The form of the argument we are about to propose is to show that the position we reject has implications which are simply untenable. The proposition that life is only instrumentally good implies that the human person or some parts of the human person are one thing and that a person's living body is quite another thing. This implied position is dualism, and dualism is false.

Some who hold that life is only instrumentally good explicitly embrace dualism. We saw in chapter three, section E, that Joseph Fletcher sharply divides the person and personal goods from the body and physical nature, which he considers to be "out there" and "over against us." In another work Fletcher asserts his dualistic view again:

> The right of spiritual beings to use intelligent control over physical nature, rather than submit beastlike to its blind workings, is the heart of many crucial questions. . . . To perceive this is to grasp the error lurking in the notion—widespread in medical circles—that life as such is the highest good. This kind of vitalism seduces its victims into being more loyal to the physical spark of mere biological life than to the personality values of self-possession and human integrity. The beauty and spiritual depths of human stature are what should be conserved in our value system, with the flesh as the means rather than the end.[12]

Although, as we have argued already, Fletcher is mistaken in thinking that one who does not treat life as a merely instrumental value must regard it as the highest good, we think he is quite right in holding that dualism and the thesis that human life is only an instrumental good of persons are necessarily connected. In fact, the view that life is a merely instrumental good implies dualism, as we shall now demonstrate.

As we explained already, the goods which constitute human flourishing are not entities apart from human persons. The basic human goods are not ideals beyond humankind nor are they states of affairs to be reached in the future nor are they objects to be acquired and possessed. Rather, these goods are the realization in human persons of their potentialities to be and be more fully. These potentialities are realized by actions in which persons participate in these goods. Thus, human flourishing is at least a part of the person; it is that part of the person which the person realizes by his or her own choices and actions. More adequately, human flourishing is the part of persons which individually and communally is realized by their own choices and actions, including their care for one another and cooperation with one another.

This conception, as we have seen, gives a precise meaning to the dictum that persons are ends in themselves. Human flourishing is the principle toward which human action is rightly directed, and human flourishing is not extrinsic to persons but is at least one part of them.

Now, if the instrumental view of human life is correct, then human life cannot be identified with the human person insofar as the person is the end of human activity. Life is instrumental by hypothesis on this theory and so cannot be part of the person as end in himself or herself. The human person, thus, must be divided into the part which is end and the part which is not end. According to Fletcher's concept in human individuals there is a personal component, but there is also a distinct, bodily component, which is part of physical nature "out there."

The distinction between these two parts or components must be a distinction between two entities. Clearly, the living organism is an entity. If the person as end is to be distinct from the entity which is the living organism, then the person also must be an entity—for example, as Fletcher suggests, a spirit. If the person is not also an entity, what else could it be? Clearly, the person cannot be merely the activity of the living organism. For if it were, the living organism would be that which is acting, and that which is acting is no mere instrument of its own activity. Nor can the person as end merely be activity which is not the activity of the living organism or of anything else, for then there would be nothing to have the potentiality of which this activity is the fulfillment.

The proponent of the instrumentalist view of human life might try to argue that although the living human organism is one entity and the person is another entity, still these two entities together constitute one something—one human individual or one complete self. But the suggestion that one something is made up of two quite distinct entities seems hardly intelligible.

Furthermore, this attempted escape invites one to stress either the unity or the duality of this odd "self." If one stresses its duality, then all the difficulties to be evaded recur. If one stresses its unity, then the merely instrumental reality of life once again merges into the reality of person as end.

A very philosophical attempt to escape from the dilemma takes the following form. Perhaps the human self is in theoretical truth only one entity but for practical purposes has to be regarded as two entities—a living organism and a person, the former merely instrumental and the latter an end in itself.

The difficulty with this attempt is that if one treats as two in practice what one maintains to be one in theory, there seems to be no single perspective to use in distinguishing and relating the theoretical and the practical perspectives. If one says that what is existentially many is *really* one, then moral life seems to rest upon a false assumption, a kind of fiction at odds with reality. If one says that the two perspectives are *equally valid* and merely distinct, the question arises how they can be distinct enough to avoid being incompatible while being unified enough to allow oneself or any self to think of and talk about "my life" and "my dignity."[13]

We conclude that those who hold that human life is merely an instrumental good of the person must accept some form of dualism. Either one distinguishes two entities within the self, one personal and the other merely organic, or one distinguishes life in some other way from what fulfills the person as end of activity. But any distinction will raise the difficulty of unity and duality, either by being insufficient to separate merely instrumental life from personal flourishing or by being all too sufficient—that is, sufficient to destroy the unity of the human person.

Our next point is that the dualism to which an instrumentalist view of life inevitably leads is false. Many have tried to hold some version of dualism, but it is an untenable position.

Both classical and contemporary authors—and among the latter philosophers from both the analytic and phenomenological schools—have pointed out the many problems of dualism.[14] If one thinks of the human individual as made up of a duality, how are the two parts to be distinguished? Where is one to draw the line between the person as end and the person as mere means? A reader who is impatient with philosophical speculation is likely to suspect that any question about line drawing is merely an academic distraction. But in the present case we ask where the line is to be drawn as a way of leading to the clearer understanding that no line can be drawn.

Life is not merely one process among others, which might be distinguished from breathing, feeling pain, choosing, talking, and administering treatments. The life of a living entity is indistinguishable from the very reality of the entity—a reality which pervades and includes all that the entity does. Breathing, feeling pain, choosing, talking, and administering treatments can all be enlivened and real by one and the same life of one single individual, and all these activities are parts of the individual's whole life process. For any organism to exist is for it to live, and all of its activities are part of its life. The same is true for human individuals.

Thus, human activities, including those which seem most distinctively personal, those which no one denies to be intrinsic constituents of human flourishing, are not separate from a person's life. Life is not a characteristic of one part of a whole, and these activities properties of some other part of it.

Rather, life pervades these activities or they lack reality—unless one supposes them to have reality altogether apart from the living body one also calls "mine." And one's human life includes one's activities. They perfect oneself, but they are not distinct from one's life as an end is distinct from an instrument used to realize it.

Thus, the underlying, pervasive, and inclusive character of life with respect to all of a person's activities is a fact, and this fact is inconsistent with any form of dualism which would try to separate life as merely instrumental from persons as ends in themselves. There are other data which also tell against dualism.

First, there is the experienced unity of oneself. Human persons are aware of themselves as unified wholes; they are not conscious of being aggregates of entities organized into some sort of system. This awareness is especially clear in carrying on purposeful human acts. Lawyers examine cases, engaging hands and eyes, memory and thought; they plan and prepare briefs, engaging all aspects of themselves in the work. When the trial comes, perhaps a lawyer feels slightly hung over but pulls himself or herself together to do the best for the client, fulfilling a lawyer's duty by thinking, remembering, talking, and so on. Lawyers experience all of these activities as their own; they are directly aware of what they are doing as integrated action, as part of their single and only life.

In general, the constituting of oneself through one's human acts is a realization of the potentialities which belong to and are characteristic of one's given self. The given self is oneself; its flourishing in activity is not a different thing from the unfolding of oneself. If the person as already given, as a basis for morally significant acts, were something distinct from the person as end, then this conception of human activity would be false. What, then, would unite these two principles? Are we to say that there is a third something—the real self—which unites the given self with the person? This proposal only complicates matters, for now it is necessary to ask what this third something has to do with the other two, how it unites them while remaining distinct from them, and so on.

The point we are making about the unity of the human individual can be illustrated precisely with reference to the problems considered in this book. An argument for voluntary euthanasia is that persons would be able to dispose of their lives autonomously, to avoid unnecessary pain and suffering and the indiginity of slow deterioration, loss of control of themselves, and so on. But pain and loss of control befall the organism, which on a dualistic account is quite distinct from the person as end. How, then, can what befalls the organism detract from personal dignity? Consistent dualists should say that their own living bodies simply have nothing to do with personal dignity. Pain and suffering, deterioration and loss of control, machinery and probings, discussions by those who find one "a good case"—these are indignities to the dying. But why would they be indignities if they bore not upon what has dignity—the agent and action—but only upon something instrumental: a living and dying organism which has somehow been once connected with the flourishing of a human person?

The dualist wants a distinction between person and life in order to treat life as merely instrumental, wants to treat life as merely instrumental to justify subordinating it as mere means to "higher" and "personal" values, wants to subordinate life to protect the person's dignity, but conceives of the person in a fashion that makes what befalls the organism irrelevant to dignity.

We conclude, therefore, that dualism is indefensible. It is a theory which is at war with the experience all persons have of themselves as unified wholes, as unified self-actualizing entities, whose potentialities are given but whose flourishing is a unique challenge, and whose life pervades and includes both. And since dualism is false, so is the instrumentalist conception of human life which implies dualism.

The argument we have presented regarding the view that human life is only an instrumental good of persons is very important for the light it throws on the issues discussed in this book. Like consequentialism, this dualistic view underlies most of the positions we reject. If consequentialism and the theory that human life is only an instrumental good are both admitted to be false, then the rationale of the proponents of euthanasia is almost wholly destroyed.

For example, Robert M. Veatch obviously presupposed that human life as such is only instrumental to the being and well-being of persons when he argued that "consciousness or the capacity for embodied social interaction" is needed to qualify a human body as living. He rejects a more traditional criterion of death as too animalistic. He does not see life as a direct aspect of personal flourishing.

Likewise, in chapter eight we reviewed the views of several authors who deny personhood to living human individuals who fail to meet additional conditions. Here, too, the life of a human individual is not considered a personal good, for if it were, the mere fact that a human being still lives would be enough to assure anyone that this individual is a person.

Similarly, we reviewed a number of arguments in favor of suicide and euthanasia which propose that life becomes a disvalue when one in certain respects undergoes more disvalue than enjoyment. These arguments would not make sense if life itself were not assumed to be a mere condition, which does not count as intrinsically good regardless of what else one can do or enjoy.

If life indeed is, as we have argued, an intrinsic aspect of the flourishing of persons, then all of these arguments are unsound. The ethics we are proposing is based upon the contrary view of human life. Life is not only a condition which is necessary if a person is to achieve higher values. It is an intrinsic aspect of human flourishing; it directly contributes to the full dignity of the human person. Hence, although human life is not an absolute, superior to all other personal goods, neither is it merely instrumental.

The view that human life is merely an instrumental good, while it might seem to be based upon a higher, more spiritual view of the human person, in reality undermines all respect for human persons as they in fact are. For to be a person is to be a living body, with potentialities for self-determination and participation in a multitude of goods which no other living body can share in and enjoy. Still, the most spiritual activities of human persons are pervaded by and included in the one life, which is the reality of the person and every personal activity.

As we pointed out in the introduction to this book, lack of respect for human life has had and continues to have terrible effects in the contemporary world. The lives of human persons are treated as if they were something apart from truly personal goods, are regarded as expendable in the interests of greater liberty, an ideally just society of the future, or other goods. Thus abortion, wars of mass destruction, terrorism, and finally nuclear deterrence have been rationalized. The theory that human life is merely an instrumental good has in practice borne fruit in treating millions of persons as expendable for nationalistic objectives. Contemporary men and women are learning well that if human life is not an intrinsic aspect of human flourishing, if it is merely instrumental, then it has a price. And if human life has a price, it is remarkably cheap.

12. Moral Responsibilities toward Human Life

A. The Distinction between Acts and Results

If the ethical theory which we outlined in chapter eleven is to be of help in resolving the moral perplexities which people feel with respect to the questions treated in this book, we first must clarify how the basic principle of morality and the various modes of responsibility can be brought to bear upon human action. Questions such as the following must be answered.

Are particular human acts the principal entities which are to be shaped by moral norms? Or should morality focus rather upon intentions and motives, or perhaps upon states of character? Whether or not the focus ought to be on particular acts, how are intentions and motives related to what one does?

It might be supposed that everyone knows exactly what is meant by the phrase "what one does." But further questions make clear that the exact reference of "what one does" is far from clear. Does "what one does" include all the effects of one's behavior? Does it include only those effects which one foresees? Or does it include only part of the effects which one foresees?

No matter how these questions are answered, there are still further questions about omissions. Are one's omissions part of what one does, even though one who omits seems rather not to be doing something than to be doing anything? If omissions are not part of what one does, why is one morally responsible for omissions as well as for actions?

Questions like these could be multiplied indefinitely. But we have listed enough of them to make our point: An account of human action is needed as a basis for any discussion of moral responsibilities toward human life.

For several reasons we begin our account with a consideration of choice.

First, it is plain from common experience that people seek moral guidance when they are faced with two or more alternatives, each appealing or interesting in its own way, and a choice among possibilities seems to be necessary. The conscientious person wonders, "What is the right thing to do?" Such wonder does not arise if there are no practical alternatives, if no choice seems to be called for.

Second, what one does by choice is in the clearest and fullest sense done voluntarily. What is done by choice is voluntary not only in the sense that it is willingly done but also in the sense that it is willingly undertaken, although it might not have been done. This is so because when a person chooses to do a certain act, he or she can choose either to do it or not to do it. Only what is voluntary—what is done voluntarily and its consequences—can fall within one's moral responsibility; no one is morally responsible for what really cannot be helped. Moral norms shape one's moral responsibilities. Hence, moral norms certainly must bear upon choices, although they also will shape in various ways whatever else falls within one's responsibility to the extent that it is voluntarily accepted or omitted.

Third, one's choices are the vital link between actions, intentions, and states of character. This point requires explanation in a little detail.

Choices clearly are principles of one's actions, since one chooses precisely to do one thing or another or perhaps not to act or to delay acting. If there is nothing one can do at all about a certain situation, one has no choice in the matter. Actions considered possible and interesting by individuals are deliberated about very much as motions which members put forward are debated by a deliberative body. The adoption of a proposal for action is a choice. The action executes the choice, very much as an executive carries out what a legislative body has decided to do.

Choices depend upon motives or intentions. Motives are the goods embodied in alternatives which make them seem interesting, which make them living options with practical appeal. If there were no motive for doing something, even if it were possible, one would never consider it. Once one adopts a certain proposal by choice, the motive which made it interesting has the status of the good one intends.

Choices also are closely related to states of character. Clearly, if a person has an established character of a certain sort, further choices will likely be in line with this character. Character itself is of the order of potentiality; it does not present itself for direct observation but appears only in one's choices and actions. But by these fruits character shows itself and is known.

Even more important, one's choices form one's character. The moral significance of human acts, as we explained in chapter eleven, is not simply in their measurable consequences. A person who sincerely tries to do what is right is a good person, although such a person might be mistaken or might fail to accomplish a good purpose through accident, the interference of another, or simple incapacity to bring about the good which was intended. In morality good will—if it is genuine and persistent—is infinitely more important than good results. The reason is that choice is self-determination. In choosing to adopt one or another course of action one not only sets oneself into motion for the measurable time the action takes and one not only commits oneself to the use of a certain amount of energy and possessions. One also, and first of all, makes oneself be a certain sort of person, a person who would do that kind of thing.

If one chooses to allow a defective infant to die of hunger and thirst rather than to carry out a simple operation which would save its life, one does something much more significant and permanent to oneself than appears as one signs the order to withhold fluids and nourishment or pushes the crib over to a far corner of the nursery. One makes oneself a certain sort of person. One takes a certain stance toward human life and other goods. One establishes an important facet of character which might appear in numerous later choices and actions, when one's choice in this first instance will cause one to see human life as a limited, instrumental good which must give way to other goods now regarded as significantly personal in a way that mere life is not regarded as personal.

The importance of choices in determining oneself can be hidden for two different reasons.

On the one hand, those who already have determined themselves by choice and who act in mere consistency with character formed in this way are said to be "choosing" on later occasions, even when the determination of which alternative will be adopted is a foregone conclusion. On this basis character might appear to be the pivotal factor. But those aspects of character which arise apart from one's own choice, from nature and nurture, heredity and environment, are not considered by anyone to make a person morally responsible for what follows from them, unless at least one could have chosen to reform oneself and failed to do so.

On the other hand, people often choose to do certain acts and even carry out certain choices without being altogether clearheaded and wholehearted about what they are doing. In cases of this sort people sometimes change their minds and regret—perhaps repent of—their choice and do not confirm themselves in being the person their choice implies they are. Such confirmation requires the integration of every facet of the personality with the choice.

Nevertheless, choices are pivotal in the formation of character. Any choice, if it really involves some free self-determination which settles one's stance toward human goods, is a fundamental option provided that one persists in the choice and integrates one's whole self with it. The great saints and heroes of every culture have recognized this fact very clearly when they refused firmly to compromise on matters which seemed to others of very little practical—consequentialist—importance. A Socrates or a Thomas More knows that when he chooses, he holds his soul, his very self, in his own hands, and that if he does not choose rightly, his self will be lost like water trickling between fingers not held tightly enough together.

After our lengthy discussion of ethical theory in chapter eleven, it might appear a simple enough matter to determine the moral quality of choices. Those choices by which one promotes a human good (or some such goods) and in which one respects all the human goods will be morally right. Other choices will be morally wrong. But it is more difficult than at first appears to determine the moral quality of a choice. The difficulty begins to come to light when one asks precisely what a choice is.

For the most part choices are not mere mental acts, mere volitional allegiances to human goods. To make a choice is something more than to be a person of good will—or of bad will. By one's choices one determines oneself by committing one's potentialities for doing things, for carrying out individual instances of certain possible patterns of human behavior. In other words, one chooses to act or to refrain from acting in certain definite ways. Also, one chooses a concrete act, an individual doing at a certain place and time. Thus one's chosen act must be distinguished from other events and processes which occur or go on at approximately the same place and time. Hence, we must ask: Precisely what is it that one chooses to do when one chooses to act?

As we have explained in chapter eleven, section C, one makes a choice only when there are two or more incompatible possible courses of action between which one is hesitating. These alternatives come under consideration only because each of them is interesting or appealing, and none of them is irresistible. If there were no appealing or interesting alternatives, one would not hesitate and deliberate; one would do nothing (if there were no motive for acting) or would spontaneously act without hesitation (if there were a motive for doing only one thing). If any possibility were irresistibly attractive, one would not hesitate; when it came to mind one would respond to the cogency of the irresistible appeal. Thus there would be no occasion for choice were it not for the multiplicity of interesting possibilities, their incompatibility, and their common resistibility. One who deliberates is sensitive to multiple, non-compelling appeals.

What is it which appeals? It is something promised by the possible course of action—something embodied in it which makes it seem worthwhile or valuable. In other words, one who is deliberating sees—or, at least, seems to see—something in each course of action under consideration. What is seen is either an aspect in which the action will be suited to the agent and fulfilling in itself or some way in which it will lead to an ulterior goal.

In other words, one finds possible courses of action interesting when they either offer the possibility of participating in basic human goods (which are ends) or hold out promise of leading to such a participation and thus appear as means to ends. In either case reflection promotes a possibility for choice, proposes it for the good it promises directly or indirectly. As we explained in chapter eleven, section C, choice is possible and necessary because the promised goods are diverse in kind and incommensurable. Whichever choice one makes, one makes it for the sake of the good one hopes to realize by the execution of the choice.

This clarification of what is involved in choosing enables us to state more clearly precisely what people are committing themselves to when they choose to do something. If one always chooses for the sake of the good one hopes to realize, it follows that one chooses to carry out a certain performance insofar as the performance is a way of realizing the hoped-for good. This good might be in the state of affairs which is the performance itself, or it might be in some ulterior act. Thus one in choosing is committing oneself to bringing about the state of affairs only insofar as it either embodies or is a necessary condition for ulteriorly realizing the good in which one is interested.

The good in which one is interested is much more limited than the entire state of affairs which one actually causes. For example, if two boys play a game of catch, the good in which they are interested is the playing of the game itself. Their play might unexpectedly call their parents' attention to the fact that they have leisure and thus lead to their being given some chores to do. Not thought of, this possible consequence is no part of that to which they are committed. Perhaps they have been told not to play catch, and they foresee that they will be caught and punished for having been disobedient. This consequence of playing catch, although understood to be part of the state of affairs their behavior will bring about, is not precisely what they are committed to.

It might be thought that the foreseen consequence lies outside the precise boundaries of their choice only because it is something which follows by parental fiat rather than by natural consequence from what they are doing. But this would be a mistake. If the boys are thoughtful, they also realize that in playing they are wearing out their ball and their gloves. Sometime in the future new equipment will have to be purchased. Even if they consider this natural consequence of using their equipment, it is no part of that to which they commit themselves when they decide to play. They are interested in the good of play, not in the wear and tear on equipment which is inseparable from this good.

Similarly, if a girl accepts jobs baby-sitting in order to earn money, not because she particularly likes to take care of children, she commits herself to the work just to the extent that she must in order to obtain the money she wants. Her commitment does not extend to the unforeseen effect that she will be away from home while the rest of her family enjoys a midnight snack. Her missing out on the treat is a consequence of her choice but no part of her action. But even if she knows that her family will enjoy a midnight snack and that she will miss out on it if she is busy elsewhere, she commits herself by choice to what is required to earn money, not to forgoing other satisfactions she might enjoy if she did not accept the work.

In general, if a person chooses to do something because the very action is a way of participating in a human good, this person brings about a very extensive state of affairs but only does that by which the good is participated in. And if a person chooses to do something as a means to an ulterior end, this person also brings about many consequences but only does that which is instrumental to the desired end. Deliberation concerns proposals for action. The proposals are shaped by hoped for goods. Action is expected to realize potential goods directly or indirectly. Thus, to choose to do something is to adopt a proposal by which one commits oneself to trying to realize a state of affairs just insofar as this state of affairs will embody a hoped for good.

If "what one does" is defined narrowly by what one chooses, what one in fact brings about is always much wider than what one does. One brings about an indeterminate and indeterminable sequence of processes and events, many of them unforeseeable, some which only could be guessed at, and comparatively few which could be predicted with any degree of confidence. Not even everything which can be predicted with confidence is included in the proposal one adopts, since much of what one foresees is incidental and perhaps unwanted in relation to what one does. One is only committed to a small part of what one brings about in acting—namely, to the carrying out of the proposal one has adopted and to what is necessarily included in this. The entirety of what one brings about cannot define what one is doing, since the whole sequence of processes and events considered together lacks the character of something worthwhile or useful, and without this character one cannot wish to bring into reality the possibility one envisions in deliberation.

If human acts are defined by what one does in the sense we have explained, then it is possible to distinguish a person's acts from the consequences of these acts. A person's acts, what he or she does, consist precisely in the execution of proposals the person has adopted. The consequences of a person's acts include all the processes and events which the person in any way causes in acting, apart from the acts themselves.

Thus the boys' act is playing catch; the consequences include being punished for disobedience, wearing out their equipment, making thumping noises, frightening birds from the path of the ball, displacing a certain amount of air, and so. on and on. The girl's act is taking care of the children in the manner necessary to earn her fee; the consequences include missing out on treats at home, having to change the baby's diaper, wearing the carpet slightly when she walks the infant, learning by practical experience how to care for babies, and so on and on.

Someone is likely to object that in making the distinction between human acts and their consequences as we do, we are drawing a morally irrelevant line and perhaps distracting attention from a morally more relevant line. Precisely what one wishes to accomplish can be distinguished from all that one in fact causes, but—the objector will insist—one voluntarily brings about more than what one wishes to accomplish. If they realize that they may be punished, the boys not only voluntarily play catch but also voluntarily disobey and run the risk of punishment; if she realizes she may miss out on a treat at home, the girl not only voluntarily baby sits and earns income but also voluntarily forgoes the treat she might enjoy at home. Since at least the foreseen consequences of one's acts—at a very minimum those foreseen with high probability or practical certainty—are voluntarily brought about, one cannot consider oneself wholly without responsibility for them.

This objection is based upon an undeniable truth. One does voluntarily bring about the foreseen consequences of one's acts. Although they are not part of one's proposal, such consequences are within one's awareness as one deliberates and chooses. One might not want them, but one does accept them. Thus in executing one's proposal one also causes consequences which have been willingly accepted. To this extent the objection makes a sound point. But the objection also depends for its force upon a false assumption— namely, that what is included in the proposal one has adopted and what is outside the proposal and merely accepted are both voluntary in the same way. Thus the objection concludes that responsibility for acts and for their consequences arises in the very same way.

We grant that persons are not wholly without responsibility for the consequences of their acts, even if these consequences are unwanted. But we hold that certain basic truths about human choice and about morality in making choices require that differences in the voluntariness of acts and their consequences be recognized and borne in mind, and that these differences will mark out different grounds of responsibility for what one does and for the rest of what one brings about. As it will become clear, we are not saying that one's responsibility for what one merely accepts is necessarily any less grave than is one's responsibility for what one really wishes to accomplish. But there is an important distinction between the two, which we shall now try to clarify.

As we have explained, the practical reasoning and existential attitude of a person involved in deliberation and choice relate in different ways to a proposal and to other aspects of what one might cause. What is involved in a proposal is considered good; one identifies with it. Other aspects of what one causes might be matters of complete indifference or even factors in spite of which one acts. In any case, one does not identify oneself with all that one causes but only with what one considers good, either as intrinsically worthwhile or as useful for attaining what is worthwhile in itself.

This difference in practical reasoning and in attitude does have some moral significance. As we explained in chapter eleven, section F, morality is primarily in the relationship between a person's choices and basic human goods. A choice is upright if it is in harmony with the entire set of basic human goods; it is immoral if it responds to some of these goods at the expense of another or others. Moreover, one in choosing does constitute oneself, maintaining openness to more abundant flourishing or stunting oneself.

Thus the proposals which moral agents adopt and undertake to carry out do determine in a primary and very special way the moral quality of their activity. The agent is committed to the proposal and must accept its content not only as somehow good but as self-defining and—if the proposal is an immoral one—as self-limiting in an unnecessary way.

As we argued in chapter eleven, section C, the consequentialist is mistaken in thinking that the morality of acts can be determined by weighing off the benefits and harms they will bring about. For the consequentialist the distinction we are making between acts and consequences would be irrelevant. But since consequentialism is unworkable, we also saw that a sound teleological ethical theory gives sense to the dictum that evil may not be done that good might follow from it—the end does not justify the means. We are now supplying a clarification of action which allows the necessary distinction between the end and the means.

One who lives hygienically (means) for the sake of health (end) might avoid contact with a patient under his or her care (bad means) for the same end. One who gives opiates (means) to relieve pain (end) might instead kill the patient (which we will argue shortly to be a bad means) to relieve pain. One who takes good care of patients (means) to earn a living (end) might perform unnecessary surgery (bad means) for the same end. In cases in which a bad means is chosen, one who chooses it is committed to it and identified with it, not insofar as it is bad, but insofar as it is a useful good. To make such a commitment the violation of a human good must be rationalized and the person who is willing to violate it stunted in responsiveness to what in itself is humanly appealing.

States of affairs which are not included in one's proposal but are merely foreseen to follow from one's causality are not willed in the same way that means are willed. One does not directly define one's moral character by reference to those effects which one causes apart from one's proposals. One's will is not set upon the realization of such effects. Since one accepts such states of affairs, one does have a moral responsibility in respect to them, but this responsibility is quite different from that which one has for what one wishes to accomplish.

This difference in the origin of moral responsibility makes possible some differences in moral evaluation. When one undertakes to execute one's adopted proposal, precisely what one is doing is an act which either respects all the basic human goods or does not respect them. If it does not, then nothing can make the act good, although many things can make it more or less evil. When one merely foresees certain effects of one's effort to execute one's adopted proposal—effects which themselves are no part of this proposal—one does not in the same way determine oneself in relation to all the basic human goods.

One accepts the effects which one foresees, and so one must consider how these effects might bear upon various basic human goods. In some cases one might have a most grave moral responsibility not to accept certain effects, and a person who truly loves all the basic human goods would not accept them. But in no case can one who is accepting effects do evil that good might follow from it. Accepting effects of one's action simply is not the same thing as trying to reach an end by executing a proposed course of action as a means to that end.

Thus, for example, if Jane Doe is a surgeon who does unnecessary surgery to earn large fees, she adopts a proposal which involves mutilating another person. This appears to her to be a useful good; she rationalizes what she is doing by the good purpose to which she will put her earnings. By contrast, if John Roe is an experimenter who foresees that his experiment might have side effects which would seriously harm persons subjected to it, he need not adopt a proposal involving this harm. No matter what additional considerations are introduced, Doe's acts cannot be justified; precisely what she does is incompatible with the basic human good of life and health. Roe's act cannot be so directly appraised; its moral quality depends upon what the basic human goods require by way of other modes of responsibility.

On the one hand, if there is no compelling need for the risk, if the subjects do not give informed consent, or if other conditions are not met, then perhaps Roe's accepting of the risk of harm expresses an attitude just as careless about human goods as do Doe's activities. Here Roe's action might be seen wrong by the fact that it violates the golden rule; he would not want others to treat him as he treats his experimental subjects. Or the experiment might violate reasonable regulations of experimental procedures and thus contravene the experimenter's communally defined duties.

On the other hand, if there is an urgent need to carry out the experiments, if the subjects give their informed consent, if Roe proceeds as he would if the subjects were persons for whom he cared very deeply, if he is careful to abide by all reasonable regulations which define an experimenter's duties, then perhaps his accepting of the risk of harm to the experimental subjects is morally blameless and even commendable. Harm to the subjects is no part of Roe's proposal, only an accepted effect which he causes. Hence, in the strict sense the harm, even if foreseen, is not included in his action, in what he does. The morality of accepting this harm, therefore, depends upon the conformity of this accepting with other modes of responsibility which mediate Roe's stance toward basic human goods and this accepting. It simply is not possible that his proposal to learn by experiment can be directly against the good of life and health, for possible harm to these goods is no part of this proposal.

In sum, one is primarily responsible for one's choices. What one does, most properly, is what precisely executes the proposals one adopts in choosing. What one does constitutes oneself and shapes one's character directly. One is secondarily responsible for the effects one causes in carrying out one's actions. These effects are consequences of one's acts, not part of them. If these effects are foreseen, they are voluntary in the sense that they are accepted. But voluntarily accepted effects of one's behavior must be distinguished from chosen means to one's ends. Means are considered useful goods; they are included in one's proposals; one identifies with them. A means which is incompatible with any of the basic human goods cannot be adopted clearheadedly without immorality. Effects which are only accepted are in themselves neither compatible nor incompatible with the basic goods.

Yet in many cases effects have a bearing of great importance upon these goods. Although in some cases one might without immorality accept effects which significantly inhibit or damage some human good, this possibility is limited by various forms of responsibility. If one really is as concerned with all of these goods as one ought to be, one will not be partial to some people in accepting harmful effects. Nor will one permit effects it is one's duty to prevent. Hence, although one is not responsible for the effects one accepts in exactly the same way one is responsible for one's actions, responsibility for the former can be just as grave as responsibility for the latter.

B. Actions and Performances Distinguished

We have clearly distinguished what one does in a strict sense—one's action as an execution of a proposal adopted by choice—from the effects one causes other than one's action. Without disturbing this distinction, we now wish to distinguish in people's behavior certain patterns which usually would be considered actions of a particular kind, but which are not so on our account.

What we have in mind are performances which are shaped consciously and purposefully, so that they outwardly appear to be executions of proposals directed toward some obviously relevant goods. But in fact these performances do not execute adopted proposals directed toward these goods. In some cases they execute no proposal at all but follow spontaneously without deliberation and choice from an irresistible impulse which arises and draws a person into behavior or performance which in one sense is an action or a deed but is not an action (what one does) in the strict sense we have defined. In other cases these performances do execute a proposal, but not the one which appears to be executed; the actor adopted some antecedent proposal which now seems to require the performance, and no alternative to following through comes to mind.

Examples will help to clarify these points. Imagine a wife arriving home to find her husband in bed with another woman. Deeply enraged, the wife conceives the idea of killing this rival. Normally alternatives would come to mind. But let us assume that the wife has had a few drinks and is not thinking very quickly. Let us also assume that she has a gun handy. Perhaps no alternatives come to mind; the desire to kill this interloper is compelling, the motive of venting rage irresistible. The wife gets her gun and does the deadly deed.

By our strict definition the wife in this instance does no act of killing; what one does is limited by what one brings about *in executing proposals adopted by choice*. But there is no proposal to kill, no choice to kill, and so no act of killing. The proposal might have been to have drinks, to keep a gun in the house. The pattern of behavior which seems an act of killing is only an effect which the wife brings about. The morality of her deed depends on the extent to which it was voluntarily involved in what was done or accepted or in some other way within the wife's responsibility.

Next let us imagine a young man who is a normally patriotic and responsible citizen of a country not worse than most. The young man has been brought up with the belief that killing the innocent is wrong, but killing in warfare can be right. The nation is brutally attacked by a thoroughly malicious enemy—or so the young man is told and sincerely believes. All of those he considers upright encourage the young man to answer the call of duty and to fight for his country. The young man does not think of refusing to serve. In training he is taught to do a soldier's job, which is explained to him in terms of killing enemy soldiers as efficiently as possible. Again the young man does not think of alternatives to doing the job. And so he goes forth to do deadly deeds.

But he has not adopted a proposal to kill. He did not choose to kill for the simple reason that although he is executing some proposal and the execution involves causing death, the young man never considered any alternative to this pattern of behavior. What proposal is he executing? It is hard to say: perhaps the commitment to be a good citizen; perhaps even the commitment to be a good person, an obedient son of his church, or something of the sort. In making these commitments he implicitly accepted the duty of a citizen to fight for his country and to kill the enemy. But he did not think of this implication when he made his commitments, and he did not think of any alternative to doing what seemed his duty when it came to killing. The pattern of behavior of the young man in battle involves deadly deeds but no acts of killing. But he is doing something—for example, his duty as a citizen. The morality of the deadly deeds is affected by the fact that the young man has not voluntarily taken or accepted a stance incompatible with a sincere and unrestricted love of all of the basic human goods including life.

Performances of the kinds we are exemplifying do not break down the distinction between acts in the strict sense and effects one causes other than acts.

Some of these performances which look like acts are merely effects, but they are effects of a motivating conscious purpose, and in this respect they not only outwardly look like acts but also are partly similar in psychological genesis to the acts they resemble. This is the case with the deadly deed of the enraged wife.

Other of these performances do execute a proposal; they are acts. But they do not execute the proposal they might seem to execute, for that proposal was never an explicit object of choice, considered in comparison with live alternative possibilities and adopted by self-determining commitment. This is the case with the deadly deeds of the upright young man doing his duty. Whatever he is, the young man is not a killer, although he voluntarily does deadly deeds, and the deaths he causes are within his intention—for example, to do his duty as a citizen, to be an obedient son of his church, or whatever.

Nevertheless, instances of the sort exemplified by the enraged wife and the dutiful youth do demand that when conventional categories of actions are subjected to close moral scrutiny, instances usually grouped together be segregated into three types, not two. First, there will be instances which are actions in the strict sense; what is done executes a proposal adopted by choice deliberately shaped in view of the end assumed. Second, there will be instances which are not actions in the strict sense, but which are deeds analogous to actions of that kind in the way in which either the enraged wife's or the dutiful youth's deadly deeds are analogous to acts of killing. Third, there will be instances which are neither acts in the strict sense nor deeds analogous to such acts, but effects of other acts. In this third case the actor brings about a result in terms of which his or her performance is described, even though this result is not an execution of a proposal adopted by choice or even the carrying out of a consciously projected design which never was chosen by the actor.

C. The Morality of Killing: General Considerations

Having clarified these points, we are now in a position to begin to apply the normative theory articulated in chapter eleven to the kinds of killing with which we have been concerned in this book.

In chapters three through ten our concerns with killing were jurisprudential. Now our concern is ethical. The two accounts do not jibe in all respects.
This lack of complete agreement between law and morality will be discussed
in chapter thirteen.

In considering the morality of killing we deal first with cases in which
something is done to bring about death. Omissions will be considered after
some further clarifications concerning them. Also, we save for later consideration the question of cooperation by one person in the deadly deeds of
another.

From the normative theory articulated in chapter eleven it follows that
many performances which would ordinarily be described as "killing a human
individual" ("homicide") are immoral.

In the strict sense one kills a person when, having considered bringing
about a person's death as something one could do, one commits oneself to
doing it by adopting this proposal instead of some alternative and by undertaking to execute it. By definition killing in the strict sense is an action
contrary to the good of life. The adoption of a proposal to bring about someone's death is incompatible with respect for this good. Thus every act which
is an act of killing in the strict sense is immoral. No additional circumstance
or condition can remove this immorality.

This definition and moral characterization of killing in the strict sense make
no distinction between intent to kill, attempt to kill, and the consummation of
the undertaking by successful execution. These distinctions, which are legally
significant, are morally irrelevant. If one commits oneself to realizing a certain state of affairs, by the commitment one constitutes oneself as a certain
type of person. If one commits oneself to killing a person; one constitutes
oneself a murderer. This remains true even if one is prevented from attempting to execute one's purpose—for example, if someone else kills the intended
victim first. Even more obviously it remains true if one attempts to execute
one's purpose but fails—for example, if one shoots to kill but misses the
intended victim.

Although everything which is an act of killing in the strict sense is immoral,
not every deadly deed is an act of killing in this sense. As we have explained,
some deadly deeds carry out a consciously projected design, but the performance is not the execution of a proposal adopted by the actor's choice to
bring about the death of a human individual. The examples of the enraged
wife and the dutiful soldier belong here. In what follows we call this type of
performance a "deadly deed" to distinguish it from a killing in the strict
sense.

Finally, there are other cases of causing death, such as some killing in
self-defense, which are neither killing in the strict sense nor deadly deeds as
here defined. The proposal adopted or the consciously projected design car-

ried out by persons defending themselves might not extend beyond incapaci-
tating the attacker, but this can result in the attacker's death if the only
available and adequate means to incapacitate the attacker also will result in
mortal wounds.

Deadly deeds and death-causing behavior which are not killing in the strict
sense might or might not be immoral. The fact that killing in the strict sense
always is immoral does not mean that other acts which result in someone's
death are morally acceptable or less immoral than killing in the strict sense.
What is distinctive about deadly deeds and death-causing behavior is that
their morality is not settled by the kinds of acts they are, whereas the morality of killing in the strict sense is settled by the kind of act it is.

Of course, ordinary language, which heavily relies upon observable behavior in classifying acts, does not embody the distinctions we have made. Thus,
to evaluate the morality of various classes of acts which result in death, we
begin from the ordinary conceptions of these acts which are described by
ordinary language and then apply our analysis to the morally significant distinctions in the subject matter.

It is worth noticing that our approach here would be quite impossible in the
law, where actions must be determined by factors about which evidence is
possible. But morality is not primarily a matter of making judgments about
actions, still less a matter of one person judging the actions of another.
Rather, morality is a matter of shaping one's own life toward its fullness.
Hence, distinctions which individuals can respect or ignore in the hidden
depths of their own consciences can be extremely important to morality,
although totally unrealistic as instruments of social control, and so wholly
irrelevant to the law.

In chapter seven we considered cases of killing in self-defense, in war, as
capital punishment, and in cases of necessity to maximize the likelihood of
survival by some persons when two or more are in common peril. Under the
latter we considered the possibility of a nondiscriminatory statute permitting
abortion when the life of the mother is imperiled by continuing pregnancy.
We shall first take up the other cases, and then abortion.

D. Killing in Self-Defense

A self-defensive act which causes death can be killing in the strict sense. A
merchant, for example, might decide to discourage robberies by arming himself with a shotgun and planning to blast at point-blank range the next person
or group who attempt to rob his business. His idea is that the word will go
around among potential robbers who will be deterred by his readiness to kill.
Here the proposal clearly is to kill as a means to preventing future robberies.

Such self-defensive killing is immoral, since the proposal includes as an integral part the bringing about of the death of the next persons who attempt robbery.

A self-defensive performance which causes death can be a deadly deed which is not a morally significant act in itself at all. A mother, for example, might be driven to distraction by her husband's abuse of herself and her children, conceive and carry out the project of poisoning him, yet proceed in such a state of mind that she thinks of no alternative (perhaps having tried many alternatives unsuccessfully in the past), and is moved to act by an irresistible impulse to put an end to her own misery and anguish for her children.

Closely related to self-defense is killing by police officers and prison guards in the line of duty. Like the dutiful young soldier, a police officer or guard might accept this employment without considering that it might imply a demand to cause death. Once in the job the officer or guard might be told that under certain circumstances it is proper to shoot to kill. Without considering alternatives—the contingencies which will require the execution of the policy might seem remote and unreal at the time of training—the officer or guard might accept and carry out this requirement as part of the job. A deadly deed at some point is called for, and the call of duty is obediently answered. Here the conscious project is to bring about death, yet there is not an act of killing in the strict sense, for the officer or guard never considers the proposal to kill and adopts it by a deliberate choice.

It is not at all easy to evaluate the morality of what such a person does. The policy of shooting to kill perhaps involves some ambiguity; it might be imagined to be authorizing something not much different from state-authorized capital punishment or a morally acceptable act of self-defense. One is tempted to say that dutiful guards or officers should make their own conscientious, personal evaluation of the official policy, should make it an alternative to be chosen or rejected, should not obey so docilely.

That is what is generally thought of Nazi functionaries who put people to death in the concentration camps. Perhaps there is a moral defect in someone who does not think of alternatives to killing whenever killing human individuals is required as part of a job. It is hard to imagine anyone considering the interests of others impartially, not merely regarding them as objects to be dealt with, who would not ask, "Is this the right thing to do? Ought I to shoot to kill according to the policy?"

In addition to the moral responsibility of an individual who follows such a policy there is a question about the morality of the act of formulating and adopting a policy of shoot to kill. Perhaps there is a lack of clarity in the thinking of those who make the policy. But there is less room for confusion here than in the minds of individuals who accept it without thinking. If the point is that killing some individuals is a necessary means to limiting the damage they and others will or might do if they are permitted to live (and others not deterred by their example), then the proposal is to bring about death. The making of the policy is immoral. Yet lack of clear understanding, an erroneous opinion that the state has a right to contravene morality, and a sincere desire to promote the public good can combine to mitigate this immorality.

A final set of cases of self-defensive acts which cause death are those, already mentioned by way of example, in which the proposal adopted is simply to defend oneself or others, and the death of the attacker is an accepted effect of the method of self-defense which alone is available and adequate to stop the damage expected from the attack.

Here the act is not killing in the strict sense. Yet it can be immoral. If the attack can probably be evaded by retreat but the defender prefers to repel it with force, then the defender seems to care too little for the attacker's life. If the attack does not threaten death or serious harm, then the defender hardly seems to consider matters impartially if deadly force is used to repel the attack rather than the attacker permitted to cause the harm.

Indeed, in some cases one who is attacked might act immorally by violating a special duty if the evil the attacker threatens is not suffered patiently. Some Christians believe they have a duty to offer no resistance to evil threatened to themselves but may justifiably act only in defense of others. Such persons have a duty to fulfill which precludes self-defensive acts, especially those which might cause death, which could be licit for others.

It was in connection with self-defensive acts which cause death that Thomas Aquinas developed the famous analysis which evolved into the classical doctrine of double effect. In our present treatment we do not talk about "double effect," although the distinctions we have articulated in the present chapter express our own interpretation of the relationship between the moral agent and various states of affairs resulting from the agent's behavior, and we believe our interpretation to be an accurate account of the same thing Aquinas was talking about. We have dealt with the doctrine of double effect elsewhere and will not elaborate here on this subject.[1]

E. Killing in War and Capital Punishment

Turning from self-defensive acts, we next consider killing with public authorization in war and as capital punishment.

Much killing in war clearly has been killing in the strict sense. If the individual soldier perhaps sometimes does deadly deeds without killing in the strict sense—since soldiers might not by choice adopt a proposal to bring about death rather than some alternative proposal—still the soldier very often does realize that there is an alternative to doing deadly deeds, considers the alternative, and for various reasons, such as fear of punishment, rejects it. Moreover, those who plan and lead wars often clearly consider various proposals and deliberately adopt the destruction of enemy personnel as a means to victory. The body counts of the Vietnam war were by no means unique.

Nuclear deterrent strategy, to which the United States remains committed, rests in significant part on the set purpose to retaliate against enemy population centers in the event the United States is attacked. This willingness to retaliate, of course, is conditioned upon the other side attacking, and it is hoped that the deterrent will prevent this occurrence. But the event on which the will to attack is conditioned is not within the power of the United States, and so this condition is a limit, not upon the will to kill, but only upon the execution of the proposal already adopted by the deterrent strategy.

According to the ethics we have proposed and argued for, killing in the strict sense is morally indefensible. Warfare involves much such killing and in particular the nuclear deterrent involves it. Therefore, warfare as it has ordinarily been carried on is immoral. The nuclear deterrent strategy of the United States, a present and continuing national act, is immoral.

Consequentialists are likely to object that moral condemnation of killing in the strict sense in war and in nuclear deterrence is unrealistic. They will argue that the deterrent is justified because it is necessary; if it were given up, the Soviet Union probably would dominate the world, with consequent loss of liberty and other human values for millions of people.

Like all consequentialist arguments, this one attempts to compare incommensurable goods. Millions of human lives are put at risk by the continuation of the balance of terror. A huge part of the world's wealth is expended in maintaining and developing weapons systems which it is hoped will never be used. What is more important, America's willingness to kill millions with H-bombs to protect freedom has been followed by the willingness to kill millions by abortion in the name of liberty. We do not believe that this relationship is a mere coincidence.

Moreover, one need be no marxist nor in any way naive about the vicious consequentialism which marxist leaders use in rationalizing their own brutal methods in pursuit of their utopian purposes to notice that the capitalist world has been and continues to be corrupted by tremendous injustices. These injustices provide marxism with the real reason for its appeal; these injustices, as much as the blessings of liberty, are protected by the military power of the United States and other Western nations, and in particular by the nuclear deterrent.

How can one make up a balance sheet to prove the consequentialist thesis that the evils the maintenance of the deterrent prevents are greater than the evils it involves and helps to maintain?

A nonconsequentialist might point out that traditional Judaic-Christian ethics, which certainly is not consequentialist, on the whole justified war under certain conditions, including killing in the strict sense within the context of war. We admit that war seems to be justified in the Old Testament, and that Christian theologians have argued that it can be justified, although we note that the New Testament does not seem to endorse the justification of war and that a minority position throughout the Christian tradition has been pacifist.

It is not our business here to enter into exegetical and theological arguments. But Christian theologians could consistently have treated war as many of them treated divorce, which was accepted as an institution in the Old Testament but not in the New. Today, Jewish and Christian moralists could conveniently treat publicly authorized killing in the strict sense as they now treat slavery, which was taken for granted in the Old Testament, never clearly condemned in the New, and accepted with many misgivings almost to the present. But slavery now is universally condemned by religious moralists as contrary to the fundamental conceptions of human dignity and equality which are rooted in the Judaic-Christian tradition itself. War could be condemned in the same way.

Apart from the weight of the religious tradition the most forceful nonconsequentialist argument in defense of the justification of war, we think, is one which grants a special moral status to political society. Killing in war is different, according to this view, because it is authorized by law and is necessary not for selfish reasons but for the protection of the common good of society as a whole.[2]

The trouble with this approach is precisely that it treats the political society as if it had a special moral status. If the state were a kind of organism having a life and flourishing of its own, then this assumption might be correct. Individuals would have to be subordinate to the survival and well-being of political society, as parts of one's body are subordinate to one's whole self.

But the organic theory of the state seems to be at odds with the facts. While human persons cannot flourish apart from community, their community can take many forms, of which political society is only one. All of these various forms of community are rooted in the basic human goods and find their justification in their contribution to the flourishing of these goods in persons. Hence the common good is not superior to the goods of individuals but is one aspect of their well-being.

Of course, in their official capacity leaders of a political society can do many things which it would be wrong for individuals to do as private citizens. But this distinction between public and private capacities is merely a matter of the roles and duties of officials, all of which derive from a common commitment to basic human goods, and so none of which can authorize the violation of these goods, which are the principles of political societies no less than of other associations and individual lives.

For one who has been brought up within a particular society, who has been formed in character largely by the demand of the duties of the role of a member of the society, the requirements of moral goodness and of citizenship might appear to be the same, or the former might seem to be wholly defined by the latter. But if one considers the variety and perversity of political societies other than one's own, then it is clear that one who is merely a dutiful citizen of an imperfect polity falls far short of the full moral possibility of humankind. While persons in community can pursue human goods in many ways in which individuals by themselves could not pursue them, no person as a public official or dutiful member of society can be justified in doing what he or she as a person maintaining respect for all the basic human goods would not do.

While we reject every effort to justify killing in the strict sense, we do not embrace as an ethical requirement the demand of total pacifism. Apart from killing in the strict sense there are other acts which might involve a legitimate proposal, as self-defense sometimes does, which can be adopted by the leaders of a community and its soldiers. Such a legitimate proposal could be to impede the unjust use of force by the minimally adequate, available means, even though this means would have as an accepted effect the death of some of those applying or supporting this unjust use of force.

If any warlike acts can be justified in this fashion, they would be essentially defensive acts. The fact that an attacking force might not kill if its unjust objectives could be attained without killing would make the defensive characterization of resistance no less genuine. Those using force unjustly can be resisted by force; meeting resistance, they begin to threaten lives—those resisting are in peril. The defenders who have not generated the conflict and who cannot retreat without conceding the goods they legitimately defend are then justified in using the necessary force to incapacitate the attackers, even though this force is likely to cause fatalities.

But on this account acts of war can be justified only if they are effective against means of force actually being unjustly used or being prepared for unjust use. To demand unconditional surrender would be unjust. To seek by force to overcome evil which is not itself using force also would be unjust. To attack noncombatants—those who are not involved in the unjust use of force—would be killing in the strict sense. The use of terror, torture, and reprisals also would be immoral, for the effect of these techniques would be attained only by means of their destructiveness of human life, which therefore would have to be part of the proposal to adopt them.

A soldier on a battlefield could use weapons available to him with the intent to incapacitate enemies, cause them to surrender, or capture them, even though these weapons might have the effect of killing. But killing would have to be avoided, not sought, whenever possible. A military camp, a supply depot, or a factory producing munitions could be attacked—for instance, with aerial bombardment. But an enemy city as such could not be attacked.

If the problem of nuclear deterrence is considered from this point of view, one can imagine that the United States might design a deterrent which threatened only the military capability of potential enemies. If the proposal whose threatened execution constituted the deterrent included, not the killing of people or the useless destruction of property, but only the destruction of military capacity being or about to be unjustly used—in the process of which deaths and other damage might incidentally be caused—then the threat could be justifiable. (It is a question of fact, beyond the bounds of our present concern, whether such a limited deterrent would be effective and technically feasible.)

The problem with the deterrent strategy as it exists is, not that it deters the unjust use of force by readiness to oppose it, but that the proposal adopted in establishing this policy includes the killing of people as a means to deter potential enemies. Morally this killing already is done, although the hope is never to execute the adopted proposal; ironically, if the proposal ever is executed, this will be because the threat has failed and the actual bringing about of deaths will be pointless.

Capital punishment under modern conditions clearly executes a proposal to kill someone as a means of punishment. However punishment is conceived— whether as a restoration of the balance of justice or as deterrent—the death penalty cannot be carried out without killing in the strict sense. Hence this form of punishment is immoral.

Much of the argument about warfare might be repeated at this point. One factor peculiar to the moral argument about capital punishment is worthy of special mention, however. Many critics of the practice attack it on bases which assume that punishment as such is morally indefensible, that justice does not require that those who voluntarily violate the rights of others and the peace of society pay the price of losing some of their own privileges.

We are not making any such assumption. No doubt, some who are dealt with as criminals bear little or no moral responsibility for their misdeeds and should be treated with the compassion due their helplessness. But some freely choose to violate the rights of others and social order, and they should pay for such violations. Our point with respect to capital punishment simply is that taking the life of a criminal is not an appropriate way of exacting payment due, since those who take the life must themselves voluntarily violate a basic human good. Capital punishment is a bad means to a good end: just punishment.

It will be objected that in chapter seven we did not wholly exclude the possibility of capital punishment as just. It is, at the least, very different from nonvoluntary euthanasia, especially if capital punishment is understood as punishment according to a retributive theory and not according to some consequentialist theory as deterrence or the most effective social method of control of deviant behavior.

We admit that the criminal can reasonably be considered to surrender rights against other members of society as such. A murderer can even be reasonably regarded as surrendering with respect to the society whose law the murder offends the right to equal protection of the law of homicide. Thus, if a murderer is subjected to the death penalty, there might be no unfairness involved in this treatment.

But even if certain criminals have no social right not to be killed and other members of society have no social duty to refrain from killing them, still their lives keep the inherent dignity of the basic human good which they are. Thus killing in the strict sense is excluded as immoral even when it is not unfair, as might be the case when death is inflicted as a penalty, and a grave penalty is truly deserved.

One can imagine a more primitive situation than modern society in which the possible ways of controlling persistent troublemakers are very limited. In such a situation social self-defense might seem to require the certain and permanent incapacitation of the worst offenders for the sake of the safety and peace of others. Whether such troublemakers were morally guilty or insane would be irrelevant, just as the subjective disposition of an individual against whom one might defend one's children is irrelevant. Perhaps no other means of permanent and secure incapacitation would be available than a means which also would cause the death of the offenders.

In such circumstances death might be caused by a society without an act of killing in the strict sense. But a rationale along these lines hardly can be developed in modern society. Still, perhaps some such rationale partly explains the historical origins of practices which have persisted and evolved into socially sanctioned killing in the strict sense, which can never be morally justified.

F. Abortion: Usually Killing in the Strict Sense

We turn now to cases of necessity in which one or more members of a group of persons in common peril are killed in order to maximize the average probability of survival of some members of the group. From a moral point of view such cases must be judged in the first instance on the basis of whether the killing is such in the strict sense or not.

To kill one member of a party in order to cannibalize him or her clearly involves the adoption of a proposal to bring about the victim's death. This is killing in the strict sense; it cannot be justified.

But to adopt a proposal to lighten a sinking lifeboat by tossing overboard some of the passengers only brings about death as an effect of the act; it is foreseen but not included in the proposal. A sign of this is that if the passengers forcibly ejected managed to find other means of surviving, this would in no way thwart the purpose of throwing them overboard. Still, if this is not killing in the strict sense, it can be immoral because of unfairness. This is the point of the argument that passengers have a right to secure passage to which the dutiful sailors must yield and that everyone has a right to fair processes of selection if some must be dealt with in a way likely to cause death.

Other imaginary cases of killing in a situation of necessity can be dealt with similarly. But most interesting is the problem of the morality of abortion. This matter having been dealt with at length elsewhere, however, we offer here only a summary treatment.[3]

A fundamental issue to be disposed of at the outset is the question whether the unborn are morally to be considered persons whose lives are instances of that human life which is a basic human good and principle of morality. No amount of criticism of countertheories, which are erected upon speculative metaphysical premises, can demonstrate that these theories are false. It is not logically impossible that at some state of development the unborn are not persons, that their lives are not univocally called "human lives."

However, as a matter of biological fact human life does not begin; it is continuously transmitted. At conception a new human individual emerges; sometimes this new individual subsequently divides into two or more (identical twins). Our argument against dualism in chapter eleven, section H, removes most of the grounds which are proposed for imagining that such incipient human individuals are not persons. There is a prima facie basis for thinking that they are, and this basis cannot be overturned by any contrary speculation. Hence, for moral purposes the unborn ought to be considered persons, their lives instances of the good of human life which is inviolable, from conception onward.[4] To be willing to kill what for all one knows or ever can know is a person is to be willing to kill a human person. Speculations to the contrary are not logically absurd but they are morally irrelevant.

In a great many cases the proposal to have or to do an abortion includes the bringing about of the death of the unborn, and thus abortion is in such cases killing in the strict sense, which cannot be moral. This is clearly so when abortion is promoted as a method of population control or of family limitation, when abortion is justified by arguing that it is cheaper and perhaps safer to eliminate unwanted babies early in pregnancy than to permit them to be born alive, perhaps then to become welfare recipients.[5]

Through 1963 the Planned Parenthood Federation of America issued a pamphlet, *Plan Your Children for Health and Happiness,* which included an explanation of the difference between contraception and abortion: "An abortion requires an operation. It kills the life of a baby after it has begun." The 1964 revision omitted this explanation. As even proponents of abortion and other killing on consequentialist grounds have admitted, ludicrous semantic gymnastics have been employed in recent years to rationalize abortion as something other than what it is:

> The process of eroding the old ethic and substituting the new has already begun. It may be seen most clearly in changing attitudes toward human abortion. In defiance of the long held Western ethic of intrinsic and equal value for every human life regardless of its stage, condition, or status, abortion is becoming accepted by society as moral, right, and even necessary. It is worth noting that this shift in public attitude has affected the churches, the laws, and public policy rather than the reverse. Since the old ethic has not yet been fully displaced it has been necessary to separate the idea of abortion from the idea of killing, which continues to be socially abhorrent. The result has been a curious avoidance of the scientific fact, which everyone really knows, that human life begins at conception and is continuous whether intra- or extra-uterine until death. The very considerable semantic gymnastics which are required to rationalize abortion as anything but taking a human life would be ludicrous if they were not often put forth under socially impeccable auspices. It is suggested that this schizophrenic sort of subterfuge is necessary because while a new ethic is being accepted the old one has not yet been rejected.[6]

In other words, the need for rationalization demands that abortion not be recognized as what it generally is: killing in the strict sense.

In the 1973 *Abortion Cases* the United States Supreme Court proceeded on the assumption of fact that there was strong public support for the view that human life does not begin until birth. But public opinion sampling in 1975 showed that only 8 percent of women and 12 percent of men believe this, while the majority of people continue to consider the fetus a human life or human person even at conception or very early in the gestational period.[7] Moreover, anyone familiar with the medical literature on abortion techniques knows that an important consideration in choice of timing and technique is to avoid the unwanted outcome of a live-born and viable infant. The best technique is one which guarantees the death of the unborn as well as other desiderata. This makes clear that typically abortion is killing in the strict sense: It executes the immoral proposal, adopted by choice in preference to other possibilities considered deliberately, to kill human individuals whose lives are judged undesirable.

It is important to notice, however, that while those who advocate and perform abortions to exterminate the unwanted can hardly be clear of an act of killing in the strict sense, some women who undergo abortions very likely either are not morally responsible or are not responsible in the same way for the killing of their unborn children. It is quite possible that many women, especially those who are young and unsophisticated, are more or less completely deceived by propaganda into thinking that they are only accepting another form of contraception when they are in fact accepting some form of abortion.

It also is possible that some women, again especially those who are young and unsophisticated, accept abortion without adopting the proposal by their own choice, because they act under emotional strain and the pressure of other people, such as parents, social workers, physicians, religious counselors, and so on. While there might be elements of self-deception in some such cases and while the situation might have been shaped by previous wrongful acts for which such a woman had some moral responsibility, she would not be morally responsible for killing in the strict sense. In a society in which killing becomes accepted and even made a duty in order to solve various problems those who shape opinions, attitudes, and institutions bear responsibility for killings which less sophisticated members of society immediately effect, but effect rather as half-conscious instruments than as fully responsible principals.

In some cases the termination of pregnancy is brought about by the removal of a nonviable unborn child without the adoption of a proposal which is or includes the bringing about of the death of the child, but rather in the carrying out of a proposal which does include the removal of the child from the mother. In such cases an act of abortion in the strict sense is done, but such an act of abortion is not an act of killing in the strict sense. The causing of death is not part of the abortional act but is a consequence of it.

Cases which have been considered indirect abortion by those applying a traditional double-effect analysis are instances in which the death of the unborn is caused as a consequence of an act without being included in the proposal carried out in the act. For example, if a cancerous pregnant uterus is removed to stop the disease, the death of the unborn is foreseen and accepted as an effect of the operation but is not chosen as a means or part of a means to any desired end. A sign of this is the fact that in case the same operation were indicated for a nonpregnant woman, it might be done with the same purpose and carried out in the same way.

Traditional double-effect analysis, however, tended to identify direct abortion with a subclass of killing in the strict sense. Thus, a tubal pregnancy, it was argued, might be removed because of the pathology of the tube itself; an embryotomy could not be justified because the operation physically directly attacked the baby.[8]

Our analysis would classify the removal of a tubal pregnancy from its inappropriate site of development in the tube as an act of removal, which could be chosen for the sake of preventing otherwise inevitable damage to the mother by the continuing development of the fetus with almost no hope of its survival. The death of the growing child who is removed in such a case would be foreseen and accepted but would not need to be included in the proposal adopted, and thus killing in the strict sense need not be done. We think that embryotomy can be analyzed similarly.[9]

In criticizing a previous statement of our approach Paul Ramsey argued that it would not *justify* certain instances of removing a fetus which seem, intuitively, to be little different from the cases which it can be used to justify. The cases Ramsey mentions are ones in which surgery is needed to remove a displaced, diseased appendix or a damaged aorta in a pregnant woman, and the only feasible approach to the site of the problem is through the pregnant uterus, with the inevitable death of the unborn child prior to the subsequent act of surgical repair of the primary problem.[10]

In reply we point out first that whether the removal of the fetus is justified in such cases is one question; whether its removal is killing in the strict sense is another. On our analysis the proposal to remove the unborn baby from its natural site, the site required for its survival, need not include the proposal to kill the baby or to bring about its death, even though its death is foreseen as an inevitable consequence of its removal. Removal here has a different purpose: access to the site for needed surgery. The fact that the removal of the fetus is a distinct act from the subsequent surgery does not mean that this distinct act, precisely as an act which is a means to an end, is an act of killing. In the cases Ramsey suggests, the death of the child can be voluntary in the limited sense only that it is accepted as a foreseen effect.

We also point out in reply to Ramsey that our analysis does not include a thesis which he mistakenly thought to be part of the earlier analysis: abortional acts which are not acts of killing in the strict sense are automatically ethically justified. The earlier analysis included this discussion of abortion in cases in which a woman conceives as a result of rape:

> But what about the rare case in which a woman is raped and conceives a child of her attacker? She has not had a choice; the child has come to be through no act of hers. Moreover, it is not clear that her precise concern is to kill the child. She simply does not wish to bear it. If the artificial uterus were available, she might be happy to have the baby removed and placed in such a device, later to be born and cared for as any infant that becomes a social charge. Now, clearly, one could not object if that were done. May the death of the child that is in fact brought about by aborting it actually be unintended [that is, outside the proposal] in this case? I believe that the answer must be yes.
>
> But this answer does not mean that abortion in such a case would be ethically right. I fail to see what basic human good is achieved if the

developing baby is aborted. The victim of rape has been violated and has a good reason to resent it. Yet the unborn infant is not the attacker. It is hers as much as his. She does not wish to bear it—an understandable emotional reaction. But really at stake is only such trouble, risk and inconvenience as is attendant on any pregnancy. To kill the baby for the sake of such goods reveals an attitude toward human life that is not in keeping with its inherently immeasurable dignity. One of the simpler modes of obligation is violated—that which requires us to do good to another when we can and there is no serious reason not to do it.[11]

Ramsey judged that an analysis admitting a distinction between removal of the fetus and killing in the strict sense allowed almost all abortions to become cases of removal. He also thought that the argument against removal in the second paragraph amounted to no more than an appeal to a duty of charity.[12]

We do not deny that in an argument before an imaginary moral tribunal a great many abortions might be rationalized as removal of the unborn and denied to be killing in the strict sense. But ethics is not a matter of judgments before moral tribunals, real or imaginary. It is a question of shaping one's own life, and in responding to this question rationalization gets one nowhere but deep into the quicksand of false conscience. In actual fact, as we have pointed out, many abortions are carried out precisely by way of executing proposals to get rid of unwanted children. Even those having and doing such abortions must admit that the proposal they execute to get rid of a child amounts to a proposal to kill it. These are in fact killings in the strict sense for all those concerned who by choice adopt a proposal to kill the unwanted as a solution to the problems their survival would entail.

The second paragraph of the passage quoted above should have warned Ramsey that even in cases in which abortion is not killing in the strict sense the justification of abortion is a further and distinct question. The mode of obligation cited is what we would regard, not as a matter of charity, but as a form of responsibility even more elemental than the duties which belong to persons because of their roles in established relationships, defined by the accepted institutions of society. From the latter derive the system of rights and duties which articulate the requirements of justice, but there is much more to morality than justice, and many moral responsibilities which do not pertain to justice are more fundamental and stricter than those which do.

Still, in some cases in which abortion might be considered as a proposal which would not include or amount to the bringing about of the death of the unborn child, duties would preclude the moral justifiability of adopting the proposal. A woman who willingly engages in sexual intercourse, knowing that she might become pregnant, certainly implicitly accepts the role of mother, and a primary duty of this role is to care for and protect one's children. It is true that like other duties arising from a role, this duty only binds under the condition that one is not prevented by some other obligation from fulfilling it. A woman, especially if she is already a mother, has an obligation to preserve her own life, and this obligation might reasonably seem to her to require that she consent to the removal of a cancerous uterus or surgery to repair a damaged aorta, even though such procedures would make it impossible to fulfill her motherly duty to her unborn child. But in the absence of some compelling obstacle to fulfilling a parental duty an unborn child has a moral right to the care, support, and defense of both parents who have willingly taken part in initiating its life.

Similarly, even if the proposal of abortion is not a proposal to kill the unborn, the golden rule or principle of universalizability would preclude in most instances moral justification for abortion. No one would wish others to prefer their comfort and convenience to one's own life, but most who propose abortion consider the interests of the unborn with just such a partial and biased perspective. Likewise, in any sincere moral reflection considerations of the health of the mother, when life is not truly threatened, could not be accepted as a warrant for a removal of the fetus which is foreseen to cause its inevitable death.

The narrowness of the class of cases in which the proposal to abort (justifiable or not) is not equivalent to a proposal to kill the unborn can be made clearest perhaps by imagining the situation which would obtain if an artificial uterus, capable of sustaining an infant's life at any time after conception, were widely and cheaply available. The uterus would be used in cases of removal of the unborn when the intent was not to kill the child. It would not be used when the point of the abortion was to exterminate the unwanted as a solution to the problem they present.

Of the approximately one million abortions carried out in the United States each year, how many would be placed in the artificial uterus? Very few, for the unwanted baby would not be cared for in this manner. Such care would frustrate the whole point of aborting unwanted babies: to get rid of them so that they shall not live to make their claim upon their parents and upon society at large.

G. Suicide and Causing One's Own Death

We turn now to the consideration of cases in which one brings about one's own death. Even in ordinary language some ethically significant distinctions are made in speaking of this, for one does not call "suicide" all cases in which someone causes his or her own death. Most people who consider suicide immoral do not class martyrs and heroes as suicides, since "suicide" suggests an act of killing oneself.[13] Yet not all who commit suicide do a moral act of killing in the strict sense.

In cases in which suicide is an act of killing in the strict sense the proposal to kill oneself is among the proposals one considers in deliberation, and this proposal is adopted by choice as preferable to alternatives. For example, a person who for some reason is suffering greatly might think: "I wish I no longer had to suffer as I am suffering. If I were dead, my suffering would be at an end. But I am not likely to die soon. I could kill myself. But I fear death and what might follow after it. I could put up with my misery and perhaps find some other way out." One thinking in this way is deliberating. In saying "I could kill myself" suicide is proposed. If this proposal is adopted, one's moral act is killing in the strict sense. As in other instances this act is incompatible with the basic good of human life, and it cannot morally be justified, regardless of what else might be the case.

One can propose to kill oneself without saying to oneself "I could kill myself." One might say something which one would accept as equivalent in meaning: "I could destroy myself," "I could rub myself out," or something of the sort. Again, one might say something which one would admit amounts to "I could kill myself" although not equivalent in meaning to it, such as "I could shoot myself," when what one has in mind is shooting oneself in the head and thereby causing death, not merely shooting oneself to cause a wound.

From such suicidal acts which clearly are cases of killing oneself in the strict sense we distinguish deadly deeds people do upon themselves which are not cases of killing in the strict sense. Some of these suicidal deeds are not moral acts at all; others are acts which execute some choice other than a proposal to kill oneself.

A person who is suffering severe psychological stress, even though not mentally ill, can reach a point at which deliberation and choice become impossible. Perhaps the thought of suicide has come back again and again, and the proposal has been rejected as often as it has returned. But at some point the possibility of a deadly deed against oneself can become obsessive. Without one's own choice every alternative is blocked from consciousness. Only one thought remains: "I will kill myself." A person in this state of mind is not necessarily insane. Moreover, the performance which follows carries out a conscious project. But it is not a moral act of killing in the strict sense, because the project is not a proposal adopted by choice. It is an obsessive thought whose appeal draws the individual into its execution without a personal commitment.

Someone with intimate knowledge of suicidal thinking is likely to point out that we are oversimplifying the complexity of such thinking. We agree, but our purpose is not to supply a phenomenology of suicide.[14] Perhaps unconscious determinants play as large a role as conscious ones in the genesis of the deadly deed against oneself. Moreover, even when one is conscious of what one is doing, the proposal can involve a certain ambiguity. One who thinks "I could take the pills" might not be certain whether the pills will be deadly or not, and might not be clear whether the proposal amounts to "I could kill myself if the pills are deadly" or only to "I could make everyone see how much I am suffering." We are not excluding any of this complexity and ambiguity by the distinctions we are making. Rather, we are suggesting how complex and ambiguous cases must be understood by reference to clearer cases in which either a suicidal proposal is adopted or a deadly deed against oneself clearly carried out without any commitment.

While the suicidal commitment which is killing oneself in the strict sense cannot be morally justified, the deadly deed against oneself without commitment cannot be morally blameworthy in itself, for it is not a morally significant act at all. If there is any responsibility for it on the individual's part at all, this responsibility is for earlier acts or failings, in which for instance, available help was voluntarily refused when it could and ought to have been accepted. But this responsibility is far from being identical with that for a suicidal commitment, and in the case of a deadly deed against oneself probably is minimal, since most people do take care of themselves if they can.

As for the more complex and confused states of mind from which suicidal behavior usually emerges, no one can begin to judge the moral quality of another and hardly can begin to judge oneself. A person who is upright certainly will not lightly play with thoughts of suicide and will not easily adopt any ambiguous proposal which could imply that one's own death be brought about. One who has come to disrespect human life in other instances, however, might easily do so.

The impossibility of judging, it should be noticed, is double-edged. People who have killed themselves ought not to be condemned and despised. But people who are contemplating killing themselves ought not to be reassured that such a deed would carry no grave moral responsibility. The innocence of the latter can be ascertained no more than the guilt of the former.

Some deadly deeds against oneself execute choices which are not suicidal choices. One might believe that some fundamental commitment one previously made demands that one here and now kill oneself; perhaps one has so perfectly integrated this commitment that one proceeds with no further deliberation and choice to do what seems necessary and inevitable. For example, a person who believes in God might believe that God is here and now commanding suicide. Given sufficiently blind faith, such an individual might not think of disobeying. Similarly, those in certain cultures where ritual self-destruction is expected in certain situations perhaps carry out the ritual without considering breaking with received customs.

In cases such as these the morally relevant choice and the locus of responsibility is not in respect to the self-destructive deed, about which there was no choice at all, but in respect to the acceptance of the religion or culture which demands such deeds. And even this acceptance might have been voluntary not by being the content of a proposal adopted by choice but only by being uncritically accepted by a person who could and should have examined more carefully the cultural forms which were handed down.

In addition to properly suicidal acts and to deadly deeds against oneself which are not acts of killing in the strict sense, there are still other cases in which individuals contribute to the causation of their own deaths by acts which are morally significant but which in no way execute proposals which are properly suicidal. Typical martyrs lay down their lives. The death could be avoided if the martyr were willing to do something believed wrong or to leave unfulfilled some duty which is accepted as compelling. But the martyr refuses to avoid death by compromise or evasion of duty. Such persons do only what they believe to be morally required; the consequent loss of their own lives is willingly accepted by martyrs, neither sought nor chosen as a means to anything.

The martyr reasons somewhat as follows: "I would like to please everyone and to stay alive. But they are demanding of me that I do what I believe to be wrong or that I omit doing what I believe to be my sacred mission. They threaten me with death if I do not meet their demands. But if I were to comply with their threat, I would be doing evil in order that the good of saving my life might follow from it. This I may not do. Therefore, I must stand as long as I can in accord with my conscience, even though they are likely to kill me or torture me into submission."

Someone who does not understand the martyr's reasoning is likely to consider the martyr a suicide. But martyrs who reason thus do not propose to bring about their own deaths. The martyr bears witness to a profound commitment, first of all before the persecutors themselves. The latter can and in the martyr's view should accept this testimony and approve the rightness of the commitment. The martyr's refusal to give in does not bring about the persecutor's act of killing; the martyr only fails to win over the persecutor and to forestall the deadly deed.

Not all who cause their own deaths as a demonstration of commitment are typical martyrs. A war protestor might propose: "I wish to make clear the horror of war. I could douse myself with gasoline and set myself afire." Someone entertaining this proposal might admit that it is suicidal. If so, the execution of the proposal, adopted by choice, would be an act of killing in the strict sense. But if the suicidal character of this proposal were not admitted, the clearheadedness of deliberation might be questioned. The very point of the proposal seems to be that the horror of this manner of dying will emphatically communicate the horror of the war being protested. If this is so, the proposal is to kill oneself in the service of peace, and the adoption of this means cannot be consistent with respect for the good of human life. Of course, it is quite possible for an upright person to be terribly confused.

Certain nonsuicidal acts which bring about an individual's own death would be held to be morally wrong by most people. For example, a daredevil might accept very high risks of death carrying out performances which do not involve great skill or other excellent qualities. He might do this in order to create a sensation by pandering to morbid curiosity and hoping to acquire great wealth with little effort.

While not proposing to kill himself, while indeed hoping to survive to enjoy the wealth, the daredevil seems clearly to have an immoral attitude toward the good of human life. If he brings about his death, he is not a suicide, but he bears a grave moral responsibility because of his disregard for the goodness of his own life.

In what ways might acts which are not suicidal but are self-destructive in results be immoral?

In the first place, such acts remove an individual from human community and in doing so are likely to leave behind some unfulfilled responsibilities. The shock of anyone's death always creates a certain burden and hardship for others, especially when the death comes about violently and seems avoidable. Moreover, the example of disrespect for life affects other people who are tempted to destroy themselves or to kill others. Bringing about one's own death, in other words, serves as a bad example.

In the second place, those who unnecessarily cause their own deaths are taking an irreversible step into darkness. A nonbeliever will not accept concerns about an afterlife. But nonbelief cannot eliminate Hamlet's perhaps: "perhaps to dream." It is presumptuous to suppose that one knows that there can be nothing to fear after death.

In the third place, even if there is no offense against others in bringing about one's death unnecessarily and even if the act is not the execution of a suicidal proposal, still such an act seems to undermine morality in a radical way. In bringing about one's death one removes oneself from the range of the primal demand: to serve human goods, to do what one can, to communicate human meaning to every aspect of life and the world. Perhaps this point is what Wittgenstein—himself tormented by a temptation to commit suicide—meant when he wrote that if suicide is allowed, everything is allowed, and he added, "This throws light on the nature of ethics, for suicide is, so to speak, the elementary sin."[15]

Of course, we hold that suicide which is killing in the strict sense is necessarily immoral simply because it violates the basic good of human life. One who deliberately chooses to end his or her own life constitutes by this commitment a self-murderous self. But considerations which tell against even nonsuicidal acts which bring about a person's own death also argue against the moral justifiability of suicidal acts, which execute a proposal to destroy one's own life.

H. Active Euthanasia: Voluntary and Nonvoluntary

Considering matters from a moral point of view and from the side of the one whose life is to be ended, voluntary euthanasia is not significantly different from other cases of suicide. The proposal is to bring about death as a means to ending suffering. This proposal, if adopted and executed, is an instance of killing in the strict sense. It can never be morally justified.

Of course, a person who is in severe pain and who seeks death to escape it is likely to have mitigated responsibility or even to be drawn into acceptance without a deliberate choice, just as is the case with others whose suffering drives them to a deadly deed against themselves.

However, if an individual plans to seek euthanasia and arranges for it well in advance of the time of suffering, then the possibility that the demand for death is not an expression of deliberate choice is greatly lessened. The conditions which from the point of view of proponents of euthanasia are optimum for making a decision about the matter are precisely the conditions in which the decision is likely to be a morally unjustifiable act of killing in the strict sense.

Considering voluntary euthanasia from the point of view of the person who would carry out the killing, matters seem no better from a moral viewpoint. The performance can hardly fail to be an execution of a deliberate choice; the one carrying out the killing can hardly be driven to it, nor can anyone in the present culture accept the duty unquestioningly.

Of course, when a family member kills a relative under the present legal conditions, there is considerable likelihood that pressures of emotion are an important factor, and there is a possibility that no act of killing is done. But we are now thinking of the moral responsibility of someone who would carry out requested euthanasia if the practice were legalized, through acting by deliberate choice and perhaps in a professional capacity.

It might be objected that not everyone believes that human life itself is a basic good. Perhaps this belief is sincere. In such a case individuals seeking euthanasia and those providing this service would be doing nothing immoral by deliberate choice, for they would be acting upon a sincere belief, even if this belief is mistaken. After all, people are responsible, not for what they actually do, but for what they sincerely believe they are doing. How can one consider immoral the acts of those who seek or provide beneficent euthanasia in acting upon the conviction that human life is merely an instrumental good?

Our first response to this objection is that we are concerned here, not to judge anyone, but only to clarify sound guidelines for morally responsible deliberation and choice. We have argued in chapter eleven, section H, against the instrumentalist view of human life. If it is false, then those who shape their lives on this false assumption at the least are seriously mistaken about a matter of basic human concern. This mistake can hardly fail to lead to serious consequences for their attitudes and behavior toward other persons in many instances in which life is at stake.

But a further response to this objection is needed. The insight that human life is a basic good of persons is not a matter of empirical fact; it is a principle of practical reasoning. This principle underlies large areas of everyone's rational behavior. It is not easy to be mistaken about the inherent goodness of life, its inviolability, its worthiness of respect in every instance without exception. Somewhere there must be moral responsibility for a bias which hides and distorts so fundamental a truth.

This responsibility might be in an individual's own previous immoral choices. The opinion that life is not a basic good which deserves respect might be an effect of personal rationalization. Then again there is a tendency for this false opinion to attain the status of a climate of opinion by the formation of a social or cultural bias against human life. Here those who form opinion, shape the law, provide what ought to be scholarly reflection upon morality, and so on are the morally responsible agents of the moral blindness of others.

Nonvoluntary euthanasia also clearly proposes death as a treatment of choice. The act hardly can fail to be killing in the strict sense. And in addition to the violation of the good of life, the rights of those to be killed also will be violated—for example, by denial to them of equal protection of the laws. Nonvoluntary euthanasia would violate both life and justice.

On our analysis abortion is a subclass of nonvoluntary euthanasia. It is especially complicated, since in the case of abortion there are instances in which the child's death results from some act which is not itself the execution of a proposal that the child should die. In cases in which the retarded, the insane, the senile, or others would be terminated by nonvoluntary euthanasia it is difficult to think of circumstances in which their deaths would be caused otherwise than by the carrying out of the proposal that they should die, on the rationalization that their lives are not worth living and that they will be better off dead.

It will be objected that some who carried out nonvoluntary euthanasia—or who now promote it—might be motivated by genuine sympathy for others. We do not deny this possibility, although we suspect that the movement for euthanasia would have little political power were it not also motivated by the desire to get rid of the burden of unwanted people.

The important point is that sympathy, like other emotions, can lead to grossly immoral acts. Not all immorality is explicit egoism and self-indulgence. By sympathy one is identified with another psychologically, just as by patriotism one is identified with one's country, by racism with one's race, and so on. These emotions are morally neutral in themselves. They do permit one, however, to act immorally while to seem not to act out of self-interest. Sympathy together with a fanatical attachment to the good of avoiding pain and suffering can lead to grossly immoral violations of the good of life and rights of others in the ultimate form of paternalism: the killing of people for their own good.

Like all forms of paternalism, beneficent euthanasia would involve the arrogant presumption that one can determine on the basis of one's own scheme of values what is best for others who might well not share that scheme. And like all forms of paternalism which become institutionalized, beneficent euthanasia could easily become a mask for intentional injustices toward those whose lives were "kindly" extinguished—extinguished in the interests of others or society at large.

I. Omissions, Killing, and Letting Die

The preceding treatment has been concerned with instances in which people bring about death by an outward performance. We now turn to a consideration of cases in which individuals refuse treatment for themselves or others, or withhold treatment, or fail or neglect to give it. To apply the moral theory which we articulated in chapter eleven to such cases we must first say something about omissions.

If people act when they carry out a proposal which they have adopted by choice, certain cases of outward nonperformance must count as human actions. One can adopt a proposal and carry it out by deliberately not causing or preventing something which one could cause or prevent. One's choice not to cause or prevent something can be a way of realizing a state of affairs one considers somehow desirable. For example, one might adopt the proposal to protest against a government policy permitting the use of public funds for abortion by not paying certain taxes. In this case one aims to realize a desired state of affairs by means of nonconformance with the demands of the law. The nonconformance need involve no outward performance at all.

Omissions of this type—those in which one undertakes to realize a proposed state of affairs by not causing or preventing something—are very important for understanding the morality of withholding treatment from dying patients, refusing treatment proposed for oneself, and in general letting people die.

On the analysis of this sort of omission which we just now stated it clearly is possible to kill in the strict sense by deliberately letting someone die. If one adopts the proposal to bring about a person's death and realizes this proposal by not behaving as one otherwise would behave, then one is committed to the state of affairs which includes the person's death. This commitment, although carried out by a nonperformance, is morally speaking an act of killing. It involves the adoption and execution of a proposal contrary to the basic good of human life. Thus, any case in which one chooses the proposal that a person die and on this basis allows the person to die is necessarily immoral.

For example, if a child is born suffering from various defects and if the physicians and parents decide that the child, the family, and society will all be better off if the burdens entailed by the child's continued life are forestalled by its death, and if they therefore adopt the proposal not to perform a simple operation, which otherwise would be done, so that the child will die, then the parents and physicians morally speaking kill the child—"kill" in the strict sense clarified at the beginning of this chapter. The fact that there is no blood spilled, no poison injected, that the death certificate can honestly show that the child has died from complications arising from its defective condition— none of this is morally relevant. The moral act is no different from any other moral act of murder.

The same thing will be true in every instance in which a judgment is made that someone—whether oneself or another—would be better off dead, the proposal to bring about death by not causing or preventing something is considered and adopted, and this proposal is executed by outward nonperformance of behavior which one otherwise might have attempted.

Moreover, it must be noticed that hastening death is bringing about death; no one lives forever, and so all killing merely hastens death. The essential factor from a moral point of view is, not whether a person killed already is dying, but whether one's performance or omission executes a proposal that one bring about the state of affairs which includes the person's being dead when one thinks that otherwise they might be alive.

It is worth noting that one's adopting a proposal to bring about a person's death does not require that one regard the person's death as desirable in itself, or that one will be pleased when it occurs. One might regret that a patient is suffering from a painful and mortal disease; one might wish that a retarded, insane, or senile person were normal and vigorously healthy. One might feel deep compassion for the person to be killed; one might be very reluctant to kill the person; one might feel very sad when the person dies. Nevertheless, if one adopts a proposal to hasten death—for example, by injecting an overdose of opiates—one does an act of killing in the strict sense. The commitment contrary to the good of life is made, although it is made in a situation in which alternatives lack much of their ordinary appeal, and although it is made with great sadness and executed with great regret.

This point is not too difficult to grasp in cases of action which involves an outward performance. But the same thing is just as true when the proposed method of killing is by not causing or preventing something. The murderous quality of an omission can more easily be overlooked or rationalized, however, due to confusion between the adoption of the proposal and the emotional situation and wishes which accompany the adoption of the proposal.

One killing by omission in a case of this sort both wants and does not want dead the person who is to be killed. The wanting is the voluntary adoption of the proposal that the person be dead; this is what is morally determinative. The not-wanting is in the wishes that things might be otherwise, the feelings of sadness and so forth with which the chosen means to the desired good—for example, release from suffering—are brought about.[16]

The preceding analysis clarifies a point which has been made by James Rachels. He maintains that since most people agree that it is morally permissible to allow someone to die under certain circumstances, it is "patently cruel" to refuse to kill such a person painlessly when the process of dying would be painful.[17]

If the letting die is the execution of a proposal that the person die, then Rachels is right in thinking that it is morally worse to let a person die painfully than to kill the person painlessly. Cruelty does add to the malice of murder. But it does not follow that killing people painlessly is permissible—that there is a right to die quickly. On the supposition that the performance and the nonperformance both would be ways of executing a murderous proposal, both would have the immoral character of murder. However, as we shall make clear shortly, not every case of refusing or withholding potentially life-prolonging treatment is an action shaped by a proposal to bring about someone's death.

Michael Tooley and others also have criticized those who hold that there is a significant moral difference between killing a person and letting the person die.[18] Their criticism is that if one considers a case of killing and a case of letting die between which there is no difference except that in the one the death is brought about by a performance which causes it while in the other it is brought about by not causing or preventing something, then there is no moral difference between the two cases.

We agree. Both actions are killing in the strict sense; neither can ever be moral. However, not every instance in which someone deliberately lets another die is an action shaped by the proposal that the person whose death is accepted should die or die sooner than would otherwise be the case. We turn now to the consideration of such deliberate omissions which, considered from a moral point of view, are not acts of killing.

J. Nontreatment and Refusal of Treatment

The fundamental point about these omissions is that one can omit to do some good or prevent some evil without adopting any proposal which either is opposed to the good or embraces (as means) the evil whose occurrence one accepts. This possibility is most obviously instantiated when one must forgo doing a certain good or preventing a certain evil because one has a duty, incompatible with doing the good or preventing the evil, to do some other good or prevent some other evil.

For example, in an emergency situation in which many people are seriously injured and the medical resources—including time and personnel—are limited, those making decisions must choose to treat some and put off the treatment of others, perhaps with fatal consequences to those not treated first. The nontreatment of those who are not treated is deliberate; even their deaths might be foreseen as an inevitable consequence and knowingly accepted when the decision to treat others is made. Yet plainly the nontreatment of those who are not treated need involve no proposal that these people should die or die more quickly than they otherwise would. Provided there is no partiality or other breach of faith with those not treated, the execution of a proposal to save others does not embrace the death of those who die, and no immorality is done.

In the preceding example there is a certain lack of choice, in that the situation itself prohibits one from treating everyone. There are other situations in which someone forgoes doing something good because of the opportunity to do something else which also is good but incompatible with the adoption and execution of the first proposal. This situation arises whenever there is a choice between alternatives, any of which can be adopted without moral fault. It can arise in a specific case in which one and only one alternative would involve acting to save a person's life.

For example, physicians can refuse to accept additional patients, even though they know that their refusal will lead to a patient's earlier death, without proposing that the patient die. Physicians might simply be choosing to limit their practice at a level which permits them to take reasonable care of their children's personal needs, of their own health, their religious duties, and other legitimate concerns.

Obviously there are limits. Physicians who refuse occasionally to interrupt their recreation to tend to a severe medical emergency might not be in violation of medical ethics or any specific duty, but any person with a proper level of dedication will be generous with time and talents in the service of others, and all who are fair-minded will do to others as they would wish others to do to them and to their own loved ones. In other words, the golden rule sets a very important moral limit beyond which an upright person will not go in omitting to serve the needs of others. To violate this limit is just as immoral—and can show just as vicious a disposition—as to violate the good of life by killing in the strict sense.

There is another type of reason for forgoing doing good which involves no disrespect for the good which would be realized by the action. One might notice that doing the action good in itself will in fact bring about many undesirable consequences. And one might choose not to adopt the proposal to do the good in order to avoid accepting these various bad consequences. This situation is exemplified in a very important way in many instances in which potentially life-prolonging treatment is refused, withheld, or withdrawn—even in the case of a patient who is not dying—because of the expected disadvantages of accepting, carrying out, or continuing treatment.

In chapter nine we have articulated grounds on which someone might reasonably consider treatment undesirable: if the treatment is experimental or risky, if it would be painful or otherwise experienced negatively, if it would interfere with activities or experiences the patient might otherwise enjoy, if it would conflict with some moral or religious principle to which the patient adheres, if it would be psychologically repugnant to the patient, or if the financial or other impact of the treatment upon other persons would constitute a compelling reason to refuse treatment.

The moral legitimacy of refusing treatment in some cases on some such grounds certainly was part of what Pius XII was indicating by his famous distinction between ordinary and extraordinary means of treatment. The Pope defined "extraordinary means" as ones which involve a "great burden," and he allowed that one could morally forgo the use of extraordinary means.[19]

The conception of extraordinary means clearly is abused, however, when the proposal is to bring about death by the omission of treatment, and the difficulties of the treatment are pointed to by way of rationalizing the murderous act. If it is decided that a person would be better off dead and that treatment which would be given to another will be withheld because of the poor quality of the life to be preserved, then the focus in decision is not upon the means and its disadvantageous consequences. Rather, what is feared is that the means would be effective, that life would be preserved, and that the life itself and its consequences would be a burden.

Moreover, even when treatment is refused, withheld, or withdrawn because of an objection to the means—and without the adopting of a proposal to bring about death—there still can be a serious moral failing.

A person who refuses lifesaving or life-prolonging treatment, not on a suicidal proposal but because of great repugnance for the treatment itself, might have an obligation to maintain life longer in order to fulfill duties toward others.

For example, someone on dialysis might wish to give up the treatment because of the difficulties it involves, and some persons in this situation could discontinue treatment and accept death without moral fault. But a parent with children in need of continued care, a professional person with grave responsibilities, and many other persons who can prolong their lives at considerable sacrifice to themselves are morally bound to do so, even by this extraordinary means, because they have accepted duties which others are entitled to have fulfilled, and persons who love the goods as one ought will faithfully fulfill duties toward others at considerable cost to themselves.

Similarly, if one refuses, withholds, or withdraws lifesaving or life-prolonging treatment for another because of the grave burdens entailed by such treatment, the burdens must be grave indeed. This is especially clear in cases in which the patient is not dying—for example, cases of defective infants. One must be quite sure, at the least, that with no suicidal proposal one would in the patient's place not wish the treatment. Otherwise, one accepts moral responsibility for a very grave wrong toward the patient.

As with actions involving a positive performance, so with omissions there can be cases in which the omission results from a project which embraces the bringing about of death and yet there is no moral act of killing because the project is not a proposal adopted by choice. For example, someone undergoing treatment and suffering greatly might so hate and fear continued treatment and continued life that he or she could no longer accept or cooperate with the treatment—"could no longer" in the sense that a psychological impossibility blocked the way and rendered null the will to live.

In such a case, just as in the case of any obsessive-compulsive suicide, there can be no moral guilt for an omission about which there is no possibility of choice. Because of the inherent difficulty in doing anything, in fact, it is rather more likely that persons come to a point where they can no longer "pull themselves together" to make the effort needed to live or "endure the unendurable." If there is any moral responsibility in such cases, it is for earlier acts or omissions in which, perhaps, patients failed to care adequately for themselves or in some other way created a situation in which death was embraced too soon.

Again, people can omit treatment as part of a project to cause death without becoming morally guilty of killing in the strict sense because the project is not the proposal upon which they act. Consider, for instance, the situation of nurses who are trained—perhaps too strictly—to follow the orders of physicians. If parents and physicians conspire in the killing of a defective infant by starving it to death, and if the physicians order that neither food nor fluids are to be given the infant, a nurse might not think of disobeying. In such cases nurses do not make themselves parties to the conspiracy. Their fault, if fault it is, is in their too uncritical acceptance of the domination of their own proper sphere of activity by physicians, even when physicians no longer act in the interest of the patient and in the service of life.

Even after considering the preceding cases, we have not finished with the complex subject of omissions. So far we have discussed only deliberate omissions and omissions in which there is nonperformance as a way of carrying out some project, even if the project is not a proposal adopted by choice. It also is possible to omit something without adopting any proposal, without even thinking about what one is failing to cause or prevent. Not everything that one does not do is an omission. But people sometimes fail to do things which they could and should do and fail without even attending to the matter.

In most cases involving medical treatment where life is at stake this type of omission is only of indirect interest. The importance of life-and-death issues make it almost impossible that they not become proposals in deliberation, accepted or rejected in choice—except for cases in which one understands what is omitted but cannot choose, such as we have discussed already.

There is one thoroughly immoral way in which people can come to omit without further thought grave obligations such as those to preserve life. This is by adopting and rationalizing an immoral policy and then applying it mechanically until it becomes so habitual that cases are handled without any new reflection. For example, a hospital and its staff might adopt a policy of killing certain types of patient by omission, and this policy could become so much a part of the institution's routine that no one any longer thought about it.

In a case like this not only is the adoption of the policy immoral but the ability to act upon it without pangs of conscience is a sign of so deep and fully integrated an immoral commitment that those involved have made themselves moral monsters, deprived of normal human sensitivity. To persons like this the shocked objections of others are merely an amusing or annoying expression of silly and irrelevant compulsions and inhibitions.

There are some ways, however, in which persons can fail by nondeliberate omissions to do what they ought toward themselves and others. These omissions can occur without any such policy in the background as we have just discussed.

For example, a person might notice symptoms which could be signs of the beginning of a serious illness and yet irresponsibly fail to think about them, not deliberate about seeking an examination and diagnosis, and so never make any choice or have in mind any project bearing upon the matter. Similarly, parents or others having charge of noncompetent persons can ignore their symptoms or notice them and yet never get around to doing anything about them. This can happen without any consideration being given to doing something and so without any choice not to do what a reasonable person would nevertheless easily perceive to be called for.

Neglect of this sort, although it involves no deliberation and choice, is morally blameworthy. A person who cared enough and who was dutiful enough would notice, would deliberate, and would do what could and should be done. The voluntariness in this case is in the weak care and concern for life and health, the weak sense of responsibility for one's own well-being and the well-being of those in one's care.

Failings such as these might seem far removed from cases in which life-and-death decisions are consciously made. Yet such failings can prevent people from receiving the medical treatment they need and should have. And in some instances omissions of this same sort can have an important effect upon a developing situation. For instance, busy hospital administrators might hear rumors or have other reason to suspect that defective children are being killed by neglect in their hospital. The problem would be a difficult one to handle, and there are many other things to do, such as working on the budget. So the administrators can ignore what is going on, never discuss it, never think about it, and so never even decide to tolerate it.

Yet administrators could and should do something in cases such as this, for the problem is within their area of responsibility. If they loved human life as they should, if they were less attached to their own status as successful administrators, perhaps they would look into the matter. But the thoughtless omission goes on and perhaps is taken by the hospital staff and others to be tacit consent, toleration, and cooperation in what is being done.

In summary, omissions are less obvious than actions which involve an overt performance. But morally speaking, they present all of the same significant possibilities as other acts and a few of their own. One can kill in the strict sense by omission. One also can bring about death without proposing it by a moral act of omission, which itself can be unjustifiable because it violates some mode of responsibility other than that one may not act directly contrary to basic human goods.

At the same time, however, one also can bring about death by omission based upon a proposal to avoid other evils or to do other goods, not by way of or involving the death itself, when the choice of this proposal is morally upright. One can also bring about death by omission without personal deliberation of and choice of any proposal including this result, yet as part of a project which involves it, as in the case of the obedient nurse. One can also become so perverted that one omits without thinking to do what one ought to serve life. And one can also omit without thinking because of an imperfection of character and commitment like that of the inattentive parent and busy hospital administrator.

Attempts to determine the moral quality of all these various sorts of omission at the concrete level are even more difficult than are attempts to determine the moral quality of actions. But, once more, the point of ethical analysis is not to pass judgments, not even to pass judgment upon oneself. The significance of the analysis of the preceding cases is its use as a kind of checklist for reviewing one's responsibilities. One who wishes to do what is right not only must be careful to avoid behavior which expresses morally unacceptable proposals, but also must be attentive to avoid immoral proposals to be executed by outward inaction, to avoid failures to fulfill responsibilities, to avoid the inattention which permits one to ignore what one ought to consider.

For many psychological reasons omissions probably are not given the moral weight they deserve. What does not appear in experience—a murder with no blood spilled, with no deadly deed done—seems somehow less real and so less serious. Also, so far as the censure of other people is concerned, omissions are easy to get away with. But one's primary duty is to promote basic human goods, to work to protect life and make it flourish. And this primary duty is as much betrayed—perhaps, indeed, more often betrayed—by omissions as by actions executed by an outward performance.

K. The Morality of Helping: General Considerations

Up to this point we have considered a variety of kinds of actions and their moral quality insofar as they bear upon the good of human life. But we have almost entirely been concerned with actions in which those acting have been principals—that is, have been free to shape their action according to their own purposes.

Another set of concrete problems arises when one begins to consider the moral responsibilities of individuals who are acting in a way subordinate to the purposes and actions of another. Agents or helpers are not entirely free to shape their own actions according to their own purposes, yet their moral responsibility for what they themselves do cannot be dodged by assuming that it is nothing distinct from the moral responsibility of those they serve or help.

In traditional moral thought this topic has been treated under the title of "cooperation." But since persons who cooperate very often simply are two or more principals working together, we prefer the word "helping," which more accurately expresses the relationships in which we are interested.

Perplexities about helping have become more prevalent since abortion was legalized. Such perplexities will become still more prevalent if practices such as starving defective children become more generalized. And legalized voluntary euthanasia would create tremendous new perplexities about helping, since one could be confident that some who chose death would be morally upright themselves in making this choice, although from our point of view they would be seriously confused.

How is a moral counselor or guide to proceed when talking with persons contemplating volunteering for euthanasia? How are persons in institutions in the service of life and health to proceed as their institutions allow—or even establish as policy—various forms of killing and letting die?

Many nurses, for instance, already find themselves in considerable moral perplexity because of the legalization of abortion. Most nurses are deeply dedicated to the goods of human life and health, and they have been trained to serve patients in respect to these goods. To do the good work for which they have been trained nurses generally must work in close association with physicians, often in hospitals and other health-care institutions. But physicians in many cases are beginning to accept killing in the strict sense as part of their daily practice; hospitals in many cases provide facilities for abortions which cannot be morally justified. What are nurses to do if they work with such physicians and in such institutions?

In a broader social context many persons whose moral commitments are sound, who fully respect the good of human life, recognize that society is becoming more and more ready to accept violations of this good, and even to institutionalize such violations by establishing public policies which undertake to solve social problems by killing. This situation raises a great many difficulties.

If government itself adopts killing as a solution to problems, such as the problem of welfare dependency, what is the patriotic citizen who also is a friend of life to do? Most of those whose moral commitments are profoundly in defense of innocent life—for example, most opponents of legalized abortion—also are deeply patriotic. One reason they are so intent upon making abortion illegal once more, and preventing the legalization of other forms of immoral killing, is that they wish to save society from the corruption into which it is falling, to recall government to its own commitments to justice for all, not least for the weak and helpless.

Being patriotic, such friends of life feel a strong obligation to obey the laws and to support duly constituted authorities. But they see their very patriotism lending color of legitimacy to public policies which cannot be morally justified. Must friends of life become enemies of the state when the state makes itself an enemy of life? Or can friends of life somehow continue to support a government which more and more sanctions unjust attacks upon life, which more and more violates the liberty to stand aloof of large numbers of patriotic citizens?

The fact that many citizens are forced into a moral dilemma because of government involvement in killing—for example, by the public funding of abortions which are not necessary to save the mother's life—ought to make legislators, public administrators, and judges take notice. Even if they themselves sincerely believe there is nothing wrong in killing the unborn in order to reduce the burden of welfare dependency, public officials should have second thoughts about the wisdom of using this method. It is alienating large numbers of citizens who have strongly supported law and governmental authority.

Government never can count upon a commitment from its immoral subjects; when it alienates many of its upright subjects and compels all citizens to accept policies and methods which many deplore and abhor, any government is carelessly relinquishing legitimacy, as if its moral capital were nothing more than counterfeit money. But a government without legitimacy is no government; it is a structure of force without authority. When the highest court of a nation exercises raw judicial power, it perhaps can bring about the results its members consider socially desirable, but it cannot make upright people accept its decrees as law—that is, as expressions of the requirements of justice, which as such are to be respected and deserve to be obeyed and cooperated with.

The moral dilemma which is posed for citizens by the corruption of public authority is not the only one which members of the society face because of the alienating implications of social acceptance of activities which violate the good of life. Many community organizations which have done so much good and which upright people have continued to support through many other difficulties are losing support from those who abhor abortion because they directly or indirectly involve themselves in such killing.

If a voluntary association devotes most of its funds and efforts to uses which are morally praiseworthy but lends some small amount of aid to immoral activities against life, can one support such an association? For example, many people contribute to a United Way Appeal out of a sense of moral obligation. If the fund is allocated in such a way that contributions will assist Planned Parenthood, which is operating an abortion clinic, can one continue to contribute without helping the abortionists kill the innocent?

These difficult questions about the moral responsibilities of agents and helpers have received very little attention from moral philosophers. Sometimes it is assumed that the morality of the act of one helping is simply the same as the morality of the act which is helped, regardless of the differences in judgments and responsibilities of the principal and the helper.

Sometimes questions about the morality of helping are brushed aside as symptoms of scrupulosity. For example, it might be urged that when a certain result is going to be achieved no matter what one does, then one need not be perplexed about helping. Such perplexity, it might be suggested, will arise only if one is excessively concerned about one's own moral purity, afraid to dirty one's hands in carrying out unpleasant but necessary tasks which will be done anyway. And perhaps, it might be urged, if one does not help, someone else with less skill and moral sensitivity will help, with even worse results.

The account of human action which we have proposed in section A and the moral theory we argued for in chapter eleven show that responses like this to the moral dilemmas of helping are at least inadequate and at worst altogether wrong. One who is worried about responsibilities in helping what is immoral is not concerned merely about moral purity—keeping clean hands. Nor can concerns about responsibility be dismissed by pointing out that the results will be the same or worse if one does not help.

One who is concerned about helping what is immoral is concerned with the kind of person one makes oneself in helping. And one who is concerned about this cannot be satisfied with consequentialist considerations. Those who only helped the Nazi leadership carry out the final solution nevertheless made themselves murderers; their guilt could not be evaded because had they refused to serve, others would have done so, perhaps even with greater cruelty. Morality is less concerned with results than with good will; a person of truly good will is careful about helping, because a large and important part of any morally responsible person's life is given over to helping, to service, of one form or another.

What we have already said in this chapter provides the necessary basis for answering the questions which arise because of the moral dilemmas of helping. Here we are not going to reargue the normative conclusions we have already reached about various forms of killing and letting die. So if analysis indicates in any case that helping amounts to doing any of the things we have concluded to be immoral, then the helping will be immoral. The account of action in terms of the execution of proposals adopted by choice will be applied to some cases of helping to clarify exactly what one who helps is doing.

But the account of responsibility we have given is not limited to responsibility for what one in the strictest sense does. One also has responsibility for what one brings about. In many ways, as we shall explain, this latter responsibility becomes extremely important when instances of helping are under consideration.

There are two ways in which a person who is helping another or others adopts a proposal which is inherently immoral.

First, sometimes an individual considers the action he or she is about to do to be an immoral one. Such an individual might require help to do the action and decide to do it with help, despite its immorality. One who helps might out of friendship or some other motive consider the proposal precisely to help the person acting immorally to do the action as the principal understands it. No matter what the moral quality of the helping act might be from any other point of view, the adoption of such a proposal would be immoral.

Cases of this sort are not especially common, perhaps, and so it is important to consider some examples which will make clear what can be involved.

Let us imagine a Jehovah's Witness who believes that accepting blood transfusions is wrong. A friend who is not a Witness might think that it would be desirable if this person could be encouraged to accept the transfusion which might be indicated, precisely because this act of disloyalty to conviction would lead the Witness to become a convert to another world view considered by the friend correct—for example, to humanistic agnosticism or Roman Catholicism. Helping a Witness to do an act considered by him or her wrong, however, cannot be justified by ulterior good consequences. Moreover, the friend is not free of blame because in his or her own sincere belief the faith of the Jehovah's Witness is altogether erroneous in this matter, and there would be no fault apart from this erroneous faith if the transfusions were accepted.

This sort of case must be distinguished from one in which one helps persons who are doing something they consider wrong, but without adopting the proposal to help the principals do the act as they understand it. For instance, if a physician or nurse who is not a Witness helps a patient who is one by administering blood on the proposal to save the patient's life, although with the knowledge that the patient consented contrary to his or her own conscience, the physician or nurse could be acting in a morally upright manner.

Yet the conscience of the patient—even if it is sincere and the patient's choice is in accord with it—is not sufficient to justify the action of helping. For one who is helping can adopt an inherently immoral proposal in another way. For example, if a patient sincerely believes that suicide is morally right and wishes help in committing suicide, a physician or nurse could not adopt the proposal to bring about the patient's death as a means of helping the patient. Here, killing in the strict sense is the physician's or nurse's act. The fact that this act is intended to serve the good purpose of helping another do what he or she believes right does not make adoption of the means morally acceptable.

Even if one who is helping another adopts no inherently immoral proposal, there still are other modes of responsibility which must be satisfied by helpers if their acts are to be morally blameless. If A helps B to do something to C although A would not wish D to help E to do the same sort of thing to A or to F (for whom A cares deeply), then the golden rule is violated by A's act of helping. The act will be immoral even though A adopts no proposal which is inherently incompatible with moral rectitude.

For example, if nurses help physicians to administer treatment to a patient but would not want any other nurse to help any other physician to administer similar treatment to themselves or their loved ones if they were in similar circumstances, then the nurses act immorally, even though they adopt no immoral proposal, such as a proposal to kill in the strict sense or a proposal to help the physicians act immorally for some ulterior end, such as winning their approval and confidence.

Moreover, those who help cannot evade the fact that they have responsibilities other than those to the persons directly helped. For instance, if nurses have duties to physicians in charge of a case, they also have direct duties to patients under their care. Nurses cannot evade the latter duties by referring their acts to the former. Thus, a nurse cannot allow patients to die of hunger and thirst on the excuse that the physician in charge has ordered "No food and no fluids." Supplying such needs of patients falls within the proper duties of a nurse, and so nurses cannot abdicate their responsibilities to their patients out of deference to the authority of physicians without violating grave moral responsibilities which they assumed in becoming the nurses for these patients.

Further, if helping might otherwise be justified, there are times when it ought to be avoided because some other duty should take precedence. For instance, a person asked to do something which would help an act of killing in the strict sense might have a duty to refuse to do what is asked as a way of bearing witness to the good of human life and the evil of the act against it, even though, as we shall see, it might be possible to help without adopting the proposal to kill and without violating the golden rule, professional duty, or some other mode of responsibility.

For instance, nurses might have a duty to refuse to prepare patients scheduled for abortions, not because they could not do such preparations without executing any immoral proposal, failing in their duty, or otherwise acting wrongly, but because they have a very strong obligation, as persons dedicated to life and as professional colleagues of others involved, to set an example of how others should act, to express their moral convictions, to give testimony to the truth about abortion, and so on.

The fact that one is only helping to execute a certain proposal and that what one outwardly effects only contributes a necessary condition to the causing of the result by another sometimes tends to conceal the fact that one can hardly be doing what one does without adopting the proposal—for example, to kill someone.

Thus, if a patient would prefer to be dead and asks a physician to help by administering a lethal drug, it is clear enough that the physician cannot do what is requested without adopting the proposal to bring about the patient's death. So no one is likely to miss the fact that there is killing in the strict sense here and that a morally upright physician cannot comply. However, if a patient with a similar proposal asks for help by being provided with a prescription of sleeping pills, which in other circumstances might legitimately be provided, the physician who knows what the patient intends can hardly grant the request for the prescription without adopting the proposal that the drug be used to bring about the patient's death. The sufficient condition of death lies outside the physician's control, but the provision of the requested prescription is a necessary condition for which a physician bears special responsibility.

In fulfilling this condition physicians would do all that is in their power to bring about death in this case; the fact that other conditions must be fulfilled is no more relevant here than that other physical conditions must be fulfilled if most proposals to kill are to succeed. A hit man for the Mafia is no less a murderer morally speaking if his gun does not fire. Similarly, physicians who provide the means which they know are to be used immorally as a way of helping others to bring about the purpose the physicians would be morally forbidden to bring about by direct causality are no less immoral if the other conditions are not satisfied and the result does not come about.

As in omissions, so in helping it is important to avoid confusions which arise because of the psychological obscurities of the situation. One who is helping another might wish that the other would not do what he or she is in fact doing, might feel very badly about the situation, and so on. None of this is relevant, however, to what the helper is doing. "Good intentions" of this sort are morally the road to hell. The intentions which count are those which are defined by the proposal one adopts and by the consequences one willingly accepts.

Thus, if nurses feel very badly about administering lethal injections but nevertheless do as they are told and kill their patients, their sadness—the fact that doing this simply "tears them to pieces"—does not change the character of what they are doing. At the same time, if the act is a morally right one of caring for a patient as well as possible who has refused treatment—perhaps even wrongfully—and nurses have similar emotional reactions, these do not make what they are doing morally wrong, even if it causes them feelings of guilt because they are not proceeding according to standard and sound practice as would be required for other patients.

It also is very important to notice that many people who would not help another when such helping required the acceptance of a proposal to kill as the helper's own proposal will help another when such helping is immoral in some other way. When a proposal to kill would have to be adopted, the potential helper is likely to recognize that the act, being inherently immoral, cannot be justified by consequentialist arguments. But when the helping would be immoral for some other reasons—for example, because it involves a serious failure to do one's duty—there is a tendency to suppose that consequentialist considerations *as such* can relieve one of moral responsibility. This is not so.

For example, religious teachers might have a duty to instruct the consciences of those under their guidance, let us say with respect to the immorality of various sorts of acts against human life. They might be inclined not to fulfill this duty for fear that their followers will not accept sound teaching in these matters and will only become alienated further from them and their religious message. Although realizing that their silence could be taken as assent to false opinions spreading among their followers, such religious teachers might imagine that it is justifiable for them to help those committing immoral acts against life by tacitly condoning them, since they can do so without themselves adopting any proposal to violate this good.

However, the consequentialist justification for the failure to teach when this has become inconvenient is just as much a mere rationalization as is the same kind of justification for the physician who adopts the proposal to kill— for instance, by doing an abortion upon a woman whom the physician believes will otherwise attempt abortion upon herself, with risk not only to the unborn child but also to herself.

This is not to say, of course, that when the proposal one adopts is not itself inherently immoral, there cannot be cases in which a performance or omission which seems to be one's duty might morally be set aside because of other considerations. Religious teachers might hesitate to give moral instruction because they are not sure what moral instruction to give and do not wish to risk imposing burdens on their followers which they are not certain are demands of authentic morality.

Here the argument against teaching is not a consequentialist one. The duty to teach is to teach what is considered to be true. One who is confused and uncertain cannot fulfill the duty. Such teachers may have a duty to investigate the issues or to resign their office, but they cannot without irresponsibility assert what they are not confident is true. This is a very different case from one in which, for example, religious leaders might fail to fulfill the duty to teach the truth because they fear that carrying out this duty would be divisive, and they decide that trimming a bit is a lesser evil than losing their following.

L. Responsibilities of Moral Guides

Having discussed the problems of helping in general and illustrated principles with a few examples, we now turn to consider more systematically the perplexities which might be encountered by persons in various roles by taking into account their various responsibilities and concrete problems. We begin by considering the role of moral teacher or advisor—the person who helps another by counseling and supporting what the one helped does.

In many cases the moral requirements of one helping in this role are clear enough. A moral guide must propose what he or she believes to be moral truth about the problems under consideration. One who assumes this role and advises another to do what is always wrong shares fully in responsibility for the blameworthy act. And, as we have just said, one who takes the role of moral guide has a duty to investigate until confident that the advice to be given is sound.

But in some cases the responsibilities of the moral guide become clouded. For one thing there are various ways of giving moral guidance. The bluntest and most direct way is not always the most helpful or the most lastingly effective. It often is better gently to lead persons who need guidance through helping them to understand the truth and its implications for action rather than by simply announcing the moral requirements and insisting that they be followed.

Still, effective methods of teaching are one thing; nondirective counseling is something else. A person who approaches another in the role of moral advisor or teacher expects direction and has a right to it. The nondirective counselor plays a different role in making no claim to teach, making no claim to know anything which the client does not already know. If one who should function as a moral guide begins acting in the mode of a nondirective counselor, clients—for example, penitents—are likely to accept what the moral guide is doing as moral support for their own decision, whatever it happens to be. Thus, if in some cases moral guides fail to exercise their appropriate role, they accept responsibility for the immoral decisions of their clients—indeed, accept responsibility not only for the immoral decisions their clients do take but also for those their clients might take because of the failure to try to fulfill the duty of communicating moral truth which the role of moral guide imposes upon anyone who accepts it.

Again, in many cases a person in the role of moral guide holds this office within the framework of an established moral community with its own system of belief, including moral belief. This is the situation, for instance, of a Catholic priest hearing confessions or of any rabbi or minister who engages in counseling by which the consciences of adherents to the faith are formed. If a member of the congregation seeks advice of such a person, there is a presumption that the advice given will be in harmony with the fundamental commitments which members of the same community of faith share.

Thus, such moral guides are likely to mislead persons seeking advice if they begin offering personal opinions instead of clarifications of the implications of common commitments for moral life. Of course, it can happen that a person in such a position of leadership loses his or her faith and becomes unable any longer honestly to propose its moral teachings as moral truths. In a case of this sort such a person should resign the office within that community and not pretend to fulfill it, rather than in fact help members of the community to act in violation of their own most basic commitments and in this way to violate profoundly their own consciences.

People often overlook an interesting fact about conscience. When one is exercising one's conscience, one is trying to figure out what is the right thing to do. At this point there is no question *about* conscience; the only question is *about* what one ought to do.

Questions about conscience arise only when one is thinking about one's past actions or about someone else's actions. Then the question about conscience is relevant, because there is a possibility of comparing what is the right thing to do with what one thought or someone else thinks is the right thing to do. Conscience is what one thought was right, especially if one thought carefully and sincerely tried to see what is right. So one might admit now that one did something wrong at an earlier time or that someone else is doing something wrong now but excuse what was or is done on the basis that the action, though wrong, is in accord with conscience.

One cannot reasonably make a similar excuse with respect to one's own current acts. It does not make sense to say: This is wrong but it is all right for me to do it, because I am following my conscience. A person who talks like this either does not believe that the act in question really is morally wrong or does not believe that it is morally right to do it.

Now, when a person looks to a moral teacher or advisor for guidance, the person seeking guidance presumably wants to know what the right thing to do is. Talk about conscience at this point is altogether irrelevant. If the moral guide nevertheless does talk about conscience—for example, by saying that an individual who follows a sincere conscience is not morally blameworthy—this talk can be and is likely to be gravely misleading. Of course, it is true that all who follow their sincere consciences would be blameworthy if they did otherwise. (At the same time, the conscience, if erroneous, might not completely relieve a person following it from blame, since one can pervert one's own conscience by habitual wrongdoing and self-deception through rationalization, including consequentialist rationalization.) But the truth about conscience is not what one seeking guidance about a substantive question is asking for. The question is: What should I think I may do? The question is not: If I do what I think I should do and happen to be mistaken, then how do I stand morally?

If a moral guide, responding with what is sometimes called "pastoral intent" to the question What should I think I may do? instead talks about conscience inappropriately, this illogical, irrelevant reply is going to be misleading. As a response to a different question, one not asked, what is said about conscience might be perfectly true. As a response to the question which was asked—or to which the moral guide pretended to address himself or herself—the talk about conscience is empty. It means, in effect: If you blamelessly think that doing such-and-such is morally unobjectionable, then you are not to blame in thinking that doing such-and-such is permissible.

The trouble is that this empty—and so inherently harmless—remark is taken to be significant and is interpreted, as anyone might expect, to mean something quite different: If you think that doing such-and-such is morally unobjectionable, and if you are blameless in having come to think so, then I, as your moral guide, assure you that you may do such-and-such blamelessly. In other words, the inappropriate talk about conscience is understood as an espousal of subjectivism by the moral guide. The person looking for moral truth is implicitly told that there is none: Whatever he or she thinks is right *is* the right thing to do.

A moral guide who does not wish to assert that a certain kind of action is in truth morally excluded would do less damage by saying so frankly than by implicitly espousing and encouraging subjectivism in this way. The role of helper here might not be perverted by an honest statement of what is believed to be moral truth, but it certainly is perverted by an evasion of responsibility which implies subjectivism. A duplicitous moral guide who attempts to help people ease their consciences in this way accepts moral responsibility not only for the acts which are approved but also for the subjectivist wasteland into which this method of approval leads those who sought advice.

Moreover, it is by no means clear that the good purpose of easing the moral conflicts of those advised really is served. People given advice like this are perhaps sufficiently fortified to do what they otherwise might not have done with a clear conscience—for example, obtain an abortion or let a defective baby starve to death. But it is one thing to fortify people enough that they go through with acts of this sort; it is another thing to fortify people sufficiently that they are absolutely convinced that what is done is right. Previous teaching and a person's natural ability to understand right and wrong cannot so easily be put aside.

Thus, one who acts after receiving guidance of this sort is likely to continue to have a sense of guilt, and this sense can reflect real moral guilt, for the action was not really believed blameless but only rationalized to be so with the help of a moral guide who evaded his or her responsibility. Even if the person suffering such guilt was trying to escape from a conviction of conscience which was erroneously strict, so that what was done would have been blameless if it had truly been seen to be morally permissible, the moral guide has succeeded in leading those who sought guidance to act without sincere conviction. Weak consciences were not cured and strengthened; they were permanently set in crookedness and deformity.

Because of this possibility a moral guide bears very heavy responsibility for the guidance given. There might be times when even a moral guide must be silent, when the imparting of information is not a duty and could be an imposition of an unbearable burden. But such times will be few and far between. Questions are not asked unless there is some unease about them. Truly sincere persons whose consciences are blamelessly mistaken do not start asking questions about the rights of erroneous conscience and do not even think of asking questions about the matters with respect to which their moral judgment is blamelessly in error. Moreover, a moral guide must consider more goods than the moral uprightness of the person needing guidance.

This last point too often is overlooked. Human life, for example, is itself a basic good. Its destruction always is a great evil. If a person's life is lost by accident, there is a tragic loss of human good. If a person's life is lost by the act of another erroneously but sincerely thought to be morally upright, the loss is no less. And if this morally blameless act is preventable by another, the person whose life is lost has some claim upon the one who could prevent it. If the act could be prevented and should be prevented but is not, the person whose life is lost is unjustly sacrificed to some other good.

Hence, since humankind's primary moral calling is to promote and protect human goods, not merely to avoid immoral acts, moral guides have a heavy responsibility to lead those they guide to what is truly right, not merely to relieve them of moral guilt. Moral guides who care more about the client with whom they are in immediate contact, with whom they develop a personal relationship and bond of sympathy, than about others who are affected by their client's actions are proceeding with an immoral partiality. It is sentimentality, not charity, to help another by reassurance to do unto others what one would not wish done unto one for whom one had as much sympathy. The unselfish, nonegoistic character of such wrong guidance does not negate its grave immorality.

M. Responsibilities of Service Personnel

A very different sort of helping is involved if we consider the activities of service personnel, such as janitorial help, maintenance workers, cleaning persons, security guards, electricians, plumbers, letter carriers, typists, and the like. Such persons might be working in a building where there is an abortion clinic, supplying their service to a hospital where defective infants are allowed to starve, or in other ways helping to bring about death. Obviously, their help is quite remote, but it is help in the sense that those more directly involved would find it more difficult and perhaps even impossible to do the evil they do without a great deal of such help.

Service personnel very often supply their service not only to those who are doing evil insofar as they are doing it but to many who are doing good, and to those who are doing evil insofar as they are customers or tenants or the like, who also are doing good. Moreover, service personnel very often work simply for their wages. They do not adopt as their own the purposes of those for whom they work; very often they do not even think about these purposes. And if they do think about them, it seldom if ever comes to mind that there is anything to be done. Clearly, people in positions of this sort can do their jobs without adopting any immoral proposal, even though they happen to know that doing their jobs helps to create or maintain conditions in which immorality is done.

It also must be noticed that service personnel generally can continue to do their ordinary work in cases such as we are considering without violating the principle of universalizability or any duty of their role. Indeed, if the principals in the situation were doing good, the work of the service personnel would go on just as it does and would help that good. Thus their duty to those toward whom evil is done would be the same, and in continuing to do their ordinary work they are discharging this duty so far as they can. A baby starving in a hospital nursery would not be better off if the stationary engineer did not fire the boilers which provide heat to the nursery.

But persons working in such capacities also have an obligation to give testimony to what is good and to moral truth, to give good example, to promote consciousness of the evil which is being done, and to avoid involvement in it so far as possible. Therefore, it seems to us that there is some positive responsibility for service personnel to lodge their protests about what is going on and to try to find alternative places of employment.

Persons who are friends of life should help service personnel to find work which does not help maintain the conditions for immorality, should help them with legal counsel if it is needed, and so on. If there is a unionized group of service personnel who abhor the activities to which their good work lends help, such a union could do much in bringing what is being done to public consciousness. Obviously, if in particular cases service personnel have no alternative employment possibilities, can achieve nothing by protests, and so on, then they can very likely continue to do their jobs which in fact help bring about evil without in their hearts becoming conspirators in it.

Traditional moral treatises on cooperation tended perhaps too quickly to absolve service personnel. Slaves and others working in such capacities did not in the past have the liberty which modern workers do. Unions which have given many service personnel power to obtain better wages, hours, and working conditions for themselves also have given them the power to separate themselves more perfectly from activities which they find morally abhorrent. Not to use this power today for the latter purpose but only for the former would be irresponsible.

Furthermore, traditional moral treatises perhaps were too concerned about one mode of responsibility: that one not act directly against a good. Service personnel clearly are not doing this in most cases and need not do it in any. But the responsibility to do what one can to express one's commitment to the good of human life, to give testimony to moral truth, and to avoid even remote involvement in evil is a real one, though not one so well-defined as other responsibilities.

N. Responsibilities of Nurses

Nurses provide auxiliary services which often are necessary if proposals of physicians to kill or wrongfully to allow to die are to be executed. For this reason nurses often are perplexed about their responsibilities. Their activities are necessary conditions for immoral acts; in this sense they help these acts. Yet often nurses do not adopt the immoral proposals of physicians who, for example, are performing abortions or starving defective infants to death.

The first thing to notice is that it is entirely possible that nurses adopt as their own the immoral proposals of physicians or patients. For example, a nurse might wholeheartedly agree with the death-dealing purpose of the abortifacient procedure, having accepted the principle that no unwanted baby should ever be born. In such cases nurses are not merely helping to perform abortions; morally speaking, they are principal agents of acts of killing in the strict sense. Their responsibility is no less than that of the physicians who physically cause the death of the unborn.

The same thing can happen in a more subtle case. A pediatric unit might have adopted a policy of selecting some babies for nontreatment, with the intent that they should die, so that they will not survive with a poor quality of life. The execution of this policy is not by any one overt act. Rather, it is carried out by an extensive set of omissions by a whole group of physicians, nurses, hospital administrators, parents, and others who know about and are collectively responsible for the care of these individuals. Since the activities which are omitted by nurses in such cases will be ones which it is normally their duty to patients to perform, it is difficult to see how these activities can be omitted without the nurses adopting as their own the policy of the unit. Even if they accept this policy for some ulterior purpose which is morally blameless—for example, to earn a living to support their own children—the acceptance of the policy, however reluctant, is morally a commitment to the act of killing in the strict sense.

Nevertheless, it is possible that nurses do almost everything asked of them, even in a context in which killing in the strict sense is being done, without adopting the proposal to kill and becoming principal agents in killing. A woman who is having an abortion or a patient who has refused treatment with suicidal intent still needs ordinary nursing care, and nurses can give such care—feeding, comforting, administering pain-killing drugs—without adopting any proposal that the unborn or the suicidal patient should die. It is even possible to imagine situations in which nurses might prepare patients for operations in which killing in the strict sense is carried out and help physicians by handing them instruments with which they kill and yet not themselves adopt the proposal.

How could this be? Consider the instance of very poor nurses who are in desperate need of money to support their own families and who have no other way of obtaining it. Or consider the instance of nurses compelled under threat of physical violence to do these things. In such cases nurses might realize fully that what they do very proximately helps to carry out immoral proposals, yet they might do what they do not as a means to carrying out these proposals but only as a means to earning income or avoiding bodily harm.

The distinction between cases such as these and those in which the immoral proposal is adopted is a very fine and subtle distinction indeed. Nevertheless the distinction is real. The nurse's activities in assisting do help; that is what a nurse is paid for. But although nurses are only paid insofar as their activities do help accomplish immoral purposes, it does not follow that they help only if they make the immoral purpose their own.

It is possible that they help for reasons of their own and that the goods they have in view are equally achieved whether their help contributes causally to the bringing about of a state of affairs which cannot be proposed as a goal without immorality. If they do not adopt the immoral purpose as their own, nurses might possibly blamelessly help physicians who are carrying out killings in the strict sense, such as abortions aimed at killing the unborn and injections used for active euthanasia.

Of course, if nurses themselves undertook to perform the death-dealing behavior—for example, by administering the injections—they would no longer be helping but would be executing the proposal that death be brought about, and they could not do this without adopting the proposal.

But although it is possible that nurses do almost everything asked of them even in a context in which killing in the strict sense is done without adopting the proposal to kill, still nurses can gravely fail in moral responsibility without becoming principal agents in immoral acts. In discussing in section K the general principles of cooperative or helping activities, we have already indicated several ways in which nurses might be morally at fault without becoming killers in the strict sense. These ways were indicated as examples.

First, nurses might violate the golden rule or principle of universalizability by doing something to help another bring about an effect upon someone in a case in which they would not wish another nurse to bring about a similar effect upon themselves or someone for whom they cared deeply. Second, nurses have their own duties to patients and in respect to these duties cannot exempt themselves from responsibility by wholly subordinating their judgment and activity to that of physicians and others. Third, there is an obligation every bit as serious as the duties of one's profession: the obligation to oppose serious wrongs. Nurses ought in most cases to refuse help in cases in which something immoral is done, to impede the wrong, to give good example, to express their own moral convictions, and to give testimony to the truth about the goodness of life and the evil of acts against it.

There is one other area in which nurses have a special responsibility that we fear has been slighted too often. Nurses see and hear a great many things which ought to be kept private. Normally they rightly maintain high standards of confidentiality by protecting patient privacy and also avoiding publicity of innocent imperfections of physicians and others which would have a bad effect upon patient confidence and do no one any good. But there are times when a usual custom of maintaining confidentiality can lead to failure to speak up, speak out, or communicate information to authorities who should have it.

If nurses observe that unlawful activities are being done, they have the same duty as any other citizen to report this fact to officers of the law. If they know that it is common practice, for example, to kill aborted babies born alive either by action or by omission of ordinary medical care which would surely not be denied a wanted child, nurses have a duty to bring the facts to light. In some cases they cannot do so without risking their own positions. But in many cases there should be no difficulty in communicating the facts to officers of the law and to the public at large by means of journalists who are friends of life. Too little of what is going on and is spoken about privately is coming to light. Nurses have a special opportunity and so a special responsibility to make clear what is happening as exterminative medicine is more and more widely adopted.

O. Responsibilities of Health-Care Institutions

Hospitals and other health-care institutions also can encounter perplexities about the extent to which they can blamelessly allow death-dealing acts to be carried on with their help and facilities. Obviously there is no perplexity when the institution itself adopts proposals to kill—for example, sets itself up as an abortion facility. The problem arises rather in the case of institutions which find activities going on in various services without the institution itself having planned or made policies specifically furthering these activities, when the activities are judged to involve killing in the strict sense or other acts involving immoral proposals, and when there are possible ways in which the administrators of the institution might restrain the physicians or others engaged in the immoral activities.

This situation is a very difficult one for administrators of institutions who are personally friends of life. They realize that their institutions provide many essential services to the community. They would like to eliminate or restrict as much as possible immoral acts facilitated by the fact that their institutions exist and provide conditions necessary for a variety of activities, most of which are good. But in the present legal and moral climate how can health-care facilities not allow killing in the strict sense—for example, abortion—and other immoral activities to go on with their help?

The answer to this vexing question is in a clear understanding of what it means for a health-care institution to "allow" certain procedures to take place within its facilities.

In one sense everyone who helps another who is doing evil accepts the bad consequence and allows what is evil to be done. In this sense busy administrators might continue to keep the physical plant running well while knowing that morally blameworthy operations are done in their hospital, not intervening to try to compel staff physicians to conform to hospital policies forbidding such operations.

In another sense one allows something by making specific provisions for it. For example, a hospital administrator might allow abortions or other immoral acts to be done by scheduling certain facilities and personnel for these specific purposes. This latter kind of allowing is more than accepting bad consequences; it is making policy to organize activity precisely in view of these purposes.

Thus, in the latter case the administrator in setting policies defines the institution's purposes, establishes the proposals it will help to realize, makes it the sort of institution it is. A hospital which allows euthanasia and abortion in this latter sense of "allows" makes itself an accomplice in the immoral acts it facilitates—for example, makes itself an abortion mill.

The implications of this analysis are important. A hitherto praiseworthy and truly humanitarian institution—such as a charitable hospital—corrupts itself as soon as it makes provision for activities which execute immoral proposals. Nor is this corruption lessened, but rather intensified by hypocrisy, if the sponsors of such an institution express their personal rejection and institutional disapproval of the activities which they nevertheless facilitate.

There can be cases in which hospital administrators, like others, help someone who is executing an immoral purpose without themselves adopting the purpose, yet act in a morally blameworthy way. For instance, if a court orders a hospital to permit killing in the strict sense in its facilities, an administrator might do only what the court specifically mandates without adopting the proposal which is morally excluded. Yet the administrator might have a moral responsibility to resist the court's order. The fact that the institution can comply without becoming an accomplice in the immoral acts it facilitates does not cancel responsibilities which arise, for example, from the obligation to stand for principle, to carry out the intentions of those who have supported the institution in the past, to offer good example, and so forth.

If an ecclesiastical body were threatened with the loss of its most valuable real property by a judicial decision denying its title to the property, those who are leaders of the body certainly would launch appeals, obtain the services of the most able attorneys, seek every possible avenue to avoid losing the property. If the leaders of an ecclesiastical body act with less energy and determination in defending the institutions under their jurisdiction when these institutions are ordered by courts to help carry out antilife activities, then such leaders clearly manifest what they treasure and where their hearts are.

P. Responsibilities of Citizens at Large

Citizens whose governments are committed to the execution of immoral purposes also face perplexity. On the one hand, few if any governments fail to carry out many good and necessary activities which deserve the support of all citizens. On the other hand, cooperation with a government—for example, by paying one's full taxes—unquestionably helps to facilitate all its activities, including those which carry out morally objectionable proposals. Whether or not citizens should resist government—for instance, by openly or covertly withholding taxes or in other nonviolent ways—is a difficult question to which there can be no general answer. Concrete circumstances, especially the personal duties of such citizens, always play an essential part in reaching sound moral judgments in these matters.

It is not always immoral to pay taxes which one knows are being used in part for immoral purposes such as funding abortion and maintaining the nuclear deterrent. Those who pay taxes knowing that they thereby help such purposes need not adopt the immoral proposals which governmental policies involve. One may pay taxes for many reasons, such as a desire to further the good things government also does and such as a desire to avoid the seizure of one's assets which would only contribute more to the government's immoral acts and at the same time deprive one's dependents of the support they require.

A person who pays taxes for reasons such as these need not adopt any immoral proposal which shapes the government's policy, even though the taxpayer knows that the payment will help fund the execution of the immoral policy. To say this is not to defend an attitude of conformism to the immoral demands of a political society. Rather, it is to recognize that very often it is difficult, if not impossible, to resist the power of government which is bent upon executing immoral proposals.

At the same time a person who finds it possible to withhold taxes or other support from such a political society might well be justified in withholding support to the extent that the society is corrupt. The failure to meet obligations both to other members of the society as such and even to one's family and others would be, not part of one's proposal, but rather an unwanted but inevitable side effect of a principled refusal to cooperate in the doing of evil and to tolerate the infringement of one's liberty to stand aloof.

Every person has a real and strong obligation to avoid helping to promote evil, and only other serious responsibilities justify one doing what in fact does help evil. In some situations the protest value of refusing to pay certain taxes might be significant, and the consequences of refusal to pay minor. Some people might be in a position to accept the costs and inconvenience of fines and imprisonment for demonstrating their deep resistance to immoral governmental policies by refusal to pay taxes or in other ways. Such persons could have a duty to resist.

Those who have taken the side of life in the debate on abortion have only begun to face these issues. Those who are eager to compel public participation in killing have hardly begun to think about them. As the movement to legalize killing gains ground, the question of the legitimacy of government will more and more be raised. The responsibility to resist will become clearer.

When one turns from the support of political society through taxes and in other ways to support for voluntary associations which adopt policies which further immoral purposes, the issues about cooperation become less perplexing. In general one should not support any organization which conducts or shares in immoral activities.

The reasons for withholding support here are similar to the reasons for withholding support from corrupt proposals of a government, but for one essential difference. Unlike the case in which one must engage in civil disobedience or some other form of unlawful resistance to avoid cooperating in evil, one always can refuse to join or contribute to purely voluntary associations without doing anything unlawful. One's moral obligations to support charities and voluntary associations do not arise in the same way and have the same specificity as one's moral obligation to support a just government. And the leaders of a voluntary association such as the United Way or the March of Dimes do not have the same power to make one's dependents suffer if one refuses cooperation as do the judges and police who enforce the immoral programs of political society.[20]

This is not to say, of course, that one has no obligation to support some purely voluntary community activities. But one does not have an obligation to support particular voluntary associations.

If there is evidence that calls into question the moral quality of the activities of such organizations, one is well justified in withholding support until all questions are satisfactorily answered. It is for those who manage such voluntary activities to prove that what contributors are helping is morally above question. It is not for those with doubts to prove the contrary. The consistent following of this approach by all who are friends of life can only have a salutary effect in discouraging involvement of voluntary associations for community purposes in the immoral activities of those who take advantage of liberty to attack life and other basic human goods.

Moreover, the responsibility many people feel to contribute something to voluntary community activities presupposes that there is a genuine community to which everyone belongs. But if the so-called community activities are directed toward executing proposals one considers immoral, then one either becomes immoral or becomes alienated from the supposed community. A community is based upon shared purposes. Those who are trying to solve problems of defective children, of the sick, and of others by killing them—no matter how beneficently—cannot claim community support from those who are friends of life and cannot complain if friends of life deny help to organizations which only now and then support a little killing.

Thus the fact that one can support a United Way appeal or a March of Dimes drive without adopting all of the proposals which recipients of funds from these organizations have adopted does not mean that one can in good conscience continue to support such organizations if there is doubt about some of their projects. Friends of life will have no difficulty in finding voluntary organizations which need and deserve their support and should help no others.

13: Justice and the Ethical Foundations of Jurisprudence

A. Introductory Remarks

Throughout our treatment of jurisprudential questions in chapters three through ten we assumed as sound the view of government articulated in chapter two. In other words, we assumed that a jurisprudence which bases laws upon commonly accepted principles of liberty and justice is ethically defensible. Many readers might hold on ethical grounds that a less libertarian conception of government would be preferable.

Some will maintain that the basic personal good of human life should be accepted as a substantive purpose of political society, so that the sanctity of life will be protected in every instance—even, for example, against an individual who wishes to commit suicide. Others will maintain that a utilitarian jurisprudence ought to be accepted and that laws and public policies generally should be based upon quality-of-life considerations. In this final chapter we shall show that the ethical theory we explained in chapter eleven and applied in chapter twelve also can be used to defend the jurisprudence which we articulated in chapter two as the American proposition and which we assumed in chapters three through ten.

To show that this jurisprudence is ethically defensible, we shall argue that—assuming our theory of moral norms and human actions—a morally upright person *may* wholeheartedly accept this jurisprudence in practice and cooperate in a political society which bases its laws and policies upon it. We also shall show that a jurisprudence which would base laws directly upon the sanctity of human life does not comport well with our ethical theory but rather is inconsistent with it. As for a utilitarian jurisprudence, there is obviously no need to restate the criticism of its foundations made in chapter eleven, sections C and D. But a utilitarian jurisprudence *also* is incompatible with the philosophy of government which we outlined in chapter two.

This inconsistency between the jurisprudence of liberty and justice which we have assumed in this book and a utilitarian jurisprudence arises because utilitarian theory cannot permit liberty and justice to have the status they must have if they are to be the object of the sort of consent which gives moral legitimacy to government. One consequence of the inability of utilitarian theory to allow liberty and justice the required status is that utilitarian jurisprudence can offer no basis for law other than utilitarian morality itself. Thus utilitarianism, the philosophical foundation of most of the proposals we have argued against throughout this book, not only is bad ethics; it also is bad jurisprudence. This will become clear when utilitarian jurisprudence is examined in the light of the assumptions concerning liberty and justice which underlie the American conception of government and law—assumptions we shall show to be ethically defensible.

B. Utilitarianism and the American Proposition

The proponents of the legalization of killing on quality-of-life grounds, who are our main opponents in the euthanasia debate, are consequentialists in ethics; in legal theory they often owe much to the utilitarianism of Bentham and Mill. They often say—in fact, loudly and insistently proclaim—that law and morals must be separated. What they mean is that law must be separated from traditional morality to the extent that traditional morality is embodied in the laws of those nations which were shaped by Christian civilization. But they by no means object to legislating morality. They precisely want the law to permit and encourage what they consider morally acceptable and to establish as public policy what they consider morally required.

The coincidence between the legal and moral standards accepted by proponents of euthanasia is evidenced in many ways. In general they discuss law and morality at once and make no clear distinction between the two domains. Any reader of Glanville Williams, Joseph Fletcher, Marvin Kohl, and other proponents of euthanasia will notice this fact. Very often they argue for changes in the law by arguing against traditional moral positions, as though the falsity of the latter, if it were proved, would justify the former.

Suicide must not be a crime. Why not? Because, they say, it is not always immoral and is sometimes the best way out. Voluntary euthanasia must be permitted. Why? Because, they answer, objections against it are rooted in traditional morality, and many people today consider it a demand of dignity that a person be permitted to be killed by choice. Nonvoluntary euthanasia must be permitted, they argue, since it is beneficent to kill painlessly those who otherwise would live wretched lives of poor quality. These are ethical arguments for legal policies. These arguments are the very same ones a utilitarian would propose in an attempt to justify the choices of individuals in the same matters.

The coincidence between the legal and moral standards defended by our consequentialist opponents is no accident. Their whole approach compels them to merge into one the two domains which we carefully distinguish. We shall now explain why this is so.

To begin with, the consequentialist claims that the right thing to do is what will yield the greatest net good. It follows from this principle that if consequentialism were workable at all—which we have shown it is not—then in any given situation there would be only one right act which could be chosen from among all the alternatives. This would be the act which would maximize net benefits. (A utilitarian might maintain that in some cases two or more acts would have equal utility, superior to any alternative, and so any one of these two or more acts, taken at random, could be considered the morally right thing to do.) Corresponding to the right act would be the best state of affairs to be brought about by a given agent or set of agents. For this agent or set of agents it would be more or less seriously immoral to bring about any other state of affairs.

It follows that on any consequentialist theory the class of permissible but nonobligatory acts tends to be empty. The only such acts are those which are members of a set of alternatives equal in net utility, only one of which can be obligatory. Apart from this case the act promising maximum net benefit will be obligatory, and every other possible act will be morally forbidden. Considered as an ethics, a consequentialist theory—if it were workable at all—would be extremely strict; it would not leave morally upright persons any extensive set of morally permissible possibilities from which to choose and so would leave them almost no room for morally permissible maneuver.

When a consequentialist theory of morality becomes a utilitarian jurisprudence, this strictness remains, and it has antilibertarian implications. When utilitarians see something which seems to them good for society, they tend to want to set up a public program which will promote the good, regardless of the reluctance of many members of the society to have government engage in that particular sphere of action. Analogously, there is a strong tendency to remedy social evils by means of governmental methods of social control. However, for various reasons the antilibertarian implications of utilitarian jurisprudence are mitigated in practice, so that using it as a basis of law does not appear to be as incompatible with the American proposition as it really is.

In the first place, the utilitarian will take into account the costs of the government's intervention. When government undertakes to promote a good by a public program or to remedy an evil by some official method of social control, the government's activity itself has consequences. Although the utilitarian policy maker might consider intervention desirable almost everywhere if its costs were ignored, costs cannot be left out of account. In many cases it will be felt that the consequences of intervention will be mostly harmful; this will most likely be so when there is widespread public opposition to government involvement in a certain area. Hence, the utilitarian policy maker often urges that the government *not* undertake to promote some social good or to control some evil. In practice much seems best left to private initiative and to informal methods of restraint. With respect to such matters utilitarians can then present themselves as libertarians.

We are not suggesting that utilitarians are insincere in claiming to be libertarians. They can like liberty as much as anyone and regard it as a very useful good. Liberty can be seen as a necessary means to individual self-fulfillment. As such, restrictions upon liberty can be considered in general undesirable, a factor of disutility which must be taken into account whenever possible public policies are weighed. When this appraisal of the usefulness of liberty plays an important part in the utilitarian's judgment that a matter would be best left to private initiative and informal methods of control, the utilitarian can quite sincerely consider this judgment truly libertarian.

In the second place, utilitarians are limited in legislating morality according to their own views by the very generality of law. When individual acts are under consideration, all of the circumstances can be taken into account, and so, for example, a utilitarian might decide that in some cases infants afflicted with spina bifida should be killed and in others not. But when public policies are framed, they must be formulated in general terms which cannot take account of all the diverse circumstances present in the various situations to which the policies must apply. Thus, the utilitarian who thinks that some defective infants ought to be killed might advocate permissive legislation and yet not insist on a public program of nonvoluntary euthanasia, since it is hard to write such a program into a statute or even into a set of administrative regulations.

Again, because of this limit utilitarians can present themselves as libertarians who favor permissive legislation rather than public intervention. Such restraint certainly can include some regard for liberty. But this is not the essential factor. What is essential is that the enterprise of making and executing public policy has its own built-in constraints, which a utilitarian jurisprudence, as much as any other, must respect. The result is that utilitarians accept another limit upon their tendency to legislate their morality.

The two limits upon utilitarian jurisprudence which we have described might not be the only ones. There could be others like them. But whatever the limits, they will restrict the public domain and leave certain matters to private discretion only to the extent that utilitarian calculations demand that these limits be recognized and respected. This fact has several implications.

First, the private domain has no secure boundaries. The boundaries are set by the disutility of public intervention, the limits of administrative practicability, or the like. These factors can change. For example, although public opposition might rule out compulsory abortion at present, the costs of intervention might be judged less than the disutility of forgoing such a program if more welfare recipients resist the urging of welfare workers and agencies that they voluntarily terminate their pregnancies. Similarly, although it might be practically impossible to write the handbook of administrative regulations for a program of nonvoluntary euthanasia for defective infants, such a program might be legislated and the bureaucrats given the impossible task of administering it fairly if socialized medicine is adopted more widely and the medical costs for certain classes of infants becomes a target in a cost-cutting drive.

Second, although utilitarians might appeal to liberty as a value weighing in favor of public restraint, they regard it as only one value among many. No consequentialist ethics can treat liberty as if it were an absolute which could exclude the application of cost-benefit analysis to any problem. Liberty might be a benefit to be taken into account, and its infringement a cost to count on the debit side when a public policy would restrict liberty. But the benefit of liberty is only one good among others and its infringement only one cost among others. Liberty always can be outweighed. Liberty has a certain value, perhaps even a considerable value. But it is not a blessing to be held sacrosanct.

This abstract argument showing the incompatibility between the American proposition—in which it is one of the ends of government to preserve the *blessings* of liberty—and a utilitarian jurisprudence helps to clarify several features, which we have noted previously, of the movement for euthanasia.

For example, it helps to clarify why consequentialists argue directly from their moral views to their legislative proposals without the slightest hesitation over whether there might be something intolerant in taking this direct step. Faced with opponents who insist upon the sanctity of life, utilitarians might tolerate what seems to them this irrational position. But they will not tolerate it because the liberty to hold it and to advocate its implementation is a basic principle of American society; rather, they will tolerate such opposition because this residue of traditional religious morality, although irrational, cannot easily be removed. (As we shall point out in section D, we ourselves question the justice of attempting to base public policy directly upon a morality of the sanctity of life, but we have no reservations about the right of those who hold either traditional morality or a utilitarian quality-of-life morality both to hold their positions *and to advocate* their implementation.)

The preceding argument also helps to explain why public officials who accept a utilitarian ethics can hardly limit the full impact of their own personal moral opinions and hierarchies of value when they undertake their official tasks of making laws, executing laws, and reaching judicial decisions. Put into positions where they have more options than most people, such officials will have to do what seems to them best under the circumstances, all things considered; to do less would seem to them immoral. Thus their personal values will become principles of legality to the extent that they can get these values established—that is, to the extent that they have political power. Supreme Court justices, thinking of themselves in this way, will see what has to be done—"has to be done" in the light of their own values—and will do it.

The consequentialist approach does not necessarily lead to totalitarianism. As we have explained, it often will be decided that the greatest good for the greatest number will be achieved by letting people do as they please; sometimes it will be decided that public action is undesirable because the good it could accomplish is outweighed by the costs it will impose. Still, the fact that everything is subject to weighing and balancing and that any consideration in favor of governmental restraint can be outweighed will tend to make prevalent moral views and legal requirements coincide. Minority moral views will influence law significantly only when the minority is powerful enough or determined enough to make it too costly for the majority to legislate its own morality, execute what it legislates, and call the result "justice."

The preceding considerations make clear why a utilitarian jurisprudence based upon a consequentialist method in ethics has implications which are incompatible with the high regard for liberty—a regard which amounts almost to reverence—characteristic of the American proposition. We shall now show that a utilitarian jurisprudence not only is inconsistent with a just respect for liberty but also is inconsistent with other demands of justice.

As we mentioned in chapter eleven, section C, many critics of consequentialism have attacked this method of moral judgment because there often are cases in which most people's intuitions are that justice would require one sort of action while it seems clear that the results of a consequentialist calculation would demand another. If the greatest good for the greatest number is to be attained, then it seems individuals might rightly be considered expendable in the common interest. If individuals have any unalienable rights whatsoever, then there are some absolutes which may not be violated regardless of consequences.

Justice generally is admitted by utilitarians to be a necessary means to promoting other aspects of well-being. The consequentialist points out, for example, that inequality or inequity creates envy and perpetuates misery. Thus consequentialist theories set up an ideal of equality as an almost absolute condition for achieving peace among members of a society and the greatest happiness of the greatest number.

In an attempt to make plausible the claims of justice when consequentialist considerations would seem to require injustice in particular, exceptional cases, many consequentialists have argued in favor of rule consequentialism.

On this view rules are justified by the fact that they would conduce to better consequences than alternative rules, and acts are judged by their conformity to rules.

If the distinction between rule and act consequentialism could be maintained, it would permit utilitarians to make a more serious distinction than they actually can between just law and morally right action for individuals. But the distinction cannot stand up, since on a consequentialist theory all the consequences of an act are equally relevant. Thus, the particular act of making a rule is only one act among others; the rule cannot be made broader and more unexceptionable than will conduce to the best consequences. At the same time, as we already have explained more fully in chapter eleven, section C, any particular moral judgment will express a rational determination which will stand as the only reasonable rule for cases of precisely the same sort. Thus, rules of law and ad hoc decisions will tend to merge into one another.

When people who have adopted consequentialism think that they should do something, they quite naturally think—in accord with their theory—that their judgment reflects what is objectively the socially right thing, the greatest good for the greatest number. When a majority thinks it should do something, it quite naturally thinks that the minority who disagree are benighted or selfish or both. Only the stupid could miss seeing what is the greatest good, since it is a simple matter of calculation to determine it, and only the selfish could resist so beneficent a plan, which alone promises the greatest good for the greatest number.

The majority sharing and reinforcing one another in such convictions will work its will if it can, thus to tend to tyranny. This tendency will be concealed, however, by loud and persistent appeals to the democratic rights of the majority to pursue the common welfare as they see fit. Objections from any minority can be dismissed as obstructionist and self-serving. To oppose the tyranny of the majority—or even of a minority in power and convinced by consequentialist rationalizations that it is in the right—will be derided as morally absolutist and condemned as an attempt to impose a nonconsequentialist morality upon the society as a whole.

The legalization of abortion is a case in point. Opponents appealed to justice, which would require the equal protection by law of the lives of the unborn. Proponents appealed to the good consequences to be achieved by legalization—fewer back-alley abortions, reduced costs for welfare programs, and every mother a willing mother with a wanted child. The proponents of legalized abortion also used the language of liberty and justice yet showed in practice that they used this language to express social policies they preferred on other grounds.

Liberty for women was demanded, but liberty for the public to stand aloof from abortion is still very widely attacked. Justice for the poor is demanded, but not more justice than would be needed to eliminate poverty by killing the children of poverty. Opponents of abortion are attacked on the basis that they are trying to impose an outdated, religious morality of sanctity of life upon a secular society innocent of the obscurantism of those who think legalized abortion is slaughter of the innocent. But proponents of abortion who control powerful media of communication refuse to treat their opponents fairly either in reporting news or in contending for influence on public opinion.

C. The Correct Relationship between Morality and Law

By contrast to this utilitarian jurisprudence we have in this book carefully avoided mingling moral and jurisprudential considerations. In considering what the laws should be with respect to euthanasia and related questions, we have not argued from our ethical theory to justify jurisprudential positions. Rather, we carefully began with a clarification of the American proposition, extracted common principles of liberty and justice from it, and argued on the basis of and within the limits of these principles. To make this point clear, it is worthwhile reviewing the difference between our legal proposals and our moral prescriptions.

In chapter four we argued that a legally competent person should be at liberty to refuse medical treatment and that this liberty should be subject to very few restrictions. The permissible restrictions would be for the sake of the public health, welfare, and safety, for the protection of dependents, and for the protection of persons at least temporarily noncompetent. We also suggested means by which the law could—and we argued for the sake of liberty should—facilitate every competent person's wishes with respect to his or her own care during a future time of noncompetence.

The minimal limits built into our proposal would allow competent persons to choose policies for themselves inconsistent with what we argued in chapter twelve is the morally required respect for the good of their own lives. For example, an individual could make certain that a guardian would be appointed who would under agreed upon conditions decide that life was no longer worth living—that the person would be better off dead—and order treatment discontinued on this basis. In this case the refusal of treatment would be intended to bring about death; it would thus be killing in the strict sense and so, according to our view, inevitably immoral. Even without directing that treatment be discontinued precisely to bring about death, a person would be at liberty to arrange for the discontinuation of treatment in morally irresponsible ways which a person with due regard for the good of life would carefully avoid. For example, an individual could appoint as guardian a relative or friend who lacked practical wisdom.

In chapter five we argued that suicide and attempted suicide ought not to be considered crimes, and that although the law should not facilitate such acts, it should take care to avoid interfering with competent adults who freely choose to kill themselves. For example, people who choose to commit suicide by refusing to eat should not be force-fed provided that they are found to be competent. Clearly, just such suicides as the law in our judgment should not interfere with will be instances of killing in the strict sense and so, as we have argued, inevitably immoral.

In chapter six we argued against the legalization of voluntary euthanasia, as previously we argued against the legalization of assisted suicide in general. But these arguments were not based upon an assumption of the sanctity of life. Rather, they were based upon the interests of others than those who would be killed: their interests in safety on the one hand or, on the other, in standing aloof from activities they abhor. Morally speaking, we found both the person who volunteers to be killed and the one who does the killing to be engaging, ordinarily, in moral acts of killing in the strict sense, which can never be right, regardless of considerations about the interests of anyone else.

In chapter seven we argued that under certain conditions killing in self-defense and in war can be justly considered legal, particularly because under appropriate conditions the killing defends the legal order itself and prevents it from being overridden by brute force. But from a moral point of view much such killing probably will be done by way of executing a proposal that an aggressor be destroyed, and such killing will morally be excluded on the ethical theory we defend, although not on most traditional theories of justifiable killing.

As to capital punishment, we consider it an immoral violation of the good of human life. But we did not argue against it in chapter seven on this ground. Rather, we pointed out that such killing need not be regarded as unjust but is objectionable jurisprudentially on the basis of the violation it involves of the liberty to stand aloof of all the members of the society who find this practice abhorrent, regardless of the moral ground on which they find it so.

We also argued for an equitable rule permitting killing when necessary to maximize the probability of the survival of some persons when two or more are subject to a common peril. In many cases killings permitted by such a rule would be morally justified as well. But it is clear that as a rule permitting abortion to save the mother's life, a statute along the lines we defended in chapter seven, section G, would in practice permit abortion in any case in which it would be impossible to prove beyond reasonable doubt that the abortion was not done for this purpose. And so this legal rule, even if just, would permit many abortions precisely aimed at killing an unwanted child and other abortions which we are convinced a morally responsible person would not approve—for example, on the ground that a pregnant woman should be willing to run a serious risk to protect her unborn child.

In chapter eight we argued against the legalization of killing in nonvoluntary euthanasia. Here our absolute exclusion of the permissibility of legalizing such killing coincides in result with the moral judgment that such killing cannot be chosen without violation of the good of life. But the jurisprudential argument, once more, was not framed in terms of the sanctity of life. Rather, the basis of the jurisprudential argument was equal protection of the laws. To kill the noncompetent on the judgment that they will be better off dead or that they are nonpersons is to discriminate against them and arrogantly to usurp a prerogative for making value judgments on their behalf on principles they need not accept if they were competent.

In chapter nine we argued for legal safeguards for the rights of noncompetent persons to medical treatment. These safeguards are such that they would never require anyone to make an immoral choice in this matter. But they are not by any means adequate to preclude immoral choices, including some which would be the adoption of proposals to bring about death. The legal safeguards we outlined would embody presumptions about the justice of decisions under certain conditions. For example, a dying, noncompetent person whose physician and next of kin agree that treatment be discontinued would be presumed to consent to the discontinuance. In many cases such a presumption would be correct, but in some it would not, and in some it would be used by those legally permitted to decide as a legal shelter for disposing quickly of dying persons, such as the severely retarded or the demented, who with care might enjoy several months of life as good as any they were ever capable of. The problem is that when omissions are consistent with justice, the law should not try to enforce actions which moral uprightness would certainly demand.

Throughout our treatment of various questions we tried to make certain that the prerogatives of the medical profession would be safeguarded. For example, nothing in our legal treatment of the issues demands that a physician accept a patient who needs care or that a physician continue to treat a patient who exercises the liberty to refuse consent. In many cases physicians can and do abuse these prerogatives by failing to give the service which true dedication to the goods of life and health would demand, refusing to care for patients who choose to exercise their right to make decisions limiting their own treatment.

Thus it is clear that the jurisprudential arguments we have developed in chapters three through ten do not proceed directly from the ethical theory we presented in chapter eleven. The basis for our jurisprudential arguments is in the common principles of liberty and justice which we call the "American proposition"—principles located in the American consensus and articulated in chapter two. This basis for jurisprudential judgments has a normative status for Americans who engage in civil debate of public policy issues.

The principles of liberty and justice cannot easily be set aside by anyone who wishes to participate in such civil debate. Certainly they cannot be set aside as if they constituted a sectarian morality, insistence on which in the formation of public policy would constitute an unjust imposition of morality. Indeed, the charge that one or another party is seeking to impose morality has force only because all Americans regard tolerance and pluralism as important. These values in turn are considered important because liberty is accepted as normative, and any sign of its infringement by the establishment of any one set of deeply held conscientious views is universally regarded as a most serious threat to justice.

At the same time, the common principles of liberty and justice can be explained and defended within various ethical frameworks. To offer such an explanation and defense does not transform the American proposition into the particular ethics which someone uses to explain and defend it. But to offer such an explanation and defense does provide an ultimate moral foundation upon which those who accept the ethics which is used can take part in building the common structure of political society. Hence, we offer our explanation and defense of the common principles of liberty and justice by using the ethics articulated in chapter eleven, without hereby conceding the non-neutrality of the principles upon which the jurisprudential arguments in chapters three through ten are based.

We do not accept the common principles of liberty and justice as sufficient principles for jurisprudence for mere strategic or rhetorical purposes. So far as we are concerned, the positions for which we have argued in chapters three through ten in no way represent a compromise between our moral principles and the hard realities of the euthanasia debate. Rather, we believe that morally upright citizens ought to be satisfied if public policies are shaped by considerations of liberty and justice alone. Our defense of this jurisprudence is as follows.

The ethical theory articulated in chapter eleven entails that actions of certain kinds are always wrong. Whether these actions are done by private individuals or by persons associated in communities, including political societies, does not alter this general point of normative ethics. The kinds of actions which are always wrong are those which include a proposal to violate some basic human good. Justice is one of the basic human goods. Actions which violate it, including public policies which violate it, are always wrong.

Of course, it is not always easy to discern what constitutes justice and what acts would violate it. But when this is determined, a political society ought never to violate it and ought never to perpetuate injustice in its laws, policies, and structures. Justice demands that due respect be given to liberty and that the range of liberty be very wide. Only justice itself, and no mere pragmatic considerations about what could usefully promote the common good, can limit the claims of liberty.

To understand why liberty is so important and why it is so firmly protected by justice, we offer a brief account of how liberty can be understood in terms of our ethical theory.

Liberty means the absence of imposed constraints to pursuing one's own purposes in one's own way. Persons are constrained whenever they must do or refrain from doing something for the sake of purposes which they do not share. A boy playing as he wishes is at liberty; his liberty is restricted if he is required to do chores before he is permitted to play and if he considers the chores as no more than an imposed service to his parents. A girl is at liberty if she is studying courses which interest and appeal to her, so that she finds satisfaction in them and is happy to work at them; her liberty is restricted if she must take required courses which she would not otherwise take in order to obtain a diploma, necessary for a job or other purpose she desires.

Slavery is an extreme infringement of liberty, because slaves must work constantly to achieve purposes with which they are not in the least identified. The purposes are those of the master. The slave's labor is alienated to the master's use. The slave only suffers this situation for the sake of survival and what security in the necessities of life being owned by another offers.

The maximum of liberty in a social situation exists where a group of persons voluntarily cooperate together in working for an objective dear to all of them, a purpose in which all share and find their own identities and fulfillment. One might think of children playing together simply for the joy of the game and one another's companionship as a model case of liberty. No one is making them do anything.

One must contrast with liberty as we have just defined it a false concept which is rather widely held. According to this false concept the essence of liberty is individualism. One way in which this concept arises is by starting to think of social relationships from an essentially negative point of view. If one assumes that human persons are naturally selfish and tend to be wicked, one might suppose that government is primarily a constraint upon individual excesses. Ideally, on this assumption, there would be no law, no authority, no one ever giving direction to another. But, sadly, wickedness must be limited by force, and so laws must be made, the rule of law enforced, and those too blind or too selfish to pursue the greater good compelled to do so. Since on this theory government is no more than a necessary evil, the limitation upon government, which is liberty, is regarded as a good. Liberty is the residue of individuality which survives social control.

On our definition the children playing together are not less at liberty than they would be engaged in some solitary activities. In order to play they must recognize and respect some minimum of rules, but they see these rules, not as impositions upon their spontaneity, but as a plan for doing together what they wish to do. Captains might be elected and their judgments accepted if the game calls for this; submission is not a restriction upon liberty but a way of participating in the common activity which one wishes to engage in. Similarly, on our view people can exercise their liberty in forming a political society. They can be seeking not simply to repress evils but to cooperate in pursuing a good—justice.

Since there are many human goods and many possible morally good courses of action in most situations, even the most upright people must in their own individual lives make many choices among good possibilities. One might enter this profession or that and cannot in fact do both. Usually the need for choice is dictated, not by the immorality or the lesser goodness of one or the other alternative, but by factual limitations. Likewise, many people who attempt to live together will wish to pursue many good purposes. Even if there were no moral failings at all, their upright acts in many cases would conflict in practice—two groups of children cannot play in the same area at the same time.

If all who live together are to have peace, if their pursuit of goods is to be carried on as smoothly as possible, these factual conflicts must be resolved. Such harmonization of activities would make laws necessary even in a community of perfect saints. And those who made laws—whether the whole people assembled or some few chosen for their special talent in this particular work—would have governmental authority. The difference between this ideal community and the actual one is not that there would be no laws, but that people would not willingly violate the laws, since they would see in them a plan for living together in peace, in mutual respect, in cooperation fulfilling to all.

Thus, we hold that liberty is not essentially individualistic. It is not necessarily contrasted with the directions of law; these need not be felt as constraints at odds with one's own purposes. Precisely in willingly forming or participating in a society committed to a purpose with which one identifies a person exercises liberty, not accepts constraint.

But it follows that if people accept a social order for the sake of goods to which they are committed, and the society then uses its methods of control—especially the coercive methods of political society—to compel people to act for other goods to which they are not in fact committed, then the process of government does infringe liberty. Not finding their identity and fulfillment in the ends to which the laws compel them, people are alienated from the law and regard authority behind the law as a mere power which one has to submit to, attempt to evade, or defy at a very high personal price. Even committed members of such a society are compelled to accept constraints; they go where they do not wish and are forbidden to go where they would.

We do not regard liberty as a basic human good. Liberty, however, is closely related to the realization of all of the basic human goods. It is an aspect of one's actions insofar as they are one's own. Unfortunately, liberty is not always justly used. In such a case, because liberty is not an absolute moral principle, it can be limited without immorality.

Sometimes people who are blind or selfish will set themselves to pursue their own purposes with total disregard of the harm they inflict upon others. The bully will demand to be captain despite his ineptness for the role. In cases like this the society cannot help infringing upon someone's liberty. Either the other children will play under conditions they only reluctantly accept, conditions which substantially damage the goods of play and companionship to which they are committed, and thus their liberty is infringed; or the bully is excluded from the game or refused the role of captain which he covets, and so he does not play as he would like, and his liberty is infringed. If people whose initial desires are incompatible are not pleased to please one another and so accommodate one another, then someone's liberty must be infringed, for some cannot do as they please.

It is worth noticing that liberty does not seem in any ordinary sense to be a means to attaining other goods. One can be at liberty and can exercise liberty while damaging goods—for example, while committing suicide. And one can be at liberty yet do nothing to make use of the opportunity liberty offers for action. Liberty is only the absence of constraint. As such, it is entirely negative and effects nothing whatsoever.

Yet from a moral point of view liberty is very important. People constitute themselves by their own actions. If they have not liberty, then their actions are not in the fullest possible sense their own. Their lives are of necessity constituted otherwise than they wish; they are alienated from their very selves. Only with liberty can persons act in such a way that the selves which they constitute in action are the selves in whom they find their own fulfillment.

Of course, even with liberty an immoral person constitutes a self which cannot be in self-harmony, a self whose integration is a form of self-mutilation and disintegration. But without liberty even a morally upright person is barred from becoming the person he or she wishes to be, a person wholly at peace with himself or herself. The whole point of existing as a human person who lives in the moral domain is to constitute oneself.

Without liberty this process is blocked except to the extent that one becomes able to rise above the limits of one's condition and to make even slavery into a challenge joyfully accepted for the sake of some basic human good such as the nobility of the defiance of Sisyphus or the holiness of the obedience of Jesus—neither of which would be possible for a person whose liberty was not infringed. But not everyone is a Sisyphus or a Jesus. For most people liberty is vital, and for a person's active realization of a great many human goods in a morally upright way it is an indispensable condition.

Thus, on our view liberty must be respected by political society, almost as an absolute, limited only by the demands of justice. For the sake of liberty evil must be tolerated which could be prevented if only the attainment of good consequences were important, and if the constitution by their own acts of persons living their own lives were not important.

A political society does not infringe liberty at all if it makes its reasonably necessary demands upon its consenting members in order to promote their willing cooperation in the pursuit of the goods for which they constituted the society. And it does not infringe liberty wrongly if it makes similar demands upon those who resist them unjustly, who want the benefits of society without helping to bear its burdens, who want to enjoy rights and to evade duties. But a political society infringes liberty wrongly if it must coerce its upright members, for it will be unnecessary to do this unless the demands which are made either are not reasonably necessary for the goods to which they are committed together or are not directed to these goods at all, but rather to some private purpose which not all members of the society share or ought to share.

On our view there are spheres of life into which political society has in principle no business in intervening. Liberty of conscience and belief are of central importance, because they are so basic to the self-constitution of persons. Liberty of communication about matters of conscience and belief is equally vital, because this liberty is essential for persons to constitute themselves together into morally significant communities of love and friendship.

There is widespread agreement in societies with roots in the Christian tradition that these liberties ought to be accepted, although the nations which have adopted marxist ideals and consequentialist methods attack them. However, too many theorists in the liberal democratic nations can offer nothing stronger than considerations of practicability and expedience in terms of good consequences for respecting even these basic liberties.

We do not say it is expedient to respect liberty. We say, rather, that attempts to coerce conscience and fundamental world view are inherently wrong and can never be right. Conscience can be immoral and perverse, but even the immoral and perverse conscience must be respected by law. To attempt in this fundamental sense to enforce morality is simply wrong and could never be just, regardless of consequences.

Consequentialists might say that they cannot imagine any situation in which the infringement of such basic liberties could be justified by any conceivable benefits which could outweigh the harms such infringement would entail. But what a consequentialist cannot imagine today will become imaginable tomorrow, and by the day after tomorrow a once liberal society will despise the blessings of liberty as obstacles to progress toward a better-adjusted world of men and women whose behavior is better and more efficiently conditioned, a society beyond freedom and dignity.

If political society must respect liberty as nearly an absolute and avoid infringing upon certain fundamental liberties absolutely, it must be completely absolutist with respect to justice. For political society justice is not simply one value among others which are to be pursued; justice is a good which should never be put upon a scale and weighed against good consequences of any sort. Morally speaking, justice is one of the basic human goods. It is always wrong directly to act contrary to it. Harmony and friendship among people is the fuller good of which justice is a part. But justice is not only a means. It is an intrinsic condition, never surpassed, of peace and genuine friendship.

Justice means that the roles of people in relation to one another are determined by the possibilities and necessities of the goods to which they are jointly committed. It means that requirements that each member do certain things and forbear from doing certain things, claims that each member receive certain things and be immune from certain things, form a system which has its reason for being in a common purpose. And this system also must be reasonable in the sense that all members of the society who are truly committed to the common purpose can reflect upon it and honestly say that they would be willing to have someone for whom they had deep affection and sympathy fulfill any of the society's roles, being bound by its duties and satisfied with its rights.

This conception of justice is based upon the principle of universalizability or the golden rule. Universalizability does not assume or demand equality in some other sense. Rather, it defines a certain, very important moral sense of equality. Everyone is a person with duties to do and rights to fulfill. Everyone shares personal dignity and deserves the same respect. Everyone enjoys certain rights which truly are unalienable, such as the right to fundamental liberties. And so everyone is entitled to equal protection of the laws. There is no natural caste system, for differences in various valued qualities do not make one more or less a person or make one's life more or less worth living. Precisely as members of political society, as persons before the law, all are equal.

Consequentialists who do not and cannot understand this sense of equality try to define justice in terms of equality in some other sense, whereas we define the relevant sense of equality in terms of justice. What this equality can be and ought to be, consequentialists do not agree. In any case, it is only one good among others, always in danger of being outweighed.

We hold that justice is the basis of all good law, not only in the sense that the law ought to be just, but that it primarily should be for the sake of justice. Thus, for example, we hold that political society must have a law of homicide, not only because most people want their own lives protected but also because universalizable maxims which permit killing must be very closely limited, as we argued at length in chapters seven and eight. Given a law of homicide, it is a matter of justice—equal protection of the laws—not to exclude from the protection it offers those whose lives are judged by others to be not worth living, those who are unwanted by others, those who are a burden to others.

Living justly together is not merely a means to some other good; it is an important aspect of the self-fulfillment as human persons of all those who are dedicated to it. Thus, for political society the demands of justice are sufficient to exclude most attacks upon human life. It is not essential for the state to be prolife. But it is essential and also sufficient for the state to be just, for it to protect life indiscriminately in the defective, the weak, the retarded, the insane, and the senile as well as in the normal, the strong, the bright, the well-balanced, and those in the prime of life.

In summary, justice is a basic human good. Justice requires due respect for liberty which, while not itself one of the basic human goods, is a necessary condition for the active, human realization of any of these goods. We believe, therefore, that morally upright persons may consent to a government based upon a jurisprudence in which liberty and justice are the sole overriding principles and in which the claims of liberty are restricted only by the demands of justice. Such consent is morally upright because this jurisprudence can be accepted and applied without the adoption of any immoral proposal.

No one who accepts such a jurisprudence is committed to doing anything incompatible with any basic human good. The very libertarianism of this jurisprudence offers protection against pressure to engage in any immoral act. A person who accepts this jurisprudence will foresee, of course, that respect for liberty will require toleration of a great deal of immorality, but the proposal to accept the jurisprudence need not include the proposal that any of this moral evil be done. The good of liberty, not its abuse, is what one proposes; the abuse is only accepted.

Finally, the acceptance of this jurisprudence does not require that one immorally absolutize the goods of liberty and justice, so as to deny the irreducible goodness of other basic human goods, such as life. Life and the other goods are not less good than liberty and justice; the latter can be accepted as the proper basis for political society without in the least denigrating the former. To commit oneself to some goods is not to violate others unless one turns against these other goods in making the commitment.

D. Respect for Life Not an Independent Principle

Many readers who agree with us in most of our substantive positions concerning euthanasia and the related issues will object that our refusal to accept any direct limitation upon liberty except justice does imply some disregard for the other goods. If other basic human goods, such as human life, were recognized as direct elements of the constituting purpose of political society, they would justify certain constraints upon the abuse of liberty. From this point of view our refusal to put constraints upon liberty in favor of life will appear to betray a disregard for this good, since such constraints would justify the prevention of certain violations of this good.

We oppose this attempt to introduce the good of human life as a fundamental principle of political society. Moreover, our proposition is not based merely upon a conviction that this approach is bad strategy and bad rhetoric, which is likely to guarantee more victories for the consequentialist proponents of euthanasia than the political appeal of their positions would otherwise win for them. Rather, our opposition is principled. We do not believe that an ideal political society would allow reverence for life to directly constrain liberty. We have several reasons for taking this position.

In the first place, the view that human life is a constituting purpose of political society sometimes is held as part of a theory that all of the basic human goods are included in the constituting purpose of political society. This theory is plainly paternalistic and potentially totalitarian. It also seems to us morally indefensible.

A political society constituted according to this theory would necessarily order and rank the various basic human goods, since it is impossible to promote all of them at the same time and with the same level of commitment. Choices will have to be made and priorities set. These choices will establish one common, public style of life, which will inevitably conflict with the styles of life which otherwise would be chosen by various morally upright persons. The self-constitutions of such persons will be compromised; their liberty will be violated.

This violation of the liberty of citizens is a direct consequence of such a theory of the state. The common good on this conception is all-inclusive. The pursuit by citizens of their own goods in their own ways is necessarily subordinated to the common good. Such a view of the state might have seemed defensible to the Greeks. But to all who have understood that human dignity requires that each person establish his or her own disposition toward God (or whatever each person considers ultimate in reality) by a free and uncoerced choice, this classical view of the state is unacceptable. Personal dignity demands that the most important concerns of individuals transcend the state and be free of its political control and coercive sanctions. If the state claims control in these areas, it oversteps its proper bounds, and mortal conflict ensues.

Of course, one who holds that human life ought to be accepted as an element of the constituting purpose of political society need not hold the theory of the state just criticized. Such a person can hold that human life, because of its special status—perhaps because it is a necessary condition for all the other human goods—must be promoted and protected by the state.

We think that not even this position can be sustained. If human life is an element of the constituting purpose of political society, it would follow that life should be promoted by the state's power. Programs to sustain life and promote health will have to take priority over other public programs—for example, in the field of education. The spending of public funds on the arts or on recreation, when they could be spent on preventive medicine, will be unjustifiable. The use of the resources and power of the state to promote human life will lead to conflicts with the personal preferences of even those citizens who would never violate human life, but who do not consider its promotion more vital than the pursuit of other basic human goods.

Morally upright citizens need not put life high in the hierarchy of goods in their own self-constitution, but if the state is committed to promoting life, they will be coerced into accepting this priority. Again, their liberty will be violated. Moreover, the liberty here violated is not the liberty of the potential suicide, but the liberty of the upright person who simply prefers to spend more on education than on health or who would like to engage in risky mountain climbing which a state committed to life might well outlaw. If life is a good to be promoted by the state, the legitimate exercise of the liberty of upright persons to make different choices will be compromised. This compromise would not necessarily be immoral in itself, but its imposition upon persons who are both morally upright and unwilling to accept it will be unjust.

Those who wish to limit the exercise of liberty by the good of human life might accept the foregoing criticism as valid and limit their thesis to the claim that although the state need not actively promote life, it must uniformly protect it. Such a position would avoid our criticism yet provide a strong enough basis on which to overturn the policy we have argued is jurisprudentially justified on certain matters, such as suicide and the nearly absolute liberty of competent persons to refuse medical treatment. It also would provide a basis for a much more direct argument against the legalization of voluntary euthanasia than the complex argument we constructed in chapter six.

However, if the state is not obliged to promote life, then why must it protect it absolutely, even when justice is at stake neither directly nor indirectly? If the good of human life is a principle of political society, then promotion of this good would be required. If it is not a principle, then a policy of extending absolute protection to human life does not seem to be required, and it is difficult to see how any such policy can be justified. Simply to stipulate that all killing, even killing of oneself, is to be held illegal would be arbitrary. Of course, the common law tradition did forbid all killing. It did so precisely because the common law tradition reflected the Christian morality of the sanctity of life. But a just regard for liberty in a pluralistic society forbids any such appeal to Christian moral norms to justify public policies.

E. The Adequacy of Justice

A state which is as limited as one which can be justified on the jurisprudence we have defended might seem to be seriously impoverished. It might be a just society, but would it be a very good society?

In considering this question one ought to be careful not to identify the state with society, even with the society which is materially coextensive with—that is, which has the same individuals in it as—the state. If the state were minimal, this would not mean that society at various levels and by various associations would be barred from promoting and protecting any and all of the basic goods of persons. A society need not be irreligious because the state avoids establishing religion or preferring any religious or irreligious world view to any other. And if the society is irreligious, it is not clear that state action would help matters. The same thing, we suspect, is true of other human goods.

It should not be concluded that a state committed solely to justice as its proper good and concern will be the sort of state so-called rugged individualists wish for. In the first place, many who are called rugged individualists want all sorts of benefits from the state but do not wish to make proportionate contributions. In other words, they are people whose demands are unjust and who use libertarian language as a cloak for their disregard of the rights of others.

In the second place, rugged individualism often means a theory of property which we think could be shown to be incompatible with justice. Since this is not the place to begin an investigation of the question of what justice requires in the economic domain, we simply assert our view that much of what is wrong with the modern welfare state has developed because the radically social character of the just control of property has not been recognized and legally established by the state as it should be. If the state truly established justice, other societies at various levels would have broad scope for more adequate and more humanly satisfying ways of caring for the helpless, helping the poor, and doing the other things the welfare state rather feebly attempts to do.

Finally, we are convinced that many friends of life who are anxious that the state recognize the sanctity of life and treat life as a direct and independent good of political society really are concerned that on any other conception the state must adopt a policy allowing unjust violations of human life. Our entire argument in this book has tried, among other things, to allay this concern.

What is necessary and sufficient is that the state establish and protect justice, which includes respect for the just claims of liberty. If this is done, while immoral acts against human life will be permitted, the state will not itself engage in such acts and it will not stand by and permit the killing of the innocent in the name of beneficence. The wider conception of the purpose of the state, not the narrow one which restricts it to justice, is the enduring threat to all the basic human goods.

While to some extent the present involvement of various levels of political society in the welfare of private individuals and families—public social insurance and relief—can be defended in terms of the demands of justice, we think that the dynamics of the commitment of the state to welfare funding is a significant cause of the unfolding attack upon innocent human life. In earlier centuries such expenditures were largely a function of families for their own members, of voluntary associations, and of private charities. They became matters of public relief first on the local level; then gradually at the intermediate, state level of American political society, where criminal laws are made and enforced; and only finally at the national level where constitutional decisions are handed down.

The costs of social welfare programs are larger than anyone ever expected. Selfish members of society do not wish more and more to bear these costs. Thus what appeared originally to be a vast accomplishment of humanitarian idealism is becoming an important motive for mass killing. Already a major reason why abortion is legalized is to save the state the costs of caring for unwanted children as they carry on a tradition of dependency. We think it is clear that the poor would be safer if the state which has the power to authorize killing them did not also have the expense of supporting them.

Our conclusion, then, is that the state should protect human life, not because life is a basic human good, but because justice both is such a good and is the good to which the state is committed insofar as it is a genuine community. And justice requires very extensive protection for human life, as it also requires much else which the state does, more or less well, under other titles, such as promoting the general welfare.

No one ought to suppose that the analysis we have proposed in this chapter would separate legal from moral considerations. The noncoincidence between the standards of law and the standards of morality is not a sign of some sort of impossible divorce between the two. Rather it expresses the fact that legal standards only depend upon some few moral standards, not all of them. The moral standards expressed by law are the moral demands of a group of persons who form a good state, among other societies, upon themselves and one another as members of this state, and upon the state itself as their common way of pursuing together the good of justice.

The demands of justice are never surpassed in human relationships, not even in intimate ones. Other relationships are established for the pursuit of other goods; they flesh out the skeleton of justice and make a full-bodied life. But the requirements of justice are not transcended. They remain always. If they are not visible in many relationships, if they are never felt to be present, this is not because they are absent or unnecessary. A person stands erect without protruding bones and aching joints. This person is well. The skeleton becomes visible and is felt only when there is injury or disease.

This will be true in all relationships other than the state itself. In the state, the common tent in which a people live, the skeleton of justice always is exposed. It is the indispensable framework over which is stretched the fabric which protects moral men and women from brute force. If this framework does not stand, the people are exposed to the natural forces of the struggle of all to survive, a struggle in which the fittest to survive are those who survive, but the fittest to live with human dignity are more than others likely to die.

Notes

1: INTRODUCTION

1. Matter of Quinlan, 70 N.J. 10, 355 A.2d 647 (1976), at 654–655, 657–658, and 670–672.

2. *In the Matter of Karen Quinlan,* vol. 1 (Washington, D.C.: University Publications of America, 1975), p. 57.

3. Robert M. Veatch, *Death, Dying, and the Biological Revolution: Our Last Quest for Responsibility* (New Haven and London: Yale University Press, 1976), pp. 21–23.

4. Willard Gaylin, "Harvesting the Dead," *Harper's,* 249 (September 1974), pp. 23–30.

5. B. D. Colen, *Karen Ann Quinlan: Dying in the Age of Eternal Life* (New York: Nash Publishing Co., 1976), pp. 74 and 94–95.

6. U. S. Bureau of the Census, *Statistical Abstract of the United States: 1976,* 97 ed. (Washington, D.C.: Superintendent of Documents, 1976), p. 72, No. 104 and No. 105.

7. Claire F. Ryder and Diane M. Ross, "Terminal Care—Issues and Alternatives," *Public Health Reports,* 92 (1977), pp. 20–29.

8. Odin W. Anderson, "Reflections on the Sick Aged and Helping Systems," in Bernice L. Neugarten and Robert J. Havinghurst, eds., *Social Policy, Social Ethics and the Aging Society* (Washington, D.C.: Superintendent of Documents, 1976), pp. 89–95.

9. Byron Gold, Elizabeth Kutza, and Theodore R. Marmor, "United States Social Policy on Old Age: Present Patterns and Predictions," in Neugarten and Havinghurst, eds., *op. cit.,* pp. 9–21.

10. U. S. Bureau of the Census. *Statistical Abstract,* p. 293, No. 459 (calculations from table supplied by subtracting from total federal expenditures expenditures for veterans programs and education, computing the remainder as a percentage of the total, and multiplying this factor by the percentages of GNP and total federal outlays stated in the table); for defense, p. 326, No. 513.

11. See Anderson, *op. cit.,* p. 94; Robert A. Derzon, administrator, Health Care Financing Administration, Memorandum to the Secretary, U. S. Department of Health, Education, and Welfare, "Additional Cost-Saving Initiatives—ACTION," June 4, 1977, pp. 8–9. Helge Hilding Mansson, "Justifying the Final Solution," *Omega,* 3 (1972), pp. 79–87, reports the chilling results of a social psychology experiment in

which large numbers of university students agreed that the unfit should be killed by society as a final solution to problems of overpopulation and personal misery.

12. See Herbert B. Eckstein, Geoffrey Hatcher, and Eliot Slater, "Severely Malformed Children," *British Medical Journal*, 2 (1975), pp. 285–289.

13. Ronald W. Conley, *The Economics of Mental Retardation* (Baltimore and London: Johns Hopkins University Press, 1973), p. 87.

14. *Ibid.*, pp. 78–79; Morton Kramer *et al.*, *Mental Disorders/Suicide* (Cambridge, Mass.: Harvard University Press, 1972), p. 64.

15. *Developments in Aging: 1976; A Report of the Special Committee on Aging, U.S. Senate, pursuant to Sen. Res. 373* (March 1, 1976), 95th Cong., 1st Sess., p. 46; Bernard A. Stotsky, "Extended Care and Institutional Care," in Ewald W. Busse and Eric Pfeiffer, *Mental Illness in Later Life* (Washington, D.C.: American Psychiatric Association, 1973), p. 172.

16. Walter W. Sackett, "Statement," in *Death with Dignity: An Inquiry into Related Public Issues: Hearings before the Special Committee on Aging, U. S. Senate*, 92nd Cong., 2nd Sess., part 1 (August 7, 1972), p. 30.

17. U. S. Bureau of the Census, *Statistical Abstract*, p. 86, No. 136; Conley, *op. cit.*, pp. 96–97.

18. U. S. Bureau of the Census, *Census of Population: 1970; Subject Reports: Persons in Institutions and Other Group Quarters* (Washington, D.C.: Superintendent of Documents, 1973), p. 61, table 28; *Statistical Abstract*, p. 86, No. 136.

19. U. S. Bureau of the Census, *Census of Population: Persons in Institutions*, p. 44, table 25; *Statistical Abstract*, p. 109, No. 168; *Developments in Aging: 1976*, p. 46.

20. *Developments in Aging: 1976*, p. 43; *Census of Population: Persons in Institutions*, p. 11, table 6; *Statistical Abstract*, p. 85, No. 133.

21. *Developments in Aging: 1976*, pp. 44–47; Conley, *op. cit.*, pp. 360–362.

22. Conley, *op cit.*, p. 39.

23. *Developments in Aging: 1976*, pp. 4 and 33.

24. U. S. Bureau of the Census, *Statistical Abstract*, p. 433, No. 700, shows consumer price inflation at 4.6 percent per year average 1966–1970, 7.4 percent per year average 1971–1975; p. 305, No. 479, shows investment income and profit/loss on sales of investments for all private pension funds other than those managed by insurance companies at less than 4 percent per year.

25. *Financing the Social Security System: Hearings before the Subcommittee on Social Security of the Committee on Ways and Means, House of Representatives*, 94th Cong., 1st Sess. (May 7 to June 19, 1975), p. 185 (report of the quadrennial advisory council).

26. *Ibid.*, pp. 369–379 (statement of John A. Brittain, Brookings Institution), pp. 102–103 (statement of W. Allen Wallis).

27. *Ibid.*, pp. 13–17 (reply by Social Security administration) gives the history of the actuarial estimates; Gold, Kutza, and Marmor, *op. cit.*, p. 13, explicitly ask: "whether a diminishing number of workers, through higher taxation, will be willing to support the steadily growing numbers of retirees."

28. *Financing the Social Security System*, p. 181 (report of the quadrennial advisory council).

29. *Ibid.*, pp. 392–393 (statement of Conrad Taeuber).

30. *Ibid.*, pp. 102–103 (statement of W. Allen Wallis), pp. 275–276 (report of the quadrennial advisory council), p. 382 (statement of Martin Feldstein).

31. *Developments in Aging: 1976*, pp. 26–32; Derzon, in the memorandum cited in

note 11 above, estimates fraud in Medicaid alone at 800–900 million dollars per year (p. 2).

32. *Financing the Social Security System,* p. 113 (statement of J. W. van Gorkum), pp. 199–200 (report of the quadrennial advisory council), p. 419 (remarks of Congressman James A. Burke, chairman of the subcommittee).

33. *Medicine and Aging: An Assessment of Opportunities and Neglect: Hearing before the Special Committee on Aging, United States Senate,* 94th Cong., 2d Sess. (October 13, 1976), p. 13.

34. *Training Needs in Gerontology: Hearing before the Special Committee on Aging, United States Senate,* 93d Cong., 1st Sess. (June 19, 1973), pp. 15–17 (statement by George Ebra).

35. *Developments in Aging: 1976,* p. xix; Theodore R. Marmor, in Neugarten and Havinghurst, eds., *op. cit.,* p. 24.

36. Anderson, *op. cit.,* p. 94.

37. For the history of the legalization of abortion see Germain Grisez, *Abortion: The Myths, the Realities, and the Arguments* (New York and Cleveland: Corpus Books, 1970), pp. 185–266. For the Soviet attitude toward nuclear war see Richard Pipes, "Why the Soviet Union Thinks It Could Fight and Win a Nuclear War," *Commentary,* 58 (July 1977), pp. 21–34.

38. See Grisez, *op. cit.,* pp. 117–150.

39. See John M. Ostheimer and Leonard G. Ritt, "Life and Death: Current Public Attitudes," in Nancy C. Ostheimer and John M. Ostheimer, eds., *Life or Death—Who Controls?* (New York: Springer Publishing Co., 1976), pp. 286–289.

40. "History of Euthanasia in U.S.: Concept for Our Time," *Euthanasia News,* 1 (November 1975), pp. 2–3. The following paragraph (p. 3) is of special importance: "Legislative initiative had all but ceased and it was decided that there was no chance of getting any bills passed until there was a massive educational effort. By the end of the '60s there were two significant events: the Euthanasia Educational Fund was established in 1967 to disseminate information concerning the problem of euthanasia, and Luis Kutner suggested the Living Will at a meeting of the Society." Kutner published his proposal in an article concerned primarily with active euthanasia which switched with practically no transition to the proposal of the "living will": "Comments: Due Process of Euthanasia: The Living Will, a Proposal," *Indiana Law Journal,* 44 (1969), pp. 539–554, especially pp. 548–550.

41. "Society Names New President," *Euthanasia News,* 1 (February 1975), p. 1.

42. Cf. the list inside the back cover of *Death with Dignity: Legislative Manual,* 1976 ed. (New York: Society for the Right to Die, 1976), with the list on the back cover of *Death and Decisions: Excerpts from Papers and Discussion at the Seventh Annual Euthanasia Conference* (New York: The Euthanasia Educational Council, 1976).

43. Cf. "Model Bill," *Death with Dignity: Legislative Manual,* pp. 95–96, with the New Mexico statute, 1977 N. M. LAWS, ch. 287.

44. CAL. HEALTH & SAFETY CODE §§7185–7195 (1976).

45. 1977 N. M. LAWS, ch. 287; 1977 ARK. ACTS, act 879; 1977 N. C. LAWS, ch. 815; 1977 IDAHO LAWS, ch. 106; 1977 TEXAS LEGISLATIVE SERVICE, S.B. 148; 1977 OREGON LEGISLATIVE ASSEMBLY, S.B. 438; 1977 NEVADA LEGISLATURE, Assembly Bill 8.

46. See note 43 above.

47. The 1969 British bill is printed in A.B. Downing, ed., *Euthanasia and the Right to Die* (London: Peter Owen, 1969), pp. 201–206. Both this bill and the California statute contain similar safeguards: the requirement that one's terminal condition be certified by two physicians for one to become a *qualified patient,* the prescription that a

legal form be used for the *directive to physicians,* a fourteen-day *waiting period* after one is qualified before the directive becomes fully effective, and a penalty for *homicide* specified for anyone forging a directive or concealing its revocation. From one point of view such safeguards may be admirable, but they are precisely the machinery needed for active euthanasia.

48. See James M. Gustafson, "Mongolism, Parental Desires, and the Right to Life," *Perspectives in Biology and Medicine,* 16 (1973), pp. 529–557.

49. See Dennis J. Horan, "Euthanasia, Medical Treatment and the Mongoloid Child: Death as a Treatment of Choice?" *Baylor Law Review,* 27 (1975), pp. 76–77.

50. Anthony Shaw, "Dilemmas of 'Informed Consent' in Children," and Raymond S. Duff and A. G. M. Campbell, "Moral and Ethical Dilemmas in the Special-Care Nursery," *New England Journal of Medicine,* 289 (October 25, 1973), pp. 885–890 and 890–894.

51. John M. Freeman, "Is There a Right to Die—Quickly?" *Journal of Pediatrics,* 80 (1972), pp. 904–905.

52. Raymond S. Duff and A. G. M. Campbell, "On Deciding the Care of Severely Handicapped or Dying Persons: With Particular Reference to Infants," *Pediatrics,* 57 (1976), p. 492.

53. James Rachels, "Active and Passive Euthanasia," *New England Journal of Medicine,* 292 (1975), pp. 78–80.

54. John A. Robertson, "Involuntary Euthanasia of Defective Newborns: A Legal Analysis," *Stanford Law Review,* 27 (1975), pp. 217–244.

55. Cf. Harvey A. Stevens and Richard A. Conn, "Right to Life/Involuntary Pediatric Euthanasia," *Mental Retardation,* 14 (1976), pp. 3–6.

56. Joseph Fletcher, "The Right to Die: A Theologian Comments," *Atlantic,* 221 (April 1968), p. 63.

57. See Robert A. Burt, "Authorizing Death for Anomalous Newborns," in Aubrey Milunsky and George J. Annas, eds., *Genetics and the Law* (New York and London: Plenum Press, 1976), p. 441.

58. Joseph Fletcher, "Indicators of Humanhood: A Tentative Profile of Man," *Hastings Center Report,* 2 (November 1972), p. 1.

59. See Eliot Slater, "Assisted Suicide: Some Ethical Considerations," *International Journal of Health Services,* 6 (1976), pp. 321–330.

60. John A. Robertson, "Organ Donations by Incompetents and the Substituted Consent Doctrine," *Columbia Law Review,* 76 (1976), pp. 48–78.

61. Case cited note 1 above, at 664.

62. Cf. Glanville Williams, *The Sanctity of Life and the Criminal Law* (New York: Alfred A. Knopf, 1957), p. 16 (where he claims, falsely, that Christians objected to infanticide mainly because of concerns about baptism), p. 193 (where he makes the same claim about abortion), pp. 254–257 (where he maintains the horror of suicide is religious), p. 312 (where he holds that euthanasia, *since condemned by religious opinion,* must not be prohibited by criminal law).

2: LAW, LIBERTY, AND JUSTICE

1. One of the more adequate treatments is that by Lon L. Fuller, *The Morality of Law,* rev. ed. (New Haven and London: Yale University Press, 1964), pp. 33–94. Fuller's conception of law as a purposeful enterprise (pp. 145–151) and his clear dis-

tinction between managerial direction and law (pp. 200–224) seem cogent and are taken for granted in the present chapter.

2. The classic and influential conception of the doctrine of consent, which certainly influenced the American Founding Fathers, was that of John Locke, *Two Treatises of Government,* ed. Peter Laslett, 2nd ed. (Cambridge: Cambridge University Press, 1967), *The Second Treatise,* chapters 6–8 (pp. 321–367). Our account of consent differs from Locke's by as much as is necessary to meet the objections which have been cogently made against his theory, but we take as our project the articulation of the American proposition as it has unfolded historically in the nation's public philosophy and law.

3. Cf. Alexander Hamilton, James Madison, and John Jay, *The Federalist Papers,* ed. Clinton Rossiter (New York, Scarborough, London: New American Library, 1961), No. 49 (pp. 313–314), No. 78 (pp. 467–468), No. 84 (p. 513), and *passim.*

4. J. R. Lucas, *The Principles of Politics* (Oxford: Clarendon Press, 1966), pp. 279–301, offers sound arguments, including a development of the point we make here, against the minimum state. Robert Nozick, *Anarchy, State, and Utopia* (New York: Basic Books, 1974), p. 351, note 1, rejects one of Lucas's arguments against the minimum state, beyond which Nozick argues (pp. 149–231) one cannot justly go. But Nozick does not deal with the whole of the case Lucas articulated. Moreover, Nozick recognizes only liberty as a per se ground of legitimacy; he fails to see that consent itself would provide no basis for legitimacy if the consent were a mere fact, not a justified act rooted in goods which deserve impartial respect. As soon as justice is made primary, much of Nozick's ingenious argument loses its plausibility.

5. *Federalist Papers,* No. 84 (pp. 512–513).

6. *Annals,* 1st Congress, 1st session, pp. 435–439, in Charles S. Hyneman and George W. Carey, eds., *A Second Federalist: Congress Creates a Government* (New York: Appelton-Century-Crofts, 1967), pp. 266–271.

7. With our discussion of religious liberty cf. John Courtney Murray, *We Hold These Truths: Catholic Reflections on the American Proposition* (New York: Sheed & Ward, 1960), pp. 45–78.

8. John Rawls, *A Theory of Justice* (Cambridge, Mass.: Belknap Press of Harvard University Press, 1971), pp. 22–27, makes the familiar point against a utilitarian conception of government. For an extensive critique of all forms of utilitarianism see Germain Grisez, "Against Consequentialism," *American Journal of Jurisprudence,* 23 (1978), forthcoming.

9. On the limitations of the concept of equality in efforts to clarify the concept of justice see Lucas, *op. cit.,* pp. 233–261. See also George Sabine, "The Two Democratic Traditions," *Philosophical Review,* 61 (1952), pp. 451–474, for a clarification of the historical difference between the implications of the egalitarian and the status-respecting conceptions of democracy. The latter, based upon the tradition of the British common law, has fared far better by the test of historical, political experience in providing stable and (in our view) just principles of constitutionality.

10. Since the conception of justice proposed here is somewhat like that proposed by Rawls, it may be helpful to clarify some respects in which the reasonable participant of our account differs from the rational contracting party in the original position as Rawls describes (*op. cit.,* pp. 118–150) such a party. Like Rawls's contracting party, our reasonable participant is rational in limiting prescriptions to those which can be universalized. But we do not assume mutual disinterestedness, nor do we assume that there are preferences to be ordered lexically. Our reasonable participant considers the substantive purposes of society and everything which enters into the constitution, not merely possi-

ble ordering principles, as a foundation for justice. Our reasonable participant proceeds with many fewer specifications than does Rawls's rational contracting party; our reasonable participant can consider at each juncture what can be prescribed universalizably by one committed to the common purposes of the society. On our view it is what underlies and justifies the intuitions of the reasonable participant, not what is pronounced in accord with them, which is the core of the concept of justice. The pronouncements of Rawls's rational contracting party, by contrast, are supposed to define political justice.

11. The strain of trying to interpret Fifth Amendment protections on a utilitarian theory is evident in many cases, such as those cited by Yale Kamisar, "Some Non-Religious Views against Proposed 'Mercy Killing' Legislation," *Minnesota Law Review*, 42 (1958), pp. 1038–1041. Herbert Packer, *The Limits of the Criminal Sanction* (Stanford, California: Stanford University Press, 1968), pp. 149–173, contrasts the "due process model" with the "crime control model" of criminal law procedure. See also Gertrude Himmelfarb, *On Liberty and Liberalism: The Case of John Stuart Mill* (New York: Alfred A. Knopf, 1974), p. 323.

12. Although we are concerned here with equal protection of the laws as a standard for legislation rather than as a judicial principle of constitutional law, we suggest as helpful a classic article by Joseph Tussman and Jacobus tenBrock, "The Equal Protection of the Laws," *California Law Review*, 37 (1949), pp. 341–381.

13. Once more we are concerned with the ideal of justice expressed by the phrase. In constitutional law the privileges or immunities clause was rendered practically null by the U. S. Supreme Court decision in the *Slaughter-House Cases*, 83 U.S. (16 Wall.) 36 (1873). It has not yet been revivified, although the due process clause was drafted into service in its place. Cf. Normand G. Benoit, "The Privileges or Immunities Clause of the Fourteenth Amendment: Can There Be Life after Death?" *Suffolk University Law Review*, 11 (1976), pp. 61–112.

14. H. L. A. Hart, *The Concept of Law* (Oxford: Clarendon Press, 1961), pp. 181–195, formulates a minimalistic concept of "natural law," which has become widely assumed; we do not consider it adequate as an account of natural law or of the natural foundations of law.

15. In *On Liberty* Mill did not claim liberty to be a moral principle independent of utility. But Mill considered liberty to be a good which makes its own categorical demand for respect and recognition. Indeed, Mill tended to absolutize this demand of liberty. In this Mill was inconsistent; cf. Himmelfarb, *op. cit.*, pp. 3–139.

16. Louis Henkin, "Morals and the Constitution: The Sin of Obscenity," *Columbia Law Review*, 63 (1963), pp. 401–414, proposed a standard of utilitarian rationality, to the exclusion of any alternative standard, as the norm for acceptable legislation aimed at control of behavior.

17. Griswold v. Connecticut, 381 U.S. 479, 85 S.Ct. 1678 (1965) at 1681–1682.

18. *Ibid.*, at 1682–1690.

19. *Ibid.*, at 1690–1691.

20. *Ibid.*, at 1694–1707.

21. Stanley v. Georgia, 397 U.S. 557 (1969) at 564.

22. Eisenstadt v. Baird, 405 U.S. 438, 92 S.Ct. 1029 (1972) at 1038.

23. Roe v. Wade, 410 U.S. 113, 93 S.Ct. 705 (1973) at 726–728.

24. *Ibid.*, at 756–759.

25. Louis Henkin, "Privacy and Autonomy," *Columbia Law Review*, 74 (1974), pp. 1424–1431.

26. John Hart Ely, "The Wages of Crying Wolf: A Comment on *Roe v. Wade*," *Yale Law Journal*, 82 (1973), pp. 932–933.

27. Henkin, "Privacy and Autonomy," p. 1427.

28. Archibald Cox, *The Role of the Supreme Court in American Government* (London, Oxford, New York: Oxford University Press, 1976), pp. 51–55 and 112–115, takes a less negative position than Ely's toward the Court's work but demands that the Court act in a principled manner beyond mere pragmatism, because a Court which is completely pragmatic will lose status as an impartial arbitrator, become enmeshed in the political process, and so become unable to function effectively. See also Arnold H. Loewy, "Abortive Reasons and Obscene Standards: A Comment on the Abortion and Obscenity Cases," *North Carolina Law Review,* 52 (1973), pp. 223–234; Richard A. Epstein, "Substantive Due Process by Any Other Name: The Abortion Cases," 1973 *Supreme Court Review,* pp. 159–185; Norman Viera, "Roe and Doe: Substantive Due Process and the Right of Abortion," *Hastings Law Journal,* 25 (1974), pp. 867–879; Robert A. Destro, "Abortion and the Constitution: The Need for a Life-Protective Amendment," *California Law Review,* 63 (1975), pp. 1250–1351, especially p. 1304. Perhaps the most significant attempt to rationalize the Court's decisions in the *Abortion Cases* is Laurence H. Tribe, "Foreword: Toward a Model of Roles in the Due Process of Life and Law," *Harvard Law Review,* 87 (1973), pp. 1–53; Tribe's effort was effectively criticized by Joseph W. Dellapenna, "Nor Piety Nor Wit: The Supreme Court on Abortion," *Columbia Human Rights Law Review,* 6 (1974), pp. 379–413, especially pp. 384–389. See also Michael J. Perry, "Abortion, the Public Morals, and the Police Power: The Ethical Function of Substantive Due Process," *U.C.L.A. Law Review,* 23 (1976), pp. 692–693; Frank R. Strong, "Bicentennial Benchmark: Two Centuries of Evolution of Constitutional Processes," *North Carolina Law Review,* 55 (1976), pp. 96–105; Robert G. Dixon, Jr., "The 'New' Substantive Due Process and the Democratic Ethic: A Prolegomenon," *Brigham Young University Law Review* (1976), pp. 84–87.

29. On the motorcycle and snake cases see Norman L. Cantor, "A Patient's Decision to Decline Life-Saving Medical Treatment: Bodily Integrity Versus the Preservation of Life," *Rutgers Law Review,* 26 (1973), pp. 246–247; "Notes: Informed Consent and the Dying Patient," *Yale Law Journal,* 83 (1974), p. 1644, note 73. Cf. Henkin, "Privacy and Autonomy," pp. 1425–1433.

30. Basil Mitchell, *Law, Morality and Religion in a Secular Society* (London, New York, Toronto: Oxford University Press, 1967), expounds and masterfully criticizes the views of H. L. A. Hart, Lord Devlin, and others; his own conclusions differ little from the view we articulate on this point.

31. Cf. Lucas, *op. cit.,* pp. 162–167.

32. In declaring religious liberty Vatican II, *Dignitatis Humanae,* 11, explicitly recognizes that this liberty is abused and asserts that it is a divinely revealed truth that this evil ought to be accepted. The rational argument in favor of religious liberty, *ibid.,* 3, is the same as that proposed above: coerced acts of this sort are not conducive to participation in the good of religion.

3: DEFINITION OF DEATH

1. Cf. Carl E. Wasmuth, Jr., "The Concept of Death," *Ohio State Law Journal,* 30 (1969), pp. 41–44; Daniel J. Conway, "Medical and Legal Views of Death: Confrontation and Reconciliation," *St. Louis University Law Journal,* 19 (1974), pp. 176–178.

2. See Gunnar Biörck, "When Is Death?" *Wisconsin Law Review,* 1968 (1968), p. 493; Wasmuth, *op. cit.,* pp. 34–38.

3. The technique of feeding is described in Matter of Quinlan, 137 N.J. Super. 227, 348 A.2d 801 (1975) at 808; 70 N.J. 10, 355 A.2d 647 (1976) at 655. Karen Quinlan entered hospital 15 April 1975; the New Jersey Supreme Court decided her case 31 March 1976, and at this time remarked (*ibid.*) that she had lost 40 pounds, yet as this is written in March 1978 she has not yet died.

4. See Biörck, *op. cit.,* pp. 491–492 and 495; cf. Ronald Converse, "But When Did He Die?: *Tucker v. Lower* and the Brain-Death Concept," *San Diego Law Review,* 12 (1975), pp. 424–435, makes graphically clear in the circumstances of a particular case the relationship between the definition of death debate and transplant surgery, in particular transplantation of the heart.

5. Cf. Paul Ramsey, *The Patient as Person: Explorations in Medical Ethics* (New Haven and London: Yale University Press, 1970), p. 83; David W. Louisell, "Transplantation: Existing Legal Constraints," in Gordon Wolstenholme and Maeve O'Conner, eds, *Law and Ethics of Transplantation* (London: J. A. Churchill, 1968), pp. 91–93.

6. See Luis Kutner, "Due Process of Human Transplants: A Proposal," *University of Miami Law Review,* 24 (1970), pp. 799–803; for an illustration of the problem see "Uniform Anatomical Gift Act—Death Construed by Court Consonant with Medical Standard of Brain Death—*New York City Health & Hospitals Corp. v. Sulsona,*" *Rutgers Law Review,* 29 (1976), pp. 484–498.

7. Willard Gaylin, "Harvesting the Dead," *Harper's,* 249 (September 1974), pp. 23–24, 26–28, and 30.

8. Ramsey, *op. cit.,* p. 103.

9. Robert M. Veatch, *Death, Dying, and the Biological Revolution: Our Last Quest for Responsiblity* (New Haven and London: Yale University Press, 1976), p. 32, splits the seam between Ramsey's view and ours by saying that it is wrong to change the definition because of benefits to others, but right *to undertake consideration* of the definition, which Veatch nevertheless does not consider to be a matter of fact for this reason.

10. Cf. *ibid.,* p. 23; Ramsey, *op. cit.,* pp. 98–101; H. A. H. Van Till, "Diagnosis of Death in Comatose Patients under Resuscitation Treatment: A Critical Review of the Harvard Report," *American Journal of Law and Medicine,* 2 (1976), pp. 1–5 and 31–38.

11. American Medical Association, *Opinions and Reports of the Judicial Council* (Chicago: American Medical Association, 1977), p. 23.

12. Cf. Van Till, *op. cit.,* pp. 29–30; Veatch, *op. cit.,* pp. 55–61; Alexander Morgan Capron and Leon R. Kass, "A Statutory Definition of the Standards for Determining Human Death: An Appraisal and a Proposal," *University of Pennsylvania Law Review,* 121 (1972), pp. 92–101.

13. "A Definition of Irreversible Coma: Report of the Ad Hoc Committee of the Harvard Medical School to Examine the Definition of Death," *Journal of the American Medical Association,* 205 (August 5, 1968), pp. 337–340.

14. *Ibid.,* pp. 337 and 340; this interpretation is confirmed by the separate article of the chairman, Henry K. Beecher, "The New Definition of Death: Some Opposing Viewpoints," *International Journal of Clinical Pharmacology,* 5 (1971), pp. 120 (note summary, item 2) and 121.

15. "A Definition of Irreversible Coma," pp. 337 and 340.

16. Beecher, *op. cit.,* pp. 120–121 (italics his).

17. "A Definition of Irreversible Coma," p. 339.

18. Cf. Van Till, *op. cit.*, pp. 15–16; Ramsey, *op. cit.*, pp. 89–109; and the bitter reply to his critics by Beecher, *op. cit.*, pp. 122–124.

19. "A Definition of Irreversible Coma," pp. 337–338. An extensive critique of these criteria with references is in Van Till, *op. cit.*, pp. 12–20. Mainly in defense of the Harvard criteria is: "Refinements in Criteria for the Determination of Death: An Appraisal: A Report by the Task Force on Death and Dying of the Institute of Society, Ethics, and the Life Sciences," *Journal of the American Medical Association,* 221 (July 3, 1972), pp. 48–53. The latter relies (pp. 50–51) on an unpublished report of 128 autopsy studies of the brains of individuals who had met the criteria—all were found to have been destroyed—and on reports collected by Daniel Silverman *et al.,* "Irreversible Coma Associated with Electrocerebral Silence," *Neurology,* 20 (1970), pp. 525–533, from 279 electroencephalographers which showed that of 2,650 patients with presumed isoelectric EEGs of up to 24 hours duration, only three, outside the Harvard criteria, *recovered cerebral function* (p. 533). But this proves nothing whatever about death unless it is assumed that one who is permanently unconscious is dead even if otherwise wholly independent of machinery and apparently merely in a deep sleep. Gerald M. Devins and Robert T. Diamond, "The Determination of Death," *Omega,* 7 (1977), p. 285, summarize evidence indicating that EEG is of little value in most cases and could be contraindicated in some.

20. See Van Till, *op. cit.*, pp. 20–25; Veatch, *op. cit.*, p. 47 and the works he cites.

21. Robert S. Morison, "Death: Process or Event?" (Paper delivered at a symposium at the AAAS meeting in Chicago, Ill., 29 December 1970), *Science,* 173 (20 August 1971), pp. 694–698.

22. Leon R. Kass, "Death as an Event: A Commentary on Robert Morison," *Science,* 173 (20 August 1971), pp. 698–702.

23. Roger B. Dworkin, "Death in Context," *Indiana Law Journal,* 48 (1973), pp. 623–639.

24. Alexander Morgan Capron, "The Purpose of Death: A Reply to Professor Dworkin," *Indiana Law Journal,* 48 (1973), pp. 640–646.

25. On the person and the law see Germain Grisez, *Abortion: The Myths, the Realities, and the Arguments* (New York and Cleveland: Corpus Books, 1970), pp. 402–410; on the confusion which results from uncertainty see Kutner, *op. cit.*, pp. 793–803.

26. William C. Charron, "Death: A Philosophical Perspective on the Legal Definitions," *Washington University Law Quarterly,* 1975 (1975), pp. 979–1005.

27. *Ibid.*, p. 983.

28. See two representatives of the distinct major types of contemporary philosophy: P. F. Strawson, "Persons," in G. N. A. Vesey, ed., *Body and Mind* (London: George Allen & Unwin, 1964), pp. 403–424; Gabriel Marcel, *The Mystery of Being,* vol. 1, *Reflection and Mystery* (Chicago: Henry Regnery, 1960), pp. 127–153.

29. Joseph Fletcher, *Morals and Medicine* (Boston: Beacon Press, 1960), p. 211 (italics his).

30. Joseph Fletcher, "New Definitions of Death," *Prism,* 2 (January 1974), p. 14.

31. *Ibid.*, p. 36.

32. Hans Jonas, *Philosophical Essays: From Ancient Creed to Technological Man* (Englewood Cliffs, N.J.: Prentice-Hall, 1974), p. 139.

33. In addition to the book, Veatch has presented his view on this matter somewhat more simply and straightforwardly in an article: "The Whole-Brain-Oriented Concept of Death: An Outmoded Philosophical Formulation," *Journal of Thanatology,* 3 (1975), pp. 13–30.

34. Veatch, *Death, Dying,* p. 25.

35. *Ibid.,* pp. 25–42, quotations at 42; Veatch's use of "animalistic" here reveals that although he rejects the old-fashioned dualism, he falls into the modern type.

36. *Ibid.,* pp. 36–38, 46–47 and 53; cf. idem, "The Whole-Brain-Oriented Concept of Death," pp. 23–28.

37. Veatch, "The Whole-Brain-Oriented Concept of Death," pp. 20–23; idem, *Death, Dying,* pp. 38–42.

38. Veatch, *Death, Dying,* pp. 48–50 and 53; however, on the limitations of EEG see Devins and Diamond, *loc. cit.*

39. Veatch, *Death, Dying,* p. 36.

40. *Ibid.,* pp. 72–76.

41. Ibid., p. 30.

42. Van Till, *op. cit.,* pp. 8–11.

43. Veatch, *Death, Dying,* p. 36.

44. See David Jensen, *The Principles of Physiology* (New York: Appleton-Century-Crofts, 1976), pp. 44–50; see also Kass, *op. cit.,* p. 699.

45. One of Veatch's arguments in "The Whole-Brain-Oriented Concept of Death" (pp. 13–14 and 23) is that if one is going to move away from the traditional view, one may as well go further than the whole brain. This makes sense only if there is no reason in principle to stop with the whole brain, but our argument is that going this far and no further is not a matter of choice, as Veatch thinks it is, based on one's evaluation of characteristics, but rather is a matter of clarifying an existing concept by applying a sound biological theory to the facts.

46. Van Till, *op. cit.,* pp. 21–25; cf. Peter McL. Black, "Criteria of Death: Review and Comparison," *Postgraduate Medicine,* 57 (February 1975), pp. 69–74.

47. KAN. STAT. § 77–202 (1970); cf. MD. CODE ANN. PUB. GEN. LAWS § 54 F (1972).

48. See Ian McColl Kennedy, "The Kansas Statute on Death—An Appraisal," *New England Journal of Medicine,* 285 (1971), pp. 946–950; Capron and Kass, *op. cit.,* pp. 108–111; Veatch, *Death, Dying,* pp. 62–68.

49. See items cited in note 46, *supra.*

50. CAL. HEALTH & SAFETY CODE § 7180 (1974). Cf. ALASKA STAT. § 09.65.120 (1974); N. M. STAT. ANN. § 1–2–2.2 (1973); VA. CODE § 32–364.3:1 (1973).

51. MICH. COMP. LAWS § 336.8b (1975); cf. GA CODE ANN. § 88.1715.1 (1975); ILL. ANN. STAT., ch. 3 § 552b (1975); OKLA. STAT. ANN. tit. 63 § 1–301g (1975); 1975 OK. LAWS, ch. 565; W. VA. CODE § 16–19–1c (1975); LA. REV. STAT. ANN. § 9:111 (1976); 1976 IOWA ACTS § 208.

52. "House of Delegates Redefines Death, Urges Redefinition of Rape, and Undoes the Houston Amendments," *American Bar Association Journal,* 61 (1975), pp. 463–464.

53. McCarthy DeMere, "Report of the Committee on Medicine and Law," *The Forum,* 11 (1976), pp. 300–316.

54. *Ibid.,* p. 302.

55. TENN. CODE ANN. § 53–459 (1976); cf. 1977 IDAHO SESS. LAWS ch. 130; 1977 MONT. LAWS, ch. 377.

56. N. C. SESS. LAWS, ch. 815 (1977).

57. Matter of Quinlan, 70 N.J. 10, 355 A.2d 647 (1976) at 671.

58. Katzenbach v. Morgan, 384 U.S. 641, 86 S.Ct. 1717 (1966) at 1722; see also Robert A. Destro, "Abortion and the Constitution: The Need for a Life-Protective Amendment," *California Law Review,* 63 (1975), pp. 1288–1289 and 1332–1333; Joseph D. Cronin, "Private Hospitals that Receive Public Funds under the Hill-Burton Pro-

gram: The State Action Implications,'' *New England Law Review,* 12 (1977), pp. 573–574.

4: THE LIBERTY TO REFUSE MEDICAL TREATMENT

1. Schloendorff v. Society of New York Hospital, 211 N.Y. 125, 105 N.E. 92 (1914) at 93.
2. Angela Roddey Holder, *Medical Malpractice Law* (New York, London, Sydney, Toronto: John Wiley & Sons, 1975), pp. 225–234; Norman L. Cantor, ''A Patient's Decision to Decline Life-Saving Medical Treatment: Bodily Integrity Versus the Preservation of Life,'' *Rutgers Law Review,* 26 (1973), pp. 236–237.
3. Nancy Rice, ''Informed Consent: The Illusion of Patient Choice,'' *Emory Law Journal,* 23 (1974), pp. 503–522.
4. Robert M. Veatch, *Death, Dying, and the Biological Revolution: Our Last Quest for Responsibility* (New Haven and London: Yale University Press, 1976), pp. 204–248; Milton D. Heifetz with Charles Mangel, *The Right to Die* (New York: Berkley Medallion Books, 1975), pp. 17–21.
5. Anonymous, ''Notes: Informed Consent and the Dying Patient,'' *Yale Law Journal,* 83 (1974), pp. 1645–1647.
6. See Robert M. Byrn, ''Compulsory Lifesaving Treatment for the Competent Adult,'' *Fordham Law Review,* 44 (1975), p. 31; John J. Paris, ''Compulsory Medical Treatment and Religious Freedom: Whose Law Shall Prevail?'' *University of San Francisco Law Review,* 10 (1975), pp. 25–28.
7. 61 Am. Jur. 2d, § 159; Holder, *op. cit.,* p. 227; Kenney F. Hegland, ''Unauthorized Rendition of Lifesaving Medical Treatment,'' *California Law Review,* 53 (1965), pp. 863–864.
8. 61 Am. Jur. 2d, §§ 159 and 161; cf. Byrn, *op. cit.,* pp. 14–15.
9. Holder, *op. cit.,* pp. 40–64; cf. Matter of Quinlan, 137 N.J. Super. 227, 348 A.2d 801 (1975) at 818.
10. Luis Kutner, ''Comments: Due Process of Euthanasia: The Living Will, a Proposal,'' *Indiana Law Journal,* 44 (1969), pp. 547–548; Thomas H. Sharp, Jr., and Thomas H. Crofts, Jr., ''Death with Dignity: The Physician's Liability,'' *Baylor Law Review,* 27 (1975), pp. 100–102: Byrn, *op. cit.,* pp. 29–31; ''Notes: Informed Consent and the Dying Patient,'' pp. 1649–1650.
11. Richard A. McCormick and André E. Hellegers, ''Legislation and the Living Will,'' *America,* 136 (March 12, 1977), pp. 210–211.
12. Matter of Quinlan, 137 N.J. Super. 227, 348 A.2d 801 (1975) at 806, 813–814, 817–819, 824; 70 N.J. 10, 355 A.2d 647 (1976) at 666–669.
13. In addition to ''Notes: Informed Consent and the Dying Patient'' and the studies of Cantor, Byrn, and Paris, cited in notes 2 and 6 above, see Veatch, *op. cit.,* pp. 116–163, and Peter J. Riga, ''Compulsory Medical Treatment of Adults,'' *Catholic Lawyer,* 22 (1976), pp. 105–137.
14. Natanson v. Kline, 186 Kan. 393, 350 P.2d 1093 (1960) at 1104.
15. Jacobson v. Massachusetts, 197 U.S. 11 (1905); cf. Byrn, *op. cit.,* p. 35.
16. Cf. Riga, *op. cit.,* pp. 112–113.
17. *Ibid.,* pp. 122, 126–127; Byrn, *op. cit.,* p. 30.
18. Veatch, *op. cit.,* pp. 156–159.

19. Cf. places cited in notes 17 and 18; also Cantor, *op. cit.,* pp. 231–233 and 251–254.

20. Byrn, *op. cit.,* p. 25; Riga, *op. cit.,* pp. 123–126; Veatch, *op. cit.,* pp. 152–156.

21. John F. Kennedy Memorial Hospital v. Heston, 58 N.J. 576, 279 A.2d 670 (1971) at 672; Application of President and Directors of Georgetown College, Inc., 331 F.2d 1000 (D.C. Cir.) at 1009, *cert.den.,* 377 U.S. 978 (1964). In both of these cases questions also were raised about the current competency of the patients, yet in both it seems clear that the patients did refuse treatment when competent.

22. Byrn, *op. cit.,* pp. 16–22; Riga, *op. cit.,* pp. 123–126 and 135; Cantor, *op. cit.,* pp. 234, 242–249, and 254–258; Paris, *op. cit.,* pp. 22–25.

23. Byrn, *op. cit.,* p. 18.

24. Cantor, *op. cit.,* pp. 254–258.

25. United States v. George, 239 F. Supp. 752 (D. Conn.1965) at 754; cf. Paris, *op. cit.,* p. 25.

26. The best treatment is in Byrn, *op. cit.,* pp. 22–33; also see Cantor, *op. cit.,* pp. 233 and 250–251; Paris, *op. cit.,* pp. 25–28.

27. In re Yetter, 62 Pa. D. & C. 2d 619 (C.P. Northampton County Ct. 1973) at 623.

28. John F. Kennedy Memorial Hospital v. Heston, *loc. cit.*

29. Matter of Quinlan, 70 N.J. 10, 355 A.2d 647 (1976) at 662–665, 669–670.

30. *Ibid.,* at 664.

31. Veatch, *op. cit.,* pp. 164–186, considers several methods.

32. CAL. HEALTH & SAFETY CODE § 7185–7195 (1976); 1977 TEXAS LEGISLATIVE SERVICE, Senate Bill 148; 1977 OREGON LEGISLATIVE ASSEMBLY, Senate Bill 438; 1977 IDAHO LAWS, ch. 106; 1977 NEVADA LEGISLATURE, Assembly Bill 8; 1977 NORTH CAROLINA GENERAL ASSEMBLY, ch. 815; 1977 NEW MEXICO LEGISLATURE, ch. 287; 1977 ARKANSAS GENERAL ASSEMBLY, act 879.

33. Kutner, *op. cit.,* p. 552.

34. Scott R. Cox, "The Qualified Right to Refuse Medical Treatment and Its Application in a Trust for the Terminally Ill," *Journal of Family Law,* 13 (1973), pp. 153–163.

35. Michael T. Sullivan, "The Dying Person: His Plight and His Right," *New England Law Review,* 8 (1973), pp. 197–215.

36. Jeffrey Alan Smyth, "Antidysthanasia Contracts: A Proposal for Legalizing Death with Dignity," *Pacific Law Journal,* 5 (1974), pp. 738–763.

37. Veatch, *op. cit.,* pp. 184–186.

38. *Ibid.,* pp. 199–202.

39. Cf. G. Emmett Raitt, Jr., "The Minor's Right to Consent to Medical Treatment: A Corollary of the Constitutional Right of Privacy," *Southern California Law Review,* 48 (1975), pp. 1417–1456; Richard Gosse, "Consent to Medical Treatment: A Minor Digression," *University of British Columbia Law Review,* 9 (1974), pp. 56–84.

5: SUICIDE AND LIBERTY

1. Suicide does sometimes serve as a do-it-oneself euthanasia. See, for example, Norman L. Farberow, Edwin S. Shneidman, and Calista V. Leonard, "Suicide among Patients with Malignant Neoplasms," in Edwin S. Shneidman, Norman L. Farberow, and Robert E. Litman, eds., *The Psychology of Suicide* (New York: Science House, 1970), pp. 325–344.

2. Thus Glanville Williams, *The Sanctity of Life and the Criminal Law* (New York: Alfred A. Knopf, 1957), pp. 248–283, in discussing suicide spends more space on criticism of traditional moral conceptions than on examination of properly jurisprudential considerations; his argument is typical and especially important because his work has influenced many others.

3. See Wayne R. LaFave and Austin W. Scott, Jr., *Handbook on Criminal Law* (St. Paul, Minn.: West Publishing Co., 1972), pp. 568–569; 83 C.J.S. 781–782; Robert M. Byrn, "Compulsory Lifesaving Treatment for the Competent Adult," *Fordham Law Review,* 44 (1975), p. 16. It should be noticed that in ordinary language not every self-killing is "suicide"; proponents of legalization and tolerant attitudes toward suicide often tendentiously classify the deeds of martyrs and heroes as suicides, but this is linguistically arbitrary stipulation. See David Daube, "The Linguistics of Suicide," *Philosophy and Public Affairs,* 1 (1971–1972), pp. 387–437, especially 433–437, for the limits of "suicide" and related expressions in several languages.

4. LaFave and Scott, *op. cit.,* p. 569; 83 C.J.S. 783; R. E. Schulman, "Suicide and Suicide Prevention: A Legal Analysis," *American Bar Association Journal,* 54 (1968), p. 856.

5. Byrn, *op. cit.,* pp. 20–22; the case cited is Hales v. Petit, 75 Eng. Rep. 387 (C.B. 1562).

6. See LaFave and Scott, *op. cit.,* p. 569; Williams, *op. cit.,* pp. 273–283 and 288–290; Norman St. John-Stevas, *The Right to Life* (New York, Chicago, San Francisco: Holt, Rinehart and Winston, 1964), pp. 67–70.

7. St. John-Stevas, *op. cit.,* pp. 71–77; Williams, *op. cit.,* pp. 276–286; George Rosen, "History," in Seymour Perlin, ed., *A Handbook for the Study of Suicide* (New York, London, Toronto: Oxford University Press, 1975), pp. 19–26; David F. Greenberg, "Involuntary Psychiatric Commitments to Prevent Suicide," *New York University Law Review,* 49 (1974), pp. 227–236.

8. Cf. Glanville Williams, "The Right to Commit Suicide," *Medico-Legal Journal,* 41 (1973), pp. 26–29; Richard Delgado, "Euthanasia Reconsidered—The Choice of Death as an Aspect of the Right of Privacy," *Arizona Law Review,* 17 (1975), pp. 474–494.

9. E.g., Delgado, *loc. cit.;* William H. Baughman, John C. Bruha, and Francis J. Gould, "Euthanasia: Criminal, Tort, Constitutional, and Legislative Considerations," *Notre Dame Lawyer,* 48 (1973), pp. 1237–1252; Morris D. Forkosch, "Privacy, Human Dignity, Euthanasia—Are These Independent Constitutional Rights?" *University of San Fernando Law Review,* 3 (1974), pp. 18–25.

10. Greenberg, *op. cit.,* pp. 237–242.

11. Williams, *Sanctity of Life,* p. 292.

12. N. Y. PENAL LAW § 35.10 (McKinney).

13. ARK. STAT. ANN. § 41–505.

14. PA. STAT. ANN. tit. 18 § 508 (d) (Purdon).

15. WASH. REV. CODE ANN. § 9.11.040 (6).

16. Williams, *Sanctity of Life,* pp. 292–293.

17. Greenberg, *op. cit.,* pp. 227–269; the argument is persuasive because he shows that if one assumes, as is reasonable, that the burden of proof is upon those who would take away an individual's liberty, then it really cannot be shown that detention gives significant protection to the potential suicide or anyone else. It is important to bear in mind that the fact of suicide does not rebut the presumption of sanity; see 31 C.J.S. *Evidence* § 147 (1964). A fortiori, the fact that someone threatens or attempts suicide does not rebut this presumption. Since diminished responsibility of itself would not

have rendered suicide noncriminal and since this result was desired in a context in which the unalienable character of life could not be directly attacked, those seeking the practical decriminalization of suicide during the past one hundred years or so tended to overstate the mental unbalance of suicides and potential suicides. This was an unfortunate rationalization with negative implications for the basic right of liberty. Since life is no longer regarded as a substantive principle as it used to be, suicide can now be admitted as noncriminal merely because it does not violate justice, and the detriment to liberty can be removed.

18. Cf. Williams, "The Right to Commit Suicide," p. 26.

19. Farberow, Shneidman, and Leonard, *op. cit.*, p. 334; Robert E. Litman and Norman L. Farberow, "Suicide Prevention in Hospitals," in *The Psychology of Suicide*, pp. 461–473.

20. Henry A. Davidson, "Suicide in the Hospital," *Hospitals: Journal of the American Hospital Association*, 43 (November 16, 1969), pp. 55–59.

21. *Ibid.*

22. See Williams, *Sanctity of Life*, pp. 286–304; LaFave and Scott, *op. cit.*, pp. 569–571.

23. See Helen Silving, "Euthanasia: A Study in Comparative Criminal Law," *University of Pennsylvania Law Review*, 103 (1954), pp. 369–386.

24. *Model Penal Code, Proposed Official Draft*, May 4, 1962 (Philadelphia: The American Law Institute), § 210.5 (1).

25. PA. STAT. ANN. tit. 18, § 2505; N. Y. PENAL LAW § 120.35 (McKinney).

26. Suicide Act, 9 & 10 Eliz., 2, c. 60 (1961); cf. St. John-Stevas, *op. cit.*, pp. 76–77; William Ll. Parry-Jones, "Criminal Law and Complicity in Suicide and Attempted Suicide," *Medicine, Science, and the Law*, 13 (1973), pp. 110–119.

27. *Time*, September 5, 1977, p. 21; *MCCL Newsletter*, September 1977, p. 4.

28. *Ibid.*

29. *Model Penal Code, Proposed Official Draft*, § 210.5 (2). For a discussion of aiding and abetting suicide at common law and in American law to 1920 see 13 A.L.R. 1259–1264.

30. N. Y. PENAL LAW § 120.30 (McKinney).

31. FLA. STAT. ANN. § 782.08 (West); cf. MO. ANN. STAT. § 559.080 (Vernon); MINN. STAT. ANN. § 609.215 (West).

32. CAL. PENAL CODE § 401 (West).

33. See Silving, *op. cit.*, pp. 376–377.

34. Williams, *Sanctity of Life*, p. 309.

35. *Model Penal Code, Tentative Draft No. 9*, May 8, 1959 (Philadelphia: The American Law Institute), comments on section 201.5, p. 57.

36. See LaFave and Scott, *op. cit.*, pp. 568–571; Schulman, *op. cit.*, pp. 855–862; 83 C.J.S. 781–785. The situation is so erratic that at least until recently assisting another to commit suicide ranged from murder in some jurisdictions to no crime at all in at least one—Texas.

6: VOLUNTARY ACTIVE EUTHANASIA AND LIBERTY

1. See Nancy Lee Vaughan, "The Right to Die," *California Western Law Review*, 10 (1974), pp. 613–615; Arval A. Morris, "Voluntary Euthanasia," *Washington Law Review*, 45 (1970), pp. 242–243.

2. Marvin Kohl, "Voluntary Beneficent Euthanasia," in Marvin Kohl, ed., *Beneficent Euthanasia* (Buffalo, New York: Prometheus Books, 1975), p. 134.

3. So is the case with the two proposals most seriously debated, those considered by the British House of Lords in 1936 and 1969. The former is printed in Harry Roberts, *Euthanasia and Other Aspects of Life and Death* (London: Constable & Co., 1936), pp. 19–25; the latter in A. B. Downing, ed., *Euthanasia and the Right to Death: The Case for Voluntary Euthanasia* (London: Peter Owen, 1969), pp. 197–206.

4. Kohl, *loc. cit.*

5. Sissela Ann Bok, *Voluntary Euthanasia,* unpublished Ph. D. Dissertation, Department of Philosophy, Harvard University, 1970, pp. 87–109.

6. *Ibid.,* p. 94.

7. *Ibid.,* pp. 110–114.

8. See Yale Kamisar, "Some Non-Religious Views against Proposed 'Mercy Killing' Legislation," *Minnesota Law Review,* 42 (1958), pp. 970–971; Edward J. Gurney, "Is There a Right to Die?—A Study of the Law of Euthanasia," *Cumberland-Samford Law Review,* 2 (1972), pp. 238–240; Jerry B. Wilson, *Death by Decision: The Medical, Moral, and Legal Dilemmas of Euthanasia* (Philadelphia: Westminster Press, 1975), pp. 142–145; Helen Silving, "Euthanasia: A Study in Comparative Criminal Law," *University of Pennsylvania Law Review,* 103 (1954), pp. 352–353 and 379; *On Dying Well: An Anglican Contribution to the Debate on Euthanasia* (London: Church Information Office, 1975), pp. 51–58.

9. Wilson, *op. cit.,* pp. 142–143; Kamisar, *op. cit.,* pp. 970–971, note 9; William H. Baughman, John C. Bruha, and Francis J. Gould, "Survey: Euthanasia: Criminal, Tort, Constitutional and Legislative Considerations," *Notre Dame Lawyer,* 48 (1973), pp. 1204–1206.

10. Joseph Sanders, "Euthanasia: None Dare Call It Murder," *Journal of Criminal Law, Criminology, and Police Science,* 60 (1969), pp. 351–359; Vaughan, *op. cit.,* pp. 613–615; Morris, *loc. cit.;* Wilson, *op. cit.,* pp. 148–155; Baughman *et al., op. cit.,* pp. 1213–1215; Silving, *op. cit.,* pp. 353–354.

11. Kamisar, *op. cit.,* pp. 971–972.

12. People v. Roberts, 178 N.W. 690, 211 Mich. 187, 13 A.L.R. Ann. 1253 (1920) with annotation at 1259–1264; cf. 25 A.L.R. Ann. 1007–1008.

13. E. g., Morris, *op. cit.,* pp. 240, 244, 247–248; Joseph Fletcher, "The Patient's Right to Die," *Harper's Magazine,* 220 (October 1960), pp. 139–140; Marvin M. Moore, "The Case for Voluntary Euthanasia," *University of Missouri at Kansas City Law Review,* 42 (1974), pp. 332–333; *Parliamentary Debates, House of Lords* (5th ser.), 300 (25 March 1969), col. 1196 (Lord Soper), cols. 1203–1204 (Lord Platt).

14. Baughman *et al., op. cit.,* p. 1205 and notes 22–23.

15. Moore, *op. cit.,* p. 337; James Rachels, "Active and Passive Euthanasia," *New England Journal of Medicine,* 292 (Jan. 9, 1975), pp. 78–80; Edward M. Scher, "Legal Aspects of Euthanasia," *Albany Law Review,* 36 (1972), pp. 692–694; Elizabeth Barkin and Sally B. Macdonald, "The Option of Death! Euthanasia: An Issue for the Seventies," *University of San Fernando Law Review,* 4 (1975), pp. 305–309; Walter W. Steele, Jr. and Bill B. Hill, Jr., "A Plea for a Legal Right to Die," *Oklahoma Law Review,* 29 (1976), pp. 332–333, 335–336, 339–340.

16. See Glen William Argan, "The Killing/Letting-Die Controversy: An Aspect of the Morality of Euthanasia," unpublished M. A. Thesis, Department of Philosophy, University of New Brunswick, 1977.

17. See Philippa Foot, "Euthanasia," *Philosophy and Public Affairs,* 6 (1977), pp. 100–102; Norman L. Cantor, "A Patient's Decision to Decline Life-Saving Medical

Treatment: Bodily Integrity versus Preservation of Life," *Rutgers Law Review,* 26 (1973), pp. 260–261; David W. Louisell, "Euthanasia and Biathanasia: On Dying and Killing," *Catholic University Law Review,* 22 (1973), pp. 739–744; George P. Fletcher, "Prolonging Life: Some Legal Considerations," in Downing, ed., *op. cit.,* pp. 75–83.

18. Baughman *et al., op. cit.,* pp. 1207–1210; Kamisar, *op. cit.,* pp. 982–983, esp. note 42.

19. Morris, *op. cit.,* pp. 251–254; *A Plan for Voluntary Euthanasia* (London: Euthanasia Society, 1962), pp. 5–9; C. Killick Millard, "The Case for Euthanasia," *Fortnightly Review,* 136 (December 1931), p. 712; Parliamentary Debates, House of Lords (5th ser.), 103 (1 December 1936), col. 474 (Lord Denman), col. 499 (Earl of Listowel); 169 (28 November 1950), cols. 569–570 (Lord Horder, commenting adversely); Glanville Williams, " 'Mercy-Killing' Legislation—A Rejoinder," *Minnesota Law Review,* 43 (1958), pp. 1–2; idem, "Euthanasia and Abortion," *Colorado Law Review,* 38 (1969), p. 182; Richard Delgado, "Euthanasia Reconsidered—The Choice of Death as an Aspect of the Right of Privacy," *Arizona Law Review,* 17 (1975), p. 479; Marvin Kohl, "Understanding the Case for Beneficent Euthanasia," *Science, Medicine & Man,* 1 (1973), p. 113 and p. 119.

20. Morris, *op. cit.,* pp. 262–264; Glanville Williams, *Sanctity of Life and the Criminal Law* (New York: Alfred A. Knopf, 1957), p. 325; *A Plan for Voluntary Euthanasia,* p. 20; *House of Lords* (1950), cols. 589–590 (Earl of Huntingdon); John Hinton, *Dying* (Harmondsworth, England: Penguin Books, 1967), pp. 65–78.

21. Morris, *op. cit.,* pp. 249–250; Williams, " 'Mercy-Killing' Legislation," p. 2; idem, "Euthanasia and Abortion," pp. 179–180, 183–184; idem, *Sanctity of Life,* pp. 311–315, 317–318; Kohl, "Understanding the Case for Beneficent Euthanasia," pp. 111–112; Antony Flew, "The Principle of Euthanasia," in Downing, ed., *op. cit.,* pp. 32–33; Arthur A. Levisohn, "Voluntary Mercy Deaths: Socio-Legal Aspects of Euthanasia," *Journal of Forensic Medicine,* 8 (April–June 1961), pp. 71–74. Much of this argument commits the fallacy of the circumstantial ad hominem ("poisoning the wells") by attempting to dismiss *all* antieuthanasia argumentation as religious and so as illegitimate.

22. *A Plan for Voluntary Euthanasia,* pp. 5–9.

23. Steele and Hill, *op. cit.,* pp. 333–334; Moore, *op. cit.,* p. 333; Williams, "Euthanasia and Abortion," pp. 181–182; idem, *Sanctity of Life,* pp. 338–339 and 345; Charles Wilshaw, *The Right to Die: A Rational Approach to Voluntary Euthanasia* (London: British Humanist Association, no date), pp. 3–4 and 17–18; Lord Raglan, "The Case for Voluntary Euthanasia," *The Problem of Euthanasia* (Cockenzie, Scotland: Contact Ltd., 1972), p. 11.

24. Kamisar, *op. cit.,* pp. 984–985; *The Problem of Euthanasia* (London: British Medical Association, 1971), p. 2.

25. Williams, *Sanctity of Life,* pp. 334–338; the same interpretation was already advanced in the debate itself: *House of Lords* (1936), cols. 497–498 (Earl of Listowel), cols. 502–503 (Lord Ponsonby); *House of Lords* (1950), col. 558 (Lord Chorley, who was challenged on this by Lord Haden-Guest), col. 561 (Lord Denman, claiming that Lord Dawson said more outside the formal debate).

26. *House of Lords* (1936), col. 483.

27. *Ibid.,* cols. 484–487.

28. *Ibid.,* col. 492.

29. *House of Lords* (1950), col. 568.

30. *House of Lords* (1936), cols. 467–468.

31. *On Dying Well*, pp. 63–65; Hugh Trowell, *The Unfinished Debate on Euthanasia* (London: Institute of Religion and Medicine, 1971), pp. 26–29 and 58–60.

32. Lael Tucker Wertenbaker, *Death of a Man* (Boston: Beacon Press, 1974), p. 175, says that her husband took fifteen grains of morphine, which is just twice the maximum dose at the highest estimate cited by Trowell, *op. cit.*, p. 59.

33. Trowell, *op. cit.*, pp. 27–28.

34. Glanville Williams, "Euthanasia and the Physician," in Kohl, ed., *op. cit.*, pp. 146–147.

35. Roberts, *op. cit.*, p. 10; *On Dying Well*, p. 60.

36. Baughman *et al.*, *op. cit.*, pp. 1229–1231; Williams, *Sanctity of Life*, p. 328; Luis Kutner, "Comments: Due Process of Euthanasia: The Living Will, A Proposal," *Indiana Law Journal*, 44 (1969), pp. 542–543; Sheila Schiff Cole and Marta Sachey Shea, "Voluntary Euthanasia: A Proposed Remedy," *Albany Law Review*, 39 (1975), p. 834; Silving, *op. cit.*, p. 354; Kamisar, *op. cit.*, pp. 971–973, answers this sort of argument.

37. Kamisar, *op. cit.*, pp. 971–974; Silving, *op. cit.*, pp. 387–389, urges a lesser punishment rather than legalization of such killing.

38. Joe P. Tupin, "Some Psychiatric Issues in Euthanasia," in Kohl, ed., *op. cit.*, pp. 194–197, outlines with unusual clarity what would be involved in informed consent.

39. *House of Lords* (1936), col. 500 (Earl of Crawford).

40. Elisabeth Kübler-Ross, *On Death and Dying* (New York: Macmillan Publishing Co., 1970), pp. 112–137 and 157–180; *Questions and Answers on Death and Dying* (New York and London: Macmillan Publishing Co. and Collier Macmillan, 1974), pp. 52–73 and 86.

41. Kamisar, *op. cit.*, pp. 993–1013; Trowell, *op. cit.*, pp. 50–52; *Problem of Euthanasia* (British Medical Association), p. 6; Laurence V. Foye, Jr., "Statement," in U. S. Senate, Special Committee on the Aging, 92d Cong., 2d Sess., *Death with Dignity: An Inquiry Into Related Public Issues*, part I, pp. 22–25.

42. Millard, *op. cit.*, p. 717.

43. Tupin, *op. cit.*, pp. 194–197; Kamisar, *op. cit.*, pp. 985–993; Scher, *op. cit.*, pp. 690–692; Kutner, *op. cit.*, p. 545; *House of Lords* (1936), col. 485 (Archbishop of Canterbury); *House of Lords* (1950), cols. 564–565 (Archbishop of York).

44. Steele and Hill, *op. cit.*, pp. 341–342.

45. See "Res Ipsa Loquitur, Parts I–VII," *Journal of the American Medical Association*, 221 (1972), pp. 537, 633, 1201, 1329, 1441, and 1587; 222 (1972), p. 121. Persons working in hospitals tell tales of even more horrendous mistakes which never reach a court—the survivors remain ignorant or the case is settled.

46. In Roberts, *op. cit.*, pp. 21–25.

47. *House of Lords* (1950), col. 596.

48. Williams, *Sanctity of Life*, pp. 339–341.

49. *Ibid.*, p. 345.

50. Moore, *op. cit.*, p. 339.

51. In Downing, ed., *op. cit.*, pp. 201–206.

52. *House of Lords* (1969), cols, 1152–1155.

53. *Ibid.*, cols. 1171–1172.

54. *Ibid.*, cols. 1234–1235.

55. *Ibid.*, cols. 1240–1241.

56. Morris, *op. cit.*, p. 259.

57. Walter W. Sackett, "Statement," in U. S. Senate, *Death with Dignity*, p. 36.

58. Kamisar, *op. cit.*, pp. 976–977.

59. Bruce Vodiga, "Euthanasia and the Right to Die—Moral, Ethical and Legal Perspectives," *Chicago-Kent Law Review*, 51 (1974), p. 8.

60. Marvin Kohl, *The Morality of Killing: Sanctity of Life, Abortion and Euthanasia* (Atlantic Highlands, N.J.: Humanities Press, 1974), p. 17.

61. Williams, " 'Mercy-Killing' Legislation—A Rejoinder," pp. 3–4.

62. Millard, *op. cit.*, pp. 708–709; Roberts, *op. cit.*, pp. 22–23; Kamisar, *op. cit.*, pp. 978–979, on both British and American bills; *Plan for Voluntary Euthanasia*, p. 15; Moore, *op. cit.*, p. 338, note 72; Levisohn, *op. cit.*, p. 70; Cole and Shea, *op. cit.*, pp. 842–844, 854–855; Joseph Fletcher, *Morals and Medicine* (Boston: Beacon Press, 1960), pp. 187–188; New South Wales Humanist Society, *Euthanasia* (Winston Hills, N.S.W.: 1973), p. 4; O. Ruth Russell, "Moral and Legal Aspects of Euthanasia," *The Humanist*, 34 (July/August 1974), p. 26; *House of Lords* (1969), col. 1164 (Lord Newton).

63. Objections to what the schools are doing are registered in a vast literature, of uneven quality. But the literature does show the extent of dissatisfaction. The following items are taken as examples: Onalee McGraw, *Secular Humanism and the Schools: The Issue Whose Time Has Come* (Washington, D.C.: The Heritage Foundation, 1976); John Steinbacher, *The Child Seducers* (Fullertown, California: Educator Publications, 1970); Russ Walton, *One Nation Under God* (Old Tappan, N.J.: Third Century Publishers, 1975), pp. 100–134; Susan M. Marshner, *Man: A Course of Study—Prototype for Federalized Textbooks?* (Washington, D.C.: The Heritage Foundation, 1975); United States General Accounting Office, *Report to the House Committee on Science and Technology by the Comptroller General of the United States: Administration of the Science Education Project "Man: A Course of Study" (MACOS)* (October 14, 1975), pp. 1–10, includes descriptive information about the program and its wide use; Barbara M. Morris, "A Parent's Guide to Understanding and Recognizing the Religion of Humanism in Public Schools," mimeograph, Ellicott City, Maryland, 1976; Virginia L. Gray and Timothy L. Hastings, "Humanistic Education in Southern Illinois," mimeograph, West Frankfort, Illinois, 1977; Brief of Appellant, Hobolth v. Greenway, filed in the Court of Appeals, State of Michigan, October 15, 1973. Arguments that the exclusive grip of the public schools on public support of education chills the exercise of religious liberty are presented by Joseph F. Costanzo, *This Nation Under God: Church, State and Schools in America* (New York: Herder and Herder, 1964), pp. 211–212, 294–296, and *passim;* Virgil C. Blum, S.J., *Catholic Parents: Political Eunuchs* (St. Cloud, Minnesota: Media + Materials, 1972), pp. 43–58. See below, chapter ten, section D.

64. Kamisar, *op. cit.*, pp. 980–981; Roberts, *op. cit.*, pp. 14–15, saw this difficulty clearly; see *House of Lords* (1936), cols. 475–476 (Viscount Fitzalan of Derwent), cols. 482–483 (Lord Dawson of Penn), col. 489 (Lord Horder).

65. Kamisar, *op. cit.*, pp. 1015–1030 and 1030–1041.

66. *Ibid.*, especially pp. 1015–1019.

67. See Sackett, *op. cit.*, pp. 30–39; cf. David Mall, "Death and the Rhetoric of Unknowing," in Dennis J. Horan and David Mall, eds., *Death, Dying, and Euthanasia* (Washington, D.C.: University Publications of America, 1977), pp. 654–656.

68. Kamisar, *op. cit.*, pp. 1019–1025.

69. Williams, "Euthanasia and Abortion," pp. 184–187; Vaughan, *op. cit.*, pp. 614–615 and 622; Steele and Hill, *op. cit.*, 337–338; Morris, *op. cit.*, pp. 242–243; Moore, *op. cit.*, pp. 331–333; Levisohn, *op. cit.*, p. 66; Baughman *et al.*, *op. cit.*, pp. 1204, 1206, and 1213–1215; Cole and Shea, *op. cit.*, pp. 832, 836; Fletcher, "The Patient's Right to Die," p. 139; Downing, ed., *op. cit.*, pp. 20–21; Kutner, *op. cit.*, pp. 540–541; Barkin and Macdonald, *op. cit.*, pp. 303–304; Rowine Hayes Brown and Richard B. Truitt, "Euthanasia and the Right to Die," *Ohio Northern University Law Review*, 3

(1976), pp. 616–621; Daniel C. Maguire, *Death by Choice* (New York: Schocken Books, 1975), pp. 23–26, 150, 173–177; Marya Mannes, *Last Rights* (New York: Signet, 1975), pp. 92–99; *House of Lords* (1969), col. 1218 (Earl of Huntingdon), cols. 1222–1223 (Lord Ritchie-Calder), cols. 1244–1245 (Lord Segal).

70. Kamisar, *op. cit.*, pp. 1024–1029.

71. Joseph Fletcher, "The Right to Die: A Theologian Comments," *Atlantic*, 221 (April 1968), pp. 63–64; idem, "Ethics and Euthanasia," *American Journal of Nursing*, 73 (1973), p. 674; Williams, "Euthanasia and Abortion," p. 182; idem, " 'Mercy-Killing' Legislation—A Rejoinder," pp. 9–12; idem, "Euthanasia," *Medico-Legal Journal*, 41 (1973), pp. 23–24; idem, "Euthanasia and the Physician," pp. 154–157; Kohl, "Understanding the Case for Beneficent Euthanasia," pp. 112–113; Sackett, *op. cit.*, pp. 30–39; Maguire, *op. cit.*, pp. 173–177; Moore, *op. cit.*, pp. 335 and 339; Steele and Hill, *op. cit.*, pp. 343–346; Ronald P. Kaplan, "Euthanasia Legislation: A Survey and a Model Act," *American Journal of Law & Medicine*, 21 (1976), pp. 69–70 and 93–94; New South Wales Humanist Society, *op. cit.*, p. 6; Russell, *op. cit.*, p. 26.

72. Williams, *Sanctity of Life*, pp. 314–315.

73. Kamisar, *op. cit.*, pp. 1030–1031 and 1038–1039.

74. Williams, *Sanctity of Life*, pp. 315–316; idem, "Euthanasia and Abortion," p. 181; idem, " 'Mercy-Killing' Legislation—A Rejoinder," pp. 9–11.

75. Kohl, "Understanding the Case for Beneficent Euthanasia," pp. 113–114.

76. Arthur Dyck, "Beneficent Euthanasia and Benemortasia: Alternative Views of Mercy," in Kohl, ed., *op. cit.*, pp. 120–122 and 128.

77. Fletcher, "Ethics and Euthanasia," pp. 670–675; Williams, *Sanctity of Life*, pp. 316–317; idem, " 'Mercy-Killing' Legislation—A Rejoinder," p. 11; Kohl, "Voluntary Beneficent Euthanasia," in Kohl, ed., *op. cit.*, pp. 139–140; Richard Brandt, "A Moral Principle about Killing," in Kohl, ed., *op. cit.*, p. 113; Steele and Hill, *op. cit.*, p. 328; Sackett, *op. cit.*, pp. 30–39; about Sackett see Kaplan, *op. cit.*, pp. 47 and 54; Eliot Slater, "Assisted Suicide: Some Ethical Considerations," *International Journal of Health Services*, 6 (1976), pp. 323–324; against this view see Paul Ramsey, "The Indignity of 'Death with Dignity'," in Horan and Mall, eds., *op. cit.*, pp. 306–313. In *House of Lords* (1936), col. 479, Lord Dawson of Penn clearly formulated the principle of the priority of quality of life; perhaps this is the reason why Williams and others assumed he was proeuthanasia, although their conclusion was not his. Almost every proeuthanasia author quite explicitly accepts some form of quality-of-life ethic which would justify nonvoluntary euthanasia; the places cited in this note are merely a sampling which could be augmented endlessly.

78. This is the point of view of those who see no distinction at all between the concept of euthanasia and that of assisted suicide; their point is that all and only those who choose to be killed should be at liberty to be killed "on demand" for whatever reason and by whomever they wish. The only restriction a view such as this would accept would be in the definite public interest—e.g., to protect others from being killed incidentally.

79. Curiously, several contributors to Kohl, ed., *op. cit.*, present elements of a view of this sort; see Robert Hoffman, "Death and Dignity," p. 78, for a libertarian concept of dignity; Bertram and Elsie Bandman, "Rights, Justice, and Euthanasia," pp. 90–96, for a defense of the libertarian principle of consent against fanatical kindness; Baruch Brody, "Voluntary Euthanasia and the Law," pp. 228–229, for a formulation which excludes the patient's condition and the agent's motives as irrelevant.

80. Morris, *op. cit.*, pp. 254–255, offers a libertarian argument, but then (pp. 266–271) establishes obviously arbitrary limiting conditions; Cole and Shea, *op. cit.*, pp.

838–841, have obvious difficulty in trying to justify limits; Steele and Hill, *op. cit.*, p. 343, fail to ground limits, since obviously anyone who wishes to die is in some sort of distress; *On Dying Well,* p. 6, points out the general indefensibility of limits proposed; Barbara Yondorf, "The Declining and Wretched," *Public Policy,* 23 (1975), pp. 480–482, argues that the key condition is simply wretchedness or misery, which is not necessarily related to terminal illness or other easily specified conditions.

81. The argument from animals is especially prevalent in the British debate: *House of Lords* (1936), col. 473 (Lord Denman); (1950), col 556 (Lord Chorley); answered, cols. 585–586 (Lord Webb-Johnson); nonvoluntariness emphasized, cols. 594–595 (Viscount Jowitt); (1969), col. 1186 (Lord Ailwyn); answered, cols. 1191–1192 (Earl of Longford). Wilshaw, *op. cit.*, p. 7, uses the argument; Trowell, *op. cit.*, p. 18, answers it. Those who use the argument from animal to human euthanasia would do well to study the latter with some care; see, e.g., Modern Veterinary Practice Staff, "Euthanasia: An Act of Compassion or One of Expediency?" *Modern Veterinary Practice,* 56 (June 1975), pp. 395–400; "Report of the AVMA Panel on Euthanasia," *American Veterinary Medical Association Journal,* 160 (1972), pp. 761–772. From a veterinary point of view euthanasia is simply killing the animal in a way which is relatively painless for it. In most instances the animal to be killed is not suffering antecedent pain but has simply served its purpose, and the mercy is in killing it painlessly rather than in an unnecessarily painful way. Obviously, if people are going to be killed, euthanasia in this sense is preferable to torture. But should people be killed?

82. A leading case is Strunk v. Strunk, 445 SW2d 145 (Kentucky, 1969), 35 A.L.R. 3d 683, with annotation 692–695; followed by Hart v. Brown, 29 Conn. Sup. 368, 289 A2d 386; opposed by In re Richardson, 284 So.2d 185 (Louisiana, 1973); and by In re Guardianship of Pescinski, 67 Wis.2d 4, 226 N.W.2d 180. The problem is discussed and substitute consent *for organ transplants* defended by John A. Robertson, "Organ Donations by Incompetents and the Substituted Judgment Doctrine," *Columbia Law Review,* 76 (1976), pp. 48–78. We shall see in chapter nine that Robertson argues against infant euthanasia. Some case can be made for transplants with substitute consent largely because here the damage and danger is not great, *and it is a kind of act which the law approves for competent persons themselves.* The implications if voluntary euthanasia is legalized are obvious.

83. In the Matter of Quinlan, 70 N.J. 10, 355 A.2d 647 (1976). The decision is definitely based upon substitute consent (662–664); the Court suggests Miss Quinlan's right of privacy is to be exercised for her. No right to die is asserted; the right to refuse consent to treatment is assumed and, as we explained in chapter four, unnecessarily couched in terms of privacy.

84. Superintendent of Belchertown State School v. Saikewicz, Mass. 370 N.E.2d 417 (1977) at 427–429.

85. John M. Freeman, "Is There a Right to Die—Quickly?" *Journal of Pediatrics,* 80 (1972), pp. 904–905; James Rachels, "Active and Passive Euthanasia," *New England Journal of Medicine,* 292 (1975), pp. 78–80.

86. Kohl, "Understanding the Case for Beneficent Euthanasia," p. 118, assures his readers that he is not for but rather against "any theory that solely or ultimately rests upon a principle of economic utility."

87. U.S. Department of Health, Education, and Welfare, *Improving Family Planning Services for Teenagers* (Washington, D.C.: 1976), pp. 5 and 77. This report was done on contract, and the title page carries a disclaimer of the official status of the views in it, but the text makes clear why the report was contracted and published by the department. (*Family* planning?)

88. Roe v. Wade, 410 U.S. 113 (1973) at 116; see below, chapter ten, section C.

89. The drive to institutionalize abortion as a publicly supported act and to compel even private institutions to participate willy-nilly in it is evident in Harriet F. Pilpel and Dorothy E. Patton, "Abortion, Conscience, and the Constitution: An Examination of Federal Institutional Conscience Clauses," *Columbia Human Rights Law Review,* 6 (1974–1975), pp. 278–305. Two survey articles are Marc D. Stern, "Abortion Conscience Clauses," *Columbia Journal of Law and Social Problems,* 11 (1975), pp. 571–627; Jane Finn, "State Limitations on the Availability and Accessibility of Abortions after *Wade* and *Bolton,"* *Kansas Law Review,* 25 (1976), pp. 87–107. Two particularly important cases are: Doe v. Charleston Area Medical Center, 529 F.2d 638 (1975), in which a U.S. Court of Appeals held that since abortion is legal, a *private* hospital must allow it; Doe v. Bridgeton Hospital Association, 71 N.J. 478, 306 A.2d 641 (1976) in which the New Jersey Supreme Court held (with one dissent) that a statutory conscience clause was unconstitutional in respect to *private* hospitals. In both of these cases the fact that private hospitals receive public funding was an important consideration. If a "right to die" became similarly legalized and institutionalized, it is doubtful that many who abhor the practice could avoid some specific participation in it.

90. Doe v. Rampton, 366 F.Supp. 189 (1973). This case is peculiar, and it should be noted that while one of the three judges rejected the conscience clause in principle, the second only rejected it as inseverable and the third would have accepted it.

91. Planned Parenthood of Central Missouri v. Danforth, 428 U.S. 52, 96 S.Ct. 2831 (1976) at 2842–2844.

92. Beal v. Doe, 97 S.Ct. 2366 (1977); Maher v. Roe, 97 S.Ct. 2376 (1977); Poelker v. Doe, 97 S.Ct 2391 (1977). These three cases, decided June 20 by a majority of six to three (Blackmun, Brennan, and Marshall dissenting), only say that the states are not *compelled* to fund and facilitate abortions. The dissenting opinions make clear that economic considerations play a very important part in thinking on abortion within the Court. See below, chapter ten, section C. For commentaries on the 1977 cases see John T. Noonan, Jr., "A Half-Step Forward: The Justices Retreat on Abortion," *The Human Life Review,* 3 (Fall 1977), pp. 11–18; Robert M. Byrn, "Which Way for Judicial Imperialism?" *The Human Life Review,* 3 (Fall 1977), pp. 19–35.

93. See "A Five Year Plan: 1976–1980, for the Planned Parenthood Federation of America, Inc.," mimeograph, approved by the PPFA Membership, October 22, 1975, Seattle, Washington, pp. 2–3, 6–7, and 16; "A Guide to Sources of Family Planning Program Assistance," *Population Reports,* series J, number 15 (March 1977), J 267, 269, 271–272; "Abortion Funds Ordered," *Washington Post,* 22 April 1978, p. 1; "Taxpayer's Guide to Federal Anti-Life Programs," *Pro-Life Reporter,* 5 (Spring 1977), pp. 6–13; Randy Engel, *A Pro-Life Report On Population Growth and the American Future* (private publication, 1972), pp. 1–16.

94. Testimony of Harriet F. Pilpel on behalf of the New York Civil Liberties Union before the Committee on Health, New York State Assembly (mimeograph), March 7, 1966; cf. Martha Robinson, Jean Pakter, and Martin Svigir, "Medicaid Coverage of Abortions in New York City: Costs and Benefits," *Family Planning Perspectives,* 6 (Fall 1974), pp. 202–208; see below, chapter ten, section C, for comments by Leo Pfeffer and analysis. The importance of keeping the right appearances is noted by James E. Allen, "An Appearance of Genocide: A Review of Governmental Family-Planning Program Policies," *Perspectives in Biology and Medicine,* 20 (1977), pp. 300–306; a negative view of the antilibertarian implications of the legalization of abortion is proposed by George S. Swan, "Compulsory Abortion: Next Challenge to Liberated Women?" *Ohio Northern University Law Review,* 3 (1975), pp. 152–175.

95. Richard Delgado, "Euthanasia Reconsidered—The Choice of Death as an Aspect of the Right of Privacy," *Arizona Law Review*, 17 (1975), pp. 479–480; cf. R. F. R. Gardner, "A New Ethical Approach to Abortion and Its Implications for the Euthanasia Dispute," *Journal of Medical Ethics*, 1 (1975), pp. 129–130.

96. Sackett, *op. cit.*, p. 30.

97. "Memorandum, Department of Health, Education and Welfare, Health Care Financing Administration," June 4, 1977, from Robert A. Derzon, administrator, Health Care Financing Administration; to The Secretary (photocopy), pp. 8–9.

98. Silving, *op. cit.*, pp. 386–389; Wilson, *op. cit.*, pp. 162–166; Sanders, *op. cit.*, pp. 357–358, considers and rejects; Scher, *op. cit.*, pp. 675–677, views as a step toward legalization; Kamisar, *op. cit.*, pp. 970–971 and 979–980, prescinds from the question; Baughman *et al., op. cit.*, pp. 1229–1237, claim a dilemma in the present situation which would point toward mitigation, but (pp. 1257–1260) offer no solution to their dilemma.

99. Ramsey, *op. cit.*, pp. 305–330.

100. Elizabeth A. Maclaren, "Dignity," *Journal of Medical Ethics*, 3 (1977), pp. 40–41, is suggestive; note the repeated and noncognitive use of "dignity" in idem, "A Plea for Beneficent Euthanasia," *Humanist*, 34 (July/August 1974), pp. 4–5.

101. Edward F. Dobihal, "Statement," in U.S. Senate, *Death with Dignity*, part 3, pp. 129–136; Sonya Rudikoff, "The Problem of Euthanasia," *Commentary*, 57 (February 1974), p. 67; Fletcher, "The Patient's Right to Die," p. 141.

102. Ronald Koenig, "Dying vs. Well-Being," *Omega*, 4 (1973), pp. 181–194; Richard Schulz and David Aderman, "How Medical Staff Copes with Dying Patients: A Critical Review," *Omega*, 7 (1976), pp. 11–21.

103. C. Condrau, "The Dying Patient—a Challenge for the Doctor," *Hexagon (Roche)*, 3 (1975), pp. 15–24.

104. Kübler-Ross, *On Death and Dying*, pp. 269–276; Hinton, *op. cit.*, pp. 111–125; the ethics of this was spelled out by Paul Ramsey, *The Patient as Person: Explorations in Medical Ethics* (New Haven and London: Yale University Press, 1970), pp. 124–157, but (pp. 161–164) he arbitrarily allows active euthanasia in certain cases which could never be distinguished from a continuum of cases, and the exceptions seem to include nonvoluntary euthanasia. Good nursing has always aimed at appropriate care; see Virginia W. Kasley, "As Life Ebbs," *American Journal of Nursing*, 38 (1938), pp. 1191–1198; Ned H. Cassem and Rege S. Stewart, "Management and Care of the Dying Patient," *International Journal of Psychiatry in Medicine*, 6 (1975), pp. 293–304.

105. Thomas P. Hackett, "Psychological Assistance for the Dying Patient and His Family," *American Review of Medicine*, 27 (1976), pp. 371–378; G. Gail Gardner, "Childhood, Death, and Human Dignity: Hypnotherapy for David," *International Journal of Clinical and Experimental Hypnosis*, 24 (1976), pp. 122–139; Rita Jean Dubrey and Laura Amy Terrill, "The Loneliness of the Dying Person: An Exploratory Study," *Omega*, 6 (1975), pp. 357–371.

106. Robert E. Neale, "Between the Nipple and the Everlasting Arms," *Archives of the Foundation of Thanatology*, 3 (1971), pp. 21–30; Cicely Saunders, "Living with Dying," *Man and Medicine*, 1 (1976), pp. 227–242; Richard Lamerton, *Care of the Dying* (London: Priory Press, 1973); Dobihal, *loc. cit.;* "Oct. 1976 Report/Rapport," Royal Victoria Hospital, McGill University, Montreal, Palliative Care Service/Service de Soins Palliatifs. For discussion see Claire F. Ryder and Diane M. Ross, "Terminal Care—Issues and Alternatives," *Public Health Reports*, 92 (1977), pp. 20–29.

107. *House of Lords* (1969), col. 1146.

108. Lamerton, *op. cit.*, pp. 43–61, is the best summary of the procedures, although Saunders, *loc. cit.*, conveys more the spirit of hospice-care.

109. Robert G. Twycross, "The Use of Narcotic Analgesics in Terminal Illness," *Journal of Medical Ethics*, 1 (1975), pp. 10–17; Lamerton, *op. cit.*, pp. 105–113; cf. Kamisar, *op. cit.*, 1008–1011. What the work of the hospices shows is that not only the sensation of pain but many annoying symptoms can be removed, and the suffering of dying can be greatly mitigated.

110. British Medical Association, *Problem of Euthanasia*, p. 5. The U. S. Senate, *Death with Dignity*, hearings ought to have led to a legislative program along the lines suggested, but they did not.

111. Cf. *On Dying Well*, pp. 44–50.

7: KILLING WHICH IS CONSIDERED JUSTIFIED

1. See Germain Grisez, *Abortion: The Myths, the Realities, and the Arguments* (New York and Cleveland: Corpus Books, 1970); at common law, abortion was murder if the unborn was delivered alive and subsequently died as a result of the abortive procedure (pp. 186–193, 375–376); by statute in eight states (1965) the willful killing of an unborn quick child was manslaughter, a provision first enacted by New York in 1829 (pp. 376–377); an Oregon Supreme Court decision held abortion manslaughter even if the child was not quick: State v. Ausplund, 86 Ore. 121, 167 P. 1019 (1917), *error dismissed* 251 U.S. 563 (1919).

2. See Yale Kamisar, "Some Non-Religious Views against Proposed 'Mercy-Killing' Legislation," *Minnesota Law Review*, 42 (1958), pp. 994 and 1017; he refers to *New York Times*, February 14, 1939, p. 2, col. 6.

3. Foster Kennedy, "The Problem of Social Control of the Congenital Defective: Education, Sterilization, Euthanasia," *American Journal of Psychiatry*, 99 (July 1942), pp. 13–16.

4. Walter W. Sackett, "Statement," in *Death with Dignity: An Inquiry into Related Public Issues: Hearings before the Special Committee on Aging, United States Senate*, 92nd Cong., 2d Sess. (August 7, 1972), p. 30.

5. William G. Lennox, "Should They Live? Certain Economic Aspects of Medicine," *American Scholar*, 7 (1938), pp. 454–458. Lennox's approach to epilepsy would have destroyed many people who have been enabled during the intervening four decades to lead normal lives due to improved pharmacological treatment of the disease, with drugs such as mycelin and dilantin with phenobarbital (which are used by a personal friend of one of the authors who has had the disease for over twenty years).

6. Robert H. Williams, "Our Role in the Generation, Modification, and Termination of Life," *Archives of Internal Medicine*, 124 (1969), p. 232.

7. Robert H. Williams, "Number, Types, and Duration of Human Lives," *Northwest Medicine*, 69 (1970), pp. 493–496.

8. Richard Trubo, *An Act of Mercy* (Los Angeles: Nash Publishing, 1973), p. 153.

9. Glanville Williams, " 'Mercy-Killing' Legislation—A Rejoinder," *Minnesota Law Review*, 43 (1958), p. 11.

10. Marvin Kohl, *The Morality of Killing: Sanctity of Life, Abortion and Euthanasia* (Atlantic Highlands, N.J.: Humanities Press, 1974), p. 109.

11. See John Connery, S.J., *Abortion: The Development of the Roman Catholic Perspective* (Chicago: Loyola University Press, 1977), pp. 284–303, for the Catholic

position, which since the nineteenth century was the strictest of any large group; here abortion was regarded as morally permissible if it were not direct, that is, if it were not precisely what one proposed in acting. This position permitted certain acts which the law would have considered intentional abortions to save the mother's life.

12. Cf. Daniel C. Maguire, *Death by Choice* (New York: Schocken Books, 1975), pp. 209–216.

13. Thomas Aquinas, *Summa theologiae,* 2–2, qu. 40, art. 1.

14. See Franziskus Stratmann, O.P., *The Church and War: A Catholic Study* (London: 1928), pp. 52–80, for a discussion of the development and weakening of the theological account of the justifiable war.

15. See Myres S. McDougal and Florentino P. Feliciano, *Law and Minimum World Public Order: The Legal Regulation of International Coercion* (New Haven: Yale University Press, 1961); Wolfgang Friedmann, *The Changing Structure of International Law* (New York: Columbia University Press, 1964); and Julius Stone, *Legal Controls of International Conflict* (New York: Rinehart, 1959).

16. Wayne R. LaFave and Austin W. Scott, Jr., *Handbook on Criminal Law* (St. Paul, Minnesota: West Publishing Co., 1972), p. 391.

17. *Ibid.,* pp. 397–399.

18. *Ibid.,* pp. 399–402.

19. *Ibid.,* pp. 402–403 and 406–407.

20. *Ibid.,* p. 405.

21. Hugo A. Bedau, *The Case against the Death Penalty,* a pamphlet published by the American Civil Liberties Union (New York: January, 1973), p. 2. The same organization's statement, "Policy Statement of the American Civil Liberties Union on State Laws Prohibiting Abortion," was issued March 25, 1968; it marked a turning point for the proabortion movement by outlining the position that the United States Supreme Court enacted into law the same month Bedau's pamphlet defending sanctity of life in the case of criminals was published.

22. The deterrent effect of the death penalty—or the lack of it—was discussed at length by the justices in Furman v. Georgia, 408 U.S. 238, 92 S.Ct. 2726 (1972). Marshall, 345–355, 2780–2785, provides an extensive and useful survey of the literature; Burger, 395–396, 2807, says the debate is a "stalemate" or an "unresolved factual question." Powell, 446, 2841, note 63, quotes the Report of the President's Commission on Law Enforcement and the Administration of Justice, *The Challenge of Crime in a Free Society* (1967) in stating that it is "impossible to say with certainty whether capital punishment significantly reduces the incidence of heinous crimes." A thorough study of the deterrent question is Ezzat Abdel Fattah, *A Study of the Deterrent Effect of Capital Punishment with Special Reference to the Canadian Situation,* Research Centre Report 2, Department of the Solicitor General (Ottawa: 1972).

23. See John T. Noonan, Jr., "Why a Constitutional Amendment?" *Human Life Review,* 1 (Winter 1975), pp. 26–30.

24. Cf. Baruch Brody, *Abortion and the Sanctity of Human Life: A Philosophical View* (Cambridge, Mass. and London: MIT Press, 1975), pp. 6–12.

25. Judith Jarvis Thomson, "A Defense of Abortion," *Philosophy and Public Affairs,* 1 (1971), pp. 47–66.

26. United States v. Holmes, 1 Wall. Jr. 1, 26 Fed. Cas. 360, No. 15, 383 (C.C.E.D. Pa. 1842).

27. R. v. Dudley and Stephens, L.R. 14 Q.B.D. 273 (1884).

28. LaFave and Scott, *op. cit.,* pp. 381–388. Rex v. Bourne, 1 K.B. 687 (1939), often is cited as an application of the defense of necessity. But it is not; rather it is a

case of arbitrary exegesis of a statute which did not mention any exception by means of another statute which did, and the stretching of "had not acted in good faith to preserve the life of the mother" to include preservation of health, and this to include aborting a pregnancy consequent upon rape in the instant case. The background of *Bourne* is interesting as an example of how far proabortionists will go in exploiting a victim of rape and contriving adjudication to achieve their ends; see Grisez, *op. cit.*, pp. 220–222.

29. Glanville Williams, *Criminal Law: The General Part* (London: Stevens & Sons, 1961), pp. 741–745, comments on this judicial opinion, and criticizes it upon his own assumptions that the function of law is to deter and that this could not be accomplished in a case of this sort. Even he admits that there is a problem in determining who should be the victim. It seems not to occur to him that hanging Dudley and Stephens would have perhaps deterred some persons in the future from arbitrarily resolving a difficult situation of this sort by killing the youngest, the weakest, and the most unresisting—a point much emphasized by the decision against Dudley and Stephens. The law deters in difficult situations too by making desperate persons think: I may as well be fair about this even if it costs my life, for if I am not fair I shall surely be hanged anyway. (This is not to argue for the death penalty, but this was the law's specified penalty for Dudley and Stephens, though it was commuted.)

30. Cf. LaFave and Scott, *op. cit.*, pp. 384–385.

8: NONVOLUNTARY EUTHANASIA AND JUSTICE

1. John A. Robertson, "Involuntary Euthanasia of Defective Newborns: A Legal Analysis," *Stanford Law Review*, 27 (1975), pp. 217–244.

2. Glanville Williams, "Euthanasia," *Medico-Legal Journal*, 41 (1973), p. 22.

3. Glanville Williams, *Sanctity of Life and the Criminal Law* (New York: Alfred A. Knopf, 1957), pp. x and 312.

4. Joseph Tussman and Jacobus tenBrock, "The Equal Protection of the Laws," *California Law Review*, 37 (1949), pp. 341–381. It is especially important to note several points: the concept of equal protection rests on a theory of legislation distinct from that of pressure groups (p. 350); there are classifications which are forbidden or suspect (pp. 353–361); and while underinclusiveness may be acceptable in regulatory legislation, it is not similarly defensible when basic human and civil rights are in question (p. 373). In effect, the argument we offer in this chapter is against admitting as a rational principle of classification the deficiencies on the basis of which nonvoluntary euthanasia is considered justified as an exception to the present law forbidding homicide.

5. Roe v. Wade, 410 U.S. 113, 93 S.Ct. 705 (1973) at 156–164, 728–732.

6. Marvin Kohl, *The Morality of Killing: Sanctity of Life, Abortion and Euthanasia* (Atlantic Highlands, N.J.: Humanities Press, 1974), p. 96; pp. 74–76 on consent as a criterion.

7. *Ibid.*, p. 81. Kohl does not draw the conclusion that involuntary euthanasia would be justified, but he supplies the premises for it. His respect for liberty is minimal in comparison with his regard for what he considers kind.

8. Williams, *Sanctity of Life*, p. 316.

9. Williams, "Euthanasia," pp. 22–24.

10. A. R. Jonsen, R. H. Phibbs, W. H. Tooley, and M. J. Garland, "Critical Issues in Newborn Intensive Care: A Conference Report and Policy Proposal," *Pediatrics,* 55 (1975), pp. 760 and 767.

11. *Ibid.,* p. 762.

12. Richard A. McCormick, "To Save or Let Die: The Dilemma of Modern Medicine," *Journal of the American Medical Association,* 229 (1974), p. 175.

13. Richard A. McCormick, "A Proposal of 'Quality of Life' Criteria for Sustaining Life," *Hospital Progress,* 56 (September 1975), p. 79.

14. Joseph Fletcher, "The Right to Die," *Atlantic Monthly,* 221 (April 1968), pp. 63–64.

15. Joseph Fletcher, "Indicators of Humanhood: A Tentative Profile of Man," *Hastings Center Report,* 2 (November 1972), p. 1.

16. Joseph Fletcher, "Four Indicators of Humanhood—The Enquiry Matures," *Hastings Center Report,* 4 (December 1974), p. 7, but note section III, pp. 5–6.

17. Michael Tooley, "Abortion and Infanticide," *Philosophy and Public Affairs,* 2 (1972), pp. 37–65, especially 44–48.

18. H. Tristram Engelhardt, Jr., "Euthanasia and Children: The Injury of Continued Existence," *Journal of Pediatrics,* 83 (1973), pp. 170–171.

19. H. Tristram Engelhardt, Jr., "On the Bounds of Freedom: From the Treatment of Fetuses to Euthanasia," *Connecticut Medicine,* 40 (1976), pp. 51–52.

20. Williams, "Euthanasia," p. 24.

21. Richard Lamerton, "Vegetables?" *Nursing Times,* 70 (1974), pp. 1184–1185.

22. Robertson, *op. cit.,* pp. 253–254.

23. Kohl, *op. cit.,* p. 103.

24. The most interesting such case is Gleitman v. Cosgrove, 49 N.J. 22, 227 A.2d 689 (1967). For discussion of this and other cases see Germain Grisez, *Abortion: The Myths, the Realities, and the Arguments* (New York and Cleveland: Corpus Books, 1970), pp. 397–402.

25. See Russell L. Ackhoff, "Does Quality of Life Have to Be Quantified?" *General Systems,* 20 (1975), pp. 216–218; Lewis H. LaRue, "A Comment on Fried, Summers, and the Value of Life," *Cornell Law Review,* 57 (1972), pp. 621–631. LaRue provides a good example of a military leader who accepts greater risk of loss of life for his men to preserve loyalty. Some proponents of euthanasia simplistically claim that since individuals are willing to spend only a certain amount to prevent a risk of death, therefore they have quantified the value of life. But how much people will spend depends greatly on how much they have; by this criterion a Rockefeller's life would be worth a lot more than the life of the ordinary poor person who lacks medical insurance. This seems questionable. What people will accept as a risk also depends upon many nonquantifiable factors; people do not gamble rationally.

26. Persons afflicted with this condition vary greatly in their capacity to learn and to live satisfying lives. One case of mongolism, admittedly unusual, was a girl of normal intelligence: Frank R. Ford, *Diseases of the Nervous System in Infancy, Childhood, and Adolescence,* 5 ed. (Springfield, Ill.: Charles C. Thomas, 1966), p. 182; another was a boy who attained the linguistic ability of a seventh-grade student and who was anything but lacking in personal quality: May V. Seagoe, *Yesterday Was Tuesday, All Day and All Night* (Boston and Toronto: Little, Brown and Co., 1964). Many persons having Down's syndrome achieve less, yet their lives seem to be quite meaningful and satisfying to themselves.

27. See Germain Grisez, *Beyond the New Theism: A Philosophy of Religion* (Notre Dame and London: University of Notre Dame Press, 1975), pp. 152–180.

28. Glanville Williams, " 'Mercy-Killing' Legislation—A Rejoinder," *Minnesota Law Review*, 43 (1958), p. 12.

29. Richard Trubo, *An Act of Mercy* (Los Angeles: Nash Publishing Co., 1973), pp. 154–155.

30. Thus James Rachels, "Active and Passive Euthanasia," *New England Journal of Medicine*, 292 (1975), pp. 78–80. Rachels both ignores the fact that in law the omitting of treatment can be criminal homicide and misrepresents the extent to which the AMA statement he criticizes condones omitting treatment. Note reactions in "Correspondence," pp. 863–867.

31. Robertson, *op. cit.*, pp. 217–218; Yale Kamisar, "Some Non-Religious Views against Proposed 'Mercy-Killing' Legislation," *Minnesota Law Review*, 42 (1958), pp. 982–983.

32. Cf. Clifford T. Morgan and Richard A. King, *Introduction to Psychology*, 3 ed. (New York: McGraw-Hill Book Co., 1966), pp. 419–441.

33. John Rawls, *A Theory of Justice* (Cambridge, Mass.: Belknap Press of Harvard University Press, 1971), pp. 504–512.

34. Joseph M. Boyle, Jr., "That the Fetus Should Be Considered a Legal Person," *American Journal of Jurisprudence*, 24 (1979), forthcoming. See also Grisez, *Abortion*, pp. 361–442; Dennis J. Horan *et al.*, "The Legal Case for the Unborn Child," in Thomas W. Hilgers and Dennis J. Horan, eds., *Abortion and Social Justice* (New York: Sheed & Ward, 1972), pp. 105–141 and 301–328; Robert A. Destro, "Abortion and the Constitution: The Need for a Life-Protective Amendment," *California Law Review*, 63 (1975), pp. 1250–1292 and 1331–1341; Joseph W. Dellapenna, "Nor Piety Nor Wit: The Supreme Court on Abortion," *Columbia Human Rights Law Review*, 6 (1974), pp. 389–409; Robert M. Byrn, "An American Tragedy: The Supreme Court on Abortion," *Fordham Law Review*, 41 (1973), pp. 807–862.

35. Grisez, *Abortion*, pp. 186–193 and 374–397.

36. Roe v. Wade, 410 U.S. 113, 93 S.Ct. 705 (1973) at 133–137 and 148–153, 718–721 and 724–726.

37. In addition to the work cited in note 35 see Destro, *op. cit.*, pp. 1267–1292; Byrn, *op. cit.*, pp. 815–839. Nowhere other than in its careless acceptance of proabortion propaganda as historically determinative is the Court's bias and irresponsibility more evident.

38. Grisez, *Abortion*, pp. 361–402; Horan *et al.*, *op. cit.*, pp. 109–127.

39. Roe v. Wade, 410 U.S. 113, 93 S.Ct. 705 (1973) at 160–163, 730–731.

40. U.S. Constitution, art. 1, § 2; see James Madison, No. 54 of Alexander Hamilton, James Madison, and John Jay, *The Federalist Papers*, Clinton Rossiter, ed. (New York and Scarborough, Ont.: New American Library, 1961), pp. 336–340, in which Madison avoids arguing for this provision by putting its defense into the mouth of a fictional southerner. Cf. Destro, *op. cit.*, pp. 1284–1289; Joseph Parker Witherspoon, "Impact of the Abortion Decisions upon the Father's Role," *Jurist*, 35 (Winter 1975), pp. 41–47. Dee Brown, *Bury My Heart at Wounded Knee: An Indian History of the American West* (New York, Chicago, San Francisco: Holt, Rinehart & Winston, 1970), pp. 351–366 and *passim*, shows how the rights of American native people continued to be violated even after the ratification of the post-Civil War amendments and how they continued to be treated as semipersons.

41. Roe v. Wade, 410 U.S. 113, 93 S.Ct. 705 (1973) at 160–163, 730–731. See comments by Byrn, *op. cit.*, pp. 809–814 and 840–852; Destro, *op. cit.*, pp. 1263–1267; Baruch Brody, *Abortion and the Sanctity of Human Life: A Philosophical View* (Cambridge, Mass. and London: MIT Press, 1976), pp. 127–129.

42. See Trubo, *op. cit.*, pp. 141–158. Norman Podhoretz, "Beyond ZPG," *Commentary*, 53 (May 1972), pp. 6 and 8, already argued that if abortion entailed infanticide, as some argued, this should weigh against abortion. F. Raymond Marks, "The Defective Newborn: An Analytic Framework for a Policy Dialog," in Albert R. Jonsen and Michael J. Garland, eds., *Ethics of Newborn Intensive Care* (San Francisco and Berkeley: University of California, 1976), p. 102, notes that the Court's decision in Roe v. Wade embodies a fiction that the unborn is not a person and thus conceals the adoption of quality-of-life criteria for preferring other lives to its, but Marks argues (pp. 106–125) on the assumption that abortion is now accepted and so infanticide also must be accepted. It is frightening to notice that *at every stage* of its unfolding the control of life movement has insisted very strongly upon the utter difference between its immediate objective and the next step, and at every stage it has used its achievement as a step toward that next step—notably in using the acceptance of contraception to promote abortion and using liberalization of restrictions upon private activities to promote public programs of contraception and abortion.

43. See Grisez, *Abortion*, pp. 403–431; and other works cited in note 34, above. See also Joseph L. Lewis, "Homo Sapienism: Critique of *Roe v. Wade* and Abortion," *Albany Law Review*, 39 (1975), pp. 856–893.

44. Roe v. Wade, at 162–163, 731–732.

45. Arval A. Morris, "Voluntary Euthanasia," *Washington Law Review*, 45 (1970), pp. 264–265; Lucy Dawidowicz, in "Biomedical Ethics and the Shadow of Nazism," *Hastings Center Report*, 6, Special supplement (1976), p. 3.

46. Kohl, *op. cit.*, pp. 98–100.

47. Williams, "Rejoinder," pp. 10–11; idem, "Euthanasia and Abortion," *University of Colorado Law Review*, 38 (1966), p. 181.

48. Dawidowicz, *op. cit.*, p. 17.

49. Kamisar, *op. cit.*, pp. 1031–1034.

50. See Frederic Wertham, *A Sign for Cain: An Exploration of Human Violence* (New York: Macmillan Co., 1966), pp. 153–191, especially 161–163, 167–169, 175, and 178–180.

51. Maximilian Koessler, "Euthanasia in the Hadamar Sanatorium and International Law," *Journal of Criminal Law*, 43 (1953), pp. 736–737.

52. Karl Binding and Alfred Hoche, *Die Freigabe der Vernichtung Lebensunwerten Lebens* (Leipsig: Felix Meiner, 1920), tr. with commentary by Robert L. Sassone, *The Release of the Destruction of Life Devoid of Value: Its Measure and Its Form* (Santa Ana, Cal.: Life Quality Paperback, 1975). Note (p. 4) reference to this work in war crimes trials.

53. This point is stressed by Wertham, *op. cit.*, pp. 153–191.

54. See James Hitchcock, "The Roots of American Violence," *Human Life Review*, 3 (Summer 1977), pp. 17–28.

55. C. P. Blacker, " 'Eugenic' Experiments Conducted by the Nazis on Human Subjects," *Eugenics Review*, 44 (April 1952), p. 12.

56. "Resolutions Passed at First American Birth Control Conference," *Birth Control Review*, 6 (January 1922), p. 18.

57. Margaret Sanger, "The Morality of Birth Control: Address of November 18, 1921 at the Park Theater," *Birth Control Review*, 6 (February 1922), p. 25.

58. See Grisez, *Abortion*, pp. 60–65. Also see references to Raymond Pearl, *ibid.*, pp. 55–56. William G. Lennox, "Should They Live? Certain Economic Aspects of Medicine," *American Scholar*, 7 (1938), pp. 457–458, cites with approval Pearl's remarks in favor of disposing of idiots and monsters. Lennox's own statements are full of

eugenicist ideas; he remarks with respect to birth control: "This principle of limiting certain races through limitation of offspring might be applied *intra*nationally as well as *inter*nationally. Germany in time might have solved her Jewish problems in this way" (p. 461).

59. Frank W. Notestein, "The Importance of Population Trends to the Birth Control Movement," *Birth Control Review,* 22 (April 1938), p. 76.

60. See Joseph M. Boyle, Jr., *loc. cit.*

61. Lewis, *op. cit.,* p. 892. It is worth noticing that even if one did not hold that the Supreme Court's decision violates arbitrarily the right to life of the unborn, one might still hold that the decision by the Court was lawless because legislative rather than interpretative; thus John Hart Ely, "The Wages of Crying Wolf: A Comment on *Roe* v. *Wade,"* *Yale Law Journal,* 82 (1973), p. 947: The decision "is bad because it is bad constitutional law, or rather because it is *not* constitutional law and gives almost no sense of an obligation to try to be." If the Court should legislate euthanasia, this act also would be doubly unjust, both as a substantive violation of rights and as a procedural abuse of its own power.

9: JUSTICE AND CARE FOR THE NONCOMPETENT

1. See John A. Robertson, "Involuntary Euthanasia of Defective Newborns: A Legal Analysis," *Stanford Law Review,* 27 (1975), pp. 217–218, and the works cited in his note 28; also see Jerome Hall, *General Principles of Criminal Law,* 2nd ed. (Indianapolis and New York: Bobbs-Merrill Co., 1960), pp. 190–205.

2. Hall, *loc. cit.,* correctly stresses that a legal duty to act does not specifically distinguish crimes by omission from other crimes, but he seems to ignore the point intended by those who stress this requirement for a crime in the case of omissions: that absent a duty to act, all other conditions of a crime by omission being given, no crime can be imputed to the potential agent who does not act. In addition to Robertson, *loc. cit.,* and the works cited by him, an especially helpful discussion is presented by George P. Fletcher, "Prolonging Life: Some Legal Considerations," in A. B. Downing, ed., *Euthanasia and the Right to Death: The Case for Voluntary Euthanasia* (London: Peter Owen, 1969), pp. 78–83. See also Otto Kirchheimer, "Criminal Omissions," *Harvard Law Review,* 55 (1942), pp. 617–636, on questions of causality and the relevance of duty.

3. Robertson, *op. cit.,* pp. 217–244.

4. See James M. Gustafson, "Mongolism, Parental Desires, and the Right to Life," *Perspectives in Biology and Medicine,* 16 (1973), pp. 529–557; Dennis J. Horan, "Euthanasia, Medical Treatment and the Mongoloid Child: Death as a Treatment of Choice?" *Baylor Law Review,* 27 (1975), pp. 76–85 (discussion of a case in a Catholic hospital in Illinois); David H. Smith, "On Letting Some Babies Die," *Hastings Center Studies,* 2 (1974), pp. 37–46.

5. John A. Robertson, "Discretionary Non-Treatment of Defective Newborns," in Aubrey Milunsky and George J. Annas, eds., *Genetics and the Law* (New York and London: Plenum Press, 1976), p. 460, cites a survey of Massachusetts pediatricians. An influential article favoring the withholding of necessary treatment in such cases is Anthony Shaw, "Dilemmas of 'Informed Consent' in Children," *New England Journal of Medicine,* 289 (1973), pp. 885–890.

6. See Robertson, "Involuntary Euthanasia of Defective Newborns," pp. 213–217; Robert M. Veatch, *Death, Dying, and the Biological Revolution: Our Last Quest for Responsibility* (New Haven and London: Yale University Press, 1976), pp. 134–136. We are ignoring here a number of distinctions in respect to the condition which are needed for medical accuracy but not relevant to our present purpose. See John Lorber, "Ethical Problems in the Management of Myelomeningocele and Hydrocephalus," *Journal of the Royal College of Physicians,* 10 (October 1975), pp. 47–52, for brief historical information about the phases of treatment and nontreatment and the results of each; see also G. Keys Smith and E. Durham Smith, "Selection for Treatment in Spina Bifida Cystica," *British Medical Journal,* 4 (1973), pp. 189–197, who present a great deal of information about outcomes and who evaluate the results more optimistically than Lorber.

7. See P. P. Rickham, "The Swing of the Pendulum: The Indications for Operating on Myelomeningoceles," *Medical Journal of Australia,* 2 (1976), pp. 743–746, for a frank expression concerning the motives for selection.

8. See Mary D. Ames and Luis Shut, "Results of Treatment of 171 Consecutive Myelomeningoceles—1962–1968," *Pediatrics,* 50 (1972), pp. 466–470; Smith and Smith, *op. cit.,* p. 189, exclude 27 percent; John Lorber, "Early Results of Selective Treatment of Spina Bifida Cystica," *British Medical Journal,* 4 (1973), pp. 201–204, excludes 68 percent; Rickham, *op. cit.,* pp. 743–744, who points out that the selection is based upon probabilities.

9. Lorber, "Ethical Problems," p. 55; Rickham, *op. cit.,* p. 744; John Lorber, "Selective Treatment of Myelomeningocele: To Treat or Not to Treat?" *Pediatrics,* 53 (1974), p. 308; John M. Freeman, "To Treat or Not to Treat: Ethical Dilemmas of Treating the Infant with a Myelomeningocele," *Clinical Neurosurgery,* 20 (1973), pp. 135–137.

10. Lorber, "Ethical Problems," pp. 54–55.

11. Smith and Smith, *op. cit.,* pp. 195–196; M. F. Robards, G. G. Thomas, and L. Rosenbloom, "Survival of Infants with Unoperated Myeloceles," *British Medical Journal,* 4 (1975), pp. 12–13.

12. John M. Freeman, "Is There a Right to Die—Quickly?" *Journal of Pediatrics,* 80 (1972), pp. 904–905; idem, "The Short-Sighted Treatment of Myelomeningocele: A Long-Term Case Report," *Pediatrics,* 53 (1974), pp. 311–313.

13. Freeman, "To Treat or Not to Treat," pp. 143–146; Raymond S. Duff and A. G. M. Campbell, "On Deciding the Care of Severely Handicapped or Dying Persons: With Particular Reference to Infants," *Pediatrics,* 57 (1976), pp. 487–493.

14. Lorber, "Ethical Problems," pp. 57–58, considers the distinction important; J. Engelbert Dunphy, "Annual Discourse—On Caring for the Patient with Cancer," *New England Journal of Medicine,* 295 (1976), p. 317, stresses it; Raymond S. Duff considers it a quibble in Beverly Kelsey, "An Interview with Dr. Raymond S. Duff: Which Infants Should Live? Who Should Decide?" *Hastings Center Report,* 5 (April 1975), p. 7.

15. Raymond S. Duff and A. G. M. Campbell, "Moral and Ethical Dilemmas in the Special-Care Nursery," *New England Journal of Medicine,* 289 (1973), p. 893; Charles L. Paxson, Jr., "To the Editor," *New England Journal of Medicine,* 290 (1974), p. 518.

16. See Geoffrey Hatcher and Eliot Slater, "Severely Malformed Children," *British Medical Journal,* 2 (1975), pp. 285–286.

17. Rickham, *op. cit.,* p. 746; D. A. De Lange, "Selection for Treatment of Patients with Spina Bifida Aperta," *Developmental Medicine and Child Neurology,* 16, supp. 32 (1974), pp. 27–30.

18. Rickham, *op. cit.*, p. 744; Duff and Campbell, "Moral and Ethical Dilemmas," pp. 890–894.

19. With respect to the elderly cf. Michael B. Miller, "Challenges of the Chronic Ill Aged," *Geriatrics*, 25 (1970), pp. 102–110; in general, Joseph Fletcher, "Ethics and Euthanasia," *American Journal of Nursing*, 73 (1973), pp. 670–675.

20. See "Editorial: A New Ethic for Medicine and Society," *California Medicine*, 113 (1970), pp. 67–68. Duff and Campbell, "Moral and Ethical Dilemmas," and Shaw, *op. cit.*, brought into the open the killing by omission of defective infants just nine months after the decision in Roe v. Wade. See also the sociological remarks of Diana Crane, "Decisions to Treat Critically Ill Patients: A Comparison of Social versus Medical Considerations," *MMFQ/ Health and Society*, 53 (1975), pp. 29–30. F. Raymond Marks, "The Defective Newborn: An Analytic Framework for a Policy Dialog," in Albert R. Jonsen and Michael J. Garland, eds., *Ethics of Intensive Newborn Care* (San Francisco and Berkeley: University of California, 1976), pp. 101–103 and 106, uses *Roe* and *Doe* to justify infanticide.

21. Marks, *loc. cit.*; Philip B. Heymann and Sara Holtz, "The Severely Defective Newborn: The Dilemma and the Decision Process," *Public Policy*, 23 (1975), p. 392; explained by Robertson, "Discretionary Non-Treatment of Defective Newborns," pp. 435–436; cf. Warren Reich, "What Rights Have the Newborn?" *Origins* (July 4, 1974), pp. 89–91. John Fletcher, "Abortion, Euthanasia, and Care of Defective Newborns," *New England Journal of Medicine*, 292 (1975), pp. 75–78, makes one of the few attempts to distinguish abortion from infanticide, yet even he admits (p. 78) death as a "good outcome" in some cases and considers acceptable the withholding of treatment precisely to bring about death. Lorber, "Ethical Problems," pp. 57–58, argues most strongly for the continuity between abortion and infanticide yet rejects active euthanasia and favors killing by omission, although he admits: "There is a major inconsistency and perhaps hypocrisy here, yet I, for one, uphold this principle." His reason for drawing the line where he does seems primarily to be the great possibility of abuse of active euthanasia and secondarily the repugnance he would feel toward actively causing the death of an infant. Various cases such as *Edelin* and *Waddill* have focused attention on the close relationship between abortion and infanticide, because in such cases the indistinctness of the dividing line between the two types of killing becomes painfully obvious. A defense attorney in *Edelin* has argued that the point of abortion is to deliver a dead fetus; he holds that any state attempt to limit this is "interference," but even he admits that once the child is live-born, it should be protected: Benjamin B. Sendor, "Medical Responsibility for Fetal Survival under Roe and Doe," *Harvard Civil Rights/ Civil Liberties Law Review*, 10 (1975), pp. 444–471. The practice of allowing aborted viable babies to die is reported to be widespread; various states have tried to prevent this by special legislation. See Joseph P. Witherspoon, "The New Pro-Life Legislation: Patterns and Recommendations," *St. Mary's Law Journal*, 7 (1976), pp. 661–668, for examples of such legislation and discussion, Witherspoon also cites evidence of the killing of persons born alive as a result of abortion, including an affidavit of Dr. Baker, Abele v. Markel, Civil No. B-521 (D. Conn., July 27, 1972), concerning the practice in Yale-New Haven Hospital, where Duff and Campbell report similar practices in the special-care nursery.

22. Especially Duff and Campbell, "On Deciding the Care of Severely Handicapped or Dying Persons," pp. 490–492; idem, "Moral and Ethical Dilemmas," pp. 890–894; in Kelsey, *op. cit.*, p. 7; "To the Editor," *New England Journal of Medicine*, 290 (1974), p. 520. The last contains the remarkable assertion: "The family more than anyone loves the patient and is most likely to know intimate details of the patient's personal and social life

and his preferences or probable preferences for care." This position is in defense of allowing unwanted babies to die—or seeking "early death as a management option, to avoid that cruel choice of gradual, often slow, but progressive deterioration of the child who was required under these circumstances in effect to kill himself"—in the special-care nursery of the Yale-New Haven Hospital. Is this double-think?

23. Robertson, "Involuntary Euthanasia of Defective Newborns," pp. 213–244, seems to overlook this point in his otherwise admirable analysis; see Veatch, *op. cit.*, p. 135, note 41.

24. Bryan Jennett and Fred Plum, "Persistent Vegetative State after Brain Damage," *Lancet*, 1 (1972), pp. 734–737, describe several more or less similar conditions, in some of which the patient is conscious. Edward J. Leadem, " 'Guidelines for Health Care Facilities to Implement Procedures Concerning Care of Comatose, Non-Cognitive Patients'—A Perspective," *Hospital Progress*, 58 (March 1977), pp. 9–10, describes efforts to implement the decision narrowly; B. D. Colen, *Karen Ann Quinlan: Dying in the Age of Eternal Life* (New York: Nash Publishing, 1976), p. 74 and *passim*, exemplifies the tendency to extend a decision to cases in which treatment is withdrawn from paralyzed, conscious patients without the patient's consent.

25. F. Patrick McKegney and Paul Lange, "The Decision No Longer to Live on Chronic Hemodialysis," *American Journal of Psychiatry*, 128 (1971), pp. 267–274.

26. Superintendent of Belchertown State School v. Saikewicz, Mass. 370 N.E.2d 417 (1977); cf. Kathleen A. Corbett and Robert M. Raciti, "Witholding Life-Prolonging Medical Treatment from the Institutionalized Person—Who Decides?" *New England Journal on Prison Law*, 3 (1976), pp. 53–56, 65, and 73.

27. For example, in cases of anencephaly; see K. M. Laurence, "Abnormalities of the Central Nervous System," in A. P. Norman, ed., *Congenital Abnormalities in Infancy* (Oxford: Blackwell, 1963), pp. 22–24; for a medical judgment from an ethically conservative viewpoint see Edward J. Kilroy, "To Treat or Not to Treat," *Linacre Quarterly*, 43 (February 1976), p. 4.

28. Pius XII, "The Prolongation of Life," *The Pope Speaks*, 4 (1957–1958), pp. 395–396 (*AAS*, 49 [1957], pp. 1027–1033 at 1030). He perhaps thought the distinction was descriptive; his language in the original French hovers between the descriptive and the frankly moral. In any case, the formulation is vague and at least partially circular, and so of little help unless one can assume an established context of moral principles and practices, as in the Catholic Church.

29. Matter of Quinlan, 70 N.J. 10, 355 A.2d 647 (1976), at 658–660, although the Court is careful to say that it does not make the Catholic position a precedent for New Jersey Law; 1977 ARKANSAS GENERAL ASSEMBLY, Act 879.

30. Paul Ramsey, "Prolonged Dying: Not Medically Indicated," *Hastings Center Report*, 6 (1976), pp. 14–17; Richard A McCormick, "A Proposal for 'Quality of Life' Criteria for Sustaining Life," *Hospital Progress*, 56 (September 1975), pp. 76–79. The latter errs in our judgment in merging considerations about the *means*—whatever "extraordinary" and "ordinary" might signify—into considerations about the prospective quality of life if the individual survives, thus to justify homicide by omission in some cases.

31. A. R. Jonsen, R. H. Phibbs, W. H. Tooley, and M. J. Garland, "Critical Issues in Newborn Intensive Care: A Conference Report and Policy Proposal," *Pediatrics*, 55 (1975), p. 763.

32. Eliot Slater, "Death: The Biological Aspect," in A. B. Downing, ed., *op. cit.*, p. 59, argues for death as good for the species; idem, "Wanted—A New Basic Approach," *British Medical Journal*, 2 (1973), pp. 285–286, considers human aspects, but

still the society more than the individual; Duff and Campbell, "Moral and Ethical Dilemmas," pp. 890–891, consider family economic interests and feelings very important; Freeman, "To Treat or Not to Treat," pp. 135 and 141–142, argues on the basis of social costs and various qualitative criteria against both child's right to life and the unwillingness of others to kill it; Lorber, "Ethical Problems," pp. 52–53, stresses cost and impact on the family; Richard E. Harbin, "Death, Euthanasia and Parental Consent," *Pediatric Nursing,* 2 (July–August 1976), pp. 26–28, stresses the interests of everyone but the infant, even including the hospital nursing and house staff; Robert E. Cooke, "Whose Suffering?" *Journal of Pediatrics,* 80 (1972), pp. 906–907, points out that there is more concern about others than about the infant.

33. H. Tristram Engelhardt, Jr., "Ethical Issues in Aiding the Death of Young Children," in Marvin Kohl, ed., *Beneficent Euthanasia* (Buffalo, N.Y.: Prometheus Books, 1975), pp. 183–184, does not consider infant a person and weights the judgment in favor of the parents.

34. Crane, *op. cit.,* pp. 20 and 26, makes clear that wantedness by the parents makes a substantial difference to the actions of physicians.

35. See Robertson, "Involuntary Euthanasia of Defective Newborns," p. 242, note 179.

36. E.g., 29 U.S.C. § 794; 42 U.S.C. § 6705; cf. "Helping the Handicapped," *Time,* December 5, 1977, p. 16.

37. Cf. Robertson, "Involuntary Euthanasia of Defective Newborns," pp. 255–256.

38. *Ibid.,* pp. 257–258; Philip R. Lee and Diane Dooley, "Social Services for the Disabled Child," in Jonsen and Garland, eds., *op. cit.,* pp. 64–69, describe available services but also point out (pp. 70–74) the need for better coordination and improvement of assistance.

39. Robertson, "Involuntary Euthanasia of Defective Newborns," p. 219, note 37.

40. See Patricia W. Hayden, David B. Shurtleff, and Arline B. Broy, "Custody of the Myelodysplastic Child: Implications for Selection for Early Treatment," *Pediatrics,* 53 (1974), pp. 253–256.

41. Anonymous, "Scarce Medical Resources," *Colorado Law Review,* 69 (1969), pp. 658–659.

42. *Ibid.,* p. 661; Paul Ramsey, *The Patient as Person: Explorations in Medical Ethics* (New Haven and London: Yale University Press, 1970), pp. 242–252; Harry S. Abram, "Survival by Machine: The Psychological Stress of Chronic Hemodialysis," *Psychiatry in Medicine,* 1 (1970), pp. 38–39; James F. Childress, "Who Shall Live When Not All Can Live?" *Soundings,* 53 (1970), pp. 344–346.

43. Anonymous, "Scarce Medical Resources," pp. 643–644.

44. See the works by Lorber, Smith and Smith, Ames and Shut, Freeman, and Duff and Campbell, cited in notes 6, 8, 9, 12, and 13 above.

45. Robards *et al., op. cit.,* p. 13, speak of those who would have "a quality of life so poor as not to merit survival"; Jonsen *et al.,* "Critical Issues in Newborn Intensive Care," pp. 760–761, would have court weigh quality of life; McCormick, *op. cit.,* pp. 77–78, proposes to redefine the benefit of means to the patient in terms of quality of life expected because of *already* existing conditions; Gustafson, *op. cit.,* pp. 553–554, who rejects letting Down's syndrome baby starve, draws the line at monsters, without distinguishing, for example, siamese twins from those which cannot survive regardless of treatment.

46. Robertson, "Involuntary Euthanasia of Defective Newborns," p. 254; William B. Hobbins, "What Is a Day of Life Worth?" *National Magazine for Nurses,* 38 (April 1975), pp. 33–34.

47. Duff and Campbell, "On Deciding the Care of Severely Handicapped or Dying Persons," p. 488; however, they also argue (p. 492) that society should interfere with what the parents and physicians are doing only if they not only harm the baby and there is a better alternative available but if they also can expect social support in carrying through the unwelcome choice! On this basis anyone who wanted to do armed robbery should go unpunished unless society was willing to provide robbers with bank rolls.

48. *Ibid.*, p. 492; Herbert B. Eckstein, Geoffrey Hatcher, and Eliot Slater, "Severely Malformed Children," *British Medical Journal*, 2 (1975), pp. 286–289; Freeman, "To Treat or Not to Treat," pp. 140–146.

49. Freeman, "Is There a Right to Die—Quickly?" p. 905.

50. Heymann and Holtz, *op. cit.*, pp. 409–414, note the discrimination but assume that the distinction justified subordinating newly born persons.

51. Smith, *op. cit.*, p. 46.

52. Jennett and Plum, *loc cit.*; on "vegetables" see Helen Creighton, "Choose Life or Let Die?" *Supervisor Nurse*, 6 (August 1975), pp. 12–14, including letter of Sondra Diamond, which appeared in *Newsweek*, December 3, 1973.

53. See Leslie S. Libow, "Pseudo-Senility: Acute and Reversible Organic Brain Syndromes," *Journal of the American Geriatrics Society*, 21 (1973), pp. 112–120.

54. McCormick, *op. cit.*, pp. 78–79; cf. Richard A. McCormick, "To Save or Let Die: The Dilemma of Modern Medicine," *Journal of the American Medical Association*, 229 (1974), pp. 174–175.

55. Matter of Quinlan, at 655, 657, 663, 667; cf. *In the Matter of Karen Quinlan*, 2 vols. (Washington, D.C.: University Publications of America, 1976), vol. 2, pp. 28, 219, and 225–226.

56. Matter of Quinlan, at 664.

57. *Ibid.*, at 663.

58. Angela Roddey Holder, *Medical Malpractice Law* (New York, London, Sydney, Toronto: John Wiley & Sons, 1975), pp. 40–64.

59. See Marks in Jonsen and Garland, eds., *op. cit.*, p. 109, who reports a proposal that euthanasia could become gradually accepted by practice.

60. Lorber, "Ethical Problems," p. 52; idem, "Early Results of Selective Treatment," p. 202.

61. Cf. Virginia Henderson, "The Nature of Nursing," *American Journal of Nursing*, 64 (August 1964), p. 63.

62. See Leon R. Kass, "Regarding the End of Medicine and the Pursuit of Health," *The Public Interest*, 40 (1975), pp. 13–14; Joseph M. Boyle, Jr., "The Concept of Health and the Right to Health Care," *Social Thought*, 3 (Summer 1977), pp. 7–9. In view of the problems with which we are concerned here, the notion of mental health can be set aside, since treatment for psychological problems is only distantly related to questions of euthanasia.

63. Kass, *op. cit.*, pp. 36–37, urges the need for more preventive medicine; Charles Fried, "Equality and Rights in Medical Care," *Hastings Center Report*, 6 (February 1976), p. 33, refers to the medical profession as a tight and self-protective guild; Anonymous, "Scarce Medical Resources," p. 641, holds that the Veterans Administration care of nonservice-related problems is discriminatory; George W. Paulson, "Who Should Live?" *Geriatrics*, 28 (1973), p. 134, makes clear that the patient's demand, the sympathy of the physician for the patient, and the patient's ability to pay make significant differences in how hard physicians try to cure the patient or prevent death.

64. Anonymous, "Scarce Medical Resources," pp. 688–689, stresses the need for priorities and the inevitability of an absolute limit; Fried, *op. cit.*, p. 31, makes the

point very clearly; Boyle, *op. cit.*, pp. 14–15, clarifies the ethical grounds of such a limit; Smith, *op. cit.*, p. 46, stresses the unavoidability of limits while rejecting the quality-of-life solution; Ramsey, *Patient as Person*, pp. 268–269, points out that even the most adequate medical resources are scarce in comparison with needs.

65. Ramsey, *Patient as Person*, pp. 240–252; Anonymous, "Scarce Medical Resources," p. 652; Smith, *op. cit.*, pp. 45–46; Kass, *op. cit.*, pp. 12 and 39–40.

66. Anonymous, "Scarce Medical Resources," pp. 662–663; Boyle, *op. cit.*, pp. 12–15; Gene Outka, "Social Justice and Equal Access to Health-Care," *Journal of Religious Ethics*, 2 (1974), pp. 21–25; Bernard Williams, "The Idea of Equality," in Joel Feinberg, ed., *Moral Concepts* (London and New York: Oxford University Press, 1970), p. 163.

67. See Robertson, "Involuntary Euthanasia of Defective Newborns," pp. 258–259.

68. Heymann and Holtz, *op. cit.*, pp. 403–405, argue very effectively that to refuse to use available resources on behalf of one individual when not used for another on the excuse of cost would be frightening abandonment. Clearly, where costs must be limited, this must not be done by making resources unavailable to some identified beforehand.

69. Paulson, *op. cit.*, p. 133.

70. Smith, *op. cit.*, p. 44.

71. De Lange, *op. cit.*, p. 29.

72. H. Richard Beresford, "Who Should Decide to Withhold Care in Chronic Coma?" *Archives of Neurology* (Chicago), 33 (1976), p. 371.

73. Dunphy, *op. cit.*, p. 315.

74. See works cited in notes 1 and 2 above.

75. Superintendent of Belchertown State School v. Saikewicz, Mass. 370 N.E.2d 417 (1977).

76. *Ibid.*, at 426.

77. *Ibid.*, at 431–432.

78. McKegney and Lange, *op. cit.*, pp. 269–272; Abram, *op. cit.*, pp. 42–49.

79. Miller, *op. cit.*, p. 104, provides good examples.

80. See Robertson, "Involuntary Euthanasia of Defective Newborns," pp. 222 and 232; James A. Baker, "Court Ordered Non-Emergency Care for Infants," *Cleveland-Marshall Law Review*, 18 (1969), pp. 298 and 306–307.

81. Cf. Robertson, "Involuntary Euthanasia of Defective Newborns," pp. 216 and 263.

82. Milton Viederman, "Saying 'No' to Hemodialysis," *Hastings Center Report*, 4 (September 1974), pp. 8–10; John E. Schowalter, Julian B. Ferholt, and Nancy M. Mann, "The Adolescent Patient's Decision to Die," *Pediatrics*, 51 (1973), pp. 97–103.

83. For example, by Crane, *op. cit.*, pp. 30–31.

84. Melvin D. Levine, "Disconnection: The Clinician's View," *Hastings Center Report*, 6 (February 1976), pp. 11–12; Paulson, *op. cit.*, p. 136; against: Smith, *op. cit.*, p. 39; Daniel C. Maguire, *Death by Choice* (New York: Schocken Books, 1975), pp. 177–184; Stanley Hauerwas, "Selecting Children to Live or Die: An Ethical Analysis of the Debate between Dr. Lorber and Dr. Freeman on the Treatment of Meningomyelocele," in Dennis J. Horan and David Mall, eds., *Death, Dying and Euthanasia* (Washington, D.C.: University Publications of America, Inc., 1977), pp. 241–242. See Veatch, *op. cit.*, pp. 168–173, against the physician as competent to make moral decisions for patient who can make them; the argument suggests that also in the case of the noncompetent the problem ought to be viewed as finding a suitable person to make decisions *for the patient*, and there is no special reason to put a physician in this role.

85. Marks, *op. cit.*, in Jonsen and Garland, eds., *op. cit.*, p. 122, on the model of abortion; this approach is criticized by Robertson, "Involuntary Euthanasia of Defective Newborns," pp. 262–264.

86. George G. Annas, "In re Quinlan: Legal Comfort for Doctors," *Hastings Center Report*, 6 (June 1976), pp. 29–31, criticized the New Jersey Supreme Court decision on this matter; Shaw, *op. cit.*, p. 886, mentions that a committee was set up at Johns Hopkins following the famous case but questions the point of such a body; Corbett and Raciti, *op. cit.*, pp. 69–73, also question the *Quinlan* decision in this matter in pointing out that the committee does not protect the individual. Veatch, *op. cit.*, pp. 173–176, points out that a medical committee has most of the disadvantages of the individual physician plus some additional ones.

87. See Corbett and Raciti, *op. cit.*, pp. 65–68.

88. *Ibid.*, pp. 69–73 and 79.

89. 1977 Arkansas General Assembly, act 879.

90. 1977 N. M. Laws, ch. 287.

91. Matter of Quinlan, at 666.

92. *Ibid.*, at 662–664.

93. *Ibid.*, at 668–669.

94. *Ibid.*, at 671. Harold L. Hirsch and Richard E. Donavan, "The Right to Die: Medico-Legal Implications In Re Quinlan," *Rutgers Law Review*, 30 (1977), pp. 267–303, point out that neither for the future nor even for the instant case are the implications of the decision clear. The decision (at 651) uses the ordinary-extraordinary means distinction, which leads to uncertainty about what may be done.

95. Matter of Quinlan, at 657, 667.

96. *Ibid.*, at 672.

97. *In the Matter of Karen Quinlan*, vol. 1, pp. 486 and 504.

98. Leadem, *loc. cit.*; William F. Hyland and David S. Baime, "*In Re Quinlan:* A Synthesis of Law and Medical Technology," *Rutgers-Camden Law Journal*, 8 (1976), 58–60. The latter note the ineptness of the attempt of the Court to legislate and the tragic effect this attempt has in putting a false constitutional block in the way of more competent action by the legislature.

99. Matter of Quinlan, at 668–669; cf. Karen Teel, "The Physician's Dilemma: A Doctor's View: What Should the Law Be," *Baylor Law Review*, 27 (1975), p. 9. The Court deletes Teel's remarks beginning with, "However, it has its drawbacks." Teel is sensitive to the point that the family might reasonably question whether this group has any right to make decisions, as might the physician.

100. Cf. Veatch, *op. cit.*, pp. 137–143 and 173–176.

101. Matter of Quinlan, at 669.

102. Superintendent of Belchertown State School v. Saikewicz, at 432–435.

103. *Ibid.*, at 432.

104. William J. Curran, "Law-Medicine Notes: The Saikewicz Decision," *New England Journal of Medicine*, 298 (1978), p. 500.

105. Arnold S. Relman, "The Saikewicz Decision: Judges as Physicians," *New England Journal of Medicine*, 298 (1978), pp. 508–509.

106. George J. Annas, "The Incompetent's Right to Die: The Case of Joseph Saikewicz," *Hastings Center Report*, 8 (February 1978), pp. 21–23. Even this sympathetic commentator's article is published with a title which suggests an irrelevant claim to a "right" to die.

107. See Alan Sussman, "Reporting Child Abuse: A Review of the Literature," *Family Law Quarterly*, 8 (1974), pp. 245–313; Lon B. Isaacson, "Child Abuse Report-

ing Statutes: The Case for Holding Physicians Civilly Liable for Failing to Report,'' *San Diego Law Review,* 12 (1975), pp. 743–777.

10: THE CONSTITUTION, LIFE, LIBERTY, AND JUSTICE

1. Louis Henkin, ''Morals and the Constitution: The Sin of Obscenity,'' *Columbia Law Review,* 63 (1963), p. 408. Henkin makes clear (pp. 407–411) that he considers utilitarian reasons to have an exclusive claim on rationality.

2. Torcaso v. Watkins, 367 U.S. 488, 81 S.Ct. 1680 (1961); note the holding at 495–496, 1683–1684, and the dictum in footnote 11.

3. U.S. v. Seeger, 380 U.S. 163, 85 S.Ct. 850 (1965) at 184, 863. The fact that the Court interprets a statute in this case does not make it less significant for constitutional law, since the alternative clearly would have been to find the statute unconstitutional; cf. Robert L. Rabin, ''When Is a Religious Belief Religious: *United States* v. *Seeger* and the Scope of Free Exercise,'' *Cornell Law Quarterly,* 51 (1966), pp. 240–244.

4. Welsh v. U.S., 398 U.S. 333, 90 S.Ct. 1792 (1970), at 340, 1796.

5. *Ibid.,* at 342–344, 1798. The prevailing opinion was held by only four members of the Court. The majority was formed by the concurrence of Justice Harlan, whose separate opinion rejected the opinion's construction of the statute. Yet Harlan held with the others that an unconstitutional establishment of religion could be avoided and religious neutrality nevertheless maintained by the government only if theistic and nontheistic religious beliefs and comparable secular views were treated alike (at 357, 1805).

6. Paul Ramsey, ''Some Terms of Reference for the Abortion Debate,'' manuscript of a paper delivered at the Harvard-Kennedy Conference on Abortion (Washington, D.C.: September 6–8, 1967), p. 7.

7. John Hart Ely, ''The Wages of Crying Wolf: A Comment on *Roe* v. *Wade,*'' *Yale Law Journal,* 82 (1973), p. 947.

8. See James L. Buckley, ''A Human Life Amendment,'' *Human Life Review,* 1 (Winter 1975), pp. 7–20; John T. Noonan, Jr., ''Why a Constitutional Amendment?'' *Human Life Review,* 1 (Winter 1975), pp. 26–43; Robert M. Byrn, ''A Human Life Amendment: What Would It Mean?'' *Human Life Review,* 1 (Spring 1975), pp. 50–76 and 102–103; David W. Louisell, ''The Burdick Proposal: A Life-Support Amendment,'' *Human Life Review,* 1 (Fall 1975), pp. 9–16; Robert A. Destro, ''Abortion and the Constitution: The Need for a Life-Protective Amendment,'' *Human Life Review,* 2 (Fall 1976), pp. 30–108; Jesse Helms, ''A Human Life Amendment,'' *Human Life Review,* 3 (Spring 1977), pp. 7–42.

9. Byrn, *op. cit.,* pp. 51–53; Helms, *op. cit.,* pp. 24–26.

10. Roe v. Wade, 410 U.S. 163, 93 S. Ct. 705 (1973) at 732.

11. See Dennis J. Horan, ''Abortion and the Conscience Clause: Current Status,'' *Catholic Lawyer,* 20 (1974), pp. 297–302; Germain Grisez, *Abortion: The Myths, the Realities, and the Arguments* (New York and Cleveland: Corpus Books, 1970), pp. 32–33.

12. Davenport Hooker, ''Early Human Fetal Behavior, with a Preliminary Note on Double Simultaneous Fetal Stimulation,'' in Davenport Hooker and Clarence C. Hare, eds., *Genetics and the Inheritance of Integrated Neurological and Psychiatric Patterns,* Research Publications: Association for Research in Nervous and Mental Disease, vol. 33 (Baltimore: Williams and Wilkins Co., 1959), pp. 49–67.

13. Peter G. Guthrie, "Proof of Live Birth in Prosecution for Killing Newborn Child," 65 A.L.R. 3d, pp. 413–428.

14. Planned Parenthood of Central Missouri v. Danforth, 428 U.S. 52, 96 S.Ct. 2831 (1976) at 2847–2848.

15. Hodgson v. Lawson, 542 F.2d 1350 (1976) at 1355.

16. Ibid., at 1360; Planned Parenthood of Central Missouri v. Danforth, at 2855.

17. Joseph P. Witherspoon, "Statement," Proposed Constitutional Amendments on Abortion: Hearings before the Civil and Constitutional Rights Committee of the Judiciary, House of Representatives, 94th Cong., 2d Sess., part 1 (1976), pp. 17–20.

18. Cf. Grisez, op. cit., pp. 410–423.

19. See Byrn, op. cit., pp. 62–67. It seems to us that there can be no better protection for the unborn than to make clear in the Constitution that they are persons and to exclude any reference to them in laws respecting homicide, for in this case the latter will allow minimal exceptions.

20. Leo Pfeffer, God, Caesar, and the Constitution: The Court as Referee of Church-State Confrontation (Boston: Beacon Press, 1975), p. 96.

21. Ibid., p. 97.

22. Ibid., pp. 99–100.

23. Ibid., p. 101.

24. Ibid., p. 104.

25. Ibid., p. 111.

26. Jane Finn, "State Limitations upon the Availability and Accessibility of Abortions after Wade and Bolton," Kansas Law Review, 25 (1976), pp. 87–107.

27. Beal v. Doe, 97 S.Ct. 2366 (1977), the Pennsylvania case, was not decided on constitutional grounds; Maher v. Roe, 97 S.Ct. 2376 (1977), the Connecticut case, was.

28. Poelker v. Doe, 97 S.Ct. 2391 (1977).

29. Cf. John T. Noonan, Jr., "A Half-Step Forward: The Justices Retreat on Abortion," Human Life Review, 3 (Fall 1977), pp. 11–18; Robert M. Byrn, "Which Way for Judicial Imperialism?" Human Life Review, 3 (Fall 1977), pp. 19–35.

30. Brennan, dissenting, in Beal v. Doe, at 2376.

31. Blackmun, joined by Brennan and Marshall, dissenting in Beal v. Doe, Maher v. Roe, and Poelker v. Doe, at 2398–2399.

32. Marshall, dissenting in Beal v. Doe, Maher v. Roe, and Poelker v. Doe, at 2395–2396.

33. See above chapter six, notes 88–94 and accompanying text. Those urging the institutionalization of abortion have argued for an extremely inclusive concept of state action, so that the acts of any private entity which receives public funding would be state action. See Jane Finn, loc. cit.; Harriet F. Pilpel and Dorothy E. Patton, "Abortion, Conscience and the Constitution: An Examination of Federal Institutional Conscience Clauses," Columbia Human Rights Law Review, 6 (1974–1975), pp. 279–305; and especially Marc D. Stern, "Abortion Conscience Clauses," Columbia Journal of Law and Social Problems, 11 (1975), pp. 571–627. Their point was to require abortion cooperation on the theory that anyone involved in state action could not abridge the woman's "right" to an abortion. Our point is that on their theory most abortions involve state action: the people at large are compelled to cooperate in what many regard as murder of unborn persons. This is an infringement on liberty to stand aloof.

34. See above, chapter six, note 63 and accompanying text. A widely used text for values clarification is Sidney B. Simon, Leland W. Howe, and Howard Kirschenbaum, Values Clarification: A Handbook of Practical Strategies for Teachers and Students (New York: Hart Publishing Co., 1972). An official state publication which exemplifies

the typical, consequentialist approach of the new value instruction is *Valuing: A Discussion Guide* (Albany, New York: The Board of Regents, 1976). A revealing work directed to teachers is Ronald G. Havelock, *The Change Agent's Guide to Innovation* (Englewood Cliffs, N.J.: Educational Technology Publications, 1973), portions of which were developed under Contract No. OEC-0-8-080603-4535 (010), Office of Education, United States Department of Health, Education and Welfare. For a statement concerning the impossibility of neutrality, the way in which the school teaches values even by trying to be neutral, and the new directions in value formation see Robert D. Barr, ed., *Values and Youth* (Washington, D.C.: National Council for the Social Sciences, 1971), pp. 21–24; this book as a whole also contains much illuminating material about the new values education. It would be an interesting but endless task to demonstrate precisely what is going on in the values courses by examining the books in use. An interesting example of the genre, taken from a book which on the whole is not a horrible example, is a little section "What are value theories?" in a high school textbook, Carl A. Elder, *Making Value Judgments: Decisions for Today* (Columbus, Ohio: Charles E. Merrill Publishing Co., 1972), pp. 16–17. Boards of education have considerable power; parents have objected unsuccessfully to secular humanist content in the public school curricula; see Kenneth A. Schulman, "Parental Control of Public School Curriculum," *Catholic Lawyer,* 21 (1975), pp. 197–210, concerning Williams v. Board of Education, 388 F.Supp. (S.D.W.Va. 1975), aff'd, Civil No. 75-1455 (4th Cir., Dec. 3, 1975). The values clarification approach in sex education is exemplified by Eleanor S. Morrison and Mila Underhill Price, *Values in Sexuality* (New York: Hart Publishing Co., 1974). In this field the Sex Information and Education Council of the U.S. (SIECUS), formed in 1964 and closely related to Planned Parenthood, has had great influence. Much revealing material exists: for example, a manual in which many of the leaders of the organization wrote specialized articles to form the educators: Carlfred B. Broderick and Jesse Bernard, eds., *The Individual, Sex, & Society: A SIECUS Handbook for Teachers and Counselors* (Baltimore and London: Johns Hopkins Press, 1969). Of special interest in this book is the chapter by Lester A. Kirkendall and Roger W. Libby, "Trends in Sex Education," pp. 5–21, where the predicament of the teacher who must deal pro or con with premarital intercourse is discussed, and the solution of letting students decide for themselves is suggested—one makes one's point more effectively if one does *not* overtly make it. Even the annotated bibliographies in this volume are revealing.

35. See Annotation, "Sectarianism in schools," 5 A.L.R. 866, 141 A.L.R. 1144.

36. Leo Pfeffer, "Uneasy Trinity: Church, State, and Constitution," *Civil Liberties Review,* 2 (1975), pp. 145–146; cf. idem, *God, Caesar, and the Constitution,* pp. 168–179.

37. See Annotation, "Sectarianism in schools," 5 A.L.R. 879–884; 141 A.L.R. 1148–1153; 68 Am. Jur. 2d 617–623.

38. Everson v. Board of Education of Ewing Tp., 330 U.S. 1, 67 S.Ct. 504 (1947).

39. McCollum v. Board of Education, 333 U.S. 203, 68 S.Ct. 461 (1948).

40. Pfeffer, *God, Caesar, and the Constitution,* p. 195.

41. Engel v. Vitale, 370 U.S. 421, 82 S.Ct. 1261 (1962); School District of Abington Township v. Schempp, 374 U.S. 203, 83 S.Ct. 1560 (1963).

42. Jackson, dissenting in Everson v. Board of Education, at 23–24, 515.

43. Jackson, concurring in McCollum v. Board of Education, at 236, 477.

44. *Ibid.,* at 237–238, 478.

45. The briefs *amicus curiae* of the American Ethical Union and of the American Humanist Association in Abington School District v. Schempp are printed in Philip B.

Kurland and Gerhard Casper, eds., *Landmark Briefs and Arguments of the Supreme Court of the United States,* vol. 57 (Washington, D.C.: University Publications of America, Inc.), pp. 809–856. See pp. 813, 828–829, and 847 (p. 2 of the Ethical Union brief; pp. 1–2 and 20 of the Humanist Association brief).

46. *Ibid.,* pp. 815–816 (pp. 4–5 of the Ethical Union brief).

47. *Ibid.,* pp. 829–830 (pp. 2–3 of the Humanist Association brief).

48. See above, notes 2–6 and accompanying text. It is worth noticing that the Court's holding that nontheistic world views are religions is not a sudden, recent development but goes back at least to Vidal v. Girard's Executors, 2 How. 205 (1844), in which deism was held to be a sect along with Judaism and "any other form of infidelity"; Chief Justice Hughes, dissenting in United States v. McIntosh, 293 U.S. 605 (1931), said that "cosmic consciousness of belonging to the human family" is a "religious" belief. A person's fundamental world view thus is his or her religion.

49. See John Dewey, "My Pedagogic Creed," *The School Journal,* 14 (January 16, 1897), pp. 77–80, a uniquely clear, succinct, and important summary by the man himself. The creed is divided into five articles, and each of these into brief paragraphs beginning "I believe" and setting forth Dewey's whole educational philosophy. The fifth article sets out the role of education as the highest duty of society and the mode of social progress and reform, for which the child is to be trained. The final paragraph gathers the whole together in religious language: "I believe that in this way the teacher always is the prophet of the true God and the usherer in of the true kingdom of God." The emphasis here should be on "true"—that is, the this-worldly, social reality of which Dewey has been speaking. A sympathetic but informative history of the progressive education movement, which has entrenched secular humanism in the public schools, and of Dewey's important role in it is Lawrence A. Cremin, *The Transformation of the School: Progressivism in American Education, 1876–1957* (New York: Alfred A. Knopf, 1961), especially pp. 100, 115–126, and 234–239.

50. Abington School District v. Schempp, at 225, 1573.

51. See James D. Smart, *The Cultural Subversion of the Biblical Faith* (Philadelphia: Westminster Press, 1977), pp. 21–29 and 100–104; Russell E. Richey and Donald G. Jones, eds., *American Civil Religion* (New York, Evanston, San Francisco, and London: Harper & Row, 1974); Perry C. Cotham, *Politics, Americanism, and Christianity* (Grand Rapids, Mich.: Baker Book House, 1976), esp. pp. 127–179.

52. Abington School District v. Schempp, Brennan concurring, at 241–242, 1582.

53. Board of Education v. Allen, 392 U.S. 236, 88 S.Ct. 1923.

54. Lemon v. Kurtzman, Earley v. DiCenso, Robinson v. DiCenso, 403 U.S. 602, 29 L. Ed. 2d 745 (1971), at 752–763.

55. *Ibid.,* Douglas concurring, at 766–772.

56. *Ibid.,* Brennan concurring, at 776–781.

57. *Ibid.,* White dissenting, at 784–789.

58. Cf. *ibid.,* Douglas concurring, at 766.

59. The argument that public funding of separate schools is constitutionally *required* has been made by Virgil C. Blum, S.J., *Freedom of Choice in Education,* rev. ed. (Glen Rock, N.J.: Paulist Press, 1963). Many careful legal analyses have shown that the Court is giving undue weight to and misinterpreting the Establishment Clause to the great detriment of Free Exercise for those who wish to avoid indoctrination in their local public school and Equal Protection for those who pay to support private schools in which their children are taught in ways which better comport with their religious beliefs than they would be taught in the public schools. On the interpretation of the Establishment Clause see Jesse H. Choper, "The Establishment Clause and Aid to

Parochial Schools,'' *California Law Review,* 56 (1968), pp. 260–341, especially pp. 283–295; Alan Schwarz, ''No Imposition of Religion: The Establishment Clause Value,'' *Yale Law Journal,* 77 (1968), pp. 692–737, especially pp. 727–737. An excellent statement of the case that the Court is overemphasizing the Establishment Clause and disregarding the competing demands of the Free Exercise and Equal Protection clauses is Paul G. Kauper, ''The Supreme Court and the Establishment Clause: Back to *Everson?*'' *Case Western Reserve Law Review,* 25 (1974), pp. 107–129. It also has been argued effectively that the ''tests'' used by the Court are not reasonable interpretations of the constitutional requirements; in addition to the preceding articles see John E. Nowak, ''The Supreme Court, the Religion Clauses, and the Nationalization of Education,'' *Northwestern University Law Review,* 70 (1976), pp. 883–909, especially pp. 900–909. Alexander Bickel, *The Supreme Court and the Idea of Progress* (New York: Harper and Row, 1970), pp. 121–125 and 136–137, has suggested that the Court's decisions concerning schools have been intended to further social-policy objectives favored by the justices themselves; this view, if correct, would explain the straining of the Establishment clause evident in the decisions. The political background of the Court's early decisions is briefly summarized by Richard E. Morgan, *The Supreme Court and Religion* (New York and London: The Free Press, 1972), pp. 81–90; this summary makes clear that the post-World War II decisions were a calculated blocking of public aid to parochial schools. Consistency with any set of principles is hard to find in nearly contemporary decisions; this point is made with regard to some of the more recent decisions by James L. Underwood, ''Permissible Entanglement under the Establishment Clause,'' *Emory Law Journal,* 25 (1976), pp. 17–62.

60. In Wisconsin v. Yoder, 406 U.S. 205, 92 S.Ct. 1526 (1972), at 1536, the Court has admitted that regulations neutral on their face may offend the constitutional requirement of neutrality by unduly burdening the free exercise of religion. In Yoder, Amish parents wished to avoid sending their children to high school, and the Court accepted their position. In an earlier case, Sherbert v. Verner, 374 U.S. 398, 83 S.Ct. 1790 (1963), the Court held that unemployment benefits could not be denied a person who could not work on Saturday because of religious convictions. These decisions have breathed considerable life into the Free Exercise clause but would not likely be followed to their logical conclusion: Children in religious schools cannot be denied public funding simply because they cannot in conscience attend the established schools. The Ohio Supreme Court has taken one further step in this direction by holding that children attending one of the Christian schools—a development of Evangelical Protestants who object on grounds of conscience to the public schools—could not be forced by the state's school attendance regulations into the public schools, although their religious school did not meet the state's minimal standards in a number of respects: State v. Wishner, 47 Ohio St. 2d 181, 351 N.E. 2d 750 (1976). The issue resolves to the ultimate one: What is to be done about liberty when money is at issue? We do not doubt that if the parents of separate school students were not being forced to carry both the burden of their own children's education and their share of the burden of the education of those attending the established schools, thus to provide a tremendous subsidy for the dominant groups in American society, the true status of education as always embodying some form of religion or another would long since have been admitted by the Court.

61. A clear and extensive argument for the proposition that Free Exercise requires a general recognition of the right of conscientious objection is articulated by J. Morris Clark, ''Guidelines for the Free Exercise Clause,'' *Harvard Law Review,* 83 (1969), pp. 327–365.

11: THEORIES OF ETHICS

1. Three introductions to twentieth-century ethics, each from a somewhat different viewpoint and valuable for its special approach, are W. D. Hudson, *Modern Moral Philosophy* (Garden City, New York: Doubleday & Co., 1970), G. J. Warnock, *Contemporary Moral Philosophy* (London, Melbourne, Toronto, New York: Macmillan, St. Martin's Press, 1967); Ronald Lawler, *Philosophical Analysis and Ethics* (Milwaukee: Bruce Publishing Co., 1968).

2. For an exposition and critique of Kant's ethics by a sympathetic scholar see Lewis White Beck, *A Commentary on Kant's Critique of Practical Reason* (Chicago: University of Chicago Press, 1960), esp. pp. 176–208; for the present authors' critique of Kant's attempted compatibilism see Joseph M. Boyle, Jr., Germain Grisez, and Olaf Tollefsen, *Free Choice: A Self-Referential Argument* (Notre Dame and London: University of Notre Dame Press, 1976), pp. 110–121.

3. Thomas Aquinas, *Summa theologiae*, 1–2, q. 94, a. 2; cf. Germain Grisez, "The First Principle of Practical Reason: A Commentary on the *Summa theologiae*, 1–2, Question 94, Article 2," *Natural Law Forum*, 10 (1965), pp. 168–201.

4. For a classification of many forms of utilitarianism see William K. Frankena, *Ethics*, 2nd ed. (Englewood Cliffs, N.J.: Prentice-Hall, 1973), pp. 34–39. David Lyons, *Forms and Limits of Utilitarianism* (London: Oxford University Press, 1965), argues at length that all the more interesting forms of utilitarianism amount to the same thing.

5. See John Rawls, *A Theory of Justice* (Cambridge, Mass.: Belknap Press of Harvard University Press, 1971), pp. 22–27.

6. The critique of consequentialism is developed more fully in certain respects in Germain Grisez, "Against Consequentialism," *American Journal of Jurisprudence*, 23 (1978).

7. See Joseph M. Boyle, Jr., "Aquinas and Prescriptive Ethics," *Proceedings of the American Catholic Philosophical Association*, 49 (1975), pp. 82–95.

8. See Dan W. Brock, "Recent Work in Utilitarianism," *American Philosophical Quarterly*, 10 (1973), pp. 241–269, for a telling survey and criticism of efforts to deal with the perennial difficulties of consequentialist theory.

9. For an interesting thought experiment against any form of hedonism see Robert Nozick, *Anarchy, State, and Utopia* (New York: Basic Books, 1974), pp. 42–45.

10. Thomas Aquinas, *Summa contra gentiles*, 3, chs. 121–122, maintains that nothing offends God which is not contrary to human good. He quotes St. Paul, "Let your service be reasonable" (Rom. 12.1) in support of the view that divine law demands of humankind only what is rationally required; see also idem, *Summa theologiae*, 1–2, q. 19, aa. 9 and 10.

11. The maxim is derived from Romans 3.8, where St. Paul rejects the contradictory. Christians, he says, were falsely accused of justifying evildoing. It is noteworthy that this point is in the context of a discussion of divine providence: God permits evil for a good he draws from it. If both this conception of providence and consequentialism were correct, Christians would have a simple ethics: When in doubt, try it! So Paul rejects consequentialism. Joseph Fletcher, *Moral Responsibility: Situation Ethics at Work* (Philadelphia: Westminster Press, 1967), pp. 21–23, as well as in other works, denies the principle which he regards as an unwarranted absolutization of Paul's "remark" by asserting that the end does justify the means. However, Fletcher never takes the trouble to clarify the traditional meaning of the maxim derived from Paul, and he takes the saying that the end does not justify the means as if it meant—what obviously is absurb—that one can act without any end in view.

12. Fletcher, *op. cit.*, pp. 151–152.

13. For a development of this argument see Boyle, Grisez, and Tollefsen, *loc. cit.*

14. See Thomas Aquinas, *Summa theologiae*, 1, q. 75, a. 4; q. 76, a. 1; P. F. Strawson, "Persons," in G. N. A. Vesey, ed., *Body and Mind* (London: George Allen & Unwin, 1964), pp. 403–424; Gabriel Marcel, *The Mystery of Being*, vol. 1, *Reflection and Mystery* (Chicago: Henry Regnery, 1960), pp. 127–153. It can be argued that Strawson's argument itself is too Cartesian, but if so, there are other, more recent analytic critiques of dualism which remedy the defect—for example, B. A. O. Williams, "Are Persons Bodies?" in Stuart F. Spicker, *The Philosophy of the Body: Rejections of Cartesian Dualism* (New York: Quadrangle/New York Times Book Co., 1970), pp. 137–156. Religious readers might be concerned that a firm rejection of dualism will undercut the belief in life after death. However, it is important that for many Jews and for the common Christian tradition the key to personal existence beyond the present life is in the resurrection of the body. This would make little sense if the person were not, in fact, a bodily reality. Thomas Aquinas, commenting upon St. Paul, states that the soul is *not* the person (he regards the soul after death as immaterial remains of a person): "homo naturaliter desiderat salutem sui ipsius, anima autem cum sit pars corporis hominis, non est totus homo, et anima mea non est ego; unde licet anima consequatur salutem in alia vita, non tamen ego vel quilibet homo" (*Super primam epistolam ad Corinthios lectura*, XV, lec. ii).

12: MORAL RESPONSIBILITIES TOWARD HUMAN LIFE

1. Germain Grisez, "Toward a Consistent Natural-Law Ethics of Killing," *The American Journal of Jurisprudence*, 15 (1970), pp. 64–96; Joseph M. Boyle, Jr., "Double-effect and a Certain Type of Embryotomy," *Irish Theological Quarterly*, 44 (1977), pp. 303–318; Joseph M. Boyle, Jr., "Toward Understanding the Principle of Double Effect," forthcoming.

2. Cf. Thomas Aquinas, *Summa theologiae*, 2-2, q. 40, a. 1; q. 64, a. 2; *Summa contra gentiles*, 3, ch. 146; Aristotle, *Politics i* (1253a19–28); *Nicomachean Ethics i*, 2 (1094b7–11); *x*, 7–8 (1177b26–1178b23); *Metaphysics xii*, 9 (1074b15–34).

3. Germain Grisez, *Abortion: The Myths, the Realities, and the Arguments* (New York and Cleveland: Corpus Books, 1970), pp. 273–346; Boyle, "Double-effect and a Certain Type of Embryotomy."

4. Eike-Henner W. Kluge, *The Practice of Death* (New Haven and London: Yale University Press, 1975), pp. 8–9, erroneously assumes that Grisez argues from the genetic structure of the fertilized ovum to its potential personhood. Grisez's argument has nothing whatsoever to do with "potential personhood," whatever that is, but rather is from the facts which provide no ground for distinguishing the unborn from already born without unprovable metaphysical or theological assumptions to the reasonability of a presumption that the unborn are persons, and hence to the ethical mandate that they be treated as such. When one is killing something which might be a person and has no way of knowing that it is not, one has a moral obligation to be very careful—not to kill it—since otherwise one is willing to kill a person if this happens to be one.

5. See the remarks of Harriet Pilpel in a telecast "Firing Line," broadcast by Public Broadcasting System the week of Nov. 4, 1977, published in Appendix C, *Human Life Review*, 4 (Winter 1978), p. 98; Roe v. Wade, 410 U.S. 149, 93 S.Ct. 725 (1973), especially note 44.

6. "Editorial: A New Ethic for Medicine and Society," *California Medicine,* 113 (September 1970), pp. 67–68.

7. Judith Blake, "The Supreme Court's Abortion Decisions and Public Opinion in the United States," *Human Life Review,* 4 (Winter 1978), pp. 72–73.

8. See John Connery, *Abortion: The Development of the Roman Catholic Perspective* (Chicago: Loyola University Press, 1977), pp. 284–303.

9. Boyle, "Double-effect and a Certain Type of Embryotomy."

10. Paul Ramsey, "Abortion: A Review Article," *The Thomist,* 37 (1973), pp. 212–218.

11. Grisez, *Abortion,* p. 343.

12. Ramsey, *op. cit.,* pp. 224–226.

13. See David Daube, "The Linguistics of Suicide," *Philosophy and Public Affairs,* 1 (1971–1972), pp. 433–437.

14. See Edwin S. Shneidman, Norman L. Farberow, and Robert E. Litman, *The Psychology of Suicide* (New York: 1970), pp. 3–93, 227–304, and *passim.*

15. Ludwig Wittgenstein, *Notebooks, 1914–1916,* trans. G.E.M. Anscombe (New York and Evanston: 1961), p. 91e.

16. See Gerald Hughes, "Killing and Letting Die," *The Month,* 236 (1975), pp. 43–44.

17. See James Rachels, "Active and Passive Euthanasia," *New England Journal of Medicine,* 292 (1975), pp. 78–80; for a critique: Joseph M. Boyle, Jr., "On Killing and Letting Die," *The New Scholasticism,* 51 (1977), pp. 433–452.

18. See Michael Tooley, "A Defense of Abortion and Infanticide," in Joel Feinberg, ed., *The Problem of Abortion* (Belmont, California: Wadsworth Publishing Co., 1973), pp. 84–85; see Boyle, "On Killing and Letting Die," for discussion of this and other relevant literature.

19. Pius XII, "The Prolongation of Life," *The Pope Speaks,* 4 (1957–1958), pp. 395–396 (*AAS,* 49 [1957], pp. 1027–1033 at 1030).

20. United Way fund raising contributes to diverse purposes in different places. Some programs might contribute to objectionable causes, but we by no means suggest that all do. The March of Dimes has supported prenatal genetic screening. As a matter of well-established fact, genetic screening primarily is a means used as part of the execution of proposals to abort infants found defective. See Tabitha M. Powledge and Sharmon Sollitto, "Prenatal Diagnosis—The Past and the Future," *Hastings Center Report,* 4 (November 1974), pp. 11–13; Philip Reilly, "Genetic Screening Legislation," *Advances in Human Genetics,* 5 (1975), pp. 354–368. (The latter looks forward to compulsory prenatal screening and government controls of procreation in case defects are found.) Since prenatal screening is used as it is, anyone who says that support of it is not helping to execute abortive acts is either naive or dishonest.

Index